Dirty War, Clean Hands

DBS Library

31362

Dirty War, Clean Hands

ETA, the GAL and Spanish Democracy

DBS Library
13/14 Aungier Street
Dublin 2
Phone: 01-41775

This book is due for return on or before the last date shown below.

9 - SEP 2008

First published in 2001 by

Cork University Press
Crawford Business Park
Crosses Green
Cork, Ireland

© Paddy Woodworth 2001

All rights reserved. No part of this book may be reprinted or reproduced
or utilized in any electronic, mechanical or other means, now known or
hereafter invented, including photocopying and recording or otherwise,
without either the prior written permission of the Publishers or a licence
permitting restricted copying in Ireland issued by the Irish Copyright
Licensing Agency Ltd, The Irish Writers' Centre, 19 Parnell Square,
Dublin 1.

British Library Cataloguing in Publication Data
A CIP catalogue record for this book is available from the British
Library.

ISBN 1 85918 276 3 (HB)

A CIP record for this publication is available from
the Library of Congress

Printed by MPG Books Ltd., Cornwall
Typeset by Phototypeset Ltd., Dublin

CONTENTS

Part III: Placing Blame:
Investigating The Investigators

Part IV: Conclusions:
Cleaning Up After A Dirty War

LIST OF ILLUSTRATIONS

1. Segundo Marey at his home, on the day he was released by the GAL 14 December, 1983. (Reproduced courtesy of Jesús Uriarte).

2. The mothers of Joxean Lasa and Floren Aoiz, Herri Batasuna leader, lay wreaths before his portrait outside La Cumbre Palace in August 1995. ETA members Lasa and Joxi Zabala had been held and interrogated by the GAL in this building in 1983–4. (Jesús Uriarte).

3. *Ertzainas* (Basque police) baton-charge family members at the funeral of Lasa and Zabala in Tolosa cemetery, 21 June 1995. (Jesús Uriarte).

4. Izaskun Ugarte, widow of GAL victim and ETA member Mikel Goikoetxea Elorriaga (*Txapela*), touches her husband's ashes with one hand and with the other raises ETA's symbol, the axe (for strength) and serpent (for cunning) at his funeral ceremony in St-Jean-de-Luz in January 1984. The Herri Batasuna leader Santiago Brouard, who was shot by the GAL later the same year, stands behind the ashes. On the right is José Manuel Pagoaga Gallastegi (*Peixoto*). (Reproduced courtesy of Perrin/FSP/GAMMA).

5. The Kayetenia Bar in Bayonne after the shooting of Ramón Oñederra (*Kattu*) on 19 December 1983. The banner accuses the Spanish Socialist Party and Spanish police of killing him. (Reproduced courtesy of Eric Verdier/SIPA).

6. The mothers of ETA members Bixente Perurena (*Peru*) and Ángel Gurmindo, (*Escopetas / Stein*), killed by the GAL in Hendaye on 25 February 1984 hold their ashes during their funeral. In the right foreground, looking away, is Herri Batasuna leader Txomin Ziluaga. (Jesús Uriarte).

7. ETA member Xabier Pérez de Arenaza is carried dead from his car after a GAL attack in a Biarritz petrol station, 23 March 1984. (Jesús Uriarte).

8. Veteran ETA leader Tomás Pérez Revilla (right) and the refugee priest Román Orbe in the immediate aftermath of a GAL bombing in Biarritz in June 1984. Pérez Revilla, who was already ill with leukaemia, died 43 days later. (Reproduced courtesy of Corbis).

9. Relatives of Joxean Lasa and Joxi Zabala visit the site where they were buried in quicklime in Busot, Alicante. The banner reads 'Freedom for the Basque Country!' (Reproduced courtesy of Joaquín de Haro/*El País*).

10. Militant mourners at the funeral of Herri Batasuna leader Santiago Brouard in Bilbao, 22 November 1984. The banner in the foreground carries the symbols of HASI, the revolutionary party which Brouard led, and KAS, a shadowy committee which appeared to link Herri Batasuna and ETA. (Reproduced courtesy of Luis Alberto García/*El País*).

11. The bodies of two of the four victims of the GAL shooting at the Hotel Monbar in Bayonne, on 25 September 1985, lie covered in sheets while anti-GAL protesters begin a silent demonstration. (Reproduced courtesy of Goitia/SIPA).

12. Former Spanish police superintendent José Amendo, already convicted for two GAL attacks and one kidnapping, attends a court hearing in Bilbao, during the protracted investigation of Santiago Brouard's murder, in July 1999. (Reproduced courtesy of Alfredo Aldai/*El País*).

13. Laura Martín, widow of the GAL's last victim, Juan Carlos García Goena, who had no links to ETA and was killed by car bomb in July 1987. 'I want the truth, all of it, all of it.' (Jesús Uriarte).

ACKNOWLEDGEMENTS

Individual authorship is a kind of fiction. All books are, to a greater or lesser degree, works of collaboration – though the author bears exclusive responsibility for the final result.

This book could not have been written without the active collaboration of survivors of the dirty war, and relatives and friends of those who did not survive. They shared their painful memories with me willingly and generously, despite the reopening of wounds which this process inevitably involved. While they may not – and probably will not – agree with all that I have written, I hope I have kept faith with their versions of the events they lived through. In the order in which they appear in the narrative, they are: Emile Muley, Jean-Louis Humbert, Mikel Mari Lasa, Juan Mari Zabala, Izaskun Rekalde, Prudencio Oñederra, Arantza Ganbara, Izaskun Ugarte, Edurne Brouard, Ramón Basáñez, Fernando Egileor, Karmen Galdeano, Karmele Martínez Otegi, Txetx Etcheverry and Laura Martín. To them all, my humblest thanks.

Several lawyers who represented GAL victims gave me valuable insights, some of which are directly quoted in these pages, while others were helpful for background. My thanks to Iñigo Iruin, Iñigo Goioaga and Juan Mari Bandrés.

I am particularly grateful to Karmelo Landa, a member of the national executive of Herri Batasuna, who willingly opened many doors for me, despite sharp differences in our political perspectives.

I would also like to thank two men convicted for GAL crimes, Rafael Vera and José Amedo, who were willing to talk to me at length about the view from their side of the dirty war. If others associated with the GAL had been as forthcoming, the complexity of these events might have been better reflected in this book, but their reticence tells its own story. My thanks to the lawyers for Amedo and Vera, Jorge Manrique and Manuel Cobo del Rosal, respectively, for facilitating these contacts.

I owe a debt of gratitude to three of the figures involved in the investigation of the GAL, Baltasar Garzón, Javier Gómez de Liaño and, in particular, Jesús Santos. They were helpful and patient in giving an outsider to the Spanish legal system a wealth of contextual information. Two journalists at *El País*, José Yoldi and Julio Lazaro, also helped guide me through this maze. Their own court reports are models of clarity, and are frequently quoted here. Ignacio Montes Pérez and Patrick O'Reilly made helpful suggestions on 'Some Notes on the Spanish Constitution, Judiciary and Legal System'. My thanks to all of them; in this field, as elsewhere, any errors which may remain are mine alone.

Thanks are due, too, to a number of politicians, peace activists, commentators, writers and journalists who shared their knowledge and opinions with me: José Luis Barbería, Patxo Unzueta and Javier Pradera at *El País*; Santos Juliá; Margarita Robles; Fernando López Agundín;

Manuel Vázquez Montalbán; Mario Onaindia of the Spanish Socialist Party, and formerly of Euzkadiko Ezkerra; Joseba Azkarraga, former parliamentary deputy for Eusko Alkartasuna (a party formed by dissident Basque Nationalist Party leaders in 1986); Cristina Cuesta of Gesto por la Paz; Xabier Arzalluz, president of the Basque Nationalist Party; Pepe Rei, formerly of *Egin*; and Manuel Cerdán and Antonio Rubio of *El Mundo*. To those who did not want to be mentioned, my thanks also.

The archives of *El País* are a treasure house of exceptionally well-organised information, and I am grateful to the newspaper for allowing me unlimited access to them. The courtesy and warmth with which my endless queries were received by the staff made working there a pleasure. A very special thank-you is owed to the archives director when I first worked there, Maite Elola, whose exceptional professional and personal qualities made the early phases of my research much easier. Among her staff, Ana Lorite and Isabel Órtiz both gave me exceptional assistance. More recently, Jesús Alborey's invaluable research went very far beyond the call of duty. Thanks, also, to Maite's successor, Juan Carlos Blanco, for accepting my subsequent hurricane visits to his department with such good grace. Terry Otero was always most helpful in picture research, and I am very grateful to Jesús Uriarte and Luis Alberto García for the images which give this book many of its illustrations. John Cassidy of *The Irish Times* studio did a fine job on the maps. In *El Mundo*'s archives, Miguel Gómez also gave me generous assistance.

A long-standing debt is due to Luis Rodríguez Aizpeolea, who guided my first steps in journalism in the Basque Country in 1979, and, through many amicable – and, for me at least, profitable – discussions, has been a constant reference point ever since. His wife, Oliva María, has been a delightfully dissident participant in many of these debates, sometimes supplying lavish meals out of nowhere to accompany them.

Friendship and hospitality can be as valuable to a writer as intellectual support. Not only has Txomin Artola supplied me with many pleasurable insights into Basque culture and music over many years, but he and his wife, Mertxe Ezeiza, and their *cuadrilla*, have also provided a haven of rest and relaxation in their exquisitely situated home in Iparralde, when I needed it most. In Madrid, Jane Walker's warm hospitality, beautiful flat, splendid dinners and generosity with her contacts sustained me through many difficult weeks. I am grateful to Pamela O'Malley for her continuous encouragement and wise counsel. Ciarán Benson, Orla Brady, Ana Carrigan, Pat Donlon, Lynn Geldof and Emer McNamara gave me the faith to keep going at various critical moments. Ricardo and Belchu Cristóbal diverted and supported me on several occasions when I would otherwise have drowned in files and transcripts. So did John Holmwood and Maribel Benito, Bill and Olivia Roxby, María Pages and José Sánchez and Pancho, Catherine Kavanagh, Brendan McCaul, Teri and Stephen Meyer, and Kristina Bolger. Tom Burns tried to warn me off the whole topic of the GAL, and when he failed gave me welcome encouragement. Ed Owen gave valuable time when my laptop crashed. Adela Gooch helped me with contacts in Madrid. Aurora Díaz-Rato and Ignacio Montes Pérez helped me in ways too numerous to mention, not least by consistently challenging my point of view. To John de Courcy Ireland, whose inspired and passionate teaching first aroused my interest in history and politics, I owe a great deal.

I am directly indebted to two meticulous readers and a first-class editor for many improvements to the book. Professor Richard Gillespie's notes went far beyond the usual brief of an academic reader, and were tremendously helpful. His subsequent support at a difficult moment in the book's development was crucial. Miguel Ángel Bastenier's deeply critical engagement forced me to rethink many points. If, as Blake said, opposition is true friendship, Miguel Ángel is a friend for life. They were followed by Finbarr O'Shea, whose close attention to detail saved me many blunders, and whose empathy with the text made a difficult process most enjoyable. Once again, the remaining faults are all my own work. Thanks are also due to Nora Artola for her excellent transcriptions of interviews, and to Judith Crosbie for standardising references.

Without Cork University Press, its courageous publisher, Sara Wilbourne and her staff, this book would not now be in your hands. Many thanks, too, are due to Ania Corless for her generous advice on dealing with British, Irish and Spanish publishers. Helen Meany, Caroline Walsh and James Ryan also gave welcome counsel and support in this and related areas. Geraldine Creamer kindly helped with financial planning. Tom Murphy and Marc Cabal both provided contacts with publishers at moments when I might otherwise have abandoned the project. Karl Meyer, editor of the *World Policy Journal*, gave much appreciated help in promoting the book in the USA.

This project would have been neither started nor finished without the support of the editor of *The Irish Times*, Conor Brady. Allowing his arts editor to go off on paid sabbatical to write about state terrorism in another country is a small but clear example of the kind of lateral thinking that has made the newspaper so successful under his editorship. He then granted me a further year's unpaid leave to finish what I had assured him was three months' work, and never chided me when no visible results were forthcoming on my return. I greatly appreciate his indulgence, and hope that this book is worthy of such trust. Twenty years earlier, acting in his capacity as foreign editor, Conor Brady had commissioned the first pieces I ever wrote from the Basque Country. Paul Gillespie, who succeeded him in that position, commissioned dozens more articles over subsequent years, providing invaluable nurture for an area of coverage which many other newspapers ignored. Gerald Barry and his colleagues in the newsroom at RTÉ played a similar role for this writer on the airwaves. Patsey Murphy and Deirdre Falvey have been most receptive to proposals related to this book in The *Irish Times* weekend supplement. Picture editor Dermot O'Shea and his staff were helpful in facilitating the transmission of illustrations from abroad. My thanks, also, to my colleagues, past and present, on the foreign desk Seamus Martin, Patrick Comerford, Peter Murtagh, Declan Burke-Kennedy, Angela Long, Enda O'Doherty, David Sholdice and David Shanks and sub-editors too numerous to mention here, for their support, professionalism and camaraderie. To anyone I have inadvertently omitted, in any of the above categories, my apologies.

The final debts are personal, and cannot be adequately registered here. They are to the memory of my late father, Dudley Woodworth, who taught me that justice is a fundamental value, and of my late brother, David, whose death curtailed the publication of at least three of his own books and whose advice on this project I sorely missed. To my mother, Phyllis Woodworth, whose ninety-second year has neither blunted her intelligence nor diminished her fortitude, for enduring my long absences with good humour. To my sister, Elizabeth Wallers and the extended Long and Woodworth families, for their warm support. To Trish Long, *compañera de mi vida*, to whom this book is dedicated, for so very many wonderful things for which I can find no adequate words, but especially: for graciously taking the bad with the good during the repeatedly extended gestation of *Dirty War, Clean Hands*, but taking no bullshit; and for never letting me forget that there are worlds to explore and share outside the covers of this book.

Paddy Woodworth
March, 2001

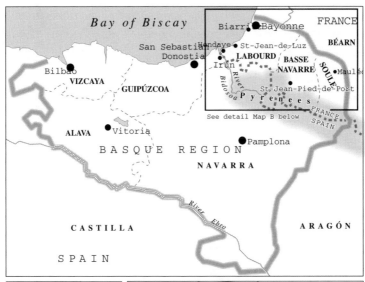

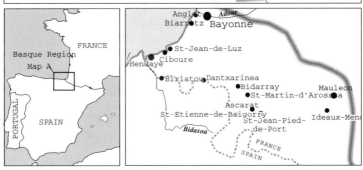

GAL ATTACKS IN THE FRENCH BASQUE COUNTRY

Hendaye: José Mariá Larretxea kidnapping; Segundo Marey kidnapping; Ángel Gurmindo Izarraga (*Escopetas / Stein*) and Bixente Perurena Telletxea (*Peru*) killed; Jean-Pierre Leiba killed; Juan Carlos García Goena killed.

Biriatou: Christian Olaskoaga killed; Claude Olaskoaga wounded.

Ciboure: Emile Weiss and Claude Doerr killed; Bar Bittor attack (Ramón Basánez wounded).

St-Jean-de-Luz: Mikel Goikoetxea Elorriaga (*Txapela*) killed; Javier Galdeano killed; Bar La Consolation attacks (Ramón Basañez wounded in 1986 attack).

Biarritz: Xabier Pérez de Arenaza killed; Tomás Pérez Revilla killed, Román Orbe injured; Robert Caplanne killed.

Anglet: Attacks on Fernando Egileor.

Bayonne: See Map of Attacks in Bayonne.

St-Etienne-de-Baigorry: Rafael Goikoetxea killed, Jesús Zugarramurdi (*Kixkur*) wounded.

Ideaux-Mendy: Eugenio Gutiérrez Salazar (*Tigre*) killed.

Ascarat: Juan Mari Otegi Elizegi (*Txato*) killed.

Bidarray: Christophe Matxikotte and Catherine Brion killed.

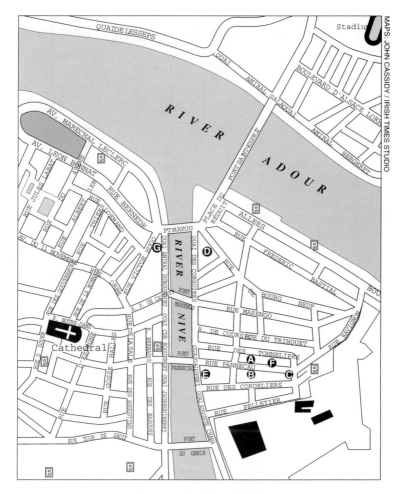

GAL ATTACKS IN BAYONNE

A. Car Park, Rue des Tonneliers: Joxean Lasa and Joxi Zabala kidnapped, 16 October 1983.

B. Hotel Monbar: Joxe Mari Etxaniz (*Potros*), Inaxio Asteasuinzarra (*Beltza*), Agustín Irazustabarrena (*Legra*), Xabin Etxaide (*Eskumotz*) shot dead, 25 September 1985.

C. Café des Pyrénées: Benoit Pecastaing killed, Kepa (Pedro) Pikabea seriously hurt, 29 March 1985.

D. Bar Kayetenia: Ramón Oñederra (*Kattu*) shot dead, 19 December 1983.

E. Bar Batxoki: Karmele Martínez Otegi and her daughter Nagore (3), Juan Luis Zabaleta and his daughter Ainitze (5), and Frédéric Haramboure wounded, 8 February, 1986.

F. Bar Lagunekin: Gotzón (Ángel) Zabaleta and Josu Amantes seriously wounded, 4 March 1985.

G. Bar Victor Hugo: Santos Blanco shot dead, 27 June 1985.

Dirty War, Clean Hands

To Trish,
With Love and Gratitude

Prologue:

the view from a Basque balcony

This is a political story, but it has personal roots. Since its subject, political violence, is bitterly contentious, it may be helpful to try to expose those roots at this stage, so that the reader will have some idea where this writer is coming from.

As far as I can tell, the roots of this book began to grow in a taxi in Barcelona in 1995, when I heard on the radio how the broken, tortured bones of two young Basque radicals had been identified in Alicante. They had been unearthed from a quicklime grave ten years earlier, and had lain in a mortuary ever since, until a bright policeman linked them to a 'disappearance' in the Basque Country. The dirty war of the 1980s, waged by a shadowy group known as the GAL, suddenly became a story I felt compelled to find out about, and write about.

If that was when the roots of the book began to sprout in my mind, the seeds had been sown well before the GAL death squads began to make their grim mark on Spanish politics. I remember in particular one grey afternoon in the Basque city of Bilbao, in the early spring of 1976.

That afternoon, fires had been lit on the bridge leading into central Bilbao from the student quarter of Deusto. I was teaching English there at the time, and sharing a flat with half a dozen student revolutionaries of one kind or another. They belonged to rival but friendly groups – communists, Maoists, socialists and anarcho-hippies. Such domestic alliances were quite common among Spanish students at that time. I had only just graduated from a left-wing student background in Dublin, and I felt pretty much at home in this company.

I was aware, however, that one key element of the anti-Franco opposition was missing from our little fraternity: there were no Basque nationalists among us. And there were no supporters of ETA (Euskadi Ta Askatasuna – Basque Homeland and Liberty), the best known and most controversial of all the organisations fighting the dictatorship. A chasm divided Basque leftists into *españolistas* ('pro-Spanish', those who saw Madrid as their capital) and *abertzales* ('patriots', who saw the Basque Country as a completely separate entity). This divide was not easily bridged, even in the flexible camaraderie of a student flat.

On 3 March, a few days before the afternoon in question, Spanish police had shot dead five striking workers in Vitoria, another Basque provincial capital. They had first used tear-gas and rubber bullets to flush the strikers out of the church where they had peacefully assembled, and finished the job with lead bullets on the church steps. The first post-Franco government was showing itself to be as contemptuous of elementary democratic principles as the old dictator, who had died the previous November.

The fires in Bilbao were part of a countrywide effort by demonstrators to draw the heat from Vitoria, which had been under a virtual state of siege by the police since the massacre. Our fourth-floor flat was less than five minutes' walk from the bridge, and though the bridge itself was out of sight, the black smoke from burning tires was clearly visible from our balcony. I was standing out there, watching the smoke with a flatmate called Julián, when we noticed that some youths were attempting to build a barricade in the street almost directly below us. They were laboriously dragging parked cars into position to break the wave of riot police which, sooner rather than later, would come surging through the *barrio*.

A hundred yards away, a municipal policeman also saw what the youths were up to. He began to amble towards them, tugging rather hesitantly at his clumsy white pistol holster. The municipal police were not usually directly involved in the maintenance of what the regime called public order. The democratic opposition called it repression. Generally speaking, the municipal police, with their absurd white Keystone Kops helmets, were only concerned with minor theft and parking fines.

This man, however, clearly felt he could not stand idly by while barricades were being built. Yet his reluctance to intervene was palpable from his start-stop approach. The demonstrators ignored his warning shouts, and continued to lug, lever and bounce the stationary cars across the road. The policeman continued his shuffling advance, and would soon pass directly under our feet. At this point my flatmate did something which put the heart across me.

For some reason, the heavy steel hub of a car wheel was among the items on our balcony. To my amazement, Julián picked it up and raised it above his head, making as if to throw it down on the hapless policeman's head. When I tried to dissuade him – or at least persuade him not to decapitate the unfortunate man until I had had a chance to escape from the flat – he melodramatically declared: 'If he shoots, I'll give it to him.'

'Julián,' I said, 'he's not going to shoot. He can hardly get his gun out, for God's sake. He's only bluffing . . . '

Happily, at about this point the demonstrators opted for discretion over valour, and conflict was averted. Oblivious to the threat from above his head, the policeman buttoned up his holster and headed off to quieter streets, no doubt relieved that words had sufficed to uphold public order on this occasion. Julián put the hub back down, while I berated him for putting all of us at risk for the sake of a futile and potentially lethal gesture.

This anticlimax made the incident appear less dramatic, and a lot less frightening, than a number of other encounters I had with street violence during those turbulent years. Yet it nagged at the back of my mind for long afterwards, precisely because it made so little sense. Of all the student revolutionaries I knew, Julián was the least overtly militant. He was some sort of bright spark in the local Socialist Party, but they were the least violently inclined left-wingers around.

The radical Basque nationalists of ETA were demonstrably and efficiently committed to armed struggle. I had little doubt that one or two of our Maoist friends would crack a policeman's skull happily enough in the heat of a street battle. Even a mainstream Communist might forget his party's national reconciliation policy under pressure, and throw a brick with the best of them. But neither Julián nor his Socialist Party colleagues had much reputation as heroes of the barricades. He was, then, the last person I would have expected to see ready to maim or kill. It would take me a long time to learn how wrong I was, to learn that terror can come from many directions, for many reasons.

Over the years, as I learned more about Julián's real loyalties, I began to wonder whether his behaviour that afternoon reflected the suspicions that some of our friends had quietly expressed about him. One or two people had whispered to me that, on the rare occasions when the police raided Socialist Party meetings locally, Julián always seemed to have left a few minutes earlier. Was it possible that Julián was that mythical beast, the *agent provocateur*, testing the presence of violent inclinations in his Irish flatmate? It seemed far-fetched; it still does. It would take a series of much more far-fetched and terrible incidents, at which I was fortunate enough *not* to be present, to put that scene on the balcony into context.

I returned to Ireland that summer, and Julián and his girlfriend paid me a visit. I remember very little about their stay except that my parents surprised me by according the couple a remarkable privilege, which neither I nor my Irish friends would have dreamed of asking for at the time. They were allowed to share a room. Even for my relatively liberal parents, any whiff of unmarried cohabitation, at least under their own roof, was sulphurous. But they spontaneously applied different criteria to Julián. Was it because Julián was foreign, and therefore not subject to our customs, or was it because he was simply so good at getting away with things? He had an easy charm which exuded innocence and sincerity. I imagine my parents simply assumed that he and his girlfriend would sleep chastely in separate beds.

In 1978 I moved back to Spain or, more precisely, to the Spanish Basque Country. I taught English in Fuenterrabía, a fishing and holiday village on the mouth of the Bidasoa estuary. This river separates – or unites, depending on one's point of view – the French and Spanish Basque Countries. I also began to report for *The Irish Times* on the tense and volatile Basque conflict.

At the time, Spain as a whole was going through a remarkable transition, more by consensus than conflict, from dictatorship to democracy. A new Constitution had been painstakingly drawn up. It somehow encompassed both the conservative concerns of Franco's political heirs and the democratic aspirations of his enemies, including Spain's remarkably moderate Communist Party. The right to private property was safeguarded, there would be 'co-operation' with the Catholic Church, and the state would take the form of a monarchy. It would be a parliamentary monarchy, however, with an unequivocal commitment to popular sovereignty, democracy and what the Spanish call the *Estado de Derecho* – roughly translatable as 'the rule of law'.[1] This last concept was the touchstone of the transition: after forty years of capricious and arbitrary government, the Spanish wanted the same laws to apply to their rulers as applied to ordinary citizens. This book is an examination of how that admirable dream panned out against reality over the next twenty years.

Vexed questions were carefully balanced in this Constitution. For the consensus to work – with the unthinkable prospect of a replay of the Civil War if it didn't – it was often necessary to have it both ways. Thus, the sentence which proclaimed 'the unity of the Spanish Nation' was qualified by the recognition of minority 'nationalities' (like the Basques and Catalans). These peoples were guaranteed the right to form autonomous governments with extensive regional powers. Ominously, however, in the view of many, the armed forces retained a 'mission' to defend the territorial integrity of Spain, defined in the Constitution as 'indissoluble' and 'indivisible'. At first sight that might seem innocuous, even axiomatic. What else do armed forces do, after all? To Basque nationalists, though, it had the smell of giving the army the role of a government in the shadows, not directed at external enemies, but a last bastion to prevent regional self-government going too far. The autonomy promised to the Basques under this Constitution was anathema to the Right generally, and to the army in particular, but it fell short of what most Basques wanted: the right to self-determination, with an option on full independence.

The crucial referendum on the new Constitution took place on 6 December 1978. The Spanish people as a whole approved it by a significant majority, almost two-thirds of the electoral census. In sharp contrast, less than one-third of Basques voted 'Yes'.[2] Abstention, actively campaigned for by most Basque nationalist groups, was 55 per cent among the Basques, close to twice the national average. The Basque 'No' vote, as a percentage of participants, was triple the overall 'No' result. Among the minority of Basques who did turn out to vote, the 'Yes' option still had a comfortable three-to-one majority, but the massive level of abstention cast a heavy shadow over the legitimacy of the new Constitution in the Basque Country. A fissure had opened up between Basque nationalists and the rest of the Spanish state at the dawn of the new democracy. This fissure has had consequences for that democracy's healthy development, which are still unresolved.

Basque radicals could argue – as they do to this day – that the Constitution has not been endorsed by the majority of their people. In their view, therefore, ETA's violent campaign is a legitimate, even necessary, form of resistance to the 'undemocratic' imposition of an alien state structure. Meanwhile, the vast majority of Spanish democrats, including many Basques, hold that the Basques should abide by the decision of the overall majority within the existing state borders.

Moreover, abstention being a double-edged weapon, they point out that only a quarter of the Basques who did go to the polls actually cast their vote *against* the Constitution. They also argue that, since a majority of Basques voted in favour of a Statute of Autonomy based on this Constitution in another referendum only ten months later, the 1978 Constitution has been retrospectively ratified in the Basque Country.[3]

Far-Right elements in the armed forces, their political power now stripped away, found the intransigent Basques a convenient excuse for continuing in their old ways. It was not just that Basque demonstrators would continue to be treated with an iron fist more appropriate to the fascist past than the democratic future. Rightist die-hards also waged a full-scale dirty war against ETA's escalating terrorist campaign.[4] Only fifteen days after the constitutional referendum, José Miguel Beñarán Ordeñana (*Argala*),[5] an ETA leader living in the French Basque Country, switched on his car and blew himself to bits. The explosive charge wired to his ignition allegedly came courtesy of the Spanish security forces, acting through a death squad made up of right-wing foreign mercenaries.[6] Five years earlier, almost to the day, Beñarán Ordeñana had personally wired the bomb which blew Franco's hard-line Prime Minister and designated successor, Carrero Blanco, over an apartment block. Franco's most loyal supporters were carrying a legacy of vengeful memories, and a potent paramilitary infrastructure, into the new democracy.

In 1974, within a year of Carrero Blanco's assassination, a significant split occurred in ETA. One group, the 'political-military' faction of ETA, or ETA(p-m), accepted that the basic conditions of democracy had been created. Its leaders embarked on policies which would, by the early 1980s, bring most of its members home from underground, exile or prison, and into normal politics. The other group, the 'military' faction of ETA, or ETA(m), insisted that ETA was involved in a justified war of independence against Spanish occupation. Its response to a hard-won amnesty which finally emptied every Spanish jail of Basque prisoners in December 1977 was the killing of a municipal councillor.[7] Needless to say, the jails soon filled up again. In pursuit of the withdrawal of the 'occupation forces', and a referendum on self-determination, ETA(m) dramatically stepped up the rhythm of its attacks. Its list of 'legitimate targets' grew longer and longer, including many civilian 'agents of the state' as well as the security forces. All the elements of a long and continuing political tragedy were in place.

As I covered these developments, I occasionally wondered what had happened to Julián. I had heard that he was, with many of his contemporaries, racing up the fast track of the Socialist Party bureaucracy, but no one I knew seemed to see him any more.

The only time I saw him again myself for many years was at a funeral in October 1979. A young Socialist welder and trade unionist, Germán González López, had been killed by a splinter group from ETA, the Comandos Autónomos. They accused him of being a police informer. He was the first victim of terrorism after the referendum in which the Basques had approved the Statute of Autonomy, and the Comandos Autónomos attacked all the parties that had supported the statute in the communiqué which claimed the killing.

Aware that this attack on a party member – and on the political process itself – was a potentially dangerous escalation from the targeting of the security forces, all the democratic political parties active in the Basque Country turned out for the ceremony. The funeral Mass in the fishing village of Zumaia, with anthems in the ancient and mysterious Basque language, was conducted in a baroque cavern of a church meshed in candlelight and shadow. It was deeply moving, as was the subsequent demonstration. The mourners marched around the village to the victim's home, and sang both the *Internationale* and the Basque Civil War song *Eusko Gudariak* in heart-breaking harmonies, before dispersing in silence into the night.[8]

I turned away into a narrow street, and there was Julián. Stouter than I remembered him, dressed in a sober gabardine and accompanied by big men in similar garb, he looked prosperous and somehow *serious,* a man already at home in the grown-up world of power. He had moved on, I had heard, from being private secretary to the Basque Socialist leader to becoming the mayor of an industrial town. He greeted me solemnly, as befitted the occasion, about which we exchanged polite banalities, and he moved on, with his entourage.

Many years later, I would learn that his stewardship as mayor had been a stormy one, on at least two counts. These were allegations never substantiated, that he had been, at the very least, careless with the municipal cash register, whose contents had slipped into his pockets in greater quantities than the amounts agreed on his payslips. And he had been indiscreet, to the point of recklessness, in making belligerent comments about ETA. 'I would sort [ETA] out in four days, practising "two for one",' he used to say. His fellow councillors understood this to mean killing two ETA members for every one of ETA's victims.[9] He made it clear to his intimates that he wasn't talking about upping the conviction rate for terrorism. He was contemplating fighting fire with fire.

That decision would indeed be his to take, and sooner than most people expected. On 28 October 1982, the Socialist Party, led by the forty-year-old Felipe González, swept away the disintegrating coalition of reconstructed Francoists and Christian Democrats which had ruled Spain since 1977. It was a landslide victory, and a landmark: the long-haired generation of the Sixties had come in from the streets and taken over the national parliament. This was the youngest government Spain had ever had, and one of the youngest in Europe. Not one of its members could be tarred with the ugly brush of the dictatorship. This was to be a real new start.

Julián Sancristóbal seemed to fit this mould perfectly, and the election victory catapulted him up a dizzying number of rungs in the state administration. On 28 December, before his thirtieth birthday, he was appointed Civil Governor of Vizcaya, the richest and most populous of the Basque provinces, whose capital is Bilbao. His inaugural reception, contemporary accounts tell us, shocked the police on duty on the doors. Many of the guests, it was said, had only previously been in the governor's imposing headquarters through another entrance, to pay political fines. They included the author of a savagely accurate biography of Franco which the new governor's predecessors would have burned in the street.

It may have been more significant, however, in terms of the sinister reputation that Sancristóbal was soon to acquire, that Luis Olarra was also on the guest list. Olarra was a leading member of the Bilbao business community who had prospered famously under Franco, and who now made no secret of his view that ETA's violence should be repaid in kind by the state. If the state would not get its hands dirty, he used to boast, there were private individuals who would.[10]

This was not the only contrast evident to a keen observer that evening. For the first time, the Basque national flag, the *ikurriña,* the object of fetishistic persecution by the police less than a decade earlier, flew alongside the Spanish flag outside the building. This seemed like welcome progress to many of the moderate Basque nationalists present. But some of them could not help asking themselves why they had to have a Civil Governor at all.

Along with the parallel figure of Military Governor, the position was redolent of a centralist and authoritarian administration. Its incumbents had been generally loathed under the previous regime, and especially so in areas like the Basque Country. The control of the police and the enforcement of the central government's wishes, both highly contentious matters in Vizcaya, figured high among the Civil Governor's responsibilities. The local nationalists, moderate and radical, did not have long to wait until they found out how the young Socialist wine would taste when poured from the old conservative cask.

Sancristóbal came to the job with a reputation as a skilful negotiator, a man of dialogue, but these qualities were not much in evidence in the thirteen months before he was called to even higher service. His concept of authority seemed rigid, in major and minor matters. He ordered the removal from a Bilbao plaza of a commemorative plaque to the ETA leader – and early death squad victim – Beñarán Ordeñana. He imperiously overruled Bilbao city council's democratic decision not to fly any flags during the city's fiestas. This decision had been taken to avoid conflict in what had become an annual 'battle of the flags', in which radicals tried to tear down Spanish flags which, according to the Constitution, should fly alongside Basque flags in public places. It seemed that the new Julián preferred conflict to compromise.

It was said that he was deeply influenced by certain police officers in making these unpopular decisions. In retrospect that is not surprising: it now seems probable that, behind the scenes, he was already at the heart of a security forces conspiracy to launch a dirty war against ETA, which would involve kidnapping, misuse of public funds, torture and murder.

This conspiracy called itself the GAL (Grupos Antiterroristas de Liberación – the Anti-terrorist Liberation Groups). Over the next four years, the GAL would claim twenty-seven mortal victims, nine of whom had no connection whatsoever with ETA. As many again would be injured, including very young children. Three months after the campaign started, Julián Sancristóbal was appointed Director of State Security, in charge of all the Spanish police forces, with special responsibility for anti-terrorist strategy. Eight months after the GAL campaign was wound down, he would be removed from this position. But, with a little help from his

Socialist colleagues, he would become almost immediately a very wealthy director of private financial enterprises.

He would soon fall much further than he had risen. His nemesis would be a former police officer with whom he had had a long and obscure relationship. According to some accounts, Sancristóbal was already a paid informer for this officer on that strange afternoon I had spent with him many years earlier, on that balcony in Bilbao. Superintendent José Amedo had been a flamboyant scourge of student revolutionaries in the 1970s, but when Julián became his boss in the 1980s, he found a role he really savoured, running some of the GAL death squads. In 1991 he and his deputy were sentenced to 108 years in prison for GAL operations. At first, he confidently expected a state pardon and maintained a wall of denial and silence. When he realised he had been scapegoated, he began to spill the beans on his superiors. The GAL cases were reopened, and after initial outraged denials, several successive links in the chain of command cracked, up to the former Director of State Security.

Nearly twenty years after Julián Sancristóbal had made as if to kill a municipal policeman from a balcony in Bilbao, he confessed to having organised the first action acknowledged by the GAL, the kidnapping of a middle-aged, terrified and completely innocent man. He told a judge that, knowing that his mercenaries had seized the wrong target from France, he decided to keep holding their unfortunate victim in miserable conditions, for reasons of political expediency. More sensationally, he said that he had asked for – and received – the blessing of the Minister for the Interior for this decision. And he added that such a blessing could not have been given without the knowledge and approval of the Spanish Prime Minister, Felipe González. The spectre of state terrorism was returning to haunt the most successful democratic government in Spanish history.

A few months before Sancristóbal confessed, I was attending a cultural conference in Barcelona. That was the moment when I heard, on the taxi radio, the news that two bodies had been identified in Alicante as those of Joxean Lasa and Joxi Zabala. These were two young ETA members who had disappeared or, as the Latin Americans tellingly put it, 'had been disappeared' in Bayonne some weeks before the GAL's first acknowledged kidnapping. No one had ever been charged with this crime, but the quality of the GAL's subsequent intelligence led their comrades to suspect that Lasa and Zabala had been interrogated by a GAL death squad, and then killed.

Unknown to their families, their bodies had been found, buried in quicklime, in the Alicante countryside, only two years later. The local coroner had never bothered to check missing persons outside his own province, 800 kilometres from the Basque Country, and decided that the bodies were the result of a shoot-out between international drug gangs. He wanted them buried in a common grave. The local pathologist, however, insisted that the remains be kept refrigerated. He was uneasy: the victims had not only been shot; there was strong forensic evidence that they had been brutally tortured, and that this torture had been accompanied by the use of psychoactive drugs. Ten years later, an Alicante policeman was reading newspaper reports of the reopening of the GAL trials and made a startling connection. Dental records were checked, and they matched up. The first victims of the GAL's dirty war had finally come to light.

I could not help wondering what my charming student friend Julián knew about this sort of operation. I decided to see what sense I could make of death squads operating under a democracy. The nature and consequences of those operations are the subject of this book.

***   ***   ***

Since we will be venturing into fiercely contested territory, where I do not believe that complete neutrality is either possible or desirable, I should first make my personal position clear on some of the main issues involved.

I accept that the Basques have the right to constitute themselves as a nation. The political form which that nation takes – autonomy or total independence – should, I believe, be decided democratically by the people who live in the Basque Country. (This, as usual in Basque politics, is far less simple than it sounds. If we are talking about a referendum, would it include Navarre and the French Basque provinces, or should they hold separate referenda? Basque nationalists themselves are often ambiguous, perhaps deliberately so, on this issue.)

I am opposed to the aggressive Spanish and French nationalisms which attempt to portray the Basque Country as just one more region of a greater nation, and which denigrate Basque culture as inferior to their own.[11] The existence and shape of the Spanish and French nations are not eternal verities, any more than the existence and shape of the Basque nation are. All nation-states are constructed politically by their inhabitants over time, and can legitimately be reconstructed (or even deconstructed) by their inhabitants, over time, through democratic means.

However, I am also opposed to the exclusive Basque nationalism which attempts to define citizenship on the basis of race, language or, more recently, political allegiance. All citizens of the Basque Country, regardless of ethnic origin or political views, have a democratic right to be considered Basque, and to participate fully in Basque democracy.

Terrorism is a term which will crop up on almost every page of this book. It is a very highly charged word, but I think it can be defined quite simply. I understand terrorism as the use of violence for political ends, in a situation where the essential democratic liberties – the rule of law and the freedoms of speech, association and representation – are in operation. I believe that the use of violence can be justified when such liberties are suppressed by the state, as was the case in apartheid South Africa. The violence of the African National Congress (ANC) under those conditions can no more be properly called terrorism than could the actions of the Resistance in Nazi-occupied France.

Some commentators, and much popular opinion, add a further criterion, even under circumstances where violence is held to be justified. This is the distinction between legitimate and terrorist targets. Thus a selective ANC attack on South African security personnel would not be termed terrorism, but an indiscriminate bomb attack by the same organisation on a bar crowded with civilians would. I accept this point, but feel it does recall the ironic observation made by the Irish writer (and 1940s IRA bomber) Brendan Behan: the man with a big bomb is a statesman, while the man with a small bomb is a terrorist. There is a degree to which *all* weapons of mass destruction, great and small, could be called terrorist.

On the other hand, there is undoubtedly a case for not using the word 'terrorism' at all: 'If all sorts of murders, kidnappings, threats, civil wars, government crimes, killings by secret or underground organisations, paramilitary executions, and so on, were simply called by those names, without ever using the word "terrorism", would there be something missing in the description of the real world?' This question is asked by Joseba Zulaika and William A. Douglass in *Terror and Taboo*. It is provocatively put, but the answer may lie in the fact that these authors use the word repeatedly, though always with careful qualifications, throughout their own book.[12]

Grant Wardlaw, an Australian academic specialist in terrorism theory, argues that writers should 'apply the term terrorism even-handedly to governments, groups and individuals'.[13] This point is crucial to the thesis of this book, where 'terrorism' will be used to describe not only violence by revolutionary movements within a democracy, but also the illegitimate use of violence by the servants of the democratic state.

In the particular case of Franco's dictatorship, I once believed that ETA's revolutionary violence was justifiable as long as the dictatorship existed. With the benefit of hindsight, I am now increasingly inclined to the view that ETA's venture into armed struggle was a strategic error, which has resulted in a perilous 'sacramentalisation' of violence in Basque politics. But it was not easy to see that at the time. With the transition to democracy, I saw no justification for ETA's violence, which became clearly terrorist under the definition I have suggested. It lacked – and lacks – any democratic mandate. But, to complicate matters, it does enjoy the support of a significant minority of Basques who think of themselves as democrats.

Reprehensible as ETA's terrorism has been, I do not believe that the democratic state has any mandate to use terror against terrorism, however much it has been provoked. The state which launches a dirty war undermines its own legitimacy, and becomes the very thing which it claims to abhor. I believe that the dirty war against ETA was repugnant in principle, and disastrous in practice. It has revealed that Spain's transition to democracy, fêted as exemplary in many quarters, and certainly admirable in many respects, had a very dark side, which has still not been entirely exorcised. I agreed with the assessment made by Gabriel Jackson, writing in *El País* at the beginning of 1997: 'Between ETA and the legacy of the GAL, Spanish democracy is in serious danger for the first time since the end of Franco's dictatorship.'[14] Things do not look quite so bleak in 2000, with many senior GAL leaders brought to justice. Many questions, however, remain to be answered.

It is still too early to say whether the massive, and scrupulously democratic, response to ETA's killing of a young town councillor, Miguel Ángel Blanco, in the summer of 1997 marked a truly significant break in the corrosive dynamic of terror and counter-terror.[15] ETA's renewed terrorist campaign in 2000 suggests otherwise.

It was striking that the dominant visual symbol of those great civic expressions of revulsion against ETA was 'clean hands': thousands of demonstrators painted their palms white and raised them in a gesture of innocence. On the positive side, the refusal of the centre-Right Partido Popular government to be drawn into a dirty war response to ETA's relentless campaign against its local councillors over the ensuing twelve months strongly suggests that a lesson has been learned from the GAL debacle.[16]

On the other hand, it was depressing to note that, while peaceful anti-ETA street demonstrations in the wake of the Blanco killing were still going on, Felipe González was using the crisis to publicly thank some of his discredited former colleagues from the Interior Ministry for their 'services to Spain'.[17] These were men who, in several cases, faced very serious charges for GAL crimes, and would subsequently be convicted. Their hands were far from clean, and Felipe González has often appeared to praise them for being prepared to get their hands dirty in the name of 'Spain'. The PSOE's response to these court rulings indicates that many party leaders are still 'in denial', as it were, on the issue. The unfinished business of the GAL trials continues to fracture and corrode Spanish democratic institutions.

Within these parameters, I have tried to expose the complex narrative of these obscure events as clearly as possible, through a survey of the extensive documentary evidence now available. I have also tried to give this narrative a human voice, or rather human voices, through speaking directly to the GAL's surviving victims, and to the relatives and friends of those who were less fortunate. For the same reason, I have talked to those involved in the subsequent political, legal and media battles, as well as to those GAL protagonists who were willing to talk to me.

The GAL's war is a small entry in the annals of contemporary atrocities, but it is not a minor one. In terms of scale, it does not compare to the dirty wars in Latin America or Algeria. The GAL's twenty-seven mortal victims, and thirty-odd wounded, represent only about a quarter of the casualties caused by ETA over the same period, and a much smaller fraction of the eight hundred or so people killed by ETA since 1968. But each victim is a victim too many, and the victims of the GAL, we are now reasonably sure, were killed or injured by those from whom they should have been able to expect all the protection of the democratic rule of law. That it is possible to name most of the protagonists and all the victims, and to speak to many of them face to face, may make it possible to comprehend the significance of this black episode in Spanish democracy.

I hope that the story which follows goes some way to explaining why one of the most charismatic and talented political leaders in recent European history, the former Spanish Prime Minister Felipe González, may yet be best remembered for either tolerating or masterminding a network of death squads. And I hope it explains how and why large sections of Spanish political and public opinion, only recently liberated from a dictatorship which had systematically used torture, murder and terror against democrats, came to justify the use of terror, murder and torture in the name of democracy.

This political culture, apparently mature and sophisticated, often seemed to have only two responses to state terrorism. Some people outspokenly espoused the dirty war, explicitly endorsing vengeance and reprisal as preferable to the rule of law. Others, probably a majority of Spanish public opinion at the time, believed a blind eye should be turned to the activities of the death squads, on the principle that the end would justify the means. Both groups would modify or reverse their positions only as evidence emerged that the state's chosen counter-terrorists were sometimes inefficient and usually corrupt.

The Spanish/Basque experience shows, I believe, that when democracies break their own best rules to fight terrorism, democracies always lose, and lose badly, in principle and in practice. This is the position always defended by a small but coherent and honourable minority in Spain and in the Basque Country. But perhaps what is most remarkable in this story is how that minority, through extraordinary integrity, courage and persistence, have persuaded the institutions of democracy to apply the rule of law to the highest in the land. The dirty war was a blight on Spain's democracy, but, in bringing its protagonists to the courts, Spain is teaching the world a lesson in democratic practice.

NOTES

1 See 'Some Notes on the Spanish Constitution, Judiciary and Legal System', p. 44.

2 Nothing is straightforward in this territory, as we will see in ch. 1. The 'Basques' referred to here are the inhabitants of Guipúzcoa, Vizcaya and Álava, which ultimately formed the Basque Autonomous Community in 1980. Navarre, one of the provinces considered an integral part of the Basque Country by Basque nationalists, has a majority which does not have a strong sense of Basque identity, and has stayed outside the Basque Autonomous Community. Navarre's voting pattern in the constitutional referendum was much closer to the Spanish average than to the other three provinces. And there are another three Basque provinces in France where nationalist feeling was, until very recently, extremely muted, and which had no right to participate in a Spanish referendum in any case. The referendum results are analysed in greater detail in ch. 3.

3 The radicals' counter-argument is that, faced with a choice between autonomy and nothing, it is not surprising that most Basques voted for the Statute of Autonomy, but that this vote does not represent any retrospective endorsement of the Constitution.

4 ETA killed thirty-four people in the last eight years of the Franco period (1968–75), and 160 in the two years following the establishment of the democratic Constitution (1979–80). See Robert P. Clark, 'Patterns of ETA Violence: 1968–1980', in Peter Merkl (ed.), *Political Violence and Terror* (Berkeley: University of California Press, 1986), p. 134. One of the most puzzling and disturbing features of the Basque conflict is the fact that ETA's use of indiscriminate terrorism accelerated with every democratic reform in Spain. See chs. 2–4 for a detailed analysis of this phenomenon.

5 ETA members are widely known, even to the general public, by their *noms de guerre*. Thus *Argala* was the code-name of José Miguel Beñarán Ordeñana.

6 Ricardo Arques and Melchor Miralles, *Amedo: El Estado contra ETA*

(Barcelona: Plaza y Janés/Cambio 16, 1989), pp. 72–82, gives a detailed account of the genesis, composition and *modus operandi* of the squad which killed Beñarán Ordeñana. These details, however, have never been independently confirmed. See also ch. 3, p. 53.

7   Patxo Unzueta, 'Euskadi: Amnistía y Vuelta a Empezar', in Santos Juliá et al. (eds.), *Memoria de la Transición* (Madrid: Taurus, 1996), p. 282.

8   The singing of a left-wing anthem by conservative Basque nationalists, and of a nationalist anthem by the Socialist Party, was still possible in 1979, when the tradition of a relatively united opposition to Francoism was still a recent memory. The rift between the Madrid-based Left and democratic Basque nationalism has become so deep in the intervening years that it is inconceivable today.

9   *El Mundo,* 9 January 1995.

10   Olarra was, of course, fully entitled to attend such a reception purely in his capacity as a representative of the Vizcayan business association. There is no evidence that he ever participated in dirty war activities. But his intemperate and very public threats to hire mafiosi to avenge any successful attack on himself or his family provided a useful cover for the death squads, when they wanted to suggest that their sponsors were in the business sector rather than the Interior Ministry.

11   Such French and Spanish nationalism, while experienced as aggressive by Basque nationalists, may be quite unconscious in those who propagate it. I have often heard cultured and liberally minded Spaniards say they simply cannot understand why the Basques should want to maintain their language as a medium of daily communication. Spanish, after all, is so much more *useful.* If one suggests to these people that, for similar reasons of utility, they should abandon Spanish and speak English – or Chinese – in the twenty-first century, they are, naturally, deeply offended. Our sense of our own national identity is often only visible to us when it is under threat or challenge.

12   Joseba Zulaika and William A. Douglass, *Terror and Taboo* (London: Routledge, 1996), pp. 102–3.

13   Grant Wardlaw, *Political Terrorism,* 2nd edn (Cambridge: Cambridge University Press, 1989), p. 8.

14   *El País*, 24 January 1997.

15   Miguel Ángel Blanco was a young conservative (Partido Popular) town councillor for Ermua in the Basque Country. He was kidnapped in July 1997 by ETA, who threatened to shoot him if the government did not move its prisoners closer to the Basque Country within forty-eight hours. His killing sparked the biggest anti-ETA demonstrations ever seen in Spain.

16   Five Partido Popular councillors, and one of their wives, were killed before ETA's ceasefire in September 1998. This was one of the most sustained campaigns against the members of a political party in ETA's history. One of ETA's first actions, on renewing terrorist operations in 2000, was to kill a Socialist Party leader, Fernando Buesa, and the group has subsequently renewed its campaign against the Partido Popular as well.

17   *El Mundo*, 16 July 1997.

PART I

An Ancient People, A Modern Conflict

1

'Only 5,000 Years Ago':

a country where the past is always present

The small resorts of the Côte Basque are best known abroad as the epitome of the chic tourism of another era. The names of Biarritz and Bayonne evoke images of exquisite maritime cuisine, elegant promenades overlooking the Bay of Biscay, discreet casinos and intimate hotels. Some parts of these towns still exude the faded, padded comforts of sedate bourgeois holidays.

The area had its tourist heyday from the late nineteenth century until the 1950s, but in recent years the discerning rich have returned to the region in small numbers, and the middle classes of France and Europe fill the campsites in the pleasant green hinterland. One of the great attractions of the area is its superb food. But when you first sample *la nouvelle cuisine Basque,* you may be bewildered by some strange and very unFrench names on the menu, like *txangurro* and *txacoli.* These names are reminders of the hidden codes which lie at the roots of a bloody conflict in Spain, though many French Basques would rather ignore it.

Names like *txangurro* (spider crab) and *txacoli* (a refreshing, greenish wine, made locally) are taken from Euskera, the Basque language. Euskera is arguably the oldest and most enigmatic European language west of the Urals, and certainly one of the most difficult to learn. It is a language where *ez* means 'no' and *bai* means 'yes', where the number eight is called *bederatzi,* and where double consonants like 'tz', 'tx' and 'tp' seem to crop up twice in every sentence, and sometimes twice in the same word. Euskera does not belong to the Indo-European family of languages. It is one of several unique distinguishing marks of a people whose identity is their pride, and their Calvary, though some would say that the contemporary Basque crucifixion is self-inflicted.

The origins of the Basque people are both obscure and, to an outsider, oddly contentious. 'For few peoples of the world, and surely no other in Europe', writes Roger Collins, 'can the scholarly study of their origins and earliest history be of such direct and contemporary importance, linked at not many removes to political debate and even terrorism.'[1] His own work is the epitome of careful research, balancing scant evidence against informed speculation, but he must be well aware that such an approach guarantees no immunity in the virulent atmosphere of Basque cultural politics and political culture. 'A politicisation of normally abstruse and *recherché* anthropological arguments about the Stone Age is a distinctive feature of the ideological underpinning of modern Basque nationalism', he continues. 'Few statements relating to the people, their history and their language can be treated as politically neutral.'[2]

Few statements? None at all, would be a more accurate reflection of the painfully acute sensitivities which this topic touches. Add to these local feelings the fiercely proprietorial attitude which many foreign Basquophiles bring to their work and the mixture becomes explosive. 'There can be few parts of the world about which so many wild and inaccurate statements have been made, and so much irresponsible and unauthoritative literature has been written', Rodney Gallop fumed in *A Book of the Basques*.[3] His study is a charming if patronising account of Basque folklore which, in the nature of things, carries a few inaccuracies of its own.

Plunging into this maelstrom, this chapter seeks to give the reader some orientation in the Basque landscape, physical, cultural and political, as the essential background to the events which are the subject of this book. Two very early personal and contrasting impressions – one rural and the other urban – may help set the scene.

I first arrived in the Basque Country in the dark, off the Paris train into San Sebastián, one evening in October 1975. *En route*, I recall a long customs halt at the grimy border station of Irún, where the shadows seemed to teem with police and, just a little further back, with prostitutes. The tense gloom was almost theatrically appropriate. Franco was on his deathbed – he would die six weeks later – and all of Spain was holding its breath.

I hitchhiked out towards Bilbao early the next morning, before the unpretentious elegance of San Sebastián could make much impression on me. My first lift left me standing in the early morning sunlight in a scene that, but for the busy main road, could have been set in the Middle Ages.

Below the highway, the green fields fell away sharply to the sea, where twisted slate promontories jutted out at crazy angles into the Bay of Biscay. Between them stretched generous arcs of sandy beaches, swept by Atlantic waves. Above me, similar small but irregularly shaped fields rose steeply to a small village, dominated by a church which seemed big enough to be a cathedral. It looked like a great stone ship, moored to the hill high above the ocean. Its hollow bell tolled the hour. The sound conjured half-remembered, half-imagined worlds, drowning the even more suggestive background ripple of cowbells. In the fields, a stout little farmer was prodding a brace of oxen, linked by a colourfully tasselled wooden yoke, up an impossible slope. Another man was scything at an equally awkward angle, with a kind of stolid grace. The sharp tang of cut grass carried across the motorway, where a car was stopping to bring me to Bilbao.

Along the way I saw several very messy industrial towns in an otherwise Arcadian landscape, but nothing that could have prepared me for that megalopolis of filth and misery. Workers' apartment blocks were scattered across the hills like grubby handkerchiefs as we approached. They soon joined up to form narrow, dark streets. Glimpsed below us through the smog, the river Nervión arrived in the city a sickly green from the industries upstream. I would soon learn that, by the time it had wound its way through 15 kilometres of metallurgical effluent and poor sewerage, it would be boldly streaked with rust, finally spreading out beyond the port as a brown stain on the sea beyond. Stepping out of the car, the city's noxious air slapped its way damply into my lungs. It felt like living in a launderette where everyone smoked. Every passer-by seemed to be coughing. When night fell, the dim and patchy street lighting, combined with the saturation presence of mechanised police, made the whole place look like some film set for a fascist Hades. The idyll of the countryside seemed to belong to another world, and another century.

It did not, of course. The village I had so superficially observed was then the home of a very modern terrorist unit, which would shortly kidnap and ultimately kill a Basque industrialist. The luckier of Bilbao's inhabitants had relatives, or even second houses, in the countryside, and for many of them it was a rich source of political symbols, however remote it might be from their daily lives. The relationship of city to country in the Basque Country has long been an unusually unstable blend of conflict and interdependence.

Modern Basque nationalism developed at the end of the last century, when rapid urban industrialisation seemed to threaten the rural-based economic and cultural value system to which many Basques were deeply attached. Critics of nationalism, from both the Left and Right, point out how 'artificial' some aspects of this nationalism were. The founding father of Basque nationalism, Sabino Arana, had to invent not only a flag but also a name, Euskadi, for the country he wished to free from Spanish domination. Such critics also point out that, at no time since the eleventh century, and then only briefly, have the Basques been governed by a Basque leader in a single political unit.

This, however, is only to say that nations are constructed by their constituent peoples, and are not ahistorical absolutes handed down by God, a point the Left at least should be able to understand. Most nations look more than a little ridiculous in the first phase of construction, when the raw mortar of rhetoric and myth is most apparent. The key questions are: do the people who decide to constitute themselves as a nation have adequate building materials? Does the political weather in their region permit them to erect the structure they want? A third question is particularly relevant in the Basque Country: can non-nationalist citizens share the new national space in equal conditions with nationalists?

As we shall see, the Basques were exceptionally well endowed in the first respect, but the second and third questions have proved much more problematic. Regardless of that, Basque nationalism is now here to stay. Since 1980, nationalist parties have dominated the powerful autonomous government which runs three of the four Spanish provinces claimed by Basque nationalism.[4] Moreover, the acceptance of this autonomous structure by all the major Spanish parties is a signal concession to a key nationalist demand. The Basques, like the Catalans and Galicians, are implicitly recognised as a 'nationality' in the 1978 Spanish Constitution.[5]

That is not enough for some nationalists, who pursue total Basque independence, and reject the Constitution's prior insistence on 'the indissoluble unity of the Spanish Nation'. Over twenty years after the transition to democracy, the Basque terrorist organisation ETA, which demands a totally independent Basque state, is still supported by about 15 per cent of the electorate. When the process of nation-building fails to achieve a full consensus, the combustible nature of the building materials and the instability of the political weather both become very apparent. That is the 'Basque problem', which underlies the specific conflict described in the rest of this book.

Like many nation-builders, the early Basque nationalists chose their ethnic identity as their first building block. Sabino Arana, as we shall see in more detail later in this chapter, expressed this identity in primarily racial terms, indeed in terms which would be described today as racist in the most offensive sense. Leaving aside this mode of expression, which has been largely – though not entirely – discarded by most of his successors, the persistence of the Basque race in one region over thousands of years is itself a remarkable historical fact. It seems likely that no other European people, small or large, has inhabited the same place for so long. Quite how long, of course, is a point where we could get detained by the 'abstruse and *recherché* anthropological arguments about the Stone Age' referred to above.

These arguments turn on arcane issues, such as the extent to which a few fragments of 11,000-year-old human skulls might establish a Basque presence on the Pyrenees at that period. The idea that the Basques predate the other peoples of the Iberian peninsula, and that this copperfastens their right to nationhood, has been something of an obsession with some nationalist anthropologists and historians. They may have been influenced by a tradition in Basque studies of making extravagant and absolute claims, a tradition established long before nationalism as we know it was conceived. One sixteenth-century Basque cleric declared that Euskera was the tongue spoken in the Garden of Eden. One of his more modest successors was happy to settle for just one of the seventy languages spoken on Earth prior to the erection of the Tower of Babel.

The origin of the Basques, and of their non-Indo-European language, is still a mystery, if not a sacred one. However, linguists have tentatively established relationships with languages spoken in the Caucasus. There may also be a connection with the Berbers, so it is possible to imagine a great migration of a mountain people many millennia ago, which left remnants on the Pyrenees and Atlas ranges. For our purposes, it should be enough to point out what is *not* disputed.

The Basques have occupied an inverted triangle on either side of the north-west third of the Pyrenees for at least two thousand years, and very probably much longer. In historical times, this territory has extended roughly 160 kilometres from contemporary Bilbao to Bayonne along the coast. Inland, the southern limits run, again approximately, along the river Ebro to Tudela on the Spanish side, up to the Pic d'Anie on the Pyrenees, and then across to Mauleon in France, making a total area of a little more than 20,000 square kilometres. The Cantabrian mountains, intersecting with the Pyrenees parallel to the coast, make this a doubly mountainous region. Even the lower lying areas tend to be very hilly, the characteristic Basque rural landscape consisting of steep interlocking spurs.

Rainfall is heavy, giving the palette of most of the region a range of greens which Ireland might envy. The great exception is the flat, brownish-grey expanse of the Navarran and Álavan irrigated plain, which, geographically speaking, is part of the Castilian plateau. The earth generally is not particularly rich, but has been intensively and successfully cultivated. The coast is endowed with many good natural harbours, and the Basques have fished cornucopian maritime harvests, both locally and much further afield, for many centuries.

Very significant iron deposits around Bilbao have also been exploited for many centuries – there is a reference in Shakespeare to 'Bilbos', a name for iron swords and manacles, derived from the Basque name for the city. Dense forests provided the other vital element for a dynamic shipbuilding industry. The Basques' maritime prowess served them well. They held key positions in the Spanish imperial navy. They also took full advantage of their strategic location for trade with England and Flanders, whose advanced economies contrasted sharply with the stagnation of the Castilian hinterland. In the late nineteenth and early twentieth century, iron ore would be the basis for a major industrial revolution, closely linked to the take-off of the British steel industry. The population of the whole region today is just under three million, with less than 300,000 on the French side of the border.

The three historical provinces north of the contemporary Spanish–French border are Zuberoa, Lapurdi and Benafarroa (Soule, Labourd and Basse Navarre in French). The four historical provinces south of that divide are Bizkaia, Araba, Gipuzkoa and Nafarroa (Vizcaya, Álava, Guipúzcoa and Navarra in Spanish).

Unfortunately, that is about it, as far as generally accepted information is concerned. Almost everything else is open to question. Even the use of names is contentious. To use the Basque as opposed to the Spanish or French versions, or vice versa, is often read as taking a political position.[6] Some eagle-eyed Basque nationalists would take exception to the above reference to even geographical kinship between Navarre and Castile. Their political opponents would be quick to point out that Navarre itself is no longer administratively a part of the Basque Country at all. That said, and bearing in mind these daunting pitfalls, what follows is an attempt to give a fair synthesis of the development of Basque nationalism.

The first written reference to the Basques comes from the Roman historian Strabo, writing in about AD 7.[7] However, as I have already mentioned, the most traditional school of Basque nationalists insists that their people have lived where they live today from, quite literally, time immemorial. As is so often the case with nationalist ideology, the conviction with which this widespread belief is held is more significant than the scant evidence which supports it. As Joseba Zulaika, a Basque anthropologist, says of the people of two small villages: '[Their] identity runs in an unbroken line from the ancestors, who came from nowhere else but Urtiaga and Ekain [the villages in question], who achieved their human condition right there in those nearby underground dwellings. These caves provide for Basques the tangible context in which their imagination of the past finds its home . . . in conversations with Basques, it is not unusual to hear expressions such as "that happened *only* 5,000 B.C."[8] In this context, it is worth recalling the French historian Ernest Renan's dictum: 'Getting its history wrong is part of being a nation.'[9]

This sense of the intimate presence of the distant past is linked in nationalism with a whole series of beliefs about more historically verifiable periods. In summary, the classical nationalist canon asserts the following. Having occupied their own lands since the dawn of humanity itself, the Basques were never conquered by the Romans, the Moors, the Visigoths or the Franks. Their devastating attack on Charlemagne's rearguard, at the battle of Roncesvalles in AD 778 (the incident which gave rise to the *Chanson de Roland*) was a warning that no foreign army could cross the Basque lands at will. The basic structure of their society was egalitarian and democratic, presided over morally by a Catholic Church whose clergy were drawn from the common people, untainted by the hierarchic corruptions of the Mediterranean clergy.

Right up to the nineteenth century, this canon continues, Basque was the universal language of the region. The Basques may not have established a clearly defined unitary state, but they had a strong sense of themselves as a separate people. They ran their own affairs, entering into alliances only by their own consent with Castilian kings, each one of whom had to come to the sacred tree of Guernica to swear to uphold the charters of special rights (*fueros*) enjoyed by the Basques. These included control of their own taxation system and exemption from customs duties and from military service. When they travelled or worked elsewhere in the Spanish kingdom, every Basque citizen would enjoy important privileges, usually reserved for the nobility, such as exemption from arbitrary arrest and torture.

According to Basque nationalist orthodoxy, this long Golden Age ended abruptly in the nineteenth century, when military defeat in the two Carlist wars resulted in the abolition of the *fueros*. The four Basque provinces south of the Pyrenees were thus forcibly annexed by the Spanish empire. Spain then encouraged, as a matter of policy, the massive migration of godless Andalusian and Galician workers into the Basque region, thus diluting the ethnic, religious and linguistic purity of the Basque nation. This influx is sometimes described as a kind of genocide. Basque nationalism – according to the nationalists – was the virile answer of a proud people to invasion and suppression by a backward empire. The nationalist demand for self-determination is a progressive, democratic call which should be supported by a 'Europe of the Peoples'.[10]

Anti-nationalist historians of both Right and Left, often as ideologically driven as the nationalists, have put forward a counter-canon.[11] It runs along the following lines. The Basques are probably a vestige of a primitive people who once lived throughout Iberia. The Romans found little worth conquering in the Basque Country, though their writ did run there. In a neat reversal of interpretation of the same evidence, anti-nationalists argue that the general absence of Roman fortifications is an indication of *how little* resistance the Basques had offered the empire. The Moors set up a caliphate in the Basque city of Pamplona, and the battle of Roncesvalles was merely an ambush by brigands.

Basque social structures were often rigidly hierarchic, the anti-nationalists contend, and such elements of egalitarian democracy as did exist could often be found in other rural Spanish communities. The Basque language was never more than the primitive tongue of a marginalised peasantry, as the absence of any significant vernacular literature before the nineteenth century testifies. Latin, and later Castilian, were the languages of administration and culture.

Fueros were a common feature of the relationship between the Spanish monarchy and the regions, and the Basque Country was as integrated into the emerging Spanish state as was any other part of the kingdom. The universal nobility granted to the Basques was a device for suppressing the local overlords, whose factional wars regularly devastated the region. The Basque Country was riven by divisions and conflicting exterior alliances. It was utterly lacking in any sense of homogenous nationhood. The abolition of the *fueros* in the nineteenth century was a positive act of modernising centralism, actively supported by the progressive liberals of the Basque cities, which were never captured by the Carlists.

The immigration of non-Basque workers was the natural response of a landless peasantry to an industrial revolution. Basque nationalism was the backward-looking, reactionary response of a regional lower middle class displaced by modernisation. While respecting minority cultural rights, democrats should support the closest possible integration of the Basques into the Spanish state, itself integrated in the European Union.

As Marianne Heiberg points out, both of these conflicting histories are 'partially valid'.[12] The Basque experience has been both exceptionally distinct from those of other peoples on the Iberian peninsula and very closely connected to them. For whatever reason, the Basques had less contact with the Romans than most other Iberians had, even in the Basque Country's more accessible regions. What happened in the Basque mountains at that time is largely a mystery, though Collins suggests that even there some economic interaction with the empire probably took place.[13] The Moors did briefly establish themselves in Pamplona, and even passed through the Basque Country to meet the limits of their expansion in Aquitaine, but the fertile intermingling of cultures which seven centuries of Arab (and Jewish) presence bequeathed to more southerly parts of the peninsula is not part of the Basque inheritance.

However, the Basques did play a major part in the long, slow 'Reconquest' of Spain for Christianity. Ironically, it was this process which provided the only moment when all the Basques lived under a single Basque ruler. This was when Sancho the Great (AD 999–1035) ruled the kingdom of Navarre from Pamplona. Even then, however, it seems unlikely that the Basques had any strong sense of themselves as a political unit. 'The emergence of a kingdom which in practice embraced all of them, ruled by a monarch who may well have been a speaker of their language, was not to have any impact on their self-awareness or aspirations', Collins comments. 'No sense of racial, linguistic or cultural unity seems to have existed that could prove itself greater than their own internal divisions.' Their social structure, he notes, was apparently very loose 'at anything beyond the level of the extended family'.[14]

Sancho's kingdom was in fact far bigger than the Basque Country, stretching from Bordeaux in France to Zamora in north-western Castile, and looping more than halfway down the Pyrenees. The title he gave himself was *not* king of the Basques, but *rex Hispaniarum,* king of the Spains.[15] On his death, his four sons each inherited separate slices of the realm, and rapidly fell out with each other, the new king of Castile invading Navarre. Unlike Catalonia, therefore, the Basque Country has never had any sustained existence as a single political entity. Moreover, as the rest of Moorish Castile progressively fell to the Reconquest, it was repopulated to a significant degree by Basque warriors and settlers.[16] There is a sharp irony in the fact that many Castilians, who are now regarded as foreign oppressors by radical Basque nationalists, may themselves be of Basque descent.

For much of the later Middle Ages and beyond, the Basque Country was indeed riven by feuding, known as 'the wars of the bands'. Factional leaders entered into alliances with non-Basques as easily as with Basques. The granting of 'noble' rights to the ordinary people of Guipúzcoa and Vizcaya may have indeed been an attempt by the Spanish monarchy to undermine the authority of the fractious local aristocracy. It also provided a mechanism whereby Basques, as 'gentlemen', had easy access to positions in the Spanish imperial administration, an advantage which they pursued widely and with distinction.

Basques were also prominent participants in the creation of that empire, fighting with the *conquistadores* and, especially, opening up and maintaining sea routes. It was the Basque sailor Elcano who completed the first circumnavigation of the globe, after the death of Magellan. That most emblematic of Spanish imperial enterprises, the voyage to the 'Indies' led by Christopher Columbus, had as one of its leaders the Vizcayan cartographer and master mariner Juan de la Cosa, captain of the *Santa María.*[17]

Nevertheless, it is also true that the Basques maintained a powerful sense of distinctness. Their *fueros* were more extensive than those of any other region apart from Catalonia, which lost them 150 years before the Basques. The issue of charters of special local or regional rights is a complex one, made more complex in the Basque case by the charter being determined individually in each province, and sometimes each city or even village. (The Catalans had had a single charter for their whole region.[18]) Among the more singular Basque privileges was an exemption from compulsory military service. Their two most important *fueros*, however, were both fiscal.

Firstly, the Basques had the power to decide their own levels of taxation. They were therefore free of oppressive financial demands from a notoriously corrupt, stagnant and bureaucratic Madrid administration. Secondly, they were exempt from paying customs duties on goods entering the Basque Country from abroad. They could, however, impose duties on goods imported from the rest of Spain. Thus they enjoyed the benefit of cheap foreign manufactured imports, while protecting their farmers (in particular) from Castilian competition.

However, as Basque industry developed during the nineteenth century, urban employers (and employees) began to see the customs *fuero* as a severe hindrance to growth. They could not compete in either quality or price with manufactured imports from northern Europe, while their own products were subject to customs duties in their natural 'domestic' market – the rest of the Spanish kingdom. The relatively weak Basque agricultural sector, however, was in no mood to willingly accept the shifting of the customs frontier from the Ebro to the coast and the Pyrenees.

This issue crystallised an urban–rural divide that goes back many centuries. Most of the larger Basque towns became 'Hispanicised' at an early stage.[19] In some cases, this was because they were actually established by, and planted with, Castilians. Much more often, however, it was because their commercial intercourse with Spain and the outside world made urban populations more cosmopolitan than rural ones, and, crucially, largely Spanish-speaking. It is significant that the first nucleus of those who would in future oppose nationalist politics within the Basque Country were themselves mostly of Basque ethnic origin, and not 'foreigners', as nationalists often claim.

This divide became a gulf with the outbreak of the first Carlist war in 1833. The war was a civil conflict between those who supported the claim to the throne of King Ferdinand VII's brother Carlos and those who backed his infant daughter, Isabella. It was not so much a dynastic quarrel as a war between two worlds. Isabella's supporters represented 'Liberal' Spain, in favour of curbing the power of the Crown and the Church, and ardent believers in rationalised, centralist administration and free trade. Don Carlos represented the Spain of the 'Black Legend', absolute monarchy, ecclesiastical dominance, economic protectionism and – so, at least, many Basques believed – the defence of the *fueros*.

The Basque countryside, and especially Navarre, rose passionately and ferociously for God and King. The big Basque cities, and especially Bilbao, threw in their lot with Liberalism. It was an indecisive if often bloody conflict, with the Liberals unable to subdue the countryside, and the Carlists unable to capture the cities. It was settled in 1839 by a compromise which temporarily preserved the *fueros*, but a further uprising provided an excuse for their suspension in 1841. The Carlists became embroiled in yet another civil war in 1872, and the *fueros* were definitively abolished in 1876 following the Carlists' final defeat. The Basque urban Liberals were then able to negotiate a *concierto económico* two years later, which gave them the very advantageous right to negotiate annual tax deals with the central government, while enjoying the protection of the shifted tariff barriers. They had the best of the old and new worlds. The countryside sank back into sullen resignation, and, in the case of Navarre (which managed to maintain a separate *fuero* of its own), an alienation from their fellow Basques which is still palpable today.

In these favourable circumstances, Basque industry went into overdrive, in tandem with a rapidly expanding financial sector.

Phenomenal growth brought two classes to prominence: a Basque oligarchy which embraced Spanish centralism, and a proletariat which mostly came from outside the region.

The accelerating demand for cheap labour precipitated a flood of immigration from the desperately poor landless peasantry of Andalusia, Galicia and Estremadura. The population of Bilbao tripled between 1876 and 1900, making Vizcaya the most densely populated province in the state.[20] By that point, half of Bilbao's inhabitants were not ethnic Basques. The Basque language had died as a regular medium of communication in the city a century earlier. In any case, Basque has such unfamiliar grammar and vocabulary to Spanish ears that, in contrast to Catalan, it is extremely difficult to learn by casual osmosis. Even assuming the immigrant workers wanted to learn the language, to do so was far beyond their educational and financial means.

Not surprisingly, they were more interested in their own economic survival, and enthusiastically supported the newly established Spanish Socialist Workers' Party (Partido Socialista Obrero Español – PSOE) and its allied General Workers' Union (Unión General de Trabajadores – UGT). They became a powerful element in Bilbao's political and industrial life. A Basque middle class, which did not share either the enormous wealth or cosmopolitan outlook of the oligarchy, looked on in horror as Bilbao seemed to be falling into the hands of strangers. It was among this class in this city, rather than in the countryside, that Basque nationalism was born as a self-conscious political force.

Its first, most prolific and most problematic ideologue was Sabino Arana, who founded the Basque Nationalist Party (Partido Nacionalista Vasco – PNV) in 1895. The son of a Bilbao shipbuilder, who did not himself speak Basque fluently, he broke with a tradition evident in the Basque language itself by making race, in the biological sense, the key element of Basque nationality.[21] His writings have a strident, rhetorical tone familiar in similar proponents of nationalism elsewhere in Europe at this time – Patrick Pearse inevitably springs to mind for an Irish writer. He listed the distinguishing features of the Basque people in the following order: '1. race. 2. language. 3. government and laws. 4. character and customs. 5. historical personality.'[22]

These were the blocks with which he wanted to build the Basque nation, and a brief résumé will indicate that they were generally made of sturdy stuff. Even under the heading of race, which understandably makes today's readers very wary, the Basques had remarkable biological peculiarities to which he could appeal.

Many Basques have a distinctive physical appearance – significantly taller than most Spaniards, with a skull structure that often features a prominent nose. Curiously, they also have notably higher and lower percentages of certain blood groups than other European peoples. For Arana, race was so important that he initially insisted that only those with four ethnically Basque grandparents could join the PNV. This insistence became an obstacle to expanding the party, and an embarrassment to his successors, and had to be moderated even in his own lifetime. Today most nationalists reject any overt racial criterion for

'Basqueness', substituting language or simply residence in the Basque Country. But such attitudes still crop up in the rhetoric of some PNV leaders, especially the party's president, Xabier Arzalluz.

As for the second criterion, language, there is no difficulty, as we have seen, in establishing the unique qualities of Euskera. Under government and laws, Arana cited the whole range of Basque *fueros,* presenting their abolition as the curtailment of independence by an oppressive foreign power. However ahistorical this was, since many urban Basques had whole-heartedly fought for their abolition, it was an appeal of great sentimental attraction, and did hark back to a genuinely differential factor. Under the heading of character and custom, despite the lack of a Basque-language literary tradition, the impressive richness and variety of Basque cultural traditions would be an ideological (and organisational) treasure house at the service of nationalism. Basque culture is exceptionally distinctive and vital, in dance, music, oral poetry and sports. There is no space here to explore those traditions, but three examples should suffice to illustrate the point.

One of the favourite sports in Basque villages is ritualised rock-lifting, an extraordinary demonstration of sheer, unmediated muscle power. The same villages boast remarkable skills in spontaneously created oral poetry: two men will vie with each other on a given topic for hours, remaining within the same metrical structure. Finally, the fiestas which feature both activities may be opened in the early morning by the sound of the *txalaparta*, an enormous wooden xylophone about six metres long, with an uncanny percussive capacity to evoke galloping horses or thunderstorms.

While Arana did not explicitly mention religion in this list of national characteristics, rigid adherence to Catholic moral teaching was for him an essential part of the Basque historical personality. So much so that the great slogan of the PNV became '*Jaungoikua eta Lagi-zara*' ('God and the Ancient Laws'). The party's Catholicism would be both a magnet for attracting former Carlists in the countryside and a major obstacle to any alliance or even understanding with the then militantly atheistic Socialist Party. And it would baffle and infuriate Franco, when he found that such an avowedly confessional party refused to join his Catholic 'crusade against communism' in 1936. This was the moment when Basque nationalism came of age, opting for democratic politics over dogma.

Reaching that maturity, however, was a process full of growing pains. The first sign that the PNV might be more than a folkloric sect came when they were joined by a group of businessmen led by Ramón de la Sota. Though part of the Bilbao oligarchy, de la Sota saw both sentimental and practical reasons to move towards Basque self-government. The Madrid administration was bureaucratic and inept, and most of Spain remained very backward compared with the Basque Country. Marianne Heiberg makes the fertile suggestion that the real key to the success of Basque nationalism lies in the failure of Spanish nationalism. Madrid at the turn of the century, she argues, was 'unable to endow the identity of "Spaniard" with advantages and dignity that outweighed "Basque" or "Catalan"'.[23] This was, after all, the period in which Spain had just ignominiously lost most of the remnants of its empire (Cuba, Puerto Rico and the Philippines) in the 'disaster' of 1898. At the very moment when Castile was trying to fully exercise its political hegemony within Spain, Heiberg points out, its own economic power was crumbling. Meanwhile the Basque and Catalan economies at the periphery were taking off.

The PNV made another step forward when Arana himself suddenly reversed his insistence that the Basque Country must become totally independent, and advocated the pursuit of the right to autonomous government within the Spanish state. Since the article in which he indicated this shift was written while he was in jail for a minor offence, and he died soon afterwards, his motivation for writing it is a matter of conjecture. Pro-independence nationalists contend that it was a tactical manoeuvre; autonomists prefer to believe it was a change of heart. Either way, it has provided a useful catch-all ambiguity within the party's doctrine which the PNV has exploited to the full, accommodating most nationalist opinion until ETA came on the scene in the 1950s.

In the first two decades of the twentieth century, the PNV grew rapidly beyond its urban origins, to become the hegemonic party of nationalism throughout Vizcaya, Guipúzcoa and Álava. Only in Navarre did the PNV make little or no headway. Basque-speakers in that province retained a stubborn loyalty to Carlism's nostalgia for absolute monarchy and regionalist traditions, a loyalty which would ultimately lead to Navarre's remaining outside the Basque Autonomous Community today. In the French Basque provinces, lip-service to the contrary, the PNV made no serious attempt to win popular support.

The PNV's internal policy shifts made little impression, however, on their political opponents to Right and Left. The former continued to regard them as dangerous eccentrics willing to undermine the sacred unity of the Spanish state for the sake of a folkloric whim. The latter saw them as clericalist allies of the Basque bourgeoisie and, though the word was not yet current, as racist. The great Basque writer Miguel de Unamuno, who supported the Socialists, dismissed Euskera as 'a tuberculous invalid',[24] and ridiculed the PNV for its 'absurd racial virginity'.[25] He held that the core of Basque nationalism was 'above all else an hostile explosion against the Spaniard . . . who lives and works in Bilbao'.[26] (Unamuno, and the PSOE itself, gradually became more tolerant of some nationalist positions in the 1920s and 1930s.)

When the PNV attempted to challenge the Socialists on their own territory, and set up a trade union specifically for ethnic Basque workers, their mutual hostility became volatile, with shoot-outs between their members being quite frequent. But the nationalist union survived and prospered, increasing the PNV's reach across class barriers, at least within its own ethnic community, and thus its electoral viability. Its electoral performance improved steadily during the First World War, when Spain's neutrality produced a sustained boom in Basque industry. A setback followed, when both industrial unrest and the collapse of negotiations for autonomy undermined the party's credibility.

Miguel Primo de Rivera's dictatorship (1923–30) followed, a period when the PNV was able to demonstrate its remarkable ability to survive, even to thrive, underground. The fact that the PNV had always been as much a social movement as a political party meant that many of its characteristic activities – gastronomic society dinners, traditional dance festivals, mountaineering expeditions and so on – could carry on almost undisturbed by the ban on political activism.

The PNV was initially reluctant to support the developments which led to the establishment of the Second Republic in 1931, following the collapse of Primo de Rivera's dictatorship. The party was inhibited by its Catholicism from backing a secular and often violently anti-clerical movement. Meanwhile, the Republicans shared the Left's suspicions about the PNV's democratic credentials. In contrast, the Catalan nationalists were rewarded for their unequivocal republicanism with extensive powers of self-government in 1932. The willingness of the Republicans to negotiate seriously about autonomy tipped the PNV in the Republic's favour. But progress towards autonomy was painfully slow, despite a largely successful referendum in favour of a statute of self-government in 1932. (Navarre was the only province to reject it.) Spectacular outbursts of church-burning and violence against priests, largely unpunished by the Left-Republican government, did nothing to enhance Basque nationalist confidence in the administration.

Progress was interrupted altogether by the victory of the Right in the elections of 1934. As PNV radicals began to hint at independence, the new government declared: 'Faced with regionalism, understanding. Faced with separatism, executions in the public square.'[27] The PNV lurched towards the Left, but fell into confusion when the Asturian miners staged a revolutionary uprising, which was savagely suppressed by Madrid. In case the Basque nationalists did not get the message, a government minister subsequently said that he preferred *'una España roja a una España rota'* ('a Red Spain rather than a broken Spain').[28] The terrible die of the immediate future, and that of the long years of Franco's dictatorship, was being cast.

The return of the Left to power in February 1936 was quickly followed by Franco's military uprising in July, before the government could fulfil its promise to grant the Basque nationalists their long-delayed autonomy. Some sectors of the PNV, still nervous of the Left, were tempted to support Franco's 'crusade', and the leadership in Álava did so. The Carlists of Navarre gave the fascists immediate and well-organised popular endorsement. But the main PNV leadership remained loyal to the Republic and, along with their erstwhile Socialist and Communist rivals, organised the defence of Vizcaya and Guipúzcoa with courage and commitment.

The Basque Country, or what remained of it, was now an autonomous power *de facto*, since Franco's allies had cut it off from Madrid. The Republic formally recognised that reality in October, at a ceremony beside the symbolic oak tree at Guernica, where the kings of Castile used to swear to uphold Basque *fueros*. This small Vizcayan market town would soon become a symbol of another sort, as one of the first European towns to be razed by aerial bombing, providing Picasso with one of his most terrible and durable images. On 19 July 1937, General Mola's troops took Bilbao, and the PNV prevented the Socialists from sabotaging the city's heavy industry, which subsequently proved invaluable to Franco's war effort. Shortly afterwards, the Basque nationalists surrendered (to Franco's Italian allies) rather than leave their own territory to fight on for the Republic in Asturias.

If these last two actions suggest a lingering equivocation in the PNV's loyalty to the Republic, the subsequent behaviour of their conquerors did not reward them for it. The Italians broke their promise to let them leave for exile, handing them over to the Francoists who imprisoned them under terrible conditions, executing many nationalists, including priests. And the new mayor of Bilbao, José María de Areilza, made a chilling speech which was more significant than he knew: 'Bilbao . . . has been conquered by the army . . . Bilbao is a city redeemed by blood . . . Spain, united, great and free, has triumphed. The horrible and sinister nightmare called Euskadi has fallen defeated forever. Vizcaya is again a piece of Spain through pure and simple military conquest.'[29]

Forty years earlier, Sabino Arana had said that the Basque Country was suffering under forcible occupation by a foreign power, Spain. To all but his devotees, this seemed like an eccentric political fantasy. Ironically, Franco's dictatorship was to make that fantasy a grim reality in the perception of many Basques. The enduring result of that experience was the transformation of a youth section of the PNV into ETA, a revolutionary group committed to 'liberating' all seven Basque provinces by force of arms.

NOTES

1 Roger Collins, *The Basques,* 2nd edn (Oxford: Blackwell, 1990), p. 1.

2 Ibid., p. 3.

3 Rodney A. Gallop, *A Book of the Basques* (London: Macmillan, 1930), p. 4.

4 This picture is changing. Elections since 1998 have shown a growth in support for non-nationalist options, especially the conservative Partido Popular. In July 1999, a non-nationalist coalition took control of the city council in Vitoria, seat of the Basque government, and the Partido Popular outvoted the Basque Nationalist Party in all three Basque capitals in the general elections of March 2000.

5 Spanish Constitution, 1978, Article 2: 'The Constitution is based on *the indissoluble unity of the Spanish Nation,* the common and indivisible fatherland of all the Spaniards, and recognises and *guarantees the right to autonomy of the nationalities* and regions which are part of [the Spanish Nation] and mutual support between all of them.' My translation and emphasis.

6 I will generally use the French and Spanish versions of the names of these provinces from here on. Where there is a familiar English version (for example Navarre for Navarra), I will use it. For cities and towns I will use the French and Spanish versions, even where the Basque name is again in common use, unless the latter is used in a text or quotation. Thus I will refer to Bilbao and not to Bilbo, to St-Jean-de-Luz and not Donibane Lohizune. In the case of smaller towns, not well known to the English-speaking reader, I will generally use the Basque name where it is now in common use, for example Lekeitio and not Lequeitio.

7 Collins, op. cit., p. 31.

8 Joseba Zulaika, *Basque Violence, Metaphor and Sacrament* (Reno, Nev.: University of Nevada Press, 1988), p. 24.

9   Quoted in E.J. Hobsbawm, *Nations and Nationalism since 1780,* 2nd edn (Cambridge: Canto, 1992) p. 12.

10 The reader may well ask where the three Basque provinces now in France fit into this scenario. The reality is that they rather tend to get left out, despite the slogan, ubiquitous in nationalist bars and political clubs, which declares that 'Seven are One' (*Zazpiak Bat*). Their omission is due to three factors. Firstly, the Spanish–French border was established more than three centuries ago, in 1659, so that the two regions inevitably face more towards Paris and Madrid than towards each other. French Basque participation in two world wars in the twentieth century, while their fellows south of the border remained, perforce, part of neutral Spain, copperfastened their orientation northwards. Secondly, the centralising policies of revolutionary France were much more successful than Spain's halting steps towards a modern nation-state in the nineteenth century. Thirdly, the smaller and much poorer French Basque region has experienced emigration rather than immigration, and Basque nationalism has never taken strong root there. This is ironic, because the Basque cultural traditions are still very strong on the French side of the border. In some respects, the rural Arcadia yearned for by Spanish Basque nationalists finds its most dynamic contemporary form in French Basque communities where their politics find little echo.

However, the French Basque Country has been of great significance as a refuge for Spanish Basques, first for the Carlists, then for the generation exiled by the Spanish Civil War. More recently, as we shall see, it would become a crucial infrastructural base for ETA, a fact which conditions the events of this book.

11 Some of the most brilliant of the currently dominant left-wing school of Basque revisionists are former members of ETA themselves, who deconstruct their formative ideology with all the zeal of the converted. The contemporary doyen of this group is Jon Juaristi, author of the bible of anti-nationalism, *El Bucle Melancólico* (Madrid: Espasa-Calpe, 1997). The following extracts may give a taste of its pungent, ironic flavour: 'Basque Nationalism knows only one thing, but it knows it very well: that it is necessary to lose in order to win, to keep the [sense of] injury alive so that the sacrifice of successive generations may be politically profitable . . . A great part of the success of nationalism derives directly from its incorporation of modernity in homeopathic doses, which has always produced in its followers a healthy reaction against the culture of modernity' (p. 19). See also Mario Onaindia, *Guía para Orientarse en el Laberinto Vasco* (Madrid: Temas de Hoy, 2000), Mikel Azurmendi, *La Herida Patriótica* (Madrid: Taurus, 1998), and Patxo Unzueta, *El Terrorismo: ¿Qué era? ¿Qué es?* (Barcelona: Ediciones Destino, 1997). Unzueta's regular columns in *El País* are another useful source. These writers acknowledge a debt to the revisionist school of Irish historical writing, and especially to Conor Cruise O'Brien.

12 Marianne Heiberg, *The Making of the Basque Nation* (Cambridge: Cambridge University Press, 1989), p. ix.

13 Collins, op. cit., pp. 52–3.

14 Ibid., p. 180.

15 Ibid., p. 182.

16 Ibid., pp. 168–9.

17 Columbus, of course, was himself not Spanish but Genoese.

18 Heiberg, op. cit., p. 20, and Collins, op. cit., p. 266.

19 Collins, op. cit. pp. 182–3, Heiberg, op. cit., pp. 13–14, and Martín de Ugalde, *Sintesis de la Historia del País Vasco,* 4th edn (Barcelona: Ediciones Vascas, 1977), p. 152.

20 Heiberg, op. cit., p. 42.
21 Until Arana coined the neologism Euskadi ('land of the Basque race') the only words in Euskera for 'Basque Country' and 'Basque person' were Euskal Herria and Euskaldun, meaning respectively 'land of Basque-speakers' and 'possessor of the Basque language'.
22 Quoted in Gurutz Jáuregui Bereciartu, *Ideología y Estrategia Política de ETA*, 2nd edn (Madrid: Siglo XXI de España, 1985), p. 16.
23 Heiberg, op. cit., p. 6.
24 Quoted in ibid., p. 79.
25 Quoted in Raymond Carr, *Spain 1808–1975*, 2nd edn (Oxford: Clarendon Press, 1982), p. 556.
26 Quoted in Heiberg, op. cit., p. 79.
27 Quoted in ibid., p. 84.
28 This was José Calvo Sotelo, whose murder by radicals was one of the precursors of the 1936–9 Civil War. Quoted in ibid., p. 85.
29 Quoted in Francisco Letamendía, *Historia del Nacionalismo Vasco y de ETA*, 3 vols. (San Sebastián: R&B Ediciones, 1994), vol. 1, p. 204, and Heiberg, op. cit., p. 89. The rhetoric of *Spanish* nationalism, in the Basque context, finds one of its quintessential expressions in this speech.

2

Boys Become Giant-Killers:
the making of ETA

If Sabino Arana considered Euskadi to be an occupied country,
Francoism made that occupation real and effective.

José María Garmendia[1]

From one perspective, the whole story starts like this: José Pardines, a young *guardia civil*, was checking cars near Villabona, between San Sebastián and Tolosa. Something, perhaps the false number plate on their car, drew his attention to Juan María Etxebarrieta (*Txabi*), a leading member of ETA aged twenty-three, and Iñaki Sarasqueta, a nineteen-year-old provincial leader. Both were armed. They stopped as Pardines indicated, and while the *guardia civil* was examining the car, Etxebarrieta drew his pistol and shot him several times. ETA had claimed its first victim.

Etxebarrieta and Sarasqueta went on the run, but they were stopped by a pair of *guardia civiles* near Tolosa. The first *guardia civil* somehow missed the pistol stuck in Sarasqueta's belt as he searched him, but Etxebarrieta was not so lucky. 'It was like a scene from the Wild West,' as Sarasqueta tells it today. 'Trying to see who would shoot first.'[2] In fact, he didn't wait to see, and made his escape, while Extebarrieta was shot dead. ETA now had something even more crucial than its first victim: it had its first martyr. A dynamic had been kick-started which would continue, unbroken and relentless, for thirty years.

Of course, the story started long before 1968. ETA was born, like many revolutionary movements, not in a moment of drama but in an obscure study group. The nucleus of the organisation which would shake the Francoist state to its foundations, and repeatedly threaten Spain's transition to democracy, was a handful of restless, intellectually curious young men. They were hardly more than boys.

This group began to meet, in great secrecy, in Bilbao in the early 1950s. The purpose of their studies was, essentially, to resolve the dilemma presented by their parents' generation. On the one hand, nationalism retained a remarkable degree of vitality in Basque society a decade after it had been militarily defeated and politically suppressed. On the other, the PNV appeared unable or unwilling to channel that vitality into effective opposition to Franco's dictatorship.

The PNV had bet almost all its cards on the defeat of Hitler. The party assumed that the victorious allies would punish Franco for his political affinity with the Nazis. They even imagined that, in allied foreign policy, commitment to democratic principles would take precedence over international *realpolitik*. The Spanish dictator had, however, steered skilfully through the labyrinth of wartime diplomacy. He had stayed reasonably cosy, in the early years of the war, with his former mentors in Berlin and Rome, but he had done nothing to give the Western allies an urgent *casus belli*.

There were some gestures of support for the PNV from the allies in the immediate postwar years. Armed Basque units were permitted to exercise close to the French–Spanish border in 1946, and a US army colonel was despatched to train 150 Basque fighters near Paris;[3] more realistically, there were moves to isolate Franco diplomatically and economically.[4] The Cold War put an end to all that: Franco might not be a democrat, but his anti-communist credentials were impeccable. The US led the way in offering his regime the dollar credits which permitted the Spanish economy to start growing again after the grim, hungry years of postwar paralysis.

The PNV found itself between a rock and a hard place. The party's devotion to the Western allies was such that some of its members had begun to work with the Central Intelligence Agency (CIA). They even provided information against their Communist partners in the Second Republic's exiled institutions, who were attempting to maintain a guerrilla war against Franco within Spain.[5] Once the US swung behind the dictatorship, the PNV was left isolated and exposed. The small stock of international influence enjoyed by the Basque government-in-exile was crushed under the big wheels of the broader conflict which was defining the postwar world.

The PNV's influence within the Basque Country remained considerable, however, and was stimulated by Franco's ruthless cultural, political and economic authoritarianism. The regime's repression fell most heavily on Guipúzcoa and Vizcaya, officially declared to be 'traitor provinces' by Franco because of their clear-cut support for the Republic. Navarre and Álava, which had either actively or passively supported his insurrection in 1936, had it rather easier.[6]

One of the first acts of the Francoist Military Governor of Guipúzcoa was to prohibit the public use of the Basque language in all territory under his control.[7] Even in villages where the whole population used Euskera as its first (and often only) language, Spanish, the 'language of Christians, language of the empire', had to be spoken in the street. Priests were forbidden to use Euskera in their sermons. Eleven years later, in 1948, the Francoist censor was still banning Basque-language writing in seven Guipuzcoan periodicals.[8] Even in the early 1970s, when the laws had been considerably liberalised, and a network of private Basque-language primary schools operated legally, young people were periodically arrested for speaking Euskera in the street.

Such prohibitions were, inevitably, erratically applied, even in the early years. But they enormously reinforced the sensation that the Basque Country was now occupied by a foreign, hostile power, as Sabino Arana had contended. Francoism had turned the nationalist thesis of an occupied homeland into a kind of lived reality.[9] Parents were forbidden to give their children Basque names, and all the symbols of Basque nationalism, including the *ikurriña*, were prohibited.

Political parties were, of course, banned throughout Spain under the dictatorship, and the rights of freedom of association, assembly and expression were severely curtailed. The PNV survived these conditions better than many other parties (as it had in the Primo de Rivera dictatorship) through its extensive social networks of choirs, hill-walking clubs and gastronomic societies.[10] It had also suffered rather less savage repression than the other defeated parties of the Republic, though the executions (including sixteen nationalist priests) and privations of the early 1940s were severe enough to give the surviving *gudaris* (Basque soldiers) an aura of martyrdom.

Survival was one thing, however, and resistance was something else. Stripped of meaningful allied support, the PNV was in danger of becoming an emperor without clothes in full view of the next generation of nationalists. It had no clear strategy to end the dictatorship, but the ferocity of Franco's economic repression gave the party an opportunity to seize an unlikely role as instigator of industrial unrest. The cost of living had risen 400 per cent since the start of the Civil War, but wages had stayed the same.[11] Following a period of spontaneous, desperate stoppages by workers whose unions had been shattered by fascism, the Basque government-in-exile, led by the PNV, called a general strike for 1 May 1947.

The strike was widely supported and was a propaganda success, but the PNV was never a party of the Left and could not sustain this role. Nor had the party the discipline and security required for clandestine revolutionary activity. In 1950, its student organisation was dismantled by the police, who were clearly well acquainted with its membership.

It was in this atmosphere of confusion, fear and lack of direction that the long gestation of ETA began. Several university students started holding secret study sessions in 1952, at first focusing on the Basque language, then on nationalist themes, and finally on a wide range of political issues. The name they chose for themselves was significant: EKIN, in Euskera, means 'to act'.[12] For all their intellectual seriousness, action against the dictatorship was what these young men desperately wanted. Though they were slow starters, the cult of activism, and later militarism, would become the hallmark of the organisation they went on to establish.

Over the next few years, it seemed that they would simply be the Young Turks of the PNV. They formed good relations with the PNV's leadership in exile, and merged EKIN with the party's youth branch, giving the EKIN members an almost professorial role. But tensions arose almost immediately, and were heightened by the senior EKIN members' patent lack of respect for the PNV's leadership in the 'interior' (the Spanish Basque Country), and their horror at its lax security measures. The definitive split came in 1958, and EKIN took many young PNV militants with it. A year later, on the anniversary of Sabino Arana's foundation of the PNV, 31 July, Euskadi Ta Askatasuna (Basque Homeland and Liberty) was chosen as the name of the new organisation.

ETA was more radical, on several levels, than the PNV. While it also based itself on Arana's teachings, it opted unequivocally for full independence for the seven provinces it claimed as Basque, and rejected autonomy as a political goal. It shifted away from the traditional emphasis on race and ethnicity as the foundation of the nation, instead making the use of the Basque language the touchstone of Basque nationality.[13]

ETA's activism first found expression through painting nationalist graffiti, a perilous enough activity in a state patrolled by Franco's trigger-happy police. But its members wanted to go much further than this. While the new organisation initially put great emphasis on propaganda, recruitment and education, the dramatic means it employed in pursuit of its policies would ultimately be as definitive as the ends themselves. Within its first year, ETA had established a military wing.

The first indication of how potent this development might be came in July 1961, when ETA attempted to derail a train carrying Francoist veterans to a Civil War commemoration. The attack failed, apparently because ETA had taken so many precautions to avoid risk to human life.[14] The consequences were still dramatic enough: more than a hundred activists were arrested, and many of them were tortured and jailed; overnight, ETA had become a respected name, not just in nationalist circles, but in the anti-Francoist underground generally. A violent action had provoked an indiscriminate state response, which would in turn generate popular support for further action. ETA's revolutionary model of the spiral of 'action–repression–action' had been demonstrated in practice, years before the group fully elaborated the theory.[15] Meanwhile, ETA's first leadership took refuge from the repression by crossing the border into exile. Another of ETA's distinguishing characteristics – a leadership operating out of what was to become the group's 'French sanctuary', the French Basque Country – had taken shape.

The 1960s saw ETA go through a rapid political development, but a surprisingly slow military evolution, given its subsequent violent profile. Deeply influenced by the anti-imperial successes of British and French colonies in this period, and in particular by the liberation struggles in Algeria and later Vietnam, ETA defined itself first as anti-colonialist and then as socialist. The victory of Castro's guerrillas in Cuba was also a major inspiration to ETA, and a plank in the platform which legitimised the use of violence for political ends. While most of ETA's members were middle class or lower middle class in origin, the organisation became increasingly preoccupied with its relationship to the working-class movement.[16]

Since the most militant sectors of the Basque working class were often of immigrant origin, this produced a further shift away from the anti-immigrant bias, explicit or implicit, of the PNV. It was a move towards a sense of solidarity and a redefinition of Basque identity. This is not to say that ETA did not continue to imbibe, like mother's milk, as it were, some of the quasi-racist attitudes which traditional Basque nationalism accepted as normal. But it did mean that there was a new and critical debate among young nationalists as to what constituted 'Basqueness'.[17]

The definition had already moved from an ethnic to a linguistic basis, and now became increasingly socio-economic. Many early (and later) members of ETA came from seriously religious backgrounds, and many of these were ex-seminarians. The Basque clergy had been a guardian of the repressed nationalist culture, and the repression they had suffered as a result had radicalised many of them. They were especially open to the ideas of social commitment which were endorsed by Vatican II, and which fostered the worker-priest and liberation theology movements across the world. Christ, Che Guevara, Sartre and Mao seem to have been held in equal respect in many Basque parochial study groups at this time.[18] Revolutionary, often utopian, Leftism blended with existentialism and with Christian ideas of redemption through martyrdom to form the complex psychological make-up of many ETA members.[19]

These debates crystallised around 'assemblies' of ETA, each of which tended to define a particular stage in its evolution. So close was the relationship with the Catholic Church that the assemblies were sometimes held in monasteries. In the late 1960s, by the end of the crucial Fifth Assembly period, which gave rise to the predominantly militarist grouping known as ETA-V, prototype of today's ETA, certain elements were set in stone. ETA defined itself as a 'Basque Socialist Movement of National Liberation'. It was a 'revolutionary nationalist' force, and the vanguard of its revolution was the *'Pueblo Trabajador Vasco'*. This ambiguous phrase can be roughly translated as 'Basque Working People'. It became a convenient formula which seemed to include or exclude the immigrants, depending on the taste of the person who used it. Eventually, the radical nationalist movement would come to accept as Basque anyone 'who lived and sold their labour in the Basque Country', a definition which, if rigorously interpreted, would – and did – exclude the Basque nationalist bourgeoisie.[20]

It would be wrong to draw the conclusion that such developments were absolutely clear-cut, or that the acceptance of new definitions of nationalism erased all traces of the old ones. They do indicate, however, that ETA had positioned itself to reinvent Basque nationalism by the late 1960s, a moment in which a new generation of young people was uniquely receptive to this heady, explosive cocktail of tradition and liberation.[21]

In the course of these debates, many ETA members and supporters began to question the whole basis of nationalism, and took up purely Left positions, ranging from anarchist to Maoist, and from Trotskyist to mainstream Communist. A series of splits in ETA resulted, with many of the brightest and, some would say, the best departing to form or join other Left groupings. Such groups would be dismissed by those who remained in ETA – a minority, on occasions – as *españolistas*, because they inevitably entered into alliances with parties whose headquarters were in Madrid. Those who remained in ETA were generally still characterised by their radical nationalism and by passionate activism. But it was only after the Fifth Assembly that the 'Military Front' finally seized the initiative, and embarked on a campaign which marked ETA as an organisation inextricably linked to violence.

The campaign began with the bombing of Francoist statues and emblems, then ubiquitous features of Spanish cities and villages. ETA also began to carry out bank robberies. Both activities required members to carry arms. It was only a matter of time before the long-heralded 'revolutionary war' claimed its first victims.

The Rubicon was crossed, almost by accident, with Extebarrieta's killing of José Pardines on 7 June 1968, and his own death in action shortly afterwards. This was the year in which so many definitive Sixties events occurred: the Paris student rebellion, the Tet offensive in Vietnam, the invasion of Czechoslovakia, the civil rights marches in Northern Ireland and the shootings of Martin Luther King and Bobby Kennedy in the US. It must have seemed like a propitious moment to start a revolutionary war.

Things suddenly began to move very quickly. There were huge attendances at funeral Masses in memory of Etxebarrieta, now affectionately known in nationalist circles by his *nom de guerre, Txabi*. ETA appeared to have moved abruptly to the forefront of the anti-Franco struggle. It was certainly the only group using arms against the dictatorship.[22] Even those democrats who disagreed in principle often felt some private admiration for young men daring enough to challenge the fearsome repressive machine which the old man had at his disposal. The actions of ETA in the late 1960s provoked the regime into using this machine at full power, after a period of relative liberalisation.

The next blow fell in August. Melitón Manzanas, chief of the political police in Guipúzcoa, who enjoyed (the word is probably not inappropriate) public notoriety as a torturer, was shot dead outside his home in Irún. The killing was interpreted by the public as a response by ETA to the killing of Etxebarrieta; in fact, it had been already planned under his leadership.[23] In any case, ETA had demonstrated that it could strike at the heart of the state apparatus. The repression which followed was a textbook vindication of the radicals' thesis.

A state of emergency was imposed on Guipúzcoa, accompanied by the application of a Decree on Military Rebellion, Banditry and Terrorism. The former removed the few civil rights which late Francoism had conceded to the populace. The latter categorised political opponents as mutineers, and penalised them accordingly. Mere membership of an opposition group could carry a twenty-year jail sentence. The leaders of such groups risked sentence of death.[24]

The experience of mass repression radicalised much of Basque society, nationalist and non-nationalist alike. The thesis that Euskadi was occupied by enemy forces again became the lived experience of much of the population. Most people suffered the humiliation and irritation of endless checkpoints and searches by security forces who, almost entirely, came from outside the region and were encouraged to regard the Basques with suspicion and downright hostility. Nor did the police differentiate between 'immigrant' and 'ethnic' Basques. Inevitably, many people who had no political involvement became acquainted with abuse, arbitrary arrest and ill-treatment. The systematic practice of torture bred a widespread loathing for the so-called 'forces of public order'. The fact that the Basque Country was the main target of such measures, in the turbulent final years of Francoism, further confirmed the perception that it was the object of foreign domination.[25]

Most of the original leadership of ETA-V was already on the French side of the border by mid-1968. In early 1969, virtually the entire remaining leadership was arrested. In an act of extraordinary hubris, the regime decided to try sixteen of them collectively, by a military tribunal; the prosecution demanded death penalties for six of them and 700 years in aggregate jail sentences for the rest. ETA had been handed an unprecedented national and international propaganda platform. The organisation used it to the full.

The Burgos trial in December 1970 became a test of strength between an increasingly senile Francoism and the entire democratic opposition. Many democrats disagreed with ETA's aims and methods, but they passionately opposed the regime's use of summary military 'justice' against any anti-Francoists. There were huge demonstrations, general strikes and protests from the clergy (two priests were among the ETA defendants) and intellectuals. Internationally, this charismatic group of young, hirsute and defiant revolutionaries acted as a magnet for all kinds of defenders, from Pope Paul VI to Jean-Paul Sartre.[26] Three hundred Catalan notables, including the painters Joan Miró and Antonio Tàpies, locked themselves into the monastery at Montserrat, where they declared their support for 'the national rights of the Basque people'.[27]

In the court itself, the ETA leaders did themselves proud. They used no conventional defence. Instead, they used the dock to launch manifestos for the Basque right to self-determination, for socialism and for international solidarity.[28] At the end of their formal declarations, they instructed their lawyers to withdraw, sang revolutionary songs, and virtually provoked a riot in the courtroom. Some of the military judges entered this spirit of political theatre by drawing and brandishing their ceremonial sabres.[29]

Three days after Christmas Day, 1970, the tribunal gave its verdict. Instead of the six death sentences demanded by the prosecution, it handed down nine. In the face of appeals by nine governments, including France, Germany and the Vatican,[30] Franco commuted the sentences to thirty years' jail three days later. He was also influenced, apparently, by large, stage-managed demonstrations in favour of the *status quo*. These proved, he said, that the regime was safe.

In fact, the trial, and the mass reaction in support of the prisoners, had provoked a sudden resurgence of militant fascism among right-wing Spaniards. This also manifested itself in outbursts of 'uncontrolled' violence against opponents of the regime, especially clergy. The seeds of the first dirty war against ETA were sown at this time, as various groups began to feel that the state apparatus alone no longer was sufficient to stem the rising tide of opposition.[31]

Burgos was undoubtedly a propaganda triumph for ETA, 'a trial of the regime as much as of the terrorists themselves', in the words of Raymond Carr.[32] Outside the courtroom, however, the organisation was in some disarray. The intense repression, while beneficial politically in broad terms, had greatly reduced the ranks of active militants on the ground. Those who remained tended to become immersed in political debates, and most of this generation of ETA (known as ETA-VI, from the Sixth Assembly) ended up in 'Spanish' left-wing parties. Military action actually declined in this period – ETA carried out no killings in 1970 or 1971. Hard-liners within the organisation began to draw a conclusion which would be deeply influential on ETA for the next quarter-century. Every time the group ceased to prioritise armed struggle, ETA's irredentists noted balefully, it tended to abandon nationalism and decant to the non-nationalist Left.

The remnants of the 'Military Front' of ETA-V regrouped, and were joined by a raft of new recruits from the youth section of the PNV. With the demise of ETA-VI as a credible force, and the most politicised members of ETA-V in prison, nationalist 'activism' once again became a defining characteristic of ETA. There would be one more crucial split in the organisation, between the 'military' faction and the 'political-military' faction, in 1974. But the dynamic for the future had now been firmly established. As the historian Antonio Elorza puts it, from this point onwards, 'when military and political logics collide, and the latter tries to act on its own account, the "armed wing" will impose its law'.[33] The gun was now seen as more eloquent, and much less treacherous, than the word.[34]

Despite its militarism, however, the first major actions of the regrouped ETA-V, under the leadership of a former seminarist, Eustaquio Mendizábal (*Txikia*), had a distinctly 'Leftist' gloss. These were the kidnappings, in 1972 and 1973, of two industrialists, not just to raise money for the organisation, but also to impose a favourable solution to industrial disputes in which they were involved. Both kidnappings were successful, in both respects. While ETA filled its war chest, it enjoyed the considerable prestige of playing Robin Hood to striking workers. In the same period, ETA lost several activists, including Mendizábal, in shoot-outs with the security forces.

In 1972, ETA began to plan a much more ambitious kidnapping. Their target was Admiral Luis Carrero Blanco, Franco's right-hand man and intended political heir. Though already elderly, and a close associate of Franco's since the Civil War, Carrero Blanco represented not only the past and present of the regime, but its future. He was the man entrusted by the dictator to keep affairs 'tied up, and well tied up' after his death, which now seemed imminent. Old age and Parkinson's disease were increasingly evident in Franco's every public appearance.

Carrero Blanco had also recognised the degree to which the Francoist state was in crisis. The formal machinery of repression was no longer sufficient to stem the flood of opposition activism. He was, according to some sources, secretly setting up channels to direct the 'uncontrolled' violence of Rightist groups into a coherent strategy of counter-revolutionary violence. If these accounts are true, Carrero Blanco was the father of state terrorism in modern Spain, and of the dirty war against ETA, though he would not live to see his plans come to fruition.[35]

ETA had planned to kidnap Carrero Blanco and barter him for prisoners. But when, in June 1973, Franco made him Prime Minister, relinquishing the post himself for the first time, ETA decided to go further.

An ETA unit, or *comando*,[36] named *Txikia* in honour of Mendizábal, dug a T-shaped tunnel under a narrow street in central Madrid, through which Carrero Blanco passed *en route* to Mass every morning. On

20 December 1973, just as a major trial of Communist trade union leaders was about to begin, the *comando* detonated three dynamite charges. Carrero Blanco and two of his bodyguards were blown to bits, and so were Franco's plans for the continuity of his regime.

Opposition parties formally condemned this spectacular assassination, and there were well-founded fears that it could lead to a blood bath by the infuriated military. Many democrats, however, privately applauded the killing. Ironically, given ETA's revolutionary intentions, the removal of Carrero Blanco from the scene may ultimately have facilitated the decidedly non-revolutionary reform of the regime in the years which followed. Either way, ETA had changed the course of Spanish history before the eyes of the world. The operation was, in the words of the usually sober historian Raymond Carr, 'one of the most brilliantly planned [assassinations] in the history of terrorism'.[37]

ETA's prestige among the Basque youth soared. The boys of the 1950s had become the giant-killers of the 1970s. The organisation had shown, incontrovertibly, that violence could be a very powerful political weapon. It was a lesson which would not be unlearned easily, even when the political conditions in the Spanish state had changed utterly.

The killing of the Prime Minister was celebrated in a Basque tune which became known as 'The Waltz of Carrero'. From that killing onwards, the dance of 'action–repression–action' speeded up into a deadly *pas de deux* between the Spanish security forces and ETA. The code-name for the action was 'Operation Ogre', but in destroying one monster, ETA had conjured up others.

NOTES
1   José María Garmendia, *Historia de ETA* (San Sebastián: R&B Ediciones, 1995), p. 41.
2   Sarasqueta gave a less than heroic account of this historic shoot-out to *El Mundo*, on the thirtieth anniversary of the killings. He claims that Etxebarrieta was high on amphetamines, and that he killed Pardines in cold blood despite Sarasqueta's request to disarm him and tie him up. He adds that the amphetamines also contributed to a fit of panic on Etxebarrieta's part, which led them into the second confrontation. There is no way of corroborating Sarasqueta's account at this stage. But his story suggests that, as in so many other wars, human error and human weakness played a larger part in ETA's armed struggle, even at this relatively innocent stage of the campaign, than is generally acknowledged by the group's admirers. *El Mundo* (colour supplement), 14 June 1998.
3   Francisco Letamendía, *Historia del Nacionalismo Vasco y de ETA*, 3 vols. (San Sebastián: R&B Ediciones, 1994), vol. 1, p. 211.
4   See Sagrario Morán, *ETA entre España y Francia* (Madrid: Editorial Complutense, 1997), ch. 1, for details of the evolution of the Western powers' relationship with Franco's Spain.
5   Letamendía, op. cit., vol. 1, pp. 210–12.
6   In many Navarran villages, the speaking of Basque had no nationalist connotations, and was tolerated and sometimes fostered under the Franco regime – strictly as a quaint piece of 'Spanish' folklore.
7   Morán, op. cit. p. 49.
8   Mario Onaindia, *La Lucha de Clases en Euskadi* (San Sebastián: Hordago, 1979), p. 39.

9   See the epigraph that heads this chapter.
10 The PNV survived better as a social organisation, which was both its strength and its weakness; the party *was* society for many of its members. But they were not well organised or active politically, which was a key reason why the next generation of nationalists founded ETA. The Communist Party and the Socialist Party, despite the heavier repression they suffered, had more active political organisations than the PNV in the Franco period.
11 Gurutz Jáuregui Bereciartu, *Ideología y Estrategia Política de ETA*, 2nd edn (Madrid: Siglo XXI de España, 1985), p. 52.
12 Among the founding members of EKIN were José Luis Álvarez Emparanza (*Txillardegi*), Julen Madariaga, Benito del Valle and José Manuel Aguirre, several of whom would remain prominent figures in, or close to, ETA for many years.
13 This shift in emphasis was an implicit rejection of the biological racism inherent in the PNV's traditional position, and a move towards a conception of nationality as something that can be 'constructed'.
14 Letamendía, op. cit., vol. 1, p. 259.
15 The model of 'action–repression–action', as related to the Basque Country, was first articulated by Federico Sarrailh de Ihartza (under the pseudonym Federico Krutwig) in *Vasconia* (Buenos Aires: Norbait, 1962). This book was very influential in ETA's development, and the theory of 'action–repression–action' was formally adopted by ETA at its Fourth Assembly in 1965. It is expressed in an internal ETA report, *Bases Teóricas de la Guerra Revolucionaria,* which was written by José Luis Zalbide and was debated at the Fourth Assembly, and which is possibly the most influential document in the history of the organisation. It marks the point at which ETA sheds some of its romantic idealism, and seeks to find a practical application for 'Third World' revolutionary theories in the concrete conditions of the Basque Country under late Francoism. Zalbide proposed that a dialectical spiral of violence would operate along the following lines: (1) ETA carries out a provocative action against the political system; (2) the system responds with repression against 'the masses'; (3) the masses respond with a mixture of panic and rebellion, whereupon ETA embarks on a further action which brings the masses a step further along the road to revolution. This grim motor shifted into gear when Juan María Etxebarrieta killed José Pardines, and its momentum has proved very difficult to halt ever since. See Jáuregui Bereciartu, op. cit., pp. 245–7; Letamendía, op. cit., vol. 1, pp. 298–300; Antonio Elorza (ed.), *La Historia de ETA* (Madrid: Temas de Hoy, 2000), pp. 228–9; John Sullivan, *ETA and Basque Nationalism* (London: Routledge, 1988), pp. 41–5.
16 See Sullivan, op. cit., for a sceptical view of ETA's discovery of the working class as a revolutionary vanguard, given the social composition of its membership.
17 This double sensibility produces a kind of schizophrenia, whereby ETA supporters, even those of immigrant origin, will use words like 'Spanish' pejoratively. In the experience of this writer, however, naked racism is more common among PNV supporters, who have never had this debate, or among non-affiliated cultural nationalists. I heard one senior Basque cultural figure, in the 1970s, speak with contempt of the miserable overcrowding in immigrant tenements. 'No Basque,' he said, 'would live the way the immigrants do.'
18 See Joseba Zulaika, *Basque Violence, Metaphor and Sacrament* (Reno, Nev.: University of Nevada Press, 1988) for detailed insights into the intimate relationship between the junior Basque clergy and the dissemination of radical ideas in the 1960s.

19 Complex, and, of course, contradictory. The fact that some of these elements blend so badly goes some way to explaining ETA's many splits, and the mutual hostility between the resultant groups.

20 See Sullivan, op. cit., pp. 55–62, for a lucid account of the ambiguities inherent in the concept of *Pueblo Trabajador Vasco.*

21 For full accounts of the remarkably complex debates which characterised ETA in the 1960s, see Elorza (ed.), op. cit., Letamendía, op. cit., Sullivan, op. cit., and especially Jaúregui Bereciartù, op. cit.

22 It is true that the Spanish anarchists unsuccessfully tried to maintain a commitment to armed struggle, and Maoist groups like FRAP and GRAPO would develop significant terrorist fire-power in the 1970s. But ETA had the field more or less to itself in the late 1960s, and undoubtedly holds the dubious distinction of remaining the pre-eminent terrorist group from then on.

23 Letamendía, op. cit., vol. 1, p. 331.

24 Ibid., p. 332.

25 Many other areas, particularly Madrid and Catalonia, also suffered indiscriminate repression in this period. But nowhere was it so intense, or so sustained, as in the Basque Country. (See Letamendía, op. cit., vol. 1, p. 332 – of eleven states of emergency from 1956 to 1975, all but one affected the Basque provinces, and five of them were applied exclusively to the Basque provinces.) Nor was there any other part of the state where the security forces were so often felt to come from 'outside', from another country.

26 Sartre wrote a remarkably badly informed prologue to a book on the trial. See Letamendía, op. cit., vol. 1, p. 367.

27 Ibid., p. 353.

28 Letamendía (ibid., p. 352) makes the point that the various speeches from the dock represented different tendencies within ETA. Several of the defendants went on to become leading members of the two divergent parties which represented opposed sectors of ETA in the late 1970s and early 1980s. Mario Onaindia and Eduardo Uriarte were founders of Euskadiko Ezkerra, born of the 'political-military' faction of ETA, and Jokin Gorostidi and Itziar Aizpurua played a similar role in Herri Batasuna, political front for the 'military' faction. Several of their lawyers also became prominent figures in radical nationalism.

29 Ibid.

30 The Pope had asked Franco for 'measures of grace' even before the sentence was dictated.

31 Letamendía, op. cit., vol. 1, p. 356.

32 Raymond Carr, *Spain 1808–1975,* 2nd edn (Oxford: Clarendon Press, 1982), pp. 733–4.

33 Antonio Elorza, 'Foreword', in Garmendia, op. cit., p. 35.

34 Letamendía (op. cit., vol. 1, pp. 373–7) gives an interesting analysis, from a radical nationalist point of view, of the development of militarism as the guiding principle of ETA.

35 The most detailed account of Carrero Blanco's role in establishing a dirty war apparatus is Ricardo Arques and Melchor Miralles, *Amedo: El Estado contra ETA* (Barcelona: Plaza y Janés/Cambio 16, 1989), pp. 72–82. As pointed out on p. 13, n. 6, their account has never been independently confirmed, and many of the protagonists are now dead. However, it is based on first-hand interviews. Writers with different perspectives from these authors, like Victorino Ruiz de Azúa, 'Las Manos Sucias', in Santos Juliá et al. (eds.), *Memoria de la Transición* (Madrid: Taurus, 1996), p. 580, and Patxo Unzueta, *El Terrorismo: ¿Qué era? ¿Qué es?* (Barcelona: Ediciones Destino, 1997), pp. 36–7, broadly endorse their account.

36 For an explanation of the use of the term *comando* see Glossary, p. 453.

37 Carr, op. cit., p. 734.

3

The First Dirty War:

Warriors of Christ the King and the Basque Spanish Battalion

Instead of lying down, Emile Muley stood up. To this day, he does not know whether this instinctive reaction saved his life and those of his wife and two children. They were enjoying a Sunday evening drink in the Bar Hendayais, a few hundred yards on the French side of the Spanish border, when he saw two men approach the door and thought he heard a firework go off outside.

The Hendayais is a small bar, and was smaller in November 1980 than it is now. 'There were about forty people inside,' says Muley, 'it was packed. My brother-in-law, a hunter, immediately realised that the banging sound was a gun, not a firework. He shouted at us to lie down. My wife pulled my daughters down to the floor by the wall, but for some reason I stood up.

'As I did so, I got a shotgun blast in my shoulder, and as I went down again a burst of machine-gun fire hit me in the knees. The strange thing is that I remember the attack quite differently from what I'm telling you. I thought that all the firing happened when I was already on the ground. I was told later that it was actually all over by then.'[1]

His wife and daughters, aged two and five, were unhurt, but a hole in the wall above where his wife lay showed how close the call had been. Muley thinks that, had he not stood up, he might have taken that shot in the head. And he thinks that the bullets he took in the legs could have killed his wife and children had he not inadvertently stopped them. 'I knew my wife was alright, but I thought I was paralysed. I was suffering, bleeding a lot. I was pretty disorientated, but I remember the firemen taking me to an ambulance, and then moving me to another one. The pain was so great I wished I was unconscious.'

Muley was relatively lucky. After three weeks in one hospital and three months in another, he was able to walk again. Built like an ox, and with a remarkably sunny disposition, he was busy running a small engineering business close to Hendaye when I met him in 1997. His wife, he says, suffered worse than he did, and for years she felt compelled to look under their car before they got into it. She used to refuse to cross the border to

Spain, which she had good reason to associate with the attack. The children only remember the smell of cordite. 'When fireworks go off, they say "that smells like Hendaye", but they don't seem traumatised.' Survival, he says, 'is a matter of personality'.

Two of the other clients in the Hendayais that night got no chance to survive at all. José Camio and Jean-Pierre Haramendi died on the spot. Nine others were seriously injured. Only two of the injured and neither of the dead men had any connection whatsoever with ETA.

In the summer of 1997, I had found Jean-Louis Humbert, another innocent bystander, taking his morning coffee in the revamped Hendayais. The new owner, who asked not to be named, did not like to be reminded of the attack. It has made his establishment emblematic of the first dirty war in the French Basque Country, a tag which has very little marketing value. But he was an amiable man and agreed to point out any patrons who might have witnessed the events in question.

The trauma of the attack is much more legible in the lines and nervous tics of Humbert's face than in Muley's. He doesn't want to talk about the attack at first, but then agrees to introduce me to several other victims and eye-witnesses, including Muley, and takes a lot of trouble to do so. 'I do what I can,' he says, rather enigmatically, when I thank him.

Humbert was shot in the stomach, and has been in and out of hospital ever since. He can work only periodically. 'They took out a metre of my big intestine. Food gets to my stomach very quickly, it digests very quickly, and then I have to go to the toilet very quickly,' he says, half wryly, half as though it is something to be ashamed of.[2]

He is convinced that the men who shot up the Hendayais timed their raid deliberately, to hit as many innocent people as possible. The refugees from the Spanish side of the border, he says, always went to the bar at an earlier hour. Ordinary French Basque citizens, like himself, were usually the only customers there at the time of the shooting. 'Those mercenaries were butchers,' he says, 'and then they ran off to Spain with their noses in the air.'

The Hendayais attack has become as notorious for the manner in which the attackers escaped as it was for the indiscriminate carnage they had left behind them. By all accounts, the two gunmen ran to a green Renault 18 parked nearby, where a third man drove them off at speed towards the border. Minutes later, an identical green Renault 18 drove straight through the French control post on the International Bridge across the Bidasoa, and crashed into a stationary car on the Spanish side.

Surrounded by armed police and *guardia civiles*, three men emerged with their hands up. One of them was brandishing a Madrid phone number and claimed that they were doing a job for the Spanish police. While some of the police were finding a rifle, four pistols and magazines in the Renault,[3] another policeman was helpfully calling Madrid. The number turned out to be that of Manuel Ballesteros, head of police intelligence and director of the newly established Unified Counter-terrorist Command (Mando Único para la Lucha Contraterrorista – MULC).[4] Ballesteros was regarded as the force's leading expert on ETA, and had served as a police chief in Bilbao and San Sebastián.

His instructions were succinct: 'Let the matter drop. No one has seen or heard anything.'[5] Despite the vociferous protests of the French police, just a few yards away, the men were driven away into the obscurity from whence they had come. They have never been officially named, or charged. Officially, in fact, they have never been seen again.

The Hendayais case became a major scandal, provoking angry exchanges in the French and Spanish parliaments. It is a paradigm for the way in which the Spanish state, under conservative and Socialist governments alike, would do everything in its power to protect both those accused of participating in death squads and those high functionaries accused of covering up for them. Before looking at the details of the case, however, we need to return to the moment in which the decision was made to unleash a dirty war against ETA, and against Basque nationalism generally.[6]

The rising tide of militant opposition to the dictatorship in the early 1970s had provoked a resurgence of the Spanish ultra-Right. As well as open political forces like Blas Piñar's Fuerza Nueva (New Strength), which promised to be more Francoist than Franco, clandestine groups began to emerge. They operated outside the legality of the Francoist state, but were either tolerated or sponsored by the state apparatus. One of the earliest such groups was the Guerrilleros de Cristo Rey, the Warriors of Christ the King, who specialised in beating up 'Red priests'. Those who believed that Franco's insurrection had been a Christian crusade against communism were outraged to find that the younger clergy were now often taking up the cause of workers' rights and ethnic minorities, and that their bishops were sometimes supporting them.[7]

Painful as the Church's 'betrayal' was for Franco and Carrero Blanco, something rather more fundamental was wrong. Repression was no longer working. No amount of conventional police activity was capable of stemming the flood of strikes, demonstrations and, in the Basque Country, armed attacks by ETA. Carrero Blanco seems to have decided that two things were necessary: a central intelligence agency should co-ordinate information about 'subversion';[8] and this service should become the nerve centre which would control and direct the 'uncontrolled' violence of the Right into a coherent weapon of state terror.[9]

Carrero Blanco, however, had barely set up the innocuously named Central Documentation Service for the Presidency of the Government (Servicio Central de Documentación de Presidencia del Gobierno – SECED) when ETA put a violent end to his career.[10] It was apparently left to elements in this intelligence service to establish the network that would operate the first dirty war (1975–81), and have a major influence on the second dirty war (1983–7), waged by the GAL. In terms of ultimate responsibilities for state terrorism, however, it is significant that the service which set up the network reported directly to the 'President of the Government'; under the Spanish system, that means it reported to the Prime Minister.[11]

The organisational principle of a dirty war is the inverse of the ideal in any normal military strategy, or indeed in any enterprise involving a hierarchy. James Selfe, in a study of the dirty war waged by the apartheid governments of South Africa, identified this principle as 'the need *not* to know'.[12] A similar principle was described to Javier García, a journalist who has written extensively about the aftermath of the assassination of Carrero Blanco. An anonymous source in the Interior Ministry during the Suárez governments explained to him: 'We agreed that the police should sort things out between themselves, and that matters like *Argala*'s death should not be the concern of those responsible for those departments [the French and Spanish Interior ministries]; we politicians should not know about these things, because we are indiscreet, and there are questions of State which are untellable.'[13]

Unlike conventional military commanders, the organisers of a dirty war protect themselves by knowing as little as possible about the details of the operations on the ground. This gives them 'deniability' should any embarrassing facts come to light. In order to achieve this, the use of surrogates rather than direct subordinates is desirable.

Potential surrogates were quite thick on the ground in the Spain of the 1970s. The Franco dictatorship was a magnet for anti-democratic activists from other parts of the world. There were Italian neo-fascists, from groups like Ordine Nuovo (New Order) and Avanguardia Nazionale (National Vanguard), on the run from their own authorities after their terrorist campaign at home had failed to attract popular support. There were French veterans of the Organisation de l'Armée Secrète (OAS), the 'secret army' which had opposed the settlement of the Algerian conflict and had been crushed by de Gaulle when it attempted to subvert the French state.[14] There were Latin American zealots like the 'Triple A', the Alianza Anticomunista Argentina, who could practise their trade as exterminating angels comfortably in any Spanish-speaking country.[15] And there was the Spanish ultra-Right, which drew many of its militants from the police and the armed forces, who could act as conduits from the state apparatus.

All of these groups had several advantages over the use of purely mercenary gangsters. Right-wing 'dirty warriors' had a degree of ideological commitment which made them more reliable than underworld figures motivated only by money. Moreover, many of the foreigners owed the police favours for residence permits or for overlooking extradition orders, which made them more reliable still. Finally, they generally had better military training, especially in the use of explosives, than ordinary criminals.

Jean-Pierre Cherid was the prototype for those who were picked to do the dirty work for the Spanish state. Cherid was the quintessential right-wing mercenary, a man whose skill, discretion and ruthlessness were legendary among the lowlife elite that served the Spanish state apparatus. Like many dirty warriors, he had first seen action in the Algerian War of Independence, as a sergeant in the French paratroops. Then, as de Gaulle moved towards an accommodation with the Algerian independence movement, he joined the illegal OAS, and was sentenced to thirty years in prison in Toulouse in 1963 for his activities. He managed to escape to Franco's Spain in 1964, where the dominant ideology suited him very well. He also fought as a mercenary in the Nigerian/Biafran war, where he lost half his left hand.

It is appropriately symbolic, given the neo-Nazi ideology of many of those involved, that the initial action usually attributed to the first dirty war was the bombing of a bookshop, the Mugalde, in Bayonne in April 1975.[16] There were no casualties. Businesses, cars and houses associated, however loosely, with the exiled nationalist movement became regular targets of arsonists and bombers over the next few years.

Forty-five days after the attack on the Mugalde, on 5 June, the dirty war began in earnest, but, rather characteristically, with a cock-up. Michel Cardona, a former comrade of Cherid's in the OAS, died in Biarritz when the bomb he was trying to place exploded in his hands. The other members of his group were arrested by the French police. Their target had been José Antonio Urritikoetxea (*Josu Ternera*), one of ETA's top leaders and a future chief of staff. They told a French court they were working on the orders of a Captain Cándido Acedo of the Guardia Civil.[17]

Domingo Iturbe Abásolo (*Txomin*), another senior member of ETA, and also a future chief of staff, was targeted in Biarritz in November 1975, but he also escaped unhurt. Franco died a few days later, on 20 November, but the dirty war continued into 1976, with a machine-gun attack on the car of a third ETA leader, Tomás Pérez Revilla, in St-Jean-de-Luz in March. He was uninjured, but his wife, Felicia Ziluaga, was very seriously wounded.

These actions, and the more minor sabotage attacks in between, were usually claimed by the Batalión Vasco Español (BVE), the Basque Spanish Battalion. Other colourful cover names were also employed, such as Anti-Terrorismo ETA (ATE, an inversion of ETA's acronym) or Acción Nacional Española (ANE), but the BVE appears to have been the main organisational framework for this dirty war.[18] A characteristic of these death squads was that they operated on both sides of the border, though probably with different personnel. They were responsible for two deaths in the Spanish Basque Country in 1975, and another in 1977. Apart from the latter, however, the dirty warriors seem to have hung up their guns between the attack on Pérez Revilla and the summer of 1978, an interval of more than two years.[19]

What caused this pause in operations? In the absence of hard evidence, any explanation must be speculative, but the political context offers some clues.

This was a period of exceptional political turbulence, in which the Spanish transition from dictatorship to democracy was formulated and put into practice. The last year before Franco's death had been characterised by severe repression. It culminated in the execution by firing squad of two members of ETA and three other young revolutionaries on 26 September 1975, only two months before he died.[20] The two members of ETA, Juan Paredes Manot (*Txiki*) and Ángel Otaegui, became enduring symbols of radical Basque martyrdom.[21] The furious reaction in the Basque Country was echoed by large demonstrations in many parts of the world. The Spanish embassy in Portugal was burned down, and there were calls for Spain's expulsion from the United Nations.

Franco was replaced as head of state, as expected, by Juan Carlos de Borbón, son of the Bourbon claimant to the Spanish throne. The prince had been regarded as a cipher of the dictator, who had virtually brought him up, and his first few months as king seemed to bear this out. He reappointed Carlos Arias Navarro, the man with whom Franco had replaced Carrero Blanco, as Prime Minister. Arias proceeded to vacillate between timid reform and rigid authoritarianism.

Arias had previously been Director of State Security and Interior Minister. He was reputed to keep a tight control on the intelligence services,[22] so we may assume he was at least *au fait* with the progress of the dirty war, which had entered its active phase under his first premiership. The killing of five striking workers by police, outside a church in Vitoria in March 1976, showed just how limited his conception of reform actually was.[23] The King told *Newsweek* that his own Prime Minister was 'an unmitigated disaster'.[24]

In May, two democrats were shot dead in separate incidents at a right-wing rally on a Navarre mountainside. The shootings took place in full view of press cameras and under the noses of dozens of *guardia civiles*, who did not intervene either to stop the attacks or to arrest those responsible. This incident probably forced a brake on the dirty war, because the killers were seen to be among a party of Italian and Argentinian ultra-Rightists, the very same individuals who were suspected of forming the anti-ETA death squads. 'The Government is a prisoner', one of the more liberal ministers wrote in his diary, 'of the intelligence services.'[25]

A few weeks later, the King accepted the resignation of Arias, who was sixty-eight, and jumped a political generation by appointing the forty-five-year-old Adolfo Suárez as his successor. Suárez's brief from the King was clearly to modernise, and therefore democratise, the Spanish state. After his appointment, there would be no dirty war actions in France for more than two years.[26] It is at least plausible to suggest that the new Prime Minister insisted that the intelligence services kept their dirty warriors on a tight leash while he attempted the infinitely tricky task of tightrope-walking from dictatorship to democracy.

Within a year, Suárez had legalised most political parties, including the Communist Party, in the teeth of opposition from the army. He called general elections in June 1977, Spain's first multi-party poll since 1936. With 165 seats, as against 118 for Felipe González's Socialists, Suárez was able to form a reasonably comfortable minority government with his reinvented Union of the Democratic Centre (Unión del Centro Democrático – UCD).[27]

After forty years of dictatorship, the Spanish electorate had plumped firmly for the safest middle ground, leaving the Communists and the conservative Right with just twenty and sixteen seats respectively, and the real extremists out of the frame altogether. The scene was set for a reform of the old system from within, rather than the radical rupture with the past which many democrats would have preferred. This reform process arguably saved Spain as a whole from the unthinkable prospect of a replay of the Civil War. However, it left many of the old institutions, and the men who ran them, firmly in place. This made the conflict in the Basque Country, which had a dynamic of its own, much more difficult to resolve.

Since the assassination of Carrero Blanco in 1973, ETA's killing rate had climbed steeply. Eighteen people died at ETA's hands in 1974, three times as many as the previous year. This figure includes the twelve civilians who died in the bombing of the Cafetería Rolando in Madrid's Calle Correo, a savage act of indiscriminate terrorism never acknowledged by the group, but almost certainly its responsibility.[28] Internal dissension over the bombing hastened the process whereby the organisation split one more time, into 'military' and 'political-military' factions, in 1974. These were known as ETA(m) and ETA(p-m).

The 1977 elections in the Basque Country showed that the PNV, despite its lack of activism, was still the dominant political force in the region. It took eight seats, against just one for Euskadiko Ezkerra (Basque Left), a coalition hastily thrown together to front for ETA(p-m). Its rivals in ETA(m) did not field any party in these elections. In 1978, ETA(m) backed the establishment of Herri Batasuna (Popular Unity), which has represented its policies in the political arena ever since.[29]

ETA(p-m) was initially the dominant group, both politically and militarily. But the thesis that, in any split in ETA, the most militarist faction will ultimately impose its will was once again confirmed. ETA(p-m) abandoned armed struggle and became a purely political movement in the early 1980s. From then on, ETA has been synonymous with ETA(m). In the meantime, the combined violence of these two ETAs reaped a terrible harvest: sixty-eight deaths in 1978, seventy-six in 1979 and ninety-one in 1980.[30] In these same years ETA lost, respectively, seven, four and six members in combat, including dirty war victims.[31]

At first sight, ETA's escalation of terrorism at this moment in its history is rather baffling. After all, these were the very years in which Spain elaborated and endorsed a democratic Constitution. This was done by a remarkable process of consensus, a kind of 'peace process' which reconciled the traditionally lethal enmities between Right and Left. These were the years in which the rule of law was firmly established and the fundamental freedoms of speech, expression and association were consolidated.[32] These were the years when every single member of ETA was released from jail, under a series of amnesty arrangements.[33] These were the years in which the Basques voted in favour of a Statute of Autonomy which gave them more self-government than they had ever previously enjoyed, a degree of regional power almost unprecedented in Europe. How was it that ETA responded to these developments with violence rather than dialogue?

The full answer to that question lies well beyond the scope of this book, but I would suggest there are three main reasons. One lies in the nature of ETA itself.

The organisation has its origins in a deeply religious culture, with a highly developed sense of commitment. This admirable quality can become distorted into a craving for apocalyptic martyrdom. Correspondingly, this culture has a poorly developed sense of negotiation and compromise.[34] ETA's long attachment to 'activism' made it overvalue 'revolutionary' – that is, military – options for their own sake.

ETA's suspicion that purely political activity led inevitably to an abandonment of nationalist aspirations had become a dogma. It seemed to be borne out by the 'pro-Spanish' tendencies followed by most of those groups who had split from the organisation. The core members of ETA were convinced that any compromise on full independence was tantamount to betrayal, or even to collaboration with 'genocide'. The idea of 'genocide' is linked to the precarious situation of the Basque language, which was also sometimes cited as a factor in making terrorism seem 'necessary': only the urgent achievement of independence could prevent the language dying in the current generation, some radicals argued.

The lack of any real democratic reform within the security forces was another major factor in maintaining popular support for ETA's violence. The Guardia Civil and the police continued to unleash violent, undisciplined and indiscriminate repression in the Basque Country, long after democracy had been established. This made it relatively easy for ETA to convince its supporters that their homeland was still occupied by a foreign and oppressive government. The experience of the GAL's dirty war would greatly assist in reconfirming that impression for the first generation to grow up under democracy.

There was, however, at least according to ETA's supporters, a further, and more objectively based, justification for launcing a terrorist offensive in a developing democracy. This is the fact that the Spanish transition to democracy failed to offer the Basques a clear choice as to whether or not they wanted to be part of the freshly constituted Spanish state. The Basque nationalist majority remained outside the remarkable consensus which endorsed the 1978 Constitution, though the PNV played a part in its elaboration, and only withdrew at the last minute.

The Constitution recognises Basque 'nationality' and the Basque language, and makes relatively generous provision for Basque autonomy. Crucially, however, the Spanish consensus had co-opted the Basques as part of a larger unit, to which many of them felt they did not belong. Basque nationalists felt they had been betrayed by Spanish democrats. The PSOE, for example, had explicitly supported self-determination for the minority nationalities only a few years earlier, but had ditched that principle by the time the Constitution was negotiated. This switch in strategy can be attributed to 'centralism', indeed to 'Spanish nationalism', on the part of the Socialists. It was also a pragmatic recognition of the fact that a referendum on independence for the Basque Country might have been a bridge too far for the army, which was already rattling its sabres over the introduction of democratic reforms. Either way, however, Basque nationalist aspirations were not recognised, or, at least, not to the extent demanded by the Basque nationalists themselves.

The rift between Basque nationalists and the rest of Spain was made dramatically visible in December 1978, when the Constitution was subjected to referendum. It was supported, in Spain as a whole, by a clear majority of the total Spanish electorate (59 per cent) and by an overwhelming majority of those who voted (88 per cent). In the Basque Country, in sharp contrast, only 31 per cent of the electorate voted 'Yes' to the Constitution.[35] This still represented 75 per cent of those Basques who did turn out, but the high rate of abstention (55 per cent, nearly double the Spanish average of 32 per cent) undermined the legitimacy of this pro-Constitution majority. The 'No' vote in the Basque Country, campaigned for by ETA(p-m) supporters and some backers of ETA(m), garnered the support of 10 per cent of the electorate (compared to 5 per cent for Spain as a whole) and 24 per cent of voters (three times the Spanish average of 8 per cent).[36]

Constitutional Referendum, December 1978 (%)		
	All Spain	Basque Country
'Yes' vote as percentage of electorate	59	31
'No' vote as percentage of electorate	5	10
Abstention	32	55
'Yes' vote as percentage of participants	88	75
'No' vote as percentage of participants	8	24

While the 'No' vote was significantly higher than in the rest of Spain, it was the level of abstention which really made the pattern in the Basque Country quite different from that in any other region.[37] Given that both the PNV and the biggest sector of ETA(m) supporters had campaigned for 'active abstention', it was possible to contend that the Constitution had been rejected, or at least not accepted, by a majority of Basques. Spanish democrats drew the opposite conclusion. They argued that, since 75 per cent of those who had *not* abstained had voted 'Yes', the Basques had actually endorsed the new dispensation. They also claimed that much of the abstention indicated no particular political intention. They (wrongly) attributed all the rest of the abstention to the PNV.[38] They assumed that this abstentionist sector would be steered back into the democratic consensus through the negotiation of the Statute of Autonomy.[39]

However Spanish centralists interpreted the figures, the gap which had opened up between Basque nationalism and Spanish democracy was a real one. This was demonstrated by general elections less than three months later. Standing for the first time, ETA(m)'s new political front, Herri Batasuna, which explicitly refused to recognise Spanish democracy as such, took nearly 10 per cent of the vote. This was despite the fact that Herri Batasuna refused to participate in Spanish political institutions.

As Spanish democrats had predicted, however, both the PNV and ETA(p-m)'s supporters in Euskadiko Ezkerra appeared to legitimise the Constitution after the fact. In 1979, both parties campaigned for the introduction of a Statute of Autonomy for three Basque provinces (excluding Navarre, against the nationalists' wishes). This charter for regional self-government was supported in a 1979 referendum by over 90 per cent of those who voted.[40] This represented 53 per cent of the total electorate, and gave the Statute of Autonomy, commonly known as the Statute of Gernika, democratic legitimacy. This in turn could be considered a retrospective legitimisation of the 1978 Constitution in the Basque Country, since the statute fell within the limits to self-government set by that document.[41]

For ETA(m) and its supporters in Herri Batasuna, however, the transition's failure to recognise a Basque right to self-determination invalidated all subsequent legislation. In their view, the Statute of Autonomy, like the Constitution, was an undemocratic 'imposition', which should be resisted by force and by politics.[42] Which is what they continued to do. The formidable 'rejection front' represented by Herri Batasuna still had a strong constituency in Basque society. It was sufficient sea, in Mao Zedong's famous saying, to give ETA(m) swimming space for another twenty years and more. Herri Batasuna's share of the vote rose to 16.5 per cent in the first elections to the Basque autonomous parliament in March 1980, just as ETA's offensive went into overdrive. With fairly marginal fluctuations, Herri Batasuna has maintained this level of support through two decades of increasingly extensive self-rule by Basque autonomous institutions. These institutions have been dominated by the moderate nationalists of the PNV throughout this period.

Meanwhile, for some people in the Spanish security apparatus, the rule of law was not enough to contain the violent dissidence of ETA. The option of a dirty war was exercised again, this time under a government most citizens regarded as fully democratic.

Before the referendum campaign on the Constitution had even started, the dirty warriors went back into action in France. In July 1978, a car driven by Juan José Etxabe, a former ETA leader who had left the group, was machine-gunned by the BVE in St-Jean-de-Luz. He was severely wounded, and his wife, Agurtzane Arregi, was almost cut in half by the fusillade and died on the spot. Four days earlier, José María Portell, a journalist and ETA specialist, had been killed by ETA near Bilbao. Questions raised about the relationship between these two killings have never been satisfactorily answered.

The BVE's next attack was the spectacular booby-trap which killed José Miguel Beñarán Ordeñana (*Argala*), the day after the fifth anniversary of Carrero Blanco's death. This bombing, which scattered Beñarán Ordeñana's body over a 150-metre radius in the little French Basque town of Anglet, may also have aimed to derail possible talks between Madrid and ETA. Beñarán Ordeñana was widely believed to represent the tendency in ETA(m) best disposed to a negotiated settlement at the time. What is undeniably true is that his death left 'an enormous vacuum at the core of ETA Militar; above all in regard to its capacity for theoretical analysis', in the words of Letamendía.[43]

It may be, however, that the main motivation for killing Beñarán Ordeñana was simply revenge. Those who sent out the death squads seem to have had an obsession with hunting down the men directly responsible for the killing of Carrero Blanco.

According to Arques and Miralles, the group directly responsible for killing Beñarán Ordeñana was a microcosm of the BVE. Commanded by Jean-Pierre Cherid, the former OAS militant referred to above, it also included an Italian neo-fascist and a veteran of the Argentinian 'Triple A'.[44]

Only three weeks later, the BVE seriously injured another ETA leader, and (reputedly) also a member of the *comando* who killed Carrero, José Manuel Pagoaga Gallastegi (*Peixoto*). In the following months there were two further failed attempts on the life of Domingo Iturbe Abásolo (*Txomin*), who had replaced Beñarán Ordeñana as ETA's top man, and would run the organisation for the first half of the 1980s. As ETA's armed campaign in Spain continued to intensify, the death squads picked off another three victims in France in the course of 1979.

This year also saw a resurgence of killings claimed by the BVE inside Spain itself, including Herri Batasuna's deputy mayor of San Sebastián, Tomás Alba. In 1980, which was ETA's bloodiest year, right-wing terrorism on the Spanish side of the border also reached its climax, with seventeen victims, most of whom seem to have been chosen at random.

This was also the period during which a majority of Basques re-entered the democratic process through endorsing the Statute of Autonomy and electing their first autonomous government, under terms laid down by the Spanish Constitution, as we have seen.

Against this unstable background, the BVE's 1980 campaign was particularly indiscriminate on the Spanish side of the border. Bombs were left outside a bar (killing four) and a playschool (killing three people including a gypsy child and her pregnant sister). In the cases of two female victims, rape preceded death. It seems that this campaign may have been as much a gut reaction from ultra-Rightists, both to the consolidation of democracy and to ETA's ongoing attacks, as a strategically planned dirty war by the security forces. To some degree, at least, it seems to have been a genuinely 'uncontrolled' phenomenon. But what is also evident is that the authorities made very little attempt to control it, as the notorious case of the 'triangle of death' illustrates very clearly.

At least ten killings were claimed by the BVE in the triangle formed by San Sebastián, Rentería and Andoain between 1979 and 1981. The names of two of the killers, Ignacio Iturbe and Ladislao Zabala, were well known to many people in the area, but the police took no action against them. A French court issued an arrest warrant against Zabala in October 1980, but still no action was taken. Only after two more people were killed and another wounded did the police act, and then only because local politicians were threatening to expose them for complicity. The police officer responsible for this extraordinary piece of procrastination was Jesús Martínez Torres. Far from suffering for his laxity, he was promoted to head up the police intelligence services by the Socialists, as soon as they came to power in 1982.[45]

The man he replaced was Manuel Ballesteros, whom we last met at the beginning of this chapter, ordering the release of the suspects for the Bar Hendayais massacre. His subsequent legal history is a template for the treatment of dirty war crimes by successive governments over the next fifteen years, as Spanish democracy became, supposedly, fully mature.[46]

In the first place, Ballesteros (as well as three other policemen and a *guardia civil*) simply ignored requests for their attendance at French court hearings on the Hendayais killings. France was officially outraged by the affair; the Minister for Foreign Affairs had called in the Spanish ambassador to Paris for an explanation. The Spanish Interior Minister, Juan José Rosón, told the Madrid parliament that he accepted

Ballesteros' version of events: the three men who had fled across the border minutes after the shooting had no connection with it, but they were police informers whose identities had to be protected.

The French government, and the Spanish opposition, led by the Socialists, declared these explanations unacceptable. Rosón himself was visibly embarrassed by the affair when it was raised in parliament, but he continued to support his man. The first dirty war, however, petered out within months of the Hendayais killings. There were other factors involved, as we shall see, but it seems likely that the clash between the newly acquired democratic values of the Spanish government and the decidedly undemocratic values of the unreformed police forces had temporarily been resolved in favour of the former.

What is more surprising is the fact that the Socialists, who had so righteously demanded explanations from Rosón in 1980 and 1981, did a complete U-turn on the Ballesteros/Hendayais case once they came to power in 1982. José Barrionuevo, who replaced Rosón as Interior Minister, made it clear from the beginning that he was 'not in favour of reopening cases inherited from the previous administration'.[47]

While Ballesteros was initially sidelined to a bureaucratic position under the new administration, he would be very well protected by the Socialists, and ultimately regain much of his power and influence in Interior. In 1985, after ignoring six Spanish summonses to appear in court, he was finally compelled to attend a hearing on the Hendayais case in San Sebastián. A few days before this court appearance, he was invited to a lunch in his honour at the Ministry of the Interior. The guests included the minister, Barrionuevo, the former minister, Rosón, Barrionuevo's deputy, Rafael Vera, and various police chiefs including Jesús Martínez Torres – Ballesteros' replacement as chief of police intelligence.[48]

Despite this intimidating show of support, the San Sebastián court found Ballesteros guilty of refusing to assist the justice system, since he would not reveal the names of the three suspects. The court's sentence was relatively light: he was barred from serving in the police for three years. This sentence was appealed to the Supreme Court in 1986, and, after some irregular legal manoeuvres, he was found not guilty. The senior court gave rather extraordinary grounds for his acquittal: he had refused to give the names 'in the erroneous belief' that it was more important to preserve the identity of his informers than to give information to the courts. Barrionuevo promptly reinstated him in a top police intelligence position, where he remained until 1994.

The San Sebastián court believed the Supreme Court absolution carried a condition: since he had been informed, by the highest legal authorities, that his interpretation of his duty was erroneous, he should now give the names of the suspects to the court. When he again refused, in 1994, he was sentenced to six years' disqualification from public service, for the slightly different crime of 'dereliction of duty'. He again appealed to the Supreme Court, where there were once again remarkable legal manoeuvres. The prosecutor, while formally presenting the charges brought by his colleagues against Ballesteros, exercised his 'freedom of speech' to make a comprehensive defence of the man in the dock. The Supreme Court ruled that the San Sebastián court had tried him twice for the same offence, and again found him not guilty.

By a strange coincidence, the Supreme Court ruled in this case on 16 December 1994, just three days before most of the rest of the anti-terrorist high command were imprisoned as part of the investigation into the second dirty war, which had been conducted under the Socialist administration between 1983 and 1987. The relationship of Suárez's UCD administration, and of his security forces, to the first dirty war has never received such an investigation. The silence of Ballesteros has been a stone wall which has never been breached.

I asked Emile Muley, survivor of the Hendayais attack, how he felt about the apparent complicity of the Spanish authorities in covering up a crime which had riddled him with bullets and nearly wiped out his entire family. He replied with a wry French pun, which expressed both resignation and condemnation: 'Affaire d'État,' he said, 'rien à faire.' ('It's a question of state, nothing can be done about it.')

The conviction that citizens *could* do something about questions of state, when the state was involved in crime, has motivated those who investigated the second dirty war, against all the obstacles the state put in their way.

NOTES

1 All quotations from Emile Muley in this chapter are from an interview in Hendaye, June 1997.
2 Interview with Jean-Louis Humbert, Hendaye, June 1997.
3 *El País*, 11 May 1995, quoting French court documents.
4 This was the committee that co-ordinated counter-terrorist activity in the various security forces.
5 Ibid. The source is the police telephone record book which, after being mislaid for some years, was successfully recuperated by a San Sebastián court.
6 A comprehensive account of the first dirty war is to be found in Ricardo Arques and Melchor Miralles, *Amedo: El Estado contra ETA* (Barcelona: Plaza y Janés/Cambio 16, 1989), pp. 72–149; other versions can be found in Victorino Ruiz de Azúa, 'Las Manos Sucias', in Santos Juliá et al. (eds.), *Memoria de la Transición* (Madrid: Taurus, 1996), ch. 22; Patxo Unzueta, *El Terrorismo: ¿Qué era? ¿Qué es?* (Barcelona: Ediciones Destino, 1997), pp. 35–9; and *Egin*, 'Guerra Sucia' series, January/February 1995, nos. 1–3.
7 A 1974 Pastoral Letter from the Bishop of Bilbao, Antonio Añoveros, which called for the recognition of Basque national rights, provoked an unprecedented crisis in the formerly intimate relations between the Catholic Church and the Francoist state. The government wanted to expel the bishop from Spain; the Vatican indicated that this would result in the excommunication of the government, and Franco backed down. See Juan Luis Cebrián, 'La Agonía del Franquismo', in Juliá et al. (eds.), op. cit., p. 18.
8 Each branch of the armed forces, and the various police forces, had their own intelligence branch. Rivalry was intense, and information was rarely shared. On occasions, their undercover agents ended up shooting at each other, rather than at their targets.
9 This account again follows the version of the origin of the dirty war given by Arques and Miralles, op. cit., pp. 72–82.
   '*Violencia incontrolada*' was a term used as a euphemism for right-wing terrorism in the press of the late Franco years. '*Incontrolados*' became the

shorthand for the individuals, whether police or right-wing civilians, who carried out such activities.

10 The SECED was later replaced by the Centro Superior de Información de la Defensa (CESID – Higher Information Centre for Defence), which was set up by Suárez's deputy Prime Minister and Defence Minister, Gutiérrez Mellado, in 1977–8.

11 Arques and Miralles, op. cit., p. 73. The CESID, under the PSOE governments, reported directly to the deputy Prime Minister. Under the Spanish political system, the Prime Minister was, and is, referred to as the 'President of the Government'. The head of state is the King, but his functions are largely ceremonial. The Spanish system has been described as 'semi-presidential', recognising the weight the Prime Minister carries relative to the rest of the executive, and to parliament. (See Paul Heywood, *The Government and Politics of Spain* (London: Macmillan,1995), pp. 88–102.) The term *Presidente* will generally be translated as Prime Minister in this book, but the title has a particular significance for our subject, because an abbreviation ('Pte') on one CESID document has been alleged to refer to *Presidente*, as in the former Prime Minister, Felipe González.

12 Quoted in Allister Sparks, *Tomorrow is Another Country* (Sandton, South Africa: Struik Book Distributors, 1994), p. 160. My emphasis.

13 *El País*, 10 November 1986.

14 These included both 'pieds noirs', from a white settler background, and 'harkis', Algerian Arabs with French loyalties. Both played a major part in both dirty wars.

15 The 'Triple A' was also known, in Spain, as the 'Alianza Apostólica Anti-comunista'.

16 It is a sad reflection on the political degeneration of ETA supporters that, in the mid-1990s, they would become involved in repeated attacks on a left-wing bookshop (the Lagún) in San Sebastián, because the owners were firmly opposed to ETA's use of terrorism in a democracy.

17 Arques and Miralles, op. cit., p. 76. Cándido Acedo has featured repeatedly in allegations about dirty war operations, but has never been convicted. He provided an alibi for General Galindo in the Lasa and Zabala trial (see chs. 5 and 19). *El País,* 10 February 2000.

18 Francisco Letamendía, *Historia del Nacionalismo Vasco y de ETA*, 3 vols. (San Sebastián: R&B Ediciones, 1994), vol. 2, pp. 230–1, attributes the killings up to 1976 to the ATE, and those from 1978 to 1980 to the BVE. Arques and Miralles, however, describe all these 'organisations' as 'the same dogs with different collars'. Op. cit., p. 74.

19 ETA was not the only target of the dirty war in this period. Antonio Cubillo, a leader of a separatist movement in the Canary Islands, was the victim of an assassination attempt linked to the Spanish security forces while in exile in Algeria in April 1978. See Patxo Unzueta, *El Terrorismo: ¿Qué era? ¿Qué es?* (Barcelona: Ediciones Destino, 1997), p. 37.

As well as the attack on Cubillo, there were other instances of the dirty war being carried to third countries. Arques and Miralles document a double killing of ETA supporters by the BVE in Venezuela in 1980, and one in the US in 1982. Op. cit., pp. 89–96 and 139.

20 Several other left-wing groups turned to armed struggle in the last years of Franco's regime. These included the Maoist group FRAP; the other three young revolutionaries executed were members of this group. Antonio Elorza (ed.), *La Historia de ETA* (Madrid: Temas de Hoy, 2000), p. 168.

21 ETA published an account of Paredes' execution, which has him singing the Basque national anthem in the face of death, even after the first volley was

fired. (Letamendía, op. cit., vol. 1, pp. 412–14.) Paredes was a first-generation immigrant from Estremadura, Otaegui an indigenous Basque. If Franco had wanted to indicate that ETA had succeeded in winning over immigrant workers to the radical Basque cause, he could not have chosen a more appropriate symbol.

22 See Carlos Elordi, 'El Largo Invierno del 76', in Juliá et al. (eds.), op. cit., p. 128.

23 See prologue, p. 2.

24 Elordi in Juliá et al. (eds.), op. cit., p. 128.

25 Elordi in Juliá et al. (eds.), op. cit., p. 128. The minister was José María de Areilza (Foreign Affairs 1975–6). The first Francoist mayor of Bilbao (see ch. 1, p. 30) he had broken with the regime by the 1960s and was an advocate of democratic reform in the 1970s.

26 There were two killings claimed by the BVE in the Spanish Basque Country within this period. As we shall see, however, these were the responsibility of a very maverick group, whose unfortunate victims rarely had any political significance whatsoever.

27 This impromptu party, which had not enjoyed much success until Suárez made it his personal vehicle, now included modernising former Francoists, opportunistic regional 'barons' of the old regime, and Christian Democrats in search of a political home. Its lack of political coherence pulled it apart in the early 1980s, but it served an essential function as the key vehicle for the reform of the Francoist system.

28 Letamendía, op. cit., vol. 1, p. 395.

29 For a fuller account of the origins and early years of Herri Batasuna, see ch. 9, pp. 129–31.

30 Ministry of Interior figures cited in Juliá et al. (eds.), op. cit., p. 290, and corresponding details in José María Calleja, *Contra la Barbarie* (Madrid: Temas de Hoy, 1997), appendix. The figures for the intermediate years are as follows: 1975 – sixteen; 1976 – seventeen; 1977 – twelve. Some sources give significantly higher figures, as high as 110 for 1980, but this is probably due to the inclusion of the victims of other terrorist groups.

31 *Punto y Hora de Euskal Herria* (hereafter *Punto y Hora*), 13 July 1984, pp. 29–30.

32 Of course, the dirty war conducted in much of this same period gave ETA the argument that the rule of law was not being applied to the Basques, an argument that would gain even more force during the GAL campaign in the 1980s.

33 The Suárez government finally yielded to the clamorous demand for a full amnesty covering all ETA members in October 1977. Days later, ETA killed the President of the provincial govenment (*Diputación*) of Vizcaya and his two bodyguards. See Patxo Unzueta, 'Euskadi: Amnestía y Vuelta a Empezar', in Juliá et al. (eds.), op. cit., pp. 275–83.

34 For a full and challenging exposition of this 'cultural' argument, see Joseba Zulaika, *Basque Violence, Metaphor and Sacrament* (Reno, Nev.: University of Nevada Press, 1988).

35 The same caveat about the use of the term 'Basque Country' applies here as when this issue was discussed in the prologue; see p. 12, n. 2.

36 Juan J. Linz, *Conflicto en Euskadi* (Madrid: Espasa-Calpe, 1986), pp. 226–8; Letamendía, op. cit., vol. 2, pp. 219–20; Soledad Gallego-Díaz y Bonifacio de la Cuadra, 'La Constitución', in Juliá et al. (eds.), op. cit., p. 315; and Basque government website www1.euskadi.net.

37 It is noteworthy that the Catalans, whose claim to national identity is as strong as the Basques, identified strongly with the Spanish constitutional process. Ninety per cent of Catalan voters, and 61 per cent of the Catalan

electorate, voted 'Yes'. Only 5 per cent of Catalan voters voted 'No'. All these figures were actually more pro-Constitution than the Spanish national average. See Linz, op. cit., pp. 226–8, and Letamendía, op. cit., vol. 2, pp. 219–20.

38 The substantial vote which Herri Batasuna consistently achieved in subsequent elections suggests that at least 15 per cent of the abstention represented the political supporters of ETA(m).

39 See *El País*, 8 December 1978.

40 Letamendía, op. cit., vol. 2, pp. 342–3.

41 While the PNV has not only recognised but administered the autonomous institutions, the party has always maintained a distance from the Constitution, a distance which became explicit with the signing of the Lizarra Pact for Basque self-determination in 1998.

42 Herri Batasuna had called for abstention in the referendum, in which participation was just under 60 per cent, as against 45 per cent in the 1978 plebiscite. The level of abstention was hardly a victory for the radicals, but it did indicate that their constituency was rock solid. Indeed, it seems likely that a number of PNV supporters heeded Herri Batasuna's call.

43 Letamendía, op. cit., vol. 2, p. 228.

44 Arques and Miralles, op. cit., p. 73.

45 Iturbe and Zabala were convicted of seven murders and two attempted murders after their arrest in 1981. They were rank-and-file right-wingers, and among the few BVE members to be prosecuted in Spain. For accounts of this case, see *Egin*, 'Guerra Sucia' series, January/February 1995, no. 3; Arques and Miralles, op. cit., pp. 139–41, and Ruiz de Azúa in Juliá et al. (eds.), op. cit., pp. 579–88).
    There were more examples of lack of enthusiasm for finding the culprits: the police officer instructed to investigate the bar bombing that killed four people in 1980 was José Amedo Fouce, later convicted as an organiser of the GAL. Unsurprisingly, he identified no suspects.

46 Among the best sources for the Hendayais/Ballesteros affair are Arques and Miralles, op. cit., pp. 96–103, Ruiz de Azúa in Juliá et al. (eds.), op. cit., pp. 579–88, and *El País*, 19 May 1981, 11 May 1985 and 17 December 1994.

47 Ruiz de Azúa in Juliá et al. (eds.), op. cit., p. 584.

48 Arques and Miralles, op. cit., p. 100.

PART II

A Dirty War Run by Democrats

4

Clean Hands in Government:

provocation, response and the French connection

Spanish democracy swung vertiginously from terror to celebration between the beginning of 1981 and the end of 1982. Since the start of the transition, the threat of a military coup had shadowed Spanish politics. Each dramatic advance – the legalisation of the Communist Party, the negotiation of the Constitution, the establishment of autonomous governments in Catalonia and the Basque Country – was made to the sound of sabres rattling offstage.

The savage escalation of ETA's campaign over this period inevitably exacerbated extremism within the armed forces and the police. Rank-and-file members of the security forces suffered appalling losses in 1980. ETA killed six *guardia civiles* in a single shoot-out in Ipaster in February. On 15 June three national policemen were killed in a bar, and two *guardia civiles* were shot dead in similar circumstances the next day. Four *guardia civiles* were killed while having lunch in September, and five more died in an attack on the bar where they were relaxing in November. This force alone lost a total of thirty-two members in the course of the year.

The victims also included senior officers, often retired men who were very soft targets. The list of civilian victims grew longest of all. They ranged from politicians to alleged informers, from company directors to unfortunates who found themselves in the wrong place at the wrong time. A thirteen-year-old boy was killed by a bomb left in a sports holdall. Those who wanted to blame democracy for the chronic collapse in 'public security' were being given plenty of excuses, wrapped in body bags, courtesy of ETA.

Meanwhile the Union of the Democratic Centre, Adolfo Suárez's governing party, had begun to fall apart at the seams. The Socialists, who had been expected to win the general elections of 1979, and nearly did, were snapping at UCD's heels. The party had always been an unlikely coalition, and its regional grandees were permanently embroiled in unseemly squabbles. In January 1981, Suárez resigned. Though he has always denied yielding to pressure from the army, the military was still being described as a *poder fáctico,* a *de facto* and unconstitutional political power in the land. The rattling of sabres grew to a crescendo.

On 23 February Suárez's successor, Leopoldo Calvo Sotelo, was about to be sworn in as Prime Minister when the parliamentary chamber was seized by dozens of *guardia civiles*. They were led by Antonio Tejero, a lieutenant-colonel with a comic opera moustache. In one of the most extraordinary pieces of live television in European history, bursts of submachine-gun fire raked the ceiling while Tejero, brandishing a pistol like a demented John Cleese, ordered the deputies to 'Sit down, fuck it!' There were courageous exceptions, including Suárez, but most of the parliamentary deputies took cover under their seats.

The longest night in recent Spanish history followed. At first it seemed that the coup was going to succeed. Lieutenant-General Milans del Bosch brought armoured cars out onto the streets of Valencia. General Alfonso Armada, second in command of the army, and a former secretary general to King Juan Carlos, also actively backed the coup from behind the scenes. Democratic Spain endured its worst nightmare in humiliating impotence.[1] It could only wait to see what the King, as commander-in-chief of the armed forces, would do.

After seven hours of silence, which have never been fully explained, the King went on national television at 1 a.m. the following morning. He wore military uniform as Captain-General of the army. He repudiated the coup and demanded support for the Constitution. The coup fizzled out, and Tejero surrendered. The King's position as guarantor of democracy was copperfastened. There were massive, and peaceful, demonstrations in support of democracy throughout Spain, but everyone knew it had been a close-run thing.

Calvo Sotelo's new government had been born limping, and never walked tall. It was widely believed that he was operating only by the grace and favour of the army.[2] Two of his major initiatives suggest that this was so. He took Spain into NATO, at the time a deeply unpopular move with the Spanish populace, but one which gave the long-isolated army a new and prestigious international role. He also introduced a controversial law, backed by the Socialists, which sought to severely curtail the autonomous powers just granted to the Basques and Catalans. The perfectly constitutional moves towards self-government by these regions were anathema to the generals, perhaps even more so than ETA's offensive.[3]

However, Calvo Sotelo did ensure the trial of the coup conspirators, who received heavy jail sentences. There was also some further liberalisation in the form of Spain's first divorce law. Meanwhile, the remarkable process known as 'social reinsertion' was largely negotiated under this government. This was the scheme whereby a sector of ETA(p-m) abandoned armed struggle. In return, it got its prisoners out of jail and its exiles home, and became integrated in normal democratic politics through Euskadiko Ezkerra.[4]

This process left the field of 'armed struggle' almost entirely in the hands of ETA(m). Most people believed that ETA(m)'s acceleration of violence had been at least partly aimed at provoking a coup, something ETA has always denied. In any case, Tejero's assault on parliament did not even make ETA pause to reconsider its strategy. The group killed a policeman within two weeks of the coup attempt, and killed two colonels within a month. In May, ETA seriously injured the general in charge of the royal barracks, killing his three escorts. But the organisation never again achieved the terrible intensity of its 1980 operations, and its killing rate dropped by about two-thirds during Calvo Sotelo's premiership.

It is also notable that the dirty war ceased almost as soon as Calvo Sotelo had appointed his first cabinet. The virtual absence of death squad activity under his premiership is one of the strongest arguments against the Socialist contention that the GAL were a direct 'inheritance' from UCD. However, that absence also suggests that UCD probably had more control of the *incontrolados* than the party's leaders like to admit. As Victorino Ruiz de Azúa puts it: 'It is implausible to attribute to hired guns or to police acting on their own account this capacity [of stopping operations], and it is more implausible the more democracy became established. Someone with sufficient power gave the order to stop, and to start again, in every case.'[5]

The uninspired leadership of Calvo Sotelo, coupled with the further disintegration of UCD, laid the ground for the extraordinary Socialist victory of October 1982. Since the beginning of the transition, the hugely charismatic and politically adroit Felipe González had moved the PSOE steadily towards the centre, ditching its commitment to Marxism in the process. The PSOE appeared as the party of youth and modernisation. It was the party whose accession to government would mean that the transition to democracy was complete, but which could be trusted not to make any very radical changes. It was also the party which anyone with an eye for the main chance was now joining. Socialist militants had probably been outnumbered by smart opportunists well before the party took power.

González's victory, then, was expected, but the scale of it astounded everyone. Ten million Spaniards opted for the PSOE, nearly 50 per cent of those who voted, in a general election with the highest level of participation in Spanish history. This first of three consecutive absolute majorities brought the Socialists as close to absolute power as the rules of democracy permit.[6] Ironically, democracy was offering Felipe González a monopoly of influence in Spanish society, a monopoly which would inevitably tend to become anti-democratic. But on that October night of champagne fizzing in the streets, of fists clenched joyously around red roses, very few people foresaw the long slide from grace which lay ahead.

The bright young men who made up González's first government seemed the antithesis of the stuffy, authoritarian past. An air of Sixties radicalism still clung to many of them, and their longish hair and lack of neckties bespoke a style which promised freedom. This was a government untainted by any connections with Francoism. This was the first Spanish cabinet in half a century to start off with clean hands. González's choice for deputy Prime Minister was Alfonso Guerra, his long-time comrade from Seville, and virtual *alter ego*. Guerra habitually played the political street-fighter, savaging internal and external enemies, while González's seductive charm remained untainted by unseemly name-calling. Guerra coined a famous phrase in 1986, which was intended to promise liberating modernisation, but took on a much more sinister reading as time revealed the real nature of *Felipismo*.[7] 'With another four years of Socialist Government,' he said, 'Spain will be unrecognisable even to the mother who gave her birth.'

Very few observers saw the PSOE establishment as sinister in 1982, however. Nevertheless, there was one appointment by González which immediately caused some consternation in well-informed circles. One of the most sensitive positions in the new government was bound to be at the head of the Interior Ministry. This was not only because of ETA's offensive, or the rising level of ordinary crime, or even the involvement of the Guardia Civil in the attempted coup. It was also because the various police forces were virtually unreformed since Franco's time. If the Socialists really wanted to establish the democratic rule of law in Spain, they would have to start with those charged with enforcing that law.

It was widely expected that Carlos Sanjuán, who had been the PSOE's Interior spokesperson in opposition, would get the job. It was Sanjuán who had tenaciously pursued Juan José Rosón over the Hendayais/Ballesteros scandal in parliament. At the last moment, however, González opted for someone else: José Barrionuevo. It was a fateful decision. The idea came, curiously enough, from Rosón himself, according to Barrionuevo's own long-serving deputy, Rafael Vera: 'In the first meeting which Felipe González had with Minister Rosón, after winning the elections and just before he was formally appointed as Prime Minister, Rosón tells him that the person who fits the bill for Minister [of the Interior] is Barrionuevo.'[8]

Barrionuevo had been deputy mayor of Madrid, in charge of the municipal police. Vera, who had first worked with him in that department, says that his boss had greatly impressed Rosón with his efficiency. As Vera tells it, González considered the appointment a 'question of state' and overrode party interests to accede to Rosón's request. Not everyone was so easily persuaded.

'When I heard the news that the Interior Minister was going to be José Barrionuevo, I put my head in my hands,' says Fernando López Agudín, who would later work in the ministry for the Socialists himself. 'He is not a bad person, but I had the feeling that he was limited politically, a man with right-wing origins . . . the man least suited to be Interior Minister.'[9]

Barrionuevo's 'right-wing origins' are a matter of record. He had been a member of the Francoist student union, where he may have come into contact with Rodolfo Martín Villa, who had been Rosón's predecessor as Interior Minister and who, according to López Agudín, also pressurised González to appoint him. His conversion to socialism came relatively late in life, and very late in the life of the Franco regime, at the age of twenty-seven in 1969. Moreover, he and Vera, who was the senior member of his team on Madrid city council, had already acquired a reputation for supporting the police against the people when the two interests came into conflict.[10]

Far from using his new position to reform the police, Barrionuevo followed his instincts in retaining officers from Franco's hated political police, the defunct Brigada de Investigación Político-Social, in senior positions. He did sideline, reluctantly according to his own account,[11] and only temporarily, Manuel Ballesteros, the intelligence chief who was refusing to divulge the identity of the alleged Hendayais mercenaries. He replaced him, as we have seen, with Jesús Martínez Torres, the man who had failed to arrest BVE members when they were killing people under his nose in the 'triangle of death'.

Carlos Sanjuán, who had reluctantly accepted the position of Barrionuevo's under-secretary, clashed repeatedly with Vera, who had been made Director of State Security and was effectively in charge of the police. Sanjuán managed to appoint some police with impeccable democratic credentials to relatively senior positions, but they found their investigations into the far Right rigidly obstructed by the unpurged state apparatus.[12]

Vera insists that there was no option but to keep the Francoist commanders in their places, and win them over to democracy: 'Those were terrible years,' he says. 'I was a Socialist, which the generals and police superintendents regarded with contempt. Starting from mutual distrust, we had to win the respect and even the admiration of those who were against us. These were the generals of Franco, the police of Franco. It was a very complicated process. You would have to have lived it [to understand it]. Yes, we tried to change the commanders, we even looked for candidates to do it. But when we saw the list [of Socialist candidates] for the Ministry of the Interior there was nobody, the list was empty.' The few police with Socialist sympathies, he claims, 'wanted office jobs. None of them wanted the responsibility of fighting terrorism. Go to Bilbao, go to San Sebastián? Not one.'[13]

If Barrionuevo and Vera really did possess any reforming zeal, ETA did not make it easy for them to exercise it. The Socialists had thought that the Basque radicals would at least give them a breathing space, a chance to show that this really was a democratic government.

'There was a rather naive analysis of what was going to happen,' Vera has said. 'In the PSOE there was the impression that with the victory of the Socialists the position of ETA would change substantially . . . we were thinking in terms of channels of contact, of dialogue with ETA. We thought there would be changes on their side, or that at least there would be a period in which ETA would permit the Socialists to make progress in the development of autonomy in the Basque Country, and in the general development of democracy in Spain. It would have given us breathing space if ETA had put its activities on hold.'[14]

ETA did not allow the Socialists to remain naive for long. Scarcely a week after the PSOE had won the elections, ETA struck at the very heart of the Spanish armed forces. General Lago Román, commander of the Brunete Armoured Division, was shot dead by motorcyclists in his official car in Madrid. The Brunete unit, one of the most important in the Spanish army, had a particular significance because it had come very close to full-scale participation in the 1981 attempted coup.

If there were still any doubts that for ETA this was business, or terror, as usual, they were dispelled when three *guardia civiles* were shot in two incidents in December. Their funerals were among the first official functions which Barrionuevo and Vera had to attend. These grim ceremonies, with grieving relatives and comrades who openly denounced the Socialist leaders as cowards, and demanded tough action against the terrorists, deeply influenced them.[15] The ETA offensive continued, at more or less the same rhythm as the two previous years, throughout the Socialists' first full year in office. The PSOE government suffered neither more nor less provocation from ETA than their predecessors, despite respective claims to the contrary by their defenders and by their critics.[16]

The PSOE's public response to this violence was the 'Plan ZEN' (Zona Especial Norte – Special Northern Zone), launched in February 1983. The title conjured up unfortunate images of US operations in hostile territory in Vietnam, and the acronym was unintentionally bizarre. In fact, the plan was a dressed-up version of a document prepared by their predecessors in government, which is hardly surprising given the continuity in Interior personnel. It ranged from proposals for psychological warfare to beefing up the military resources of the security forces. Overall, the plan simply intensified the familiar climate of heavy-handed 'occupation' in the Basque Country, and notched up the dynamic of 'action–repression–action' another few degrees. This democratic and socialist government brought nothing new, at this stage, to the battle against terrorism, a fact not lost on propagandists for the radicals.[17]

The PSOE's disappointment with ETA's failure to offer them any kind of initial truce was followed by an even ruder awakening for the new government. They found that their Socialist comrades in France, who had come to power only a year earlier, had very little interest in helping them in what they regarded as an absolutely essential task: eliminating ETA's 'French sanctuary'.

Following a long tradition among Basques who were in conflict with Madrid, ETA leaders had been taking refuge across the French Basque border since the organisation's first big military operation brought repression down on their heads in 1961.[18] Since then, the group's command structure, as well as its political, financial and propaganda headquarters, had been based between Hendaye and Biarritz. Moreover, many of ETA's *comandos* operated out of France, crossing the border to carry out a shooting and returning for rest and relaxation. In the Franco period, and, as we shall see, long beyond it, they benefited from the French policy of providing exile for political refugees. They also enjoyed the knowledge that they were not really in exile at all, since they were still in the Basque Country, their own homeland. This situation obviously gave the group an enormous logistical advantage in the struggle with the Spanish police, and infuriated successive Spanish administrations.

At first sight, it seems strange that the French Socialists did not recognise any great difference between the new Spanish Socialist administration and the conservative governments of the transition, or even the authoritarian governments of the late Franco period. France's refusal to fully accept that Spain had become a democracy by 1983, despite obvious evidence to the contrary, was one of the seeds of the GAL.

When Barrionuevo met his French opposite number, Gaston Deferre, for the first time in April 1983, he found his own admitted inexperience matched by Deferre's almost incredible ignorance. Deferre claimed not to know that the Spanish Basque provinces enjoyed autonomy – a status promised, and then denied, to the French Basques by his own party.[19] He dismissed Barrionuevo's list of *etarras* (ETA members) living in France as 'old propaganda' and told him 'you should look for them in Spain'.[20]

The roots of this huge gap in perception are complex and intertwined, and we will look at this question in greater detail later.[21] For the moment, it must suffice to say that, when the Spanish Socialists came to power, relations between the two countries were 'not bad or mediocre, but execrable', in the words of a sympathetic French diplomat.[22]

On the surface at least, they improved very little during the Socialists' first twelve months in office. And with each *guardia civil* or policeman shot down or blown up in the Basque Country, the clamour to be allowed to pursue their killers across the border grew louder and louder, not just in the armed forces, but in the new administration itself. The guns of the dirty war had been silent in the 'French sanctuary' for nineteen months when the Socialists won the October 1982 elections, and for another eleven months the dirty warriors made no moves at all. When they were unleashed again, the government of Felipe González would be firmly in charge of the state apparatus.

On 5 October 1983, a remnant of ETA(p-m) kidnapped an army medical officer, Captain Alberto Martín Barrios. The threat to his life was the trigger for the Spanish security forces, and their surrogates, to go back into action on French soil. The hands of the González administration would not look clean for much longer. But perhaps they had never been so lily-white. As early as the previous December, Barrionuevo had told the Spanish parliament about the kind of *'cambio'* (change)[23] he wanted to see in the war against ETA: 'It would not be a bad change if police officers stopped dying, even if some terrorist or other died.'[24]

NOTES

1   There were honourable exceptions. *El País* produced an unprecedented special edition in defence of the Constitution, and had it on the street outside the parliament by 8.30 p.m.

2   See David Gilmour, *The Transformation of Spain* (London: Quartet Books, 1986), pp. 254–5: 'In the aftermath of the unsuccessful coup, the democratic system virtually ceased to function . . . Fear of the army effectively prevented the exercise of democratic government.'

3   The LOAPA, the Institutional Law for the Harmonisation of the Devolution Process, was finally rejected by the Constitutional Court, to the chagrin of the Socialists, who were in power by then. Not surprisingly, this law further deepened Basque distrust of Madrid's commitment to relinquishing central power. See ibid., p. 255: 'One measure clearly designed to placate the military and assure them that the unity of Spain was not threatened was the LOAPA.'

4   The sector of ETA(p-m) which rejected this process soon disintegrated, with some of its members being absorbed into ETA(m) and others negotiating a further process of 'social reinsertion'. See María Ángeles Escrivá, *El Camino de Vuelta* (Madrid: El País-Aguilar, 1998), p. 99.

5   Victorino Ruiz de Azúa, 'Las Manos Sucias', in Santos Juliá et al. (eds.), *Memoria de la Transición* (Madrid: Taurus, 1996), p. 586.

6   The third majority, in 1989, was in fact only a *de facto* one. The PSOE won exactly half the seats in parliament (175), but had a comfortable margin

because, ironically enough, the four deputies for Herri Batasuna, ETA's political wing, refused to take their seats.

7   González's power became so personalised that his first name became synonymous with his party's policies in the 1980s and early 1990s.

8   Interview with Rafael Vera, Madrid, November 1997.

9   Interview with Fernando López Agudín, Madrid, November 1997.

10 Ángel Sánchez, *Quién es Quién en la Democracia Española* (Barcelona: Flor del Viento Ediciones, 1995), p. 64.

11 José Barrionuevo, *2,001 Días en Interior* (Barcelona: Ediciones B, 1997), p. 37.

12 Ricardo Arques and Melchor Miralles, *Amedo: El Estado contra ETA* (Barcelona: Plaza y Janés/Cambio 16, 1989), p. 130.

13 Interview with Rafael Vera, Madrid, November 1997.

14 Quoted in Eliseo Bayo, *GAL: Punto Final* (Barcelona: Plaza y Janés, 1997), p. 185.

15 Barrionuevo, op. cit., pp. 26–7.

16 Some Socialists have tried to defend the dirty war as an inevitable response to unprecedented pressure from ETA. Critics of the Socialists, like Manuel Cerdán and Antonio Rubio, in *El Orígin del GAL* (Madrid: Temas de Hoy, 1997), p. 28, say that, on the contrary, ETA were operating 'in slow motion' during the first Socialist government. In fact, ETA more or less maintained the body count of the previous two years, which was significantly below the peak of ETA's offensive in 1980, though they certainly increased tension by killing more senior army officers than previously. According to Interior Ministry figures, ETA killed ninety-one people in 1980, thirty people in 1981, thirty-eight in 1982, thirty-two in 1983, thirty-two in 1984, thirty-seven in 1985, forty in 1986, and fifty-two in 1987. See Antonio Elorza, 'La Metamonfosis de la Violencia', in Juliá et al. (eds.), op. cit., p. 290, and appendix to José María Calleja, *Contra la Barbarie* (Madrid: Temas de Hoy, 1997).

17 The EMK, a small Maoist group which gave critical support to ETA, had a quite brilliant poster-design and copywriting team. They plastered the Basque Country with powerful images under the title '*PSOE, Policía, la misma porquería*' (PSOE, Police, the same old pigshit). It summed up how many people, much less radical than the Maoists or ETA, experienced the situation on the streets.

18 See ch. 2, p. 36.

19 François Mitterrand's Socialist election programme in 1981 had promised that the French Basques could have their own *département*, instead of being subsumed into the Bas Pyrénées. This pledge was forgotten once in office. In any case, such autonomy would not have been remotely comparable to what already existed in Spain. In March 2000, the Socialist government under Lionel Jospin again turned down a very broadly based demand for a Basque *département*, on the interesting grounds that such a move would be unhelpful to Spain in the fight against terrorism.

20 See Sagrario Morán, *ETA entre España y Francia* (Madrid: Editorial Complutense, 1997), pp. 173–4, and Barrionuevo, op. cit., pp. 57–9. It is curious that Barrionuevo gives a much happier account of this meeting in his own book than he apparently gave to Morán.

21 See ch. 14.

22 Pierre Guidoni, who would become ambassador in Madrid in 1983. Morán, op. cit., p. 165.

23 '*Por el cambio*' had been the Socialist Party's simple and effective election slogan.

24 Barrionuevo, op. cit., p. 27.

5

Fear Crosses the Border:
two disappearances and a kidnapping

'There was a sense that something was going to happen,' Izaskun Rekalde says, recalling the autumn of 1983 among the radical Basque community in France.

Rekalde has lived in that community for more than twenty years, and is an influential figure within it. She was one of a handful of Spanish citizens who enjoyed official 'refugee status' in France.[1] A tall, striking woman with big, sad eyes, she looks like an icon of the dedicated revolutionary whose exile has gone on too long. Her account of the advent of the GAL is suffused with a restrained nostalgia for a once-vibrant social group that has been dispersed and diminished, in more ways than are immediately obvious.

For the previous two and half years, she points out, there had been a long parenthesis in the bombings and shootings which the refugees and their supporters had come to expect from groups linked to the Spanish security forces. But long-term residents like Rekalde felt that the uneasy peace enjoyed by the refugees was too good to be true, when all hell was breaking out in the Spanish Basque Country. 'There were more Spanish police coming here than usual, and it was a period of heavy armed activity [by ETA] on the other side of the border, where the Spanish government was carrying out very repressive policies. We knew that something was coming,' she says.

When that something came, however, many refugees did not want to recognise it. Life north of the border was not exactly Siberia for Basque radicals on the run from Spanish police in the early 1980s. The beaches and bars of the French Basque resorts have a charm to which even committed revolutionaries did not remain immune. Nonetheless, to a people so blessed and cursed with a sense of their native place as the Basques, exclusion from the daily life of their own town or village was always a real exile. If the refugee could not get to his village, however, there were ways of bringing the village to the refugee.

'We lived differently,' says Rekalde. 'We went to someone's house and stayed there. We lived with other refugees, or with French Basques who helped us. We lived on solidarity. Our families helped a lot, and not only families but friends. The village *cuadrilla*[2] brought food and money. "Visiting the refugees on the other side" became a kind of fiesta, for them and for us. The atmosphere was very attractive and very agreeable. The refugees came here to escape repression, but found themselves very protected by family, friends and *pueblo*.'[3]

At weekends, all over the Spanish Basque Country, cars would be packed to bursting point with sheep's cheeses, cider, *chorizo* sausages, dried red peppers, salted cod, Rioja wine: whatever the local cornucopia of the refugee's home town and home kitchen could pour into them. Family members and friends would squeeze in around the provisions and head for the border, rarely more than an hour away. They might be held up for thirty minutes at the frontier while the police checked their groceries, more meticulously than was strictly necessary. But the last leg of the journey was usually even shorter, and long hours of conviviality could be enjoyed before returning home.

It was during just such a weekend that the first, and arguably the most terrible, of the GAL's hammer blows fell. These blows would shatter and disperse this extraordinary community of revolutionaries, romantics, camp followers and, we must not forget, terrorists. The first victims of the GAL, Joxean Lasa and Joxi Zabala, fell into the latter category as members of ETA. We will return to their short biographies, which give some indication of how problematic that classification of 'terrorist' can be in the Basque context, later in this chapter.

Juan Mari Zabala, Joxi's elder brother, shares Izaskun Rekalde's sense that the summer and early autumn of 1983 were shadowed with foreboding. 'We used to take advantage of the longer days to go to the beach at Hendaye and San Juan de Luz. Joxi and Joxean used to point out odd things to us. "That Renault 12 is from Intxaurrondo" [the Guardia Civil barracks in San Sebastián], they used to say. Or "That man is a *guardia civil*." They were living with a refugee, who had escaped from Intxaurrondo and knew many police based there by sight. It was always *guardia civiles* that they saw.'[4]

One has the impression, however, that the increase in 'visiting' policemen did not put a stop to the gallop of the social lives of Lasa and Zabala, both still in their very early twenties. There is a picture, taken around this time, which shows the pair outlandishly dressed for a fancy dress party; the next mortal victim of the GAL, Ramón Oñederra, is also in the picture, as are several attractive girls.[5] They look like any group of young people, anywhere, eager for a night on the town. Lasa and Zabala, who were inseparable friends, don't seem to have missed many parties. This innocent weakness may explain why they ended up buried in quicklime 800 kilometres from their native place.

Joxean Lasa's elder brother, Mikel Mari, remembers Saturday, 15 October, as a 'normal day's visit'. His family, and Zabala's, went to Bayonne, where the two had lived since they had fled across the border after a botched bank raid in 1981. 'That night we had dinner with them, and stayed till about 11.30. Then we split up to go home, while they went to borrow a car.'

Lasa and Zabala wanted a car to go to the annual fiesta in the village of Arrangoitze, taking place all that weekend. They first met their flatmate, the escapee, who said he had seen more Spanish police that day.

As they were talking, a light-coloured Renault 12 stopped close by. In a rather naive attempt to scare off the suspected agents, Lasa went up to them and told them to 'go away'. They did, for the time being. Then Lasa and Zabala went for a drink in the Kayetenia bar (where their friend and comrade Ramón Oñederra would be shot two months later) before meeting two other refugees, Mariano Martínez Colomo and his wife, who were going to lend them a car.

The four of them went for a late-night stroll. Le Petit Bayonne, the area across the river Nive from the city's emblematic thirteenth-century Gothic cathedral, is a hive of little streets. The presence of hundreds of Spanish Basque refugees had given these streets something of the buzz of San Sebastián's old quarter by night. There seemed to be bars every few yards, many of them run by refugees. The southerners had imported the traditions of the *cuadrilla* and the *poteo,* whereby large groups of friends circulate together, having one drink and perhaps one *pincho* (snack) in each bar, before moving on to the next.

The four refugees started at the Kayetenia and ended up in the Café des Pyrénées, thus traversing the entire – tiny – area where the GAL would claim most victims over the next thirty months. They returned to the Colomos' house about 1.15 a.m., and stood chatting outside for fifteen minutes. A big, light-coloured car paused for longer than necessary as it took a nearby corner. Colomo remembers that it had a Guipuzcoan licence plate, and that its two occupants, one of them with a broad moustache, seemed to be watching them. They assumed, again, that they had the attention of the Spanish police, but they took no action.

The Colomos went inside, and Mariano threw the car keys down to Lasa and Zabala from an upstairs window. He saw them head off for the parking lot, just around the corner. He closed the shutters and went to bed.

Lasa and Zabala had promised to return the car on Monday morning. Their friends knew they had gone off to a fiesta, so their absence all day Sunday caused no disquiet. Nor did the Colomos notice that their Renault 4 had never been moved from the parking lot. When the two failed to return the keys the next morning, however, Colomo found his car was still where he had left it. One of the front doors was unlocked, and the maroon anorak which Zabala had been carrying was still in the back seat. Colomo tried to hot-wire the car, but found that the battery switch had been removed. Then he found Lasa's and Zabala's personal papers in the glove compartment.

Meanwhile, his wife had noticed that the back door of the car was also unlocked, and that, on the floor, there was a hank of human hair, apparently pulled out by the roots. Yet the French police later reported that they could find no evidence of a struggle in the car, though they did say that a cigar in Zabala's anorak pocket was broken in two and partly crushed.[6]

Word ran quickly around the Bayonne refugee community that the pair seemed to have disappeared. The French police had no record of their detention, and no one had seen them at the fiesta in Arrangoitze. Izaskun Rekalde remembers a general sense of denial, despite the omens.

'At first, everyone said "They're staying in someone's house, they're at such and such a fiesta, they'll turn up, they'll turn up" . . . but the days passed.'

Nevertheless, a friend formally reported them missing to the French police on the Monday, and the families were contacted. 'We went down to Bayonne that very night,' says Mikel Mari Lasa. 'We went to the Kayetenia bar, where Ramón Oñederra worked as a waiter, and we realised something was very wrong.'

Fourteen years later, sitting in the comfort of a new hotel in Tolosa, the brothers of the two friends still automatically act out the see-sawing of hope and despair which afflicted their families until 1995, when the bodies, or rather the dismembered skeletons, of the two *etarras* were at last identified.

'You never lose hope,' says Juan Mari Zabala, 'that somehow or another they will turn up.'

'I did,' Mikel Mari Lasa interrupts very quietly. 'On the Monday night, with friends of theirs in Bayonne, people very close to ETA, I still remember the thought hitting me: "I'm never going to see my brother again." I don't know why.'

'I felt the same,' says Juan Mari Zabala, appearing to contradict himself. 'The anguish we felt in those days was indescribable. I can't express it, you try to hope . . .'

'But you know it's impossible,' Mikel Mari Lasa repeats.

'And if it's the worst,' continues Juan Mari Zabala, 'at least you hope that the bodies will turn up, especially for your parents. It's much harder for them if the bodies are not found.'

In this situation, says Mikel Mari Lasa, there is no 'final point' for the family, no moment when they can let themselves grieve freely. 'You can hope for a month, two months, even a year,' he concedes, 'but knowing the political situation in the country, not more than that. My mother used to cry constantly.' For both families, finding the bodies became an obsession, but despite hopes raised briefly by two false trails, both in 1988, there seemed to be nowhere to look.

First, Daniel Fernández Aceña, a particularly flaky member of the GAL, offered a story which ultimately turned out to be a garble of fact and fiction. From his prison cell in Madrid, where he was doing time for one of the group's 'mistaken identity' killings, he declared that Lasa and Zabala had indeed been kidnapped by the GAL. According to his account, based on gossip with his fellow mercenaries, they had been taken by boat to a fishing village on the Spanish side of the border. They had been given psychotropic drugs, beaten and tortured. The torture, he said, 'had got out of hand', and they had been killed, burned with car tyres and buried in quicklime near a frontier pass in the Pyrenees.[7] Aceña was near the mark about the manner of their deaths, but well wide of it on their location, so nothing came of his story except further anguish for their relatives.

Then the Guardia Civil came up with the rather bizarre idea that they were buried in the cave where their ETA *comando* used to hide arms near their home town. The cave turned out to be empty. This episode raised a sickening issue for their brothers. The most likely sources of information on the location of the cache, they say, were Lasa and Zabala themselves, because it had been kept secret from the other members of the *comando*. The hypothesis that they had been tortured was now confirmed, as far as the families were concerned.

What the Guardia Civil should have known, had they had any real interest in pursuing the case, was that the bodies had actually been found three years earlier. On 18 January 1985, an old man walking his dog disturbed a human leg bone in rough countryside near Busot in Alicante, on Spain's Mediterranean coast, nearly 800 kilometres from Bayonne. He was too scared to tell the police, but two days later a hunter came across the same remains, and a mound of quicklime, poorly covered by soil, nearby.[8]

He told the Guardia Civil, who found two skeletons buried together in a single grave under 50 kilos of quicklime. Though only bones and a few bandages remained, they bore signs of torture, and of the causes of death. The two young men had been stripped naked but for the bandages on their wounds, gagged and blindfolded, and shot at close range in the back of the neck.[9]

Despite this dramatic forensic evidence, the local Guardia Civil made remarkably little effort to identify the bodies, limiting themselves to posting a notice to other Guardia Civil units.[10] They did not compare them with lists of missing persons, or contact the other police forces. The case, however, caused a small sensation in the area at the time, and an Alicante journalist did speculate, under the headline THEY WERE TORTURED BEFORE THEY DIED, that the bones might belong to 'the two *etarras* who disappeared in the south of France some years ago'.[11]

He floated the idea more than once, but no one, in the police or in the media, picked up his suggestion. Even stranger is the fact that there was no follow-up of any kind to a call to Radio Popular de Alicante, several days after the bodies were discovered: 'I am calling for the GAL. You are mistaken. They are Lasa and Zabala. We tortured them and we killed them. They were dogs and they deserved it.'[12]

The call was noted but not recorded, and was never broadcast. Sources in the station explained this lapse to *El País*, ten years later, as the result of both lack of credibility and 'real fear', two motives for dropping the story which seem to contradict each other. The coast of Valencia, the region to which Alicante belongs, was and is a favourite haunt of some of the least savoury elements of the Spanish extreme Right.[13] So the station's staff probably had good reason not to stick their necks out too far.

In any case, no echo of these events reached the distraught relatives in the Basque Country. Today, Juan Mari Zabala takes a tolerant view of the human failures involved. The journalists had to think of their families. 'That's human.' If they had been able to stand up the story, 'it could have caused them a lot of problems'.

The judge handling the post-mortem made enquiries about matching the bones to the medical records of missing persons, but limited the investigation to Alicante and the surrounding provinces. When there was no response, he declared that the killings were 'probably a settling of accounts between international gangsters'. He then shelved the case, and apparently ordered that the remains should be disposed of in a common grave or ossuary.[14]

But the provincial pathologist did not agree. Antonio Bru Brotons could never shake off the sensation that 'something very big' lay behind the poor bundle of bones he had examined. Besides, he was a diligent man and this was the only time in his career when he had failed to identify a body. That failure irritated him like a stone in his shoe, even after his retirement. He insisted that the bones be preserved at an appropriate temperature (10 degrees below zero) in a drawer in the city morgue. Thanks to his diligence, or obsession, the macabre evidence remained safely in cold storage for another ten years. Its rediscovery would shock the nation, and bring a Socialist Civil Governor and a Guardia Civil general to trial for torture and murder, and a deputy Interior Minister to trial for covering up the killing.

Evidence of another type was already emerging, back in 1983, which indicated that Lasa and Zabala had not only been tortured, but tortured 'successfully'. We have already seen that their friend Ramón Oñederra was the GAL's next mortal victim, but the GAL would have needed no special intelligence to find the public bar where he worked every day.

However, on 28 December, Mikel Goikoetxea, allegedly one of ETA's most prolific hit men, and certainly a very senior figure in the organisation, was shot with surgical precision as he left his wife and young daughter home. According to his wife, Izaskun Ugarte, his personal security arrangements were such that practically no one else in ETA knew where he lived. Nobody, that is, except the two very junior members who had helped them move house earlier in the autumn – Joxean Lasa and Joxi Zabala.

The following month, the Guardia Civil carried out an exceptionally large raid in the Tolosa region of Guipúzcoa, arresting many suspected members of the two factions ('military' and 'political-military') of ETA then operating. It was unusual for the police to direct big operations against both groups simultaneously.[15] Tolosa was Lasa's and Zabala's home town, and though they were members of ETA(m), they would have known at least some people in the rival group locally. Indeed, it seems they may have at some stage considered joining it, and so had a foot in both camps. It also appears that the Renault 4 they had intended borrowing had been used by ETA(p-m) on occasions, and this may explain why they were the GAL's first victims, something which baffled many people at the time, and still baffles Izaskun Rekalde today.

'They were just lads, very young, barely twenty. I used to see them because they were from my town. They were at all the fiestas. Nobody would have thought that anyone, starting such a monstrous operation [as the GAL], would go after them, with such a simple, short record. There were thousands and thousands of kids like them in Euskadi.'

It is possible, therefore, that the GAL was starting as it would often go on, with a case of mistaken identity, and that Lasa and Zabala had simply chosen the wrong car to go partying in.

In 1983, ETA(p-m) was on its last legs, most of its members having already opted for a deal with the Spanish government which effectively offered them an amnesty in exchange for giving up armed struggle.[16] Those who rejected this deal were uncompromising hard-liners who would soon be absorbed by ETA(m). In a last, hamfisted effort to regain a high profile, this rump group had kidnapped an army medical officer, Alberto Martín Barrios, in early October, as we saw in the last chapter.

They threatened to kill him unless the Spanish government agreed to a national TV broadcast of a statement condemning Spanish military courts, which were then trying some of their comrades. The kidnap victim won the massive sympathy of the Spanish public, rather as Miguel Ángel Blanco did in 1997.[17] The kidnapping also aroused fury in the military establishment, sparking rumours of another coup. The Socialist administration felt that ETA was putting them under unendurable pressure.

It may well be that this kidnapping was the stimulus which persuaded them to uncork the genie of the dirty war. If so, the origins of the GAL reveal a bitter historical irony: a desperate action by a group of terrorists in the process of dissolution provoked a democratic government to unleash its death squads. The barbarities committed by the death squads, in their turn, would legitimise the future actions of the remaining terrorist group in the eyes of a new generation of its wavering supporters.

Just after Lasa and Zabala had disappeared, an ETA(p-m) leader was involved in a bizarre incident which clearly revealed the active role which the Spanish security forces were now playing, uninvited, on foreign soil. José María Larretxea was riding a scooter down a quiet street in Hendaye on 18 October. A white Ford Talbot came up rapidly behind him, and knocked him off balance. Its occupants leapt out, covered his head with a hood and began to beat him and drag him towards the car. The chance arrival of the French police interrupted them, and quite possibly saved Larretxea's life. The aggressors turned out to be a Spanish police inspector, accompanied by a captain and two sergeants from a crack anti-terrorist squad, the Special Operations Groups (Grupos Especiales de Operaciones – GEO), whose members are known as GEOs.

They were charged with assault, but the Spanish government insisted that they had only been looking for information, since they were unarmed, and that their encounter with Larretxea was really a traffic accident. Most uncharacteristically, the Spanish administration accepted responsibility for the incident. The four were visited in Pau by Francisco Álvarez, then chief of police in Bilbao and a senior 'counter-terrorist' who would ultimately admit to involvement in the GAL.

Long before he made that admission, Álvarez publicly defended the Larretxea operation on 'humanitarian' grounds. His officers, he said, had simply wanted to talk to the ETA leader in the hope of finding a way to save Martín Barrios' life. The men were released on bail, having sworn on their honour as Spanish police officers to return to face trial. They broke their bond, and were sentenced in their absence, but they have never faced any disciplinary action in Spain, where they went back to their units.[18]

If the kidnappers of Lasa and Zabala had hoped to extract information about Martín Barrios' whereabouts from their victims, they must have been severely frustrated. And the two young *etarras* must have endured some of their worst moments attempting to persuade their tormentors that they could not, rather than would not, reveal information which they did not have. In any case, ETA(p-m) announced the 'execution' of Martín Barrios only two days after Lasa and Zabala were seized, so there was no further reason to pursue that line of inquiry. Yet, according to a 1996

Spanish judicial investigation, they were held for three months before being driven to Alicante, shot and buried in quicklime on or around 20 January 1984.[19]

Their most ardent defenders do not imagine that they were so heroic that they kept back the little information they had for this whole period. This is not just because the forensic evidence suggests that they suffered extreme torture, involving burnings, beatings and possibly the administration of mind-warping drugs. It is also because ETA has always had a curiously pragmatic attitude to its members' duties when faced with cruel and unusual interrogation methods.

Unlike other resistance groups under the Franco regime, ETA's practice was to assume that arrested militants will not hold out very long under questioning. Torture was standard practice in Spanish police stations under Franco, and, regrettably, has been a recurrent, though declining, feature of police detention since Spain became a democracy. The view in ETA seemed to be that a pragmatic approach was best: tortured members should try to hold out for a couple of days, or at least yield only misleading information which takes time to check out. This would give any comrades who might be affected a chance to make themselves scarce. After that, there was no great shame in 'breaking'. Militants who had been kidnapped, as opposed to arrested, would have known there was no legally imposed time limit on their interrogation. They would be expected to break even more easily.

Mikel Mari Lasa remembers the ghastly moment when he saw his brother's bones: 'We always knew they had been tortured, but to see them without fingernails, burned, destroyed . . . To get a person to talk, once they know they are kidnapped and in whose hands they are, it is not necessary to torture in this way. This is rage, fury, vengeance.'[20]

'Why didn't they just shoot them?' ponders Zabala's brother. 'They knew they weren't leaders with useful information. We'll never know what really happened to them. I often wonder if a human being can inflict so much damage on another, however great your hatred. The truth is the evidence says, yes, it happens every day. If people can be tortured in a democracy, imagine what can be done to people who have been kidnapped. You would tell [your torturers] anything, including things you know nothing about.'

What made these two young men, who seemed to have such a zest for life, choose a road that would lead them to such an early and terrible death, a road which, of course, also meant that they themselves must be prepared to kill? Their brothers tell stories that could fit the biography of ETA's Everyman.

Lasa and Zabala were brought up in Tolosa, a Guipuzcoan town then famous for its malodorous paper mills, mostly since closed down. It is also the place where ETA's first 'martyr', Juan María Etxebarrieta, met his death at the hands of the Guardia Civil in 1968.[21]

The town lies along the bends of the river Orio, surrounded by steep hills, about 20 kilometres inland from San Sebastián. Zabala was brought up in the town, while Lasa lived in the very different world of the countryside, though only a few kilometres away. The Lasa family run a *sidrería,* a cider brewery which also operates as a bar and restaurant for part of the year. Initially, the Zabalas lived in an outlying *barrio*, much nearer to the *sidrería*, and both boys became close friends early on.

Both families were Basque-speaking and strongly nationalist in sentiment. A relative of Lasa's mother had been in ETA and was killed in a shoot-out in Bilbao, but as Juan Mari Zabala says: 'At that time you always knew someone who had been involved. This was one of the hottest zones in the country. Tejero was captain of the Guardia Civil here.'[22]

When the two boys reached their early teens, the Basque Country was passing through its most dramatic days since the Civil War. The ageing Franco imposed something approaching martial law in the region in the early 1970s. He outraged international opinion by ratifying death sentences on two members of ETA, and three Maoists, only weeks before he collapsed into his final illness in the autumn of 1975. The subsequent transition to democracy, when the boys would have been in their mid to late teens, was almost equally stormy, as experienced on the streets of Tolosa.[23]

'When they were growing up, things were difficult for young people in every sense,' Juan Mari Zabala says. 'It was hard to get work, there were constant strikes, and political strikes got mixed up with labour strikes. Demonstrations were repressed in a very brutal manner. For three months at a time, the police would be stationed in the centre of the town, with their armoured jeeps and so on, it was like a total state of emergency. I remember, for example, a train arriving in the station, and the police immediately began to beat the people getting off the train. Their reasons for beating up these people? Absolutely none, it was just a way of letting off steam.

'There are people who are not prepared to be trampled on like that. So you took sides, you had to do something against it. But it is very difficult to tell you what motives our brothers had in opting to join the military wing of ETA. I was affected by the same political system, but what I thought I could contribute against it was very different to Joxi. Perhaps, being younger he was more prepared to take risks; perhaps, because his ideas were a little more radical than mine, he gravitated towards ETA.'

But both men say that, while their brothers discussed their ideas in the family circle, no one else had a clue that they were actually part of an ETA *comando.*[24]

Looking back, however, Mikel Mari Lasa can see things he missed at the time. 'Joxean left school as early as possible, at the same time as Joxi, and took a job in the town. I told him he should stay in school, I couldn't understand why he left. Now I see that, working away from home, he had more independence for his . . .' His soft voice peters out, as if he fears that he could still incriminate his brother. A job in town would be especially attractive, Juan Mari Zabala points out, for an independent-minded teenager growing up on a Basque farm, where family members are expected to put in most of their spare time on collective chores.

Mikel Mari Lasa also remembers seeing Joxean jotting down copious notes in bed at night, and being vaguely puzzled that he never saw the notebooks in the morning. He now assumes that these related to tasks for ETA which Joxean naturally wanted to keep hidden.

While Joxi Zabala was by far the more extrovert of the pair, neither of the teenagers allowed their militancy in ETA to curb their social lives. 'The fact that you are having a bad time politically does not mean that you have to repress your *joie de vivre*,' says Juan Mari Zabala. 'Your militancy is part of your life, but not all your life. The fact that you can't enjoy life as you would like may be what leads you to being a militant in the first place. My brother needed to express himself by having fun.'

In late October 1981, however, the moment came when all the fun stopped, at least in the short term. Mikel Mari Lasa remembers it like this: 'One day Joxean didn't turn up at the farmhouse at the usual time. He rang several times that day and asked if the car was available, but he never came to pick it up. Then the police came looking for him, and we realised what had happened. He was really calling to find out if the police were on to him. His *comando* had robbed a bank, and got the money out, but one of them was then arrested in a shoot-out. It was a great shock, but not a great surprise. Afterwards, I realised I had kind of guessed it. I began to think of all those times he had come home late, of all those notes he took.'

On the assumption that their captured comrade would give their names to the police, Lasa and Zabala had gone into hiding, prior to seeking refuge across the border. Mikel Mari Lasa thinks his brother hid in a farmhouse in a nearby valley for several weeks, possibly months. On one occasion he got a message to go and meet him, not in the farmhouse but in a bar, a fair indication of how the hectic round of the Basque *poteo* can enable militants to hide in plain sight.

Oddly enough, this episode comes as news to Juan Mari Zabala, during our interview. He had always thought that both brothers had headed across the border within days, and Mikel Mari Lasa explains that crossing the border illegally required a lot more preparation than that. It then emerges that Juan Mari Zabala has good reason to be unclear about the details of that period, because he was doing his military service in the Canary Islands at the time.

When our formal interview was over, Juan Mari Zabala and Mikel Mari Lasa invited me to drive out of town, to see a monument to their dead brothers. After a couple of kilometres, they stopped at the edge of an outlying *barrio*. It was late now, but there was still enough streetlight to see a large, handsome plaque, welded to a big pedestal. The two heads are sculpted in relief, against a background of mountains and the sea. A verse in Basque is carved above the inscription, which says they 'disappeared in Bayonne'.

The families erected the plaque less than two years after the kidnapping, and long before they knew what had really happened. It was an attempt to give them a focus for their grief. The site was close to the house where Joxi Zabala was born, and the building beside it had been the school which he had attended with Joxean Lasa. This building was now used as a church and social centre, and their mothers liked to leave flowers at the plaque after attending morning Mass.

Very early one morning, the brothers told me, a resident of the *barrio* looked out her window and saw that some *guardia civiles* had put a chain round the monument. They had attached the other end of the chain to an armoured car and were trying to drag it down off its pedestal. The neighbour phoned the Basque autonomous police, who, in an exchange one would love to have on record, persuaded the *guardia civiles* to desist. This would not be the last ghastly tug of war over the remains, symbolic or otherwise, of Joxean Lasa and Joxi Zabala.

***   ***   ***

The GAL left no clear signature on the kidnapping of Lasa and Zabala at the time, so no one in the refugee community could at first be sure whether it was a once-off action or whether they were facing a full-scale renewal of dirty warfare. However, the attempted kidnapping of Larretxea boded ill, and confirmation would soon follow that someone in Spain wanted the war brought home to ETA's French headquarters.

Lasa and Zabala had been low-profile targets for the dirty warriors, but the GAL's next victim should not even have figured in their shooting range. Segundo Marey belonged to a much earlier (and very different) generation of refugees than the *etarras*. His Socialist parents had brought him across the border from Irún as a four-year-old in 1936, as the right-wing insurgents swept down from Navarre towards the Basque coast at the start of the Civil War. They settled in Hendaye, just across the Bidasoa river.

They never returned to live in Spain, though Marey maintained dual citizenship. He was a shy, private man with no political affiliations, though Sokoa, the business for whom he sold office furniture, did turn out to be deeply implicated with ETA. Like many of its employees, Marey almost certainly had no knowledge of this link.[25] He would also have known refugees close to ETA, both through his job and through other residents in his neighbourhood, but such contacts were a commonplace part of social life in Hendaye at this time.

Marey was quietly married with two young daughters, and his main public activity was playing the saxophone in the municipal band. He also had a keen interest in bullfighting, and he occasionally wrote on the subject for a Spanish weekly. Neither brass bands nor bulls rate highly among the hobbies of ETA's camp followers. As a fellow-worker from Sokoa put it, 'he was the least typical of us, on account of his age, his manner, his way of dressing, and everything else.'[26]

Somehow, however, the motley group of mercenaries employed for the GAL's first acknowledged operation managed to mistake this balding fifty-one-year-old for a thirty-seven-year-old ETA veteran with a full head of hair. Mikel Lujua, their real target, was responsible for smuggling *etarras* back and forth across the border. His only link to Marey was that he also lived on the Rue Aizpurdi, a sleepy residential street in the heart of middle-class Hendaye. The pristine whiteness of its houses, most of them small villas, is almost antiseptic, a strange setting for the scenes of violence it would witness over the next few months.

On Sunday, 4 December 1983, Segundo Marey and his wife, Marta, were having dinner when their doorbell rang. Marta answered it, and found three strangers outside, one of whom asked her if she was the owner of the Citroën 2CV parked outside. He claimed he had just damaged the car, which aroused Marta's suspicions, as she herself had been responsible for the dent he was pointing out. Seeing her distrust, they tried to silence her; Marey came out to see what was going on, and the men attacked him. He lost his carpet slippers and glasses in the struggle, which went on until his assailants used a tear-gas aerosol spray to knock him out and get him into their car, a grey Peugeot 504.[27]

For the next ten days there was no clear news of Marey himself. The Red Cross received a phone call which said he would be killed unless the police officers who had assaulted Larretxea were released from French custody. One of his captors was arrested, driving the grey Peugeot alone, by the French police on the night of the kidnapping. He was trying to cross the border at the quiet frontier post of Dantxarinea. (Marey had evidently been transferred to another car.) Pedro Sánchez, Spanish-born with French nationality, was a former member of the French Foreign Legion, known to the French police as a pimp and a far Rightist.[28] In his possession were a tear-gas aerosol, a baton, rope, several dozen photographs of Basque refugees, and the phone number of Francisco Álvarez's office in Bilbao police headquarters.[29]

Marey and his abductors appeared to have vanished into Spain, but the Spanish authorities in the neighbouring province of Guipúzcoa did not undertake any searches. Julen Elgorriaga, the Socialist Civil Governor of the province, who would be charged thirteen years later with the murder of Lasa and Zabala, had a bureaucratic defence. He told *El País* on 6 December that 'in his jurisdiction, up to now, there has been no request, or official initiative, to conduct the kind of inquiries usual in kidnapping cases'. He said that the Spanish police had put checkpoints on the border as soon as they heard the news, but were not co-ordinating with the French police, though the Guardia Civil in Navarre did claim to be doing so.[30]

Whether Elgorriaga knew it or not, Marey was already in the jurisdiction of his colleague, the Civil Governor of Vizcaya, Julián Sancristóbal. More precisely, he was in Sancristóbal's custody. On Sancristóbal's orders, and those of Francisco Álvarez, a Spanish police officer called José Amedo had arranged to have Marey kept in miserable conditions in a shepherd's hut in the hills inland of Laredo in the province of Santander.[31]

The organisers of the GAL already knew he was not the man they wanted – they had known that since the mercenaries handed him over just beyond Dantxarinea – but they had decided to hold him anyway, 'to put the French under pressure'.[32] The GAL had a dual agenda from the start: to eliminate ETA members, but also to 'persuade' Paris to act more forcefully against the refugees, by bringing the reality of terrorism home to French soil. Making a virtue of a monumental cock-up, the kidnappers realised that an innocent French citizen might serve even better than a Spanish Basque terrorist to make the second point.

This is the argument Sancristóbal now claims to have put, successfully, in a phone conversation to the Minister of the Interior, José Barrionuevo, on the night of the kidnapping.[33] It is this claim by Sancristóbal, above all, which brought the former minister to the dock in 1997, charged by an investigating magistrate of the Spanish Supreme Court with 'setting up an armed gang'. In December 1983, the existence of this armed gang was only just coming to light, and its leadership would remain a mystery for many years, though well-educated guesses were already being made.

At 4.20 on the morning of 14 December, an anonymous phone call brought the French police back to the isolated frontier post of Dantxarinea. It is a well-wooded area, and it took them until 6.30 a.m. to find their man, propped up against a tree beside a lane leading to a quarry.

Segundo Marey presented a pathetic, distressing sight. *El País* reported his condition thus: 'Emaciated and with several days of growth of beard, he had remained in the same place shivering with cold, with his hands on his head, and so terrorised that he had not taken off the blindfold which had covered his eyes.'[34]

Marey has never fully recovered from the psychological and physical shock of his ordeal. Like ETA's own kidnap victims, he was kept in a small space, and deprived of any news of the solidarity demonstrations taking place on his behalf in the French Basque Country during his captivity. He could not remember, or was afraid to say, whether his captors spoke French or Spanish. But they had left a note in his breast pocket, in stilted but all-too-comprehensible French, which spoke volumes:

> Because of the increase in the murders, kidnappings and extortion committed by the terrorist organisation ETA on Spanish soil, planned and directed from French territory, we have decided to eliminate this situation.
>
> The Grupos Antiterroristas de Liberación (GAL), founded with this object, put forward the following points:
>
> 1 Each murder by the terrorists will have the necessary reply, not a single victim will remain without a reply.
> 2 We will demonstrate our idea of attacking French interests in Europe, given that its Government is responsible for permitting the terrorists to operate in its territory with impunity.
> 3 As a sign of goodwill and convinced of the proper evaluation of the gesture on the part of the French Government, we are freeing Segundo Marey, arrested by our organisation as a consequence of his collaboration with the terrorists of ETA.
>
> You will receive news of the GAL.[35]

Incorporating a cruel libel of an innocent and now broken man, the GAL'S dirty war had been officially declared.

NOTES

1   Izaskun Rekalde has repeatedly denied reports in the Spanish media that she is herself a senior member of ETA, and stressed that point to this writer when she unexpectedly offered an interview for this book in Bayonne, in June 1997.
        All quotations from Rekalde in this chapter are taken from that interview. While formal refugee status was never granted to more than a small group of Basque political activists by the French, the term 'refugee' was loosely applied to all ETA supporters who moved to France. Its use was naturally anathema to the Spanish authorities, who categorised this community as criminal rather than political.
        Rekalde's husband, Santiago Arróspide Sarasola (*Santi Potros*), who certainly was a leading member of ETA, had also enjoyed official 'refugee status' in France, until shortly before his arrest in September 1987. He had allegedly been in charge of all ETA's underground *comandos* at the time of some of ETA's bloodiest actions. A Paris court sentenced him to ten years in prison in July 1990 for membership of a criminal organisation and illegal possession of arms. He became a key figure in the Spanish battle to persuade the French to extradite top *etarras*. See Sagrario Morán, *ETA entre España y Francia* (Madrid: Editorial Complutense, 1997) for an account of Arróspide's judicial history.

2   A *cuadrilla* is a tightly knit group of friends, the people with whom one has grown up. It is a central strand in the Basque social fabric, second only to family, with bonds that often last a lifetime.

3   *Pueblo* conveniently translates both as 'people', as in 'the Basque people', and as 'village'.

4   All quotations from Juan Mari Zabala and Mikel Mari Lasa in this chapter are from an interview in Tolosa, June 1997.

5   Shown to the author by Ramón Oñederra's parents, June 1997.

6   Some of the details of this account of Lasa's and Zabala's last days in Bayonne were originally published in *Egin*, 'Guerra Sucia' series, January/February 1995, no. 5, and in *El País*, 22 March 1995. They were confirmed in the prosecution writ against General Galindo and others, Audiencia Nacional, Madrid, 27 May 1996, and by the final judgement in that trial, 26 April 2000. I have also drawn on details provided by Juan Mari Zabala and Mikel Mari Lasa. See also Ricardo Arques and Melchor Miralles, *Amedo: El Estado contra ETA* (Barcelona: Plaza y Janés/Cambio 16, 1989), p. 156.

7   *El País*, 6 and 25 March 1988.

8   *El País*, 22 March 1995.

9   Interview with the pathologist who originally examined the bodies, Antonio Bru Brotons, in *El País*, 22 March 1995. See also prosecution writ against General Enrique Rodríguez Galindo and others, Audiencia Nacional, Madrid, 27 May 1996, p. 5.

10   *El País*, 23 March 1995.

11   *El País*, 27 March 1995.

12   *El País*, 22 March 1995.

13   A death squad which operated both before and during the GAL period, run by the mercenaries Gilbert and Clement Perret, had had a kind of 'rest-and-recreation' base at Castellón, on the Valencia coast well to the north of Busot. ETA had killed Clement Perret there in 1985. See Arques and Miralles, op. cit., pp. 110–11.

14   *El País*, 22 March 1995.

15   *El País*, 22 March 1995.

16   See ch. 4, p. 64.

17   See prologue, p. 10–11.

18 The Larretxea kidnap attempt is the only dirty war action for which the Socialist Interior Ministry accepted full responsibility, and its details were very widely reported. They form part of the Supreme Court judgement in the Marey case, Madrid, 29 July 1998, p. 31. One of the participants in this operation gave evidence in the Marey trial, and claimed that, on their return to Spain in 1983, the GEOs had received telegrams of support from a member of the Supreme Court and even from the royal family. See ch. 23.

19 See prosecution writ against General Enrique Rodríguez Galindo and others, Audiencia Nacional, Madrid, 27 May 1996, p. 5. The trial judgement considered they had probably been held for a much shorter period before being shot.

20 When the bodies were first discovered, the separation of their fingernails from the remains of their fingers suggested that they had been torn out by their torturers. This was the view of the pathologist who examined the bones in 1985, and he repeated this gruesome point to *El País* (22 March 1995) and other papers. Later forensic examination indicated that the separation was due to the natural process of decomposition, as Mikel Mari Lasa conceded later in our interview. But the image became a symbol of Lasa and Zabala's fate.

21 See ch. 2, page 33.

22 Antonio Tejero, the Guardia Civil lieutenant-colonel who became notorious for holding the Madrid parliament at gunpoint on 23 February 1981. See ch. 4, p. 64.

23 Like many Basque radicals, Juan Mari Zabala made it very clear to me that he believed that no real transition had taken place, at least as far as the Basque Country is concerned. He is a computer programmer, smartly dressed and highly articulate, every inch a 1990s urban European. Mikel Mari Lasa, on the other hand, is very much a countryman, slower moving and self-effacing in conversation. Even when sorrow and anger move him to speak, he remains quiet-spoken and hesitant. The pair are a living illustration of the range of support radical Basque nationalism attracts.

24 While there might be a natural reluctance, even today, to admit to having had such knowledge, hermetic secrecy has always been a characteristic of ETA members, even in the company of close friends who would vote for ETA's political wing, Herri Batasuna.

25 Marey's relationship to Sokoa, which the defence for his kidnappers unsuccessfully used to link him to ETA in their 1998 trial, is described thus by *El País,* 20 December 1994: 'He was the representative in the border area of an office furniture company, and as such had a relationship with the Sokoa chair factory, where the police found a large ETA arsenal on 5 November 1986, almost three years later.'

26 *El País*, 7 December 1983, 20 December 1994, 5 April 1997.

27 *El País,* 20 December 1994; Arques and Miralles, op. cit., pp. 163–71; Supreme Court judgement, Marey case, Madrid, 29 July 1998, p. 33.

28 *Punto y Hora*, 9/16 December 1983.

29 Arques and Miralles, op. cit., p. 164; *Diario 16,* 6 December 1983.

30 *El País*, 7 December 1983.

31 By a curious irony, Amedo was president of Bilbao's prestigious Vista Alegre bullring, where Marey was a regular *aficionado.*

32 Evidence of Julián Sancristóbal to investigating magistrate Baltasar Garzón, 17 July 1995, cited in Garzón's report to the Supreme Court, 22 August 1995. Sancristóbal later withdrew this element of his evidence, but a majority of Supreme Court judges held that he only did so to in order to avoid a longer jail sentence. See chs. 23 and 24.

33 Marey may also have been a useful pawn in a smaller game, according to the original evidence of Sancristóbal and others to Garzón in July 1995. While he

DBS Arts Library

was in illegal Spanish custody, the four Spanish police officers held legally in Pau for attempting to kidnap Larretxea were released on bail by Judge Svahn, a man who was to be particularly helpful in putting suspected members of the GAL back on the streets over the next two years. Whether there was in fact any causal connection between the kidnapping and these releases was a matter of contention between Supreme Court judges when the Marey case finally came to trial in 1998. See chs. 23 and 24. The majority verdict argued that there was.

34   *El País,* 15 December 1983.
35   *El País,* 15 December 1983.

6

Under Siege in the Sanctuary:
decapitating ETA

There are many entirely innocent reasons to cross the border from the south into the French Basque Country. In a culture so dominated by gastronomy, shopping for food is one of them. Pâté, cheese and cakes are all reckoned to be better, cheaper, or both, north of the Bidasoa.

In the winter of 1983, shoppers sometimes found that they were less welcome than previously. Small groups of refugees would stop strangers on the streets and demand to know their identities and their business. Arabs, in particular, came in for close scrutiny. The word was out that the GAL, like their predecessors, were hiring north African mercenaries for their death squads. These 'patrols', which were never very frequent, were one of several rather ineffective responses from the radical community to the threat from the GAL.

ETA members who thought they might be targeted took to carrying shotguns in the boot of their cars. Some of them, like Ramón Oñederra, whose *nom de guerre* was *Kattu*, started carrying pistols. Even before his friends Joxean Lasa and Joxi Zabala had disappeared, he had been aware that he was being followed. He told his father that he had seen Spanish policemen watching him. He may have been aware that he figured in the picture files found by the French police in the possession of the suspected kidnapper of Segundo Marey, Pedro Sánchez.[1] Whatever the reason, he feared for his life.

Yet he continued to work in the Kayetenia bar, where he was very vulnerable. The Kayetenia is a little isolated from the nest of bars around the Rue Pannecau which form the heart of Petit Bayonne. It is only 50 metres from the main road through the city. It is very close to a police station, but Oñederra would not have derived much sense of security from the proximity of gendarmes.

Izaskun Rekalde agrees that Oñederra was not very significant in ETA. The press, she says, often exaggerates the status of some members of ETA, and underestimates that of others. '*Kattu* was very young,' she says. 'It wasn't usual for someone like him to carry a pistol, but it was also very contradictory that he should have worked in a bar. For them [the GAL] it was very easy. Anyone could go in or out at any time.'[2] For their first acknowledged kill, the GAL had chosen a very easy prey. He was twenty-three years old, a popular member of a Bayonne football team and had a steady girlfriend.

The day after Segundo Marey was released, with the GAL's threat to 'reply' to every ETA action in his pocket, ETA killed Eduardo Navarro, a national policeman, in San Sebastián. Three days later, another policeman had to have his foot amputated following a terrorist bombing near the same city. If the GAL needed any excuses, eyes taken to take eyes, ETA had not kept them waiting. The GAL struck back the next day.

Oñederra was working in the Kayetenia as usual on the evening of 19 December. It was the eve of the tenth anniversary of ETA's assassination of Carrero Blanco, and of the fifth anniversary of the retaliatory killing of the ETA leader José Miguel Beñarán Ordeñana in the first dirty war. There were no customers in the bar, and his boss was upstairs making dinner, so Oñederra was playing a game of solo chess, one of his several hobbies.

The bar owner heard several shots, but by the time he got downstairs Oñederra's killers had already made their getaway. The victim was on the floor, his head surrounded by a spreading pool of blood from at least seven, possibly ten, bullet wounds. His boss was too stunned to move, but moments later some other refugees came into the bar. They ran out shouting 'Kattu hil digutela' ('They've killed Kattu'), and within half an hour Bayonne was swept by one of the biggest, and most violent, street demonstrations it had seen in several years.

Oñederra had tried, and failed, to use his pistol. 'It was the smallest little thing, nothing really,' his father, Prudencio, told me, as though the gun had been a toy.[3] He almost certainly died within seconds of the first shots. His father thinks his attackers had intended to kidnap him, but killed him when he resisted. The next day a man claiming to represent the GAL phoned a local newspaper, speaking French with a heavy Spanish accent. He said that they had killed Oñederra, and also warned that the group was extending its list of targets to include French citizens 'who give cover to, collaborate with or employ terrorists'.

Like Lasa and Zabala, with whom he had enjoyed refugee social life in Bayonne to the full, Oñederra came from a small town, Azcoitia, in the Guipuzcoan mountains. Azcoitia is only a few kilometres from Loyola, one of the Catholic Church's great sanctuaries. Loyola was the home of St Ignatius Loyola, Basque nobleman, warrior and founder of the Jesuits, an order whose military zeal and sense of passionate commitment are to some extent mirrored in ETA's ideology.[4] Azcoitia has a handsome main street, lined with fine stone houses with bright brass fittings on iron balconies, sometimes adorned with magnificent flowering creepers and trailing plants. It is dominated by a huge Gothic church. At street level, there is the usual incongruous Basque market-town mixture: hi-tech bars and quaintly old-fashioned shops.

Taking a late-night stroll down this street after interviewing Oñederra's parents in June 1997, I found one section of the street suddenly filled with the Ertzaintza, the Basque autonomous region's own police force. They looked like refugees from *Star Wars* in their exotic red riot gear, over which their black balaclavas seemed a menacing anachronism. (The balaclavas are for their own protection. Unlike the Guardia Civil, the Ertzaintza is made up of local people, for whom individual recognition could spell intimate retaliation.)

It turned out that the youth section of ETA had just tried to burn down a bank as part of their campaign of *kale borroka* (street struggle).[5] While the Ertzaintza protected the local fire brigade from any follow-up action, drinkers continued to circulate casually from bar to bar. A street-level window in the bank had been smashed, and a Molotov cocktail had started a small fire inside. But the residents of the apartments in the same building, directly above the potential danger, chatted nonchalantly from balcony to balcony. It was just another Friday night in Euskadi.

Ramón Oñederra's parents, a delightful and most hospitable couple who should be enjoying their retirement, still live in the small flat on a steep hill above the town where they reared their only son with his two sisters. His mother, Arantza Ganbara, is elegantly turned out, and offers coffee and an array of formidable liqueurs, but finds time to participate actively in the conversation. She sometimes has to be very firm to do so, because his father, Prudencio, gets easily carried away by the force of his emotions, raising his voice and stressing his points with vigorous, angular gestures.

They say they were never members of any political party, but always felt themselves to be 'Basques and Basque-speakers, nothing more'. At school under the Franco regime, Oñederra seems to have been a natural rebel, painting the forbidden image of the Basque national flag on a school wall, but cute enough not to get caught.

'He was always conscious of being a Basque-speaker, and a lover of the Basque Country,' his father says, though he was unaware of the extent of his son's youthful involvement in politics. 'He was a Basque, and nothing more,' he says, repeating the deceptively straightforward phrase he had applied to himself and his wife. Under a system which made comprehensive and violent efforts to liquidate any non-Spanish ethnic awareness, to be conscious of one's Basqueness could very rarely imply 'nothing more'.

'We used to say to him "Don't get involved, it's dangerous,"' says his mother. 'But children don't do what their parents want. That is, I think, how life evolves,' she adds, a little tentative about the latter point. Given the consequences of her son's evolution, that is hardly surprising.

The spark which seems to have prompted this dangerous evolutionary leap for Oñederra was his notification to report for compulsory military service. 'He said he would not serve in armed forces which were crushing the Basque nation,' his father recalls. 'One night, at twenty to one or so, he came in to me and said: "Father, I am leaving. Everything for the Basque Country."[6] And he went out and never came back. He never told us he was in ETA, but once he was on the other side we supposed it.'

It is very natural for the Oñederra parents to have rose-tinted memories of their son, and of the world in which they found him on the other side of the border. They are worth quoting, I think, because they reflect a very widespread perception of ETA in radical nationalist circles, a view which is utterly baffling to those who imagine that such an organisation must be made up of psychopaths, sadists and mafiosi.

'He had very clear ideas,' says his mother. 'He could have had a good life here, but he gave it all up.' 'He was very intelligent and good-hearted,' interrupts his father. 'Let me tell you a detail. When they murdered him, a woman of eighty years or more came into the Kayetenia, crying her eyes out, asking who would now accompany her to Mass. It seems that every day he used to see her waiting to cross the road to the cathedral, and he would go and take her arm and guide her across it.'

'On the hill you've just climbed,' continues his mother, 'if he saw a woman with heavy shopping bags, he would stop and help her. He treated *gente de fuera* [people from elsewhere][7] the same way as people from here. He was a boy with a good heart, open, who wanted to help everyone. I think all those boys, those friends of his who lived on the other side, had good hearts. The first time we went there, we went with the car full of food bags. We brought them in, and he picked up all but one of them and began to take them out again. We asked where he was going and he said "I'm going to other houses where they need these more than I do." It was incredible.'

Credible or not, this picture of the refugee community as made up of people with all the virtues of the early Christians is one that many Basques carry in their minds. There was undoubtedly still something of the atmosphere of the Sixties in the air in Petit Bayonne, the exalted purity of utopian communist ideology reflected, however imperfectly, in the practice of groups of young people sharing houses, free from the restraints of parental control. This was intoxicatingly blended with the passion of a nationalism untainted by the exercise of political power, made dangerously seductive by the sacramentalisation of violence. The next few months would see the GAL bestowing the supreme virtue of martyrdom to a fellowship only too capable of accepting it, even of thriving on it.

***   ***   ***

Arantza Ganbara remembers going into her local butcher's on the evening of 19 December 1983. 'The radio was on in there, but when I entered they turned it down, right down. A neighbour said "Listen, they've said something about Ramón, they've mentioned the name Oñederra." I thought it might be something about my niece, who works for Radio Vitoria, and I ran over to some friends in another shop and asked them if they had heard anything. They had the eight o'clock news on, but there was a huge lottery win and all the talk was about that. Then this one' – she points at her husband – 'came in with his eyes looking as if he was about to be killed, and said "Come at once, Ramón's been shot." Just like that. I don't know how I got out to the street.'

By the time the Oñederras reached Bayonne, several hours after the shooting, the beatification of their son was already in progress. They had an unsatisfactory interview with the French police, who did not take kindly to the family's allegation that some of them might have assisted

Oñederra's assassins. But they were overwhelmed by the multitudinous support of the mourners and demonstrators who crammed the streets of Petit Bayonne. 'There were dances, recitals by *bertsolaris* [poets who improvise in Basque], a speech by *Peixoto* [José Manuel Pagoaga Gallastegi, a veteran ETA leader]. We began to drive around Bayonne, with lights full on and horns sounding.'

On the day of his funeral, Oñederra's body was accompanied through every town and village on the French Basque coast by 'three hundred cars, all carrying his picture, all hooting their horns,' according to his father. Then, when they reached the Spanish border at Irún, 'it all stopped'.

The Spanish police had orders to prevent a similar progress through the villages of Guipúzcoa. In grim scenes, which would be repeated many times over the next few years, the Guardia Civil effectively kidnapped the corpse, forcing the hearse to travel on the motorway, separated from centres of population and accompanied only by the immediate family.

'We were in the car behind the hearse,' says his mother, 'but they put an armoured car in between us and it, and there were guardias aiming down at us with submachine-guns all the way to Azpeitia [the last major town before Azcoitia]. Then, just before we got him home, they withdrew, and it was as if we had come alone.'

The nationalist parties on the town council had fallen out over the wording of a resolution condemning his killing. So the *capilla ardiente,* an improvised funeral chapel where the deceased is laid out for public honour, was not installed in the town hall. The Oñederra flat would have been much too small to accommodate the numbers who wanted to pay their respects. So the family installed the *capilla* in the hallway of their apartment block. The area was soon flooded with thousands of mourners from the town and much further afield. 'We didn't expect anything like it, because he was the first victim,' his parents say, adding that the presence of so many people was a support, not an intrusion. While they are adamant that they still have no political affiliations themselves, they were clearly impressed and gratified by the turnout of most of the leadership of ETA's political wing, Herri Batasuna. Prudencio Oñederra had an archetypal conversation with one of them, Txomin Ziluaga.

'*Kattu* had once confided to me that if they ever killed him, there would be one hundred *gudaris* [Basque soldiers] to take his place. And when they did kill him, and we brought his body here, I told Txomin that story. And he said, standing right here: "A hundred? No, a thousand, *more*."' Allowing for the rhetorical exaggeration demanded by the occasion, Ziluaga was right. In the 1980s, ETA would get no better recruiting sergeant than the GAL.

The leadership of Euskadiko Ezkerra, themselves recent converts from the use of terrorist violence, put out a statement on Oñederra's killing, blaming the Ministry of the Interior for creating a climate 'which justifies and applauds illegal and criminal actions. The problem with a "dirty war"', their statement concluded, 'is that we know how it begins, but not how it ends.'[8]

The Socialist Prime Minister, Felipe González, seemed to have no such concerns. At the very moment when Bayonne was full of demonstrators chanting 'González assassin, Mitterrand complice!' ('González is a murderer, Mitterand is his accomplice!') the two men were meeting in Paris. González was trying to persuade his French opposite number to act more vigorously against ETA in France. It does not appear to have been a very fruitful meeting. 'I don't deny that there are difficulties,' he said afterwards. Asked by journalists, apropos of the Larretxea kidnap attempt, if he intended to put an end to the incursions of Spanish police into French territory, he 'adopted a dry tone and said that the 500 murders committed by ETA since the 1977 amnesty worried him a lot more than the missions of the Spanish police in France'.[9] It was the first entry in a lexicon of evasive and ambiguous statements to come from González on the question of the dirty war.

On the same day, in the first of a series of fine editorials on the subject, *El País* compared ETA and the GAL in unambiguous terms: 'They are both united by their filthy cult of violence, vengeance and crime. They both substitute the values of civilised society by the principle of "an eye for an eye" and the customs of barbarism. They are both simply variants of the same terrorist phenomenon.'[10]

*** *** ***

If the GAL were operating on the general principle of 'an eye for an eye', they did not wait for ETA to kill again before claiming another victim.[11] Just nine days after Oñederra's assassination, a GAL unit shot and fatally wounded a much more significant member of ETA. Mikel Goikoetxea Elorriaga was only twenty-seven years old, but he had already acquired an almost legendary status in radical Basque circles. He started early, inheriting his *nom de guerre*, *Txapela*, from his brother Jon. In 1972, the first *Txapela* had been shot, allegedly in the back, by *guardia civiles* who had flushed him out of the convent where he had sought refuge, on the road to the border crossing of Dantxarinea.[12] His name was evocative for the *etarras* of the 1970s, since he was the second member of ETA to die in action. Most of the Goikoetxea family had to flee to France shortly afterwards, when the 'safe house' they had run for ETA was exposed.

The new *Txapela* had participated, according to the Spanish police, in the killing of twenty-seven people by the time of his own shooting on 28 December 1983. Even allowing for the exaggeration that such posthumous charge-sheets often involve, he probably was one of ETA's top hit-men in the late 1970s and early 1980s. Trained in Algeria in 1976,[13] he was one of two ETA members whose extradition was sought in a benchmark legal offensive by the Spanish government in 1979. In killing Goikoetxea, the GAL seemed to be moving towards a strategy of 'decapitating' ETA, in the sense of both eliminating its top figures individually and destroying the relative security of the organisation's 'French headquarters'.

Goikoetxea's wife, Izaskun Ugarte, had gone to live with him in the French Basque Country on 1 January of that year. Their lives, she says, bore little resemblance to those of refugees like Lasa, Zabala or Oñederra. 'There was always a category of people who could not live normally, even in the sense the other refugees did. Mikel was a person who had scarcely ever lived normally.'[14]

She is a small, wiry woman with thick, dark brown hair, beautiful features and formidably direct eyes, softened by a disarming smile. She must have needed her remarkable beauty and evident strength of character to play her iconographic role in the highly ritualised funeral ceremonies she organised for her husband. When I interviewed her in 1997, she was teaching Basque in Bilbao's Kafe Antxokia, a marvellous cultural resource which marries education, entertainment and good food. She remained quietly committed to the cause for which her husband died – and killed – nearly a decade and a half earlier.

She had, she said, no difficulty in accepting Goikoetxea's active participation in armed struggle. 'It was clear from the beginning that that was his road, and that I had to accept it if I could. At no point did I consider not doing so.'

Extracts from his letters to her were published in *Egin* two days after he died.[15] Their tone and content, I suggested to her, indicated an extraordinary idealism in his thinking. Agonising at some length about the peril that their relationship might become a bourgeois marriage, based on materialism and property relationships, he concludes: 'We have given our children names from Nature, they are called Hodei and Haize because a cloud or storm cannot be tied down, nor can the air itself, and both are necessary for life. We don't want work or money, because they oppress us, and Haize and Hodei will be whatever they want, but it will not be you and I who introduce them to the mechanisms of consumer society.'

Izaskun Ugarte, who speaks very quietly, thoughtfully and with many pauses, rejects the word 'idealism', but continues: 'I think you have to believe in something very concrete in order to be willing to give your life for it. Mikel was ready to die . . . His struggle was not just for a territory, it was for much more. It was a struggle to live in another way, so that we could be real persons, to create a way of living that is not the one we have now, a different kind of life and people.'

Less than a month after they moved in together, the French police came to their house and arrested him. 'That was my entry to refugee life,' says Izaskun Ugarte wryly, 'and the end was . . .' – her words tail off. 'You can speak of different epochs in the history of the refugees, but we never experienced a golden age there.'

He was first confined with some other leading refugees to a small village outside the French Basque Country, and then taken to jail in Marseilles to face extradition proceedings. He enjoyed the services of one of the best lawyers in France, Robert Badinter. By a strange twist of fate, Badinter had become Mitterrand's Minister for Justice at the time Goikoetxea was killed. He based his successful defence of Goikoetxea on 'recognition of the fact of Basque nationality, and of the political character of the struggle of the Basque militants'.[16] Five years later, he would refuse to meet Goikoetxea's widow on the grounds that such a meeting would break protocol.

Goikoetxea was released from prison, but he was not granted refugee status and his movements were restricted, at least officially. He was initially barred from returning to the French Basque Country. This did not prevent him carrying out several major operations for ETA in Spain, or fathering two girls with Izaskun Ugarte. Some lines from verse he wrote to her may not suggest great literary talent, but they do give a flavour of the insecurities of a life which was never settled and often clandestine:

> We go into and go out of one valley only to enter another
> We climb a mountain to descend it
> We move inside dark tunnels again and again
> And we reach the light by striking out,
> Step by step we conquer and reconquer liberty.[17]

By 1983 Goikoetxea was back in the Basque Country, with his wife and two young daughters. Life seems to have been a little more settled, and he was giving regular Basque classes in Biarritz, where they were living, and in St-Jean-de-Luz. In September they decided to move house to the latter town, and chose Lasa and Zabala to help them move their belongings. Goikoetxea was aware that he was under more than usual surveillance, and dropped his classes in Biarritz because they involved driving on an isolated road late at night. After Lasa and Zabala's disappearance, Izaskun Ugarte remembers regularly seeing 'strange people' around their apartment block, which was in a quiet, tree-lined suburb known as Le Lac.

'The situation was always very difficult, he was always being followed. It was hard to know if the people watching us were the [French] police or the GAL. Once, in front of our house, a car with four people came up suddenly, and Mikel hid under the steering wheel. "It was as though I felt the bullets hit me," he said afterwards. We lived permanently like that.'

She also thinks that Goikoetxea had a clear premonition at this stage that he had not long to live. 'One memory I will never forget. We were laying down cork tiles in the hallway, and I expected him to finish on another day. But he said he wanted to do it all at once, "because something will happen to me and I won't be able to do it any more then". He was a person who always knew he was going to die, and perhaps because of his militancy, he was ready for it.'

On 28 December, just after 8.00 p.m., the couple arrived home with their youngest daughter, who was not yet two years old. Izaskun Ugarte got out of the car, and waited while Goikoetxea spent several minutes trying to fix a broken lock on the driver's side. Just as he finished, and stood up to his full height, Izaskun Ugarte heard a 'click'.

'I looked around, I thought it was a stone, and I said "It's all right, Mikel, I don't see anything." Just then, I saw two people running away, and I realised he was on the ground. There was no phone in our house, and I had to go to a friend's house to call an ambulance.'[18] Meanwhile, her daughter had run off in the dark, and could not be found for two hours.

Goikoetxea had been hit in the neck and head by bullets so powerful that they went on to penetrate a steel shutter and a door, and embed themselves in an interior wall. That was the 'click' which his wife had heard. He was already in a deep coma when the ambulance arrived, and there was only the faintest hope that he might survive, paralysed from the neck down. He was in fact probably clinically dead when he arrived at Bayonne general hospital, where he ceased to show any signs of life on 1 January.

*** *** ***

After their bungling debut with Segundo Marey, the GAL had now shown ETA they were a force to be reckoned with. They could kill twice in quick succession with impunity. Their intelligence was good enough to track down a clandestine leader. They could kill with precision under difficult conditions. (There was little light in the car park where Goikoetxea was shot, his killers were some 13 metres away from him and he was a moving target.)

The refugee community was under severe pressure, and some French Basques were beginning, as the GAL had clearly intended, to blame the victims and to revise their generally positive attitude to the exiles. 'We think its horrible that they are killing the Spanish refugees, but that is not our problem . . . we are sick of all this trouble, and it would be better if they [the refugees] left here,' some shopkeepers in St-Jean-de-Luz told journalists after Goikoetxea was shot.[19] In their communiqué claiming the shooting, the GAL warned that 'no activist, collaborator or sympathiser with ETA will be able to escape our vengeance. Next week will represent the beginning of actions against the French set-up which protects the terrorists.'[20]

Political parties in France and Spain condemned the escalating dirty war, some of them, we now know, with rather less sincerity than others. The Basque Socialist Party leader, Ricardo Damborenea, for example, said it was 'an unfortunate initiative which is only going to make things worse'.[21] This same man subsequently ardently defended the GAL as a legitimate and effective weapon against ETA, and admitted his own role as one of the organisers of Segundo Marey's kidnapping. Two other men who since have confessed to senior roles in GAL also made statements which now sound very hollow indeed.

'I am waiting,' said Julián Sancristóbal, Civil Governor of Vizcaya, 'for information from the police . . . but as [the GAL] have not operated so far in Spanish territory, we have no data on them.' He firmly denied that the Spanish government had any part in the dirty war.[22] Francisco Álvarez, the Bilbao police chief who was already openly linked to the attempted kidnapping of Larretxea, made similar noises.[23] 'The police do not know, for the moment, what the GAL is. If we knew, we would imprison them if they were in Spain, or we would give information to the French police so that they could do so.'[24]

The Guardia Civil completed this 'see no evil' chorus. 'We have seen that these people [the GAL] are not joking, and that they are as murderous and criminal as the others [ETA], but since they are operating in France we can do nothing against them,' a spokesman said.[25] This would remain the standard excuse for Spanish inaction against the GAL long after the evidence became overwhelming that the organisation was masterminded, financed and staffed from Spanish territory. In Goikoetxea's case, the evidence was still circumstantial. A car similar to a Datsun seen leaving the scene of the crime by Izaskun Ugarte had crashed through a police checkpoint south and inland of St-Jean-de-Luz on the evening of the killing. That suggested it was heading for one of the quieter border crossings like Dantxarinea. A Datsun found burnt out in Bilbao was thought at first to be the same car, but then the police said they had linked it to a drugs operation, not to terrorism, and no more was heard of it.[26]

The Director General of the Guardia Civil, General Sáenz de Santamaría, while denying that even a single member of the security forces had any involvement in the GAL, sounded a slightly more ambiguous tone than the Guardia Civil press office. 'He who sows the wind will reap the whirlwind. Normally there are many interests damaged by the actions of ETA and ETA will receive, as is natural, the corresponding punishment from those who are so damaged. But this is a topic for the French Government.'[27] His adage about winds and whirlwinds was echoed by the leader of the conservative Alianza Popular, and former Francoist Interior Minister, Manuel Fraga, who bluntly refused to condemn the GAL, describing it as 'the logical result of the action of ETA. He who lives by the sword dies by the sword.'[28] It was a motto which Fraga might be reluctant, his critics pointed out, to apply to himself. He had firmly defended, for example, the shooting by police under his control of five unarmed workers in a church in Vitoria in 1976.

At this stage it seemed a real possibility that the GAL might be largely or wholly financed by wealthy Basque businessmen. The trail in this direction seemed clearer when Luis Olarra, Basque oligarch *par excellence*, admitted having contracted mafiosi to respond to any attack on himself or his family by ETA. 'You can only fight terrorism efficiently with its own weapons and methods; all other methods are garbage,' he said. He described the GAL as 'a soft reply to terrorism', but he conceded that 'they give the impression that they are going to succeed, that they are to be taken seriously'. (Other Basque businessmen, perhaps with less protection at their disposal than Olarra, expressed their 'surprise and stupor', through the Basque Business Council, at suggestions apparently emanating from the police that they were funding the GAL.[29]) Nevertheless, Basque PSOE leaders continued to suggest that the GAL were 'mafiosi'.[30]

Meanwhile, the Socialist Minister for the Interior, José Barrionuevo, had threatened to sue anyone who 'slandered' the Spanish security forces as participants of the GAL.[31] A much more forthright comment came from his chief of police, Rafael del Rio, who told the Spanish radio channel SER on the night of the killing that Goikoetxea was just 'one more of the many murderers who infest France'.[32]

In a prompt and clearly argued response, *El País* took him firmly to task. 'The brazenness of the chief of police in diverting to the victim the condemnation which is deserved by his executioners has a precedent in the recent declarations of the prime minister [Felipe González]. He has twice replied to journalists' questions about the *dirty war* – a euphemism to designate the crimes committed by this new armed band in the French

Basque Country – with disturbing replies about the hundreds of attacks and murders carried out by ETA. [Those attacks are] a sad and painful reality which no one forgets, but which does not absolve terrorism by the opposite side . . . The least concession in this area, even of a verbal character, would little by little result in the emptying of the house of democracy . . . only the walls of a phantasmal construction, à la Potemkin, would remain . . . our authorities have the moral and political obligation to make impossible the creation of a sanctuary in Spanish territory for the terrorists of GAL.'[33]

ETA supporters, of course, had no doubts by this stage that they were being subjected to a full-scale clandestine offensive by the Spanish security forces, as their slogans denouncing González as a 'murderer' clearly expressed. It was rather more surprising that a number of senior French Socialist politicians did not hesitate to point the finger at their Spanish opposite numbers. Jean-Pierre Destrade, Socialist MP for the region which includes the French Basque Country, demanded that France should break off negotiations with Spain on EEC entry in protest.[34] The GAL were still not getting it all their own way.

*** *** ***

Izaskun Ugarte had organised a funeral for her husband which would be a propaganda triumph for those who supported his brand of revolutionary, and violent, politics. Mikel Goikoetxea was nothing if not consistent. He appears to have been a utopian whose faith in the imminent creation of a communist society may have seemed extreme even within ETA. He had lived his entire adolescent and adult life in the heady, hothouse ambience of revolutionary politics, and he had developed equally politicised views on the appropriate rituals for his departure from that life.

The day after he died, Izaskun Ugarte told *Egin*, the newspaper which supported ETA, that 'cremation had a political-revolutionary meaning for Mikel'.[35] For all their Marxist-Leninist rhetoric, many members of ETA felt quite comfortable with, and perhaps comforted by, the rites of the Catholic Church, within which they would almost all have been baptised. But Goikoetxea felt that this was inconsistent with the struggle for a completely new, 'non-formalist' society. 'He wanted his funeral in accordance with his life,' she told me. 'He had no religious beliefs. It cost his parents a lot to understand it, that's normal.'

The cremation itself was a turning-point for her. 'You put a box into the oven, and you receive back a pile of ashes. Then you really know that someone has disappeared from the world. He doesn't exist. It's over.'

The struggle, she is quick to stress, was not. For the first half of the funeral she chose a venue which often stands right beside the church in Basque villages, a *frontón*, or pelota court. Pelota is one of the great Basque national sports, and the *frontón* very often doubles as a political arena. At the *frontón* in St-Jean-de-Luz she handed over the ashes, now enclosed in a wicker casket decorated with roses, to Santiago Brouard, a leader of Herri Batasuna who would himself be killed by the GAL later that year. Her message to the mourners was uncompromising: 'The finest homage one can pay *Txapela* is to continue the armed struggle.'[36] Over thirteen years later, sitting in a classroom in Bilbao, she still said, very quietly and very firmly, that she saw no alternative course of action for those who support Basque independence.

At the *frontón*, holding up the snake and axe which is the emblem of ETA, she continued: '*Txapela* never wanted to accept society as it is. He fought to change it, a change he only conceived as possible through a personal change in each of us in pursuit of an independent and socialist Euskadi.'

José Manuel Pagoaga Gallastegi (*Peixoto*), an ETA veteran whose walking stick and thick glasses bore witness to his own severe injuries in the first dirty war, stood by her side. '*Txapela*'s sword was liberty, and thousands of swords will take his place,' he said. The libertarian language of individual and social transformation was blending with the language of militarist resurrection, an apocalyptic ideological cocktail of intoxicating potency to many young Basques.

The casket of ashes was then brought to the pier at Hendaye, which faces the pier at Fuenterrabía, separated by the Bidasoa estuary through which the Franco-Spanish border passes. Thousands of mourners on the Spanish side watched as hundreds on the French side paraded to the end of the pier for the final ceremony. They marched to the music of the *Funeral March of Gernika*, written by Pablo Sorozabal, one of the best-known contemporary Basque composers, 'not for priests or monks, but for *gudaris* [Basque soldiers]'. Chants of 'Gora ETA Militarra' ('Long live ETA(m)') and '*Txapela* – Herriak ez du barkatuko' ('*Txapela* – the people will not pardon') rang from one side to the other.

Txomin Ziluaga and Santiago Brouard took the ashes in a boat, while children threw roses, carnations and violets after it and performed ceremonial dances. *Bertsolaris* chanted verses, and the ashes were lowered into the sea at some point where the border must dissolve, so that, in the words of the Herri Batasuna leader Itziar Aizpurua, 'the great sea of Cantabria may keep him always among us'.

This extraordinary piece of political theatre made a huge impression, not just on the immediate spectators but on those who saw its images on television or in the press. The Basque sociologist Joseba Zulaika has commented that 'folklore and ethnography abound in ritual uses of *auts* [ash] . . . *Autsak* [ashes] are invested with various religious, magical and protective qualities . . . During the winter of 1984, a new ritual development in the politics of ETA took force: on several occasions the body of a political exile assassinated by GAL in southern France was cremated and the remains vented to the air in the presence of family members, political leaders and ETA sympathizers. The photograph of the mother or wife, holding over her head a crystal box containing her ETA son's or husband's *autsak*, would make the front page of the newspapers. The commentary of the people in the street stressed the impressive solemnity of the moment. The political ritualisation of cremating a body and venting its *autsak* reproduces the traditional beliefs concerning the ritual uses of ashes. The fallout of the ashes energises the combat with ritual power.'[37]

Anyone in the English-speaking world who finds such an analysis far-fetched should consider the central role of funeral rituals in the IRA's hunger-strike campaign in the early 1980s, arguably the most successful propaganda events ever staged by that organisation.

The GAL had killed Mikel Goikoetxea, but in doing so they had created the circumstances for the spectacular ascension of *Txapela* to the pantheon of Basque revolutionary heroes. The GAL had turned him into an even more dangerous member of ETA in death than he was in life.

NOTES

1   *Punto y Hora*, no. 365.
2   Interview with Izaskun Rekalde, Bayonne, June 1997.
3   All quotations from Ramón Oñederra's parents, Prudencio Oñederra and Arantza Ganbara, in this chapter are from an interview in Azcoitia, June 1997.
4   Joseba Zulaika points out that ETA was founded on Loyola's feast day, 31 July 1959, and claims that there is 'an intimate connection between the militants and the patron saint'. Joseba Zulaika, *Basque Violence, Metaphor and Sacrament* (Reno, Nev.: University of Nevada Press, 1988), pp. 334–5.
5   The 'street struggle' strategy was the most visible part of a ferocious radicalisation within Herri Batasuna from the late 1980s, unleashing all the energies of its youth groups at every perceived manifestation of 'the system', from telephone booths to offices of other parties to, on some occasions, individuals foolhardy enough to carry openly a copy of *El País* past a bar run by the radicals. For some of the background to this development, see Antonio Elorza (ed.), *La Historia de ETA* (Madrid: Temas de Hoy, 2000), pp. 401–6.
6   It is curious that Oñederra's parting phrase, a melodramatic declaration probably pardonable in an eighteen-year-old, is a direct reflection in Basque ('Dana Euskadigatik') of the Spanish slogan 'Todo por la Patria'. Those words stand above the gate of every barracks belonging to the force whose members probably killed him, the Guardia Civil.
7   This is a euphemism for Spanish immigrant workers, which Arantza Ganbara uses almost apologetically.
8   *El País*, 21 December 1983.
9   Ibid.
10 Ibid. *El País*'s editorials on the GAL, over a period of fifteen years and with very few exceptions, have shown an exemplary understanding of the antithesis between the democratic rule of law and the practice of state terrorism. This editorial line is particularly remarkable in a newspaper which has been, often rightly, closely associated in the public mind with the thinking of the Socialist governments of Felipe González in other respects.
11 José María Calleja, in *Contra la Barbarie* (Madrid: Temas de Hoy, 1997), gives a comprehensive chronology of ETA's victims. There were none in this period.
12 Francisco Letamendía, *Historia del Nacionalismo Vasco y de ETA,* 3 vols. (San Sebastián: R&B Ediciones, 1994), vol. 1, p. 372; *El País*, 29 December 1983.
13 *El País*, 29 December 1983.
14 All quotations from Izaskun Ugarte in this chapter are from an interview in Bilbao, June 1997.
15 *Egin*, 3 January 1984.
16 *El País,* 5 April 1979.
17 *Egin,* 3 January 1984.
18 That friend was Javier Galdeano, who would himself fall victim to the GAL in 1985. See ch. 10.
19 *El País*, 30 December 1983.
20 Ironically, the vast majority of attacks against French interests over the next years would be carried out not by the GAL but by ETA itself, furious at the

increased collaboration of the Mitterrand administration with the Spanish authorities and also, allegedly, with the GAL.

21 *El País*, 30 December 1983.
22 *Deia*, 30 December 1983.
23 Álvarez was also head of the Unified Counter-terrorist Command (MULC), which co-ordinated the various security forces involved in counter-terrorism.
24 *Deia*, 30 December 1983.
25 Ibid.
26 *El País*, 5 January 1984.
27 *Diario 16*, 30 December 1983.
28 *El País*, 5 and 6 January 1984.
29 *El País*, 15 January 1984; *Egin*, 6 January 1984.
30 For example, Enrique Múgica, a future Minister for Justice in Madrid. See *El País,* 11 January 1984.
31 *El País*, 20 December 1983.
32 *El País*, 29 December 1983.
33 *El País*, 30 December 1983.
34 *Deia*, 30 December 1983. For more detail on Destrade's views, see ch. 14, p. 178.
35 *Egin*, 3 January 1984.
36 *Sud-Ouest*, 7 January 1984.
37 Zulaika, op. cit., pp. 331–2.

7

ETA Between Two Fires:

the dirty war and the diplomatic offensive

The killing of Ramón Oñederra (*Kattu*), says Izaskun Rekalde, made it clear what the GAL could do, while the killing of Mikel Goikoetxea (*Txapela*) made it clear that the refugees faced a new and sustained assault on their own doorsteps. But she insists that the uppermost anxiety in the minds of the refugees was not assassination, but extradition.[1] This anxiety was heightened by a diplomatic offensive by Madrid, aimed at persuading Paris to treat the Basque radicals as criminal suspects rather than as political refugees. One of the distinguishing features of the GAL campaign, compared to the earlier dirty war, was that the physical and legal threats to ETA began to go hand in hand.

Spectacular operations by the Basque Spanish Battalion, such as the car bomb which killed José Miguel Beñarán Ordeñana (*Argala*) in December 1978, sent waves of tension through the exile community. 'They were very strong actions, but they were isolated incidents,' Rekalde says. 'When they happened they were a great shock, but we did not feel the same fear of being in the street then, as we did when the GAL were coming at us from one side and the French police from the other.' In the 1980s, she says, 'there was no way out'.

Despite the fear, many refugees would continue to stubbornly pursue the same social life in the streets for years to come. 'The Spanish government wanted to keep us in our houses; we wouldn't let them impose that on us. But it was a little suicidal,' she concedes ruefully. Even in their houses, the refugees would not now be safe. Goikoetxea's ashes had hardly been swept into the Bay of Biscay when one of the biggest French police raids ever was launched against these increasingly unwelcome guests of the French nation.

On 10 January 1984, a hundred houses were searched and forty people arrested. (Many appear to have had some warning of the raid and gone underground.) Ten of the detainees were confined to the north of France, and six were deported to the island of Guadeloupe, and thence to Panama.

Among the latter was José María Larretxea, one of the leading figures in what remained of ETA's 'political-military' faction, and the target of the botched 1983 kidnap attempt by Spanish police.

The consequences of the French police operation were small scale compared to what was to follow, but it indicated that the French government was at last beginning to accept the Spanish position that ETA members were not refugee freedom fighters, but terrorists on the run from a legitimate democracy.

Was this shift in perception and policy a result of González's apparently abortive meeting with President Mitterrand in December? Was it produced by the 'pressure' applied by the two GAL killings in the last days of 1983? Was it influenced by Spain's progress in EEC entry negotiations? The answer remains unclear. It is quite possible, of course, that this shift was the result of all three factors.

Whatever Mitterrand's own views, it was not easy to change his party's deep attachment to the principle that France was a land of political asylum. But such a change would be facilitated if the Basque refugees became perceived locally and nationally as a political problem, rather than as a worthy cause to support. The refugees had generally been very careful to keep their noses clean and remain on good terms with their French Basque neighbours.[2] But if ETA began to be associated with terrorism on French soil, from whatever source, the price of the principle of asylum might then become too high. This was particularly true for the citizens of the French Basque Country, regardless of their sympathies. The perception that the refugees not only drew physical danger on the community where they lived but also threatened its economic prosperity was beginning to take root.

The fact that the Basque refugees were the victims, rather than the perpetrators, of the GAL outrages was already becoming blurred. A report by the French Senate, as early as the spring of 1984, had noted that 'the Basque refugees are now being perceived as a cause of public disorder'.[3] The legal mechanism under which refugees were detained and dispersed in January was that of 'absolute urgency', by which a foreigner considered a serious threat to public order can be expelled by governmental decree. The GAL campaign caused many French Basques to see the refugees in a new and unfavourable light. By their mere presence, they were causing a rapid decline in the local economy, especially the tourism business, as the news spread that the bars and boulevards of the region's coastal resorts were now the targets of a terrorist group.[4]

Egin, the newspaper which defended ETA's programme, subsequently attempted to establish that Mitterrand specifically imposed a policy of accepting the GAL as a 'lesser evil' on the Socialist leadership in the French Basque Country.[5] The evidence for this is flimsy, while the continuing angry condemnations of the dirty war by local Socialist leaders suggest that, if such an effort was made, it was not initially successful. Nevertheless, the idea that the Spanish authorities were using the GAL not so much to pressurise their French governmental colleagues as to help the latter overcome the resistance of the French public to extraditing Basques to Spain cannot be discarded out of hand. Mitterrand, after all, had no qualms about his own administration's dirty war against the relatively harmless ecologists of Greenpeace on foreign territory.[6] He might not have had any great moral problem with the killing of foreigners on French soil, particularly if they belonged to a group who were themselves using terrorist violence against a neighbouring democracy.

In any case, a second factor was conditioning French Basque public opinion against their long-term visitors from south of the border. A rather shadowy organisation called Iparretarrak (the name can conveniently mean either 'those of the north' or 'ETA of the north') had re-emerged in the French Basque Country in 1982. This group claimed aims and used means similar to ETA's in the Spanish Basque Country. Iparretarrak carried out a series of attacks in France up to March 1984.[7] Most of them were attacks on property, but there were fatalities, and in February they attempted to bomb the Paris–Madrid high-speed train. If they had succeeded, the civilian death toll probably would have made ETA's worst outrages seem minor.[8]

Their operations caused great irritation to ETA. This shows up a central contradiction in radical Basque politics. In theory, ETA was unequivocally in favour of detaching the French Basque Country from France. In practice, the organisation was not at all in favour of anything which would undermine its comfortable logistical bases in friendly, or at least neutral, territory. This was precisely the effect, in practice, of Iparretarrak's campaign, which overlapped in the public mind with the GAL's killings to create an impression that the Basque refugees were becoming a very serious nuisance.

A third factor contributed to a general weakening of sympathy for ETA throughout France in the early 1980s. This was the dramatic increase in Islamist terrorism in Europe. In Paris alone, Arab terrorists claimed 21 lives and injured 191 people in 1982. It became a little harder to see shootings and bombings in Spain as romantic actions by a legitimate liberation movement when similar attacks were shattering civilian bodies on the streets of France.

Meanwhile, whatever was really happening at government level, the GAL were still being given plenty of scope for dirty work by their masters, whoever they were. ETA, for its part, was far from intimidated by the arrival on the scene of a group which perfectly fitted the necessary role of repressor, in the model of 'action–repression–action'. For the first half of 1984, the GAL and ETA engaged in a vicious spiral of atrocity and counter-atrocity.

On 29 January, ETA shot dead Lieutenant-General Quintana Lacaci, and wounded his wife, as they returned home from Mass in Madrid. Lacaci had been a central figure in preventing the army from supporting Tejero's *coup d'état* attempt three years earlier.[9] His killing seemed designed to outrage democrats in general and the Socialist leadership, still unsure of the military's loyalty, in particular.

On 4 February, ETA picked a very different kind of victim, but an equally disturbing target for anyone who hoped the organisation really wanted a democratic resolution of the Basque conflict. Mikel Solaun had been a member of the 'military' faction of ETA, and had been imprisoned once under Franco and again in 1981. But he had accepted the programme of 'social reinsertion' which had mostly been availed of by ETA's 'political-military' faction. This provision enabled him to serve much of his sentence on parole. For such 'individualist egotism' and 'loss of revolutionary conscience' (according to an ETA communiqué), he was shot dead in front of his family in a bar in Getxo.

The 'reply' from the GAL came four days later. Angel Gurmindo Izarraga (*Escopetas* or *Stein*) and Bixente Perurena Telletxea (*Peru*) were going into the latter's house to watch a cup final between two Basque teams, Atlético Bilbao and Real Sociedad de San Sebastián. Perurena's house was on the same quiet street in Hendaye where Segundo Marey had been kidnapped, less than a kilometre from the Spanish border. His wife, who knew they had been concerned about 'strange people' in the area, heard an odd sound 'a bit like a car starting'. She ran out to find both of them dead on the street. She saw two men running to a waiting car.

According to the Spanish police, Perurena was commander of the *mugalaris*, the ETA *comando* responsible for transporting activists across the border. If this is accurate, it suggests that the GAL had very up-to-date intelligence. The previous *mugalari* commander, Mikel Lujua, the man in whose place Segundo Marey had been kidnapped, had been deported to the north of France just a month previously. The same sources described Gurmindo as a bodyguard of Domingo Iturbe Abásolo (*Txomin*), probably ETA's chief of staff at the time. He was also a close associate of Miguel Ángel Apalategui (*Apala*), the organiser of ETA's bloodiest offensive in the late 1970s.[10] Gurmindo's two *noms de guerre*, *Escopetas* (shotguns) and *Stein* (the brand name for a favourite ETA submachine-gun), probably speak for themselves. If the GAL's aim was to decapitate ETA, they were getting close to the jugular. Yet the long-term futility of such actions is clearly indicated in the case of Perurena. His daughter, Miren Argi Perurena, who had been a child at the time of his death, was arrested and investigated for ETA activities in France, thirteen years later. Released without charge, she was arrested a second time, in the company of a 'most wanted' ETA suspect, in 1999 these investigations continue at the time of writing.[11]

Two hours before their deaths, Gurmindo and Perurena had complained to the French police that they were being followed by what they suspected was a GAL *comando*. They had told their comrades they had not had a very helpful hearing.

The French press now openly and angrily asserted that the Spanish authorities were involved in the GAL. The front page of *Le Quotidien de Paris* on 10 February commented that 'the French government seems incapable of assuring the security of its guests'. The article continued: 'That the Ayatollah Khomenei or President Assad have sent their killers here one more time is not a novelty or a surprise. That the democratic and socialist Spanish government should send people to approve and advise, and perhaps to organise by remote control, police reprisal raids on this side of the Pyrenees gives plenty of pause for thought.'

In another article, however, the newspaper also pointed out that the actions of the GAL could backfire, if their intention was to pressurise France to abolish ETA's sanctuary. 'With the Hendaye killings, the GAL may be discouraging France from taking new administrative measures against the exiles, who may become martyr figures. It is like throwing a jar of boiling oil on a fire which was going out.'[12] Plausible as this scenario was at the time, this is not what happened. Far from gaining sympathy as martyrs, the refugees were, by and large, blamed for their own difficulties by the French public. In the Spanish Basque Country, however, the GAL offensive had precisely this effect of adding fuel to ETA's cooling fires.

The funerals of the Hendaye victims coincided with the start of the campaign for the second-ever poll for the Basque autonomous parliament. Under the circumstances, this election was bound to be bitterly fought. *El País* commented, noting the coincidence, that 'once the Pandora's Box of contempt for legality has been opened, the internal dynamic of the forces unleashed is uncontrollable, and is capable of undermining the stability of our democratic institutions'. Herri Batasuna, which had been expected to lose support from a populace increasingly unwilling to see ETA as heroes, was able to use the revulsion felt by most Basques towards the GAL to claw back sympathy, and to brand the entire Socialist Party as 'state terrorists'.

Then, on 23 February, three days before polling day, something happened which caused unprecedented stupor and despair, even in this brutalised society. Enrique Casas, the Socialist Party's leading candidate for Guipúzcoa, and a man with a personal reputation for decency and moderation, was shot dead on his doorstep. Up to this point, all sides had generally avoided the assassination of top political figures, perhaps realising that such acts could make any negotiated resolution of the conflict virtually impossible. As it was, the situation probably only remained under control because it turned out that the killers of Casas were not from ETA, but the Comandos Autónomos, an ultra-radical fringe group with no political stake in the elections.

Herri Batasuna condemned the killing, accusing the Comandos Autónomos of acting as a 'credit card' for the GAL. According to this argument, they had given the GAL an excuse to kill Herri Batasuna members. The PSOE accused Herri Batasuna of rank hypocrisy, alleging, almost certainly wrongly, that the Comandos Autónomos was simply a front name to acknowledge work that was too dirty even for ETA. More to the point, *El País* wondered if Herri Batasuna was trying to invert Max Weber's dictum that the democratic state has a monopoly of legitimate violence, and was claiming a monopoly of *illegitimate* violence for ETA.

Forty-eight hours later, the GAL struck back in dramatic fashion, not at Herri Batasuna or at the Comandos Autónomos, but at one of the securest enclaves in ETA's sanctuary. The action demonstrated a combination of military expertise, excellent intelligence-gathering and sheer daring that chilled the blood of the refugees.

Ideaux-Mendy is hardly even a village, more a townland with a church, surrounded by a scattering of farmhouses. It is in the district of Mauleon, itself the smallest and poorest of the French Basque capitals, but an area where a very high percentage of the dwindling population speak Basque as their first language. The area attracted few refugees, but the isolation of the small hamlets among the rolling hills of Zuberoa afforded them a certain security. Strangers are much more quickly spotted here than in the crowded coastal resorts, and the houses, often hundreds of metres from the road, are not easily told apart.

One of these houses, a former presbytery with the huge curved dark slate roof and white frontage typical of the area, had been rented by a group of about twenty refugees. They were using it as a centre for intensive Basque language courses. It is easy to assume that language classes were a cover for more sinister activities. Without ruling that possibility out, the fact is that, quixotically enough, being a fluent Basque speaker is almost as important to an ETA member as being proficient in arms.

They seem to have been well liked in this secluded neighbourhood. A neighbour fondly recalled that they came around offering to clean up when their Doberman soiled his courtyard, and that the large group of young people caused no disturbance.[13]

One of the refugees was Eugenio Gutiérrez Salazar (*Tigre*), a lathe operator from near Bilbao. An ETA activist, he had gone into exile a year earlier, when he suspected that the police had detected his membership of a *comando* operating in the city. He was taking a mid-morning break with his comrades on Saturday, 25 February, when he heard the Doberman barking. The students had noticed the passage of many strange cars in the area, and were concerned enough to have set up a rota for night security. But Gutiérrez Salazar felt sufficiently confident in broad daylight to take his sandwich out onto the patio alone.

A moment later, he was staggering back into the house, shot through the heart, dying on the floor where he fell. His comrades slammed the doors and shutters, assuming the attackers were close by, and saw nothing. Afterwards, it was possible to establish that the shot came from a high-powered rifle, probably fired from the main road more than 100 metres away,[14] by a marksman who may have used his own getaway car to steady his aim. If the GAL unit was returning to a base in Spain, the driver faced a difficult mountain drive of more than 40 kilometres to reach the border.

In any case, according to Begoña Clemente, a refugee who was also on the course, the French police did not exert themselves about the killing. They took half an hour to arrive at the house, and showed more interest in the identity of the victim than of his killers. She also claims that more sympathetic police, who arrived subsequently, told them that of the list of sixteen 'strange' number plates the group had recorded, nine were false and one was based in the local Spanish consulate in Pau.[15] Whatever their connections on both sides of the border, the GAL seemed able to kill at will, whenever and wherever they chose. In strictly military terms, they were looking like a major success. So much so that there was much speculation, among their admirers and their detractors, that the GAL were using SAS or Mossad operatives and training.

This, however, is to assume, quite wrongly, that there were no groups within the Spanish security forces capable of operating abroad and taking out an unarmed man at a hundred metres. Curiously, *Egin* reported receiving a phone call from the GAL on the evening of Gutiérrez Salazar's death, which ended with a cry of 'Viva el GAL! Viva la Guardia

Civil!'[16] But whether this was a piece of remarkably stupid self-incrimination, or a piece of black propaganda by the radical newspaper, must be a matter for speculation.

While the GAL now looked good in military terms, it was already becoming evident that, from almost any anti-ETA viewpoint, they would be a political failure. True, they could claim some credit for squeezing concessions out of the French on the issue of controlling the refugees. But in the elections south of the border, the day after Gutiérrez Salazar was shot, Herri Batasuna increased its vote to 14.5 per cent, reversing a decline in the previous year's municipal elections. It was not easy to argue that ETA was just a gang of isolated criminals, if 150,000 people were still voting for them in a democracy. Within the next month, the GAL's military brilliance would also begin to look tarnished, recalling the clumsily bungled kidnapping of Segundo Marey, but with more deadly results.

*** *** ***

Like border towns everywhere, Irún has its fair share of smugglers, pimps, drug dealers, fixers and bent cops, sometimes all incarnated in the same human being. As a Spanish border town, controlling one of Iberia's two main land thoroughfares to the rest of Europe, it is a favourite posting for both the most corrupt and the most passionately fascist elements of the Guardia Civil. Again, these are not mutually exclusive categories.

Daniel Fernández Aceña was an ideal vehicle for their interests. He lived in Irún, but worked across the border in the railway station complex in Hendaye. He was one of sixty employees in a maintenance unit, amongst whom there were about a dozen Spanish Basque refugees. Aceña held far-Right political opinions and displayed fascist insignia on the locker where he kept his tools and working clothes. Political tension between the workers often soured the atmosphere, and took a nastier turn when little painted coffins began to appear on the lockers of refugees. But the Basques took Aceña for a braggart and were not too concerned about his posturing. No one seems to have remembered that he used to work directly alongside Joxi Zabala, one of the first two victims of the GAL.[17]

Hendaye's important railway network is a full-scale spaghetti junction, with tracks switching and overlapping over many hundreds of metres. This maze of rails was still obscured by darkness early in the morning of 1 March, when three refugees were making their way across it to go to work. A young French colleague, Jean-Pierre Leiba, was walking close to them. Suddenly, a man opened fire with a pistol from behind a railway wagon, killing Leiba on the spot. The refugees gave chase to the killer and his companion, who made for the border. A third man may have run in the opposite direction, but vanished.

One pursuer nearly caught the first pair, but had to pull back when threatened with a gun. The border was only a couple of hundred metres away, another inhibiting factor for the refugees, who risked immediate arrest if they crossed it. The killers, splitting up and crossing by two adjacent bridges, got past the French checkpoints. The Spanish police, alerted by the refugees' shouts, arrested Mariano Moraleda Muñoz as he tried to slip through the heavy vehicles' entry point. This was the first of several occasions when refugees or bystanders were instrumental in the detention of GAL members.

The second man, who turned out to be Daniel Fernández Aceña, somehow got through the border, but gave himself up two hours later.[18] Two other men were arrested in connection with the killing, and released without charge. A fifth suspect, the businessman and right-winger Víctor Manuel Navascués Gil, believed to be the brains of the operation, evaded the police for seven months, before also turning himself in.

There was enormous public interest in the identity of the detainees. These were the first members of the GAL to be arrested since Pedro Sánchez, and the only ones to be captured so far in Spain. Perhaps the secrets of this mysterious organisation would at last be revealed.

But almost immediately assertions were made that Leiba's killers were not in the GAL at all, despite the detainees' admissions of membership. The next day, Felipe González's deputy Prime Minister, Alfonso Guerra, made the extraordinary statement that he 'had the impression that these are people who want to prove their worthiness to join the GAL, but do not belong to that organisation'.[19] As a Herri Batasuna leader put it, if Guerra knew who was *not* in the GAL, then it was legitimate to wonder if he knew who was.

A day later, a caller purporting to represent the GAL told several news media that the organisation had no link with the killing. Since the GAL had not set up any code with the media to authenticate their claims, there was no way of verifying the call.

Jean-Pierre Leiba was the GAL's first fatal 'accident'. He had no connection whatsoever with ETA, apart from the fact that he worked alongside refugees. He was not even thought to have mild Basque nationalist sympathies. It is possible that he was shot because he saw the attackers and warned his colleagues, or that Aceña was afraid he would recognise him. It is just as likely that Muñoz, who did the actual shooting, just could not make out his targets properly in the dark.

As fate would have it, Leiba was the nephew of the proprietor of the Bar Hendayais, where one of the bloodiest attacks of the previous dirty war had taken place. Several observers commented on the similarity between the two incidents: the victims had no terrorist connections, and the attackers fled directly to the border, into the arms of the Spanish police. The difference was that, on this occasion, they were arrested, and not permitted to vanish into thin air. They were not, however, extradited to France, where the authorities might have been more zealous in investigating their backers.

In December 1985, Aceña and Muñoz were both sentenced to thirty years in jail despite having changed their original statements to deny both membership of the GAL and any part in the killing. Matters came close to farce when they even tried to deny knowing Navascués, who freely admitted knowing both of them. Navascués himself was found not guilty. The fertile references that both convicted men had made, in their early statements, to links between the Guardia Civil in Irún, the Spanish army and the GAL were not pursued. Once convicted, Aceña became a kind of hired interviewee on every aspect of the GAL, mixing fact and fiction bewilderingly, as we have seen in his comments on the fate of Lasa and Zabala.[20]

It seems quite likely that the GAL would not have been demoralised just because they had killed the wrong man in Leiba's case. The spilling of innocent French blood might well be more effective in persuading Paris (and the local population) to get tough on the refugees than the killing of suspected terrorists. Where the Leiba debacle was really embarrassing, from the GAL's point of view, was that it was a pretty pathetic cock-up. Muñoz was a small-time criminal with a string of convictions, Aceña was a bar-room Nazi, and the planning of the operation was a parody of the practice of their alleged mentors in Mossad or the SAS.

The victim of the next GAL operation, another Jean-Pierre as it happened, was far from innocent, but that did not make the outcome any happier for the group.

On 19 March in Biarritz, a powerful bomb, intended for a large group of ETA members according to one account, exploded prematurely.[21] Quite literally hoist with his own petard, the man who had been manipulating it was gruesomely dismembered, some of his body parts landing burnt and mangled on the roof of a nearby house. Only a driving licence, which had somehow remained undamaged, provided a clue to his identity. The name, of course, was false, as were the number plates on the shattered car, but the photograph was genuine. For several days there was speculation in the press as to his true identity. Two days later, the GAL revealed Jean-Pierre Cherid as the real name of one of their leading activists.

Cherid was one of the key men picked by Carrero Blanco's 'Documentation Service' for unorthodox operations, according to the most extensively investigated Spanish account of the first dirty war.[22] He went on to lead the team which, among other grim achievements, avenged Carrero's death by wiring Beñarán Ordeñana's car to a bomb in Anglet in 1978. He had been a natural choice to lead the GAL's hired guns when the dirty war was revived in 1983.

It surprised many of his associates that someone so experienced with explosives should blow himself up. The supplier of the explosive was allegedly a *guardia civil*.[23] There was already some rivalry between the various groups which constituted the GAL, but it seems most likely that Cherid was simply the victim of bad luck on this occasion. His death was a double blow to the GAL. It demonstrated, for the second time in a month, that the organisation was not quite as formidable as it had appeared. Secondly, Cherid himself was a veteran operative, a respected commander of small units and a rich source of mercenary contacts. He would be hard, but not impossible, to replace.

March was to be a bloody month all round. Two nights after the GAL acknowledged Cherid's identity, a group of GEOs (the crack Spanish anti-terrorist police unit, two of whose members had attempted to kidnap Larretxea) moved into Pasajes de San Pedro. This port on the margins of San Sebastián's industrial belt is very picturesque, if you can screen out the pollution. It stands on the edge of a particularly narrow inlet, and the GEOs took up a 'U' formation above the port, covering all entering shipping.

Their decoy was a young woman called Rosa Jimeno, who they sent down, roped by her ankle, to a small beach. She signalled with a flashlight, as agreed, and a light on an incoming motor launch responded. On board were six members of the Comandos Autónomos, the group which had killed the Socialist leader Enrique Casas on the eve of the February elections.

The launch drifted in silently towards Jimeno's winking signal. Abruptly, the watching GEOs opened up with a withering crossfire, which they sustained until the boat and its occupants were peppered with high-velocity shotgun pellets. There was only one survivor.

Rosa Jimeno insists that she only agreed to participate on the understanding that her comrades would be arrested, not killed, when they landed. The GEOs claimed that they had shouted a warning, and that the terrorists opened fire in response. There is no independent evidence for either police assertion, both of which were rebutted by Jimeno and other witnesses. The judicial inquiry was inconclusive and eventually shelved.[24]

The Pasajes massacre was widely interpreted as direct revenge for the killing of Casas by the Comandos Autónomos, but it was never considered a GAL operation. In this case, the Spanish security forces openly acknowledged their participation, and invited journalists to view the wreck of the launch, riddled like a colander, the next day. The attack was carried out on Spanish territory, exclusively by official Spanish forces, and they were engaging a terrorist unit actively taking part in an illegal operation. The GAL favoured the liquidation of 'off-duty' terrorist suspects on foreign soil, usually with the assistance of irregular or mercenary elements.

At the time, the GAL were busy preparing an operation elsewhere, as if to show that the loss of Cherid would not slow the rhythm of the hammer blows which were falling on ETA. This time their target was Xabier Pérez de Arenaza, the brother-in-law of the senior ETA leader Domingo Iturbe Abásolo (*Txomin*). He had shared a flat with Iturbe Abásolo until the GAL's activities drove the latter further under cover, and the GAL may have imagined they could still find this cherished target in Arenaza's company. Arenaza himself was, according to *El País,* considered to be one of Iturbe Abásolo's 'senior staff officers'.[25] On 23 March, Arenaza was going on a fishing trip and pulled into the petrol station near his home in Biarritz to fill the tank of his Citroën 2CV. Like many of his comrades in ETA, for security purposes he now was always accompanied by a friend when going out, but on this occasion his friend had had to do something else at the last minute.

He paid for his petrol and got back into the car. A man on a scooter, who had been waiting nearby, pulled up beside him. He took out a pistol and fired five shots, two of which hit Arenaza in the face and killed him instantly. A scooter hardly falls into the category of great getaway vehicles, but there was no one to give pursuit, and the assailant was never seen again. It emerged later that a next-door neighbour of Arenaza's, Jean-Pierre Bounin, who was arrested in connection with a subsequent GAL attack, had a similar scooter, but he was released for lack of evidence.[26]

Dirty War, Clean Hands

El País warned whoever was organising and financing the GAL that they were approaching a point of no return, 'a vendetta within society which will make the climate of civil discord and confrontation between communities definitively irreversible'. They were prophetic words.[27]

Such discord and confrontation were, of course, part and parcel of ETA's own strategy of 'action–repression–action'. The radicals accelerated the rhythm of their operations in the weeks after Arenaza's death, as if to show that the GAL were incapable of matching their killings with appropriate 'replies'. On 27 March they killed a municipal policeman, and in April they killed three national policemen, one *guardia civil*, one retired army major and one civilian.

It is not clear whether the GAL were unable or unwilling to keep up in this macabre competition. They suffered a further setback in April, probably as a result of information found at Cherid's Toulouse apartment. A complex French police surveillance operation led to the arrest of no less than ten suspected members or collaborators of the GAL, including Mohammed Khiar, a veteran mercenary who had allegedly seen service with the Basque Spanish Battalion.[28] Most of the detainees were associated with criminal gangs based in Bordeaux and Paris, and several were of north African origin, though they were all French nationals.[29]

Despite strong evidence against several of them (Khiar had a note with the name of a refugee, and a map of the man's house, in his possession when he was arrested), they were all released in May and June, on the grounds of 'defects of procedure'. The local press described the whole episode as a 'fiasco'.[30] They were freed by the deeply conservative Judge Michel Svahn, who operated on the curious principle that 'to suppress the GAL, you must suppress ETA'.[31] Since the latter aim was not within his remit, he seems to have felt no obligation to attempt the former, which was. Svahn had been responsible for the temporary release of Pedro Sánchez, and for freeing the Spanish policemen who had tried to kidnap Larretxea. He would also release a very senior GAL activist, Jean-Philippe Labade, later in 1984. The French Supreme Court would reverse Judge Svahn's ruling on the ten detainees a year later, but by that time most of them had vanished into that large and unmapped country known as 'whereabouts unknown'.[32]

During this same period, a number of 'GAL exposés' began to appear in the Spanish media, in which hooded figures who claimed to be GAL mercenaries gave 'exclusive interviews' about the organisation's *modus operandi*. While this material must be treated with scepticism, as it mixes fairly wild speculation with a rehash of the GAL's operations to date, it is interesting that the interviewees tend to stress the 'bounty hunter' aspects of the GAL. Specific members of ETA had specific prices on their heads, with Iturbe Abásolo among the most lucrative at approximately 20 million pesetas, according to these accounts. One mercenary claimed that the organisation was funded by a 'patriotic tax' on businessmen, a sort of voluntary equivalent of ETA's 'revolutionary tax'.[33]

If the GAL really did participate in these interviews (and some of them brought along files on ETA members to prove their bona fides), they probably had two motives. The major one could have been standard black propaganda, to maintain the largely false image of the GAL as a 'freelance' operation with no connections to the state apparatus. The minor one may have been to supplement their incomes from cheque-book journalism, as April was a quiet rather than a cruel month for the GAL in 1984.

Two of the GAL suspects arrested in France in April told the press that they were victims of a 'cosmetic' operation, designed to calm the French public with a semblance of police diligence after the wave of GAL attacks in February and March. If some of the detainees were involved in the GAL, even their temporary detention must have been a setback, and may explain the group's inactivity during April. But it may also have been that the organisation felt its interests were better served, at this stage, by occasional operations with carefully selected targets – and carefully planned escape routes. In any case, the GAL waited until early May, and then struck at a point where, despite the precedent of Ideaux-Mendy, they were probably least expected.

*** *** ***

St-Martin-d'Arossa is a village of fewer than five hundred inhabitants, tucked in under the Pyrenees and well inland, off the main road between Bayonne and St-Jean-Pied-de-Port. It used to be the home of a furniture factory called Denek, a co-operative based on the inspirational model of the great Basque co-operative at Mondragón. The company was founded in 1979 by, among others, Jesús Zugarramurdi. Under the *nom de guerre Kixkur*, this man was believed by the Spanish police to have played a major role in the assassination of Carerro Blanco, and therefore had probably been high on the list of dirty war targets for a long time.[34]

In March 1984 the Spanish magazine *Tiempo* drew attention to the possibility that, given Zugarramurdi's participation, Denek had a clandestine function in laundering funds raised by ETA through the 'revolutionary tax'. *Tiempo* pointed out that the company certainly raised a lot of its capital in the Spanish Basque Country.[35] However, the co-operative employed only a handful of refugees along with about fifty local workers, and the magazine could offer no proof of its allegations. If it was a front company it was cleverly organised, because the jobs it offered were desperately needed in a rural area beset by chronic unemployment and emigration.

Unlike most of the GAL's previous victims, neither Zugarramurdi nor his colleague Rafael Goikoetxea seems to have had any sense that they were under immediate threat. They took no particular precautions, leaving the factory as usual at 5.00 p.m. on 3 May, with Goikoetxea driving a Citroën Dyane belonging to another refugee. They took the minor road towards their homes in the dramatically situated village of St-Etienne-de-Baigorry.

This village is a favoured haven for hillwalkers. It is also one of the main stops along the French Basque 'cheese route', which lures less energetic tourists into the hidden skirts of the mountains. The approach road is quiet and fairly narrow, with a nasty double curve just before a level crossing. As the two men were taking these bends, Goikoetxea suddenly saw a big motorbike speeding up behind them.

'Where did that come from?' he exclaimed to his companion, as the bike manoeuvred out, parallel to the car. The pillion passenger fired five pistol shots into the car, hitting the driver in the chest, and Zugarramurdi in the leg and elbow. With Goikoetxea slumped over the wheel, the car ploughed into the right-hand verge.

'I could see that the bike was doing a U-turn a hundred metres up the road,' says Zugarramurdi. 'I thought they were coming back to finish us off, so I crouched down as low as possible, but they passed at top speed and disappeared back towards St-Martin-d'Arossa.'[36] Another car driven by Denek workers arrived and raised the alarm, but Goikoetxea was dead on arrival in hospital.

A native of the Guipuzcoan town of Hernani, one of ETA's main fiefdoms, Goikoetxea joined the Communist Party at the age of fifteen, but shifted towards ETA about three years later, and he was famous in a small way for several exploits, including the robbery of a lorry load of explosives. He was reported as having been commander of the *mugalaris* (border-crossing units) at one stage, but is said to have been fairly inactive in ETA at the time of his death.

Nevertheless, he had a hero's funeral in Hernani, with full honours from the town council, attended by three thousand people, many of whom chanted the usual slogans in favour of ETA. The funeral had been preceded by rioting, and stone-throwing attacks on the local Socialist Party headquarters. Goikoetxea had asked his mother, 'if anything happened to him', to make sure he was not cremated. He wanted a burial ceremony in his home town. He was, his parents say, 'a friend of everybody's', as parents in such circumstances often say. His adolescent obsession, ironically enough, was motorbikes.

The motorbike from which he was shot was found a few days later, in an abandoned shepherd's shelter on the road back to Bayonne. The refugees lodged the now-familiar complaints that the French police had mounted only the most desultory search for the killers, who have never been identified. Local people interviewed at the time were outraged that political violence had penetrated their quiet world, and quietly wondered what effect it would have on their meagre but vital tourist trade.

On the afternoon before Rafael Goikoetxea was killed, ETA kidnapped a minor businessman, Ángel Rodríguez Sánchez, near San Sebastián, and shot him in the back of the neck the following day. Within the space of a few hours, and of 50 kilometres, two men had been executed without trial. The perpetrators of one killing were revolutionary terrorists. The authors of the other were, it is almost certain, the agents of a democratic state.

Later in the summer of 1984, Denek suffered the first of several arson attacks, which would eventually close it down. Today, rusting rolling-stock at the tiny railway station is one of the few reminders of a prosperous, but politically suspect, factory in St-Martin-d'Arossa. The GAL had maintained a spectacularly high profile in the first few months of 1984. Madrid's political campaign to persuade Paris to collaborate effectively against ETA had been much less visible. But diplomats and Interior Ministry officials had been assiduous in pursuing this end, and their efforts were about to bear fruit. The pincer movement of the dirty war and the diplomatic offensive would transform ETA's 'French sanctuary' into hostile territory for the radicals within eighteen months of Rafael Goikoetxea's death.

NOTES

1   Interview with Izaskun Rekalde, Bayonne, June 1997.

2   Ramón Oñederra's mother's story that he used to help a little old lady across the road to Mass (ch. 6, p. 90) may not be entirely apocryphal. The refugees had a widespread reputation for assisting the local community, which seems to have extended to a degree of discreet vigilante activity – though nothing comparable to the notorious and brutal 'community policing' which is a hallmark of Irish paramilitaries. That would have attracted unwelcome attention from the French police. In any case, the ETA refugees could never have controlled street territory in France in the way the IRA and its loyalist counterparts do in the Belfast ghettos where they were born and bred. However, the refugees are said to have protected some small shops from thieves. The simple presence of a large, cohesive group of fit young people with a strong commitment to their own sense of social justice and discipline made the streets of Petit Bayonne unhealthy for petty criminals. 'We lived better when the refugees were here' is a not uncommon refrain in the French Basque Country. This goodwill, however, was not enough to outweigh the fear generated by the GAL campaign.

3   Sagrario Morán, *ETA entre España y Francia* (Madrid: Editorial Complutense, 1997), p. 187. See also Francisco Letamendía, *Historia del Nacionalismo Vasco y de ETA*, 3 vols. (San Sebastián: R&B Ediciones, 1994), vol. 3, p. 24, and *Egin,* 'Guerra Sucia' series, January/February 1995, no. 5.

4   *El Periódico*, 28 August 1984; *Le Monde*, 3 April 1985.

5   *Egin,* 'Guerra Sucia' series, January/February 1995, no. 6.

6   On 10 July 1985, French secret service agents bombed the Greenpeace vessel *Rainbow Warrior* in New Zealand waters. One crew member was killed. The French Defence Minister, and the head of the secret service, eventually had to resign, as the French media, the New Zealand courts and the UN all traced responsibility to Paris. Mitterrand subsequently decorated the disgraced minister, and agents implicated in the bombing were promoted. See *El País,* 9 February 1995 and 10 July 1995.

7   Letamendía, op. cit., vol. 3, p. 25. Iparretarrak has made periodic reappearances up to the recent past.

8   *Deia*, 25 February 1984, Morán, op. cit., p. 148.

9   Antonio Elorza (ed.), *La Historia de ETA* (Madrid: Temas de Hoy, 2000), p. 289.

10 *El País,* 9 February 1984. For Apalategui's role in that offensive, see David Gilmour, *The Transformation of Spain* (London: Routledge, 1985), pp. 223–5.

11 *El País,* 20 October 1997 and 1 October 1999.

12 In 1996, the former French ambassador to Spain, Pierre Guidoni, used a sophisticated version of this argument in an attempt to demonstrate that the Spanish government could have had no part in the GAL. Felipe González's cabinet, he asserted, had had an active interest in preventing, rather than promoting, a dirty war at this delicate point in their negotiations with France regarding EEC entry.

This is undoubtedly the former Spanish Prime Minister's best theoretical defence. But it signally fails to explain why he took no measures against the very senior people in his administration who clearly were promoting the GAL at the time. Nor does it explain why he has consistently defended each and every one of them since, far beyond the call of duty, when very serious charges were brought against them. Only when they themselves have confessed, or been found guilty, has the mantle of González's solidarity and protection been abruptly withdrawn.

Moreover, the language he has used in discussing the dirty war has been, right up to the time of writing, laced with blatant ambiguities. González has become a master at indicating a permissive rather than a censorious attitude to the GAL, while carefully avoiding accepting any responsibility for their actions.

13 *Sud-Ouest*, 27 February 1984.

14 Not, it must be said, a very busy one. Ten years later, I waited ten minutes for another car to pass this spot. Nevertheless, the risk of discovery was undoubtedly high, and indicates a very cool nerve – or a sense of impunity –-on the part of the sniper.

15 *Egin,* 'Guerra Sucia' series, January/February 1995, no. 6.

16 *Egin,* 26 February 1984.

17 *Punto y Hora*, 13 December 1985.

18 Ibid.

19 Ricardo Arques and Melchor Miralles, *Amedo: El Estado contra ETA* (Barcelona: Plaza y Janés/Cambio 16, 1989), p. 178.

20 See ch. 5, p. 74.

21 *Cambio 16*, May 1994.

22 Arques and Miralles, op. cit., pp. 72–82.

23 Arques and Miralles, op. cit., p. 85. According to these authors, the French police found, among his possessions, phone numbers for members of the Guardia Civil, and for the Interior Ministry's special operations and intelligence committee, directed by the former Bilbao police chief Francisco Álvarez (p. 88). They also report that his widow claimed a pension from the Spanish Interior Ministry when he died (p. 773).

24 One of the most convincing accounts of the Pasajes ambush can be found in José María Calleja, *Contra la Barbarie* (Madrid, Temas de Hoy, 1997) pp. 85–6 and 94–5. It is convincing not only because the author, a journalist, was a witness to the aftermath of the shootings, but because his stated intention in this book is to expose the brutality of ETA's terrorism. See also Arques and Miralles, op. cit., pp. 85–6 and 180, and *Libération,* 7 April 1984.

25 *El País*, 5 April 1984.

26 *El País*, 24 March 1984, *Egin,* 'Guerra Sucia' series, January/February 1995, no. 7, Arques and Miralles, op. cit., p. 180.

27 *El País*, 24 March 1984.

28 *Le Monde*, 20 May 1984; *Punto y Hora*, 2 November 1984; Arques and Miralles, op. cit., pp. 180–1.

29 *Libération*, 14 and 15 April 1984.

30 *Sud-Ouest,* 20 May 1984.

31 *Le Monde,* 18 September 1985.

32 *El País*, 16 February 1985. Svahn was the subject of a two-page investigation by *Libération* on 11 January 1985.

33 *Cambio 16*, 21 April 1984. The 'revolutionary tax' was levied by ETA, with considerable success and remarkably accurate intelligence, on Basque business people, ranging from industrialists to shopkeepers. Those who did not pay up faced assassination.

34 *El País*, 4 April 1984.

35 *Tiempo*, 26 March 1984.

36 *Egin,* 4 April 1984. Zugarramurdi was described as an 'extremely lucid' witness of the attack in *Sud-Ouest,* 4 May 1984.

8

Bombing Biarritz:

keeping ETA under pressure

N aked but for his torn underpants, T-shirt, shoes and socks, a man is standing in a pleasant street in bright sunshine. He is looking back towards the camera, with an expression that is very hard to read, but seems to convey puzzlement or anxiety. For a moment, it is very difficult to grasp what is happening in this photograph, published in *Tiempo* magazine in September 1984.[1] Then recognition dawns, as if in slow motion, because of the ghastly contrast between the setting and the action. The man has torn his clothes off because they are on fire, but the flames still lick around his body. In the foreground another man, his bare and lacerated back pouring blood, is starting to run.

The Spanish media's prurience about death and violence, coupled with ETA's cult of martyrdom, have both ensured that many gruesome images have illustrated press accounts of the dirty war. The macabre piles of bones which are all that remain of Lasa and Zabala have been used in a thousand newspaper and magazine images. But even they cannot compare to the impact of this extraordinary picture, taken on a Friday evening in a fashionable and busy area of Biarritz. The men are the veteran ETA leader Tomás Pérez Revilla and the refugee priest Ramón Orbe Etxeberria. A small bomb has just exploded right beside them.

The previous evening, 14 June 1984, the Spanish Minister for the Interior, José Barrionuevo, and his French counterpart, Gaston Deferre, appeared to make a breakthrough on Franco-Spanish co-operation against ETA. Their communiqué contains a phrase that ultimately unblocked the way towards a complete reversal of France's policy on extradition: France explicitly recognised that 'a terrorist is not a political refugee'.[2] It was reported by the agency France Press, though never confirmed, that 'well-informed Parisian sources' said that Deferre had demanded that Barrionuevo bring the GAL to heel in exchange for this historic shift.[3]

Yet the very next afternoon, two Basque refugees blaze like human torches after a GAL *comando* detonates a bomb placed on top of a motorbike in one of France's best-known resorts. Several French policemen and a photographer from the Sygma agency were there to record the incident. Either Barrionuevo had no control over the GAL or he thought that they still had a function as a 'persuader' of French political and/or public opinion.

Since the death of Rafael Goikoetxea six weeks earlier, ETA had killed three policemen in Spain, without any 'reply' from the GAL. Bombs had been used in two of the killings, and in a fourth on 14 June, marking a shift to more indiscriminate tactics by ETA, which imposed a terrible toll of both civilian and military deaths in the years to come. Barrionuevo attended the funeral of the last victim, *guardia civil* Ángel Zapatero Antolín, on 15 June in San Sebastián. The 'reply' came later the same day, in the form of the Biarritz bomb, which would lead to the detention of an entire GAL *comando*.

According to Ramón Orbe, he and Pérez Revilla had spent some time that afternoon in the Bar du Haou. It was a favourite haunt of refugees in Biarritz at the time. (Today, like several other sites of GAL attacks, it has a strangely antiseptic atmosphere, as if history had been airbrushed out of it.) They had noticed a French police officer in the vicinity, and had commented that a raid might be under way. They each left the bar separately on different occasions, leaving and returning each time in the company of other individuals.

When they left together, and unaccompanied, just after 5.30 p.m., they had only walked a few metres down the adjoining Avenue Carnot when the bomb, fixed to a Kawasaki motorbike, was detonated by remote control. The explosion enveloped them in flaming petrol, and tore a hole in Revilla's foot. The blast also set two cars on fire, smashed windows up and down the street, and shattered the frontage of the bar. Though the junction at which the bar stands was thronged with pedestrians, the only other victims were clients of the bar, who suffered minor injuries. Somehow, Orbe and Revilla both retained consciousness, tore off their clothes and staggered to another bar nearby, convinced they were about to be finished off by gunfire.

But the GAL members, who had been watching from a nearby van, had already made their getaway. Their van had been spotted by the police, and led them to the other members of the *comando*. The police told the subsequent court hearing that they had had a tip-off that there would be an attack in the area, but they did not know where it would come from and had assumed that only guns would be used.[4] This scenario, in which police stalked counter-terrorists who were stalking terrorists, would have belonged in a comic farce, if the denouement had not been so bloody. Furthermore, the use of a bomb beside a bar, on a busy street, was an indicator that the GAL were now just as callous about risking civilian lives as ETA had become.

Orbe recovered from his injuries, but Revilla was not so lucky. The victim of an earlier dirty war attack in 1976, in which his wife and child were also injured, he seems to have been somewhat sidelined from ETA after that, and emigrated to Venezuela in 1980. But he was suffering from leukaemia, and two years later he returned to France for an operation. The trauma of the bombing exacerbated his condition, and he died after forty-three days.

One of the men the police had detained after the attack, Patrick de Carvalho, was a former sergeant with explosives training in the French paratroops. His army career had ended with a drunk driving incident in which a man was killed. He ran a sleazy restaurant with his girlfriend in Pau, where he was known as *El Padrino*, the Godfather.[5] He admitted organising the attack and detonating the bomb, corroborating Orbe's account that he had done so only when the two refugees alone were in close range. The other man at the scene of the crime, Roland Sanpietro, was an ex-boxer, working as an upholsterer, with a suspected involvement with drugs.[6] He admitted driving the van, but denied knowledge of Carvalho's intentions.[7]

A minor political scandal erupted in France when *Sud-Ouest* published a photograph showing that both men had recently acted as bodyguards to Simone Veil, a leading candidate for the Gaullist/Giscardian centre-Right coalition, while she was campaigning for elections to the European parliament.[8] These men seemed to be unlucky with photographers.

Their flight in the van also led the police to Jean-Philippe Labade. Labade turned out to be the man chosen to replace Jean-Pierre Cherid in the GAL's mercenary structure. His career with the GAL would have been a short one, had not Judge Michel Svahn released him the following November, because of 'irregularities in the investigation'. He did this in spite of the fact that Labade had also been implicated in the murder of Arenaza. Labade broke his bail and left the country, and would organise more GAL attacks in due course. While the French police seemed to be getting better at capturing members of the GAL, the French justice system seemed to have great difficulty keeping them in prison.

The release of Labade was particularly surprising, given that the French police had been tailing him before the bombing and had observed one especially significant incident. On 22 May, he was seen talking to two individuals at the Col d'Ibardin, a quiet border crossing close to the coast. The Citroën GS which these individuals were driving had a number plate registered with the Spanish security forces.

The summer of 1984 in the French Basque Country was more tranquil than the refugees had reason to expect, though the growing convergence between Paris and Madrid on expelling ETA suspects filled the quiet days with a different kind of menace for them. However, although the GAL claimed no mortal victims for more than five months from the Biarritz bomb, this was hardly for want of trying. The GAL's failure to inflict any serious physical damage during this period might be attributed to the death of Cherid and the enforced idleness of Labade. On the other hand, we can now be fairly certain that other, and better, units, with more intimate links with the Spanish security forces, were readily available. In any case, there were several actions with potentially fatal consequences. The Spanish authorities who were guiding the extradition negotiations with some success were either unable or unwilling to apply a brake to the dirty war.

Another bombing, in St-Jean-de-Luz, came within inches of causing a minor massacre. The Bar La Consolation (now a rather sterile pizzeria) had a big refugee clientele, and on the night of 10 July a Spanish Basque was managing the place for the French owner. Customers has complained of aggressive surveillance from a French police van during the evening. At 11.30 p.m., just after a group of refugees had entered the bar, the van drove off. Only seconds later, according to some witnesses, a motorbike roared up. The pillion passenger tossed a bomb against the glass frontage of the bar.

The bomber's heavy sheepskin jacket seems to have impeded the force of his (or her) throw, so that the bomb bounced back and exploded on the pavement. Some shrapnel and glass penetrated the interior, causing three refugees moderate injuries. Some witnesses thought the passenger was a woman. If this is correct, the inappropriately named Consolation, which would be attacked again in 1986, may have marked the debut of one of the GAL's two female activists. Straight out of bad *film noir,* the notorious *Dama Negra* (Black Lady) and *Rubia Asesina* (Blonde Assassin) figured in a series of attacks in 1985.[9]

The motorbike, it turned out later, belonged to Rafael López Ocaña, who participated in one of the GAL's most sensational killings four months later.[10] At the time, no one was arrested for the Consolation bombing. The GAL communiqué claiming the attack had three, by now familiar, characteristics. The caller spoke French with a slight Spanish accent; he repeated that ETA attacks would be reciprocated; and he used the laconic sign-off: 'You will have news of the GAL.'

In fact, ETA would kill at least ten people before the GAL managed to cause another fatality, though there were several more near-misses. In August, a GAL *comando* burnt out part of the Denek factory at St-Martin-d'Arossa (where Rafael Goikoetxea had worked). Later in the month, the GAL machine-gunned a bar in Bayonne owned by the radical nationalist Etxabe family. Juan José Etxabe was one of ETA's senior leaders from the 1960s. His wife had been killed in a Basque Spanish Battalion attack on his car in 1978. On this occasion, four customers sustained slight injuries. No arrests were made, but in September, in one of the only pieces of preventive police work in a GAL case, two mercenaries were detained as they were about to machine-gun a bar in Biarritz.

There would be no more 'news of the GAL' for another two months. The threat of extradition, however, had loomed larger and larger over the summer months, and became a reality in September. On 6 August, Barrionuevo had his first meeting with Gaston Deferre's replacement as Minister for the Interior in Paris, Pierre Joxe.[11] The shift in the French attitude to ETA was copperfastened. Two days after the meeting, extradition proceedings opened against four refugees in Pau. On 21 September, the French court of appeal confirmed the extradition of seven Basques. Four of them were expelled to the African republic of Togo, a procedure which had first been used the previous January with the expulsions of refugees to Panama.

Such deportations to third countries became a favoured instrument of French policy towards the refugees. From here on, the Spanish government actively co-operated with it, negotiating aid deals with developing countries in exchange for their 'supervision' of Spanish Basque deportees from France. Generations of ETA leaders were effectively sentenced to open prisons in the sun, where they generally lost touch politically, and more so operationally, with their comrades who were still active in France and Spain.

DBS Arts Library

This policy often suited the Spanish authorities better than extradition to Spain itself. It meant that these senior ETA figures could not have access to the organisation's network within Spanish prisons, which interacted quite dynamically with the revolutionary movement on the outside. On several occasions, Madrid also attempted to utilise some of the deportees as 'bridges' for informal negotiations with the ETA leadership.

The French took an even more significant decision, however, with the other three refugees whose extradition sentences were confirmed in September. For the first time ever, they extradited them to the Spanish authorities.[12] This was an act of great symbolic importance. It confirmed that Madrid's powerful neighbour fully accepted the bona fides of Spain's transition to democracy. It shattered the relative security which the refugees had enjoyed on French territory. While the course of French–Spanish policy on anti-ETA collaboration was still far from smooth or settled, this was the first trickle of a coming flood.[13] It would ultimately give the Spanish police unprecedented opportunities to interrogate people they suspected of carrying out dozens of ETA attacks.

This apparent diplomatic and security triumph for the Socialists did not meet with universal approval among Basque democrats. The Basque Nationalist Party, and Euskadiko Ezkerra, strongly opposed extradition. As they saw it, each border hand-over would provide a dramatic new focus for Herri Batasuna demonstrations, and boost support for the radicals. Hundreds of families with relatives 'on the other side', and their larger network of cuadrillas, would be drawn actively into the conflict. The continuing operations of the GAL made extradition even more emotive. Nor did the moderates have much faith in the conversion of the Spanish police to democratic practices. Allegations of torture by extradited suspects would be manifold. Even if only a few of them stood up in court, the impression that Francoism still lurked in the security apparatus would be strengthened, once again, in the Basque Country.

Basque nationalist democrats believed that the whole emphasis on a 'police solution' to ETA was absolutely mistaken. The way forward, they argued, was the rapid transfer of powers to the Basque autonomous institutions, demonstrating in practice that many nationalist demands were being won by peaceful means. Unfortunately, the Socialists were choosing to stall on precisely this issue. They seemed much more concerned to show the armed forces that they had no intention of 'dismembering Spain' than to accommodate legitimate nationalist demands. Their huge parliamentary majority in Madrid meant that democratic nationalists had no way of exercising parliamentary pressure at this time, so the Socialists' chosen 'road of repression', as their opponents called it, remained wide open.

*** *** ***

During the autumn, a new name, that of Superintendent José Amedo of the National Police, began cropping up in the Spanish media in association with the GAL. The loquacious Daniel Fernández Aceña, awaiting trial in Madrid for the murder of the GAL's first 'accidental' victim, Jean-Pierre Leiba, was beginning to spill beans. On 9 November, the Basque radical magaine *Punto y Hora* reported Aceña as saying that a French Basque, Joseph Couchot, had given shelter to Victor Manuel Navascués Gil, the businessman accused by Aceña of being the brains behind the botched Leiba operation.[14] Navascués had certainly hidden out for months before giving himself up, but would eventually, and controversially, be absolved of any connection with Leiba's death.

Couchot lived in Irún, and was wanted in France on smuggling charges. He did not take kindly to having his name bandied about as a member of the GAL, and on 16 November *Punto y Hora* published a letter from him, which said he would hold the director of the publication responsible for anything which might happen to him as a result. That very afternoon, as he ate his lunch in an Irún restaurant, two men and a woman walked in and shot him six times, finishing him off with a *coup de grâce* as he lay on the floor.[15]

Four members of ETA were subsequently convicted for this killing, and ETA acknowledged the operation, referring to Couchot's alleged membership of the GAL in its communiqué. One of the GAL's French mercenaries, Christian Hitier, had a different story. He told the French police that the killing was an internal GAL affair, organised by José Amedo. However, it seems likely that this allegation was simply an attempt to damage Amedo by a disgruntled former colleague.[16]

In any case, the GAL apparently organised a fast 'reply' to the killing. Less than forty-eight hours later, only a few kilometres across the border, Christian Olaskoaga and his brother Claude were shot as they left a car park in Biriatou. This tiny village is perched over the Bidasoa, just where the Pyrenees start to rise on the French side of the border. It enjoyed some rather folksy fame as a haunt for smugglers in pre-EU days, but today is best known for a couple of comfortable restaurants with picture windows overlooking sleepy pastoral scenes.

Apart from these, the heart of the village consists of little more than a large *frontón*, a church and an *herriko etxea*, a town hall which looks absurdly large for such a micro-community. Most of the households belonging to the village are hidden away individually in the maze of lanes that meander into the surrounding hills. Below the *frontón*, which doubles as the village square, there is a small, neatly organised car park on two levels. This area marks the effective end of the road which sweeps up in broad curves from the direction of Hendaye. Except for the lanes to the surrounding homesteads, Biriatou is a dead end, which says a lot about the confidence of anyone who would carry out a killing there. The only quick way out is the way you came in.

The Olaskoaga brothers, Christian and Claude, both in their early twenties, were getting out of their car at about 1.30 a.m. on Sunday, 18 November. They were heading for the village fiesta, though Claude, who was the captain of a local rugby team, had a match in the morning and did not want to stay too late.

Two men in balaclavas appeared out of the darkness, and pointed pistols at them. The brothers thought it was a joke, until one of the assailants stuck his pistol in Claude's chest. Claude, a burly fellow, knocked that attacker down, but the other one shot his brother in the heart, and wounded Claude, who was fleeing by now, in the leg. Claude made it to a nearby bar, and called for an ambulance and police, but Christian was already dying. The attackers had vanished, unseen by anyone else, leaving behind a Smith and Wesson pistol, some cartridge shells and a tiny radio listening apparatus.[17] There is a border crossing to Irún less than five minutes away by car.

The Olaskoaga family comes from Ciboure, a French Basque fishing town which faces St-Jean-de-Luz across a bay. The brothers had decided to come up to Biriatou at the last minute, and had told no one of their intentions. Since they had no connection with politics, despite a rash declaration to the contrary by politicians,[18] there is no reason to believe that they were followed. Their attackers may have mistaken them for someone else, or they may simply have inadvertently disturbed them as they prepared an ambush for another target. There is also a strong possibility that, as the local French newspaper *Sud-Ouest* speculated, 'some organisation' might now simply be picking targets at random, in order to create a climate of fear and mistrust in the French Basque Country.[19] The refugee community complained that, in describing the Olaskoagas as 'innocent' victims, the press were implying that victims who were refugees were somehow 'guilty'.[20]

The GAL never acknowledged the killing, though it was widely interpreted at the time as revenge for the shooting of Couchot. In February 1985, the French police announced that ballistic tests showed that one of the guns used was the same as the one with which the GAL had killed the ETA members Gurmindo and Perurena in Hendaye the previous February. Suspicion now rests on Guardia Civil elements in the GAL for both attacks.[21] The Guardia Civil would also come under scrutiny in relation to the GAL's next operation, which came only two days later and had a more dramatic impact than anything the GAL had done before, or since.

NOTES

1   *Tiempo*, 3 September 1984.
2   Francisco Letamendía, *Historia del Nacionalismo Vasco y del ETA*, 3 vols. (San Sebastián: R&B Ediciones, 1994), vol. 3, p. 28.
3   Ricardo Arques and Melchor Miralles, *Amedo: El Estado contra ETA* (Barcelona: Plaza y Janés/Cambio 16, 1989), p. 193.
4   *Egin*, 'Guerra Sucia' series, January/February 1995, no. 8.
5   *El País*, 1 July 1984.
6   Ibid.
7   *Egin*, 'Guerra Sucia' series, January/February 1995, no. 8.
8   *El País*, 1 July 1984. According to the same report, a leading Spanish right-wing politician commented to reporters, off the record, that 'bodyguards are not exactly recruited from among the Little Sisters of Charity'.
9   There is a strong possibility that these two melodramatic figures were one and the same person. See ch. 10.
10 Arques and Miralles, op. cit., p. 192, and *Egin*, 'Guerra Sucia' series, January/February 1995, no. 8. López Ocaña was one of the material authors of the murder of Santiago Brouard; see ch. 9.

11   Sagrario Morán, *ETA entre España y Francia* (Madrid: Editorial Complutense, 1997), pp. 198–9, Letamendía, op. cit., vol. 3, p. 28, Miralles and Arques, op. cit., p. 193.

12   Morán, op. cit., pp. 199–201. Previous hand-overs were on the basis of the 'procedure of urgency', which did not require the same level of political and judicial endorsement as extradition. Mitterrand's own Justice Minister, Robert Badinter, was opposed privately to this change in policy, and the future French Prime Minister, Lionel Jospin, and intellectuals like Simone de Beauvoir expressed strong public opposition.

13   The ups and downs of French–Spanish relations on this issue, described by one observer as 'as sharp as the peaks and valleys of a *sierra*', would not be ironed out until 1986, the year in which the GAL effectively ceased to operate; 1985, in particular, would see a virtual reversion to the 1982 position on the part of France. For a fuller account see ch. 14, pp. 179–183; Morán, op. cit., pp. 198–201; and Letamendía, op. cit., vol. 3, p. 28.

14   This story first surfaced in the Madrid magazine *Tiempo,* 3 September 1984, but it was not picked up by the Basque radical press until *Punto y Hora*'s piece on 9 November 1984.

15   *El País,* 17 November 1984.

16   Arques and Miralles, op. cit., p. 205.

17   *El País*, 19 November 1984; *Egin,* 19 and 20 November 1984; *Sud-Ouest*, 19 November 1984; Arques and Miralles, op. cit., p. 205.

18   *Egin*, 'Guerra Sucia' series, January/February 1995, no. 9.

19   *Sud-Ouest*, 20 November 1984.

20   *Egin,* 'Guerra Sucia' series, January/February 1995, no. 9. Taking a different angle, a French anti-terrorist police superintendent, Alain Tourré, had originally pointed the finger for the attack at Iparretarrak.

21   *El País*, 2 February 1985. There was one curious detail which points in another direction: Claude Olaskoaga said that the attackers spoke to them before opening fire, but in a language he could not even recognise, which might suggest they were among the GAL's north African employees. See *Sud-Ouest*, 20 November 1984.

9

A Revolutionary Doctor:
his eventful life and sudden death

The death squads, or the people who ran them, had a liking for anniversaries. José Miguel Beñarán Ordeñana was killed on the fifth anniversary, almost to the day, of the assassination of Carrero Blanco. The GAL's first acknowledged mortal victim, Ramón Oñederra, was shot within hours of Carrero Blanco's tenth anniversary. Eleven months later, on the ninth anniversary of Franco's death in bed, the GAL stunned public opinion with their first, and only, major operation on the Spanish side of the border. Felipe González himself described this action as 'a new attempt to seriously endanger peaceful co-existence in the Basque Country'.[1] It triggered a lightning strike from ETA at the heart of the Spanish army. Spanish democracy, still a sapling, was shaken to its roots, and for a few days there were real fears that it faced collapse.[2]

The killing of Santiago Brouard on 20th November 1984, while he attended an infant girl in his paediatric clinic, was savage and reckless by several standards. Brouard was not only idolised by several generations as 'Tío Santi' ('Uncle Santi'), one of the best children's doctors in Bilbao, but he was also a radical nationalist and Marxist, and a senior public representative for Herri Batasuna. His professional skills and great personal charm were appreciated by a wide circle of patients and friends, including some political enemies. His fierce commitment to an independent and socialist Euskadi ensured his credibility with ETA's leadership. If anyone could have negotiated fruitfully on ETA's behalf with the Spanish government at this time, Santiago Brouard was widely recognised as the very best man for the job.

The killing of the Socialist leader Enrique Casas in early 1984 had been a turning-point for many in the PSOE. It redefined the Socialists' relationship with radical nationalism as one of war rather than one of politics. Brouard's assassination may have been a delayed response to that killing. Whatever its specific motivation, this new killing marked a similarly bleak watershed for Basque nationalists, far beyond ETA's normal catchment area. In bringing their dirty war home to Spanish territory, the GAL had given concrete evidence to those who argued that the transition to democracy had been a façade.

Basque nationalists would now more easily believe that, behind the shifting scenes of parliamentary democracy, the same Francoist state apparatus was functioning as murderously and untouchably as ever. This viewpoint might seem absurd in Madrid or Barcelona, but in Bilbao it made sense to many people who did not feel themselves to be extremist. In a political universe which appeared to offer a Manichean choice between ETA and the Spanish state, many Basques, repelled by the latter, reluctantly refused to condemn the former.

Brouard's killing raises several unresolved questions about the political control exercised by the paymasters of the GAL. This may explain why the organisation first claimed, and then denied, responsibility for the action. Some sections of the GAL, which was beginning to look less and less like a single entity, may either not have known about the action or not have approved of it. More likely, it was simply more expedient to create confusion about its authorship. There were suggestions in the serious Spanish press that, if the Socialist administration had a part in the GAL, they were now learning the terrible lesson of the sorcerer's apprentice.

Edurne Brouard has inherited a generous portion of her father's infectious charm, and much of his sense of political rectitude. She is a big, warm woman with a round, smiling face which sometimes looks uncannily familiar from his photographs. She speaks emphatically but quietly, repeatedly using words like 'magnificent' and 'terrible' with a conviction which recalls his legendary ability to infuse political rhetoric with personal sincerity. She has a healthy appetite for vodka and orange. When she says that she has 'never let fear make me give up living', it is easy to believe her.[3]

She has known fear from a very early age. Her father, she says, was always absolutely clear about one thing: 'We had to conserve our national identity, whatever the cost.' She was just two when her parents sent her to a clandestine *ikastola* in the early 1960s, when these Basque language schools were still prohibited by the dictatorship. Based in private homes, the school would move to another house every month or so to avoid detection.

While she was still at the school, the Franco regime unbent slightly. The *ikastolas* would now be tolerated at a very junior level, under the watchful eye of a Francoist inspectorate. This was how she came to learn right-wing anthems like *Cara al Sol* before she was six. The local inspector would give his blessing to an *ikastola* only if the children could give voice to sentiments which would have stuck in their parents' throats. Ironically, when she had to move on to a Spanish language school, she would not have to sing these songs.

She tells her father's story affectionately and humorously. There is no sense that she resented, at any stage, the many crises into which his politics plunged her family. This was, she says, 'perhaps because he was very good at involving us all in what he was doing'. She describes her family as 'very nationalist, but very atypically nationalist'. Her mother, though of Basque origin, was born in the Philippines, and to this day speaks very little Basque, though she supported her husband's political commitment. The Brouard children spoke Basque among themselves and with their father, 'which is unusual because the mother's tongue normally imposes itself on the family. In that sense, I come from a rather strange *pot-pourri*.'

Santiago Brouard was born in 1920 in Lekeitio, a fishing town on the Vizcayan coast, soaked in Basque national identity and steeped in the Basque language. His father was a mechanic who had built up a local bus company. The young Santiago developed his driving skills with heavy vehicles on the impossible bends that snake back over the hills to Guernica. Edurne Brouard's account of his early life is probably romanticised, but it does give insights into his character.

When the Civil War broke out, he wanted to fight for the Republic, but was not old enough to enlist without his parents' permission. 'No mother wants her son to go war,' says Edurne Brouard, but after much discussion he persuaded his father to secretly support him. He signed up at the recruiting post, but he somehow lost his papers on his way home. A neighbour found them and gave them to his mother, who flew into a furious rage with her husband and her son. As Edurne Brouard tells it, they were still arguing when the victorious Francoist troops marched into the town.

Finding evidence that the sixteen-year-old Brouard had volunteered for the other side, the fascists gave him the relatively merciful option of fighting for them, and utilising his skills as a driver. So, according to his daughter, Brouard spent the war driving a Francoist officer and his men around battlefields in a lorry. 'If I should fall,' the officer used to tell him, 'remember how to get back to our own lines.' According to his own account, Brouard used to answer back: 'No, if you get shot, I'm driving over to the other lines, because that's the side I'm on.' As Edurne Brouard says, 'That captain must have liked him a lot, because he never reported him.' His facility for befriending enemies was showing early.

It showed again when he went to study medicine, with considerable distinction, in Valladolid. This Castilian city is notorious as a nest of fascism in Spain, so much so that the Left nicknames it 'Fachadolid', 'Facha' being a term of abuse for extreme rightists. However, Brouard not only did his degree there quite happily – having turned down an offer to play professional football for Barcelona – but he fell in love with the place.

'My father, to the last day of his life, always said the people of Valladolid were the best in the world. He said the stereotype was a lie, and would always break a lance in their favour. Up to two years before his death, he used to go there to celebrate an annual student reunion, and he loved it.'

She tells these old stories fluently, but she is unable to pinpoint precisely the moment her father became politically active under the dictatorship. 'I think he was always uneasy with the situation, but he never joined the PNV. He moved in the world of Basque culture, he had become a prestigious doctor, and he gave economic support to [Basque-language] publishing, to anything that promoted nationalism.'

The birth of ETA, she believes, had a lot to do with his involvement, though she says he never joined that organisation either. 'But he thought it was a good thing. He had developed a close relationship with the son of an intimate friend and this boy became a member of ETA. The boy's father used to say ETA was some sort of kid's stuff. My father would say "No, it's not kid's stuff, it's a serious thing, and, besides, I support it."'

The boy concerned was arrested and sentenced to seven years and one month in jail. 'The way things are now, that would be like a gift, but it was a terrible sentence then,' says Edurne Brouard. 'I think this would be the moment my father decided he couldn't continue just *watching*. This is my interpretation, that it was a point of reflection for him. I heard him say again and again, "This young boy has got seven years, I am more than forty years old and I have to help."'

'Helping' seems to have meant hiding members of ETA on the run, and, especially, giving medical aid to the sick and wounded who could not risk exposure in hospital. In 1973, he was detected while treating an activist's injuries, and he had to flee across the border to avoid arrest. He said later that, as a doctor, he would always help anyone who needed his skills, and it is said that a *guardia civil* was among his patients.

In the French Basque Country, however, the skills Brouard shared with ETA were mainly political ones. He became a personal friend of ETA leaders like Beñarán Ordeñana, Pagoaga Gallastegi and Iturbe Abásolo, and of the veteran dissident nationalist Telesforo de Monzón, who had been a minister in the Basque government during the Civil War. He also established close contact with small Marxist groups linked to ETA.

Edurne Brouard agrees that he came to socialist politics relatively late, but she thinks its roots lie in his upbringing. 'He used to say that Lekeitio made him nationalist, and also made him socialist. In Lekeitio, he said, you had only two choices: either you were absolutely egalitarian, or you were seen as siding with the people in power. He always had a sense that "this is just, and that is not just".'

Such a sense of unequivocal moral rectitude can, of course, be very dangerous. It can lead, as it did in Brouard's case, to support for the kind of black-and-white options offered by ETA, with all the bloody consequences that involved. Strange though it may sound, the espousal of revolutionary terrorism, at least under democratic conditions, can stem from a refusal to acknowledge moral complexity and ambiguity. Hence its highly righteous – and lethal – intolerance. The paradox is that terrorists and their supporters, perceived by most of society as 'evil', often perceive themselves as occupying the very highest moral ground.

Edurne Brouard remembers her father as a voracious reader, up to date on every subject. 'The cliché is that a father takes a book from his sleeping daughter and sends her to bed. In our family it was the reverse; we used to find him asleep over books in the early hours.'

He and his wife, Teresa Aldamiz, stayed in exile, living in the picturesque inland village of Ascain, and later St-Jean-de-Luz, until Prime Minister Suárez decreed the general, pre-election amnesty of May 1977.[4] Edurne Brouard calculates the dates by reference to her progress at school. The children remained in Bilbao during this period, nurtured by an extended family network, but visited their parents as often as possible. She remembers her time in the refugee community as 'a very formative period, the most formative of my life. You come to know all that pain, with your head half-focused, but it formed me a lot in how I see the world. I'm grateful for that. I have a great hatred for the people who created those circumstances, but I don't regret having gone through them.' This was also the time when, for good or ill, her father became a prominent public figure in the anti-Franco resistance.

Fear certainly must have come into sharper focus then, as this was a period of intense activity by the 'Triple A' and the Basque Spanish Battalion in the first dirty war. 'My father was clearly a target. We were exposed,' she says, 'but also protected by the community. The refugee collectives formed a night-watch which used to go to each house . . . to check for bombs at windows and doors, and to look out for any suspicious people.' To a teenage girl, the arrival of groups of young people at all hours was evidently a kind of anxious pleasure.

'In Ascain, where my parents lived in a little house outside the village, I remember the visits of the watch with a mixture of joy and terror. On the one hand, there was the fun of welcoming them with a glass of wine and lots of chat. On the other, there was the fear of what could happen if they were not there.'

Her father advocated a stoical approach to the shadow which hung over them. 'If they kill us, they kill us, but now we have to *live*. If they succeed in keeping us behind closed doors out of fear, then we are already dead.' These words are so familiar from other refugees that one feels that such sentiments must have acted as a kind of collective psychological shield against the sword of Damocles which the death squads wielded.

While in exile, Santiago Brouard became closely involved with moves to unite two hard-Left political parties, based north and south of the border. In reality, these groups were micro-parties, more like political clubs, dominated by figures originating from ETA. These were the years in which the various branches of ETA (and indeed all political movements within the Spanish state) were struggling to reinvent themselves in the context of the emerging transition to democracy. Dozens of new political parties were born, merged, split again or simply vanished, in a flurry of confusing acronyms dubbed 'alphabet soup' by the Spanish media.

Within ETA, the debate about the new situation created by the emergent Spanish democracy led to a bitter split becoming irrevocable.[5] The 'military' faction, ETA(m), suspected that the rival 'political-military' faction, ETA(p-m), was making far too many concessions to 'normal' politics in its efforts to create a political party. ETA(p-m) wanted this party to represent ETA's programme but have no organisational links to the armed group. Brouard's high status with ETA can be gauged by his attendance at the 1974 meeting when the split between the two factions of ETA became irrevocable. This was a quite exceptional privilege for someone who was apparently not subject to the discipline of either faction. The political groups with which Brouard was associated found their final form in the political alphabet as the Revolutionary Socialist People's Party

(Herriko Alderdi Sozializta Iraultzailea – HASI) in 1977, with Brouard as its first president. HASI combined a non-aligned form of Stalinism with unwavering commitment to Basque nationalist armed struggle.

'People he trusted suggested he should join this party,' says Edurne Brouard. 'He consulted the whole family, though I was only fourteen at the time, and the eldest. It seemed a magnificent idea to us.' The idea of a Stalinist leader asking his young children whether he should take up a political position is certainly a startling one, but it seems to fit with Brouard's remarkable character. It is, perhaps, part of the same conundrum that made people describe HASI's policies as 'unorthodox Stalinism', a phrase which surely deserves a special place in the lexicon of political oxymorons.

Over the next few years of frenetic political activity, HASI would become, as far as the outside world could see, the steel rod which transmitted the thinking of ETA(m) to the myriad front organisations which gave a legal or semi-legal expression to radical nationalism. In November 1977, Telesforo de Monzón called four small Basque parties, including HASI, and sundry 'independent radicals' like himself to a meeting which became known as 'La Mesa de Alsasua' ('The Table of Alsasua'). This grouping was formalised in April 1978 as the electoral coalition Herri Batasuna (Popular Unity), at a convention in Brouard's home town of Lekeitio.[6]

Mocked by its opponents as a 'Molotov cocktail' because of its explosively unstable constituents (and because of its members' penchant for street fighting), Herri Batasuna quickly showed that it was much bigger than the sum of its small parts. Herri Batasuna passed its first test at the polls, in the general election of March 1979, with flying colours. The coalition evidently had much deeper and wider roots than its immediate rival, Euzkadiko Ezkerra, the grouping supported by ETA(p-m). More significantly, its 170,000 votes were more than half those garnered by either the PNV or the PSOE, and represented more than 13 per cent of the electorate in the Basque Autonomous Community and Navarre. In the subsequent municipal elections, Herri Batasuna demonstrated its remarkable strength at local level, taking 100 more council seats than the PSOE.[7]

Since Herri Batasuna was unambiguously identified with ETA(m), the status of political violence among the Basque population had to be radically reassessed. Those who thought that, with the transition to democracy, ETA's support would dwindle to a tiny minority of malcontents had to think again. Brouard would be one of the leading visible figures (*the* leading figure after the death of Monzón in 1981) in a movement which mobilised opposition to the Spanish Constitution in the 1978 referendum, and to the Basque Statute of Autonomy in 1979.

But was Herri Batasuna really a coalition at all? It certainly absorbed a bewildering variety of 'single issue' organisations, ranging from feminist, labour and youth groups through ecologists to prisoners' support associations. In fact, Herri Batasuna became such a powerful magnet for radicalism of all kinds that it soon had a virtual monopoly of 'Left alternative' activity in the Basque Country.

It claimed to be a model of democratic practice, conceding decision-making powers to 'popular assemblies' at which 'the people' could participate without any formal party membership. The other small parties which had originally formed the coalition suspected that this was actually a mechanism to marginalise them, through the manipulation of these assemblies, by highly disciplined but 'invisible' groups controlled by ETA(m) through HASI.

'HASI acted merely as a spokesman for ETA(m), and did not develop any of the activities normally associated with a political party,' according to John Sullivan.[8] Two of the founding political parties left the coalition before the first elections to the Basque autonomous parliament in March 1980. They disappeared without trace, while Herri Batasuna took eleven out of sixty seats. Francisco Letamendía, one of the platform of prominent 'independents' which boosted Herri Batasuna's early electoral performance, now concedes that by 1983 the organisation was rigidly controlled from the top down by ETA, with political control exercised through HASI, linked to ETA by a small co-ordinating body known as KAS.[9]

The leading role of Brouard in this process can be gauged in two ways. He was prominent electorally, being elected to both the Vizcayan provincial assembly and the Basque parliament, and to the deputy mayorship of Bilbao. In the Basque parliament, he was one of the Herri Batasuna deputies who outraged Spanish public opinion by raising clenched fists and singing *Eusko Gudariak* ('Hymn of the Basque Soldiers'), a nationalist song from the 1930s which ETA has made its anthem, in the presence of King Juan Carlos and Queen Sofía in February 1981.

But he was probably much more prominent behind the scenes. Shortly before his death, he was one of two Herri Batasuna members who met the French ambassador to Spain, Pierre Guidoni, to discuss ways of resolving the Basque conflict. 'He told Guidoni there were two alternatives, war or a cease-fire on the basis of negotiations,' says Edurne Brouard. 'Guidoni said there could be no question of negotiating with terrorists. My father explained that they were not terrorists, but they were telling him what ETA wanted.'

While the discussions seemed to have ended stormily, and Brouard subsequently described the PSOE's offer of negotiations as a 'black propaganda manoeuvre', there is no doubt that he would have been expected to play a key role in any future talks. This may seem surprising in view of his uncompromising radicalism. In 1984, he denounced the Statute of Autonomy thus: 'It is not a valid instrument to facilitate the recovery of Basque national identity; rather it is the road to our extinction as a nation.' It could not work, he said, because of 'the furiously centralist spirit of Madrid, and the shameful abandonment of principles by parties which call themselves nationalist'.

It was precisely on account of such firm positions that Patxo Unzueta, one of the most perceptive Basque journalists working for *El País*, described him, two days after his death, as 'probably *the* man for a negotiated settlement'.[10]

'Experience has shown,' Unzueta continued, 'that such negotiations, if they happen, will not be the work of those who are least firm in their convictions, but rather of those who, however radical their ideas, are capable of listening to the ideas of their opponents. Brouard knew how to listen.'

*** *** ***

Santiago Brouard's listening ears were stopped on the evening of 20 November 1984, at about 6.20 p.m. He was in his clinic, wearing his blue doctor's smock, listening to an infant's heartbeat with his stethoscope. His nurse, Begoña Martínez de Murguía, was out in the reception area. She was politically as well as professionally close to Brouard. Her brother was the third member of ETA to be killed in action, shot by the Guardia Civil in Lekeitio in 1972.

Brouard had no security arrangements at the clinic. As Edurne Brouard says, it would have 'looked bad to the adults, and been bad for the children'. When the family tried to persuade a reluctant Brouard to take more precautions in general, he would always, she continues, 'say a *terrible* thing. "If they want to get me easily, they can always do it in the consulting rooms."'

The clinic officially closed at six, but his nurse was used to late callers. Nor did it strike her as odd that the two men who faced her when she answered their knock were poorly dressed and looked very dark, like gypsies. Brouard had a reputation for taking patients who could not afford his fees. She remembers that they asked for 'Dr Brouard', which was unusually formal. She noticed that they were both very nervous, so much so that one of them dropped what she thought was a folded umbrella, but was in fact a silencer. Realising that this man was wearing a wig, she shouted a warning to Brouard to stay in the surgery, and was pushed aside.

Brouard may have misunderstood the warning. Or perhaps he was simply unwilling to leave his nurse exposed to danger. In any case, he opened the surgery door, and as he did so took at least six bullets, five in the head and one in the hand, from two firearms. He died instantly.

His killers turned and raced out of the building, dropping their weapons, a Finnish parabellum 9 mm pistol and an Italian army Jager rifle, as they did so.[11] There were no fingerprints on the weapons. Apart from the nurse, the only witnesses were the young parents of the infant Brouard had been examining. Through no fault of their own, they would not be much help when the case came to trial.

'When the time came to call them to court, they were nowhere to be found,' says Edurne Brouard. 'We then discovered they had had a car accident, and the wife and child had been killed. It was terrible, terrible, terrible. To be sitting quietly in the surgery and see this . . . and then to have such an accident . . .' In a grimly Beckettian touch, the father of the child lost his sight in the same crash. 'So we had an eye-witness,' Edurne Brouard says, 'who turned out to be blind.' The blind eye-witness would prove an appropriate symbol for the investigation which followed.

The news of Brouard's death spread around the city on wings, but members of his family were among the last to know. His son, also called Santiago, was studying in a college library. When it closed at 8.00 p.m., he went for a quick drink, and left the bar still oblivious to what had happened. As he walked home, he saw a graffito which read '¡Santi Brouard, asesinado!' but he took it to be a threat, not a fact. Then he turned a corner and saw another one, and then another, and the terrible realisation dawned.

'I think,' says Edurne Brouard, 'that he had the worst experience of us all that night.' She herself suffered rather more trauma than was strictly necessary. The office where she gave Basque classes was near her father's clinic, but she had to go to a meeting elsewhere that evening. She remembers every detail of the phone conversation she had when she rang up to check the arrangements. A stranger answered the phone, and, hearing her first name, asked her if she was Edurne Brouard. When she said she was, he asked her to wait, and another voice told her: 'Edurne, everyone's gone from here . . . your father has just been shot.'

'"Where?" I asked, meaning "Where in his body?", and they misunderstood and said "In his clinic." I went over there running, and saw an ambulance, and thought "He's alive," forgetting they can send an ambulance to pick up a corpse. I found the stairs blocked by police. I told them I was his daughter, but they would not let me go up to the surgery. I asked them if they could at least tell me if he was alive or dead. The officer said "I cannot give you that information, señorita." I had to wait twenty minutes. Finally, I saw a comrade on the next landing, and shouted up to him. Hope is the last thing you lose, but when he said he was going to get Txomin, I knew my father was dead.'

Txomin Ziluaga was the general secretary of HASI, and had reached the clinic ahead of the police. He came down to Edurne Brouard, broke the news to her and told her she would have to tell her mother. The Brouard home is only around the corner from the clinic, and when she got there her mother already knew.

'She was not crying, she was furious, absolutely furious. "They will have to pay for this," she said, and then added: "At this moment, we have to do everything that the party asks, and that the people ask." She was a magnificent example for the mothers of prisoners, I remember thinking.'

Edurne Brouard took her mother over to the clinic, and a grim battle began. The police were insisting that Brouard's body should be taken straight to a hospital morgue for post-mortem, according to normal procedures. 'We didn't want him to spend the night at the hospital. We wanted to take him home, but of course what we were doing was illegal.' By now, there were thousands of angry Herri Batasuna supporters in the street outside the clinic, and hundreds of riot police, some of them exhausted from an ongoing operation against workers who were occupying the Euskalduna shipyards.

Relationships with the police were hardly likely to be amicable, but one unanswered question in particular infuriated Brouard's mourners. Where, the demonstrators demanded again and again, had the police been when Brouard was killed? It was common knowledge that he was kept under tight surveillance, but two men armed with guns had got in and out of his building undetected. Later, Herri Batasuna would claim that the one policeman who was regularly on his street guarding a consulate had been withdrawn the previous day.[12]

The police responded with rubber bullets and baton charges, but the demonstrators, chanting 'Santi urea da' ('Santi is ours'), formed a solid human shield as Herri Batasuna leaders tried to carry his coffin through the turbulent street.[13] The grimly symbolic battle over Brouard's body was close to stalemate when the pathologist arrived. According to Edurne Brouard, he had the police's confidence as a traditional right-winger, but, naturally, was also a devoted colleague of her father's. 'He behaved,' she says, 'magnificently well.'

'On my responsibility,' he told the police, 'I swear to you he will be in the morgue by six in the morning.' Santiago Brouard's remarkable fund of goodwill extended beyond his death and, with his last negotiation brokered by a personal friend and political opponent, he got to spend that last night with his family.

*** *** ***

That same night, ETA's Madrid *comando* went into organisational overdrive to prepare a non-negotiable response to his killing. The following morning, when the unmarked car carrying General Luis Rosón Pérez slowed down at traffic lights in the capital, two members of ETA were ready and waiting. They riddled the car with bullets from two sides, using a submachine-gun and a pistol. The general and his driver were very seriously wounded, but both survived. General Rosón was a senior military figure, in charge of the army's finances. He was the thirteenth general to suffer injuries or be killed in a terrorist attack since ETA killed General Sánchez Ramos in 1978, on the very day on which the Cortes was passing the democratic Constitution.[14]

The spectre of a coup loomed once more over Spanish democracy, in the eyes of some observers, but the army's discipline held, once again. The chief of staff, General Sáenz de Tejada, said that 'the army has been enduring the actions of terrorists for years, with a great sense of duty and a great sense of service to Spain'.[15]

The choice of target may have been doubly significant, as Rosón was the brother of the former Minister for the Interior, Juan José Rosón, who had negotiated the basis for the 'social reinsertion' of many members of ETA(p-m). ETA(m) regarded this policy as a dangerously seductive blueprint for betrayal. For them, it represented precisely the kind of 'capitulationist' negotiation that they, and Brouard, utterly rejected. In a communiqué, ETA played down this interpretation, insisting that the attack was simply a 'reply' to the killing of Brouard. In any case, the speed of ETA's response showed how quickly the Basque conflict could spiral out of control. Words like 'Ulsterisation' and even 'Lebanonisation' became the common currency of anxious politicians and opinion columnists.

Back in the Basque Country, Brouard's supporters would mourn as dramatically as they had organised in Madrid. Brouard had officiated at the funerals of many of GAL's earlier victims, especially at the spectacular scattering of Mikel Goikoetxea's ashes in the Bay of Biscay, but his own obsequies surpassed them all.

Many thousands of people filed past his coffin in Bilbao city council, while Edurne Brouard and her sisters and brothers took turns to stand by his body, 'so that people would never find him alone'. Many of those paying their respects were people who would not normally be found at a Herri Batasuna funeral. Brouard's charisma drew a huge wave of sympathy from the PNV, at official and unofficial levels, and for the next few months the gulf that had opened up between the moderate and radical nationalist parties narrowed significantly.[16]

Hundreds of thousands of people, probably more than half a million, turned out for Brouard's funeral procession, which began in Bilbao, stopped at Amorebieta and Guernica, and finished with a religious and civil ceremony in Lekeitio. This was probably the biggest public demonstration that the Basque Country, well accustomed to mass protests, had ever seen. It would only be surpassed, ironically enough, by the vast numbers of people who gathered in Bilbao in 1997, in solidarity with the most emblematic recent victim of ETA, Miguel Ángel Blanco.

Like much of Vizcaya and all of Guipúzcoa, Brouard's home town had experienced the strange silence of a general strike for the previous twenty-four hours. The silence was broken in Lekeitio on the morning of the funeral by the continuous megaphone broadcasting of Pablo Sorozabal's funeral march, which Brouard would have heard as he carried Goikoetxea's ashes to the sea. As his coffin was carried into Lekeitio's main church, a striking building with a series of elegant flying buttresses, a children's choir sang the heart-stopping Basque anthem *Agur Jaunak* ('Farewell, Gentlemen'). Their voices were regularly drowned, however, by the deafening roars of *'Gora ETA Militarra'* ('Long live ETA(m)') from the multitude outside. The priest conducting the ceremony, Martín Orbe, gave a homily which was as radical as anyone in his congregation. The history of the Basque Country, he said, was 'a history of repression', and he spoke of the persecution of youth for their political ideas, the persecution of the Basque language, the non-existence of a real democracy. The Church authorities, he said, should reassess their attitudes to violence, for not all violence should be condemned.[17]

This priest sang from the same political hymn-sheet as the HASI leader Txomin Ziluaga, who closed the civil ceremony in the plaza outside. 'Santi considered ETA a brother organisation,' Ziluaga declared, 'and he considered ETA militants as brothers to be respected and loved. That is what we are expressing here today.' He concluded by warmly thanking the PNV for its solidarity over the previous few days, to thunderous applause.

In killing Brouard, the GAL did not bring ETA to its knees; on the contrary, the shooting had brought ETA supporters, in their hundreds of thousands, to their feet.

***   ***   ***

But perhaps the Brouard operation did fit some convoluted logic of 'counter-terrorism'. The reports from the early police investigations into the killing read like textbook black propaganda work, along the lines indicated by the 'Plan ZEN'.[18] The police did have to admit that there was significant evidence linking the killing to the extreme Right and members of the Guardia Civil. But this evidence 'could not be confirmed', although the source was an informer. The state intelligence services to whom the informer was attached would not co-operate. Instead of pursuing this real lead energetically, the police went on to explain that they were now concentrating on the theory that ETA had killed Brouard. They produced an elaborate ideological hypothesis to justify this, purely on the basis of *Cui bono?* – who benefited from the killing?

Brouard was apparently a hard-liner, the police argument ran, but he was known to be open to a negotiated settlement. Real hard-liners feared he would betray them. As long as ETA could blame the GAL for his assassination, ETA would gain a dual benefit from killing him. Firstly, it would remove Brouard, and thus any possibility of settling for less than total victory, from the scene. Secondly, it would put iron in the souls of any wavering supporters, illustrating the intransigence of the Spanish state. Unable to contain their enthusiasm for this theory, the police even had an explanation for the 'gypsy' appearance attributed to the killers: they must have been Latin American revolutionaries, possibly paying back in kind (unspecified) services rendered by ETA in Chile.

If we ignore the fact that the Brouard assassination does not fit at all well with ETA's political *modus operandi*,[19] there is a certain geometrical purity to the police hypothesis. What it lacked, of course, was a shred of hard evidence to give it substance. Like many 'paranoid' theories in the distorting double mirror of terrorism and counter-terrorism, it can also be neatly reversed. The Spanish Right, with well-known connections in the security forces and intelligence services, had no interest in a negotiated settlement with ETA. And Brouard's killing did fit their *modus operandi* very comfortably. That was also where the concrete evidence lay, as the police themselves acknowledged. But the same report baldly states that links to the intelligence services were 'mere speculation', adding that 'there is no possibility whatsoever that [the police] will, even as a working hypothesis, follow this line of inquiry'.[20] With such an attitude, the investigation was unlikely to get very far.

Edurne Brouard remembers that, when she took her mother up to the surgery to see Brouard's body on the night of his death, the police would not let them approach it, on the grounds that they might accidentally destroy vital clues. Her mother reproached them roundly: 'Why are you making such a fuss, if you are going to do absolutely nothing about them [the clues] later?'[21]

The Brouard case became one of those terrible instances where the Spanish administration behaved almost as though it was trying to convince the Basque public of Herri Batasuna's thesis that Spanish justice was a sham. Since 1984, it has passed through the hands of a dozen investigating magistrates, who have made greater or lesser efforts to advance the inquiries. All of them have encountered a similar lack of zeal on the part of the police in unravelling the convoluted tangle of false and accurate leads which began to emerge. The first suspects arrested were drug dealers and police informants, engaged in a complex internecine feud in which one of them was killed.

At last, in 1995, a conviction was confirmed by the Supreme Court against Rafael López Ocaña, identified as one of the killers by Brouard's nurse. He was sentenced to thirty-three years in jail. Ocaña, it turned out, was the owner of the motorbike used in the GAL bombing raid on the Bar La Consolation in St-Jean-de-Luz in 1984.[22] Juan José Rodríguez Díaz, 'El Francés', who supplied the arms, got eight years. Both men were minor underworld figures. But Luis Morcillo Pinillo, a right-wing businessman accused of having contracted them, fled to Ecuador.[23] Lieutenant-Colonel Rafael Masa of the Guardia Civil, also suspected of having an organising role, was investigated but evidence given against him was withdrawn.[24]

The case was reopened in July 1997, when Luis Morcillo was arrested in Spain in possession of 100,000 tablets of Ecstasy. There is some hope that his trial may throw some light on a meeting he is said to have held prior to Brouard's killing. The other people present were, allegedly, a second businessman, a *guardia civil*, the leading GAL mercenary Mohand Talbi, and José Amedo, the police superintendent already convicted of GAL activities. The disgraced former Director General of the Guardia Civil, Luis Roldán, has volunteered that it was common knowledge among senior security figures that the killing of Brouard was 'a warning' to ETA not to target members of the PSOE.[25]

It is generally acknowledged that this case would have made no progress at all had it not been for the diligence of the family's lawyer, Txema Montero, at one stage an MEP for Herri Batasuna. Montero was one of the first Herri Batasuna leaders (a small and brave minority) to criticise ETA's campaign of violence, and fell from favour with the coalition as a result. But he remains the motor of the Brouard case, and, Edurne Brouard says, 'one of the best lawyers and a great friend always, despite personal and political differences'.

'He has clearly demonstrated,' she says, 'the implication of the state apparatus and of the Guardia Civil. But every time we get close to the "green connection"[26] we reach a dead end. When we get close, doors slam, people die. It's pretty clear what's happening if people die just when we need to talk to them.'

'Montero will kill *me* for saying this,' she continues, 'but I see very little possibility of getting much further [she was speaking before Morcillo's arrest]. We can't prove the obvious, because neither the Guardia Civil nor the police nor Interpol want to resolve it.'

Edurne Brouard herself is clearly a survivor rather than a victim of the GAL's violence. How, I ask her, does she feel about the victims of violence on the other side, those women who have lost husbands or fathers because of the actions of ETA?

'I don't believe that I suffer less, or they suffer more. We all suffer terribly. My father used to suffer terribly because *ordinary members* of the Guardia Civil, *ordinary members* of the police, were risking their lives in the Basque Country for things which it was perfectly possibly to resolve. Those who are in ETA risk their lives because it's part of our history, it's a commitment they make. But those who are in the police are deceived, they are told they will get more money if they come to work here, but for what? To trample on me, to give me a few thumps in a demonstration, and to end up dead on the side of a road. What use is that? What use is that?

'I don't believe that the wife of a *guardia civil* suffers less than I do. I sympathise terribly with this woman, but we have important things to say, and as long as we are not listened to, the conflict will go on. I don't speak as a member of ETA, but we want this to end, we want it to end absolutely. It's in their hands – not in her hands, poor woman, poor woman [referring to a police widow] – but in the hands of those in power, to end the suffering.'

Her insistence that the responsibility for the continuing violence in the Basque Country lies exclusively with the Spanish state will seem obtuse to anyone who thinks that, despite chronic aberrations like the GAL, ETA's campaign cannot be justified in a democracy. Critics of radical Basque nationalism stress the extent of democratic liberties available to the radicals themselves. Herri Batasuna, for example, has enjoyed an access to Spanish electronic media which Sinn Féin, at a similar period in its development, was denied by both British and Irish democrats. Within the circles within which Edurne Brouard moves, however, the existence of that democracy is often, in the most literal sense, simply not recognised. Despite the firmness of her position, it is possible to hear a genuine desire for real dialogue behind her words, the kind of dialogue many of his opponents believe her father was capable of.

We will never be able to calculate exactly what price the Basque Country, and Spain, have had to pay for the silencing of Santiago Brouard. Like Chris Hani of the ANC, also killed by right-wingers with shadowy backers, he was a pivotal revolutionary figure. His brutal removal from the scene was destabilising in the medium as well as the short term. Brouard gave what would be his last interview to a small magazine called *Ezkerra Marxista*.[27] Two points he makes should have given the paymasters of his assassins reason to pause. The Basque revolutionary struggle, he said, was 'more advanced' than in other parts of the state, 'fundamentally because of repression'. Those who betrayed the best traditions of Spanish democracy by killing him provided, perversely, the best justification for his own argument.

Looking to the future, he painted a hard road ahead. 'We are facing a gradual process of prolonged war, and prolonged erosion of the power and institutions of the bourgeoisie.' Bleak, uncompromising stuff, indeed. But it may not be coincidental that those who advanced similarly bleak positions on behalf of the Provisional IRA in the early 1980s are precisely those who are now involved in a real process of negotiation in Northern Ireland. In the early and mid-1990s, many observers used to lament that there seemed to be no one in Herri Batasuna with the stature and the vision to engage in a similar process in the Basque Country. It is possible that, in killing Santiago Brouard, the GAL did not just shoot a political leader; they blew up a potential bridge to peace.

NOTES

1   *El País*, 21 November 1984.
2   A point acknowledged, to a degree, by the Interior Minister, José Barrionuevo. See his memoir, *2,001 Días en Interior* (Barcelona: Ediciones B, 1997), p. 177.
3   All quotations from Edurne Brouard in this chapter are from an interview in Bilbao, June 1997.

4   John Sullivan, *ETA and Basque Nationalism* (London: Routledge, 1988), p. 177.

5   See ch. 2, p. 40, and ch. 3, p. 51.

6   Sullivan, op. cit., pp. 190 and 201.

7   Ibid., p. 229.

8   Ibid., p. 204.

9   Francisco Letamendía, *Historia del Nacionalismo Vasco y del ETA*, 3 vols. (San Sebastián: R&B Ediciones, 1994), vol. 3, p. 33. KAS stands for Koordinadora Abertzale Sozialista (Patriotic Socialist Co-ordinating Body). Confusingly, the acronym is also the brand name of a very popular Spanish soft drink company.

10   *El País*, 22 November 1984.

11   *El País*, 25 November 1984.

12   Sullivan, op. cit., p. 257.

13   *El País,* 21 November 1984.

14   ETA was the author of most of these attacks. Others were claimed by a shadowy quasi-Maoist group called GRAPO.

15   *El País,* 22 November 1984.

16   Not all mourners were made as welcome as the PNV. Euskadiko Ezkerra, the party close to ETA(p-m), was asked to keep away. There seem to be few hostilities so deep-rooted as those between former comrades-in-arms who have gone separate ways.

17   *Egin*, 23 November 1984.

18   'Zona Especial Norte', the security forces plan for the Basque Country elaborated by the first PSOE government. See ch. 4, p. 68.

19   ETA had been almost totally immune to the kind of violent feuding and internecine killing which have characterised several IRA splits.

20   *El País*, 22 March 1985.

21   *Punto y Hora*, no. 382.

22   *El País*, 30 October 1988.

23   *El País*, 31 July 1997.

24   *El País*, 5 February 1995.

25   This case is advancing quite rapidly at the time of writing, but remains plagued with confusion. Julián Sancristóbal, Director of State Security at the time of Brouard's killing, and Lieut.-Col. Rafael Masa were both imprisoned on charges of funding and organising the crime in September 1999, but released pending fresh investigations in December. See *El País*, 10 September 1999 and 17 December 1999. For updates on cases, see epilogue.

26   The Guardia Civil, known as *'los verdes'*, 'the greens', because of the colour of their uniform.

27   Published in *Egin*, 22 November 1984.

10

A Black Lady Stalks the Bars:

the GAL get trigger-happy

Blowing things up, literally as well as metaphorically, became the GAL's stock-in-trade for a brief period in late 1984 and early 1985. José Ramón López de Abetxuko, who had been named in the Spanish media as the leader of ETA's defence squads against the GAL, had a narrow escape in early December. A friend working on his car in Hendaye noticed a clothes peg attached to the front wheel. As he took cover, a booby trap exploded, injuring him slightly. Witnesses said they had seen a small, blonde woman, dressed in black, in the vicinity of the car, so this operation may have been the first to involve one of the GAL's most notorious and enigmatic killers, the *Dama Negra* (Black Lady). The GAL phoned in a claim for the bombing, and promised more of the same.[1]

They were probably as good as their word, because two more cars were booby-trapped in Bayonne in early February 1985, the second one seriously injuring the owner, Christian Casteigts. He was a French Basque with no ETA connections. He had to have both legs amputated.[2] However, the GAL do not seem to have claimed either of these attacks, and the French police suggested, unconvincingly, they were related to an internal feud between French Basque radicals.[3]

Two top members of ETA were arrested by the French at this time, immediately after a visit to Paris by Rafael Vera, Barrionuevo's deputy at the Interior Ministry.[4] But the level of French public and media opposition to the previous year's extraditions and expulsions had made an impact on the Paris government. While there were other important ETA detentions in France in 1985, there were only five expulsions to third countries, and no extraditions at all. This further halt in the stop-start march of French–Spanish co-operation against ETA may explain the next full-scale GAL offensive, which began in March and continued right through to the early autumn. Spain's accession to the EEC in June had no apparent effect on this new and vicious phase in the dirty war.[5]

The offensive was marked by an increasing tendency towards random terrorism rather than specific assassinations. The attacks were directed at bars which Basque refugees were known to frequent, but the shootings were often indiscriminate. The GAL now seemed less interested, by and large, in hitting the biggest fish in ETA, and were more concerned to make waves in the sea in which they swam. The 'collateral damage' to uninvolved individuals rose accordingly.

This campaign also coincided with the definitive debut of the *Dama Negra*, a figure straight out of a B-movie gangster plot. She fascinated the French press, who gave her other nicknames as well as the Black Lady: they also christened her the Mercenary Murderess and the Blonde Assassin.[6] On her first confirmed operation, however, she did not look very glamorous. It was her small stature that registered most on the handful of people drinking in the Bar Lagunekin, in the heart of Petit Bayonne, on the evening of 4 March.

She entered the little bar through a back entrance, and went to the toilet, carrying a large bakery bag full of long loaves of bread. She emerged without the bag, but with a shotgun. Her dark sun-glasses, and her bulky ski-jacket several sizes too big for her, made her look more ridiculous than threatening. One of the witnesses took her to be a child with a toy gun, playing a carnival joke.[7]

She then coolly fired three times at a group of refugees, wounding two of them seriously. Throwing down the gun, and the jacket, she ran off into the network of dark and tiny streets behind the bar. The police were later able to establish that the gun had been acquired in Spain.

Nine days later, a similar woman walked into a bar in Guethary, a little port between St-Jean-de-Luz and Biarritz, and fired at the three proprietors, injuring them all. None of them had any links to ETA.

Two weeks after that, Ramón Basáñez, a Basque refugee, had an amicable argument with a friend about where to take an aperitif. He wanted to go home, but his friend finally persuaded him to have a drink in the Bar Bittor, in Ciboure, a fishing village beside St-Jean-de-Luz. The drink cost him his left eye, though, as he says, it could have been worse.

The night Basáñez and I had arranged to meet in St-Jean-de-Luz, his car broke down and he missed the appointment. I saw him in the street a couple of hours later, instantly recognisable by the huge medical patch which still covers his left eye socket. Somewhat diffidently – this man had been shot in nearby bars on two separate occasions, and had good reason to be suspicious of strangers – I introduced myself. After just a moment's hesitation, he accepted my bona fides, and offered to take me for a drink in the very bars in which he had been shot.

Basáñez has not had an easy life. His brother, a member of ETA, was killed in Bilbao in 1977. The police believed he was part of his brother's *comando*, which he rather hazily denies: 'My work has been rather more in the political area.'[8]

After a period in which he was repeatedly arrested and threatened by the police, according to his own account, they told him 'that there wasn't going to be a next time, the next time I'd end up in a hole in the ground'. Then they arrested his sister and his mother, and used them to pressurise him. So he decided to go into exile in 1982. His wife and child remained in Bilbao. To add to his woes, a teenage visitor was accidentally shot dead in his French home in 1985.[9]

Basáñez seemed lonelier and more melancholic than any other exile I had encountered, but he manages a wry, downbeat sense of humour. As if it were the most natural thing in the world, he takes me to the places where he was very nearly killed, and points out the salient features. He tells his story in the Bar Bittor phlegmatically, without any heroics or any self-pity.

'I was sitting on the bar stool, one of those high ones, and it was one of those things, I don't know exactly why, perhaps because of reflections . . . well, I noticed something strange . . . I took my drink and got down from the stool and that was exactly when someone opened fire. I felt the heat of the shot, the pain . . . if I hadn't got down from the stool, it would have hit me full in the head . . . then that's the moment you begin to think "What will I do, how can I get out of here?" You have no weapon, you have nothing. You are at their mercy, no? What I did was to go towards the kitchen, and there I found I couldn't see any more. I thought "Where do I go if I'm really fucked up?"'

Temporarily blinded in both eyes, he crawled along the kitchen floor towards a rear entrance. As he did so, he heard an explosion behind him. It was a hand-grenade the attackers had thrown to cover their retreat. It had exploded outside the bar, and injured no one. His companion, José Luis Calderón, had been hit by a ricochet inside the bar, but nobody else was hurt.

There were contradictory reports, but most of the witnesses thought the small person who fired the shots was a woman, who appeared to have difficulty in managing the recoil from her rifle. If her accuracy was not remarkable, her *sang froid* was. She had walked right down the length of the bar, firing after Basáñez into the kitchen, before running back out the front and tossing the hand-grenade. Like the assailant of the Lagunekin, she abandoned her rifle on the spot. She then fled, apparently with a companion.

Basáñez staggered down the back street and his sight began to return. 'I saw a light, a little diffuse, not very clear, and that is what orientated me. I got to the Albenitz bar where I asked for help. While they were telephoning, they were very agitated, when they saw me bleeding, all over my face and my two hands.'

In hospital, he found he had lost the sight in one eye, and has suffered persistent complications since in healing the wound. His recuperation cannot have been helped by further encounters with the GAL, the first a near miss.

One evening in mid-June, he was in the Trinquet Txiki, a small bar only a short step from the Bar Bittor. He noticed some gypsies, who often drank there, playing *mus*. This card game is very popular in the Basque Country, and there was a regular tournament that night. Basáñez took a drink, but when the friend he was waiting for did not turn up, he left.

Shortly afterwards, a woman, wearing a very obvious wig and moustache to disguise her as a man, entered the bar. Minutes later, she sprayed the card players with submachine-gun fire. Two young gypsies, Emile Weiss and Claude Doerr, were killed instantly. Their killer covered her retreat with a hand-grenade, fired at a nearby bar where clients were beginning to emerge in pursuit, and ran to a getaway car. A wig, a jacket and a machine-pistol were found nearby.[10]

According to one hearsay version, the woman had entered the bar with a man, who pointed out a table with a group of refugees to her. She hesitated, and went to the toilet. While she was there, the refugees left and their places were taken by the gypsies. The woman then emerged from the toilet and simply blazed away at the 'target' table, without checking who was sitting there.[11]

Commentators began to talk of a 'second GAL', because the sloppy and indiscriminate *modus operandi* of this group seemed so different to the (usually) surgical precision associated with the GAL in 1984.[12]

A thousand gypsies (who prefer to be known as *Manouches*) from all over France attended the funeral. Caught in the crossfire of a war which seemed to have nothing to do with them, seven small children had been left fatherless by the attack. Basáñez thinks that the gypsies were singled out in the bar for a reason: 'It so happened that some refugees were living in the very same street at that time, and they were all quite sallow-skinned. I, for one, always think they were after them.'[13]

If he is right, it suggests just how crude the GAL's intelligence on ETA had become. Alternatively, it may have been that the group was no longer being instructed to decapitate ETA, but simply to make its environment uninhabitable. If this meant killing innocent bystanders, it doesn't seem to have mattered much to the GAL's paymasters. It may even have served their interests. The view that the GAL *deliberately* killed French civilians, already touched on, and relevant to the decision to hold Segundo Marey long after the GAL knew he was not an *etarra*, gains significant credibility in the pattern of their killings from 1985 onwards.

When the group issued a statement 'regretting' the killing of the gypsies, it qualified it by warning French Basques not to frequent bars used by the refugees. The GAL evidently applied the principle of guilt by association very broadly indeed.

Two weeks later, the Black Lady, or one of her surrogates, was back in Bayonne. This time her target was a refugee, Santos Blanco González, and he was shot dead while walking alone in the street at night, after a *txikiteo*[14] in Petit Bayonne. Witnesses who saw the killer run off say the silhouette was a woman's. A bag with a wig, a jacket, a Remington pistol, a Spanish military hand-grenade and, strangest of all, a pair of ballet shoes was found nearby. Perhaps Santos Blanco should have taken more care where he walked alone: he knew he was being periodically followed by 'strange characters', and he had been present at two previous GAL attacks.[15]

In her most brazen move of all, the Black Lady returned to the Bar Bittor during July. She was wearing a platinum blonde wig and, according to the press reports afterwards, was 'poured into a short skirt'.[16] This striking figure caught the eye of a young refugee, Juan Carlos Lezartua, who was sitting outside on the bar's terrace. She aroused his suspicion because, on a hot summer night, she was wearing a gabardine coat. He got up so quickly that he knocked his table over. As he did so, she took out a machine-pistol and started shooting at him. As on other occasions, she seemed to have some difficulty handling the weight of the gun, and only one of her seven shots caused him a minor injury.

She ran off, firing again at pursuers, and once more left her coat, wig and pistol scattered behind her. According to one account, she then took a taxi to Hendaye. The driver, realising afterwards whom he had been driving, said that her 'total calm . . . rendered her above suspicion'.[17]

She made one more appearance that summer. In the light of noon, on the last day of August, she knocked on the window of a house in St-Jean-de-Luz. Dominique Labeyrie, who happened to live next door to a refugee, answered. She asked him an innocuous question about his neighbour, and turned away as a pedestrian passed by. Then she turned back and suddenly started shooting at him through the window, hitting him in the hand. No gun was found in the wake of her getaway on this occasion, but a wig and coat were dropped into the frontage of a nearby basement. A shaken Labeyrie not only moved house after this incident, he also shaved his beard. He felt it made him look too much like one of those radicals from across the border.[18]

The saga of the *Dama Negra* ended, appropriately enough, with the lady simply vanishing from the scene. She did not feature in any of the GAL's final operations, but she (or they) had left a trail of three dead men and eight or nine wounded behind her. The French press wondered about her motivations: were they ideological or financial? Could it be that she was seeking personal revenge, as the widow, lover or sister of a victim of ETA? The French police had a wealth of descriptions, but seemed incapable of tracking her down.[19] This raised the usual question mark about their lack of commitment to solving GAL cases, even when French citizens were the targets.

While her profile dominated the first half of the year, she was not the only GAL activist employed during this period. She had started the March offensive in Bayonne, as we have seen, but others finished it.

*** *** ***

The Café des Pyrénées is just a few yards away from the Bar Lagunekin on the Rue Pannecau, the main thoroughfare of the Petit Bayonne maze. The café was crowded on the night of Friday, 29 March, and there were at least two groups of refugees among the drinkers. One of them, Kepa (Pedro) Pikabea, noticed somebody 'suspicious' at the door, but 'we thought they would not be willing to shoot in such a jam-packed place'.[20] It was a recklessly generous error of judgement.

The suspect loiterer withdrew, but returned with someone else, who immediately opened fire in Pikabea's direction. He defended himself with the only weapon to hand, his wineglass, which he hurled in his attacker's face. 'In that moment, without even taking aim, he began to fire in every direction.'[21] Pikabea himself was seriously wounded. The other three victims, ordinary French Basque citizens, were badly shot up. One of them, Benoit Pecastaing, died.

In striking again in the heart of Petit Bayonne, however, the GAL were now taking a huge risk. On a Friday night, the *quartier* was thronged with refugees and their families and friends from the south. And the self-defence groups formed in response to the GAL were at last beginning to function well.

The killers of Pecastaing were chased by several witnesses, the posse gathering strength with each bar it passed. They caught up with the man who did the actual shooting just after he threw one of his guns into the river. He tried to defend himself with a second weapon, but his pursuers disarmed him after his gun jammed. He was beaten and stabbed, before being handed over to a gendarme who happened to be passing by.[22]

He turned out to be a minor French gangster, Pierre Baldés. He was charged with murder and sentenced to life imprisonment, though he insisted he was a victim of mistaken identity. He gave no clues as to who had employed him.[23] It is unlikely that he would even have been arrested had it not been for the zeal of the self-defence groups. The proprietor of the Café des Pyrénées claims that the police took an hour to respond to his call for help, by which time, of course, Baldés was already in custody. His accomplice had long since escaped.

There was a large demonstration to protest against the Pyrénées attack the next afternoon. Javier Galdeano Arana, a senior journalist and commercial representative for *Egin*[24] in the French Basque Country, went along with his family. He took photographs of the protest as usual, and then returned to St-Jean-de-Luz with his two daughters. To finish off the roll of film, before putting it on the bus to San Sebastián, he suggested that they take some family snapshots, 'for my funeral testimonial'.

That black sense of humour, says his daughter Karmen twelve years later, was an essential element of their collective survival. They were a close-knit family, repeatedly sundered by political turmoil. In several ways, Karmen Galdeano's life among the Spanish Basque refugees in the 1980s reflected Edurne Brouard's experience a decade earlier. She experienced a strong sense of belonging, not only to her family, but to a wider yet still intimate community. Despite constant stress and the omnipresent threat, and reality, of death, she remembers her teenage years with nostalgic pleasure.

There were other similarities with the Brouards. Javier Galdeano was respected far beyond the circles of radical nationalism. He was well liked by many of his colleagues in other newspapers, and had friends in surprising places in Bilbao's social, sporting and business worlds. Like Santiago Brouard, too, he was clearly deeply committed to Herri Batasuna, but allegations that he was actually a member of ETA have been consistently denied by his family and colleagues.

Now in her thirties, Karmen Galdeano is a small, bubbly woman with an infectious smile. Her seemingly infinite fund of good humour rests surprisingly easily with an unshakeable sense of hard-line political certainty. She learned about commitment at the age of thirteen, in 1979, when her father was in prison for the first time. His involvement in radical nationalism, as a senior journalist and fund-raiser for *Egin*, had earned him the attention of the Spanish police, who suspected he was an ETA activist. While visiting him in Basauri jail, close to Bilbao, she learned from some prisoners that a number of them were about to be transferred out of the Basque Country to a prison in Soria, further away from their families.[25] 'Already when I was very young they used to give me messages saying: "Call the press and tell them that tomorrow they are going to move so-and-so, and tell his relatives."[26]

After several more arrests and short jail terms, her father and mother decided to go into exile across the border in early 1983. She and her elder sister, also still a teenager, continued to study in Bilbao, visiting their parents in St-Jean-de-Luz at weekends. She talks almost idyllically, in tones very similar to the Oñederras' and Edurne Brouard's, of the social life of the refugees in the period just before the GAL made their impact.

'Every week a car used to arrive, packed to the roof with food. It was shared among everyone, things were like that: no one went hungry, no one was alone, everyone could go out for a drink. I knew *Kattu* [Ramón Oñederra], we knew him from fiestas. I remember that the fiestas of Bidarrai were very popular, and we used to go along with the other refugees. *Kattu* was always in great form. At that time, well, we knew something was going to happen. And we saw strange people in the street, but since nothing had happened we just carried on, laughing, like everything was normal. Then there was the Lasa and Zabala thing, and people began to say: "Hmm, something is coming down here." But you know, it was only the beginning.'

Then the hammer blows of the early GAL campaign began to fall relentlessly. Karmen Galdeano still recalls her times in her father's house in St-Jean-de-Luz as immensely happy ones, even though she was by then aware that he must be directly under threat. She never resented the fact that her family home was always open to the refugee community. 'No, no, no way! Because it was neither private life nor public life, everything was blended, it was very attractive. We used to laugh all day.'

There was laughter, she remembers, even when her house became a kind of studio to make the sound tapes and visual images for the memorial tributes to the victims of the GAL. The elaborate ceremonies which were ETA's farewell to militants like Mikel Goikoetxea were prepared in her parents' sitting-room, and they were always prepared with a sense of humour: 'Unfortunately, we had to make light of misfortune.' Hence her father's black joke about his own testimonial that Saturday evening after the demonstration against the Pyrénées attack.

'Yes, yes he did say that. He said it thinking that it could happen, but hardly that . . . of course we weren't thinking that what actually occurred was going to happen, nor anything like that, or at least not on that day. So it was "One with you!" and "Another one with me!", and all the photos are like that, and those are the ones which were published the next day. That was it. He took the film to the bus, and when the film was on its way, it was then that they killed him.'

His daughters went off to shop for dinner while Galdeano was going to the bus station. On their return, they found a crowd gathered outside their house.

'We knew that something had happened. What we didn't know was whether it was *aita* [father],[27] or one of those who were always in the house, or whether it was Josu,[28] any one of those who came by the house,

DBS Arts Library

which was always full. When we arrived, I remember that we came down the hill running and Josu and the others were there already, and they told us it was *aita,* and that they'd killed him.'

'I remember that I sat down with him, and we were removing things,[29] and in those moments, I don't know, it was if he was still alive, I remember I was talking to him . . .'

The GAL had chosen, by chance or otherwise, the one moment that Saturday when Javier Galdeano was alone. It would have been much easier to kill him on any weekday, when his job entailed a solo 'paper run', to a fixed routine, distributing *Egin* throughout the French Basque Country. According to neighbours, the shots which killed him were fired by two men as he was getting out of his own car to go into his house. The assassins fired from a red Citroën, or possibly a Renault, driven by a third man, and fled, unpursued.

The witnesses noted the car's registration number, and gave it to the police, who located it abandoned shortly afterwards. They found an imitation Smith and Wesson .38 pistol, the fingerprints of one mercenary, and a bill from a hotel in the name of another.[30] Through tapping the latter's telephone they traced the gang to a Paris meeting with their alleged paymaster several weeks later, where the four were arrested. Their trial exposed links with two residents of the Costa del Sol with unusual relationships to the Spanish police. The failure of the Spanish government to either extradite or investigate these suspects, despite repeated French requests, blocked any effective follow-up of this potentially fruitful line of criminal inquiry.[31] This was to be a familiar story in the history of the GAL.

Karmen Galdeano says the French police were 'very correct' in all their dealings with her family after the killing. The Galdeano case is unusual in that the material authors of the crime were quickly brought to justice by the police themselves. But she believes that the French authorities were culpably negligent in dealing with the whole GAL phenomenon.

'The French police, if they had wanted to, could have stopped this happening. Of course they could. Probably the first [GAL killings] would have happened, but we would not have known the long years in which, month after month, you got up every morning saying: "What will happen today?"'

The French Basque Country is such an intimate community, she says, especially outside the tourist season, that both Spanish police and French mercenaries were visible to everyone. 'Nobody believes that mercenaries from Portugal and Marseilles could be walking around Donibane [St-Jean-de-Luz] without the police being aware of it.'

She also believes that those really responsible for her father's death have never faced trial, and the sentences handed down to the mercenaries gave her little satisfaction. 'It even used to upset me during the trial. I used to say: "But what wretched people! They don't have a friend in the world, and they will do anything. Not for principles, not for anything, how many people there are like this!" You can find people ready to kill for half nothing everywhere, and the solution is not to arrest the mercenaries, the solution is to get higher up. Who pays the mercenaries? And why?'

At the time of her father's death, Karmen Galdeano was a somewhat reluctant student of law, preferring art and history. Her father wanted her to become a lawyer, so that she could defend ETA prisoners. She remembers that, kneeling by his body on the street outside their house, she made him a promise: '*Aita*, I'm going to do it, I'm going to finish the course, I'm going to carry on.' Once again, an action of the GAL had strengthened, not weakened, the commitment of those they were attacking.

When I interviewed her, twelve years after her father's death, she was defending ETA prisoners, some of them people she knew from her father's 'open house' in St-Jean-de-Luz in her teenage years. She talked admiringly of those 'who give their all' for the Basque Country. I asked her, as I asked most of the victims of the GAL I interviewed, how she felt about the victims of ETA, like the 1987 Hipercor supermarket bomb in Barcelona in which twenty-one people, ordinary shoppers including children, died horribly.

'I imagine it must be very hard indeed,' she says, and then adds, as though it were the most natural thing in the world: 'And I know the people who bombed Hipercor, and if anyone is sorry for what happened it's them. Of course, they are two of the most delightful people, and with the purest feelings anyone could have. And of course they are incapable of doing anyone any harm.'

More than a little taken aback by this almost incredibly ingenuous statement, I could only remind her of the obvious: 'But they did do a lot of harm.'

'Yes, but they got things wrong, thinking that the police were going to give a warning. Of course, if they had known what was going to happen, I can tell you now that they would have preferred to die themselves, with the bomb in their hands, than cause the barbarity that happened afterwards.'[32] They will never forgive themselves, she continues, not for having left a bomb in a supermarket, but for having trusted the Spanish police to act promptly on their warning.[33]

Like many Herri Batasuna supporters, Karmen Galdeano is convinced that only ETA's campaign has prevented the Spanish state from 'trampling' on Basque rights over the last twenty years: 'Unfortunately there had to be deaths. Everyone legitimises the violence of one side, isn't that so? Well, if one violence is legitimate, why not the other?'

This terrible dialectic of reciprocal violence would sound wildly irrational coming from anyone who has experienced Spain as a democracy since 1978. Coming from someone whose father was killed by, in all probability, the paid agents of that democracy, it is a little harder to dismiss. Javier Galdeano's killing was another of the GAL's pyrrhic victories.

Or, as Fernando Egileor, another GAL victim, was alleged to have put it, the dirty war strategy 'which had previously terrorised ETA would, in the fullness of time, become a shield and cover for the movement'.[34]

*** *** ***

Egileor and his family know more than most about the terror imposed by the GAL. They were the targets of no less than five attacks in 1985, all of which were unsuccessful, sometimes by a hair's breadth. Egileor insists that the intense interest which the GAL showed in him did not reflect his significance within the radical nationalist movement, but rather his very normality as a refugee who had integrated successfully in French Basque life. The French government obviously took a different view, since it eventually expelled him (illegally) and he was subsequently classified by the French cabinet as a threat to the security of the French state.

Egileor is a short, stocky man in his fifties. His face shows signs of nervous strain but his dark eyes are full of fierce intensity. He digresses repeatedly from a personal account of his experience to a rather rigid political analysis of its context. He is a man who has kept the Marxist faith of his youth, and maintains it firmly in the face of all the evidence – a true believer after the death of God.

Egileor's life as a refugee in France started early, and reasonably well, under the circumstances. In 1969, there was a major ETA escape from Basauri prison near Bilbao. Learning that he was under suspicion as the organiser, he decided to cross the border, where he was granted political asylum. He concedes that, at this time, the French administration treated him 'with a certain benevolence'.[35]

He lived in Pau, outside the Basque Country and the main communities of nationalist refugees. He set up his own successful business developing new products for sport, physical education and rehabilitation. He and his wife had three children, 'and we lived in an absolutely normal situation'.

From 1978, he availed of the amnesty granted by the Spanish government the previous year to cross the border from time to time. Partly because 'the situation for us was not very clear', partly because he wanted to continue his children's schooling in the French system, and partly for business reasons, they decided to stay on in France. But in the fateful month of December 1983, just when the GAL were launching their first offensive, they moved south to Anglet, between Biarritz and Bayonne. He notified the police of his change of domicile. He was puzzled when a friendly officer advised him 'that I should think very carefully about things, because perhaps I would have cause to regret the decision I was going to take'.

Unofficially, more warnings came from the French police. He says he saw no reason why he should have been under threat, and tended to ignore them. He evades questions about his specific relationship to ETA at this stage, though he makes no secret of his continuing commitment to radical nationalism. He insists that his very normality made him a target, because he did not conform to the stereotype of the 'dangerous' political refugee. But he concedes that his refusal of persistent Spanish efforts to make him turn informer may also have singled him out. Finally, he received an official warning: his photograph was among material seized from a captured GAL death squad.

What followed was an almost incredible run of luck. On the first occasion the GAL came to call, he was renovating a house and had gone to buy some building materials. A builder saw four people walk on to the site. 'One in particular was very fat, with his hands in his pockets, with something bulky in his pockets. He [the builder] could see that they were carrying arms.' They waited for three hours, but left before he returned.

The next time the GAL moved against him, he had lent his car to a business partner. Pulling up at traffic lights, this man turned to respond to a request for directions from the car alongside, and found himself looking down the barrel of a gun. This squad was evidently more scrupulous than most GAL activists that year, because they drove off without firing when they realised they had the wrong man in their sights.

Another time, a dog drove away intruders. Vigilant neighbours saved him from a further attack. They called the police about a suspicious car outside his house, and the arrival of a squad car frightened off its occupants.

Egileor is scathing about the role of the French police. He agrees warmly that many individual policemen had no part in the GAL, and tried to warn him of danger, but insists that there was a policy of not protecting the refugees effectively under such circumstances. His own security system, he admits, was fairly arbitrary: 'Well, elementary measures, looking around every so often, looking left and right, and trusting in luck.'

Luck was with him – and with one of his young children – one more time. He was walking towards his car with his ten-year-old daughter on the morning of 16 July 1985 when he noticed a wavy line in the sandy earth, rather like the trail of a snake. 'But it was so clearly marked that I began to wonder, and I noticed that it ended just under my car. I crouched down and I saw a package under the petrol tank.'[36]

The packet contained two kilos of dynamite, attached to a remote control detonator. Egileor and his wife gathered their children at the other side of the house, and rang the police. The GAL squad, realising that they had been foiled, panicked and took off without detonating the car bomb. Their luck was as bad as Egileor's was good. The approaching squad car saw their getaway and took their number, which led to their arrest a little later. Like Galdeano's killers, they turned out to be a group of minor French gangsters. Once again, they went to prison. Once again, the man whom they claimed had recruited them continued to live unmolested in Spain for years, despite repeated extradition requests. However, in this case, Georges Mendaille was ultimately extradited, and convicted of organising this GAL unit, in 1996.[37]

Ironically, Egileor himself was subsequently expelled across the border in the opposite direction. It was a curious way for the French authorities to protect a man who was apparently a model guest in their territory, had three French-born children with French passports, and had been the object of five assassination attempts. According to his own account, Egileor was then tortured by the Spanish police while in custody. The Spanish authorities could find nothing to charge him with, however, and he was released. He says he was seriously assaulted by a group of uniformed Spanish police in the street a few months later.

Today, Fernando Egileor runs a successful sports shop, and also specialises in advising on physical rehabilitation equipment, in the old quarter of Bilbao. He remains zealously committed to a 'Marxist-Leninist' version of radical nationalism, but he seems like a character in whom instinctive generosity is in conflict with such schematic phraseology. The night before I interviewed him, he had rescued a neighbour from a blazing building, risking his life to do so.

He would not condemn ETA for attacking the Guardia Civil, but he says he would never refuse assistance to an individual *guardia civil* who came looking for rehabilitation advice. It's easy to believe him, though it's also easy to believe his promise that such a client would not leave him without paying the price of listening to one of his political sermons.

*** *** ***

For Karmele Martínez Otegi, the worst happened not once, but twice. Of all the GAL victims I encountered, including Ramón Basáñez, she seemed the most severely marked by her experiences. She seems a shy person by nature, but a much more acute pain shows in her extreme diffidence and hesitations throughout our interview, and in a nervous tic about her eyes. There is a terrible sense of loss about her, and with good reason.

She met her husband, Juan Mari Otegi Elizegi (*Txato*), an *etarra* who had crossed the border in 1975, on holiday in the French Basque Country in '1981, or 1982'.[38] They married shortly afterwards, and then moved from Bayonne to St-Jean-Pied-de-Port, well away from the refugee community on the coast. Otegi had got a job in Denek, the co-operative in St-Martin-d'Arossa where his comrades Rafael Goikoetxea and Jesús Zugarramurdi were also working.[39] She denies, however, that this company was set up exclusively to benefit ETA refugees. Most of the people who worked there, she says, were French Basques. 'And not of all them supported our side.'

Life in the interior of the French Basque Country, she says, was very different to the coast. People met in each other's houses rather than in the street. She found the difficulty of the local Basque dialect a further isolating factor, though she says her husband, a Basque-speaker from birth, integrated very well. They did not get much time to settle in, however. A year after they arrived, the GAL campaign began, and within months it became clear that there was no special sanctuary in the interior.

Eugenio Gutiérrez Salazar was shot in February 1984, in the much less accessible hamlet of Ideaux-Mendy. The focus came a lot closer in May, with the attack on Rafael Goikoetxea and Jesús Zugarramurdi on their way home from a shift in Denek.

Otegi had always made little of the threat he faced. 'He was quite laid back anyway, and I didn't feel that he was afraid. He was confident in himself,' she says. Now, however, he began to check under their car every time they used it. She feels he was a particular target because, 'rightly or wrongly', the Spanish media, and Spanish police, had identified him as the perpetrator of 'many things'.[40]

Like Egileor, they got their warning as a result of the arrest of mercenaries. Otegi's file was found in the possession of the men who killed Javier Galdeano. The file included a plan of his house, his work timetable, and a physical description of Otegi. Karmele Martínez says that the mercenaries told the French police 'something along the lines of "the next one on the list would be him"'. The police passed on the message, vaguely and reluctantly according to her. Their distrust of the authorities in general, and the officer who brought the news in particular ('he had a reputation as a bad person, quite tough, quite savage'), was such that they did not really believe it. Then it was confirmed in detail by a sympathetic lawyer.

What security measures did they take then?

'This thing about security measures,' she begins with a hopeless gesture. 'Perhaps, more attention than before, possibly that, but really . . . the only security measure would have been to stop working.'

This was what she wanted him to do. Otegi, however, was unwilling to give up his job, and not only because they needed the money. Rather cryptically, she continues: 'It's also true that the future would not have been any easier either. Possibly. When you are alive you are always faced with that, no? You don't know how things would have worked out. But he, in any case, told me that he would prefer to be killed by the GAL than handed over here [to Spain]. Well, he carried on working anyway.'

Nevertheless, Denek ran into financial trouble and had to close down temporarily.[41] For several weeks, Otegi and some of his companions worked in the safety of his home, trying to sort out paperwork and find a way to reopen. In the last week of July 1985, they started production again. A few days later, on 2 August, Karmele Martínez became anxious when he did not return from work on time.

'I was with our infant waiting for him. She was two and a half. He was always very punctual coming home from work.[42] And I began to get very anxious.'

She saw a helicopter flying low nearby, which worried her more, and she switched on the radio for news. There was nothing. 'Then a refugee came to tell me they had shot him.'

This refugee had happened to be driving along the road when he came to the scene of the shooting, just outside Ascarat, the last village on Otegi's way home from Denek to St-Jean-Pied-de-Port. A car travelling behind Otegi's had seen the attack. A white Yamaha motorbike had driven alongside him, and a pillion passenger had shot him three times in the back, before speeding off.[43] It was eerily like the killing of Rafael Goikoetxea, only a few kilometres away, fifteen months earlier.

The refugee took Karmele Martínez to Ascarat, where the police officer who had brought them the warning was waiting. The first driver on the scene had already taken Otegi to a local clinic, where his condition was so bad that she was not allowed to see him. The helicopter which she had seen had been coming in to fly him on to Bayonne for emergency surgery. 'And when we got down to Bayonne he was already dead. I never saw him alive again.'[44]

Otegi's killer or killers have never been arrested, though it was alleged that they were acting under the instructions of Georges Mendaille, the GAL recruiter who appeared to enjoy the protection of the Spanish authorities. Mendaille was ultimately convicted of recruiting the squad which attempted to kill Fernando Egileor, but was acquitted of any involvement in Otegi's death.[45]

The veteran etarra was immediately honoured as a gudari (Basque soldier) by the town council of his native Itxasondo in the nationalist heartland of Guipúzcoa. The decision was unanimous, and included councillors from the PNV and even Euskadiko Ezkerra, despite this party's hostility to ETA(m). The council proclaimed him to be a 'favourite son, faithful and honourable', and invited his family to permit his body to lie in state in the town hall. The councillors would accompany his body from the French border to the town.[46]

It was not to be. Karmele Martínez's account of her husband's funeral, hesitant and halting though it is, follows a familiar pattern.

'We crossed the frontier. They made me get out of the car which carried *Txato* because . . . the Guardia Civil . . . I did not want to get out. Then they told me: "Well, you can go with a *guardia civil* inside", and then I got out. And they took him. I arrived quite quickly, they let me pass easily. But his family still has some brothers living . . . they arrived late, that is, it was difficult for them to get there.'

'When we arrived [in Itxasondo], the car was there, with quite a few *guardia civiles*. And then, when they saw that I had arrived, a plain-clothes man opened the car and they were going to bury him. And there we were, pushing and pulling, because I didn't want them to. And in the end, they gave in, they left him there until his brothers arrived and they made us bury him anyway, they didn't give us time for a funeral or anything, they made us bury him.'

As happened several times during our conversation, she concludes her account of her husband's burial leaving several thoughts unfinished, no less eloquent for their lacunae.

'And we buried him then. It was all very under pressure. In the frontier as well . . . even when dead they didn't let him . . . what's more, [he] didn't even die in a confrontation with the police . . . supposedly all they have against you is that you are . . . they have proved nothing . . . but they are very hard, very bad.'

But Karmele Martínez had not yet experienced all that the GAL could do to her and to her family.

NOTES

1   Ricardo Arques and Melchor Miralles, *Amedo: El Estado contra ETA* (Barcelona: Plaza y Janés/Cambio 16, 1992), pp. 219–20.
2   *Sud-Ouest*, 6 February 1985.
3   *Egin*, 'Guerra Sucia' series, January/February 1995, no. 9; Arques and Miralles, op. cit., pp. 219–20.
4   They were Juan Lorenzo Lasa Mitxelena (*Txikierdi*), reputedly ETA's number two at the time, and Isidro Garalde (*Mamarru*).
5   However, Spain's entry to the EEC, with strong backing from Mitterrand, did represent full recognition from Paris that Spain was now a full member of the European family of democracies. This had an impact on public opinion and, coupled with the PSOE's success in persuading Spain to stay in NATO in the March 1986 referendum, undoubtedly facilitated the much closer collaboration against terrorism which became the norm that year, after the GAL stopped shooting. See Sagrario Morán, *ETA entre España y Francia* (Madrid: Editorial Complutense, 1997), pp. 215–23.
6   According to an informant of Arques and Miralles, two different women used this disguise. See op. cit., pp. 592–600.
7   *Sud-Ouest*, 5 March 1985.
8   Basáñez is persistently described as a member of ETA by the Spanish media, but such attributions are usually based on police sources, which are often

wildly unreliable. He certainly speaks of 'la organización Euskadi Ta Askatasuna' with great respect, and supports its political programme, but so would most members of Herri Batasuna.

All quotations from Ramón Basáñez in this chapter are from two interviews in St-Jean-de-Luz and Ciboure, June 1997.

9   *El País*, 27 November 1985. While Basáñez was in the bathroom, the youths found a 'toy' pistol which had been adapted for real use. During horseplay, one of them accidentally fired the gun, hitting the other in the head.

10 *Sud-Ouest*, 13 September 1985. It should be noted that accounts of these attacks vary from witness to witness. In the first attack on the Bar Bittor, for example, Basáñez's injured companion was certain that the attacker was not a woman, while most of the other witnesses say she was. Basáñez himself did not see his attacker.

11 This is the version given to Judge Baltasar Garzón by Inmaculada Gómez, the girlfriend of the Spanish police superintendent José Amedo. Gómez claimed that Amedo had boasted to her of his GAL exploits, and gave her this – probably highly coloured – account of the killing of Doerr and Weiss. It has not been proved in court. See Arques and Miralles, op. cit., pp. 649–50.

12 *El País*, 16 June 1985.

13 Basáñez's next encounter with the GAL was in the attack on the Bar La Consolation in St-Jean-de-Luz in February 1986. See ch. 12, p. 165–6.

14 Very roughly, the Basque for 'a few small ones'. It does not necessarily imply heavy drinking. Blanco González was shot after he had crossed the river to his home on the commercial side of the city.

15 *Egin*, 'Guerra Sucia' series, January/February 1995, no. 12. He had been in Ideaux-Mendy when Eugenio Gutiérrez Salazar (*Tigre*) was shot in February 1984, and in the Café des Pyrénées in March 1985 when Benoit Pecastaing was killed (this attack is dealt with later in this chapter).

16 *Sud-Ouest*, 13 September 1985.

17 *Sud-Ouest* and *Libération*, 10 July 1985.

18 *Libération*, 10 July 1985.

19 The assiduous Ricardo Arques traced one of the suspects, Dominique Thomas, to Andorra. She handed herself over to the French police in 1988, and was sentenced to three years' prison for criminal association in 1991. See Arques and Miralles, op. cit., pp 592–601, and *El País*, 18 October 1991.

20 *Egin*, 'Guerra Sucia', January/February 1995, no. 10.

21 Ibid.

22 *Egin*, 'Guerra Sucia', January/February 1995, no. 11.

23 *Sud-Ouest*, 31 May 1986.

24 The radical newspaper which supported Herri Batasuna's positions and was widely regarded as a mouthpiece for ETA.

25 The 'dispersion' of ETA prisoners was regarded as a security measure by the government, to prevent prison conspiracies and, above all, to separate hard-liners from those who might be amenable to 'social reinsertion'. See Robert P. Clark, *The Basques: The Franco Years and Beyond* (Reno, Nev.: University of Nevada Press, 1979), p. 371. It was regarded as a vindictive additional penalty by the prisoners and their families, who from then on had to travel hundreds, and sometimes thousands, of kilometres for every prison visit. It later became the cornerstone of PSOE prison policy from the late 1980s, with some prisoners being held as far away as the Canary Islands. It was maintained by the Partido Popular until the ETA ceasefire in 1998, and then gradually reversed, too slowly according to some observers.

26 All quotations from Karmen Galdeano in this chapter are from an interview in Bilbao, June 1997.

27 The Basque word for 'father' has passed into the Spanish spoken by many Basques.

28 Josu Muguruza was reputed to have been a leading member of ETA, though this was always denied by his family. He worked closely with Galdeano on affairs related to *Egin*. He was later handed over to the Spanish police, who ultimately released him without charges. Shortly afterwards he was elected as a parliamentary deputy for Herri Batasuna. He was shot dead in an attack by ultra-Rightists in Madrid on 20 November 1989, the fourteenth anniversary of Franco's death, and the fifth anniversary of Santiago Brouard's assassination. See ch. 16, p. 233.

29 It seems they wanted to take his address book and diary before the police arrived.

30 *El País*, 19 May 1987 and 29 March 1989.

31 See ch. 15, p. 205. The two gunmen and the driver, Jacky Pinar, Bernard Foucher and Alain Parmentier, all received twenty-year sentences. The man who allegedly paid them, Guy Cantavenara, denied all charges and was found not guilty. He in turn was alleged to have been contracted by Carlos Gastón and Eduardo Mari-Chica in Málaga, on behalf of a Spanish police officer. As we saw in ch. 5, the Spanish Mediterranean coast was a favourite haunt of dirty warriors, whether in semi-retirement or otherwise.

32 This assertion recalls an incident in ETA's early and relatively innocent days. Two bombers actually went back to remove a bomb from a building, which they had thought was empty, when they realised that there were people inside. The bomb exploded and badly injured the *etarras*. Such quixotic gestures have not, however, been characteristic of ETA in more recent times. See Patxo Unzueta, *El Terrorismo: ¿Qué era? ¿Qué es?* (Barcelona: Ediciones Destino, 1997), pp. 27–28.

33 Blaming police negligence, malicious or otherwise, for civilian victims of terrorist bombings is a familiar justification for terrorist 'disasters'. The primary responsibility for civilian deaths in terrorist bombings must lie with those who plant the explosives. It is characteristic of those who give political support to terrorist organisations to be, as it were, 'in denial' on this issue. Moreover, it is not at all certain that the Hipercor bombing was an 'accident' from ETA's point of view. It belongs to the period in ETA's campaign when (relatively) discriminate shootings were largely replaced by indiscriminate bombings, as part of a policy of 'accumulation of forces', whereby the relentless rhythm of violence was supposed to finally force the government into negotiations. For a critical analysis of this strategy see Antonio Elorza (ed.), *La Historia de ETA* (Madrid: Temas de Hoy, 2000), pp. 332–4.

34 This quotation was attributed to Egileor by José Amedo, in a letter published in the right-wing newspaper *ABC* on 21 September 1988. Egileor does not now remember the exact form of words, but recalls telling Amedo, who would soon be one of the main GAL defendants, that the ultimate effect of the GAL would be to prove to the world 'the repression which our people have been subjected to'. The context for this extraordinary conversation between a dirty warrior and one of the targets of the dirty war was, according to Egileor, an attempt by Amedo to recruit him as an informer. Amedo also confirmed this exchange to the author, and said that he himself agreed that the GAL had made ETA stronger 'in terms of propaganda, perhaps, but it would also provide the state with a justification, in a given moment, to grant an amnesty to both sides'. This conversation took place in October 1997.

35 All quotations from Fernando Egileor in this chapter are from an interview in Bilbao, June 1997.

36 *Egin*, 'Guerra Sucia' January/February 1995, no. 12.

37 Few cases illustrate the double standards which the Spanish authorities applied to the extradition of terrorists so blatantly as that of Georges Mendaille. See ch. 15, pp. 205–6.

38 All quotations from Karmele Martínez Otegi in this chapter are from an interview in Bilbao, July 1997.

39 See ch. 7, p. 112.

40 He had been named as a member of ETA(m) in a memo from the Spanish government to the French authorities in 1978, and was named again in a similar communication as one of the most dangerous members of ETA, wanted for crimes of blood, in July 1981. He was accused of participation in some of ETA's most sanguinary operations, such as the killing of the President of the provincial government of Vizcaya and his two bodyguards in 1977. See *El País*, 3 August 1985. Barrionuevo accused him of participation in the killing of six *guardia civiles* in Ipaster in 1980 in his unreliable memoir, *2,001 Días en Interior* (Barcelona: Ediciones B, 1997).

41 The factory had itself been the object of a GAL attack a year earlier, when it was partially burned down.

42 While such punctuality may have been a domestic virtue, it must have made things easier for his killers.

43 *Egin*, 'Guerra Sucia' series, January/February 1995, no. 12, *Sud-Ouest*, 3 August 1985.

44 For other accounts of Otegi's death, see *El País*, 3, 5 and 7 August 1985, and *Libération*, 3 August 1985.

45 *El País*, 30 January 1997. See ch. 15.

46 *Egin* and *El País*, 5 August 1985.

11

Massacre at the Monbar

he Hotel Monbar is a small, neat establishment, with red exterior
beams and shutters contrasting cheerfully with its white
frontage. It stands about halfway up from the river on the Rue
Pannecau in Petit Bayonne. The ground-floor café-bar opens directly
onto the street.

The narrow entrance is made narrower still by the semicircular bar on
one wall. It barely leaves space for newcomers to pass those already
seated, and reach the half-dozen small tables beyond. Seen from a normal
perspective, it is a pleasantly intimate arrangement. From another point
of view, the room has the classic structure of a trap.

Txetx Etcheverry is an intense French Basque, in his early thirties at
the time of our interview. He is a committed radical nationalist, and was
involved in the self-defence network which the refugees and their local
supporters had organised against the GAL attacks.

He was having a drink at the Alex Bar, which is next door to the
Monbar, on the evening of 25 September 1985. He saw, and participated
in, most of that night's events. In halting Spanish (it is his third language,
after French and Basque) he can tell almost the whole story.[1]

'I was having a drink and we heard what everyone thought were
fireworks. With my obsession, my paranoia about the GAL, I went outside.

'Then I saw two guys outside the Monbar, just as they were at the door
shooting at people with pistols. I shouted at my friends in the bar "Come
out! It's the GAL and they are shooting next door!" And then I looked
again, and there was one man with his body half inside and half outside
the bar. And the old guy was shooting him, finishing him off.

'They took their time to finish off the victims. Afterwards, I learned
during the trial that they were to be paid 50,000 francs for a wounded
victim, and 200,000 francs for a dead one. That was why they took their
time to kill the four of them . . .

'I went towards them, and my friends came out of the bar, and then
they [the GAL] see me and begin to go, but *walking*. And that I also
understood afterwards, at the trial. Amedo[2] had said to them: "Well,

when you carry out this operation, all the people there are going applaud you, there is no doubt at all that the whole population is on the side of the GAL."

'They went off walking, walking for 100 metres or so. When they saw that I, and the group a little further behind, were following them, they began to raise their weapons as if to shoot me, aiming at me. Then I hid. All this went on for 500 metres, moving from street to street, hiding behind cars, and it lasted a bloody long time, because they always kept walking, though walking quickly now that they saw they had people behind them.'

He followed them to the river, and there he noticed something that struck him as odd on this already very strange night. A white car, parked on the bridge, with two men inside, drove off suddenly just as the two gunmen, and their pursuers, came into view.[3]

'They were always 50 metres ahead of me. At one moment, a refugee happened to park his car close to where I was hiding. He didn't know anything about what had happened. I went to him and said: "Don't park! Start up again. There are two guys from the GAL who have just killed several people!"

'We got into his car, and meanwhile the group of friends who were with me had got a bit lost, they didn't know the *barrio*, but at that instant I saw them and from a distance I indicated to them the way they should go. The two guys from the GAL were going to the Saint Esprit bridge, which is the last bridge before Bayonne railway station . . .'

He pauses again to recall what he later learned at the trial.

'What is incredible is that the Spanish police had given them two train tickets, from Bayonne to Irún. After killing four people they were planning to calmly take the train to Irún where they had an appointment with Amedo.'

Etcheverry and the refugee saw that the two men were standing on the bridge, no longer brandishing their guns, but they could not see clearly what they were doing.

'We went at top speed in the car towards them, so that if they took out their pistols we could smash the car into them. But they didn't take out their pistols and so we got out of the car and we each grabbed one of them and . . .' Etcheverry makes punching gestures '. . . boom! boom! boom!'

Etcheverry and his companion did not know it, but the two mercenaries had in fact already thrown their pistols into the river. The two unarmed Basques were taking quite a risk in confronting two such obviously dangerous men hand to hand, though they seem to have been well prepared for the fight.

'Yes, we were afraid, of course we were afraid. I had been afraid since [I had seen them at] the Monbar. For nearly a year and a half we had lived in this obsessive climate of war. And we had seen people close to us die. Yes, but you overcome the fear.

'Well then, I had grabbed the older one, and my friend had got the younger guy. I gave the older man the biggest punch of my life. He didn't move and I carried on. And my friend gave the other man a kick right in the balls. Afterwards, he said "I haven't been able to piss in seven days." They accused *us* of torture! My friend broke his toe with the kick; he was on crutches for a month.

'We thought they still had their pistols. We kept hold of them, and just at that moment a police car arrived. We said to the police: "These are people from the GAL. They have just killed some people." The police took them off, and the refugee went with the *txakurrada*[4] to the police station. I went back with my other friends to the Monbar.'

He was greeted by a grim scene. Four men had been killed in the attack: Joxe Mari Etxaniz (*Potros*), Inaxio Asteasuinzarra (*Beltza*), Agustín Irazustabarrena (*Legra*) and Xabin Etxaide (*Eskumotz*). They were all refugees, and all reputed to be members of ETA, some of them senior activists wanted in Spain for serious crimes, including murder. Etxaniz was believed by the police to play the key role of *mugalari* leader, co-ordinating the movement of ETA members back and forth across the border.[5]

Now they all lay side by side in the same pool of blood, riddled with bullets on the floor of the Monbar. Whatever crimes they may have committed, they had been shot without trial while living openly in a country which had given them refuge. Yet when Etcheverry arrived back at the scene, the French police had still not arrived, at least fifteen minutes after the killing.

This is all the more remarkable given the fact that there is a police station less than 500 metres from the Monbar. It is even stranger that the killers chose an escape route that actually took them *towards* this police station, passing within 50 metres of it before they reached the Saint Esprit bridge. And although the owner of the hotel had called the police as soon as the attackers left, the squad car which encountered them on the bridge had received no emergency call and came upon the citizens arresting them purely by chance.

According to another witness, Fermín Muguruza, who had been in the Alex Bar with Etcheverry, and had been playing table football with the victims only half an hour earlier, the first to arrive were members of the CRS, the French riot police, who began behaving very aggressively towards the relatives and friends of the victims gathered outside.[6] Etcheverry sought out the local police chief to protest.

'I said to him: "It's about time you arrived! You are fifteen minutes late, and then the first thing you do is shove around the relatives of the dead! Are you not ashamed?" They became violent, shouting "Give us space to do our work!"'

The police forbade any demonstration or shouting of slogans. In the hypertense atmosphere, someone began to whistle the air of *Eusko Gudariak,* the PNV's Civil War song which ETA has appropriated as its anthem. The others took it up, in an eerily restrained tribute to the dead men.

Etcheverry's turbulent day was not yet over. As he walked home, two squad cars pulled up and he was arrested and taken to the police station. Here he was confronted by a furious police chief.

'He was insulting me for thirty minutes. You can hardly imagine the situation. I had arrested two guys who had killed four people, and the police chief has *me* arrested and brought to the police station so that he could insult me. Then there was a demonstration outside the station, and they let me go. It was incredible.'

The two men he had helped to arrest turned out to be minor members of the Marseilles mafia. Lucien Mattei, who was forty-one at the time, was a hard man who denied all charges against him, despite the fact that his shoes and socks were soaked in the blood of the victims. He had stood beside their bodies after they had fallen wounded, and finished them off at point-blank range. Mattei seemed to have had a good contact among his jailers. The address of another witness, who had seen the whole attack from his house on the Rue Pannecau, was found in Mattei's cell.

Pierre Frugoli, who was only twenty-two, was made of softer stuff, and confessed his role in the killings within hours of his arrest. He maintained his confession, despite open threats from Mattei. At their trial, in December 1987, he would provide dramatic, but legally inconclusive, corroboration about the participation of José Amedo in the attack. They were both sentenced to life imprisonment, later reduced to twenty years by the Appeals Court in Paris.

Etcheverry was, of course, a key witness, and he once again fell foul of the authorities in his partisan zeal for justice.

'As a witness I told them everything. And then I said: "But look, those people [the mercenaries] showed no pity or regret. They are going to get years in prison, but they understand nothing of what they have done. Those who paid them for what they did are not here. What are you going to do with the people who are really responsible . . ." And the president of the court said: "Get him out of here." The police came and threw me out.'

Etcheverry's radical nationalism does not disqualify him as a witness. His view on the absence of the real criminals from the courtroom was shared by the police themselves. A French police inspector, Roger Bosslé, told the trial: 'Our investigations on the GAL always, sooner or later, lead us to Spain.'[7]

The funerals of the Monbar massacre victims coincided with the anniversary of Franco's execution of the *etarras* Juan Paredes Manot (*Txiki*) and Ángel Otaegui in September 1975.[8] The Herri Batasuna leader Tasio Erkizia made the parallel explicit. Those who murdered these martyrs of the anti-Franco struggle, he told a meeting, 'continue operating today'.[9] The province of Guipúzcoa, of which all the victims were natives, erupted in a violent general strike, and the police intervened violently at the funerals. A commanding officer of the Guardia Civil said that 'this amounts to a military occupation'.[10] A photograph of the *compañera* of Agustín Irazustabarrena, clutching their three-month-old child in one arm while casting his ashes from a huge *ikurriña* onto a Basque mountainside, was another iconographic propaganda trophy for ETA.

One of ETA's severest critics, Patxo Unzueta, understood the dynamic well: 'Nothing has so favoured the aims of ETA as the actions of the saviours of the fatherland who direct the GAL. Nothing so favours the saviours of the fatherland and grave-diggers of public freedoms as the actions of ETA.'[11]

The Interior Minister at the time, José Barrionuevo, didn't get the point, and apparently still doesn't. In his 1997 autobiography, he refers to the Monbar killings as part of a 'bad month for ETA', and makes no comment whatsoever on the ethics of the operation. He does, however, give extensive details of the alleged criminal records of the victims. He never mentions that one of those convicted for the crime gave evidence which linked the GAL's Monbar operation directly to the Spanish police.[12]

X

1   The following quotations, occasionally slightly edited to take account of his difficulties with Spanish, are from an interview with Txetx Etcheverry in Bayonne, June 1997.

2   The Bilbao police superintendent who was accused, but not convicted, of hiring these mercenaries.

3   A refugee who came by a moment later had seen the occupants of the car clearly, and told Etcheverry that he was 'sure' that they were Spanish plain-clothes policemen. If they were, it suggests the extraordinary degree of impunity which the GAL's handlers felt. It also raises the question of why they did not go to their comrades' assistance. Perhaps, seeing the pursuit, they simply thought the risk was too great. Another interpretation is that they were quite happy to see the mercenaries get caught, because they could then pocket their fees. Another witness later told Etcheverry that he had seen the two mercenaries, before the attack, being given a tour of the bars of Petit Bayonne by a third man.

4   Offensive slang for police, based on the Basque word for 'dog'.

5   *El País*, 27 September 1985. As we have seen, the GAL repeatedly targeted *etarras* who held this key position.

6   *Egin*, 'Guerra Sucia' series, January/February 1995, no. 11.

7   Ricardo Arques and Melchor Miralles, *Amedo: El Estado contra ETA* (Barcelona: Plaza y Janés/Cambio 16, 1989), p. 230.

8   See ch. 3, p. 49.

9   *El País*, 27 September 1985.

10   *Punto y Hora*, 4 October 1985.

11   *El País*, 28 September 1985.

12   José Barrionuevo, *2,001 Días en Interior* (Barcelona: Ediciones B, 1997), pp. 227–8.

1. Segundo Marey at his home, on the day he was released by the GAL, 14 December, 1983.

2. The mothers of Joxean Lasa and Floren Aoiz, Herri Batasuna leader, lay wreaths before his portrait outside La Cumbre Palace in August 1995. ETA members Lasa and Joxi Zabala had been held and interrogated by the GAL in this building in 1983–4.

3. *Ertzainas* (Basque police) baton-charge family members at the funeral of Lasa and Zabala in Tolosa cemetery, 21 June 1995.

4. Izaskun Ugarte, widow of GAL victim and ETA member Mikel Goikoetxea Elorriaga (*Txapela*), touches her husband's ashes with one hand and with the other raises ETA's symbol, the axe (for strength) and serpent (for cunning) at his funeral ceremony in St-Jean-de-Luz in January 1984. The Herri Batasuna leader Santiago Brouard, who was shot by the GAL later the same year, stands behind the ashes. On the right is José Manuel Pagoaga Gallastegi (*Peixoto*).

5. The Kayetenia Bar in Bayonne after the shooting of Ramón Oñederra (*Kattu*) on 19 December 1983. The banner accuses the Spanish Socialist Party and Spanish police of killing him.

6. The mothers of ETA members Bixente Perurena (*Peru*) and Ángel Gurmindo, (*Escopetas/Stein*), killed by the GAL in Hendaye on 25 February 1984, hold their ashes during their funeral. In the right foreground, looking away, is Herri Batasuna leader Txomin Ziluaga.

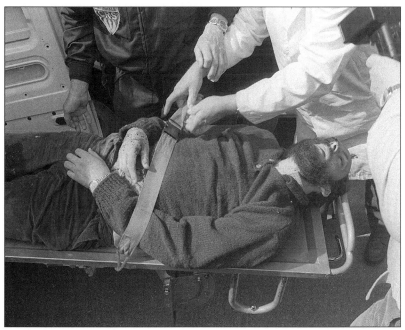

7. ETA member Xabier Pérez de Arenaza is carried dead from his car after a GAL attack in a Biarritz petrol station, 23 March 1984.

8. Veteran ETA leader Tomás Pérez Revilla (right) and the refugee priest Román Orbe in the immediate aftermath of a GAL bombing in Biarritz in June 1984. Pérez Revilla, who was already ill with leukaemia, died 43 days later.

9. Relatives of Joxean Lasa and Joxi Zabala visit the site where they were buried in quicklime in Busot, Alicante. The banner reads 'Freedom for the Basque Country!'

10. Militant mourners at the funeral of Herri Batasuna leader Santiago Brouard in Bilbao, 22 November 1984. The banner in the foreground carries the symbols of HASI, the revolutionary party which Brouard led, and KAS, a shadowy committee which appeared to link Herri Batasuna and ETA.

11. The bodies of two of the four victims of the GAL shooting at the Hotel Monbar in Bayonne, on 25 September 1985, lie covered in sheets while anti-GAL protesters begin a silent demonstration.

12. Former Spanish police superintendent José Amendo, already convicted for two GAL attacks and one kidnapping, attends a court hearing in Bilbao, during the protracted investigation of Santiago Brouard's murder, in July 1999.

13. Laura Martín, widow of the GAL's last victim, Juan Carlos García Goena, who had no links to ETA and was killed by car bomb in July 1987. 'I want the truth, all of it, all of it.'

14. Julen Elgorriaga (left), Civil governor of Guipúzcoa, and Enrique Rodríguez Galindo (then a major in the Guardia Civil) at the site of an ETA bombing in Oñate, 14 July 1987.

15. Left: Enrique Rodríguez Galindo in full dress uniform in 1992.

16. Right: Julen Elgorriaga after being questioned about the murders of Lasa and Zabala, June 1997.

17. Enrique Dorado Villalobos, former Guardia Civil sergeant, tries to avoid photographers after being questioned in a GAL investigation in Bilbao, 10 April 1994.

18. Television image of State prosecutor Jesús Santos summing up at the Lasa and Zabala trial, in March 1999: 'The GAL were morally at the same level or worse than ETA'.

19. GAL mercenary Lucien Mattei during his trial in Pau for the killings at the Monbar Hotel, 30 November 1987.

20. GAL mercenaries Patrick de Carvalho and Roland Sanpietro during their trial in Pau for the killing of Tomás Pérez Revilla 21 March 1988.

21. Investigating magistrate Baltasar Garzón: 'the State and its security is being confused with the security of certain persons and their possible criminal responsibility'.

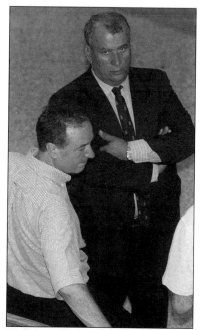

22. Former Director of State Security Julián Sancristóbal (left) with Lieutenant-Colonel Rafael Masa, just before they were remanded in custody in Bilbao during the Brouard investigation, September 1999.

23. Socialist Justice and Interior Minister Juan Alberto Belloch (standing) and Prime Minister Felipe González during a parliamentary debate on the CESID papers and the GAL, October 1995.

24. José María Aznar

Mario Conde

Pedro J. Ramírez

25. Emilio Alonso
Manglano

Juan Alberto Perote

José Antonio Sáenz de
Santamaría

26. Francisco Álvarez

Francisco Paesa

Ricardo García
Damborenea

27. Judge Eduardo Moner (centre) shakes the hand of Prime Minister Felipe González at a judicial reception in September 1995. Moner was investigating the involvement of González's administration in the GAL at the time.

28. Former Interior Minister José Barrionuevo addresses his supporters before entering Guadalajara Prison on 10 September, 1998. José Borrell is on the left, and Felipe González on the right.

29. Felipe González leads José Barrionuevo to the gates of Guadalajara Prison. Rafael Vera (in open-necked shirt) follows them.

30. Felipe González peers through the gates of the prison, on his first visit to Barrionuevo and Vera as convicts, 3 October 1998.

12

Shooting Women and Children Too:

the GAL make their exit in a blaze of shame

If Barrionuevo conceived of the war against terrorism in purely mathematical terms, September 1985 *was* a bad month for ETA. The terrorists lost one militant when his own bomb exploded, and another four at the Monbar. They claimed only two victims themselves: a US citizen unlucky enough to jog past a bomb intended for *guardia civiles* in Madrid; and a national policeman in Vitoria.

But the war against terrorism in a democracy is not a football match, and September 1985 cannot be represented by a score of 5–2 to the enemies of ETA. Not only had the GAL become an enormous propaganda boost to radical Basque nationalism, but it was becoming a major irritation to the French, and was beginning to seriously embarrass the Madrid government at home.

There was widespread public ambiguity in Spain about the GAL phenomenon. Many citizens undoubtedly still took the pragmatic view that ETA deserved a taste of its own medicine, and turned a blind eye to the betrayal of democratic principles that the dirty war involved.[1] For others, however, the increasingly credible allegations of police complicity with the death squads were slowly but steadily corroding the PSOE's reputation as a democratic party. The increasing frequency of GAL 'mistakes' made the death squads look less attractive even to those who had initially supported them. There was a growing public demand for an explanation of the impunity which the GAL seemed to enjoy. Spanish investigative journalists and French investigating magistrates were building up a body of evidence which, while not yet conclusive, leaned heavily towards implicating the Spanish state apparatus in the dirty war.

It was probably with this in mind that the GAL's organisers put together an operation which was bizarre, even by their own standards: the creation of a death squad which was designed to self-destruct. They seem to have hoped that the debris it left behind would lead the investigators in the wrong direction. An ordinary French citizen paid the price for their machinations.

On Christmas Eve, 1985, Robert Caplanne rose early and took his first coffee of the day in the Royal bar in Biarritz. A native of the town, where his parents ran a café, he was an electrician by trade, and the secretary of a social club for former sailors. He was thirty-seven years old and separated from his wife, but was hoping to celebrate Christmas with her.[2] He was well known locally as a sociable man who had no connections whatsoever with ETA.

As he walked to his car, he was shot in the chest, stomach and neck at close range by a gunman, who was driven off in a red Suzuki. The car, with an Andorran registration, was found later in the Biarritz suburb of La Negresse. Caplanne died of his wounds on 6 January. A local newspaper described the attack on him as 'an incomprehensible act'.[3]

The Suzuki contained a pistol, a submachine-gun and a lot of ammunition. The Andorran registration easily enabled the Spanish police to find the man who had hired it, Javier Rovira. He turned out to belong to a group of neo-fascists based in Barcelona. Rovira and four others were tried in Spain for the killing in 1987. They admitted membership of the GAL, but claimed that they had confused Caplanne with an alleged *etarra*, Enrique Villar Errasti.[4]

The defence at their trial argued that the *comando* had been set up as fall guys. Their detention gave the impression that the GAL were ultra-Right *incontrolados*, with no connection to the state apparatus. The stratagem backfired badly, however. The investigation revealed that the man who had recruited the group, Ismael Miquel Gutiérrez, was a police informer, who had conveniently fled the country when his comrades were arrested.[5] One of the defendants told the court: 'They told us that [our mission] was to collaborate with the police, to prevent terrorist attacks, to gather information on *etarras* . . . because, for reasons of diplomacy, the Spanish police could not go to the south of France.'[6]

In the course of the trial, the head of police intelligence, Jesús Martínez Torres, admitted that 'Interior pays police informers for the surveillance of *etarras* in the south of France'.[7] The five men claimed they had been scapegoated, but were given sentences ranging from thirty-four years to four months for their participation in the killing. Curiously, the court ruled that they were not part of the GAL, against their own admission.[8]

Meanwhile, Karmele Martínez was trying to put her life back together after her husband's death. As it happened, she had been accepted onto a French-language course in Bayonne just before he was shot. She moved there with her daughter Nagore from St-Jean-Pied-de-Port. The course went well for her, and in early February 1986 she successfully applied for work in a branch of the Banco de Bilbao in the city. By all accounts, including her own, she was not a member of ETA, and might have expected to live as normal a life as her new circumstances permitted. 'But a day or two later I was wounded in the attack on Bar Batxoki, and then I couldn't . . . it was too much.'[9]

The Batxoki is a small bar in Petit Bayonne, on the quay to the left as the Rue Pannecau reaches the river Nive.[10] Its glass frontage means that all the customers are in full view from the street. This immediate area had seen more than half a dozen of the GAL's worst attacks over the previous two years. The memory of the killings at the Monbar, less than two minutes' walk away, must surely have been fresh in the minds of everyone who lived in the refugee community.

Yet, on the Saturday night of Carnival, 8 February, around 9.00 p.m., Karmele Martínez called in there with her daughter. She was with another refugee at the bar, Juan Luis Zabaleta. Nagore, who had celebrated her third birthday just two days earlier, was playing with Zabaleta's daughter, Ainitze, who was just two years older.

What possessed people, who knew they were at risk, to continue with a social life which exposed them directly to danger? Karmele Martínez gives an answer very similar to that of Izaskun Rekalde about the situation two years earlier.[11] 'Because if we didn't go out, what would we have done? The solution was not to hide, either. I think that these sort of relations with people are what make life worthwhile.'

On this occasion, however, the resilience of the Spanish Basque social custom of the *txikiteo* very nearly brought her, and her daughter, to their deaths.

She was standing at the bar, where the owner had just poured a round of drinks, when three men appeared outside the broad glass frontage of the bar. One of them tried and failed to kick in the door, which opened outwards. Nagore, who was playing with Ainitze near the table-football machine, remembered what happened next like this, according to her mother: '"Some bad men began to throw chairs around." That is what is engraved on her memory,' says Karmele Martínez. 'Because of course chairs and so on were falling over.'

The chairs were falling over because the men outside were pumping bullets into the bar, with 9 mm automatic weapons. One fired through the door, the others through the frontage, collapsing it into flying shards of glass, and peppering the football machine, the chairs, the bar, even a small aquarium – and the clients.

'They said "On the floor" or something like that,' Karmele Martínez remembers. 'I threw myself down, or I fell, you don't think about what you're doing. Then I grabbed a little girl thinking she was my daughter, and then I stopped myself because it wasn't my daughter, but I was holding someone. After that, I noticed that my windcheater was stained.'

Then she did see her daughter. 'She was not unconscious, I could see she was still alive. She had blood on her backside . . . and her windcheater was turning pink.'

As it happened, Nagore was not as badly injured as her mother. 'She was wounded but the bullets didn't damage her bones or anything. She was about five days in hospital. I was there about a month. They had broken my tibia and fibula, they were quite shattered. The wound stayed open, they could not put the leg in plaster for seven months. Then I was several months on crutches. It took a long time.'

Eleven years later, she was still suffering balance problems, but not much physical pain. As for Nagore, Karmele Martínez thinks it is too early to tell what the impact of two bullets and some shards of glass in her thigh and buttock has really been. 'A nurse told me that she has been depressed and well, it's not easy. I think she is quite well, but she has no father, it's not clear [how she really is].'

After the Batxoki attack, Karmele Martínez returned to the Spanish Basque Country for security, but the fear stayed with her.

'I was still unnerved when I came back here. Then I became frightened. What house should I look for? It mustn't be low, because they might come in through the window. I became afraid of everything. If the other side was dangerous, it's dangerous here too. Here the same people who have the full power to . . . But fear passes, little by little, and what can you do about it?'

The gunmen hit three of the other people in the bar, including the other child, Ainitze, and her father, Juan Luis Zabaleta. A French citizen, Frédéric Haramboure, suffered the most serious wounds, with bullets in his jaw and thorax, though he, like the others, made as full a recovery as could be expected.[12]

Having sprayed the bar at will, the attackers retreated across the nearby bridge. The owner of the Batxoki, who was unhurt, managed to use a shotgun he had learned to keep behind the bar for such emergencies. He fired two shots, but missed both times. According to some witnesses, the GAL unit dumped their guns and coats with an accomplice in a black car on the other side of the bridge, and continued their successful escape on foot through the city's commercial zone.

As was becoming habitual, several refugees gave pursuit on foot. One of them claims he would have caught up with them, had the French police not arrested him as he was running up the street and ignored his claims that he was chasing a GAL unit. A special plan for such emergencies was put into action, according to the police, but, according to nationalist sources, not a single checkpoint was set up between Bayonne and the Spanish border.[13]

Anyone who argues that the GAL were not a terrorist group – an argument often made by Socialist leaders, and one which the Spanish courts have tended to endorse – should consider the Batxoki attack.[14] Apart from the basic point that those who ran the GAL already had all the resources of the law at their disposal, and were using terror as an extra-legal weapon against ETA, the Batxoki operation could also be classified as 'terrorist' in its disregard for civilian lives.[15] The killers fired completely at random into a bar, purely on the basis that they knew it to be periodically frequented by Basque refugees. Moreover, they could clearly see, through the glass frontage, children who could have no conceivable responsibility for ETA's actions.

One of the mercenaries would subsequently tell a French court that scruples about killing women and children had prevented them firing at a crowded bar earlier in the week. They had then been severely upbraided for their excessive sensitivity by the Spanish policeman who was giving them their orders. 'He said that we had done badly in not killing the women, since they were also dangerous, like the men, and also *etarras*.'[16] He added that a man who claimed to be a French policeman, who was also giving them instructions, told them that 'the men with beards who are in the bars are members of ETA, and we should not distinguish between them'.[17]

The mercenaries were sent back to Bayonne with their consciences set in order. Standing outside the Batxoki before the attack, and seeing the children within, one of them extended the moral thesis of their paymasters a little further: 'Let's hit the children too. ETA wouldn't worry about something like that. That is how they operate themselves.'[18] Neatly establishing the moral equivalence between state terrorism and its revolutionary counterpart, this Aquinas among dirty warriors gave the order to open fire.

One should probably not expect sophisticated moral philosophy from hired killers, but it was disturbing to find the mayor of Bayonne making a not dissimilar argument after the shooting: 'It is a regrettable action, but it is also a reply to the attacks carried out by ETA.'[19] These comments were an indication of how the wind of public opinion was now blowing in France.

In fact, ETA's targets over the past two months had been exclusively 'military', with the exception of two retired *guardia civiles*. They had included a general and, immediately prior to the Batxoki attack, a vice-admiral. ETA had, and would again, perpetrate attacks just as indiscriminate as the Batxoki shooting, and with worse consequences for civilians. But if the GAL's actions were supposed to be a measured reply to Basque terrorism, this one was seriously out of proportion.

Within a week, the GAL struck again, returning to St-Jean-de-Luz and a bar they had bombed in 1984, the Consolation. They also, as it happened, hit the same person for the second time. The hapless Ramón Basáñez, victim of the Black Lady in the Bar Bittor the previous March, was having a chat with friends at the Consolation at lunchtime on 13 February. He noticed two men who were not regulars coming in for a coffee. They left and returned a few minutes later.

In his usual phlegmatic fashion, he tells the story of that afternoon.

'There we were, talking and so on. Then one of them fired, and the other didn't, fortunately. They hit me. What I did was feint as if I was throwing myself on the floor, but actually went running towards the bathroom. The others got down behind the bar and threw cups and glasses.

'The police later wanted to make out that it was we who had done the shooting. It was an incredible situation, wasn't it? When you are lying like I was, in the hospital, in intensive care, and they wanted to interrogate me, as though I was the one who had opened fire. It was illogical. They were there, asking away, no matter what. One of the nurses said: "How is this possible?"'[20]

The police never found any evidence that the refugees had fired anything more potent than a heavy ashtray at their attackers. Basáñez's wounds were even more serious than those he had suffered in the attack on the Bar Bittor. He had a bullet in the elbow, another through the thigh ('just a little bit higher and it would have been *"clic"*,' he says with bleak humour, gesturing at his crotch). The three other bullets severely damaged his lungs, stomach, liver, intestines and femoral artery. When he was lying bleeding on the ground, he thought that he was dying. This most matter-of-fact man says it felt like this: 'That I was not going to see my daughter or my wife, nor the bay of San Juan de Luz, ever again.'

He finds it puzzling now that he should have been so obsessed with the beauty of St-Jean-de-Luz. He was, as we have seen, less comfortable with exile than most of his colleagues.[21] To this native of Portugalete near

DBS Arts Library

Bilbao, the French Basque Country could never really be home. 'This is also my country,' he says a little doubtfully, 'this is also Euskal Herria, but it is . . . different.'

Once the physical wounds were healed, friends took him to a farmhouse to recuperate. He still suffers considerable discomfort, and mood swings which seem to be affected by changes in the weather. He makes no secret of the fact that his nerves are not in great shape.

His attackers made off on foot. Once again they were followed, this time by a French Basque schoolteacher, Patxi Zamora. Seeing three 'strange-looking' men running headlong down the street, scattering jackets, gloves and what turned out to be pistol magazine clips, he took off after them. The thirty young pupils he was leading on an excursion were left staring in amazement.

The three GAL members split up, and the one Zamora kept after ran into the railway station, though he seemed unaware of his pursuer. This man stood on the platform in shirt-sleeves in the cold February air, but kept his gabardine over his arm. It covered the pistol he had tried, unsuccessfully, to use in the shooting, and had kept, he said later, 'as a souvenir'. Zamora called over some nearby policemen, who arrested the suspect after another short chase.[22]

Paulo Fontes Figueiredo, a young Portuguese mercenary, had decided to take a train instead of a taxi back to Spain, to save money. He had, after all, joined the GAL in order to buy a house. He was not exactly the brightest, or the toughest, man on the GAL team. His confession would not only pull in the other mercenaries with whom he had attacked the Batxoki and Consolation: it would ultimately bring to the dock the Spanish policemen who had sent them on their 'missions'.

The rapid collapse of this Portuguese *comando* did not stop the GAL's ruthless February offensive in its tracks. Another death squad was already in place, in a very different setting to the coastal resorts.

Bidarray stands on an abrupt hill beside the busy road from Bayonne to St-Jean-Pied-de-Port, about 35 kilometres inland. But it is not very accessible. The river Nive flows through an equally abrupt gorge below the main road, and the narrow route to the village has to zigzag down to a narrower Roman bridge, before climbing the vertiginous gradient to the dramatically situated church which, apart from the inevitable *frontón*, is the only real landmark.

Even by Basque standards, Bidarray is more a scattered townland than a hamlet. It is the sort of sleepy place where the bar can be closed at lunchtime, even at weekends. From the vantage point of the fine Romanesque church, the *baserrias* (Basque family farmhouses) which house much of the village's population can be seen dotted across the pastoral valleys which lead to the Pyrenees. In 1986, Spanish Basque refugees lived in two of these fine farming homesteads, some of which are three centuries old.

On the night of 17 February, a GAL squad took up an ambush position on the tortuous hairpin cul-de-sac that leads to these neighbouring farms. The road, less than three metres wide, cuts so deeply into the hillside here that a local journalist colourfully described it as 'an entrail in the mountain's flank'.[23]

When a blue Citroën 2CV came down the road in the darkness, the gunmen opened up with a sustained blast of automatic fire. They were caught in the car's headlights for an instant, and a young farmer working nearby could see that one of them had a beard. Then the driver lost control, and the car pitched over the side of the road and plunged down the embankment, turning over several times, stopping only a few metres before it reached the next loop in the road.

According to the witnesses, the gunmen escaped in a car with a San Sebastián registration, which eluded all the checkpoints the police say they set up along the routes to the border.

When the witnesses reached the car, they found a sixty-year-old man on the point of death, with several bullet wounds evident in his back. Beside him was a teenage girl, whose pathetic last words were 'Maman, je vais mourir.' ('Mother, I am going to die'.)[24] He died before an ambulance arrived; she died on the way to hospital. One panel of the car displayed fourteen bullet holes in a row.

Christophe Matxikotte was a shepherd from a nearby village, Itxassou. After working in the US, he had come back in middle age to tend his family's stock. He had some sheep on land attached to his deceased wife's farm, near the refugees' houses, which were empty at the time. The sixteen-year-old Catherine Brion was the daughter of a Parisian family who rented space for their caravan on Matxikotte's farm in Itxassou. She loved the countryside, and had gone with him that evening to help check on some new-born lambs. Neither of them had any connection with politics.

The GAL had left their unofficial signature, a discarded gun, in the river, and a day later they acknowledged the action, apologising for their 'mistake'. A local Basque nationalist group speculated that it was no mistake at all: 'These mercenaries are in fact paid, above all, to spread terror.'[25]

Whatever the GAL's motivation, the response to the killing of these almost symbolically 'innocent' victims was universal outrage in France. It was interesting to note, however, that the local Socialist MP, Jean-Pierre Destrade, who had not hesitated to blame the Spanish Socialists for the GAL in 1984,[26] had now shifted his ground.

'The terrorists of all origins, who can still move freely in our region, must be pitilessly pursued, put behind bars or chased out; right down to the last one, whether they dress up in the acronyms of GAL, ETA, or Iparretarrak.'[27]

The scene had been fully set for an equivalence between the GAL and ETA. The latter were no longer viewed in France as charming and idealistic, if misguided, radicals. They were now seen as terrorists, to be locked up or expelled, and this is precisely what began to happen.

Within a month of the Bidarray killings, a trial in Bayonne established a legal precedent, in that ETA was denominated 'an association of wrongdoers who were planning on French territory outrages to be carried out abroad'. This meant that ETA members could now be tried in France, even when there were no more specific charges against them than membership itself.[28]

French general elections in March forced the Socialist President, François Mitterrand, to 'cohabit' with a conservative Prime Minister, Jacques Chirac. The new Interior Minister, Charles Pasqua, promised to 'terrorise the terrorists'.[29] In April, ETA's most influential leader of the decade, Domingo Iturbe Abásolo (*Txomin*), was arrested and subsequently deported to Algeria, despite his possession of full political refugee status.

From July to December 1986, twenty-six ETA members were handed over directly to the Spanish authorities, under a draconian 1945 edict which permitted the immediate expulsion from the national territory of foreigners who constituted 'a threat to public order'.[30] The groundwork for this measure had been laid by the outgoing French Socialist government. From 1987 onwards, the jailing, expulsion and extradition of ETA members became systematic French practice.

If those who set up the GAL were mainly motivated by the need to remove ETA's French sanctuary, they seemed to feel they had succeeded. The GAL as such never fired another shot after the double killing on the back roads of Bidarray, though the dirty war would claim one more innocent victim in 1987.

If the GAL's chief motivation was to put an end to ETA, however, they failed miserably. ETA killed forty people in 1986, eight more than it had killed in 1983. In 1987, ETA claimed fifty-two mortal victims. Its political support in the Spanish Basque Country remained solid, undoubtedly bolstered by the black image the GAL campaign had given the young Spanish democracy in many Basque eyes. Catherine Brion and Christophe Matxikotte, like so many other victims of terrorism, had died for nothing.

NOTES

1   There is a widespread belief that the majority of Spanish public opinion actually applauded the GAL while they were active. It is probably more true to say that a majority passively accepted the GAL campaign. However, while many observers will confirm this anecdotally, an opinion poll taken at the time points in the opposite direction. See *Tiempo*, 30 April 1984, where 61 per cent of respondents said the GAL were not justified, and only 17 per cent said they were. However, one would have to bear in mind the reluctance respondents might have had in expressing their real views on such a delicate issue.

2   *Sud-Ouest*, 25 December 1985.

3   Ibid.

4   *El País*, 6 May 1987. Errasti was handed over to the Spanish authorities two months after Caplanne was shot. He was released in Spain without charge. Like Fernando Egileor, another GAL 'target' had been subsequently found to be innocent at law. How many of those '*etarras*' who died in the dirty war may likewise have had no sustainable charges against them?

5   *El País*, 6 May 1987.

6   *Egin*, 'Guerra Sucia' series, January/February 1995, no. 13.

7   Ricardo Arques and Melchor Miralles, *Amedo: El Estado contra ETA* (Barcelona: Plaza y Janés/Cambio 16, 1989), p. 232.

8   *El País*, 14 November 1987. See ch. 15, pp. 209–10, for more details on this case.

9   All quotations from Karmele Martínez Otegi in this chapter are from an interview in Bilbao, July 1997.

10   'Batzoki', spelt with a 'tz', is a common Basque word meaning 'meeting place'. The façade of this bar, however, spelt the work 'Batxoki', which is the style followed in this book.

11   See ch. 7, p. 101.

12 In terms of targeting *etarras*, the GAL had been marginally luckier, in this random attack, than they realised at the time. It was one of ETA's best-kept secrets that an 'itinerant *comando*' of French Basque citizens had been set up, and was carrying out many of their bloodiest attacks in Spain. Years later it emerged that Haramboure was a member of this *comando*. See *El País*, 14 June 1991.

13 *El País*, 9, 10 and 11 February 1986; *Egin,* 'Guerra Sucia' series, January/February 1995, no. 11.

14 See Rafael Vera's comments in ch. 25, pp. 416–7, for an account of this argument.

15 See discussion of this issue in prologue, pp. 9–10.

16 French court proceedings quoted in Arques and Miralles, op. cit., p. 250. See also *El País*, 13 June 1991.

17 *El Sol*, 14 July 1991.

18 Quoted in Arques and Miralles, op. cit., pp. 249–50.

19 *Punto y Hora*, no. 423.

20 Interviews with Ramón Basáñez, St-Jean-de-Luz and Ciboure, June 1997.

21 See ch. 10, p. 141.

22 *Egin,* 'Guerra Sucia' series, January/February 1995, no. 11; Arques and Miralles, op. cit., p. 251.

23 *Sud-Ouest,* 19 February 1986.

24 Ibid.

25 Ibid.

26 See ch. 6, p. 97.

27 *Sud-Ouest*, 19 February 1986. By a strange coincidence, Bidarray was also the scene of the assassination of two CRS men in 1982, attributed to Iparretarrak, and of the funerals of two Iparretarrak militants, who died handling a bomb, in 1980. See *El País*, 18 February 1986.

28 Sagrario Morán, *ETA entre España y Francia* (Madrid: Editorial Complutense, 1997), p. 223. This was the trial of Juan Lorenzo Lasa Mitxelena and Isidro Garalde, who had been arrested in early 1985. They were both given long jail sentences in France, and then handed over to the Spanish authorities in 1994 and 1995 respectively.

29 Morán, op. cit., p. 231.

30 Ibid., p. 327.

13

The GAL's War is Over:
but one more victim falls

Juan Carlos García Goena had no reason to fear the GAL when he walked to his car in Hendaye at 5.20 a.m. on the morning of 24 July 1987. He was a Basque refugee, but he had never been a member of ETA. In fact, he was a pacifist, a fugitive from Spanish military justice for refusing to do his military service.[1]

Besides, the GAL had not operated since the killings in Bidarray, seventeen months earlier, despite ETA's increasingly bloody and indiscriminate campaign in Spain in that period. Even when ETA killed twenty-one shoppers and seriously injured about thirty more in the horrific Hipercor bombing in Barcelona in June 1987, there was no 'reply' from the death squads. It was widely assumed that the GAL had achieved their aim of 'persuading' the French authorities to act energetically against ETA's French sanctuary, and that the organisation had been stood down.

García Goena's wife, Laura Martín, usually rose to see her husband off to work, but on this occasion she stayed in bed, something which she has regretted bitterly ever since.[2] After nearly a decade of giving interviews about the events of that day – she has been more accessible to the media than any other GAL victim – her account was still fractured, still shot through with immediate pain, when she told me the story in July 1996. She heard a loud noise just after he left, and her first thought was that the engine of their Citroën Dyane, which needed to be hill-started every morning, had somehow blown up.

'At that moment I did not relate it to a bomb. These are things you can't explain . . . you know how it was but . . . I opened the bedroom window, I couldn't see the car, and I saw him lacerated with glass. He did not scream but he moaned, he moaned . . . I ran downstairs, I don't know, I'm not even sure what I did, I went down running with the little girl . . .'[3]

She was too late to reach her husband, or what remained of him. Her neighbours were already on the street, and held her back. 'I always say that I am remorseful because I could not get to him, and the neighbours got there [first]. So many things happened that no, you don't remember what you were thinking. I thought that my little girls would be orphans, yes, I thought that a thousand times, because it was obvious.'

She is haunted by the idea that she should have been there for her husband's last moments, that perhaps he was looking for her or calling for her, but there was nothing she could have done for him. One leg and parts of his face had been torn off. The explosion was not the result of mechanical failure. A bomb had been attached expertly to the wheel of his car. It destroyed the vehicle and the driver, but the shock wave was vertical, so that neighbouring houses were hardly damaged.[4]

The GAL claimed the killing, without any apology for a 'mistake', and Laura Martín found herself in a hall of mirrors reflecting black propaganda. After years of negotiations, García Goena had been on the point of arranging their return to their home town of Tolosa with the Spanish authorities. He had always been prepared to do social service instead of military service, but was not willing to face a court martial for desertion. Through a Basque politician, Joseba Azcarraga, who was also involved in negotiating the 'social reinsertion' of ETA exiles and prisoners, an arrangement had almost been reached.

Some newspapers now suggested that ETA had planted the bomb, to show their disapproval of refugees doing deals with the Spanish government. This easily shaded into the description of García Goena as a member of ETA, who had been subjected to the same summary 'justice' as Mikel Solaun and María Dolores González Catarain (*Yoyes*), members of ETA who had accepted Madrid's offer of 'social reinsertion'.[5] This hypothesis would be repeated in court by the Interior Minister, José Barrionuevo, four years later. But González Catarain was a former 'general' of ETA, who had returned to the Spanish Basque Country against the express wishes of the new leadership. In ETA's eyes, her case would have been in no way comparable to García Goena's.

In a press conference in Paris, shortly after the killing, Barrionuevo had advanced a different hypothesis, which he repeats in his memoirs: that ETA had carried out the killing, and claimed it in GAL's name, in order to 'upset the magnificent relationship which exists at this time with the French authorities in the struggle against terrorism'.[6]

This statement is a kind of acknowledgement that the sudden silencing of the GAL's guns in February 1986 had contributed to this improved climate in Franco-Spanish relationships, with all that that acknowledgement implies. The killing of García Goena was certainly a severe embarrassment to the Spanish authorities. Well-placed French sources made it clear to the Spanish media that France's greatly improved collaboration against ETA would be drastically reduced in response to a renewed GAL campaign. Barrionuevo and Vera were virtually summoned to Paris to discuss the issue.[7]

García Goena's killing, however, was not a marker that the GAL had a future. It is much more likely that it represented a convoluted attempt to stall investigations into the GAL's past. The sordid reality behind the bombing, as far as it has emerged, will be examined in detail in later chapters. But it was revealed quite early on that García Goena's name had erroneously been included in a list of ETA members given by a French informant to the Spanish police.

This does not surprise Laura Martín. 'We had such and such a neighbour who was a refugee, for example, and automatically we had a relationship with that neighbour, and automatically it was necessary to kill us,' she says with bitter irony. 'If you went for a cup of coffee with a refugee, you were a target.' She recognises this now, but at the time she says they never felt under threat from the GAL, or at least not more than anyone living in the area might have done.

To give the case a doubly sinister twist, it seems certain that the GAL members who organised the killing were well aware that García Goena was unconnected with terrorism. He was a soft target, whom they could take out at very little risk. His ambiguous legal status as a deserter, and his Basque origins, suited their aims. The group who had warned French citizens that they were at risk if they drank in certain bars were not going to balk at killing a Basque peacenik. These people were not, however, attempting to restart the dirty war on their own account. They wanted, it seems, to remind their superiors that they still had the power to embarrass them. They suspected that the Spanish state felt tempted to scapegoat the junior officers who had done its dirty work, and keep its own hands clean.

When I met Laura Martín in 1996, her face was marked by nine years of sorrow, and nine years' frustrated struggle to make those responsible admit to their part in her husband's death. The other GAL victims who had no relationship to ETA have all kept very low profiles, but she has campaigned actively for justice. Her dramatically handsome, dark features have appeared in dozens of newspaper and magazine photographs as a kind of archetypal tragic widow. It is not a role she relishes, and while she has put her case to the media skilfully and repeatedly, she remains a reluctant interviewee.

Having first argued that everything she had to say was already on record, she finally agreed to talk to me, but insisted that she could only spare fifteen minutes. Once we began, however, it was I who had to put an end to the conversation, after nearly two hours. 'Obsessively', to use her own word, she has followed every twist and turn, and many false trails, in the tortuous investigation of the GAL.

She has seen the GAL commanders who were believed to be directly responsible for her husband's death brought to court. They were then acquitted for this particular crime in bizarrely melodramatic circumstances.[8] She has seen their superiors use weasel words to applaud or condone the dirty war and elude responsibility for its consequences.

A few weeks after her husband's killing, she found that she was pregnant. The couple already had two daughters, one five and the other fourteen months. She was so distraught that she made an appointment for an abortion, but at the last moment she accepted the child as Juan Carlos's 'last gift' to her.

She admits that there were times when she longed for revenge. There were moments when she wanted to see the perpetrators suffer as her husband must have suffered. After a few years, however, she developed a remarkably generous attitude to the people who tore her young family apart. Cristina Cuesta, founder of the peace group 'Gesto por la Paz' (A Gesture for Peace), which seeks support for, and reconciliation among, all victims of terrorism, had a big influence on her. This process has brought her into contact with the widows of *guardia civiles* and policemen killed by ETA. She has had to deal with her suspicion that their husbands might have collaborated with the GAL; they have had to overcome the stereotype that the GAL's victims were collaborators with ETA, and somehow 'deserved' their fate.

Laura Martín has been a loner among the GAL's victims and their relatives. Unlike the French victims with no ETA connections, who have remained strangely silent, she wanted to speak out strongly and pursue those responsible. But she has maintained a critical distance from victims associated with ETA, whom she sees as acting under the direction of Herri Batasuna. Her greatest hope is that she has brought up her three girls to see the futility of violence.

She no longer wishes to see her husband's killers behind bars, but she desperately wants – desperately needs – them to freely acknowledge their participation in the dirty war, and to ask forgiveness from the victims.

'All [the GAL members] began to confess [only] when there was evidence against them. Is there no one, not one of them, who suffers remorse which does not let them live? For me these people are not normal. Normal people feel guilty for the simplest little wrong thing they've done . . . and these people, who have committed barbarities, feel nothing.

'Someone should call me on the phone and say: "Look, Señora Martín, I can't live, I am eaten up with remorse" . . . and I would forgive him. If someone said to me "I put the bomb in your husband's car, but I am sorry for it, I can't live, please forgive me," I think I would forgive him. But he must say it, he must tell me. I want to know, nothing more.

'I want the truth, all of it, no? Not just for the sake of the trial for my husband's murder. All of it, eh? All of it. All of it. All of it.'

NOTES

1   Conscientious objection was a lot less popular, a lot less organised and a lot more heavily punished in Spain in the early 1980s than in the late 1990s.

2   García Goena worked in the same railway maintenance company as Jean-Pierre Leiba.

3   All quotations from Laura Martín in this chapter are from an interview in Hendaye, July 1996.

4   *El País*, 25 July 1987.

5   González Catarain was shot dead in front of her child in her home town of Ordizia, in September 1986. For the killing of Solaun see ch. 7, pp. 103–4.

6   José Barrionuevo, *2001 Días en Interior* (Barcelona: Ediciones B, 1997), p. 403.

7   *El País*, 31 July 1987.

8   See ch. 16, pp. 238, 241.

PART III

Placing Blame:

Investigating the Investigators

14

Grounds for Suspicion:
absence of proof

Everything was suspected, much was known, nothing was proved. That is the paradox at the heart of early attempts to unmask the people who hid behind the mysterious acronym of the GAL. To understand this complex unmasking process, and what it reveals about Spanish democracy, we need to retrace and review the events of the GAL's dirty war from the perspective of those who were trying to investigate it.

From the moment Lasa and Zabala went missing, many observers were certain that elements within the Spanish security forces were running this new dirty war. Some believed that the Ministry of the Interior, and indeed the entire Socialist cabinet, were directly or indirectly involved. For a long time, no one could substantiate even the former claims. But, with the 20/20 vision of hindsight, it is possible to see that the early speculation about the death squads and their paymasters was often remarkably accurate, sometimes down to quite small details. However, as the CIA might phrase it, all the known facts had deniability.

Much of that wall of deniability has now been breached. Those who have revealed the 'appalling vista'[1] that lies beyond it have mostly been investigative journalists and investigating magistrates. The role that the police might have been expected to play in investigating terrorist crimes in a democracy has been played by a combination – some would say an alliance – of the media and the courts. Yet the strings that moved the GAL have not yet been definitively traced to their ultimate puppet masters. At the highest levels of responsibility, the paradox of what is suspected, what is known and what can be proved remains as tantalising as it was in the autumn of 1983.

When Lasa and Zabala disappeared, in October 1983, their comrades in ETA had ample circumstantial evidence that members of the Guardia Civil were involved. As we saw in chapter 5, *guardia civiles* from the barracks at Intxaurrondo had been frequently spotted in plain clothes on the streets of Bayonne and St-Jean-de-Luz in the previous weeks. The refugees often had good grounds for accurate identification. The men who were now stalking them had once been their jailers, in some cases branded on their memories by the peculiar intimacy of torture or ill-treatment.

Lasa and Zabala themselves believed they were being followed by *guardia civiles* on the night they were, as we now know, kidnapped.

The evidence of ETA members and sympathisers alone would have been unconvincing, if it had not been supported by quite a few hard facts, and by the informed opinions of many who had no truck with the terrorists. Two days after Lasa and Zabala had vanished, four Spanish officers were arrested by a gendarme in Hendaye. They were attempting to drag an ETA leader, José María Larretxea, into the boot of their car. The Bilbao chief of police, Francisco Álvarez, openly acknowledged his responsibility for this incursion into foreign territory. Álvarez was also in charge of anti-terrorist co-ordination in the Basque Country. His men were finally released on bail, and failed to return to France to stand trial. When the unfortunate Segundo Marey was kidnapped in December, in the first operation publicly 'claimed' by the GAL, one of his kidnappers was arrested, in possession of dozens of French and Spanish police files on refugees. He also had the phone number of Francisco Álvarez's office in his pocket.

It did not take a rocket scientist, then, to deduce that the Spanish security forces were intimately involved in the GAL. Socialist politicians in the French Basque Country, who had no sympathy with ETA's aims or methods, were outraged by the GAL's violent disturbance of the local peace, and they immediately recognised the hand of the Spanish police in the attacks. The memory of the 1980 attack on the Bar Hendayais, where two French citizens were killed by mercenaries, was fresh in their minds. The alleged perpetrators had fled across the nearby border. They had then been arrested by Spanish police, who released them on the direct instructions of Manuel Ballesteros, head of Spanish national police intelligence.

After the release of Segundo Marey, the mayor of Hendaye, Raphael Lasallette, called on the French Ministry of the Interior to reach agreement with its Spanish counterpart to put an end to 'this tragic and intolerable' situation. The presence of plain-clothes Spanish police in French Basque towns, he said, was verifiable on a daily basis.[2] His words are a direct echo of a statement made by the French President, Valéry Giscard d'Estaing, after a Basque Spanish Battalion killing in 1979.[3] After the shooting of Mikel Goikoetxea (*Txapela*) at the end of 1983, the sub-prefect of Bayonne told *Le Monde* that the GAL were linked to the Spanish security forces.[4] The local Socialist MP, Jean-Pierre Destrade, directly attributed responsibility for the attacks to the Spanish police. He called for France to break off talks with the Spanish government on EEC entry.[5]

In so doing, he was going a step further than pointing to rotten apples in the Spanish police or army. He was implicitly accusing his Socialist colleagues from across the border of being the political mentors of the death squads. 'I believe that certain elements of the Spanish police are the effective components of the GAL,' he told the French press, 'and although the organisation may use French individuals, the resources, especially the finances, come from Spain.'[6] Such a step, however, had to be taken solely on the basis of speculation at this stage. The Spanish Socialists did not take kindly to such allegations, accusing Destrade of 'grave irresponsibility'.[7]

'THE ORIGINAL SIN WAS FRENCH': THE ROLLERCOASTER RELATIONSHIP BETWEEN PARIS AND MADRID

At first sight, it seems strange that the French Socialists failed to recognise any great difference between the new Spanish Socialist administration and the conservative governments of the transition period. Sometimes the French did not even seem to distinguish the Socialists from the authoritarian governments of the late Franco period. Ironically, it can be argued that France's culpable willingness to believe that nothing much had really changed in Spain by 1983, despite obvious evidence to the contrary, was one of the seeds of the GAL. 'You must never forget that the original sin of the history of the GAL was committed by the French,' José Luis Barbería, who was an *El País* correspondent in San Sebastián from 1980 to 1997, told me.[8]

As we saw in chapter 4, when the Spanish Socialists' first Interior Minister, José Barrionuevo, met his French opposite number, Gaston Deferre, for the first time in April 1983, he found his own inexperience matched by Deferre's ignorance. Deferre claimed not to know that the Spanish Basque provinces enjoyed autonomy – a status promised, and then denied, to the French Basques by his own party. He dismissed Barrionuevo's list of *etarras* living in France as 'old propaganda' and told him 'you should look for them in Spain'.[9]

The roots of this yawning gap in perception are complex and intertwined. Historically, the French tended to have a snobbish, superior attitude towards their southern neighbours, epitomised by the doubly racist jibe that 'Africa begins at the Pyrenees'. The Spanish, in their turn, suffer from bouts of anti-French xenophobia. There were also sharp conflicts of interest over economic issues, with France treating Spain's EEC application as a threat to its agricultural and fishing sectors, and Spain seeing France as the main obstacle to access to European markets.

The core of the immediate problem, however, was that, as Barrionuevo's deputy, Rafael Vera, puts it, 'there was no sign that [the French] saw that the reforms which the Spanish people had approved were leading to a real, true democracy. There was much underlying distrust towards the [reform] process.'[10]

Vera, who attended bilateral Interior meetings with the French over ten years, sees the origins of this distrust in the Spanish Civil War and its aftermath. Strong sentiments of solidarity bound the exiled anti-Francoists and the French anti-Nazi struggle. For many French people, ETA was the inheritor of a noble anti-fascist cause. Deferre, in his first month as Minister for the Interior, had compared the 'Basque patriots' of ETA to the heroes of the *Résistance*. (Deferre was himself a resistance veteran.) Postwar French governments had closed the border with Spain from 1946 to 1948, and strongly supported the ostracism of Spain by the United Nations until 1959.[11] Relations thereafter were more pragmatic, with a pattern emerging where the Spanish gave preference to purchasing French military hardware and other items in tacit exchange for political favours. This practice would continue when Spain became a democracy.

France's vaunted tradition as a land of asylum for political refugees, as we saw in chapter 3, strongly influenced policy on Basque political activists. Nevertheless, the view that France was at any stage a totally sympathetic sanctuary for ETA is difficult to sustain. Leading members of ETA were confined by the police to cities north of the French Basque Country, and deported to third states, even in the early 1960s, long before the organisation had claimed its first mortal victim. In 1964, one of ETA's seminal texts was banned by Paris because it advocated separatist insurrection in France as well as Spain.[12] ETA was declared illegal in France three years before Franco died. Public opinion, however, demanded that anti-ETA measures were implemented infrequently and often merely cosmetically. Extradition to Spain was unthinkable, since ETA's actions were considered to be politically motivated.

With the transition to democracy, and ETA's devastating escalation of armed actions in Spain, the French authorities did begin to take tougher measures against the refugees. But collaboration with their Spanish counterparts was hesitant and inconsistent. The abrupt ups and downs of the relationship have been well described as being 'like the teeth of a *sierra*'.[13] Under the conservative presidency of Giscard d'Estaing, co-operation peaked in early 1979, with the withdrawal of political refugee status from ETA members, the confinement of seventeen ETA leaders to an isolated area of the Alps, and the handover of seven refugees directly to the Spanish police.

It is important to note that this handover was not extradition. It was based on a little-used 'procedure of absolute urgency', whereby France could directly expel aliens considered a threat to public order. Nor did it indicate a firm policy shift: it would not be used again until 1986. In fact, in May 1979, a French appeal court refused Spanish extradition petitions against two very senior *etarras*, Mikel Goikoetxea (*Txapela*) and Miguel Ángel Apalategui (*Apala*), and released them.

The relationship between French conservative governments and their democratically elected Spanish counterparts, from 1977 to 1981, was never cordial. It was soured throughout by French agricultural priorities, which led to Giscard d'Estaing's lukewarm, when not obstructive, approach to Spain's application to join the EEC. It was periodically ruffled by disputes over fishing rights. Giscard d'Estaing was also concerned to give ETA no pretext for extending its armed campaign to France. Nor did he want to open a terrorist front in France with Iparretarrak, the French Basque organisation which ETA kept – more or less – under control.

'There was a sort of non-aggression pact [between ETA and the French authorities] and that was very difficult to break,' recalls Rafael Vera. 'ETA even gave the French police information on arms trafficking and ordinary criminal activity in the zone. [The French government feared that] French Basque terrorism would increase if there was more collaboration [between France and Spain].'[14]

In 1981, with François Mitterrand's Socialists now in power,[15] a Paris court did, for the first time, recognise that an *etarra*'s actions were criminal, not political, and recommended his extradition.[16] But it lies in the power of the French government to reject such a recommendation. After publicly wrestling with its conscience, and revealing a deep-seated conviction that extradition went against all the best French traditions, Paris turned down Madrid's request.[17] In the same year, the French Socialists restored political refugee status to a number of ETA members and supporters, including Domingo Iturbe Abásolo (*Txomin*), who was thought to have been ETA's chief of staff at the time.

As a result, when the Spanish Socialists came to power a year later under Felipe González, relations were 'not bad or mediocre, but execrable', in the words of a sympathetic French diplomat.[18]

Relations over the next five years form the backdrop to the GAL campaign and its investigation, and the following summary may be useful at this stage:

1983: Little progress towards collaboration, until the GAL come on the scene and González meets Mitterrand in late December.

1984: First big raid on ETA supporters by French police since 1979. Confinements and expulsions to third countries begin in earnest. Between January and April, seventeen refugees are expelled to third countries, and twenty-eight more confined to *départements* well away from the Basque border area.[19] González complains to the French media that he is still unhappy with the level of collaboration, but Spain agrees to buy French tanks, apparently in exchange for improved co-operation against ETA.[20] In June, Barrionuevo and Deferre sign 'Agreements of La Castellaña', in which the French explicitly acknowledge that 'a terrorist is not a political refugee'. Eugenio Etxebeste (*Antxon*), a senior member of ETA's executive committee, is expelled to Latin America in August. The French Foreign Minister, Roland Dumas, says that the Spanish government has agreed to collaborate against the GAL, and there is a lull in GAL actions after three refugees are extradited, for the first time ever, to Spain in September. The extraditions are highly controversial, and France does not extradite ETA suspects again until 1987. The total number deported to third countries during the year is twenty-eight.[21]

1985: Two senior *etarras*, Juan Lorenzo Lasa Mitxelena (*Txikierdi*) and Isidro Garalde (*Mamarru*), are arrested in France, but relations dip sharply as Paris backs off further extraditions in the face of political and media opposition. The GAL launch their biggest offensive from March through September. Spain signs up to EEC membership in June, with effect from 1 January 1986. France starts refusing to renew refugees' temporary residence permits on a large scale, but expels only five more activists to third countries during the year, and there are no further extraditions to Spain.

1986: The GAL carry out their most indiscriminate series of attacks, injuring children and culminating in the Bidarray killings. In the face of public outcry, GAL killings stop and French policy changes. ETA is legally designated as an 'association of wrong-doers' during the trial of Lasa Mitxelena and Garalde. The PSOE's U-turn on staying in NATO wins support in a referendum, promoting closer military-industrial bonding with France. Mitterrand has to 'co-habit' with conservative Prime Minister Jacques Chirac after March elections. Arab terrorism traumatises Paris. New Interior Minister Charles Pasqua says he is going to 'terrorise the terrorists'. Iturbe Abásolo is arrested in April; he is expelled to Gabon in July, and then to Algeria. New government approves extensive use of 'absolute urgency' procedure to expel militants directly to Spain, bypassing the judicial guarantees offered by the extradition process. France begins to hand over refugees on this basis in July; twenty-six are in Spanish hands by the end of the year. Pasqua's number two, Robert Pandraud, tells Vera that 'if you end this problem [GAL] and keep it under control, I assure you that from tomorrow we will begin to hand over ETA terrorists on the frontier'.[22] There are no more GAL attacks, except for one maverick killing in 1987. Many refugees go underground. ETA attacks French commercial interests in Spain. A Spanish intelligence operation leads French police to a major arms and documents find in the Sokoa factory in Hendaye, which proves beyond doubt to French public opinion that France has indeed been ETA's sanctuary and headquarters.

1987: The rhythm of expulsions speeds up, with a total of forty-one by the end of February, but most are not of significant figures. Two-thirds of them are released in Spain for lack of solid charges against them. It is rumoured that some of the expulsions are 'camouflaged reinsertions' – that is, ETA members acceding to the Spanish policy of pardon without exposing themselves to the wrath of their own organisation. Joint French–Spanish police units are set up in Paris and Bayonne. ETA's Hipercor bombing in Barcelona, with twenty-one civilian deaths and about thirty serious injuries, causes international outrage.[23] The killing of Juan Carlos García Goena in July, claimed by GAL, causes an sharp but short-lived crisis for Franco-Spanish collaboration. The arrest of Santiago Arróspide (*Santi Potros*) in September, with extensive documentation, is followed by the mass expulsion of seventy refugees, fifty-five of them to Spain. They include Miguel García (*Peque*), the first major ETA leader to be handed across the border. The first formal extradition since 1984 takes place in November, and from here on France will either extradite any known ETA leaders or jail them for offences in France before handing them over. Pandraud declares that it is 'unacceptable that terrorists should take refuge in France to be able to carry out their attacks against a friendly nation'.[24]

French policy, and public opinion, had turned around completely in the four years since the GAL had begun to operate. By the end of the 1987, the community which had nurtured ETA in the French Basque

Country had been definitively stripped away, leaving only the bones of an illegal underground organisation, and those French Basques willing to risk supporting them. Assessing this diplomatic victory for the Spanish Socialists, Rafael Vera says: 'I believe that, speaking objectively, the dirty war was a help.'[25]

The generic fingerprints of Spanish police involvement were clear enough at the scene of the GAL's crimes, though many pains would need to be taken before some of the individuals to whom they belonged could be identified. Going on to establish a link between those policemen and their new political masters would require great effort, courage and ingenuity by journalists and judges in three countries – Spain, France and Portugal – over the next fifteen years, and beyond. For many of those years the best evidence would be purely circumstantial. The catalogue of obstructions which González's government placed in the way of all investigators was perhaps the clearest indication that his cabinet had something to hide. The investigations have finally yielded the confessions of very senior Socialists, in a chain reaction which continues today, and could still reach González himself.

González's name was on the lips of pro-ETA demonstrators as soon as the GAL fired their first shots, but it is unlikely any of them imagined that his name would one day figure in a Spanish magistrate's report. The road to the indictment of the Socialist top brass would contain many detours, false trails and dead ends, and some of those who offered accurate guidance along it had – and have – very sinister motives. Nor did the road start with the Guardia Civil, the state agency which the GAL's targets had best reason to suspect. In fact, it would take twelve years for a substantial legal case to be made attributing GAL operations to elements of the Guardia Civil, Spain's most distinctive security force. The initial halting steps to the heart of the GAL were taken because other elements in the death squads behaved in an almost unbelievably slapdash fashion. Had it not been for the incompetence, arrogance and sheer greed of two middle-ranking Bilbao policemen, and the aura of impunity with which their superiors surrounded them, the political structures behind the GAL might remain a total enigma today.

The first material evidence about the GAL's structure, as we have seen, pointed immediately to Francisco Álvarez, then chief of police in Bilbao and co-ordinator of the Unified Counter-terrorist Command (MULC). He had taken responsibility for the botched operation against the ETA leader Larretxea in October 1983. He denied that the intention was kidnapping, let alone anything more sinister. He said the action was motivated by 'humanitarianism'. His men simply wanted to meet Larretxea to discuss ETA's kidnapping of a Spanish army captain, Martín Barrios, who was shot dead only days later. Things went wrong when the car in which Álvarez's men were travelling collided with Larretxea's scooter. Larretxea was being assisted, not abducted, when the French police happened on the scene, according to Álvarez's version. He received backing at the highest possible level when the Minister for the Interior, José Barrionuevo, said he took full political responsibility for the operation, a declaration Barrionuevo would repeat in court.[26]

A Spanish police officer, José Amedo, admits to having participated in an earlier operation of this nature, in which Spanish officers were also arrested by French police, and released discreetly after diplomatic intervention.[27] Naturally, the French were less amenable to diplomatic requests the second time around.

Álvarez's men were held for several weeks in Pau, but were released on bail on 8 December by Judge Michel Svahn, who was to be instrumental in freeing a number of key GAL suspects on technicalities.[28] They gave 'their word of honour as Spanish police' to return for trial. This high-sounding parole was angrily mocked by the French media when they all failed to reappear, and they were convicted in their absence. They could have been easily traced, since they had returned to active service in Spain. The Spanish authorities made no move to hand them over, responding to French requests with a single, most unhelpful, fax.

The GAL did not claim the Larretxea operation, but its timing, *modus operandi* and personnel suggest that, had it been successful, it would probably have been the group's first acknowledged action. The death squads made their public debut after the kidnapping of Segundo Marey on 4 December. This bungled operation was allegedly used to pressurise the French to expedite the bail application for the Spanish police imprisoned for the Larretxea kidnap attempt. This, at least, is the version of José Amedo, who played a major role in organising Marey's abduction: 'And it worked, because they were free within 24 hours,' he says.[29]

As we have seen, the indicators here again pointed directly to Francisco Álvarez. One of the kidnappers, Pedro Sánchez, was detained in France with the Bilbao police chief's phone number in his possession. He also had many photographs of refugees which originated from Spanish police files.[30]

There were several aspects to Sánchez's background that marked him out as a potential mercenary. He was a former member of the French Foreign Legion, was known to the police as a pimp, and had neo-Nazi sympathies. He might have been employed by the Basque industrial oligarchy to retaliate against ETA's campaign of extortion, a theory floated by police sources to the Spanish media at the time. But his links to Álvarez suggested a different employer. Álvarez was already on record as being broadly in favour of dirty war tactics against ETA. Even before he had been posted to the Basque Country, he had told a journalist that he saw no reason why a law-abiding democracy should not 'carry out illegal operations against those who use violence to undermine the State'.[31]

This kind of thinking was known to be current in police circles, where it might be expected, given the unreformed heritage of Francoism.[32] Amedo gives a fairly convincing, though no doubt self-serving, description of how legitimate anti-subversive surveillance shaded into illegal activities in the police mind-set at the time: 'At first we thought they were counter-terrorist operations, and that was as far as it would go. That was the idea I had. Little by little, month by month, they began to indicate new operations, and then you began to realise that you were involved in an affair which was going to have a certain importance, and that it was a question of state. But at the beginning, no, I didn't know what political decision had been taken. So one got involved in it, without knowing where it was going to end, or what importance it was going to have.'[33]

More surprisingly, disregard for the rule of law also found some favour among the suddenly all-powerful young *apparatchiks* of the PSOE. Julián Sancristóbal, for example, while he was still mayor of Ermua, used to tell anyone who would listen that 'I would sort [ETA] out in four days, practising "two for one"', something his fellow councillors understood to mean killing two *etarras* for every one of ETA's victims.[34] Sancristóbal's mentor, the Basque PSOE leader Ricardo García Damborenea, repeatedly used the rhetoric of fighting ETA on its own ground, with its own weapons.[35] The head of police intelligence at the time, Jesús Martínez Torres, has given evidence that Barrionuevo's ministry was 'well disposed' towards kidnapping *etarras* in France in the autumn of 1983.[36] Felipe González himself is reported to have said that 'the terrorists have to be crushed with their own hands, those of terrorism' at a private dinner in Bilbao in November 1983.[37]

Such seductively tough arguments were familiar enough in the early 1980s for *El País*, a newspaper considered to be close to the new government at this time, to feel a need to counter them. In a stinging editorial after the GAL killed Ramón Oñederra (*Kattu*), the group's first acknowledged assassination, *El País* declared: 'Some people recently arrived in public office seem, on occasions, to be affected with the sickness of "reasons of State". For these arrogant discoverers of the intestines of Leviathan, the defenders of constitutional guarantees and human rights are . . . ridiculous puritans, ignorant of the secret codes of public life. But democrats must never sacrifice the few principles on which civilised existence rests.' The leader writer called on González's government to use 'the powerful resources of the State in the pursuit of the authors, accomplices and protectors' of this 'phantasmal gang of murderers which calls itself the GAL'.[38]

It was a call that neither that government nor any of González's subsequent administrations would feel inclined to heed. And, for the time being, there was no great pressure from Spanish public opinion for them to do so. Having grown up under an authoritarian regime, the average Spanish citizen's understandable outrage at ETA's offensive may have created a general acceptance that the terrorists should be taken out by any means necessary.[39]

Javier Pradera, a Communist for many years in the Franco period, now a senior writer with *El País* and considered a supporter of the Socialists on several unpopular issues, remembers numerous conversations with PSOE leaders around this time. They never, he said, acknowledged any role in the GAL in so many words, 'but there is non-verbal communication, and from their non-verbal communication I have not the slightest doubt [of their participation]. I told them that this is a road where you know the beginning, but you don't know how it will end.'[40]

SORTING OUT INTERIOR: THE HARD MEN FROM BILBAO TAKE THE HOT SEATS IN MADRID

The Ministry of the Interior seethed with internal tensions and public scandals following José Barrionuevo's unexpected appointment as the first Socialist minister for law and order in 1982. As we saw in chapter 4, Carlos Sanjuán, the man whom many in the PSOE had wanted and expected to be minister, was a thorn in Barrionuevo's side as his number two. The minister's friend and confidant, Rafael Vera, was in trouble as Director of State Security, clashing openly and repeatedly not only with Sanjuán but with the police unions. Barrionuevo had followed his instincts in retaining officers from Franco's hated Brigada de Investigación Político-Social in senior police positions. But some of Sanjuán's appointees – policemen committed to democracy and shocked at the Socialists' failure to purge the security apparatus – were still, in Barrionuevo's view, obstructing the ministry's work.

In this context, it is worth recalling Vera's perception of the dilemma of the new administration. He insists that there was no option but to keep the Francoist commanders in their places, and win them over to democracy: 'Those were terrible years,' he says. 'I was a Socialist, which the generals and police superintendents regarded with contempt. Starting from mutual distrust, we had to win the respect and even the admiration of those who were against us. These were the generals of Franco, the police of Franco. It was a very complicated process. You would have to have lived it [to understand it]. Yes, we tried to change the commanders, we even looked for candidates to do it. But when we saw the list [of Socialist candidates] for the Ministry of the Interior there was nobody, the list was empty.' The few police with Socialist sympathies, he claims, 'wanted office jobs. None of them wanted the responsibility of fighting terrorism. Go to Bilbao, go to San Sebastián? Not one.'[41]

In early February 1984, Sanjuán resigned, on the ostensible grounds that his membership of parliament was legally incompatible with his job. The truth was that Sanjuán was ideologically incompatible with Barrionuevo's 'realists'. The minister's team believed that the threat from ETA justified the retention of experienced anti-terrorist officers like Jesús Martínez Torres (head of police intelligence), despite his unsavoury reputation as a tough anti-communist interrogator under the Franco regime.

I put Vera's pragmatic argument to Manuel Vázquez Montalbán, a novelist and acerbic social commentator who has brilliantly caricatured the 'recycling' of Francoist police in books like *Murder in the Central Committee*. He had heard a similar analysis from Felipe González himself, and he rejects it absolutely.[42]

'It had a price . . . I have friends who were tortured by the Francoist police, tortured by hand, they were craftsmen. The Socialists should have put the police under the control of democrats. They should have taken advantage of the strength of their 10 million votes, they should have explained the difficulties of exercising power . . . instead, they kept the rubbish and they had to digest it and metabolise it, and what happens when you metabolise rubbish is that you produce shit.'[43]

Nevertheless, the pragmatic view prevailed, and Barrionuevo had removed most of its critics from positions of influence within Interior by early 1984. He replaced Sanjuán with Vera in the official number two position as his under-secretary. Whether this was really a promotion or a case of getting kicked upstairs is open to question. Vera now likes to suggest he was sidelined to bureaucratic impotence at this time. Given the crimes committed by Interior appointees over the next few years, he is possibly really arguing that he was not responsible for their activities.

There is no doubt, however, that Barrionuevo gave a major slice of real power to Julián Sancristóbal, the tough young Civil Governor of Vizcaya. Sancristóbal replaced Vera in charge of all anti-terrorist operations as Director of State Security. He brought with him the Bilbao police chief and anti-terrorist co-ordinator, Francisco Álvarez, who had acknowledged his role in the Larretxea kidnap attempt and was already implicated in the kidnapping of Segundo Marey. Álvarez was made chief of a new Intelligence and Special Operations Committee (Gabinete de Información y Operaciones Especiales – GAIOE). Sancristóbal also brought to Madrid the influence of the firebrand Basque Socialist politician Ricardo García Damborenea, who would have an unofficial role as ideologue of Interior's anti-terrorist policy over the next two years. By 8 February 1984, the day on which the GAL carried out their third and fourth acknowledged killings, three of the men who have since admitted their participation in the dirty war had therefore been placed, formally or informally, at the apex of the Socialist government's anti-terrorist command structure. They would remain there until October 1986, the year in which the GAL, strictly speaking, ceased to operate.

Their period in power has been presented by Vera's own apologist, Eliseo Bayo, as a 'low-intensity coup d'état' by Basque Socialists intent on imposing a crudely belligerent policy against ETA.[44] The reality is that these hard men from the north were freely appointed by Barrionuevo, and consolidated his already established policies. They did clash with Vera on occasions, but never once – that we know of so far – on any issue related to the GAL. On the day the new men formally took up their positions, Barrionuevo attended the launch of Damborenea's book *La Encrucijada Vasca* (Basque Crossroads). In his memoir, published as recently as 1997, he warmly relates how he sat up all night reading this manifesto for belligerence against Basque nationalism, and describes it as a 'good, clear and well-conceived book'.[45]

Pedro Sánchez, held for the Marey kidnapping, was released in June 1984, again through the offices of Judge Svahn,[46] but he was quickly rearrested. In one of the most bizarre stories to emerge from the whole GAL period, one of his fellow kidnappers has alleged that a Spanish police officer[47] arranged to have Sánchez slowly poisoned, in order to stop him talking. Mohand Talbi, convicted in France for the Marey kidnapping, told a Spanish investigating magistrate that a French prison official had been bribed to administer small quantities of a cancer-inducing drug to Sánchez over a long period. This allegation has never been proved, and is probably unprovable, but Sánchez did die of cancer, without revealing any of his secrets, in December 1986.[48]

The GAL claimed the lives of seven victims in the first six months of 1984. Most of the attacks had an almost uncanny surgical precision, but there were also signs of clumsiness, resulting in arrests on both sides of the border, which would start to outline the profile of the group's foot-soldiers and field commanders. Jean-Pierre Cherid, a familiar mercenary figure from the first dirty war, died in March as he attempted to plant a bomb in Bayonne.

The man who replaced Cherid as the senior mercenary on the killing ground, Jean-Philippe Labade, was arrested with three other mercenaries after the killing of Tomás Peréz Revilla in Biarritz in June. Nearly a dozen other French mafiosi were arrested in connection with GAL crimes in April 1984, but they were all released courtesy of Judge Svahn. By the time a superior court had ordered their rearrest, in November of the following year, none of them could be found.[49] The same judge also let Labade out on bail in November 1984, whereupon he promptly made his way back to Portugal to organise new groups of mercenaries. In June 1985 Labade's former lover Jeanette Cassiede gave detailed evidence to a Bayonne judge, linking him to both the Spanish police and anti-ETA terrorism.[50]

Judge Svahn played a remarkable role in releasing GAL suspects on very minor technical grounds, a scruple he did not exercise so finely in other cases, according to his critics. The police prefect for the region, Alain Tourré, commented to *Libération* that, with nearly twenty arrests in the first few months of GAL activity, 'we have still not put the GAL totally out of action, far from it', because 'we have not been able to reach into Spain and find the commanders'.[51] Nevertheless, it must have been extremely frustrating to see suspects of the calibre of Labade, Sánchez and others walk free.[52] (Labade's second group of mercenaries launched their indiscriminate attacks on French Basque bars a little over a year after he was released.) Judge Gilbert Costeaux, who was as diligent at jailing GAL suspects as Svahn was at releasing them, gave up his job in 1985, and though he insisted that his decision was unrelated to such frustration – or to fear for his own safety – judicial sources in Bayonne believed he had been deliberately sidelined.[53]

Meanwhile, Daniel Fernández Aceña and Mariano Moraleda Muñoz, small-time ultras, had been arrested in Spain in March 1984. They were fleeing across the border after killing Jean-Pierre Leiba by mistake on the railway tracks in Hendaye. This was the occasion on which the Spanish deputy Prime Minister, Alfonso Guerra, made the curious remark that he had 'the impression that these are people who want to prove their worthiness to join the GAL, but do not belong to that organisation'.[54] Guerra seemed to betray a surprising intimacy with the membership system of a group about whom his government persistently claimed to have no information whatsoever. He has never explained the source of his knowledge.

Both detainees made allegations about the involvement of the Guardia Civil and the Spanish army in the GAL, which might have been very fertile had they been energetically investigated. But no one checked them out fully at the time, and the suspects, who in any case became notorious as unreliable witnesses, subsequently withdrew them.

The arrests of mercenaries, right-wing fanatics and gangsters, and especially the identification of the incinerated remains of the veteran Cherid, gave the GAL a public profile. It fitted very closely with the shadowy organisations which had prosecuted the first dirty war under the patronage of Francoist police and military intelligence officers. Far from clarifying matters, this profile was misleading. It failed to pinpoint what was most distinctive about the GAL: that it was a highly co-ordinated operation, involving the security forces and civil service of a state which loudly protested its full adhesion to democratic principles. The focus on the low-life soldiers of fortune who carried out *some* of the GAL's dirty work conveniently blurred the identities of those who organised *all* the group's operations, and participated directly in most of the efficient ones.

This thesis that the GAL had a unified command structure within the state apparatus has, of course, been contested, with more vigour than conviction: 'It is well said that the GAL are plural, not singular. There was no organisation behind the GAL, that's for sure,' asserts Rafael Vera. 'On the contrary, they were isolated groups, because now they are talking about a 'green GAL', a 'brown GAL' of the police and so on.[55] I believe it will be possible to demonstrate this. They were different groups, though it's true they were acting on a particular front, outside the law . . . but not within an organisation.'[56] Any disinterested reading of the evidence to date points in the opposite direction. The views of the former 'strong man' of the Ministry of the Interior have to be seen in the context of his judicial situation at the time I interviewed him: he had been indicted for *organising* the GAL.[57]

In the spring of 1984, the first major press investigations began to appear in Spain, based on 'revelations' from individuals who claimed to be GAL mercenaries. *Diario 16*, the newspaper which would investigate the GAL most successfully and courageously in the 1980s, produced the first of many dossiers in March and April 1984. 'How the GAL kills' and 'How the GAL acts' contained a mixture of fact and fantasy. Some of the latter, particularly on the group's funding, may have been deliberately planted as disinformation by the newspaper's sources. These sources were able to show the journalists weapons and copious police files on *etarras* as proof of their authenticity. *Cambio 16* published its first major GAL exposés in May, on the basis of similar sources, focusing on a detailed account of the botched operation which cost Cherid his life.

The interviewees colourfully described the GAL as 'an exterminating angel'.[58] The GAL, they asserted, 'do not kill innocent people', though Leiba's killing already gave a direct lie to such an ambiguous claim. The interviewees did, however, point out one of the critical differences between their activities and those of the previous dirty war: their predecessors had been motivated by extreme rightist ideology and targeted Basque nationalists, democrats and anti-Francoists generally; the GAL were dedicated to hunting down only members of ETA (and, by mistake or otherwise, uninvolved French civilians).[59] Those who argue that there was an unbroken continuity between the two dirty wars naturally choose to gloss over this distinction.

These articles tended to focus on the detail of GAL activity – how they falsified documents, filed gun barrels to confuse forensic experts, or 'charged for their services' – rather than the big picture. There were general references to assistance from individual Spanish police officers, but, unsurprisingly, no hard information on the group's structure. As for the French security forces, the interviewees alleged that the gendarmes were collaborating with ETA, and actively obstructing the GAL.

There was no suggestion that Spanish police, still less *guardia civiles*, were *directly* involved in GAL operations. The articles confirmed a general impression that most if not all GAL activists were bounty-hunters. *Diario 16* did, however, produce a remarkable list which, without attributing any specific role in the GAL to any of them, mentioned the names of several generals and senior Socialists. They included the Minister for the Interior, José Barrionuevo, his newly appointed Director of State Security, Julián Sancristóbal, and generals Andrés Cassinello and José Antonio Sáenz de Santamaría. These were suspicions which would take a long time to mature: all of them were investigated for GAL crimes in 1995 and 1996. No charges have been brought against either general, but Sancristóbal has since confessed to his involvement in the Marey kidnapping, and Barrionuevo, though he still protests his innocence, has been convicted for it. Ironically, Sancristóbal is quoted in one of the *Cambio 16* articles as being 'worried' by the GAL, adding that 'this administration will not tolerate anyone taking the law into his own hands'.[60]

There would be no other dramatic developments in the investigation of the GAL in 1984, though significant clues did emerge. Overall, the most striking fact was the complete absence of even a pretence at a serious investigation of the GAL by any of the Spanish authorities. When the question was raised, the stock response was that the GAL did not commit crimes on Spanish territory, so they could not pursue any leads. Julen Elgorriaga, the young Socialist Party Civil Governor of Guipúzcoa, the province closest to the GAL's killing ground, liked to indulge his rather weak sense of punning when asking about their activities.

'Los GAL?' he would say, peering myopically back at the journalist concerned, and affecting bafflement. 'Sí, los GAL que asesinan a Etarras' ('The GAL who assassinate *etarras*'), the journalist might reply. 'Ah,' Elgorriaga liked to respond, grinning broadly and putting on a thick French accent, *'Les GAL. Les GAL. Mais c'est un problème Galo.'* ('It's a Gallic problem.')[61] In 1995, Elgorriaga was charged with personal participation in the kidnapping, torture and murder of Lasa and Zabala.

Joking apart, the case that the GAL were none of Spain's business was a decidedly thin one. Most of the victims were Spanish citizens, albeit reluctant and dissident ones. There was hard evidence that GAL *comandos* were using Spanish territory as a sanctuary, confirmed by the detention of Aceña and Muñoz as they fled across the border from Hendaye. Substantial charges had been made by responsible politicians in a neighbouring country that elements of the Spanish security forces were involved, as they clearly had been in the Larretxea episode. In late 1984, the Spanish disclaimer should have collapsed altogether, when the GAL killed Santiago Brouard in Bilbao.

Yet it was the line the Spanish Socialists and their security chiefs would stick to rigidly. During the judicial investigation of Brouard's death, the police intelligence chief, Martínez Torres, was asked by the judge to produce his files on the GAL. He handed in a collection of press clippings. In 1985, General Emilio Alonso Manglano, who headed the Spanish military intelligence service, the CESID, told a closed parliamentary commission that his agency was investigating the GAL, but they 'possessed very little data on the subject'.[62] Given the mounting body of evidence in the 1990s that the CESID was directly involved in the dirty war, this declaration seems to have concealed a lot more than it revealed.

The Bilbao police again came into the frame of investigations in 1985. Le Monde reported in May that Judge Costeaux had received evidence from the French police that Labade, arrested for the murder of Pérez Revilla in June 1984, had had a rendezvous on the Spanish border shortly before the killing. The people he met were driving a car whose number plate was registered as a vehicle used by the Bilbao police's anti-terrorist intelligence service. The French judge and his Spanish counterpart confirmed this information after receiving two false identifications from Álvarez's department.[63] The province's former Civil Governor, Julián Sancristóbal, claimed in response that the number plates had been annulled in 1983, adding that he found Le Monde's publication of the information 'really disagreeable'. The paper responded with comments from French police sources dismissing this version of events. The sources added that they could not imagine why a terrorist group would choose the annulled registration of a police car for false number plates. This incident led to questions in the Spanish parliament.

The same month, Cambio 16 published a series of long articles by José Díaz Herrera and Rafael Cid which claimed to reveal the GAL's security force connections. They quoted an anonymous French judge who assured them that he had proof of Spanish police links to the GAL, and they had a verbatim account of the shooting of Eugenio Gutiérrez Salazar (Tigre) in February 1984 by a man who claimed to have participated in the operation. However, the authors focused on rehashing material from the first dirty war, sometimes confusingly implying that the GAL had also existed during this period.

The first prison sentences for GAL-related crimes were handed down, in both France and Spain, in 1985. The first convictions were relatively insignificant. Two mercenaries were sentenced to five years at a Bayonne hearing in April for criminal association and illegal possession of arms. This was one of the very few instances where the French police actually succeeded in detaining suspects before they carried out an attack.[64] In Spain, Daniel Fernández Aceña and Mariano Moraleda Muñoz were convicted, and Victor Manuel Navascués Gil found not guilty, of the murder of Jean-Pierre Leiba, at a Madrid hearing in December. Aceña and Muñoz were each sentenced to twenty-nine years.

Arrests continued, mostly in France, throughout the year. The *comando* believed to be responsible for Javier Galdeano's death in March was arrested in Paris a few weeks later. Two of the most important arrests in France in this year, however, were made by citizens, not the police. Pierre Baldés was chased and seized by bystanders after he killed Benoit Pecastaing and wounded several others in Bayonne in March. Likewise, Pierre Frugoli and Lucien Mattei were courageously and successfully pursued by a witness to the quadruple killing at the Hotel Monbar in the same city in September. Baldés and Mattei would go down for murder maintaining a vow of silence, but Frugoli would provide familiar if inconclusive evidence which pointed towards a Spanish police officer as the man who had recruited him.

In a significant development in November, three gangsters from Marseilles, charged with the attempted murder of two Basque refugees, claimed they had been paid by 'the Spanish secret services'.[65] As a result of their statements, the French would seek the extradition of Georges Mendaille from Spain. Despite his clear implication in GAL activities, the Spanish government dragged its feet on this issue for no less than ten years. This is one of a number of instances which clearly expose the mendacity of Barrionuevo's claim that 'all the requests which the French made of us were always complied with'.[66]

The year 1985 had not been a happy one for French–Spanish collaboration against ETA, despite agreement being reached over Spain's entry into the EEC in June. That same month, *El País* reported that the wave of GAL attacks during the spring had 'surprised and profoundly irritated the French Government, who had taken for granted the disappearance of these bounty-hunters from the scene'.[67] The French regional police prefect, Alain Tourré, said that the dirty war made it harder for his men to keep track of ETA members, who had been driven into deep cover by the death squads. It also appeared that, while the first wave of GAL attacks had actually dented the local population's support for ETA and the refugees, opinion was now swinging back in their favour and perceiving them as victims. In any case, French collaboration against ETA had slowed down drastically.

In November 1985, an internal source pointed for the first time at the Guardia Civil as the driving force behind the GAL. José Luis Cervero was the first of several members of the force to go public on its, and his own, involvement in the dirty war. He told Antonio Rubio and Manuel Cerdán of *Interviú*, two of the journalists who most persistently investigated the subject, that he had personal experience of the Guardia Civil's involvement in the first dirty war, and that he was certain that the whole GAL operation was directed by a *guardia civil*, backed up by staff in the Ministry of the Interior.

At the time, Cervero had been sacked from the Guardia Civil over a fraud conviction, which was later quashed. In the meantime he worked as an investigative journalist himself, under the pseudonym Jesús Mendoza. He offered to repeat the allegations made by him in *Interviú* in court or before a parliamentary commission. His offer has not been taken up.

The spate of indiscriminate GAL attacks in February 1986, starting with the shooting of two young children and a number of customers in the Bar Batxoki in Bayonne, and ending with the killing of a sixty-year-old farmer and his sixteen-year-old niece in Bidarray, prompted new demands for a Spanish investigation of the group. Even the conservative French daily *Le Figaro* reminded its readers that these killings were undoubtedly the work of a group 'closely related to the Spanish secret services and police'.[68]

'Nobody in their right mind', wrote *El País*, 'could even suggest that members of the international mafia are killing members of ETA on their own initiative, inflamed . . . by their love of the values of western civilisation. After what has been heard in various trials both in France and Spain, it is fitting to ask: Who recruits, organises, arms, supplies and pays the mercenaries of the GAL? Who gives the green light for their murders, points out their victims, and gives the order to fire? Who protects their strategic withdrawal towards the Spanish frontier? If silence is the only answer to these questions, it should not be forgotten that there are occasions when silence is the most eloquent of attitudes.'[69]

The next day, the Minister for the Interior, José Barrionuevo, broke his silence only in order to declare that he had nothing to say. He was reporting to the parliamentary justice commission on the application of anti-terrorist laws. When he was asked why the GAL did not figure in his report, he trotted out the line that 'the GAL have not acted in Spain'. He made the apparent concession that 'he did not rule out as a hypothesis that some public servants may have an involvement in terrorism'.[70] Then he made it clear he was referring to a municipal policeman accused of collaborating with ETA! He assured his listeners that no protection would be extended to any state employee involved in criminal activities. His words must be tested against the performance of his administration when the first major GAL figures came before the Spanish courts.

Outrage at the GAL's February onslaught would be complemented during the year by judicial and media revelations which consolidated suspicions that the Spanish security forces were deeply and broadly involved in the dirty war. In February 1986, Juan José Rodríguez Díaz was arrested in Madrid for supplying arms for the murder of Santiago Brouard, the starting-point in a shambles of a trial which has continued for many years, and has raised more questions than it has answered. The first prosecutor appointed, Emilio Valerio, demanded the investigation of the intelligence services of the Guardia Civil and the CESID in relation to the killing.[71] In the Madrid trial of the unit convicted for the murder of Robert Caplanne, it emerged that the leader, Ismael Miquel, had been able to abscond because of his contacts as a long-term police informer.[72] He was later arrested in Thailand on a drugs charge, trumped up, according to some sources, to keep him far away for good.

Meanwhile, some of Barrionuevo's senior functionaries got a grilling on French television in April, when the blacked-out figure of a Spanish policeman alleged that the GAL had been created at a 1983 meeting attended by the man who was about to become Chief of Staff of the Guardia Civil, General Andrés Cassinello. Also present, the anonymous policeman said, were Barrionuevo's deputy, Rafael Vera, and, hardly surprisingly, Francisco Álvarez. A notorious Francoist police officer, Antonio González Pacheco, nicknamed 'Billy the Kid', told the programme that he was 'only a small-time player, paying for the errors of my superiors'. Asked about the GAL, he told the presenters they should 'direct their questions to the Ministry of the Interior'.

Both Julián Sancristóbal and Francisco Álvarez appeared on the programme. Sancristóbal denied any connection between Interior and the GAL, and insisted that Pacheco no longer worked as an anti-terrorist advisor. Álvarez said he could neither confirm nor deny that Pacheco was connected to the GAL, 'but I can say that this gentleman has no evidence to prove that I belong to that organisation'. Asked to swear on his word as a practising Catholic, Álvarez declined, asking the presenters to be content with a simple, unsworn denial.[73]

The programme had a big impact in Spain, where its salient details were reproduced extensively in the print media, and then rebroadcast by the Catalan channel TV3. Pressure was building on the administration to investigate the GAL, with petitions from associations of lawyers, judges and academics. Embarrassing information began to emerge from court hearings in Italy, where it was established that Spanish police had protected Italian neo-fascists and employed them in the first dirty war.[74] Worse, the Socialists had refused to extradite one of them in 1984, on the grounds that the crime he was wanted for was 'political', a singular stance considering the PSOE's demand that the French should extradite suspected *etarras*.[75]

Unknown to the public, the GAL had effectively already ceased to operate at this stage. (The killing of Juan Carlos García Goena in the summer of 1987 was claimed, and probably carried out, by members of the GAL, but they appear to have been acting on their own initiative and for their own personal motives.) Yet in May 1986 the French Minister for the Interior, Charles Pasqua, made an extraordinary 'lapse', in his own words, when he described the GAL as being made up of 'persons paid by a State to come and settle accounts on our territory'. He had meant to say, he said, that the GAL were 'people paid or inspired by citizens of a foreign country'.[76] Lapse or not, the original statement must have at least rattled his Spanish opposite number.

If his words were worrying, Pasqua's deeds were a source of considerable satisfaction to Barrionuevo in this period. France's new conservative government was more amenable to anti-terrorist collaboration with Spain than its Socialist predecessors. Since coming to power in March, the authorities had detained and jailed ETA's top man at the time, Domingo Iturbe Abásolo, and would expel him to Gabon in July. A trickle of expulsions of refugees to Spain the same month was about to turn into a flood. If the GAL's main aim had been to create the conditions for such collaboration, they had made themselves redundant.

That was certainly the conclusion drawn by the journalists Melchor Miralles and José Macca in *Diario 16* in June.[77] They pointed out that ETA had killed eight people since the end of February, but that there had not been a single 'reply' from the GAL. They quoted unnamed Interior sources as confirming that France had agreed to increased co-operation on the condition that Spain made sure the GAL 'disappeared from the scene'. Though Miralles and Macca don't make the point explicitly, the fact that the GAL could 'disappear' without a single new arrest being made suggests that Interior had had a remarkable, even an intimate, degree of control over the GAL's activities. A savage summer offensive from ETA killed fourteen *guardia civiles* in two bombings in July, within a month of this article's appearance.[78] The GAL's guns still remained silent.

That same month, another former *guardia civil* who claimed to have a great deal of information about the GAL walked into the offices of *Interviú*.[79] For two months, José Velázquez Soriano assisted Cerdán and Rubio towards their second major coup in the journalistic investigation of the dirty war.

In 'I was a member of the GAL', he offered a graphic account of several of the GAL's first operations, including two foiled attempts to kidnap the leader of the Comandos Autónomos, Salegui Elorza, in the summer before the GAL first came to public knowledge.[80] Soriano said that the GAL had been made up of two distinct sections: members of the Guardia Civil on active service, commanded by officers, and international mercenaries commanded by Jean-Pierre Cherid. Both groups, he said, used the same infrastructure and intelligence sources.

He claimed he had participated personally, in a back-up unit, during the kidnapping of Segundo Marey and the killing of Oñederra and Goikoetxea. His own code-name was *Txema*, and he listed the code-names of a number of other GAL members, including *Beltza*, a senior officer.[81] *Beltza* seems to have been a blood-thirsty individual. At one point, his men had eight members of the Comandos Autónomos in their gunsights in France, and rang him to ask if they should open fire. According to Soriano, *Beltza* replied that he was 'not interested in killing eight, but rather in killing many more, and for that reason it was necessary to take their leader alive', so that they could find out where the rest of his comrades were hiding.

Days after the first *Interviú* piece was published, *Diario 16* pointedly reported that *Beltza* was the nickname given by his men to the senior commander at the barracks in Intxaurrondo.[82] Lieutenant-Colonel Enrique Rodríguez Galindo was reputed to be the most efficient, and most ruthless, officer in the field against ETA. Galindo was a man of formidable charisma and consummate professionalism, who seemed to have found himself in the right place at the right time.[83] Army officers of his stamp found welcome opportunities for 'glory' and 'honour' (and accelerated promotion) in service with the Guardia Civil in the Basque conflict. Just as the Moroccan wars had offered promotion and adventure, in the early part of the century, to men frustrated by the end of Empire in 1898,[84] so 'the northern war', as they liked to call it, offered men like Galindo stimulating careers which were generally lacking in the peacetime, democratic Spanish army in the 1980s. Galindo led Intxaurrondo as though it were a swashbuckling foreign legion outpost in hostile territory, and his men idolised him for it.

Perhaps Cerdán and Rubio were getting too close to the fire, because the second section of the five-part series they had announced appeared in truncated form, without their by-line, and the next three parts never appeared at all. According to their own account, they were called into their office at three in the morning, and asked to endorse cuts which they found unacceptable. Their editor resigned shortly afterwards.

Meanwhile, Soriano, who had previously independently verified his account to a Belgian television correspondent, was arrested, and told a judge that the whole story was an invention. He had suffered a heart attack during interrogation by his former comrades, and was constantly accompanied by several *guardia civiles* in his court appearances. The authors of the report were, however, cleared of all charges of slandering the Guardia Civil, and Soriano resurfaced as a prosecution witness in 1996, insisting that he had withdrawn his original account under duress.[85]

Despite the clues which now littered the trail to the Guardia Civil barracks at Intxaurrondo, the 'worthy ones'[86] of the Guardia Civil would not be seriously pursued in the courts until the bones of Lasa and Zabala were identified, eight years later. The investigation of the GAL, both judicial and journalistic, would turn sharply – and, it seemed for a long time, permanently – in another direction early in 1987.

NOTES

1   This phrase was used by Lord Denning, the senior English jurist, in reference to a legal action by the 'Birmingham Six', convicted for the IRA bombing of two pubs in Birmingham in November 1974 which killed twenty-one people. Lord Denning said in 1980 that if the Six were able to prove – as they ultimately were – that their convictions had been obtained through police perjury and police violence: 'This is such an appalling vista that every sensible person in the land would say: "It cannot be right these actions should go any further."' He refused them permission to take the action, and they were not freed for another eleven years. (See *The Irish Times*, 15 March 1991 and 6 March 1999.) His position seems similar to the view of much of the Spanish establishment on the dangers of revealing the truth about the GAL. The contrary view is that democratic systems are strengthened by investigations into their dark places. The British justice system, for example, is all the healthier for the vindication of the Birmingham Six, and would be healthier still had that vindication not been obstructed for so long.

2   *El País*, 15 December 1983.

3   'It is intolerable that the Spanish police should come here to settle scores on French territory.' Quoted in Francisco Letamendía, *Historia del Nacionalismo Vasco y de ETA*, 3 vols. (San Sebastián: R&B Ediciones, 1994), vol. 2, p. 325.

4   Quoted in Sagrario Morán, *ETA entre España y Francia* (Madrid: Editorial Complutense, 1997), p. 185.

5   *Egin*, 'Guerra Sucia' series, January/February 1995, no. 5.

6   *El País*, 15 July 1988.

7   Ibid.

8   Interview with José Luis Barbería, San Sebastián, June 1996. While it is easy to accept that French policy contributed to the conditions that fostered the establishment of the GAL, it does not follow that this situation justifies the dirty war or made it inevitable.

9   Morán, op. cit., pp. 173–4, and José Barrionuevo, *2,001 Días en Interior* (Barcelona: Ediciones B, 1997), pp. 57–9.

10   Interview with Rafael Vera, Madrid, November 1997.

11   Spain was formally admitted to the UN in 1955, but was not permitted to participate in all its organisations until four years later. See Morán, op. cit., p. 21.

12 The text was *La Insurrección en Euskadi*. Federico Sarrailh de Ihartza, the nationalist ideologue whose *Vasconia*, published the previous year under the pseudonym Federico Krutwig, had influenced this pamphlet, was expelled from France at the same time. See Federico Sarrailh de Ihartza (under the pseudonym Federico Krutwig), *Vasconia* (Buenos Aires: Norbait, 1962); Morán, op. cit., p. 87; Gurutz Jáuregui Bereciartu, *Ideología y Estrategia Política de ETA*, 2nd edn (Madrid: Siglo XXI de España, 1985), pp. 211–14; John Sullivan, *ETA and Basque Nationalism* (London: Routledge, 1988), pp. 41–5.

13 Journalist Ramón Acuña, quoted in Morán, op. cit., p. 195.

14 Interview with Rafael Vera, Madrid, November 1997.

15 A French Socialist politician, Guy Carcasonne, makes the interesting suggestion that there was a major element of bad faith in the French Socialist attitude to Spain, because France had not effectively supported the Spanish Republic against Franco, and, with brief exceptions, had pragmatically accepted his dictatorship. 'The French left came to power with an enormous sense of guilt towards Spain. We therefore had . . . a caricatured and quite romantic image of ETA as an anti-Francoist organisation.' Quoted in Morán, op. cit., p. 166.

16 The *etarra* was Tomás Linaza, accused of participating in the killing of six *guardia civiles* in 1980.

17 There were very sharp exchanges between the Spanish government and France on this issue. The Spanish Foreign Minister said that 'if Linaza is not extradited, France will cease to be the homeland of the rights of man and become nothing more than a refuge of assassins and terrorists'. See Morán, op. cit., p. 133.

18 Pierre Guidoni, who became ambassador in Madrid in 1983. Ibid., p. 165.

19 Ibid., p. 195.

20 This was not a popular decision with armaments experts, but it was well understood. 'At the end of the day, if the AMX-32 [tanks] can finish off ETA, they will do something which no other tank in the world can do', one Spanish tank commander said laconically. Ibid., p. 191.

21 Ibid., p. 211.

22 Interview with Rafael Vera, Madrid, November 1997. According to his own account, Pandraud warned Barrionuevo that he would 'stop it all [the expulsions] if there are anti-separatist attacks by GAL in France'. Quoted in Morán, op. cit., p. 242. There is no reference to this warning in Barrionuevo, op. cit.

23 José María Calleja, *Contra la Barbarie* (Madrid: Temas de Hoy, 1997), pp. 271–3.

24 Quoted in Morán, op. cit., p. 260.

25 Interview with Rafael Vera, Madrid, November 1997.

26 *El País*, 22 June 1991.

27 Interview with José Amedo, Madrid, October 1997.

28 Ricardo Arques and Melchor Miralles, *Amedo: El Estado contra ETA* (Barcelona: Plaza y Janés/Cambio 16, 1989), p. 161; Letamendía, op. cit., vol. 3, p. 25.

29 Interview with José Amedo, Madrid, October 1997. Amedo's statements always have to be treated with great caution. His version coincides with the sequence of events: Marey was kidnapped on 4 December, the Spanish police were released on 8 December, and Marey was released on 14 December. On the other hand, there is substantial evidence that the French had decided to release the Spanish police before Marey was kidnapped. The Spanish Supreme Court ruled that the release of the Spanish police had been a

condition for Marey's release, in a particularly controversial aspect of their 1998 judgement. See ch. 24.

30 Arques and Miralles, op. cit., p. 164; *Diario 16*, 6 December 1983.
31 The journalist was José Martí Gómez, quoted in Ángel Sánchez, *Quién es Quién en la Democracia Española* (Barcelona: Flor del Viento Ediciones, 1995), p. 29.
32 This line of argument is still influential in powerful sectors of the Spanish administration. In December 1997, the Partido Popular's Attorney General, Jesús Cardenal, caused fierce controversy by appearing to justify anti-democratic military intervention in Latin America 'to maintain the public peace'. *El País*, 18 December 1997.
33 Interview with José Amedo, Madrid, October 1997.
34 *El Mundo,* 9 January 1995.
35 Both men finally recognised their involvement in the GAL in 1995.
36 *El País*, 9 November 1995.
37 Pilar Cernuda, *El Presidente* (Madrid: Temas de Hoy, 1994), p. 292.
38 *El País* , 21 December 1983.
39 See ch. 12, n. 1.
40 Interview with Javier Pradera, Madrid, November 1997.
41 Interview with Rafael Vera, Madrid, November 1997. See also ch. 4.
42 Manuel Vázquez Montalbán, *Un Polaco en la Corte del Rey Juan Carlos* (Madrid: Alfaguara, 1996), p. 456.
43 Interview with Manuel Vázquez Montalbán, Madrid, November 1997.
44 Eliseo Bayo, *GAL: Punto Final* (Barcelona: Plaza y Janés, 1997), p. 183.
45 Barrionuevo, op. cit., p. 137.
46 Arques and Miralles, op. cit., p. 342.
47 José Amedo, who denies this story.
48 *El País*, 16 January 1994.
49 Javier García, *Los GAL al Descubierto* (Madrid: El País–Aguilar, 1988), p. 120.
50 Quoted in Garzón's questions to Amedo, no. 49, Arques and Miralles, op. cit., p. 502.
51 *Libération*, 11 January 1985.
52 Mohammed Khiar, for example, a well-known former BVE mercenary, was arrested with French mafiosi on GAL charges in April 1984 and released by Svahn.
53 *Diario 16*, 27 November 1985.
54 See ch. 7, p. 108.
55 The colours refer to the uniforms of different security forces (green for the Guardia Civil, etc.) according to self-incriminating evidence from former police chief Francisco Álvarez to a Madrid court in July 1995. (See ch. 18.) Vera in fact gets the detail wrong here. The police GAL was allegedly known as 'blue', and the 'brown GAL' was run by the CESID (military intelligence). And Vera also has the big picture out of focus: if there were separate GALs within each Spanish security service, that does not preclude their being co-ordinated by superior authorities.
56 Interview with Rafael Vera, Madrid, November 1997.
57 Vera was found not guilty on this charge of organising an armed gang in 1998, though he was convicted of kidnapping Marey and misuse of public funds. See ch. 24.
58 *Cambio 16*, 21 May 1984.
59 Ibid.
60 *Cambio 16*, 28 May 1984.
61 Interview with José Luis Barbería, San Sebastián, June 1996.
62 *El País*, 27 April 1985.
63 *Le Monde,* 9 May 1985, *El País,* 10 May 1985.

64 The mercenaries were Jean-Pierre Dauri and Ángel García Valdés. See García, op. cit., p. 124, and *El País,* 19 April 1985.

65 The gangsters included Michel Morganti and Roger Roussey. Their intended targets had been Joseph Arraztoa and Fernando Egileor. *El País,* 24 October 1985.

66 Barrionuevo, op. cit., p. 135. For a fuller account of the Mendaille case, see ch. 15.

67 *El País,* 17 June 1985.

68 Quoted in Morán, op. cit., p. 222.

69 *El País,* 19 February 1986.

70 *El País,* 21 February 1986.

71 See epilogue.

72 *El País,* 10 April 1986, quoting sentence of Audiencia de Barcelona, April 1985.

73 *El País,* 10 April 1986. Giving their word on oath, it seems, aroused particular scruples for senior figures accused of GAL activities. Nine years later, when *El País* asked Rafael Vera to give his word of honour that he had not financed the GAL, he replied: 'Why should one go that far? I simply . . . say that I did not.' Asked, in the same interview, to give his word of honour that he had not personally enriched himself with public funds, he did so willingly. *El País,* 15 July 1995.

74 *El País,* 18 April 1986.

75 García, op. cit., p. 126. In fact, Giuseppe Calzona's crime did not even have a fig-leaf of political motivation: it involved a brutal settling of scores with a man who had offended his wife. Someone in Spain must have had a vital interest in keeping him sweet. He was finally expelled from the country in 1987. For further instances of Spanish inconsistency on extradition, see references to Carlos Gastón, Eduardo Mari Chica and Georges Mendaille in ch. 15.

76 *El País,* 26 May 1986.

77 *Diario 16,* 29 June 1986.

78 ETA killed more *guardia civiles* in 1986 than in any other year. Twelve – all students at the Guardia Civil traffic section – died in a single bombing at the Plaza de la República Dominicana in Madrid on 14 July. It may not have been coincidental that this is the French national day, and that the French had expelled Iturbe Abásolo to Africa the previous day.

79 This magazine's strange combination of trail-blazing investigative journalism with photo-spreads of soft pornography and victims of violence was one of the publishing phenomena of the post-Franco media boom.

80 *Interviú,* no. 542, 1 October 1986.

81 This use of Basque-language *noms de guerre – beltza* means 'black' or 'red wine' – by *guardia civiles* was a curious piece of mimicry of their targets in ETA.

82 *Diario 16,* 5 October 1986.

83 There are conflicting assessments of Galindo's actual, as opposed to perceived, success against ETA, and his professionalism did not extend to eradicating the widespread corruption among his men.

84 The year of the 'disaster' in which Spain lost the Philippines, Cuba and Puerto Rico, the last of its major overseas colonies.

85 Manuel Cerdán and Antonio Rubio, *El Origen del GAL* (Madrid: Temas de Hoy, 1997), pp. 179–81; Arques and Miralles, op. cit., pp. 200–1.

86 The Guardia Civil traditionally enjoys the honorific 'La Benemérita', which roughly translates as 'The Worthy Force'.

15

Protecting Señor X:

the systematic obstruction of justice

I couldn't care less about the rule of law if someone wants to kill me. Because the rule of law never protected me against ETA. It never protected anyone else either. When I die, I am going to regret only one thing, not having been able to kill all the etarras, not having liquidated all of them. That would have solved problems for a lot of people.

José Amedo[1]

The news story on the GAL tilted away from the Guardia Civil and their charismatic colonel in 1987, and did not come back to them in earnest for a long time. This was partly because no *guardia civil* was ever caught red-handed in a GAL operation, and a number of mercenaries were. And the mercenaries, for the most part, seemed to have other masters than the Guardia Civil.

The possibility that more than one element in the Spanish administration was involved in the GAL had been mooted at an early stage. Some people suggested, and still do, that the GAL did not constitute an organisation at all, but were made up of entirely unconnected groups acting on their own account, using the acronym as a flag of convenience. However, the same senior names have turned up far too often in connection with the GAL for that theory to have much credence now.[2] Nevertheless, different branches of the GAL, backed by different sectors of the Spanish security forces, do appear to have used the name with a degree of autonomy. This created both strengths and weaknesses within the organisation. The full nature of the mechanism for co-ordination between them has yet to be clarified.[3]

One of the strengths of the relative autonomy of the GAL's different branches was that it spread the risk of full exposure. In 1987, the spotlight shifted to the National Police. It seemed for a long time that the focus of investigation would remain fixed on this body, and that, even within the National Police, it would not illuminate the upper links in the chain of command. Throughout that year, a series of probes by French and Portuguese judges and Spanish journalists pinpointed two Bilbao police officers, and left more significant figures in convenient obscurity.

The French investigation of captured mercenaries had persistently pointed towards Bilbao police headquarters, but the first really hard evidence linking a specific senior Spanish policeman to specific GAL operations came, oddly enough, from Portugal, a country where the organisation had never fired a shot.

The key figure in this first serious penetration of the GAL's organisational structure was Jean-Philippe Labade. The mercenary commander who replaced Cherid in the spring of 1984 was a man of few words himself, but some of the people he recruited were neither very discreet nor very bright. Labade had originally been arrested in Biarritz in June 1984, in connection with the murder, by a motorbike bomb, of Tomás Pérez Revilla. Labade admitted to the French investigating magistrate, Gilbert Costeaux, that he did 'intelligence jobs for the Spanish'.[4] According to *Le Monde,* the French police had seen him meet men driving a Spanish police car at the border, prior to the killing. Despite this, and the seriousness of the charge against him, Judge Svahn released him on bail, whereupon he promptly absconded to Portugal.

Patrick de Carvalho, convicted in France for the same crime, directly implicated Labade, but the latter continued working for the GAL in Portugal. He recruited the mercenaries for the *comandos* which carried out the attacks on the Bar Batxoki in Bayonne and the Bar La Consolation in St-Jean-de-Luz in February 1986. One of the participants in the latter, Paulo Fontes Figueiredo, was the genius who went to the local train station after the killing, still carrying his gun, and was casually waiting for a train when he was arrested by police who had been alerted by bystanders.

Fontes Figueiredo's declarations would in time be very useful in judicial investigations in Spain, but the first person they put in jail was Labade, plus four comrades who had also made it back to Portugal.[5] Labade ultimately faced a series of trials for separate terrorist offences in both Portugal and France. At a hearing in Lisbon in April 1987, Labade told the investigating magistrate: 'If I worked for the Spanish government in the "dirty war" against ETA, I would not reveal it.' However, two of the men he had employed for the Batxoki and Consolation attacks said they had been told they were working for the Spanish police, with the consent of the French police.[6]

The Portuguese authorities had already established that Labade and a fellow mercenary, Mario Correira da Cunha, had met two Spanish policemen, code-named Ricardo and Eduardo, in the Ritz hotel in Lisbon only days before the Batxoki and Consolation attacks took place. Da Cunha had worked for DINFO, the Portuguese military intelligence agency, but attempts to establish links between this agency and the Spanish police in terms of the GAL were blocked by the Portuguese government. Another tantalising trail reached a dead end when the US embassy in Portugal formally denied having trained the GAL *comando* although Fontes Figueiredo had worked as a security guard for the American diplomatic mission in Lisbon.[7]

The Portuguese investigators had been able to identify one of the Spanish policeman, who had passed himself off as a *guardia civil* to the rank-and-file mercenaries.[8] He had registered under the false name of Genaro Gallego Galindo.[9] But he had paid a (rather extravagant) hotel

DBS Arts Library

bill with his personal Visa card. The name on the card was José Amedo Fouce, a National Police superintendent stationed under the command of Francisco Álvarez in Bilbao. His real name appeared for the first time in the Spanish press in early April 1987, citing the Portuguese newspaper *Expresso*.

Amedo's name recurred repeatedly in the Spanish media over the next twelve months, until he began to personify the GAL in a public mind desperately curious to put a face to the name. He had not made things too difficult for the journalists who tried to piece together his activities over the previous three years. Superintendent Amedo was not exactly a low-profile operator.

The son of a Galician policeman, Amedo came to Bilbao as a child, where his provincial accent made him a bit of an outsider. This may have contributed to his self-conscious and rather artificial flamboyance in adult life. He followed his father, who had been a Spanish champion in Olympic target shooting,[10] into the police, though he had dreamed of being a pilot. He cut his teeth in the dying years of the Franco regime, when the democratic opposition was very active, and very actively repressed by the Brigada de Investigación Político-Social, which he had joined as an intelligence officer.

In the early 1970s, it was his duty to attempt to gather information on the various Left groups operating in the student movement in Bilbao's Deusto university. He was such an obvious campus cop, so vainly arrogant in his manner, that the students nicknamed him '*Mariflor*' – 'Sunflower'. The carelessness with which he would reveal his identity, and his profession, was unexceptional under Francoism, where police took their impunity for granted. But it was a bad habit for a cop, and a worse one for a dirty warrior. It never seems to have struck Amedo that it might have been useful to lose his bravado under democracy. It is said that, during this period, he recruited Julián Sancristóbal, then a young Socialist Party militant, to inform to the Francoist police, though Amedo denies this.[11] In a strange twist, Sancristóbal would be his boss ten years later, as Civil Governor of Vizcaya, just as the GAL campaign got under way.

In his social life, Amedo cultivated the Bilbao oligarchy, who would normally have been quite out of his league, but to whom he gained access through his presidency of the Bilbao bullring. In a time of crisis and rapid social change, a police officer must have been a comforting companion to those whose interests were most threatened by the social upheaval expected on Franco's imminent death.

Amedo had a policeman's taste for nightlife and lowlife, for sleazy dives where he could pick up information and, occasionally, women. A natty dresser, he was a well-known figure in the city's nightclubs, where he liked to make dramatic entrances, Dirty Harry fashion.[12] He was familiar, too, in its brothels, where he apparently spent most of his time chatting to the Madame, while his colleagues and collaborators were entertained more exotically. He had a strong macho streak, and was given to saying things like 'I did not come from the womb of my mother, but from the balls of my father'.[13] But he is alleged to have suffered from periods of 'sexual insufficiency'.[14] His machismo extended to the political conflict in the

Basque Country, where he claims to have offered himself as a decoy target on several anti-ETA operations. He was certainly a braggart, but not, by all accounts, a coward.

He was, then, a tabloid journalist's dream when his name surfaced in 1987, further enhanced by the fact that in recent years he had developed even more extravagant tastes. He had been seen, Spanish and Basque newspapers began to report, with extraordinary frequency in San Sebastián's Kursaal Casino. It was rumoured that his visits there coincided with those of foreigners later arrested for GAL crimes in France.

Amedo's name was often linked to that of a junior colleague, Inspector Michel Domínguez. But while Domínguez would ultimately face the same GAL-related charges as Amedo, he never had the same profile. This was partly a result of his much less flamboyant personality and partly because he played a very subordinate role to Amedo in the dirty war. However, the two men often seemed inseparable, in their social as well as their professional lives.

In the middle of May, Ricardo Arques, a ground-breaking reporter for the moderate Basque nationalist paper *Deia*, was able to report that someone using the pseudonym Genaro Gallego Galindo had stayed in a San Sebastián hotel on the same nights as Pierre Frugoli, just before Frugoli shot up the Hotel Monbar in Bayonne in September 1985, killing four people. Arques also reported that Gallego was accompanied by a police colleague of French extraction, whose first name was Michel.

A rope of suspicion was tightening around Amedo's neck. There had been a further twist a week earlier, when the French judge, Christophe Seys, who was investigating Labade asked Amedo to give evidence in Bayonne, on the basis of what had emerged from the Lisbon trial.[15] As if that were not enough, he had also been called to give evidence in the Santiago Brouard case. Within five weeks of his first mention in the press, Amedo had therefore been linked judicially to four GAL attacks (Batxoki, Consolation, Monbar, Brouard) and indirectly, through Labade, to two more (Tomás Pérez Revilla and Xabier Pérez de Arenaza). Seven people had been killed in these attacks, just over a quarter of the GAL's body count. The media and the public, anxious for quick explanations, began to cast Amedo in the role of the mastermind of the GAL.

Yet none of this seemed to have any impact on Amedo's professional situation. Not only did he remain untouched by any internal police investigation: he continued to receive minor decorations and public congratulations on his work from his superiors, as a Basque politician[16] pointed out to Barrionuevo in the Senate.

JOSÉ AMEDO TODAY: A DIRTY WARRIOR WHO LOVES THE LIMELIGHT

The middle-ranking provincial policeman investigated for GAL activities in the 1980s had become a kind of national celebrity in the Spain of the 1990s. Most of the other GAL suspects are understandably reticent about publicity, and many are unwilling to give interviews.[17] José Amedo, however, talked to me twice in three weeks, and turned up unexpectedly on a third occasion. At both interviews it was I who ran out of time.[18] Amedo would talk all night. The problem is that he has changed his story so many times: it is difficult to know whether even he himself can any longer distinguish fact from self-interested subterfuge. Sometimes he appears to be indulging in fantasy for the sheer pleasure of holding an audience.

His lawyer gave me his home phone number as a matter of course. Amedo is curt on the phone, but immediately agrees to meet. He suggests the lounge bar in the Wellington, an expensive and conservative hotel in Madrid which boasts an enormous stuffed bull, emblematic of its taurine patrons. Little groups of elderly men, clubable retired army officers and bank managers are taking their aperitifs when I arrive.

Amedo makes his entrance with a certain lupine grace, and almost every table greets him as he passes swiftly down the lounge. 'Adiós, Pepe,' the old men exclaim admiringly, using the familiar form of his first name.

He joins me with a seductive, conspiratorial smile. He is like a naughty schoolboy who cannot wait to spill the beans. Nor can he resist indicating the bodyguard he has left standing in the foyer, as if a man with a bulging jacket was some kind of status symbol. 'It's all right, you can relax, that one's with me.'

He orders whiskey and Coca-Cola. He is very slim and very fit, and wears a well-cut, expensive suit. He extends his long legs, establishing a slightly creepy intimacy by occasionally pressing his foot against mine. I would not like to be interrogated by him, I think instinctively. Happily, I am the one asking the questions, and he answers easily.

He talks in a rapid, slightly stuttering staccato, curiously devoid of any connection between feeling and emphasis. He has deep, glittering, watchful eyes and sensual lips. His face is extraordinarily flexible, like a beagle puppy's, but each new expression is another mask.

Sometimes he seems straight out of central casting as the sleazy cop. At one point he briefly but obviously loses his concentration and immediately apologises, seeking complicity: 'I was looking at that woman, heh, heh, heh.'

This man, though, is nobody's fool. His answers are clever, and curiously passionless. He clearly and self-consciously loves the interview process, blatantly playing with what he knows, what he knows I know, and what he knows I'd like to know. He gives away very little, and what gives him away are attitudes, not facts. Because any empathy with the GAL's targets, even those he knows to have had no connection with ETA, is inconceivable to him, he comes across as pitiless. More than that, he comes across as being incapable of pity, and therefore very dangerous, as much to his friends as to his enemies. His denials of the more heinous crimes attributed to him are almost off-hand, and usually coupled with an expression of contempt for the victims.

Asked about his subordinate, Michel Domínguez, whose attitude to publicity is the opposite of his own, Amedo says: 'Michel feels different, he is trying to get out of this dream.' 'Surely you mean this nightmare?' I reply. For once he says nothing, but looks at me oddly. It strikes me that he is in his element. He tells me he will publish his own book one day, and adds, proud as punch, that 'a production company of Robert de Niro's' has been in touch about a screenplay.

'When you were an ordinary policeman in Bilbao,' I suggest as we are finishing the interview, 'you could never have imagined that you would ever have this kind of national profile. How does it suit you?'

He grins broadly, like an actor who is finally getting the break he has always known he deserved. 'Stupendously well,' he says. His charm, superficial but infectious enough, can seem disingenuous. When shaking his hand, it is difficult to keep reality in focus. This is the man who, his associates have sworn in court, ordered mercenaries to fire indiscriminately into crowded bars. This is the man, if his former girlfriend is to be believed, who made Laura Martín a widow just to cover his own tracks.[19]

A few days later, I am back at the Wellington, interviewing Fernando López Agudín, a former Interior Ministry insider who has written a valuable book about the period when Amedo fell from grace with his superiors.[20] I suddenly see Amedo observing us from the bar. It is a strange moment: it is difficult, no matter who you are dealing with, not to feel guilty of some sort of obscure betrayal when you are found with someone from the other side of the story. 'If he comes over,' I say to López Agudín, 'should I introduce you?'

'Please don't introduce me at all,' he says firmly. 'That man is nothing but a common criminal. I do not wish to know him.' That is not a moral judgement which is necessarily shared, either by the select clientele of the Wellington or by some other sections of the broader Spanish public, even today.

Like Amedo, other individuals accused of GAL activities abroad also continued unmolested about their business in Spain in the late 1980s. Eduardo Mari Chica (another police informer) and Carlos Gastón were both implicated by a Paris prosecutor as the recruiters of the mercenaries who killed Javier Galdeano. Gastón, a French citizen, was also wanted in France in connection with a killing in the first dirty war. Not only were they not extradited, but their 'sauna' business in Malaga had been protected from local police investigation by superior authorities in Madrid.[21] It had become standard practice for the Spanish authorities to apply very different criteria to the extradition of GAL suspects from those which they themselves demanded should be applied to *etarras*.

This was never clearer than in the case of Georges Mendaille who, like Jean-Pierre Cherid, was one of the mercenaries who had acted as a bridge between the first dirty war and the GAL. In November 1985, the French judge who was investigating unsuccessful GAL car-bomb attacks on Joseph Arraztoa and Fernando Egileor traced the crime to four Marseilles gangsters, among them Roger Roussey. All four named Mendaille, a French citizen and former foreign legionary resident in Spain, as their recruiter. Mendaille had told them, they said, that he was acting on behalf of the Spanish and French secret services.[22] Mendaille's hand-writing was found on photographs of their targets, discovered in their car. Roussey's sister, Odette Montmigny, knew Mendaille, and said he told her that he was a GAL organiser. She also claimed that, after the arrests, she met Mendaille several times to seek help for her brother. He promised assistance, and eventually introduced her to Amedo and Domínguez, who offered her work with the GAL, which she turned down. She ratified these statements both to French courts and to an investigating magistrate in Madrid.[23]

Despite the weight of evidence against Mendaille, first the Spanish police and then the Spanish government treated French requests for his arrest and extradition with something that looked very like contempt. In 1985 and 1986, the Spanish police twice told their French counterparts that they could not find him. Then two Spanish journalists[24] easily tracked him down to Gerona on two occasions, where his phone number was in the telephone book under his own name, and his car registered with the local police.

The Guardia Civil still managed to cock up his arrest, which finally took place only at the insistence of a particularly persistent investigating magistrate, Baltasar Garzón, in February 1989.[25] The Audiencia Nacional[26] accepted the French petition for his extradition in July 1989, and rejected his appeal against that decision in September. All that was now required was the Spanish cabinet's confirmation, the government having the power to overrule the courts in such a case.[27] The following year, just before the Marseilles mercenaries were to be tried in Pau, the Spanish government formally rejected the French request for Mendaille's extradition, and released him.[28]

Once again, Barrionuevo's assertion that 'all the requests which the French made of us were always complied with' was shown to be deeply disingenuous, if not entirely cynical.[29]

'I say it loud and clear,' said the French prosecutor at the Pau trial, 'Mendaille enjoys Spanish police protection.'[30] *El País* reminded the government, to no avail, that 'reciprocity is basic to a balanced policy of co-operation between states'.[31] The Mendaille affair did some damage to French–Spanish judicial collaboration, though not as much as might have been expected.[32] Perhaps the senior French authorities were not entirely unhappy with the situation: it may have been that Mendaille knew something about French links to the GAL which they would not wish to hear in court.[33]

Meanwhile, just as judicial investigations seemed to be closing in on the GAL in France and Portugal, and journalistic investigation was making some headway in Spain, the organisation made a sudden and deadly reappearance. On 24 July 1987, Juan Carlos García Goena was killed by a car bomb, in an action claimed by the GAL. Goena, as we have seen, was a conscientious objector with no links whatsoever to ETA.[34]

Press interpretations at the time were speculative. Some said that, despite the greatly increased anti-ETA collaboration given by the French, the GAL were still trying to push them to expel more senior *etarras* to

Spain. Others suggested that rightist elements wanted to derail the negotiations with ETA which the Spanish government was in the process of setting up in Algeria.

The Spanish police let it be known that they believed García Goena had been associated with ETA, and had been killed by his own comrades, because he had wanted to return to Spain. This was a truly cynical smear, because they knew he had no ETA connections. A similar implication was repeated by Barrionuevo at a press conference, and was not withdrawn for several years.[35] One might have expected a Minister for the Interior to be better informed.

Amedo was acquitted of murdering García Goena at his trial in 1991, although his own former girlfriend accused him in court of having boasted about it. García Goena's death widowed a young pregnant woman, Laura Martín, and bereaved her two young daughters, any or all of whom could have also died in the explosion. In 1997, I asked Amedo what feelings he had towards these innocent victims. While denying, in a formal and cursory fashion, any involvement in the killing, his reply spoke volumes: 'The problem of Laura Martín is one which does not worry me. Anyway, what a place to seek refuge, where all the *etarras* are, no? If I had nothing to do with ETA, I would not seek refuge in their milieu . . . it was her problem.'[36]

Amedo's nemesis, Ricardo Arques, was becoming disillusioned with the cautious approach of his newspaper, *Deia*, to his investigations in the early summer of 1987. He was especially frustrated because he seemed to be getting close to the heart of the GAL. He had been contacted by a remarkable 'deep throat'. This man, who called himself 'Pedro', has never been identified. He had a great deal of hard information about the GAL at his disposal, with all of it pointing in one direction. When he first contacted Arques, he told him bluntly that he was a member of the GAL, and could prove that José Amedo was the leader of that organisation. He then proceeded to drip-feed the evidence, starting with the Hotel Orly registration book which put Amedo in the same San Sebastián hotel as Frugoli before the Monbar attack.

The next tip-off from 'Pedro' sent Arques to hotels in Andorra, where he was able to establish that suspected mercenaries, including a leading candidate for the role of the *Dama Negra,* and the GAL recruiter Christian Hitier, had bases. Labade was well known in one of the tackier hotels there, and Ismael Miquel had also passed through.[37] Amedo's picture was recognised by one of the bar staff. It seemed Arques had found a meeting point for the organisation.

'Pedro' then promised to direct the journalist to an arms and information cache belonging to the GAL. Such material, if valid, would be a huge advance. But 'Pedro' insisted on meeting the journalist face to face first. Arques's bosses became concerned that he was being led into a trap, with small titbits of accurate information drawing him into a major error, or serious danger. The sudden reappearance of the GAL in July made Arques himself more cautious, more concerned himself about the risk of physical danger. But when 'Pedro' got back in touch, Arques told him that he intended moving to a different newspaper to follow the story.[38] He offered his services to *Diario 16* in July. He was hired by the editor, Pedro J. Ramírez,[39] and teamed up with Melchor Miralles, another journalist who had built a reputation for investigative journalism.

In August, they met 'Pedro' face to face in St-Jean-de-Luz, in a cloak-and-dagger encounter, according to their own account, worthy of a police thriller. 'Pedro' told them he was acting on superior orders within the GAL. 'Someone in this battle is not behaving as he ought, and these things have to be paid for. Someone has got too clever.'[40] It was close to an admission that Amedo was being offered as a scapegoat, but the journalists decided to stay with their source. The lure of the cache was irresistible.

'Pedro' refused to accompany them, insisting that he could only supply them with a sketch map. Their instructions led them up a heavily wooded, winding little road on the Col de Corlecou, one of the very first foothills of the Pyrenees, only a few hundred metres on the French side of the Bidasoa river. It stands a little inland from Hendaye, where the GAL had claimed several victims, and is close to the tiny village of Biriatou, where the Olaskoaga brothers had been shot in November 1984. Reversing their two cars up a path which led into the woods, they then followed a twisting track through dense ferns and briars to a point where two fallen trees lay crossed. 'X', quite literally, marked the spot.

The cache (known as a *zulo* from the Basque word used by ETA for their arms dumps) was held in a large plastic bag, tied up with a bit of a green balloon. It was a treasure trove for the journalists. There was a box inside the bag, and then more bags. They contained photographs, files and maps on Basque refugees, including José Ramón López de Abetxuko, who had been targeted by the GAL in December 1984. Some of the refugees had already been handed over to Spain by France. There were fake identity documents, including ones made for Jean-Philippe Labade, Paulo Fontes Figueiredo and Christian Hitier. There was a woman's wig and shoes. There were pistols, ammunition and explosives, similar or identical to weapons known to have been used by the GAL, and by the Spanish police.[41]

According to the journalists' dramatic (and possibly rather dramatised) version, they were examining the explosives when a small light began to flash in what seemed to be a home-made bomb. In some disorder, as they admit themselves, they beat a retreat, but managed to take all the documents with them. They gave the Spanish authorities formal notification of their discovery before publication, but the police never followed it up. However, a Madrid judge (Baltasar Garzón) has established that the photographs of refugees are identical to those held in police files, and French judges incorporated evidence from the *zulo* into their inquiries.[42]

The story of the *zulo* raises a number of questions. What practical purpose could such a cache really have served? Given the ease with which GAL members crossed the border, would it not have been safer to keep such materials in Spain? More importantly, who was 'Pedro', and whose interests was he serving in selling Amedo down the river? This was, of course, precisely the moment when Amedo was thought by his superiors to be going out of control.[43] Yet if pointing these journalists to the *zulo* was an internal GAL attempt to expose Amedo and remove him from the scene, it risked bringing the whole organisation out into the open with him, and it may have been a significant step in that direction. Journalists who were in competition with Miralles and Arques have suggested that the *zulo* did not exist at all, but was invented as an elaborate diversion from the real source of the Miralles and Arques revelations.

Strangely, perhaps, Amedo himself roundly dismisses this hypothesis: 'That is a lie, it is absolutely false.' He claims to be the only person who knows the real identity of 'Pedro', and seems to feel no enmity for him. He will admit only that the deep throat 'came from the world of the GAL', but will not respond to speculation that he might have come from one of the rival groups involved, such as the Guardia Civil or military intelligence. 'That could give you a clue,' he says. He will only say that he has himself told Miralles that 'Your balls will fall to the floor when you finally find out who it is.'[44]

Whatever the intentions of the mysterious 'Pedro' and his superiors, the net cast by the Portuguese and French trials of mercenaries was drawing tighter and tighter around José Amedo. Now the increased pressure came from Bayonne. In November 1987, two French judges, Armand Riberolles and Christophe Seys, held a special hearing in Madrid with a Spanish anti-terrorist magistrate, Carlos Bueren. They interrogated José Amedo about allegations made against him in France and Portugal. The policeman invoked his constitutional right to silence.[45] Miralles and Arques took advantage of the French judges' visit to hand over documents from the *zulo*.

Seys gave Bueren a copy of his investigation, and the latter decided there was sufficient evidence against Amedo to ask the Audiencia Nacional to open a case against him. It immediately became clear that the Ministry of the Interior, and indeed the government, were going to stand by their man, despite the avalanche of evidence crashing down on him.

'There is nothing against Amedo,' the Secretary of State for Security, Rafael Vera, told *El País*. 'There is not the least worry in this department.'[46] The Director General of the National Police, José María Rodríguez Colorado, assured the paper that Amedo was carrying out his usual duties in Bilbao 'with complete normality'. The next day, the Prime Minister, Felipe González, issued a public reminder that those who risked their lives in the service of the state against terrorism had a right to the presumption of innocence. *El País* in turn reminded González that, while everyone had the right to be presumed innocent, no one had the right 'to an impunity incompatible with the fundamentals of a democratic State . . . the possible implication of a Spanish police officer [in the GAL] has all the characteristics of a time bomb. If it explodes, its results will be unforeseeable.'[47] The lines for the legal battle to convict significant members of the GAL in Spain had been drawn.

The precedent for a legal and ideological argument which continues to this day was also set at this time, in the Audiencia Nacional's November verdict on the GAL unit who were found guilty of killing Robert Caplanne.[48] The material author of the crime, Javier Rovira, and his closest accomplices got sentences ranging from thirty-four to twenty-six years in prison. But they were found not guilty of membership of GAL though they had admitted to such membership themselves. Nor, according to the court, did they belong to a terrorist group.

To be defined as terrorists, the judges argued, it had to be shown that they belonged to a stable organisation, and, above all, that they were dedicated to the 'destruction of the constitutional order'. Because the GAL used terror on behalf of the state, and not to overthrow it, such terror was somehow not 'terrorist'. Nor did the judges follow up or evaluate the revelation that the *comando*'s leader, Ismael Miquel Gutiérrez, who had fled the country just before his colleagues were arrested, had worked under cover for the police.[49] Not linked to the security forces, not an organisation, not terrorists: this trinity of negatives would become a familiar and continuing chorus, orchestrated from the Ministry of the Interior, as the Spanish investigation of the GAL gathered momentum.

In the conclusion of the Labade group's first trial in Portugal a fortnight later – GAL mercenaries really were going down like ninepins in late 1987 – no such fine distinctions were drawn. They belonged, said the sentence, 'to a terrorist group whose objects were kidnapping, torturing and killing'.[50] Amedo had not responded to a summons to attend the trial.

November was a dark month for Amedo, and December was blacker still. The first blows came from France. First, on 30 November, Judge Christophe Seys initiated an international search and detention order against him for the Consolation and Batxoki attacks. Once processed through Interpol, this would mean that Amedo could not travel outside Spain without the risk of immediate extradition to France. Seys made it clear that he was not insisting on Amedo's extradition from Spain itself, since Spain cannot extradite its own nationals.[51] But he fully expected the Spanish courts to try him on the basis of the evidence supplied from cases in France, invoking a bilateral judicial agreement between the two countries.

On the same day, Lucien Mattei and Pierre Frugoli faced sentencing for the quadruple murder at the Hotel Monbar. Despite the overwhelming first-hand evidence against them, the older and harder Mattei denied all the charges, while openly threatening to kill Frugoli if he talked. The younger man, however, not only admitted his responsibility, but said that their instructions had come from two Spanish policemen, 'Francis' and 'Miguel'.

In a dramatic courtroom gesture, the lawyer representing the victims produced a copy of a recent *Diario 16* investigation, 'All roads lead to Amedo', which was dominated by a large picture of the superintendent. Did Frugoli recognise him? 'I can't be sure, but I think so,' said the young gangster, 'he has a great physical resemblance to one of the people who interviewed us in Bilbao.'[52]

Judge Carlos Bueren's decision to investigate Amedo in Spain followed the next day. Then, on 3 December, in the French parliament, a rising Socialist leader, and future Prime Minister, Lionel Jospin, named Amedo and demanded his extradition to France.[53] The same day, two mercenaries charged with the kidnapping of Segundo Marey, Mohand Talbi and Jean-Pierre Echalier, insisted in court that they had been working for both the French and Spanish police. They described the progress of the kidnapping on the Spanish side of the border in some detail, an operation directed, they both said, by a Spanish police officer known as 'Pepe', which is the familiar form of Amedo's first name, José. Talbi, in an account which often seemed to ramble into fantasy, also described meeting a Spanish general and several businessmen at another meeting with 'Pepe'.[54]

A judge from the Audiencia Nacional, Francisco Castro Meije, travelled to France just before Christmas, where Fontes Figueiredo and Frugoli both confirmed their evidence against Amedo. Early in the new year, the judge's senior colleagues instructed him to continue the investigation, and he also called in Amedo's deputy, Michel Domínguez. On 5 February 1988, Castro Meije formally declared that there was evidence that Amedo was involved with the GAL.[55] Javier Solana, Minister for Culture and official government spokesperson, immediately offered the full collaboration of the executive in the investigation.[56] As we shall see, it was an offer which would not be honoured.

Just two weeks later, something happened which would transform the whole character of the judicial investigation into the GAL, and mark it to this day. Castro Meije resigned, and was replaced by a brilliant (and hungrily ambitious) young investigating magistrate called Baltasar Garzón.

Within weeks, Garzón encountered the first of many unusual hurdles which would obstruct his progress. Because of Amedo's legally privileged status as a policeman, Garzón had to refer his investigation to his senior colleagues in the Audiencia Nacional for permission to charge him. The Audiencia Nacional, in a decision which was described by one legal source as 'ridiculous word play', declared that the evidence presented amounted only to 'mere suspicion' of criminality, rather than 'categorical indications'.[57] Given the volume of verbal and documentary evidence already available, this move was widely regarded as outrageously obstructive. But Garzón was given the go-ahead to continue investigating, without bringing formal charges.

He showed his mettle by announcing that he would extend the investigation beyond individuals like Amedo to the 'institutions related to the GAL'.[58] If the Ministry of the Interior was really unconcerned about the investigation of Amedo, this decision must have rung some alarm bells. Garzón had initiated a remarkable journey which would lead him, with some tortuous diversions, to the moment in 1995 when he would ask the Supreme Court to consider charging the Prime Minister, Felipe González, as an organiser of the GAL.

Meanwhile, Jean-Philippe Labade had been temporarily extradited from his Portuguese prison to France, where he finally faced trial for organising the 1984 murders of Pérez Revilla and Pérez de Arenaza. Labade's former girlfriend Jeanette Cassiede had already provided the court with copious and decisive evidence against him, and added that he had said he was working for the Spanish police.[59] In the face of this, while denying the main charges, he conceded that he had met Spanish police at the border before Revilla's killing, though he claimed they had only discussed sport and real estate. But he gave enough information to virtually identify one of those present as Amedo's French-speaking deputy, Michel Domínguez.

Another witness was taped by the French police while talking to a man who, the phone tappers believed, was also Domínguez. But it was the evidence against Amedo which took a really decisive turn. Roger Boslé, the French police officer most actively involved in detection of the GAL units, told the court that the true identity of the GAL contact known to the mercenaries as Ricardo was undoubtedly the Spanish superintendent. The testimony of mercenaries (or their former lovers) might be tarnished by self-interest; now it was corroborated by a senior policeman.[60] *El País* pointed out that these trials were exposing to 'the most ghastly ridicule' those Spanish judges who had held that the evidence was still insufficient to charge Amedo.[61]

Labade got a life sentence in France for the Revilla and Arenaza killings, but was sent back to Portugal to face further charges there. His trigger man, Patrick de Carvalho, confessed to both crimes, admitting that it had been a mistake to fight against ETA with its own methods. He identified the aim of the GAL as forcing the French authorities to expel Basque refugees, rather than the direct annihilation of ETA. And he floated a proposal which has resurfaced several times since: reciprocal pardons could be granted to members of the GAL and members of ETA. The French state prosecutor summed up his own view of the GAL lucidly and concisely: 'They have served to justify ETA, fighting democracy in the same way. Like ETA, they represent the logic of death.'[62]

Justice was finally being done in some GAL cases in France, but it still progressed at a snail's pace in Spain – when it was not actually moving backwards. Garzón's experience of obstruction in Madrid was already familiar to the magistrates involved in the long-running investigation into the murder of Santiago Brouard in Bilbao. The Banks Council, a state body, had refused to facilitate their request for information on Amedo's finances. It pleaded that such information was private between each bank and client. Judicial sources pointed out that it had facilitated such requests in other cases. *El País* reported such sources as saying that 'the position of the council seeks to obstruct the investigation of the alleged relationship of Amedo with the GAL when, in fact, much data has already been obtained on his accounts, and especially seeks to hide the origin of the money which was lodged by the superintendent'.[63] The source of Amedo's unlikely wealth became a key and contentious issue of the whole investigation.

Back in Madrid, Garzón found himself under attack from Jorge Argote, Amedo's lawyer, who also appeared to act as legal spokesman for Interior. Argote said that the magistrate was prioritising investigating the GAL over prosecuting *etarras*. The lawyer got a dusty response from the General Council of the Judiciary (Consejo General del Poder Judicial), the body which arbitrates disputes within the legal profession and sets standards for the judiciary.

By the end of April, Garzón had finally got crucial confirmation from Amedo's superiors that his journeys to Portugal in early 1986 – where he was believed to have recruited GAL mercenaries – had been on official business. In May, Garzón travelled to France, where several mercenaries reaffirmed evidence that Amedo had been their paymaster.[64] The most serious charges were made by Mohand Talbi, convicted for the kidnapping of Segundo Marey, who repeated the (probably rather wild) allegations made at his trial about a meeting in Bilbao in 1983, in which eighteen killings were planned. He said that Amedo had organised all of them, including the assassination of Santiago Brouard.[65]

At the end of the month Garzón seemed to make another breakthrough. The Director General of the National Police, José María Rodríguez Colorado, finally admitted, after a series of obfuscations, that Amedo's journeys to Portugal had been paid for out of *fondos reservados*, 'reserved funds' used for unspecified purposes (such as payment of informers) by the Ministry of the Interior. He also said that the false name of Genaro Gallego Galindo had been officially authorised, and that the superintendent had been investigating illegal arms traffic. Garzón had asked him to say what the record showed Amedo had been doing on several dates relating to GAL attacks. Colorado replied that he could not specify Amedo's activities, but, because there was no record that he had been on leave, he could assume he had been on duty at these times.[66] Fernando Salas, making the case for the 'people's prosecution',[67] accused Colorado of 'obstructing the investigation and unconditionally and imprudently protecting Amedo'.[68]

Garzón seemed to sense that the reserved funds were probably the vein which could lead to the heart of the GAL, and promptly followed up with a request for details of how such funds had been spent in the period 1983–7, to be delivered to his court within a fortnight. Then, in early June, he notched up the temperature of the investigation yet again by summonsing five senior policemen, including Colorado, to give evidence. He advised them to bring their lawyers, in their own interests.

Days later, he finally received the Interpol international arrest order against Amedo for attempted murder, requested from Bayonne. It had been initiated by Judge Seys the previous November and formally issued by Interpol in January. Garzón had requested a copy in February, but the Interior Ministry claimed it did not reach Spain until 8 June. The Spanish press pointed out that both the French and Portuguese courts now considered Amedo's involvement in the Batxoki and Consolation attacks proven, yet the Audiencia Nacional still maintained its view that the evidence against him was 'mere suspicion'. An *El País* editorial denounced the attitude of Interior as 'a mockery of the courts and an offence to those who believe in justice'. Many people, wrote the paper, now wondered if Amedo was being protected 'because he has a lot to tell'.[69]

Colorado informed Garzón that nearly 3,881 million pesetas had been spent in reserved funds during the years the GAL was active. There had been a sudden increase of 14 per cent in 1984, the first full year of GAL operations. There was a further rise of 7 per cent in 1985. The figures had levelled out in 1986 and 1987. The real interest lay in the rise in subventions to institutions suspected of funding the GAL. The allocation to the Guardia Civil soared from 12 million pesetas in 1983 to 55 million in 1984, and the budget for Sancristóbal's Directorate of State Security rose from 509 to 549 million pesetas in the same period.[70]

Garzón wanted to know exactly how much of this money had been entrusted to Amedo. Both Colorado and the Interior Minister, Barrionuevo, refused to give any further breakdowns to the judge, though they both cited different, and obscure, legal arguments for their silence.[71] Barrionuevo insisted that he spoke in the name of the government. Garzón said that if the minister did not change his position, he would be guilty of 'a clear failure to co-operate with the courts'. The people's prosecution lawyer, Fernando Salas, described Barrionuevo's answer as 'a declaration of war'.[72] Garzón's tough response made it clear that some members of the judiciary were prepared for such a conflict.

El País reminded the minister that the funds were reserved only in that they did not have to be accounted for in detail to parliament. They were not a licence to finance criminal activity. The police, the newspaper suggested, were being permitted to break the law in the name of the law. 'As the President of the Government [Felipe González] is a lawyer, and in his day fought for democracy, the importance of these matters should not escape him.'[73] Even in the media closest to the PSOE, the implication that the GAL had been creatures of Interior, and possibly of the government, was scarcely veiled. The next day, the same paper would report that Barrionuevo had taken his position on the direct instructions of Felipe González.[74]

A magistrate consulted by the paper succinctly summed up the compelling case for disclosure: the uses of reserved funds are secret only until the moment it is suspected that those uses have contravened the law.[75] This may seem self-evident, but in fact a great gulf was fixed between those who believed that the state must be democratically accountable for all its actions and those who, explicitly or implicitly, believed that what the Spanish call *La Razón de Estado* – reasons of state – override the democratic right to information. This was the meaty bone of contention which lay at the centre of every phase of the investigation of the GAL.

Where Garzón found one path blocked, he energetically pursued another. He finally prevailed, in the same period, on the reluctant Banks Council to supply figures on Amedo's bank accounts. The superintendent had, it emerged, spent at least 27 million pesetas in the previous two years. His annual salary was just under 2 million, net.[76]

Following another lead, Garzón took evidence from the GAL mercenary Daniel Fernández Aceña, in prison in Madrid, that Amedo had contracted inexperienced mercenaries which caused great problems.[77] Today, Amedo cavalierly responds that, since the main purpose of the GAL was 'to constantly put pressure on France', it did not much matter whether they were efficient or inefficient. As long as their actions forced the French government to reassess its policy on ETA, it was not important how much the GAL cocked up, apparently.[78] Aceña also implicated the Guardia Civil's Lieutenant-Colonel Galindo, but, as always, his allegations had a most unstable bias towards fantasy.[79]

On the last day of June, Colorado and his colleagues appeared in court, where Garzón warned them that they were giving evidence not as witnesses but as suspected accessories.[80] They refused to give information on the reserved funds, citing the minister's prohibition. Sallying out in their defence, the Guardia Civil Director General, Luis Roldán, said that secrecy about the use of the funds was essential for police operations. He demanded of the public an extraordinary act of faith: 'above all there must be a conviction that those in public office respect the law'.[81] The full irony of this statement could only be appreciated ten years later, when Roldán himself was convicted of, among other crimes, personally misappropriating reserved funds to the tune of 600 million pesetas.[82]

Garzón now formally stated that he believed some reserved funds had been used to finance the GAL. Meanwhile, Felipe González went public in full defence of Barrionuevo's order. Every democratic country, he said, regulated special funds along the same lines. He went on to make a pun that became notorious: 'We have always defended and will defend *"el Estado de Derecho"* ["the law-based state", or "the rule of law"], but we will not tolerate the danger that it will become *"un Estado de desecho"* ["a shattered State"].'[83] He had not responded to the real legal arguments raised by the judge, legal experts, the media and public opinion. Instead, he had given the first of many soundbites whose main characteristic would be their evasive ambiguity. They would return to haunt him.

The investigation of the GAL was opening fissures, through which deep structural problems of Spanish democracy could now be more clearly seen. The journalist and writer Eduardo Haro Tecglen was an astute and fearless critic of the complacency which Spain's 'consensualised' transition to democracy had generated. He now reflected prophetically on this conflict between the judiciary and the government. He wondered whether a state with an executive as strong as Spain's can enjoy real judicial independence. If the relationships of 'independence and dependence' between the two powers could not be clarified, he warned, it would become a very serious problem for constitutional politics.[84]

Tecglen's colleague, Javier Pradera, is convinced that, while not minimising the damage the GAL's dirty war did to Spanish democracy, the worst was yet to come. 'What has been the overriding significance, in my judgement, about the whole GAL affair? To my mind, the fundamental aspect about the GAL was not the thing itself – that was a horrific, filthy operation, like all dirty wars. But I think the real rupture with the rule of law was produced by the Socialist government when they dedicated themselves to obstructing and impeding the investigation of the GAL.'[85]

Obstruction seemed only to spur Garzón to more decisive action. On 13 July, he summonsed Amedo and Domínguez to answer 200 questions. Amedo refused to answer a single one of them, but showed increasing signs of strain. As the tension mounted, Argote asked the magistrate to end the session. 'My client is tired and wants to leave; he is a free man,' said Argote. 'Your client,' responded Garzón, 'is a prisoner.'[86]

In his warrant for the arrest of Amedo and Domínguez, Garzón declared that they 'appeared to be the principal organisers of the so-called Grupos Antiterroristas de Liberación', recounting specifically the evidence of their participation in the recruitment and instruction of the mercenaries who carried out the Batxoki and Consolation attacks in 1986. As investigating magistrate, Garzón had the power to remand suspects in custody (known as *prisión preventiva*).[87] To justify this measure, there had to be grounds to believe that the suspects were likely to abscond, interfere with evidence or intimidate witnesses. Garzón's use of this measure was to become controversial, but *El País* praised the 'courage' of the judge. The obstruction of his investigation by Interior, said the paper, implied the espousal of the illegitimate stance that the demands of state security legitimised the commission of crimes by the state's servants.[88]

On their first full day in prison, the pair received a friendly visit from their colleagues at Bilbao police headquarters. Meanwhile, Barrionuevo, the man who had been Minister for the Interior during the entire GAL period, had moved to the Ministry of Transport, Tourism and Communications in a cabinet reshuffle announced just two days earlier. He was replaced by José Luis Corcuera, a pugnacious man who would fiercely defend his predecessor's policies.

Another resignation was more directly linked to the policemen's imprisonment. Their belligerent lawyer, Jorge Argote, moved aside for Gonzalo Casado. Argote's forte, bullying and bluster, had failed. Amedo's defence now required a sharper legal mind with a less flamboyant reputation. His imprisonment had raised the stakes on both sides.[89]

Addressing a full session of parliament towards the end of July, Felipe González tried to shrug off a series of opposition attacks on his government's failure to investigate the GAL, which had led to a public perception that it was backing the group. The most damaging comment came from former Prime Minister Adolfo Suárez, architect of the transition to democracy. Speaking in the US, Suárez declared 'I would not have created the GAL.' He appeared to insinuate, without actually stating the case, that Felipe González had done just that. Questioned about this statement, the Socialist leader's habitual gravitas cracked.

'What do you want?' he asked journalists testily. 'That I play a game of ping-pong and say that I would not have lent my support to the Basque Spanish Battalion? No way; this is a serious matter.'[90]

So serious, indeed, that he made a surprise proposal for unspecified new legislation to reinforce the security of the state. Even relatively sympathetic observers like the journalist Francisco Gor saw this move as further evidence of the 'unhidable obsession of the Socialists to strengthen the executive *vis-à-vis* the other powers and institutions of the State'.[91] The 'death of Montesquieu' became – and remains – a catchphrase for those who were disturbed by the monopoly of authority sought by the executive and the Prime Minister.[92]

On 21 July, Garzón formally proposed to his senior colleagues that Amedo and Domínguez should be tried for six attempted murders and other terrorist crimes, all related to the GAL attacks on the Batxoki and Consolation bars in 1986. In his very detailed writ, he accused Barrionuevo of obstructing justice. The state prosecutor criticised this writ on technical grounds, arguing that the evaluation of the indications of blame was a function of the superior chamber, and not of the judge proposing the trial. It would not be the last time Garzón would be accused of jumping the procedural gun.

Meanwhile, French judicial sources expressed great satisfaction at the imprisonment of Amedo. 'He is like the fuse which can put a whole electrical system in crisis,' one of them commented.[93] Garzón's decision was undoubtedly a major leap forward in the investigation. But the popular belief that Amedo was *the* key figure in the GAL (very convenient to other sections of the GAL, to his superior officers and to senior Socialists) was being reinforced by some of those who should have seen beyond it. Understandably, on the basis of the evidence available, Garzón himself overrated Amedo's role at this stage, but he was careful to emphasise that the policeman was always 'following the orders or instructions of other persons'.[94] In France, further light on the subject was expected from other suspects, especially from Dominique Thomas, an Andorran woman close to Christian Hitier who was accused of being either the 'Black Lady' or the 'Blonde Assassin' (or both).

HAVING IT BOTH WAYS: THE SOCIALIST LEXICON OF AMBIGUITY ON THE GAL

Much less light than heat was generated at a press conference given by Felipe González in late July 1988.[95] He made a series of memorable statements which became headliners in his lexicon of ambiguity about the GAL. Firstly, he asserted that, 'if it is proven that reserved funds have been used in a way radically contrary to their legal purposes', any ensuing trial should be 'preferably political'. By this he appears to have meant that such a hearing should be parliamentary rather than judicial. Judges, he said, had no legal right to 'interfere in a sovereign decision of parliament on secret use of funds for the discretional use of the government'. The corpse of Montesquieu was beginning to stink.

He denied any knowledge of GAL activities beyond that ascertained by the investigations of the Spanish police. (These had, of course, been rather minimal – indeed, the Bilbao police top brass had roundly denied carrying out any such investigation.) He repeated a rumour that a jailed mercenary had complained of being pressurised to recognise photographs of Amedo and Domínguez. Challenged on this by *Diario 16* journalists, he riposted: 'What I am saying is that there are people who have attempted to lynch, in moral terms, these two officers, who have the right and duty to feel themselves defended and supported by their government.' He also accused 'the friends of ETA' of blocking the investigation of Brouard, something the police (and the Banks Council) seemed to have done perfectly well on their own.

Rather than denying directly that the state apparatus was involved in the GAL, he said, curiously, that 'no one *will succeed in demonstrating*' that such links exist (my emphasis). His most quoted comment, however, evoked a highly ambiguous image: 'The rule of law is defended in the courts, and in the salons, but also in the sewers.' Such statements had the function of qualifying his denial of legal responsibility for the dirty war with an expression of nudge-and-wink support for such a strategy. He was having it both ways. His words were a template for most Socialist discourse on the dirty war under democracy.

Two months later the new Minister for the Interior, José Luis Corcuera, contributed to the repertoire of Socialist ambiguity about the GAL: 'ETA is not a joke, and there are some things which cannot be sorted out with flowers,' he said.[96] The Communist MP Nicolás Sartorius immediately asked him if this implied involvement with the GAL. The columnist Javier Pradera, who had so recently defended, at great personal cost, the Socialists' unpopular decision to join NATO, commented that such remarks 'belong to the tiresome genre of hints and anxious winks inaugurated with Felipe González's reference to the sewers'.[97]

Why did the Socialist leaders use this language, whose form and implied content alienated even those who, like Pradera, were personally and politically well-disposed towards them? Why would a party which had been instrumental, only a decade earlier, in re-establishing the rule of law in Spain suggest repeatedly that the law could be broken by the state? The argument of one of the masters of what we might call GALspeak is worth listening to here.

Rafael Vera was number two in Interior for many years, and has now been convicted of participating in the Marey kidnapping. In an interview in November 1997, a few months before that trial, he naturally stopped short of incriminating himself, but he gave a remarkably frank account of the Socialist predicament. I put it to him that, assuming the Socialist leadership was innocent of any role in the GAL, it was a major tactical mistake to offer so much 'defence and support' to Amedo, a man who was looking guiltier with every passing day.

'This defence has its origin fundamentally in the morale of the security forces,' Vera replies. 'I had a responsibility . . . to maintain that morale. Therefore, when the affair of Amedo and Domínguez arises, there is a kind of reaction of solidarity with them among the people who are combating terrorism in the Basque Country. That solidarity is the product of the fact that they [Amedo and Domínguez] were colleagues who were persecuted for these matters, and because there is a kind of understanding towards these irregular activities. So I have to step very carefully, above all recalling that we were generous, immensely generous, with those terrorists who accepted "reinsertion"[98] . . . There were poli-milis [members of ETA(p-m)] who had returned [from exile] who had killed police and *guardia civiles* who were not even called in to the Audiencia Nacional, who were not even tried.'

The security forces, he continues, wanted him to 'establish a kind of balance'. Hence the Socialists' support for those accused (and convicted) of torture ('the government had to pardon one of them'), and for Amedo and Domínguez: 'We gave them our backing, but not because we agreed with what they had done but because we had to respond to the police who asked us to give them at least the same treatment as "reinserted" terrorists. You may not be able to understand that from outside, you have to be inside to see it.'[99]

It seems self-evident from this analysis that Vera, and the Socialist government, were fully aware of Amedo's guilt when they took the decision to 'defend and support' them.

On 3 August 1988, Garzón got full support from the Audiencia Nacional for his decision to remand Amedo and Domínguez in custody. On the 18th, he got closely argued backing from an Audiencia Nacional prosecutor, Ignacio Gordillo. The sources of finance of the GAL, he said, were a fundamental element in the investigation. He also called for Garzón to investigate Amedo and Domínguez in relation to other GAL crimes, including the Segundo Marey kidnapping and the Monbar massacre.[100]

Any hope, however, that this indicated a sea-change in the administration's attitude to the investigation was dashed the following month. Senior figures lent credibility to a transparent – and bungled – attempt to obstruct the course of justice. Just as the Audiencia Nacional was considering whether to accede to Garzón's request to bring Amedo to trial, the conservative newspaper *ABC* produced a story which purported to exonerate him. It published letters from three of the GAL mercenaries convicted in Portugal, retracting their evidence. They claimed they had been offered release and financial help in exchange for incriminating Amedo. The Attorney General, Javier Moscoso, immediately made a public declaration that this new development was 'very important', because the evidence against Amedo was, he alleged, mainly based on their testimony. This point was refuted by prosecuting lawyers, as it would have had to be refuted by anyone with a nodding acquaintance with the case. Nevertheless, Moscoso's stance was robustly endorsed by the Minister for the Interior, José Luis Corcuera.

Moscoso might have been expected, as the senior state prosecutor, to be keen to see those accused of very serious crimes remanded in custody. Three times in two months, however, he appealed unsuccessfully to get Amedo and Domínguez out of prison. He was finally called before a parliamentary committee to explain himself. 'It is impossible to dismiss the impression that his intervention is connected with the Government's interests,' a member of Suárez's centrist party commented afterwards.[101]

Almost immediately, in any case, it became clear that the evidence offered by the 'Portuguese letters' was full of holes. The Portuguese Director of Prisons pointed out that the letters had not been properly witnessed, and lacked any legal value, something the mercenaries' lawyer must have known. Moreover, the mercenaries had had an excellent opportunity to withdraw their accusations against Amedo when Garzón interviewed them in June, but they had ratified them on that occasion. Spanish legal opinion found it hard to credit that the publication of the letters was unrelated to the Audiencia Nacional's pending decision on whether to support Garzón's decision to charge Amedo. Moreover, it soon emerged that the Portuguese lawyer who had drafted the letters believed that he had been contracted to do so by Amedo's defence team.[102]

Then two of the mercenaries did a U-turn. They had been offered release, they said, not for giving the evidence but for retracting it! The offer had come from one of the men who had recruited them. A judicial investigation found that the mercenaries had lied deliberately and that the content of the letters was false.[103] Amedo and Domínguez's new lawyer, Gonzalo Casado, denied any knowledge of the letters, and played down their significance. The manoeuvre had backfired, reinforcing the impression that powerful and shadowy elements would use any means to put the two policemen back on the street.

One of the great specialists in manoeuvring on Interior's behalf, Amedo's former lawyer, Jorge Argote, issued another letter in the same period, signed by Amedo. The policeman claimed that he had met the former ETA member (and GAL target) Fernando Egileor, in Bilbao. Egileor had told him that the dirty war strategy 'which had previously terrorised ETA would, in the fullness of time, become a shield and cover for the movement'. Trying to establish that his prosecution had been set up by ETA and Herri Batasuna, Amedo pointed out that his name had first been mentioned in *Egin* shortly after this meeting.[104] 'The strategy of falsehood,' he declared, 'is clear.' *Egin*'s source, on this occasion, was not ETA or Egileor, but the trial of Labade and company in Portugal. The strategy of falsehood would seem to have been Amedo's.

Finally, on 18 October, the game was up, at least in the short term. The Audiencia Nacional agreed to try Amedo and Domínguez for six attempted murders and membership of an armed terrorist group.[105] The senior magistrates found the evidence presented in Garzón's report 'clear and obvious'. The Audiencia Nacional writ was very detailed, and very damning. For example, it accepted Fontes Figueiredo's evidence that the two policemen recriminated with the mercenaries for failing to open fire in the Café des Pyrénées in February 1986, though the bar was packed with bystanders unconnected with ETA, including a number of children.

It was crucial that the Audiencia Nacional accepted Garzon's charge that the policemen were members of a terrorist group; otherwise it would probably have been almost impossible to try them at all, on technical grounds.[106] The Audiencia Nacional did not go all the way with Garzón, however. It postponed decisions on trying Amedo and Domínguez's superior officers, and on pursuing charges against Barrionuevo and Colorado for obstruction of justice. But it did allow him to continue investigating the mysterious reserved funds.[107]

SEÑOR X: A SYMBOL WITH A HUMAN FACE

A simple algebraic image, originated by Garzón, captured the public imagination in 1988 and has passed into common parlance in Spain. In his report to the Audiencia Nacional in July, the judge had drawn an 'organigram', a sketch of the GAL's command structure. As expected, Amedo's name connects downwards to clusters of recruiters and mercenaries, with names already familiar from the French and Portuguese trials. But the real thrust of the sketch is upwards from the superintendent, where a single 'X' indicates Amedo's unnamed *capo di tutti i capi*.

The idea of a 'Señor X', a mysterious and sinister mastermind behind the GAL, caught on. It has appeared in countless political speeches, headlines and cartoons. It became, fairly or otherwise, closely associated with Felipe González. When the GAL investigation

---

entered its second and most critical phase in the mid-1990s, the shorthand had become so familiar that the Prime Minister himself would tell a television presenter: 'It is false to say that I am Señor X, and we will sue anyone who says I am.'[108]

Garzón always insists that the X is a symbol of something unknown, and nothing more, a reliable source close to the judge told me.[109] As an examining magistrate, he always says, he can only deal in evidence, not speculation. A Spanish legal proverb says that 'What does not exist in the judicial report does not exist in the world.' That is the formal position.

I pointed out to this source that, in a later judicial report, Garzón had taken it upon himself to suggest to the Supreme Court that there was sufficient evidence to try González.[110] Surely this implied that he considered that Señor X and the former Prime Minister are indeed one and the same person? The source corrects me firmly: 'In the judicial report, Garzón says nothing. He only say what others, like Damborenea, have said to him in evidence.'

And yet, I persisted, in an interview with Manuel Vázquez Montalbán, Garzón is quoted as saying that González's role in the GAL was 'to let them do [it], to let [it] happen'.[111] That, said the source, was not a direct quote but 'a deduction of Montalbán's'.[112]

The words, however, are definitely quoted in the book. A few days later, I had the opportunity to check the source's account of Garzón's encounter with Montalbán in person. The writer was amused rather than offended by my source's apparent disclaimer, but stood firmly and precisely over his own version of events.

'I met him in the cellars of a Madrid restaurant, and he talked a great deal,' the writer told me. 'I could not tape him but I took some notes, and later I sent him the interview for him to read.'

'What did he say?'

'Well, he didn't say to me what your source said to you. That is, he left the interview practically unaltered, and only asked me [to include] one small observation. He read it before it was published, and he thought it was going to cause him a lot of problems.'[113]

Nevertheless, this most tactically astute of judges did nothing to stop its publication.

As soon as the Audiencia Nacional had decided to bring Amedo and Domínguez to trial, the police unions expressed solidarity with their imprisoned colleagues. In so doing, they cast aspersions in the same upward direction as Garzón's 'X'. They pointed out that two such officers would have neither the means nor the time to carry out the activities attributed to Amedo and Domínguez without the support of their superiors. They suggested that the case was being focused on these middle-ranking colleagues to 'avoid anything more being investigated'. More explicitly, the Communist MP Nicolás Sartorius said that 'morally speaking, this is a writ against the Government'. In Bilbao police circles, particular sympathy was expressed for Domínguez, whose only fault had been, it was said, 'to speak French correctly'.[114]

El País said that the Audiencia Nacional had put state terrorism in the dock. The writ was a victory for the independence of the judiciary; the case had become 'a test of the consistency of the structures of the democratic State'. The newspaper attacked the 'systematic and obstinate obstruction' of the Ministry of the Interior, and called for an early trial which would clear up the mystery over the 'disturbing' hypothesis of the 'X'.[115]

No sooner had the judges made the heat on Amedo and Domínguez seriously uncomfortable than journalists doubled the temperature. With impeccable timing, just two days after the Audiencia Nacional decision, Miralles and Arques of *Diario 16* broke a story they had been nurturing for nearly a year. This time their source was much more tangible than an anonymous 'deep throat'. Inmaculada Gómez and Blanca Balsategui, former girlfriends of Amedo and Domínguez respectively, had told them that the bomb which killed García Goena had been brought by the policemen to Gómez's flat.[116]

In a verbatim interview, Gómez claimed that Amedo had become deeply concerned, in the summer of 1987, about the waves of judicial and journalistic revelations that were sweeping him into the public domain. He feared that his bosses, whom she named as the Bilbao police chief, Miguel Planchuelo, and the national head of police intelligence, Jesús Martínez Torres, were going to let him go under. To show how much he could embarrass them if they did not offer him a life-raft, he had decided to kill Basque refugees who had nothing to do with ETA. He would claim the action for the now redundant GAL. Domínguez and Amedo had actually shown the two women the bomb, Gómez claimed. When she subsequently heard of García Goena's death, she had accused her boyfriend of the crime to his face. He had smilingly told her to 'shut up and change the subject'.

Shortly after her story appeared in print, Gómez confirmed this account, with abundant new and grimly colourful details about other GAL operations, to Garzón, who was able to corroborate some elements of her story.[117]

GUBU AND THE GAL, PART I: INTERIOR SENDS IN A SUPERSPY

Conor Cruise O'Brien, the Irish historian and polemicist, coined the acronym GUBU to describe the atmosphere which surrounded the controversial governments of an Irish prime minister, Charles J. Haughey. The word derives from a phrase in which Haughey himself attempted to describe a particularly embarrassing series of events in which his Attorney General had (inadvertently) given extended hospitality to a murderer on the run. These incidents were, he said, Grotesque, Unbelievable, Bizarre and Unprecedented.

There are plenty of candidates for a GUBU award among the events and characters involving the GAL, but the saga of an attempt to interfere with the testimony of Blanca Balsategui, Michel Domínguez's former lover, must be a front runner.

Balsategui was summonsed by Garzón to corroborate Inmaculada Gómez's allegations. This summons was supposed to be secret. A few nights before the appointment, she received an anonymous phone call to her home in Vitoria.[118] The caller implied that he was a friend of Domínguez's, and asked her to visit the inspector in prison before she spoke to Garzón. An envelope of bank notes was dropped through her letter-box the next day, to cover extra expenses.

Balsategui duly went to the prison in Guadalajara, where she was admitted (against regulations) and received instructions from both Amedo and Domínguez. They told her, unsurprisingly, to give a blanket denial of Gómez's story. She had been booked into a good Madrid hotel by her anonymous benefactor, who visited her there that night. He claimed that he was Alberto Seoane, a businessman, acting on behalf of 'a ministry'. He told her that what she said 'does not now affect only Amedo and Domínguez, but the government of the nation, which could fall if you tell the truth'.

The following day she gave the required version of events to Garzón, but was caught out in a lie about her last prison visit. Afterwards, she spoke to Melchor Miralles privately and revealed her predicament. With her permission, Miralles, Arques and a photographer followed her to her hotel, where they were able to photograph her with the mysterious Seoane. They were also able to track him to the Ministry of the Interior, where he spent nearly three hours, on a Sunday morning, in a meeting with persons unknown. The journalists were able to establish that he was a regular visitor to the building, but not an employee.

Miralles finally established that 'Seoane' was in fact Francisco Paesa, one of the most colourful, and most elusive, inhabitants of the shadows of Spanish public life.

A former lover of the widow of Indonesia's former President Sukarno, Paesa had had a decidedly dodgy business history. He had been the first director of the central bank of Equatorial Guinea, until the Guineans discovered that he was substituting old newspapers for legal tender in wads of dollar bills.[119] He had spent eighteen months in prison awaiting trial for fraud in Switzerland after one of his companies collapsed with enormous debts, though he was never convicted. He had links with the international arms trade, and had helped Julián Sancristóbal and the Ministry of the Interior sell electronically tagged weapons to ETA in 1986.[120] He played an obscure but probably crucial role in the capture of the fugitive former Director General of the Guardia Civil, Luis Roldán, in south-east Asia in 1995.[121]

In January 1989, however, Interior was not able to find him when Garzón charged him with interfering with a witness. His evasion of this charge involved a period enjoying diplomatic immunity as a United Nations ambassador. The Spanish media often portray Paesa as a romantic figure, a Hispanic James Bond whose success with women is as legendary as his mastery of international espionage. As a real-life figure, however, Paesa fits the category of GUBU rather more accurately than that of superspy. James Bond was never photographed by journalists while talking to a lady.

As if Amedo hadn't enough troubles at this time, two more of his agents fell into the hands of the French police in late 1988. Christian Hitier had just been extradited from Belgium to France. He added his voice to those incriminating Amedo, whom he said had contracted him in the name of the Spanish government, and he identified Dominique Thomas as the Black Lady.[122] Patrick Pironneau, a GAL associate of Hitier's, had also joined the chorus of accusations against the policemen.[123] Hitier, Pironneau and Thomas were all sentenced to three years' prison for criminal association in 1991.[124]

Important as the steady flow of interlocking evidence from the mercenaries and girlfriends was, Garzón kept a major focus of his inquiry on the funding of the GAL. This was the most likely source of documentary evidence – as opposed to hearsay accounts – leading to Amedo's superiors. The reserved funds might provide the paper trail which could lead to Señor X. In early November, it came to light that the authority to disburse these funds during the GAL period had been delegated to Bernaldo de Quirós, an accountant who happened to be the brother-in-law of Interior's number two, Rafael Vera. It further emerged that de Quirós had resigned his position shortly after Garzón began to seek information about the funds.

Contrary to what Amedo's superiors had told the courts, it transpired that there was a detailed (though non-official) documentation system for the reserved funds, including full receipts.[125] The day after this information emerged, the Audiencia Nacional gave formal backing to Garzón's demand that his investigation should receive full details of the allocation and use of these funds in the GAL period. The Audiencia Nacional refused, however, to permit him to indict Amedo's superior officers, because it had not yet been proved who had financed his operations.[126]

Despite this obstacle, Garzón kept shaking the Interior tree, and more strange fruit kept falling out of it. Jesús Martínez Torres, the head of police intelligence, admitted that he had known of the meeting, reported in *Le Monde*, between three Spanish policemen and the GAL squad leader Jean-Philippe Labade which had occurred on the frontier shortly before Labade had had Pérez Revilla killed. Yet Martínez Torres had never investigated it. Julián Sancristóbal had made a clumsy attempt to cover up these contacts when they were reported in *Le Monde* in 1985. Martínez Torres admitted that the police had carried out no investigation on the GAL. His personal curiosity appeared to have been satisfied by a phone call to the then chief of police in Bilbao, Miguel Planchuelo, who gave him the truly remarkable information that the GAL 'were a scam set up by ETA and Herri Batasuna'.[127]

In early December, the people's prosecution lawyers demanded that Felipe González should testify in the case. The Prime Minister had alleged in a press conference that witnesses against Amedo were having their statements prepared by Herri Batasuna.[128] If he had such knowledge, the prosecution argued, and had not transmitted it to the court, he would be guilty of a crime. Among the nineteen questions they drew up for him was the following: 'What does the Prime Minister mean when he says that the government backs and supports Amedo and Domínguez?'

As 1988 drew to a close, Javier García of *El País* published *Los GAL al Descubierto* (The GAL Revealed). It was a professional summary of the state of play in the investigation. There was, however, a great deal more still to be revealed than the title suggested. This was implicitly acknowledged by the author himself in his book's last words: 'The case has only just begun.'

NOTES

1   Interview with José Amedo, Madrid, November 1997.

2   This view of the GAL was often put forward, as we saw in ch. 14, by people like Rafael Vera who had a vested interest in promoting it, because they were themselves facing charges of organising the GAL.

3   The eminent lawyer Iñigo Iruin, who took the private prosecution case for Lasa's and Zabala's families, has elaborated a detailed 'organigram' of the structure of the GAL, linking the Guardia Civil, the National Police, the CESID and the Socialist Party's civil governors and other party officials. He showed it to me during our interview in June 1997. At this stage, it must still be speculative. As a veteran Herri Batasuna leader, Iruín obviously has vested interests in implicating the Socialists as far as possible, but even his political opponents concede that he is a brilliant and very well-informed investigator.

4   *El País,* 5 January 1987.

5   *El País,* 4 April 1987.

6   *El País*, 18 April 1987.

7   *El País*, 22 February 1987.

8   *El País,* 18 January 1987.

9   This false name was one of many instances of the macho sense of impunity with which GAL leaders often operated. It contained the initials 'GAL' twice in three words, the first and last names belonged in reality to senior anti-terrorist officers, and the middle name refers to Amedo's ethnic origin. It was, therefore, more like a series of clues than a cover name. Amedo's use of his personal Visa card is another instance of how certain these men must have felt that they would never be investigated.

10   *El País*, 13 June 1991; Ricardo Arques and Melchor Miralles, *Amedo: El Estado contra ETA* (Barcelona: Plaza y Janés/Cambio 16, 1989), p. 435.

11   Interview with José Amedo, Madrid, October 1997.

12   He was, in fact, a compulsive viewer of those Clint Eastwood and Charles Bronson movies where the protagonist triumphantly takes the law into his own hands.

13   Arques and Miralles, op. cit. p. 39.

14   There are several references to Amedo's sexual problems in ibid., pp. 42 and 713.

15   *El País*, 4 May 1987.

16   Joseba Azcarraga, a mainstream Basque nationalist politician who pursued the GAL issue with exceptional determination.

17   I requested interviews with more than a dozen of the senior GAL suspects linked to the Interior Ministry, ranging in rank from a police inspector to the Prime Minister. Only José Amedo and Rafael Vera agreed to meet me.

18   The interviews took place in October and November 1997. This section is based on the October interview.

19   Amedo himself of course denies this charge, and his former girlfriend's evidence was not accepted in court. See ch. 16.

20   Fernando López Agudín, *En el Laberinto* (Barcelona: Plaza y Janés, 1996). See ch. 18.

21 Arques and Miralles, op. cit., pp. 219–27; *El País*, 20 and 31 May 1987; *Diario 16*, 23 November 1987; *Interviú*, 5 August 1987.

22 *El País*, 20 and 21 June 1990.

23 *El País*, 21 June 1990; Arques and Miralles, op. cit., pp. 604–12 and 618–24. The Spanish magistrate was Baltasar Garzón.

24 Antonio Rubio and Manuel Cerdán of *Interviú*, 6 December 1987 and 11 February 1989; see also Arques and Miralles, op. cit., pp. 604–12 and 618–24.

25 *El País*, 14 February 1989.

26 Spain's special central court for serious crime, especially terrorist and drug-related offences.

27 *El País*, 6 February 1990.

28 *El País*, 20 June 1990.

29 José Barrionuevo, *2,001 Días en Interior* (Barcelona: Ediciones B, 1997), p. 135. Mendaille was not arrested until six months after Barrionuevo had ceased to be Minister for the Interior. Barrionuevo was a member of the cabinet which refused to extradite Mendaille in 1990. For further instances of the lack of reciprocity in PSOE extradition policy, see ch. 14.

30 Sagrario Morán, *ETA entre España y Francia* (Madrid: Editorial Complutense, 1997), p. 322.

31 *El País*, 20 June 1990.

32 Morán, op. cit., p. 322.

33 If this was the case, Mendaille did not betray this knowledge when he was finally rearrested and extradited in 1994, under the reforming amalgamated Justice and Interior ministry of Juan Alberto Belloch. He was sentenced by a court in Pau to twenty years on 29 January 1997, for the attacks on Egileor and Arraztoa (*El País*, 30 January 1997), but he denied all charges. There was insufficient evidence linking him to the murder of Juan Mari Otegi (*Txato*) to convict. All four mercenaries, and Odette Roussey, retracted their 1990 evidence against him at the new trial, but the court rejected their 'amnesia'.

34 See ch. 13.

35 Barrionuevo was still associating García Goena with ETA at Amedo's trial; see *El País*, 22 June 1991. His memoir, published in 1997, remains ambiguous on this question. See Barrionuevo, op. cit., pp. 37 and 403.

36 Interview with José Amedo, Madrid, November 1997.

37 Arques and Miralles, op. cit., p. 274.

38 *Deia* is the newspaper which broadly reflects the views of the Basque Nationalist Party (PNV). It seems odd that such a paper discouraged Arques's hot pursuit of the GAL story. It may simply have been loss of nerve, but it is one of the straws in the wind which can be interpreted to show that the PNV itself had something to hide regarding the GAL.

39 Ramírez is the high-profile and controversial editor who later established *El Mundo*, and whose name is inextricably linked both to the investigation of the GAL and to the manipulation of the resultant information in obscure interests. See ch. 19.

40 Arques and Miralles, op. cit., p. 293.

41 Arques and Miralles, op. cit., p. 312.

42 *Diario 16*, 18 November 1987.

43 García Goena had been killed just a month earlier.

44 Interview with José Amedo, Madrid, November 1997.

45 *Diario 16*, 18 November 1987.

46 *El País*, 2 December 1987.

47 *El País*, 3 December 1987.

48 *El País*, 14 November 1987.

49   Ibid.
50   *El País*, 27 November 1987.
51   *El País*, 1 December 1987.
52   *Le Monde*, 1 December 1987; see also *El País* and *Egin*, same date.
53   *El País*, 4 December 1987.
54   *El País*, 4 and 5 December 1987.
55   *El País*, 6 February 1988.
56   Ibid. Solana would become González's longest-serving minister, and was regarded as his likely successor until he became Secretary General of NATO in 1996.
57   *El País*, 2 March 1988.
58   *El País*, 16 March 1988.
59   *El País*, 22 March 1988.
60   Moreover, Boslé had a high reputation in Spain for his energetic implementation of tougher anti-ETA policies.
61   *El País*, 25 March 1988.
62   Ibid.
63   *El País*, 25 March 1988.
64   *El País*, 10 May 1988.
65   *El Mundo,* 24 April 1988.
66   *El País*, 26 May 1988.
67   Spanish law allows private citizens, individually or collectively, to be party to a suit relating to crimes committed by public officials with which they have no personal connection. See Vicente Gimeno Sendra et al., *Derecho Procesal Penal*, 3rd edn (Madrid: Editorial Colex, 1999), pp. 248–50. The pursuance of a 'people's prosecution' suit against Amedo by a number of public figures was a crucial factor in the development of the case. See 'Some Notes on the Spanish Constitution, Judiciary and Legal System', p. 442–44.
68   *El País*, 26 May 1988. This 'protection' was not very well organised. In several significant respects, Colorado's reply contradicted that given by Amedo's immediate superior in Bilbao, Antonio Rosinos Blanco. Colorado also denied that Michel Domínguez had accompanied Amedo to Portugal.
69   *El País*, 16 June 1988.
70   *El País*, 18 June 1988.
71   Colorado referred to a circular from the Franco period. It was a classic of bureaucratic obfuscation, which said that the only reckoning which had to be given was an assurance from departmental heads 'that they [the funds] had been assigned to the ends for which they are ear-marked in the budget'. Barrionuevo took an equally vague but more aggressive approach, ordering his subordinates to give no further information on the funds 'given the nature of the same'.
72   *El País*, 29 June 1988.
73   Ibid.
74   *El País*, 30 June 1988.
75   *El País*, 29 June 1988.
76   *El País*, 2 July 1988.
77   *El País*, 28 June 1988.
78   Interview with José Amedo, Madrid, October 1997. Once again, it must be pointed out that Amedo's response here is at least partly self-serving. Inexperienced mercenaries are cheaper than experienced ones, and the suspicion is that Amedo deliberately chose the former in order to enrich himself with the surplus. In the interview, he evaded this issue.
79   *El País*, 28 June 1988.
80   *El País*, 30 June 1988. The significance of this distinction in Spanish law is

that someone declared a suspect by a judge has the right to lie in his own defence, without facing charges of perjury. See Gimeno Sendra et al., op. cit., p. 392.

81 *El País*, 30 June 1988.

82 See *El País*, 27 February 1998.

83 *El País*, 1 July 1988. For the significance of the *Estado de Derecho* in the construction of Spanish democracy, see 'Some Notes on the Spanish Constitution, Judiciary and Legal System', p. 441.

84 *El País*, 3 July 1988. The PSOE government was at this stage enjoying its second absolute majority in the legislature, which made it particularly overbearing.

85 Interview with Javier Pradera, Madrid, November 1997.

86 *El País*, 14 July 1988.

87 See 'Some Notes on the Spanish Constitution, Judiciary and Legal System', p. xx.

88 *El País*, 14 July 1988.

89 Argote would continue to play a major role, in public and behind the scenes, in defending GAL cases. He was charged with attempting a cover-up in the Lasa and Zabala case, and was acquitted in April 2000.

90 *El País*, 21 July 1988.

91 *El País*, 24 July 1988.

92 Montesquieu was the eighteenth-century French philosopher who formulated the concept of the 'separation of powers' of the state between the judiciary, the executive and the legislature. For further discussion of this issue, see ch. 25, pp. 413–4.

93 *El País*, 24 July 1988.

94 *El País*, 22 July 1988.

95 *El País*, 30 July 1988; *Diario 16*, 30 July 1988; Arques and Miralles, op. cit., pp. 516 and 520.

96 *El País*, 29 September 1988. Corcuera was justifying the government's refusal to reveal the destination of reserved funds, even when it was suspected that they had been used for criminal ends.

97 *El País*, 2 October 1988.

98 This was the policy, initiated under the UCD and continued by the PSOE, which permitted those members of ETA(p-m) who no longer supported armed struggle to return to normal life without facing charges. See María Ángeles Escrivá, *El Camino de Vuelta* (Madrid: El País–Aguilar, 1998), for a full account of how this policy was developed and implemented.

99 Interview with Rafael Vera, Madrid, November 1997.

100 *Diario 16*, 19 August 1988.

101 *El País*, 12 October 1988.

102 *El País*, 30 September 1988.

103 *El País*, 15 December 1988.

104 Egileor recognises that this meeting took place, but at Amedo's request, and claims that the policeman was trying to recruit him as an informer. Egileor is a compulsive dialectician, and could not resist pointing out to Amedo how the dirty war policy had objectively assisted the revolutionaries at whom it was aimed. Interview with Fernando Egileor, Bilbao, June 1997. See ch. 10, p. 147 and p. 154 n. 34.

105 *El País*, 19 October 1988.

106 If the Audiencia Nacional had not accepted Garzón's view that the crimes involved membership of an armed organisation, the case would probably have been declared to be outside the particular remit of the court, and would have fallen into a legal limbo. See *El País*, 19 October 1988.

107 *El País*, 5 December 1988.

108 Interview on TVE-1 with Iñaki Gabilondo, 9 January 1995, quoted in *El País*, 10 January 1995. When a meeting with González was requested by this writer, the response of his office was to endorse this interview, and one other, as definitively representative of González's position on the GAL.

109 Interview, Madrid, November 1997.

110 This was the report sent by Garzón to the Supreme Court in which he said that he had found 'adequate evidence' that González had been a founder or leader of the GAL, based largely on the declarations of the former Socialist leader Ricardo García Damborenea. The Supreme Court prosecutor, Eduardo Moner, later rejected this aspect of Garzón's report. See chs. 17 and 19.

111 Manuel Vázquez Montalbán, *Un Polaco en la Corte del Rey Juan Carlos* (Madrid: Alfaguara, 1996), p. 299.

112 Interview, Madrid, November 1997.

113 Interview with Manuel Vázquez Montalbán, Madrid, November 1997.

114 *El País*, 19 October 1988. Domínguez's mother was French, and he had been brought up bilingually. His initial function in the dirty war was simply to translate GAL communiqués and phone them in to the French media.

115 Ibid.

116 *Diario 16*, 20 October 1988.

117 Arques and Miralles, op. cit. pp. 640–50. The details included the allegation that Amedo had accompanied the Black Lady to a bar in Ciboure, where he had pointed out a group of alleged *etarras*. The Black Lady went to the toilet before carrying out her mission, and, because people in the bar had changed places in the meantime, she shot the wrong men – the gypsies Emile Weiss and Claude Doerr.

118 The most detailed account of this episode is to be found in Arques and Miralles, op. cit., pp. 657–734. It is most unlikely that it would ever have come to light without the persistent journalistic detective work of these writers.

119 *El País*, 5 August 1990.

120 This was the operation which led to the discovery of a huge cache of ETA arms and documents in Sokoa, France. See Morán, op. cit., pp. 246–7.

121 *El País*, 12 March 1995; *Diario 16*, 12 March 1995.

122 *El País*, 14 November, 5, 19 and 22 December 1988.

123 *El País*, 30 November 1998.

124 *El País,* 18 October 1991.

125 *El País*, 4 November 1988.

126 *El País*, 5 November 1988.

127 *El País*, 19 November 1988. Planchuelo was convicted in 1998 for his part in the Marey kidnapping, and faces other GAL charges.

128 A curious aspect of the GAL investigation was that Herri Batasuna's involvement was actually quite minor at this stage. This was especially surprising given the coalition's motivation, inside knowledge and panel of legal expertise, which has always included some of the finest lawyers in the state. This reticence was interpreted by both *El País* and *El Mundo* as an indication that Herri Batasuna was using its extensive information on the GAL as a bargaining card with the Spanish government at another forum: the 'Algiers conversations' of 1986–9 which sought a negotiated solution to the conflict with ETA. See *El País*, 12 December 1988.

16

State Terrorism in the Dock:

two cops take the rap

Perhaps what is happening is that the State and its security is being confused with the security of certain persons and their possible criminal responsibilities.

Baltasar Garzón[1]

Judge Baltasar Garzón started 1989 with a very careful, very strongly worded argument, occasionally laced with irony, against the government's case on reserved funds. He insisted that his investigation represented no threat to the security of the state, but conceded that it might be a threat to particular individuals who were supposed to serve the state. The argument was addressed to three senior magistrates in the Audiencia Nacional, without whose agreement he could not proceed with this line of investigation. He did not receive an answer until April.

The government, wrote an *El País* editorialist in January 1989, 'faces the responsibility, once and for all, of demonstrating to public opinion whether or not it is in favour of letting the truth of such a murky affair be known . . . Not to provide them [the data on reserved funds] would not only be a serious obstruction of justice, but it would create impunity for very serious crimes . . . No State which really believes in the rule of law can, for whatever reason, leave [such crimes] uninvestigated and unpunished.'[2]

At the end of January, Garzón formally charged Francisco Paesa with collaboration with the GAL and obstructing the course of justice for his attempt to pressurise Blanca Balsategui. Georges Mendaille, sought by the French police since 1986, was finally arrested in Spain on 13 February. 'But I thought *you* worked for *them*,' one of his neighbours commented in amazement when the police arrived to pick him up.

Arques and Miralles published one of their dossiers, a catalogue of photographs and mini-biographies of no less than forty-six GAL suspects, in *Diario 16* in March. They revealed on the same day that previous *Diario 16* dossiers had been submitted by the police to Spanish magistrates, verbatim and without contradiction, when requested for information on the GAL. One of the dossiers was titled 'All roads lead to Amedo'.[3]

In the meantime, more evidence trickled in against Amedo from mercenaries facing long jail sentences. More tangible evidence also emerged. The magnets used in the bomb which killed García Goena were regularly available in only one shop in Bilbao: it stood just 40 metres away from Amedo's office in police headquarters. Similar magnets and explosives had been found in the *zulo* by Miralles and Arques.

Yet Amedo and his colleague continued to enjoy prison privileges available to very few people charged with such serious crimes. It may or may not have been true that, as rumour persistently had it, he and Domínguez dined on lobster and the best Castilian lamb, and were allowed to entertain women overnight.[4] But it was quite definitely true that, uniquely among all the prisoners in Spanish jails, Amedo and Domínguez were not obliged to give specimens of their handwriting, or to do fingerprinting tests. 'That would be a vexation and an offence to our honour and individual rights,' Amedo blustered successfully when he and Domínguez were requested to give their prints.[5]

Barrionuevo's successor at Interior, José Luis Corcuera, made no effort to curtail Amedo's privileges. His position on the investigation seemed identical to his predecessor's. Ignacio Gordillo, an Audiencia Nacional prosecutor who had consistently demonstrated his independence, was taken off the case. Gordillo had been repeatedly pressed by the (theoretically independent) Attorney General to demand the release on bail of Amedo and Domínguez, despite the seriousness of their alleged crimes. His parting shot was to threaten that, if he was compelled to do this, he would also publicly call for the release of ETA suspects on similar grounds.[6] He was replaced by a much more pliant senior prosecutor, Eladio Escusol.

It was not really a surprise, then, when the position of the Audiencia Nacional on the investigation of the reserved funds turned out to be absolutely supine. Garzón's superiors informed him that there was 'a collision or conflict' between the magistrate's right to investigate and the state's right to its own security. Because of this 'legal loophole', they could not support his demand for access to the financial information which was crucial to his case.[7] The main trail to Señor X had now been blocked.

'This argument is empty verbiage,' wrote *El País*, 'and hardly obscures the real motive of the decision: the impotent collapse of the judiciary before the obstructionist attitude of the government.'[8]

Legal experts rubbished the resolution. According to Enrique Gimbernat Ordeig, professor of criminal law in Madrid's Complutense University, it ran contrary to the Constitution, which he ironically suggested might be adapted as follows: 'All citizens have the right to life . . . except those who are victims of State terrorism'; 'All citizens have the right to the effective protection of the judges and the courts . . . except those damaged by criminal acts committed with public funds.'[9]

But perhaps the most memorable comment, in retrospect, came from a fast-rising judge in Bilbao, Juan Alberto Belloch: 'When there is a collision between a constitutional good, such as effective judicial protection, and another judicial value, such as the security of the State, constitutional rights always prevail.'[10] These words would return to haunt him when he himself became 'superminister' for Justice and Interior in the 'reformed' González administration of the mid-1990s, and became a late convert to the cause of state secrecy.

DBS Arts Library

Curiously, the Audiencia Nacional judges ruled shortly afterwards that the state must take financial responsibility for the consequences of Amedo's crimes, if proven, because such crimes would have been committed on active police service. To impose this responsibility on the state, while blocking the path towards clarifying if and how such responsibility might have been exercised, seemed perverse to many.[11]

State secrecy was also being invoked across the border in Portugal. The second trial of Jean-Philippe Labade and his mercenaries yielded more evidence against Amedo, but attempts to investigate the links between Labade's deputy, Mario Correia da Cunha, and Portuguese military intelligence were blocked by Lisbon on security grounds. The judges in this trial, however, specifically confirmed that Labade's men were acting on the instructions of Amedo and Domínguez.[12]

Back in Madrid, far from giving up, Garzón pursued the case more tenaciously than ever. A 'vertical' investigation – up the chain of command – was now closed off. But he retained the capacity to extend the investigation horizontally – through pursuing leads on other crimes committed by the GAL. In mid-June, he tightened the legal screw sharply with a writ charging Amedo and Domínguez, for the first time, with a consummated murder. Garzón accepted the account of the witnesses Inmaculada Gómez and Blanca Balsategui about the events which they alleged had led to the killing of Juan Carlos García Goena. The two men were also charged with interfering with witnesses. The people's prosecution went further, calling for the trial of two of Amedo's superiors for García Goena's murder. Miguel Planchuelo, former Bilbao chief of police, and Jesús Martínez Torres, the police intelligence chief, had both been implicated in the killing by Gómez and Balsategui.

It took the Audiencia Nacional only a fortnight to endorse the new charges against Amedo and Domínguez, though the court held off on the issue of trying his superiors. When Garzón formally read the charges to the policemen, Amedo insinuated that he could, if he wished to, reveal information on the real leadership of the GAL, the mysterious Señor X. It was a promise and a threat he would not fulfil for several years. Even then, he would retain the right to contradict himself. His attitude at this stage was more clearly expressed by his continued refusal to give an example of his handwriting – he limited himself to drawing a wavy line, with a little flourish of contempt, in front of the magistrate.

Ten days later, on 11 July, two of the people Amedo might well have named could breath a little more easily, as the Audiencia Nacional decided there was insufficient evidence to charge Planchuelo and Martínez Torres.

The investigative phase of the trial was formally completed on 27 September 1989, but it would be nearly another two years before Amedo and Domínguez would sit in the dock. The law delayed, and then delayed again, at the clear behest of senior politicians. There was hardly a development, or a lack of one, which did not add to the well-grounded suspicion, implicitly confirmed by Vera to this writer, that the government was doing everything in its power to continue to manipulate and obstruct the process.[13]

Despite this, the Minister for Justice, Enrique Múgica, blithely trotted out the line that 'the Amedo case is an example of collaboration between the powers of the State'.[14] Bitterly aware that the opposite was true, the people's prosecution team called, in vain, for the minister's resignation.[15]

No less than four panels of judges for the final hearing were proposed and withdrawn in as many months. Nor did the panel finally chosen inspire great confidence. The president, José Antonio Jiménez Alfaro, was well known for his protective attitude towards a former leader of the Triple A, an Argentinian terrorist group with connections to the pre-GAL dirty war.[16]

The wranglings preceding the trial were mostly as dull and fusty as the legal jargon in which they were expressed, but there were grim flashes of colour at occasional sideshows. There was the distasteful but fascinating spectacle of Amedo's superiors, called in to explain his activities. They passed the buck down the chain of command with breathtaking disregard for any conception of hierarchal responsibility. There was the desperate attempt of Amedo's lawyer to stop the publication of Arques and Miralles's ground-breaking and very well-informed book, *Amedo: El Estado contra ETA*.[17] These journalists presented a devastating case against the policeman – and the state – for the Christmas market in 1989.

For a bad moment in November, the dirty war suddenly seemed to have escaped the courts and be back in the streets. Once again striking on the anniversary of Franco's death, 20 November, masked gunmen fired at a group of diners in a Madrid hotel.[18] Josu Muguruza, a newly elected MP for Herri Batasuna and alleged to be very close to the ETA leadership, died in the attack. Another prominent Herri Batasuna leader, Iñaki Esnaola, was badly wounded. A policeman, Ángel Duce, was later convicted for the murder, but it appears that he was working for an extreme Right splinter group, and that this shooting was not linked in any way to the state apparatus.[19] In any case, it was not the start of a new campaign.

In the spring of 1990, the Hotel Monbar case, now investigated separately from the main GAL case,[20] suddenly – and briefly – got much hotter. There was evidence from a waiter at the Hotel Londres and a security officer at the Kursaal Casino in San Sebastián that Amedo and Domínguez had been seen in their establishments with the mercenaries Frugoli and Mattei before the Monbar killings. Both these witnesses suggested that the two policemen were seen from time to time with other individuals, whom they could now identify as convicted mercenaries.[21] When the two policemen put in an appearance at the tables, the casino staff used to give good odds (among themselves) that a GAL action would soon be on the news.

In one clear respect, these witnesses were better than any mercenary could have been, because they had no vested interest in accusing the policemen. In keeping with the defence that the evidence against him was a Herri Batasuna/ETA frame-up, Amedo labelled one of the witnesses as a radical nationalist. He produced nothing to substantiate this claim, but the witness in question began to qualify his evidence.[22] Amedo and Domínguez denied even knowing where the Hotel Londres was, despite conclusive evidence that they had stayed there.[23]

Despite the fact that the independent witnesses' evidence was corroborated by Frugoli's highly incriminating declarations in a French court, this case was shelved at the request of Eladio Escusol, the new Audiencia Nacional prosecutor.[24]

On 20 July, the Audiencia Nacional finally took the formal decision to set the terms for trying Amedo and Domínguez, merging the Batxoki/Consolation and García Goena cases. This writ, however, copperfastened the chamber's refusal to further investigate either the reserved funds or Amedo's superiors.

Eladio Escusol caused a wave of outrage in October, when he made his preliminary case against the two policemen to the court.[25] His evaluation was flagrantly inconsistent. He argued that the evidence of Inmaculada Gómez and Blanca Balsategui was unconvincing, and therefore he did not press the charge of murdering García Goena. Yet he did press the charge that Amedo and Domínguez had interfered with these witnesses. This most unconvincing prosecutor did not explain why the defendants should have taken the risk of doing so, if the testimony of these women was as weak as he said it was.

More strangely still, Escusol did not consider the policemen to be leaders of the GAL, despite the abundant and compelling evidence from the mercenaries they had recruited. Finally, he argued that they were not members of the GAL at all! They were, he said, members of an armed band which 'carried out actions coinciding with the illegal activities and aims of the GAL'. Since the GAL had acknowledged responsibility for the crimes for which Domínguez and Amedo stood accused, this fine distinction seemed to derive from St Thomas Aquinas – or from *Alice's Adventures in Wonderland*.

Escusol also asked for the five attempted murders at the Batxoki to be considered 'a single action', thus reducing by ninety years the potential sentence against the men he was prosecuting.

GUBU AND THE GAL, PART II: THE FUGITIVE SUPERSPY BECOMES AN AMBASSADOR

The strangest story of all, however, was that of the freelance secret agent and professional fraud Francisco Paesa. He had fled the country when accused of pressurising Blanca Balsategui to change her evidence.[26] He now turned up in Switzerland, protected from extradition by diplomatic immunity.

He had somehow become the United Nations ambassador for the tiny African island state of São Tomé and Príncipe. These islands, with a population of 120,000, receive Spanish aid totalling 15 per cent of their GDP. They obliged Spain by acting as a host country for *etarras* expelled from France. The African authorities said they were willing to revoke Paesa's new status, whose origin they could not explain, on request from the Spanish government.

His status was not revoked until 3 December 1990, and it took a further ten days to inform the court, by which time he had disappeared

---

again. A fugitive from Spanish justice appeared to have been sheltered, at one remove, by the Spanish government itself. No other convincing explanation has ever been offered.[27] Paesa, as we shall see, had even more bizarre tricks up his sleeve.

As the trial date approached, the Audiencia Nacional decided to summon three key people to give evidence: Felipe González, José Barrionuevo and José Luis Corcuera. They were, as *El País* expressed it, 'qualified witnesses', who had it in their hands to clear up, once and for all, the suspicion that Amedo and Domínguez could only have acted with support from above.[28]

Barrionuevo seemed willing, even eager, to reveal where his sympathies lay. He told a newspaper in his own constituency in April 1991: 'Amedo has undoubtedly been dealt with legally, but not justly.'[29] He would repeat a similar line in an interview after the trial.[30] Meanwhile, his party was attempting to put legislation in place which would give ordinary deputies and senators the same privileges as ministers.[31] Barrionuevo had been dropped from the cabinet in March, but this new provision would give him the same status as González and Corcuera, so that he would not have to appear in court but could reply in writing. This provision did not get through parliament, but it did not augur well for a clearing of the air at the trial.

The air looked no more translucent in May, when the court relieved the Prime Minister of the obligation to reply to twenty-two of the twenty-six questions the people's prosecution had put to him.[32] Among the rejected questions was the first: 'Did you organise the creation of the terrorist organisation, the GAL?' The Audiencia Nacional found this question 'unrelated in general terms to the ascertainment of the facts under investigation at this trial'. Nor was he to be asked to clarify his famously ambiguous statement that democracy had to be defended in the 'sewers' as well as in the 'salons'. Nor would he have to explain what he had meant by saying that Amedo and Domínguez 'have the right and duty to feel themselves defended and supported by their government'.[33] Lawyers, academics and civil liberties activists made the, by now, usual protests.

Another very large group of witnesses would not be coming at all. The twenty-one mercenaries in foreign jails, whose presence had been demanded by the prosecution, were simply going to stay where they were. Those in Portugal had turned down the invitation, and those in France had not replied, for reasons that would only become clear during the trial itself. 'Administrative and judicial difficulties make their attendance unlikely,' French sources had told *El Mundo* in February.[34] Only the convicted killer of Jean-Pierre Leiba, Daniel Fernández Aceña, would attend, because he was in prison in Madrid. And he was notoriously unreliable and given to fantasy.

The trial of Amedo and Domínguez was one of the most keenly awaited and closely observed in Spain since the fall of the dictatorship, a courtroom super-drama second only to the trial of the army officers responsible for the 1981 coup attempt.[35] The hearing before the Audiencia Nacional began on Tuesday, 11 June 1991, in the oven-dry heat of the Madrid midsummer.

The proceedings opened with a wise-cracking, cocky Amedo, clearly very conscious that he was performing on a national stage for a national audience. He denied having any connection with the GAL, whom he described as 'a group of wrong-doers, with few moral values, who sell themselves to the highest bidder'.[36] He claimed that he had been framed by Herri Batasuna and ETA.

Given the extent and weight of the evidence against him, he was distinctly short on alibis, but on the first day he produced his 'last grandmother'.[37] Like several important defence witnesses in GAL cases, she turned out to be dead. Precisely for that reason, Amedo said he could not have participated in the murder of García Goena. He had been at her funeral in Galicia on the date of the killing. He could produce no more proof of his attendance than a copy of her death certificate. His attendance would have proved very little anyway, since he was not accused of carrying out the killing personally.

Corroboration was equally lacking for his defence that the millions of pesetas he had lost at blackjack had come from 'property deals'. The anonymous Bilbao businessmen whom he claimed were his partners could not appear, he said, because of the risk of reprisals from ETA. 'I would commit high treason if I put their lives in danger,' he told the court.[38] He gave a similar reason for refusing to name the friends he said he had entertained in Portugal, the night he was accused of recruiting Labade's second mercenary *comando*. They were, he alleged, bull-fighting *aficionados* who still enjoyed trips to the bullring he used to preside over in Bilbao. 'I would rather that my innocence was questioned than give names which could cause [them] repercussions in the Basque Country.'[39]

He treated the courtroom as his theatre, and the judges allowed him to exercise his glib verbosity without restraint. Asked why a Portuguese mercenary should have been found with Spanish police issue ammunition – allegedly given to the mercenary by the defendant – Amedo joked that 'anyone can find bullets in the street'.[40] When he was pressed as to how Paulo Fontes Figueiredo had identified him in a French court, he turned on his accuser: 'But what do you want to do with me? What are you trying to do? I have told you that I do not know this person, I will not permit you to speak to me about him again. You cannot do whatever you like with me!'

As on many later occasions, the presiding judge, Jiménez Alfaro, intervened in the defendant's favour. He was equally indulgent with Domínguez, who simply refused to answer prosecution lawyers' questions on the grounds that he felt 'total antagonism' towards them.[42] For the first few days, it often seemed that Amedo was running his own trial, and directing it towards acquittal. Yet, by a strange coincidence, Fontes Figueiredo was repeating his damning evidence at his own oral hearing in Pau during these same days. He was sentenced, for some of the same crimes for which Amedo was charged, to fifteen years in prison on 13 June.[43]

The big indication that matters were moving in the defendants' favour was signalled by the court's decision to delay hearing the crucial evidence of their former girlfriends Inmaculada Gómez and Blanca Balsategui. There were already signs that Balsategui was shifting her story. Meanwhile, Amedo lost no opportunity to attempt to discredit Gómez, painting her as a resentful woman 'who did not even amount to the category of a one-night stand'. He had told her in a letter that he had 'never loved you, not even desired you, I just used you from time to time'.[44] Now, asked if he had told her about being a GAL commander, he replied, in classically ambiguous fashion, 'Absolutely not. I'm not that stupid.' He contemptuously dismissed her account of his having brought explosives to her flat. 'It's almost laughable that anyone would think that I, without having any possibility of concocting an explosive, would go on a date, dressed to kill, with a little bomb under my arm.'[45]

The impression that everything would go Amedo's way was further strengthened when his superiors, starting with the Prime Minister himself, gave evidence which favoured him. Responding in writing to the only four questions which the court had ruled admissible, Felipe González denied all knowledge of the GAL, and said that he 'could not remember' ever discussing this group with the French. Contrary to what his subordinates would tell the court, he said that the Ministry of the Interior had investigated the GAL.[46]

Memory problems afflicted every one of Amedo's superiors. They trooped into court to deny any but the most general knowledge of a group which several of them would later admit to organising. Despite their alleged ignorance of the GAL's structure, they would all insist that the GAL were not an organisation at all, but 'isolated groups, contracted from time to time'.[47] They all refused to answer questions about reserved funds, as expected, though several of them, including Vera and Barrionuevo, asked the court to accept, on faith as it were, that such funds could not possibly have been used to finance the GAL. Curiously, though he claimed that documentation on such funds did not exist, Barrionuevo also insisted that they were 'rigorously controlled'.[48]

Why did Interior not investigate the allegations against Amedo, the prosecution asked, even when the French courts began to demand his arrest? There was no need for any formal investigation, because Amedo's immediate superiors always vouched for him, said Rafael Vera.[49] He might have added that they continued to do so in court.

'There may be police who are his equals, but none who are better,' was a typical comment.[50] Exactly what Amedo had done that was so important – if it was not to run GAL *comandos* – was never explained to the court. Another of Amedo's immediate superiors in Bilbao, Antonio Rosino, made his own contribution to the lexicon of ambiguities on the dirty war when he told a television station during the trial: 'It is beyond question that the GAL have done the State a great favour, although the end does not justify the means, and the GAL must be hunted down.'[51]

This miasma of amnesia and double innuendo was thickened further by the court appearance of Barrionuevo, ten days into the case. He repeatedly refused to recognise that the GAL were terrorists. This was a point which would seriously affect the defendants' sentence should they be found guilty of membership, and was repeated by Sancristóbal and Álvarez.[52] But Barrionuevo's special contribution was to formulate a theory that would be revived aggressively when he himself came to face charges in 1996. The Interior Ministry, far from nurturing the dirty war, had investigated it so successfully that the GAL had stopped operating in 1986. How Interior had managed to this, while simultaneously claiming to know virtually nothing about the GAL, and without making a single significant arrest,[53] was an unresolved mystery. Yet the presiding judge repeatedly seemed to protect witnesses like Barrionuevo from close interrogation.

The defendants basked for days in this harmonious chorus of support. But even in these early days of the trial, independent witnesses sounded occasional dissonant notes. Court officials painstakingly delineated the trail of luxury hotels and false identities which Amedo and Domínguez had used on days coinciding with GAL attacks.[54] Handwriting experts confirmed that Amedo's signature on his Visa card corresponded to the script on Fontes Figueiredo's false ID card.[55] Employees of the Kursaal Casino and Hotel Londres in San Sebastián confirmed that the two men had been seen on their premises with others whom they now recognised as mercenaries. They said that the policemen regularly took phone calls under the same pseudonyms which these mercenaries had already identified in foreign courts.[56] These witnesses were particularly valuable, because they had nothing to gain (and, possibly, much to lose) by giving evidence.

Outside the courtroom Blanca Balsategui gave a confused and contradictory radio interview in which she retracted some of her allegations against the defendants.[57] The tactic of delaying her court appearance seemed to be bearing fruit for the defence.

But the state prosecution was coming under peer pressure to revise Escusol's extraordinarily exculpatory accusations. Escusol had been promoted before the trial began. On 12 July, his replacement, José Aranda, doubled the sentence originally demanded by Escusol. But Aranda's intervention was belated and seemed half-hearted, and his court performance was no great improvement on his predecessor's. He was yielding to the unassailable argument, firmly based on precedent, that the Batxoki attack represented five separate offences, and not a 'single action', as Escusol had tried to rule. Amedo and Domínguez now each faced up to 120 years in prison. However, Aranda maintained Escusol's position that there was insufficient evidence to convict them for the García Goena murder.[58]

That evidence was then further diminished through Balsategui's retractions, which she confirmed in a dramatic and bitter courtroom confrontation with Inmaculada Gómez. Asked about the bomb which she had previously agreed to seeing in Gómez's flat, Balsategui now said she 'didn't know if it was a bomb or a piece of cheese'. She accused Gómez of having 'lost her head', to which Gómez responded, in an exchange which reflected the catty tone of the argument, 'you never had a head to lose, unfortunately'. The confrontation attracted maximum media interest, and not only because of its legal significance. The case had heard evidence from a number of Amedo's and Domínguez's girlfriends, all striking and attractive women, and this fierce clash between two of them was an irresistible climax to the sideshow soap opera about the policemen's amatory exploits.[59]

Yet Balsategui's retraction was not really very damaging to the prosecution. Here was a woman who was suddenly denying declarations she had previously made to journalists, to her lawyer, in subsequent sworn statements to Garzón, and in private (legally tapped) phone conversations. The court accepted that Paesa, Amedo and Domínguez had pressurised her to change her evidence. Her distressed confusion was evident in court. 'By the end of this, I won't know what my name is,' she declared at the close of the confrontation.[60] An aggressive state prosecution could have torn her retractions apart. But the state seemed to have no serious interest in getting aggressive about the killing of García Goena.

The real surprise in the trial occurred by accident. Miguel Castells, the private prosecution lawyer,[61] found by chance that a letter about the mercenary witnesses from the French Ministry of Justice had been lodged in a French court. It stated that the ministry had decided unilaterally not to allow the mercenaries in its prisons to travel to the trial. The ministry said it was not willing to assume 'the risk inherent in the transfer of a group of such significant people'.[62] It had not even consulted the mercenaries themselves.

At first sight, this seemed like one more manoeuvre aimed at protecting the defendants, a collusion between Paris and Madrid to obstruct justice. If this was the motivation for the decision, which is not impossible, it backfired badly. A provision in Spanish law states that, where it is impossible for witnesses to attend the oral hearing, their previous statements to the investigating magistrate have full validity for the court. The mercenaries could not now be cross-examined by the defence, nor could they retract anything they had said, should they have wanted to.

Their lengthy, detailed statements, so assiduously collected by Garzón in visits to French prisons, were solemnly read to the court. They merged into an unbroken torrent of hours of evidence which was devastating to the defence. Here was Fontes Figueiredo's account of being upbraided by Amedo, and by his French agent, for failing to shoot indiscriminately into bars full of women and children.[63] Here were the stories about mercenaries sleeping rough in cars and taking trains instead of cars because Amedo had kept their wages in his own pocket.[64] Most of the evidence had been confirmed by the verdicts of French courts. And the same key points were repeated, again and again and again:

- Amedo and Domínguez, or their intermediaries, had contracted them as mercenaries to liquidate *etarras*.
- Amedo and Domínguez had told them – or at least implied – that their operations had the support of the Spanish (and sometimes the French) secret services.

The defendants suddenly stopped looking like the heroes of their own trial, and began to look at very long jail sentences. One part of the game of the GAL was up at last.

Or not quite. This was still a trial through the looking-glass, where things were often the reverse of what might be reasonably expected. Thus Aranda's summing up, on behalf of the state prosecution, had many of the features of a defence. He opened by enumerating the crimes committed by ETA during the oral hearing. It was a shocking catalogue, eleven killings, including five civilian victims, in five weeks. Yet it had, as he himself admitted, no legal relevance whatsoever to the matter before the court. Why, then, did he raise it? It seemed as though he was attempting to justify, retrospectively, the actions of the people he was supposed to be prosecuting.[65] Why did the court not cut him short?

When he finally listed the proofs against the defendants, he then appeared, in almost every instance, to *undermine* his own case against them, not to support it The most flagrant example was the key issue of the fingerprint on Fontes Figueiredo's false ID card. Aranda argued that it was impossible to be certain that this print was Amedo's, because Garzón had failed in his duty to fingerprint Amedo. The reality was that Amedo had refused Garzón's repeated demands to give an example of his prints. The greenest prosecutor in the world would have argued that the refusal to give decisive evidence, when easily available, can only imply guilt. Aranda, with decades of experience, chose to infer that Garzón had been sloppy and to stress that the evidence remained inconclusive.

In the context of this surrealistic 'prosecution', it was hardly surprising that he fully backed Interior's refusal to investigate the reserved funds: to do so 'would disarm society and swamp our citizens in chaos,' he argued.[66]

The people's and private prosecutions naturally took a very different line. Fernando Salas directly accused the government of creating the GAL,[67] while Miguel Castells argued that the mere existence of the GAL was 'a thousand times worse than ETA', because it undermined the legitimacy of the state itself.[68]

The defence lawyers, as was proper, had the last word, though many felt that Amedo's defenders had had the first word as well. 'It was hardly necessary,' wrote Rafael Torres in *El Mundo*, 'that Gonzalo Casado should take the floor, after the vibrant defence of the state prosecutor.' Casado's case was now numbingly familiar. The policemen were the victims of a conspiracy involving a woman scorned, a sinister politician,[69] an ambitious investigating magistrate, scumbag mercenaries and an unscrupulous press. Curiously, though he naturally insisted that his clients were not members of the GAL, he was equally at pains to insist that the GAL were not a terrorist group.

'The Truth is not a human characteristic,' commented Torres bleakly, 'and it is enough to attend a trial to see how little humankind has perfected the mechanisms for approaching it.'[70]

If the truth was in the sentence, it would have to wait until September, because Spanish legal holidays took precedence over completing it, even in a case as significant as this. There was, however, an early indication of a rather surprising outcome, given the conduct of the trial. The court decided not to allow the policemen out of prison in the meantime. Amedo and Domínguez had already served three years, the time they would have been expected to spend in jail if the sentence was less than eight years. The clear implication was that they were going to get a heavier sentence than that. Against the odds, it looked as if they were going to be found guilty on at least some serious counts.[71]

The sentence, handed down on 20 September, was 'very hard on Amedo and Domínguez, and very easy on the State apparatus', in the words of Juan Carlos Carbonell, professor of law in Palma de Mallorca.[72] The defendants were each sentenced to 108 years and eight months in prison, for six attempted murders (the Consolation and Batxoki attacks), illegal association, falsification of documents and public use of assumed names.

Their fate had been sealed once the judges decided to admit evidence from mercenaries in France as fully valid. The defendants' refusal to co-operate with such procedures as handwriting tests and fingerprinting also counted heavily against them. The Spanish judiciary might be skewed by political pressures, but it could not disregard such a coherent body of evidence.[73]

Amedo and Domínguez were found not guilty of the murder of García Goena on the grounds that, even if Gómez's story of their bringing a bomb to her flat was true, there was insufficient evidence to show that this was the bomb which killed him. The court found that the defendants had instructed Balsategui about what she should say to Garzón. But since there was no evidence that they threatened her, they were not guilty of pressurising a witness, having acted within the legitimate rights of defence according to Spanish law. Paesa, not having been a defendant at the time he spoke to Balsategui, could not have been saved by this defence, but he was, as usual, in another country.

They were found not guilty of belonging to an armed gang, or of terrorism, because their motivation was not to destroy democracy, but to defend it, 'although they used judicially reprehensible methods'.[74] This was a ruling which clearly reflected the views and interests of the government, and flew blatantly in the face of the facts. Even Vera has conceded this point, in a conversation with this writer.[75]

The court also accepted the government's argument against the investigation of reserved funds, and so the policemen were absolved of misusing public money. The same argument blocked the investigation of the structure of the GAL. 'It cannot be ascertained that this organisation effectively constitutes a parallel power operating within the State apparatus.'[76] Despite the fact that the court accepted that Amedo and Domínguez had committed their crimes while on duty, the state was absolved of any financial responsibility for damages for their actions.

The state, in fact, had been absolved of responsibility, full stop. For the moment, the buck had stopped with the two policemen. There seemed to be little possibility that it would ever move up the line again, especially as there was widespread expectation that the government would find a way of granting them a pardon. Most people in Spain were probably relieved. Insofar as an honourable effort had been made to investigate the GAL, democratic justice had done its job, without shaking the state, or the ruling party, to its foundations. It would take an extraordinary combination of circumstances to make that happen. But the 1990s turned out to be extraordinary times in Spain.

NOTES

1 Baltasar Garzón, requesting authority from the Audiencia Nacional to seek data on reserved funds, 17 January 1989, quoted in *El País*, 18 January 1989. Both Garzón and the deputy leader of the Partido Popular, Francisco Álvarez Cascos, would later use very similar arguments in pursuit of another key to subsequent GAL investigations, the 'CESID papers'. In reply to such

arguments, the Supreme Court produced an extraordinary echo of Garzón's original form of words: 'the security which the Official Secrets Act seeks to preserve is that of the State, and not of its authorities or servants who may personally find themselves related to a criminal case'. *El País*, 11 April 1997. See also ch. 21.

2   *El País*, 19 January 1989.

3   *Diario 16*, 5 March 1989.

4   This allegation was made by, among others, a police superintendent. See *El País*, 18 May 1990.

5   Ricardo Arques and Melchor Miralles, *Amedo: El Estado contra ETA* (Barcelona: Plaza y Janés/Cambio 16, 1989), p. 546.

6   *El Mundo*, 14 October 1990. He would also be removed from the Lasa and Zabala investigation in controversial circumstances. See ch. 19, p. 292. n. 22.

7   'We find ourselves,' the Audiencia Nacional argued, 'in a situation of collision or conflict between the fundamental right to effective judicial protection, which legitimises the powers of investigation of the magistrate, and the right, also fundamental, of the State to its security, to which the legal regime of reserved or secret funds corresponds; there is a legal loophole.' *El País*, 26 April 1989.

8   *El País*, 27 April 1989.

9   *El País*, 8 June 1989.

10 *El País*, 29 April 1989.

11 *El País*, 2 June 1989.

12 *El País*, 22 and 29 May, 26 June and 21 October 1989, among others.

13 See ch.15, p. 217–80.

14 *El País*, 18 June 1989. The main GAL case, known as the *Caso GAL* in Spanish, was also known colloquially in a telling synonym as the *Caso Amedo*.

15 There were shifts and overlaps between the responsibilities of the Justice and Interior ministries in the Socialist period. Broadly speaking, Justice was responsible for all matters related to the courts and to prisons and prison policy. The latter, however, sometimes formed part of the brief of the Interior Ministry, which was always responsible for internal state security, through the police and Guardia Civil, and for immigration control, civil defence, etc. The question is further complicated by the fact that the Socialists amalgamated the two departments in a single 'superministry' under Juan Alberto Belloch from May 1994 until the Partido Popular victory in 1996.

16 *El Mundo*, 14 October 1990.

17 Much of Arques and Miralles' information is, of course, now out of date and some of it has been shown to be inaccurate by the many developments since 1989. But many of those developments might never have happened had not these authors blazed such a daring and valuable trail.

18 Santiago Brouard had been killed on the same date five years earlier.

19 For a contrary view, written from the perspective of Herri Batasuna, see *Egin*, 'Guerra Sucia' series, January/February 1995, nos. 14 and 16, and Pepe Rei and Edurne San Martín, *Alcalá 20-N* (San Sebastián: Egin/Txalaparta, 1996).

20 The *Caso GAL* at this stage focused on the 1986 attacks on the Batxoki and Consolation bars, and the killing of García Goena.

21 *El País*, 17 March 1990.

22 *El País*, 20 April 1990.

23 *El País*, 5 April 1990.

24 *El País*, 23 March 1991.

25 *El País*, 10 and 11 October 1990; *El Mundo*, 14 December 1990.

26 See ch. 15, p. 222–3.

27 *El País*, 12 December 1990.

28   *El País*, 14 February 1991.
29   *La Voz de Almería,* quoted in *El Mundo*, 4 April 1991.
30   *El País*, 26 September 1991.
31   Under the Ley de Enjuicamiento Criminal.
32   *El País*, 9 May 1991.
33   See ch. 15, p. 217.
34   *El Mundo*, 19 February 1991.
35   See ch. 4, p. 64.
36   *El País*, 14 June 1991.
37   *El País*, 12 June 1991.
38   *El País*,13 June 1991.
39   *El País*, 12 June 1991.
40   *El País*, 13 June 1991.
41   *El Independiente*, 12 June 1991.
42   *El País*, 14 June 1991.
43   Ibid.
44   *El País*, 21 July 1991.
45   *El País*, 14 June 1991.
46   *El País*, 15 June 1991.
47   *El Mundo*, 19 June 1991. This was the view of police intelligence chief Jesús
     Martínez Torres. He did not tell the court who contracted these groups.
48   *Diario 16*, 16 February 1995, quoting his appearance on 22 June 1991.
49   *El País*, 25 June 1991. Barrionuevo's former deputy should have known what
     he was talking about. He remained the number two in Interior at the time of
     the trial.
50   Ibid. The source of this compliment was Miguel Planchuelo, Amedo's
     immediate superior in Bilbao police headquarters.
51   *El País*, 27 June 1991.
52   *El País*, 25 June 1991. Curiously, in an uncharacteristic slip-up, Amedo had
     referred to the GAL as 'that terrorist group' on the first day of the trial.
53   Amedo had been arrested on the instructions of an investigating magistrate.
     Mendaille was arrested only after enormous media pressure. Both men were
     subsequently protected, not investigated, by Interior. The Spanish police, as
     we have seen, arrested only mercenaries at the very bottom of the GAL's chain
     of command, and then only when they had no option but to do so.
54   *El País*, 21 June 1991.
55   *El País*, 4 July 1991. Amedo had successfully resisted court orders to give a
     handwriting sample to the authorities, right up to the opening of the trial.
56   *El Mundo*, 27 June 1991.
57   *El País*, 28 June 1991.
58   *El País*, 13 July 1991.
59   *El País*, 3 July 1991.
60   Ibid.
61   The lawyer representing the victim's interests. See 'Some Notes on the
     Spanish Constitution, Judiciary and Legal System', p. 442.
62   *El Independiente*, 10 July 1991.
63   *El Sol*, 14 July 1991.
64   *El Mundo*, 9 July 1991; *Diario 16*, 23 March 1989.
65   While ETA's unabated campaign of terror might have generated some sympathy
     for Amedo and Domínguez, it hardly said much for the *efficacy* of the GAL, since
     ETA killed more people in 1991 than in any year since 1983. With supreme
     indifference to Spanish public opinion, ETA carried out one of its worst atrocities
     just two weeks before the trial began. A car bomb in the Catalan town of Vic killed
     ten people, seven of them civilians and five of them children, on 29 May.

66 *El País, El Mundo, El Sol, El Independiente,* 16 July 1991.

67 *El País,* 17 July 1991.

68 *El País,* 16 July 1991. Miguel Castells was a senior member of Herri Batasuna at this time. However, if we eliminate his hyperbole, his conclusion is similar to that reached by the state prosecutor, Jesús Santos, in the Lasa and Zabala trial nine years later. Santos has no such radical affiliations.

69 Txema Montero of Herri Batasuna, who was alleged to have 'coached' Inmaculada Gómez in giving 'fabricated' evidence against Amedo.

70 *El Mundo,* 18 July 1991.

71 *El País,* 31 July and 20 September 1991. The magistrates were understood to have completed their deliberations before they went on holiday. Amedo and Domínguez had been so confident that they would either be found not guilty or receive a minor sentence that they had booked their own holidays.

72 *El País,* 21 September 1991.

73 Jorge Argote, the controversial lawyer linked to Interior who first defended Amedo and Domínguez, said that no court in any other European country would have found them guilty. (Eliseo Bayo, *GAL: Punto Final* (Barcelona: Plaza y Janés, 1997), p. 13.) That would be a terrible reflection on European justice, if it were true. The likelihood is rather that they would not have got off so lightly in other jurisdictions. The fact that they did not appeal to the European Court of Human Rights suggests that they, and their patrons, knew this well themselves.

74 *El País,* 21 September 1991.

75 Interview with Rafael Vera, Madrid, November 1997. For a full account of Vera's view on whether or not the GAL were terrorists, see ch. 25, pp. 416–7.

76 *El País,* 21 September 1991.

17

Recollections in Tranquillity:
the scapegoats learn to sing

'What's happening?' Rafael Vera is usually an unflappable man, but José Barrionuevo remembers getting a 'rather agitated' call from his former deputy, just before Christmas in 1994. 'They've arrested Julián Sancristóbal,' Vera continued, answering the easy part of his own question. 'He's been in Garzón's chambers for several hours.'[1]

Within a day, four police officers, all members of Sancristóbal's 1980s anti-terrorist elite, joined the former Director of State Security in jail, on the instructions of Judge Baltasar Garzón. Men who had grown used to sybaritic lifestyles saw their personal effects abruptly reduced to shaving foam, soap, toilet paper and two condoms.[2] Within weeks, Vera followed them inside. In less than twelve months, a Supreme Court judge asked for parliamentary permission to charge Barrionuevo himself with GAL offences. Unlike Barrionuevo, Vera was not an MP and enjoyed no parliamentary immunity.

While some of Spain's top counter-terrorists were being hustled behind bars, José Amedo, now a convicted criminal and once a minion of the arrested Interior top brass, was out on the town. He was regularly spotted by photographers, conspicuously eating and drinking in the best restaurants and nightclubs in Madrid. On Garzón's instructions, he took his pleasure under police protection. No wonder the Socialist establishment could not understand what was happening. Their world had turned upside down.

This was not the first shock wave to hit the PSOE leaders in the *annus horribilis* of 1994. The ground had started to shift beneath their feet the previous year, and by the end of 1995 a series of judicial earthquakes had shaken everything, even Felipe González's iron grip on power. The fault lines can be traced back, ironically enough, to the Prime Minister's inspired election campaign in 1993. González had upset all predictions at that time by snatching back victory from an opposition party which was certain it was about to cross the floor to government. The full price of his triumph has still to be calculated.

In 1993, after eleven years in office, the Spanish public had seemed to be terminally disenchanted with the Socialist Party. If, in the fateful phrase of Alfonso Guerra, Spain was now 'unrecognisable to her own mother',[3] many people were disturbed by the image their country had taken on. True, the Socialists had had spectacular successes in modernising the economy, the infrastructure and society generally, but the process had been a bruising one.

Their traditional working-class constituency had manifested its discontent as early as 1988. The trade union historically linked to the party, the General Workers' Union, had then issued a joint call with the Communist-led Comisiones Obreras for a massive general strike. An economic downturn in 1992, with three devaluations, coupled with austerity measures to converge with EU criteria for monetary union, exacerbated this divide. González's U-turns on issues like NATO membership had stripped the PSOE of most of its left-wing idealism. The conduct of the GAL cases, coupled with the growing evidence of flagrant economic corruption, had tarnished the party's reputation for honour and for honesty. Nevertheless, the PSOE had done remarkably well in the 1989 elections, missing a third absolute majority by only a single seat. That success, however, was due less to continuing enthusiasm for the outgoing government than to the persistent unattractiveness of the right-wing Partido Popular as a credible alternative.

In the early 1990s, that changed. The distinctly uncharismatic but doggedly determined leadership of José María Aznar had begun to bear fruit for the Partido Popular. He highlighted its makeover as a modern European party of the centre-Right, and understated the Francoist associations of its older members.[4] Nostalgia for the old regime among its ranks became so discreet as to be almost invisible. Since the centre had collapsed in 1982, the conservatives had seemed too right-wing for modern Spain, but Aznar gradually persuaded the public that he offered a viable democratic alternative to González.

The year 1992 was a deceptively buoyant one for the PSOE, replete with grandiose public events. The quincentennial of Columbus's voyage to America was marked by the extravagant Expo in Seville. The Olympics in Barcelona were an international public relations triumph, and a major achievement in urban renewal by the city's popular and visionary Socialist mayor, Pasqual Maragall. Meanwhile Madrid, captured from the Socialists by the Partido Popular the previous year, enjoyed rather less distinction as the annually designated European City of Culture.

The government also enjoyed a spectacular anti-terrorist success in 1992. The arrest, with significant Spanish participation, of the three top members of ETA's high command in Bidart in the French Basque Country seemed to signal a watershed in the struggle against terrorism.[5]

None of these triumphs, however, could do more than briefly sweeten the odour of corruption which fouled the Spanish political atmosphere in the early 1990s. Alfonso Guerra had had to resign as González's deputy in 1991, over allegations that his brother, Juan Guerra, had abused his connections to make a personal fortune. The PSOE's treasurer had resigned because it was emerging that a holding company, Filesa, had been financing the party through commissions paid by big business for fictitious consultancies. Senior members of the Guardia Civil in the Basque Country were allegedly deeply involved in drug smuggling.

It is true that scandals were also tainting the Partido Popular and other parties at this time, but most of the muck raked was sticking to the PSOE. The party had enjoyed a monopoly of political power at many levels in Spanish society for an unhealthily long time. It was said, not entirely in jest, that you could not become president of a village ping-pong club without having a PSOE party card in your pocket. Those excluded from this large golden circle were getting restive, and so were many who were unlikely to enjoy patronage under an establishment of a different political colour. The Spanish public did not necessarily believe that the Partido Popular would be lily-white in power. However, on the minimally democratic nineteenth-century Spanish principle that it is better to be mugged alternately by different political cliques, rather than to be permanently robbed by the same one, many voters were ready for a change.[6]

González's apparently indestructible charisma was the one asset the PSOE still had. Enormous though it was, it was insufficient to carry another election unassisted. The Prime Minister decided to look for candidates, and policies, outside the Socialist fold, among the very people who had most coherently attacked his government. The PSOE had come to power in 1982 under the slogan of *Por el Cambio* (For Change). For 1993 they produced the slogan *El Cambio del Cambio* (The Change of the Change), implying that the necessary reforming alternative could emerge from within the PSOE's natural left-of-centre constituency. González was tacitly acknowledging that something had gone wrong under his administration. But he was suggesting that it could be put right, without the risk of putting Spain back in the hands of closet Francoists whose democratic credentials had yet to be established in practice.

To implement this strategy, he sought out some of his fiercest independent critics, and asked them to run as candidates. Among them were a professor of ethics and a veteran feminist. But his boldest and most fateful coup was to enter an arena where many of his colleagues thought their party was under sustained attack: the judiciary. He emerged with three impeccably honourable judges under his belt, scourges of corruption and champions of democracy. Two of them became key players in the next phase of the GAL drama.[7]

Juan Alberto Belloch had made a name for himself as a young magistrate in Bilbao, where he was a founder of the Basque Human Rights Association and a leading member of the progressive judicial association, Judges for Democracy. He was an outspoken opponent of torture by the security forces, and had castigated the way in which the administration had obstructed the investigation of the GAL.[8] Belloch alone would have been a fine moral shield for the discredited Socialists to carry into the 1993 campaign, but González did even better than that – or so it seemed in the short term.

To be number two on the Madrid ballot list is the most coveted electoral slot in Spanish politics, after the Prime Minister's own number one position. It had been held for several successful elections by one of

González's most faithful and longest-serving ministers, Javier Solana (who subsequently became EU defence supremo). In 1993, he found himself displaced by a man whom many loyal party members would have spat at in the street. Baltasar Garzón, the indefatigable investigator of the GAL and its links to the PSOE's state apparatus, was suddenly a figurehead of the PSOE's election campaign.

The sight of González and Garzón embracing on the hustings was as much a shock to the judge's erstwhile defenders in the media as it was to his detractors in the PSOE. 'The most sceptical observers of the human condition say that everyone has a price,' wrote *El Mundo*. 'As of yesterday we know, with regret and shame, that Judge Garzón certainly has one.'[9] Many people wondered how the man who had invented the tantalising hypothesis of Señor X could have thrown himself into the arms of the politician widely believed to be the actual person signified by that symbol. *El País*, on the other hand, saw Garzón's move as the result of a salutary piece of implicit self-criticism by the PSOE, though it did wonder, prophetically enough, what the consequences would be if he chose to return to the judiciary.[10]

Garzón had a defence against those who charged him with betrayal: he argued that he could not, in conscience, have refused an invitation to help in cleaning up the corruption he had been denouncing for years. How he would act if he found that the corruption came from the top of the party remained to be seen. Most of his many critics in the PSOE kept their lips buttoned during the election campaign. Barrionuevo, however, could not resist reiterating his support for a pardon for Amedo and Domínguez, and repeating his attacks on Garzón's investigation and their 'legal but unjust' trial.[11]

The public gave both the judge and the Prime Minister the benefit of the doubt, and the PSOE won its fourth consecutive election against all the odds, though it lost sixteen seats and had to rely on support from the Catalan nationalists in order to govern. The Partido Popular gained thirty-four seats: a significant advance under other circumstances but a bitter, almost unacceptable disappointment to Aznar and his colleagues.

González's daring electoral strategy had worked in the short term, but it has come to be seen as one of the most pyrrhic victories in recent European politics. As a direct result of the success of González's strategy, three highly combustible elements – an alienated Partido Popular and two brilliant judges working against each other – came into contact during the next legislature. They detonated a series of crises which would make the scandals of the early 1990s look almost trivial.

The Partido Popular believed that they had been robbed of a victory which was theirs by right. The party's seething resentment resulted in a new style of recklessly destructive opposition. They did not have to search very hard for weapons. The zealously reforming Belloch and the soon-to-be disenchanted Garzón combined inadvertently to provide the opposition with an arsenal. They were assisted by fiercely polarised sections of the media, and a series of shady figures with dubious motivations. The sewers from which, as González had once so infelicitously claimed, democracy was defended were mined and blown open to public view.

WAITING FOR A PARDON: AMEDO AND DOMÍNGUEZ RUN OUT OF PATIENCE

While the Prime Minister was busy securing a fourth term, two people who had made those sewers their home had been sitting impatiently in their prison cells, waiting for a pardon which had been often promised but had never come. Six months after Amedo and Domínguez had been sentenced by the Audiencia Nacional, the Supreme Court had confirmed almost all the decisions of the lower court, including the crucial (and much-criticised) ruling that the policemen were not terrorists. It only corrected the Audiencia Nacional on one point: it decided that the state had 'vicarious civil liability' for their crimes.[12]

This did not mean that the Supreme Court believed that they were acting under the state's orders; it did mean that they carried out their nefarious activities on the state's time and on the state's payroll. The state therefore had to compensate their victims. This decision would have seemed all the more ironic if it had been known that the state had continued to remunerate its two former agents handsomely, from the moment they were arrested. Amedo and Domínguez's silence did not come cheap.

They shared a small cell, in an isolated gallery in Guadalajara prison. Their quarantine was for their own safety. They might now be criminals in the eyes of the law, but to the other (non-political) prisoners they were still cops. There were persistent rumours that they enjoyed special privileges. A prison spokesman, however, rejected the view that 'there is a favourable attitude towards him [Amedo] among the warders, who consider him a hero'.[13]

If the warders really saw Amedo as an ordinary prisoner, they were out of step with large sections of public opinion. The police unions collected 110,000 signatures calling on the government to pardon their former colleagues. The pair made no trouble in prison, and Amedo's good manners impressed everyone with whom he came into contact.

It was not easy to recognise the *louche* brothel-creeper and contractor of mercenaries in the eulogy of an Opus Dei priest who visited him regularly. 'Then [in 1980s Bilbao] he was single and lived that kind of life,' he told a journalist in reference to Amedo's past. 'But today he is a man of faith and great devotion . . . he is not a criminal or a thief, but an honourable man. His toughness, manliness and serenity are commendable. I respect the sentence, but I think that he has given great service to the police and to society.'[14]

Even Amedo is a little embarrassed by this eulogy today. 'I believe in God but I'm not religious in the sense that I'd want to enter a monastery. In prison I didn't have to go to church, the church came to me, no? Now I might go occasionally.'[15]

His main concern in jail, he says now, was not faith or devotion, but the traditional prisoners' preoccupation: how to get out. It should, he says, have been easy.

Even before Garzón had remanded him in custody, he says, he had told Vera and Barrionuevo, through his lawyer Argote, that he would take responsibility for what had happened. 'They were delighted, naturally. Argote passed us messages from the government saying that we would get out quickly, but the situation kept unravelling. We maintained a wall of silence for everyone. And time kept passing, and . . . they kept promising us, saying "Wait a little more, wait a little more."'

In the meantime, of course, they were receiving financial compensation. He will not explicitly reveal its precise source, but he hardly needs to. 'We were not such idiots that we would lose our jobs and go to jail to cover up for a government, and leave our families to starve, were we?'

'Did the money come from the state?'

'Well, my wife was given money, sometimes through Argote and sometimes through other people.' These payments would provide one of the crucial keys for the reopening of the investigation of the GAL.

Finally, Amedo says, he decided he would stay quiet no longer. He says he sent letters to the Interior Minister and the Prime Minister, saying 'if they didn't sort things out for us, we would make sure the whole affair blew up in their faces'.[16]

Amedo was running out of patience after the Socialist victory in 1993, though the payments to his wife kept on coming under the supposedly 'reformed' regime. Belloch had been given the Ministry of Justice, but Corcuera was still Minister for the Interior, and held all the real power over the past of the GAL and the present and future of the GAL convicts. Garzón had not been given a ministry at all, just the directorship of a new anti-drugs agency, which was initially attached to the Ministry of Social Affairs.

The *cambio del cambio* had ceased to be a priority for González once he was back in power. The principle which dominated the Moncloa Palace (the Prime Minister's residence) still seemed to be the one which the novelist Juan Benet claimed he had heard articulated there not long before: 'Corruption is the oil of the system. It lubricates the wheels so that they turn smoothly and do not screech. It is only necessary to make sure that it does not go beyond a certain level.'[17]

In the early winter of 1993, however, the tight world of the PSOE elite began to unravel very fast. Three unconnected resignations had repercussions which would interlock to bring down the whole structure of 'Felipismo', as González's highly personalised Socialist establishment was now known. Corcuera departed from Interior when his draconian proposal to give the police extra powers was found to be unconstitutional. He was replaced, not by Belloch or Garzón, but by Antoni Asunción, a former director of prisons with a tough reputation. Asunción did initiate changes, however, parting company with Rafael Vera, who left Interior after guiding departmental policy for eleven years.[18] In this reshuffle, Garzón initially appeared to have replaced Vera, being promoted to the rank of secretary of state and having his anti-drugs agency shifted into Interior. However, Asunción assumed Vera's crucial responsibility for the security forces, and kept Garzón's wings clipped.

Another senior figure connected to Interior also fell from grace in November 1993. Luis Roldán, the first civilian to be appointed Director General of the Guardia Civil, could not explain to parliament how he had rapidly become a multi-millionaire on a modest salary. Unsurprisingly, it was investigative journalism rather than the fraud squad which brought his remarkable personal wealth to public attention.

Roldán had been Government Delegate in Navarre during the GAL period, and his forced exit must have caused considerable anxiety among his former colleagues. González could take comfort in one thing only – the scandal had forestalled him from making the cardinal error of appointing Roldán as Corcuera's replacement at Interior. The parliamentary and judicial investigation of Roldán produced a series of sensational revelations over the next few months, especially relating to the once-taboo topic of reserved funds. It emerged that they had been used, without any legal basis, to pay 'supersalaries' to civil servants in Interior and the security forces, and this would clear the path to investigation of reserved funds in the GAL cases.

The third head to roll at this time had no link to the GAL scandals at this stage, but the banker Mario Conde exercised a decisive and sinister influence on revelations about the dirty war over the next few years. He made quick money faster than anyone else, flirted with politics (he was allegedly offered the leadership of Alianza Popular after Fraga) and liked to be photographed very close to the King.

His flagship bank, Banesto, was subjected to an emergency audit by the Bank of Spain in December 1993. Over 600,000 million pesetas were found to be 'missing'. Conde was out of a job and *en route* to jail for fraud, but he still had bags of money, plenty of influence, and the best private intelligence services that such money and such influence could buy. All the pieces required to checkmate González were now on the chessboard. Four months later, they moved with bewildering speed.

Felipe González's 'tragic week' began on 29 April 1994 with the news that Roldán, now under criminal investigation, had dismissed his police bodyguard and fled the country, just as a judge was ordering that his passport should be withdrawn.[19] He left behind an interview in *El Mundo* in which he threatened to wash all of the PSOE's dirty linen in public.[20] Since he had directed the Guardia Civil for eight years, it could safely be assumed he knew where a lot of it was. In a telling phrase, he told the journalists that he did not intend to be 'fooled the way they fooled Amedo'.[21] Amedo read the interview in prison, and the humiliating phrase lodged in his brain like a slow-burning fuse.[22]

Asunción felt obliged to resign the day following Roldán's dramatic departure, after only five months as Interior Minister. His predecessor, José Luis Corcuera, made a memorable comment on Roldán's transformation from police chief to most wanted man: 'How could anyone have expected that the parish priest would turn out to be the brothel owner?' It does not seem to have struck him that this was a question the

Spanish public was beginning to ask about the whole Socialist leadership. The bad apples were beginning to outnumber the good in the PSOE barrel. And it was the flawed judgement of those at the top of the party that had promoted these dubious characters to such pivotal positions in Spanish society.

González responded to the crisis, which he acknowledged as his most serious ever, with a dramatic reformist gesture. He made Belloch a 'superminister' by appointing him to Interior while leaving him the portfolio of Justice.

This move, however, only precipitated a further and more damaging resignation. Garzón now says he had already become deeply disillusioned with the PSOE's failure to deliver on its election promises. He had told the Prime Minister nearly a month earlier that he would resign unless González finally adopted serious measures against corruption. He now felt, apparently accurately, that Belloch would exclude him from any meaningful role in the new scheme of things, and gave a press conference.

'González has used me like a puppet,' he told the media, and ruefully agreed with those who had chided him for allowing himself to be used as 'an electoral scam' by the PSOE.[23] He denied that he was resigning in pique at not being made a minister. All he wanted, he said, was to be allowed to participate in effective – as opposed to cosmetic – measures to combat corruption. It was now apparent that neither Belloch nor González saw any serious role for him in this field. González's State of the Nation address a few weeks earlier, he said, 'did not reflect the attitude I hoped for, and the performance of Belloch has left a bitter and disappointing taste in my mouth'.[24]

He resigned his parliamentary seat as well as his anti-drugs position, and returned to his chambers as an investigating magistrate in the Audiencia Nacional. His return to his old position, after a passage through the ministry whose functionaries he was again going to investigate, was, and remains, deeply controversial. It naturally infuriated the PSOE leadership, but it also perturbed much less partial observers. With Garzón back in the Audiencia Nacional, and Belloch finally in Interior, the last catalysts for the explosive re-emergence of the GAL issue were in place.

The public impact of the crises unleashed by the disappearance of Roldán was very evident in the European Parliament elections in June, when the Socialists' vote dipped by 10 per cent, and the PSOE was overtaken as the most-voted national party by the Partido Popular.[25]

Meanwhile, the two former policemen in Guadalajara prison were getting ever more restless. Their campaign for a pardon had begun in earnest the previous year. In April 1993, in a meeting which would later be highly controversial, Domínguez went to Garzón's chambers.[26] His stated desire to give evidence on the Segundo Marey kidnapping was widely interpreted as a warning to his former superiors that he was considering breaking his silence.[27] In any case, it appears that, on this occasion, he told Garzón he had nothing new to say, and used the time to consult the judge on his chances of getting a pardon.

A few weeks later, Amedo caused astonishment by turning up in the Attorney General's office, supported and seconded by Julián

Sancristóbal. He demanded that his petition for a pardon should be expedited.[28] He was officially on parole to visit his sick wife. The fact that a criminal of his status was received by the state's senior law officer caused uproar in the media and among the opposition, where it was assumed that a pardon was now just a matter of course. Amedo would later state that the Attorney General had called González on the telephone during the meeting. Both Amedo and Domínguez were at this stage giving media interviews in which they made veiled threats to reveal skeletons in state cupboards. 'In this life every circumstance has a limit,' Amedo muttered darkly to *Diario 16*.[29]

At the same time, however, prosecutors at the Audiencia Nacional were looking at a case which would stall the convicts' petition for pardon. This petition could not proceed if they were facing further charges. The evidence from the mercenaries convicted in France for the Segundo Marey kidnapping had finally been translated and verified. The case would lapse altogether if it was not reopened in Spain before the ten-year statute of limitation expired in December 1993, so both former police officers were called in to give evidence in August. They denied any connection with the crime.[30]

If the road to a pardon was now blocked, Amedo and Domínguez could still follow another path out of prison. Spanish law permits convicts who have served a quarter of their sentences to accede to an open regime of privileges known as the 'third grade'.[31] All third graders have to do is sleep in prison, and sometimes they do not even have to do that. In early 1994 the Minister for the Interior, Antoni Asunción, publicly favoured this concession, and González backed him.[32] Such a procedure had the advantage, from the PSOE point of view, of being easier to defend than a pardon. 'Third grade' was a 'normal' reward for good behaviour. It could be granted at the discretion of the prison authorities, without overt political intervention.[33] A pardon generally implied that there had been some element of injustice in the original sentence, and was by definition a political decision, which had to be directly ratified by the government.

Even so, Belloch found himself having to insist in parliament that such a concession, if it was made, would not imply 'buying Amedo's silence in any way'.[34] This founder of a civil liberties group began to use arguments like 'Amedo and Domínguez are not excluded from human rights.'[35] Some of his former colleagues in the legal profession retorted sharply that, on the contrary, they were being promised an open regime much earlier than it had ever been offered before. The proposal was widely regarded as 'a pardon in disguise', though in strictly legal terms this was unfair.[36]

Opposition MPs pointed out that the open regime was usually only conceded after prisoners had expressed repentance, which meant that imprisoned *etarras*, for example, rarely benefited from it. The former policemen certainly showed no indication that they acknowledged their guilt, let alone that they wanted to atone for it. During a seven-day 'special parole' in February 1994, which was controversial in itself, Amedo gave two radio interviews in which he specifically denied any participation in the GAL. Furthermore, he continued, 'I am not the key to reveal the structure of the GAL because I can't say anything about it . . . there is no pact of silence because I have nothing to scare anyone with.'[37]

Whatever chance there might still have been of a pardon evaporated with Belloch's appointment to the 'superministry' which amalgamated Justice with Interior in May. He appointed Margarita Robles, another independent and highly regarded judge, as his deputy in this department.[38] She rapidly demonstrated that she was at least as committed to reform as her new boss was. She was also rather less discreet about it, making her opposition to a pardon for the former policemen clear and public within a fortnight. The Attorney General and the Supreme Court followed suit with formal recommendations against such a measure.[39] The 'third grade' now seemed the best option for the policemen, and, to bolster their chances, Amedo definitively changed tack. He still did not explicitly acknowledge his guilt for specific GAL crimes but, in a formal letter written in June, he came close: 'I have reached the profound and sincere reflection . . . that no end justifies the use of violent means . . . I want to show my profound repentance for all those harmful acts which I have committed against the Law and society.'[40]

It was enough to persuade the prison authorities, already well disposed by the 'impeccable conduct' of the celebrity prisoners, to grant them the 'third grade'. On 26 July they were released, and took up soft-option jobs in insurance companies run by well-wishers. For a few weeks that summer, it seemed as though the saga of the GAL was finally over. The inadvertent combination of actions by Belloch in Interior and Garzón in the Audiencia Nacional quickly shattered that illusion.[41]

Amedo's satisfaction at being back on the street was soon soured by the discovery that he had nothing to spend, or at least not as much as he had expected. Immediately after his release, he had again insisted that 'no one has bought my silence'.[42] He was being very economical with the truth, because someone in Interior had been very generous with his personal economy. While he was in custody before his trial, almost 200 million pesetas had been lodged to Swiss bank accounts for himself and Domínguez. After they had been convicted, sums of up to 2 million pesetas monthly were paid to their wives from Vera's office. But once Belloch's team had free rein to examine the channels of corruption within Interior, it was only a matter of time before the golden tap was turned off. Amedo made one last effort to have it turned on again.

According to Fernando López Agudín, who was press secretary at the ministry to Belloch and Robles, it happened like this. In late October 1994, Margarita Robles was informed by the police that José María ('Txiki') Benegas, one of the most powerful 'barons' in the PSOE, had set up a most unusual arrangement.[43] A briefcase, a key and a box number would be sent to the Justice and Interior Minister, who was to ensure that an unspecified quantity of cash would be deposited for collection by Amedo and Domínguez's lawyer. Belloch secured the unanimous backing of his ministerial team to reject this proposal, and went to see González.

'González looked him straight in the eye and replied quickly and laconically,' writes López Agudín, '"You'll know what to do."' Belloch took this to mean he had the Prime Minister's backing, and despatched no money.[44] Both Benegas and Belloch himself have denied this story, but it is indirectly confirmed by Robles. When I met her in November 1997, she initially refused to discuss the issue. 'Until the GAL trial is over, that would be very imprudent.' Then she relents: 'I contradict nothing of what Agudín's book says, which I think is telling you quite a lot.'[45]

The consequences of Belloch's new policy were momentous. Tom Burns Marañón, in *Conversaciones sobre el Socialismo,* introduces his interview with Belloch in these terms: 'As Minister for the Interior and Justice, Belloch brought into disrepute the socialist project of almost 14 years of government: his decision to refuse pardons to Amedo and Domínguez, and to stop the flow of money [to them], revealed the theme of the dirty war against ETA, of state terrorism, which, once made public, sunk the early years of González as a ruler in the most abject moral disgrace.'[46]

While Burns is coming close to saying that González's real sin was to be found out, he provokes an interesting question. Surely the Prime Minister must have realised what would follow from appointing Belloch to Interior? As we have seen, the new minister was on the record as believing that Garzón should have been allowed to investigate the financing of the GAL through reserved funds in 1989.[47] He could hardly change that position now.

How did a man of González's great intelligence and astute sense of political strategy imagine that he could honour the demand for an assault on corruption without undermining the foundations of his own power, and the integrity of his own record? Had he developed such a sense of impunity that he felt he was beyond the consequences of his own actions, or those of his closest colleagues? Did he imagine that his own reputation was such that it could survive untainted by the opening up of the sewers of the state apparatus, to which he knew Amedo had had such privileged access? Or had he fatally compartmentalised his thinking, knowing that he must clean up Interior to survive, and refusing to envisage the consequences? Was this misjudgement a consequence of the loss of his hitherto inseparable deputy and confidant, Alfonso Guerra, in 1991?

It is just possible that González could indeed have weathered whatever storm Amedo could whip up, had it not been for the conjuncture that Garzón had returned to the Audiencia Nacional. He found there, by an extraordinary coincidence, that the Segundo Marey case was on his desk. At the same time as Belloch was blocking continued payments to Amedo, Garzón was following up the leads offered by the Roldán scandal. The emergence of evidence suggesting that reserved funds had been used to pay 'supersalaries' to Interior civil servants, and to make their bosses seriously rich, had opened up new lines of inquiry. The Pandora's box of state slush money was bursting open. Huge deposits connected to Roldán had been found in Switzerland. Garzón started checking whether Amedo and Domínguez also had funds in Swiss accounts.[48]

He also reopened another GAL case, relating to the Monbar attack. The original evidence against Amedo and Domínguez from mercenaries and other witnesses had been deemed too weak to proceed in 1992. Once again, Swiss bank accounts might provide substantial clues to the financing of this GAL operation. And he asked the Audiencia Nacional to send him any information they had on the funding of the Batxoki, Consolation and García Goena operations.[49]

Before he could make much progress on any of these matters, however, the primary objects of the inquiry came knocking on his own door. Amedo and Domínguez walked into his chambers on 16 December and incriminated themselves in the kidnapping of Segundo Marey. In doing so, they told a story which directly implicated a series of their superiors in the crime. These included two Bilbao superintendents, Julio Hierro and Francisco Saiz Oceja. Rising up the ranks, their allegations reached the former Bilbao police chief, Miguel Planchuelo, and the former anti-terrorist intelligence supremo, Francisco Álvarez. And they climaxed with the former Director of State Security, Julián Sancristóbal, as well as the former Socialist leader in Bilbao, Ricardo García Damborenea.

They also linked Sancristóbal's bosses, Rafael Vera and José Barrionuevo, to the GAL, and had hearsay evidence against González himself. 'The GAL were set up by the Government,' Amedo declared. 'We did not take a single step without following orders.'[50] Three days later, Garzón imprisoned Sancristóbal and then the senior police officers, which provoked Vera's agitated phone call to Barrionuevo. In the words of a leading Partido Popular jurist, 'the pestilence of the sewers had reached the best salon in the palace'.[51]

NOTES

1 José Barrionuevo, *2,001 Días en Interior* (Barcelona: Ediciones B, 1997), p. 501.

2 Their prison conditions were, in fact, far from harsh once the initial entry procedures had been complied with. Nevertheless, for men like these, accustomed to the exercise of power, their sudden subjection to the power of others, in every detail of their lives, was a severe shock.

3 See ch. 4, pp. 65–6.

4 The previous leader, Manuel Fraga, whom Aznar succeeded in 1989, had been a prominent minister in several of Franco's governments, and had been an authoritarian Interior Minister in the first post-Franco cabinet.

5 Francisco Múgica Garmendia (*Artapalo/Pakito*), José Luis Álvarez Santacristina (*Txelis*) and José Arregui Erostarbe (*Fitipaldi*), known as the 'Artapalo collective', were detained on 29 March, in a French operation in which the Guardia Civil played a key joint role. The detentions were regarded not only as a pre-emptive strike against a campaign which ETA was expected to launch against the Olympic Games and the Expo, but also as a definitive decapitation of the organisation. It was certainly a very severe blow, but by 1995 ETA had reorganised itself. See Sagrario Morán, *ETA entre España y Francia* (Madrid: Editorial Complutense, 1997), pp. 341–6.

6 In a rather artificial attempt to make Spanish politics approximate to British democracy, the Conservative leader Antonio Cánovas del Castillo had instituted the '*turno pacífico*' (peaceful changeover) system, whereby Conservatives and Liberals alternated in government more or less automatically from 1875 to 1896.

7 The third judge, Ventura Pérez Mariño, also played a minor but dramatic role in the decline of González's last government. Disgusted by the Socialist leadership's support for colleagues facing charges in the Filesa corruption case, and by the handling of the GAL trials, Pérez Mariño resigned his parliamentary seat during the State of the Nation debate in 1995, after calling for González's resignation.

8 See ch. 16, p. 231.

9 *El Mundo*, 28 April 1993.

10   *El País*, 28 April 1993.

11   *El Mundo*, 19 May 1993.

12   *El País*, 13 and 17 March 1992.

13   *El Correo Español*, 22 March 1992.

14   Ibid.

15   Interview with José Amedo, Madrid, October 1997.

16   Interview with José Amedo, Madrid, November 1997.

17   Quoted in Fernando López Agudín, *En el Laberinto* (Barcelona: Plaza y Janés, 1996), p. 19.

18   It is a matter of contention whether Vera was pushed out or resigned voluntarily. See also n. 45 below.

19   Other events of 29 April to 5 May 1994 include: the resignation of the former Governor of the Bank of Spain Mariano Rubio, a personal friend of González's, as an advisor to the bank, over another financial scandal; and the resignation of the Minister for Agriculture, Vicente Albero, over tax evasion allegations.

20   *El Mundo*, 2 and 3 May 1994.

21   Manuel Cerdán and Antonio Rubio, *El Caso Interior* (Madrid: Temas de Hoy, 1995), p. 72.

22   *El Mundo*, 27 December 1994.

23   *El País*, 10 May 1994.

24   Cerdán and Rubio, op. cit., p. 94.

25   The often-quoted 'three million votes lost' by the PSOE in this election is relative to the general elections of the previous year, and is not a valid comparison, strictly speaking. However, the currency of the quote does reflect the panic that afflicted the Socialists, and the euphoria of the Partido Popular.

26   *El Mundo*, 1 May 1993; *El País*, 2 May 1993. This meeting took place on 21 April, a week before Garzón left the judiciary to stand for the PSOE.

27   *El País*, 20 February 1994.

28   *El Mundo*, 17 May 1993.

29   *Diario 16*, 24 May 1993.

30   *El País*, 26 and 27 August 1993.

31   Amedo and Domínguez had been sentenced to 108 years technically, but in practice Spanish law sets an upper limit of thirty years in prison. Moreover, because they had followed a regime of prison work – including the manufacture of plaster Christmas cribs! – the five years they had actually served was calculated as ten.

32   *El País*, 16 February 1994.

33   In the case of high-profile prisoners like Amedo and Domínguez, the file was in fact passed on up to the minister's desk, and Belloch took personal responsibility for it. He insisted, however, that this was an administrative, and not a political, decision.

34   *El País*, 17 February 1994.

35   *El País*, 26 February 1994.

36   *El País*, 20 February 1994. See also López Agudín, op. cit., pp. 46–7. 'Third grade' had been a contentious issue for other GAL prisoners. Two members of the *comando* which killed Robert Caplanne were offered the open regime only nine months after they were sentenced, after serving six years in pre-trial custody. See also *La Vanguardia,* 20 September 1992.

37   *El País*, 18 February 1994.

38   He had plucked her from the judiciary the previous year, when he appointed her as an under-secretary at Justice.

39   *El País,* 8 and 9 July 1994. Eligio Hernández, the Attorney General who had received Amedo in his office, had been replaced by the much more independent-minded Carlos Granados at this stage.

40 *El País*, 27 July 1994.

41 Some Socialists believed, at least for a period, that Belloch and Garzón were secretly conspiring to undermine the party from within and without. All the evidence points to the contrary. The two men had taken opposed positions on the reformability of the PSOE. But Belloch's anti-corruption policy inevitably flushed out evidence and witnesses who would objectively advance Garzón's investigations.

42 *El País*, 28 July 1994.

43 Benegas was Secretary of Organisation ('number three') in the PSOE, and the most senior Basque member of the party.

44 López Agudín, op. cit., pp. 59–62.

45 Interview with Margarita Robles, Madrid, November 1997. She also implies that, while payments may have been made in the brief period when Asunción was minister, they were made without his knowledge. 'Everything he did was absolutely legal, I can tell you that. He was the person who had it most difficult as minister, not us. For example, he sacked Rafael Vera. Vera did not resign, he was sacked.'

46 Tom Burns Marañón, *Conversaciones sobre el Socialismo* (Barcelona: Plaza y Janés, 1996), p. 419.

47 See ch. 16, p. 231.

48 *El País*, 26 October 1994.

49 *El País*, 8 November 1994.

50 *El Mundo*, 27 December 1994.

51 Ibid.

18

A Cascade of Confessions:
the sewers flood the salons

What made Amedo and Domínguez break their silence? They claimed that they 'did not want to go down in history for covering up corruption'. They were 'telling the truth in the interests of a greater stability of the rule of law'.[1] Such altruistic reflections were presumably stimulated by the refusal of the Justice and Interior Minister, Juan Alberto Belloch, to either pardon them or bankroll them. The final straw may have come in early December 1994, when it was announced that the salaries from their new jobs might be confiscated to compensate their victims.[2]

But there were other forces at work. Domínguez had been secretly meeting *El Mundo* journalists with his lawyer, Jorge Manrique, since October. There was speculation that the impending imprisonment of the banker Mario Conde on fraud charges might be germane to Domínguez's and Amedo's sudden recovery of memory. Conde was highly influential with *El Mundo*.[3] Every advance in the investigation against Conde coincided, at times uncannily, with judicial and media revelations deeply damaging to the González government. For example, a series of sensational – and arguably sensationalist – interviews with Amedo and Domínguez started publication in *El Mundo* only four days after Conde was remanded in custody on charges of corruption.[4]

Meanwhile, another disgruntled big businessman, José María Ruiz-Mateos, had developed a close relationship with Amedo and was thought to be funding him. His mega-enterprise, Rumasa, had been expropriated and dubiously reprivatised by the PSOE in the early 1980s. The GAL revelations were grist to the mill of his flamboyant campaign against the Socialists.

There was a political angle as well. The Partido Popular was at least *au fait* with developments. The opposition party's deputy leader, the bellicose Francisco Álvarez Cascos, met Amedo's lawyer more than once in that fateful month of December, for reasons which have never been disclosed. On at least one occasion, the editor of *El Mundo*, Pedro J. Ramírez, was present.[5]

If Amedo and Domínguez needed any additional encouragement to keep 'collaborating with justice', an initiative taken by Judge Baltasar Garzón provided it immediately. He adapted their 'third grade' status so that they did not even have to return to prison to sleep. He granted them permanent police protection because, he argued, they were in physical danger and were safer at home than in jail.[6] It was not an argument that the prison authorities appreciated, but Garzón gained the backing of the relevant judicial authorities, who left the power to reverse the ruling entirely in his hands.

Amedo and Domínguez undoubtedly enjoyed their best Christmas in many years. But the last ten days of the year were stripped of seasonal cheer, not only for the former anti-terrorist bosses spending the holiday in prison, but for the whole Socialist establishment. As one revelation of the charges against the detained Interior chiefs succeeded another, the government and its supporters reeled in confusion. This turmoil was reflected in the financial markets, where the peseta fell while interest rates rose.[7]

The burden of the former policemen's accusations was devastating. They alleged that their superior officers had supervised every detail of Segundo Marey's kidnapping, including the crucial decision not to free him at once when they realised they had the wrong man. Amedo even claimed that Ricardo García Damborenea and Julián Sancristóbal had wanted to kill Marey and bury him in quicklime. He portrayed himself as the man who had saved Marey's life by successfully challenging their instructions.

Moreover, the two men had documentary evidence to back up some of their accusations. Domínguez had a copy of a GAL communiqué in Miguel Planchuelo's handwriting. His former boss came up with a remarkable explanation. He acknowledged the handwriting as his own, but said he had not authored the communiqué. He had heard it on the radio, and simply copied it down for his own records. He could not explain, however, how his note came to be in Domínguez's possession.

Domínguez had another GAL document, which had allegedly been revised in Sancristóbal's hand. Sancristóbal disclaimed the handwriting, but no fewer than five graphologists consulted by the court attributed it to him. The evidence provided by Amedo and Domínguez extended beyond the Marey case to the killings of Ramón Oñederra (*Kattu*), Mikel Goikoetxea (*Txapela*) and Rafael Goikoetxea. The 'appalling vista' of many more GAL cases opened up before a half-horrified, half-fascinated public. Garzón set up a series of intensive *careos* – face-to-face confrontations between conflicting witnesses – in the days (and nights) leading up to Christmas. Audiencia Nacional sources told *El País* that the detainees, who had all denied all charges, were not coming out of this process well. 'Domínguez is walking all over them,' the sources said.[8]

Even more serious, from the government's point of view, were the allegations that Sancristóbal had conferred with José Barrionuevo over the Marey kidnapping, and that Rafael Vera had organised special (and substantial) payments to the policemen who had attempted to kidnap José María Larretxea. Amedo also alleged that Alfonso Guerra, then González's deputy, had been kept informed by Sancristóbal. (No charges have been brought against Guerra in the GAL investigations.) Vera had not been summonsed by Garzón at this stage, but the implications were obviously very serious indeed.[9] The wildest allegations of the PSOE's enemies were being confirmed out of the mouths of two policemen who had enjoyed on-the-record support from the Socialists during – and after – their prosecution.

Characteristically, Barrionuevo responded bullishly, calling on 'friends and sympathisers' of Sancristóbal to write to him, and paying him a public visit of solidarity the day after he was imprisoned. He melodramatically offered 'to share the fate of the detainees because they are people I respect'.[10] Yet he rejected demands that he resign his seat in parliament, which conferred the legal privilege that he could not be tried by the Audiencia Nacional.[11] If Garzón had directly implicated Barrionuevo at this stage, he would have had to hand over the entire investigation immediately to the Supreme Court, where it might not have been so energetically pursued.

Barrionuevo's critics accused him of hanging on to his seat in order to avoid interrogation by Garzón. Garzón's critics accused the judge of failing to charge Barrionuevo at this stage, when there was significant evidence against him, because he wanted to hang on to the investigation. Both sets of critics are probably right. Barrionuevo is not a good performer under hostile questioning, as his trial would ultimately, and dramatically, demonstrate. Garzón would probably have demolished him. Garzón prides himself on meticulous adherence to legal procedure, but his flamboyant and aggressive working methods suggest he is willing to ride roughshod over legal niceties when they would obstruct his investigation. In a word, Garzón is a magistrate who wants to get his man.

The former Interior Minister implicitly accused Garzón of putting Amedo and Domínguez under 'tremendous pressure' to 'oblige them to make such allegations'.[12] He also implied that the judge was using his judicial power 'as an instrument of political and personal vengeance'.[13] In early January, he gave a press conference in which he impugned Garzón's motivations in particularly vitriolic terms. His charges were unanimously and roundly repudiated by the legal profession's watchdog body, the General Council of the Judiciary. One of Barrionuevo's PSOE colleagues commented acidly that he had 'succeeded in something that no one else had achieved: uniting all the judges behind Garzón'.[14]

Damborenea joined the counter-attack. He told the public, with typical doublespeak, that 'the decline of ETA had begun with the intervention of the GAL, whether or not you want to recognise it', while denying any personal knowledge of the organisation. Asked if he was the ideologue of the GAL, he said 'it would be an honour for me to be considered the ideologue of anything', but that the concept of the dirty war had been invented before the GAL.[15] In another interview he denounced the 'faintheartedness' of the government in refusing to pardon the policemen. He added, setting the headline for many future attacks on Belloch, Garzón and the judiciary in general, that 'the problem is that the country is in the hands of two inquisitorial judges'.[16] Blaming the judiciary became, and remained, a standard PSOE strategy. As one newspaper columnist countered, 'the judges begin to govern when the government ceases to do so'.[17]

DBS Arts Library

Always the realist, Rafael Vera made an appeal for measures of grace to be applied to members of the GAL, 'a group which fought, or tried to fight, against terrorism, although with illicit methods'.[18]

Garzón, rather than Amedo and Domínguez, was the main target of Socialist rage. Five major charges were made against him, which would be a template for debate in the future: he was motivated by resentment, and wanted vengeance against the PSOE because his political ambitions had not been fulfilled; he abused his power to remand suspects in custody, putting witnesses under intolerable pressure, or manipulating them by favourable deals; he leaked details of secret investigations to the media; he avoided calling witnesses or suspects whose legal status would take the investigation out of his hands; he abused the privileged information he had acquired while in Interior.

It is undeniable that Garzón sailed close to the wind on at least some of these counts.[19] The central fact remained that the content of the evidence against the administration was a far more serious matter than quibbles about the form in which that evidence was judicially managed. 'He is an investigating magistrate who wants to get the facts out in the open,' says Javier Pradera. 'As for whether or not he is motivated by vengeance, look, that is a question which would have to be answered by psychoanalysts.'[20]

The general argument that judges should not enter politics and then return directly to their old positions was a strong one in theory. The great irony was that it was the Socialists who had revived this Francoist practice, abolished by the UCD, to make politics more attractive to their legal cronies. Once again, the PSOE was hoist by its own petard.

There was clear evidence of a division between the Socialist Party machine, whose first instinct was to show solidarity with its jailed comrades, and the more cautious inclinations of the government itself. While senior *apparatchiks* like José María ('Txiki') Benegas were sending Sancristóbal warm telegrams of support, González was calling for strict respect for the judicial process. He did, however, make an elaborate reformulation of one of his most notorious statements on the GAL. When Amedo and Domínguez were about to be questioned in court about the dirty war for the first time in 1987, the Prime Minister had said that 'nobody *had been able to demonstrate*' that the state apparatus was involved in the dirty war. At a press conference in 1988, he said that 'there *will be no proof*' of such involvement.[21] With that position looking more and more untenable, he shifted to higher ground. He tacitly accepted that the state apparatus might have been involved, but the cabinet was still not implicated.

'It is absolutely impossible that anyone *could be able to demonstrate* that the government has anything to do with the GAL,' he told journalists on 22 December.[22] Once again, it appeared that some curious psychological mechanism prevented González from making a straightforward denial of government involvement in the dirty war. What was impossible was not the *existence* of a GAL–government link, he seemed to be saying, but the *demonstration* of such a connection.

Against the expressed wishes of the PSOE parliamentary group, González did cautiously concede that Belloch should take parliamentary questions on the affair. Since he insisted that the government knew nothing, and Belloch had publicly supported his line, he pointed out that the minister's answers would be 'sparse'. Most of the opposition initially responded to the crisis with restraint. The pragmatic Catalan nationalists showed no sign that they would withdraw support from González.

The Partido Popular, and especially Álvarez Cascos, had been demanding that González himself should appear before parliament to explain the position of the government, but was willing to give him a breathing space. At this point the Partido Popular was relatively restrained in pushing the huge political advantage presented by the scandal. The party apparently believed that the PSOE was now totally on the ropes. Aznar wanted to demonstrate statesmanship, and let it be known that he recognised that this crisis threatened not just the government but the institutions of the state itself. But he was angry that González had leaked news of a private dinner they had had on 19 December. The leak made Aznar look vaguely complicit with González. In response, he told a party meeting that he had had to listen to 'many lies' from the Prime Minister.[23]

The public soon had an unprecedented chance to judge for themselves whether the Prime Minister was lying about the GAL. On 9 January, *El Mundo* published the first instalment of their second series of interviews with Amedo and Domínguez, entitled 'How the GAL were covered up'. It described, with a wealth of detail, how the former policemen had allegedly been financed, and claimed that reserved funds, authorised directly by Vera, had been handed over to the wives of Amedo and Domínguez by Vera's personal secretary, Juan de Justo.

A spokesman for the United Left (Izquierda Unida) coalition, Felipe Alcaraz, seized the moment to throw down the full gauntlet for the first time: 'Now it's clear: Felipe González is Señor X.' The leader of the coalition, Julio Anguita, followed quickly with only one qualification: 'By action or omission, González is Señor X.'[24] The government was now up to its neck in a sea of allegations, and González knew he had to sink or swim. He decided to do an in-depth television interview with Iñaki Gabilondo, one of Spain's most respected TV journalists. Just minutes before he went on air, he learnt that Garzón had jailed Vera's secretary, Juan de Justo.

When asked to discuss the GAL for this book, González responded through a spokesperson that he had said all he had to say on the subject in this television interview, and in another more recent newspaper one, so it is worth some close attention.[25]

'FALSIFYING REALITY': GONZÁLEZ GOES ON PRIME-TIME AND INSISTS HIS GOVERNMENT'S HANDS ARE FREE

Gabilondo went straight to the heart of the matter:
'Mr President, did you organise the GAL?'[26]
'It would never have occurred to me. I am a lifelong democrat, convinced that you can only use democratic methods to fight against crime . . . I never authorised [the dirty war] nor covered it up . . . It is untrue that I am "Señor X".'

'Did you tolerate it at any time because it turned out to be useful to you for the war [against ETA] . . .?'

The Prime Minister cut in: 'I repeat that I neither tolerated nor consented to it in any way whatsoever . . . anyone who attributes responsibility to the government [in relation to the GAL] is lying, they are falsifying reality.'

González distanced himself from those Socialist voices which, Gabilondo pointed out, had 'contextualised' the GAL, effectively justifying it, in recent weeks.[27] He pointed out that the fight against terrorism was an unequal struggle, precisely because democrats were obliged by their own convictions to use only legal methods, while the terrorists could use whatever violent methods they chose.

But how, Gabilondo insisted, could he have asserted with certainty that nothing *would be discovered* about the GAL which would damage the government? González then gave his own version of his already infamous exchange with a journalist on 22 December.

'[The journalist] said to me: "What if it is demonstrated that the government has participated in the GAL in some respect?" And I answered him: "Look, that is an impossible hypothesis, because [the government] has never done it, and it follows that it is impossible that it could some day be proved that it had."'

Gabilondo then tried to pin the Prime Minister down. At what level of seniority would the administration's implication in the GAL prove him wrong? At the level of senior police officers in the anti-terrorist high command?

'They are not the government, but civil servants who are responsible to the government . . . it seems to me that they have fulfilled their duties with absolute loyalty, with great fidelity to democracy.'

'The Director General of State Security is [part of the] State?'

'Obviously you could not say he is [part of the] government, but of course he is [part of the] State, and it seems to me that he has given great service to Spanish society.'

González conceded that Vera, as secretary of state, had a 'responsibility close to the government', and that Barrionuevo, as a former minister, would implicate the government if found guilty. He fell back, in both cases, on saying that he knew they were innocent. He insisted repeatedly that the principle of 'presumption of innocence' must be applied to all those touched by the accusations of 'two men found guilty by our justice system'. Legally, and indeed morally, this was impeccable. But in political terms it was an evasion of responsibility for a scandal in which his whole chain of command was now implicated.

It was not too long, after all, since the Prime Minister had been proclaiming the 'presumption of innocence' of precisely those two guilty men, to whom he had offered and given 'the defence and support' of his government. Indeed, Amedo and Domínguez had been eulogised at their own trial by Barrionuevo in very similar terms to those which González was now using about Sancristóbal and his subordinates. Finally, Gabilondo succeeded in coaxing the Prime

Minister to say that 'If the judges establish responsibility at whatever level, I will take the responsibility which corresponds to me.'[28]

Gabilondo pressed him on whether he had any clues at all as to the structure of the GAL. 'I know the same as you do,' replied the Prime Minister blandly, 'because there have been a lot of [press] reports on the subject.' 'But no more?' retorted Gabilondo. 'How would I know more?' responded González. It was an extraordinary remark for someone who had sophisticated security and intelligence services at his disposal, but Gabilondo did not press him on it. Nor did he query González's assertion that the police had investigated the GAL, despite their own evidence to the contrary.[29]

The interviewer went on to remind him that some people had cited international examples of dirty wars against terrorism with some admiration[30]. What was his view?

'It has no justification. It's as clear as that.'[31]

On the issue of reserved funds, the Prime Minister simply said he did not believe that they had been used to buy the silence of Amedo and Domínguez. He defended the absolute secrecy of these provisions, and then pleaded that such secrecy made it very easy for people to lie about them, as their lies could not be disproved by the government.

González was much more restrained than many of his colleagues on the question of Garzón's judicial practice, committing himself to 'respect for his actions and his independence'. While supporting Barrionuevo's right to defend himself, he criticised him for expressing the view that the judge was basely motivated.

The Prime Minister turned much of the rest of the interview into a statesmanlike defence of the capacity of the Spanish economy and Spanish society to weather the crisis calmly. He was visibly more comfortable in this role than as the target of dire allegations. He was able to conclude by quietly developing a political argument that the GAL had not facilitated French collaboration over ETA, because this collaboration had already begun by the time the GAL started to operate. This argument would not have been supported by an examination of mid-1980s PSOE statements about France's lack of support against ETA's 'French sanctuary'.[32] But it became a mainstay of the PSOE position in the future.

He also planted the germ of what would become a full-scale conspiracy theory: the scandals, including the GAL, were 'the result of the actions undertaken by the government against corruption'. The credible hypothesis that Mario Conde and others were manipulating the GAL investigation would be used, again and again, to support the much less credible hypothesis that this investigation had no basis in fact.

González put in a characteristically strong performance in television terms, though many observers noted a slight trembling in his voice during the series of flat denials with which he kicked off the interview. Javier Pradera described González's tone as 'close to authoritarian'. He commented that the broadcast might have eased the minds of those sections of the public least well informed on the subject, but other sectors 'would feel confirmed in their fears about the State's involvement in the GAL'.[33] An opinion poll showed that 52 per cent of the public did not believe their Prime Minister on this issue.[34]

González's loyalty to his subordinates – or his fear at the damage they might do him – perhaps led him to protest too much in defending their reputations. The Prime Minister had spoken of the 'impossible hypothesis' that 'the government' was involved in the GAL. *El País* argued that any hypothesis about the GAL which did *not* involve the state apparatus was 'unbelievable and absurd'.[35]

If González could stomach eating his own words, he had plenty to chew on the following July. The same anti-terrorist bosses whom he had praised for their great and faithful service to democracy would bring the 'impossible hypothesis' to the edge of his cabinet table, according to the very criteria he had expressed in this interview. González's own charisma was by far the biggest bulwark the Socialists had to shore up the battered dam of their credibility, but too many leaks were springing for him to hold it together for much longer. The six months between his television appearance and a cascade of confessions from most of the GAL defendants saw a bewildering kaleidoscope of events unfold.

In January, a month after going into jail, Sancristóbal was the protagonist of a new scandal. He gave a national television interview from prison, in which he was treated almost like a head of state. He rubbished as 'absurd' the same allegations which he would embrace as the truth the following July. His major theme, however, was that his imprisonment was part of a huge conspiracy to overthrow González. He cited Garzón as a major player in this conspiracy, which he said was organised by a 'Señor Z', whom he would not name, but whom many people took to be Mario Conde.

While the interview was technically legal, it caused outrage, and great embarrassment to Belloch. How was it possible for someone in custody on suspicion of very serious crimes to besmirch, on the evening news, the reputation of the judge who was investigating him? Once again, the accusation that GAL suspects got very special treatment was hard to refute.

Garzón did not pause for breath, however. He imprisoned Vera and Damborenea in February. Vera, in particular, mounted an energetic and sometimes ingenious campaign of legal obstruction, appealing repeatedly against every one of the judge's decisions. Those who publicly criticised the judge's actions included such very distinguished jurists as Francisco Tomás y Valiente[36] and Miguel Rodríguez-Piñero,[37] then respectively the former and current presidents of Spain's highest court, the Constitutional Court. They argued that, like Caesar's wife, a judge must not only be impartial but be seen to be impartial. However, Garzón's defenders included the Attorney General, Carlos Granados, and all Vera's appeals against the judge were solidly rejected by Garzón's peers.[38] A number of libel actions, the most potentially dramatic being the government's decision to sue the United Left leader, Julio Anguita, were threatened with great huffing and puffing, but then ran out of steam.[39]

While Spanish democracy sank into crisis, ETA did not stay on the sidelines. It had carried out a series of car bombings with multiple victims, often civilians, throughout the first half of the 1990s. The group opened 1995 with a new and particularly sinister strategy in January by killing the leader of the Partido Popular in the Basque Country, Gregorio Ordoñez. Aware that the Partido Popular was likely to come to power in the next elections, ETA seemed determined to get its retaliation in first, no doubt confident that such 'action' would provoke a politically profitable wave of 'repression' once the Right were in power.

In April, the group launched an attack whose consequences would have been incalculable had it succeeded. In a duplication of the 1973 assassination of Carrero Blanco, ETA placed a remote-control bomb under the road over which José María Aznar was due to pass. Only the armour-plating on his limousine saved the life of the leader of the opposition. He emerged virtually unscathed. His extraordinary sang-froid in the immediate aftermath of the explosion was interpreted by Spaniards as a demonstration either of great courage or of a total absence of feeling, depending on their political loyalties. A woman passer-by was seriously hurt and died months later; twenty others were injured.

The attempt to assassinate Aznar showed that ETA had recovered from the supposedly fatal blow dealt it by the arrest of its leading triumvirate in Bidart three years earlier. A new generation of ETA activists, and their supporters in Herri Batasuna, had elaborated a new strategy, called *Oldartzen Confrontation*. Based on the scarifying concept of the 'socialisation of suffering', it consisted in combining carefully targeted ETA attacks on pillars of the Spanish establishment with a virtual 'intifada' by Basque youth.[40] This *kale borroka* (street struggle) elevated acts of bullying and vandalism to the status of political activism and 'sabotage'. It was directed against moderate nationalist parties as well as the Socialists and the Partido Popular, and a number of PNV premises were attacked. The degree of conflict within Basque society was, in the view of many observers, now sharper than ever. While the rhythm of ETA attacks had undoubtedly slowed down, the organisation's support among a significant section of the population remained solid.

Parallel to this radicalisation on the streets, ETA presented a new political programme which appeared, paradoxically, to be more moderate than the one it had maintained since 1978. This so-called 'Democratic Alternative', with its focus on 'self-determination' rather than 'independence', slowly drove a wedge between the PNV and the Madrid-based parties, and contributed to the emergence of the Lizarra Pact which united all Basque nationalist forces and heralded ETA's 1998 ceasefire.[41]

The dirty war had clearly not managed to destroy ETA, and the investigation of the dirty warriors would provide rich material for an ideology which viewed the Basques as the victims of a murderous Spanish state apparatus. One could argue that the GAL *continued to fail* long after the death squads had been disbanded.

González gave a State of the Nation speech in parliament in early February, which contained the seed of an idea which would become the main root of the Socialists' political and legal defence against charges that they had organised the GAL. 'The violent activities of anti-ETA groups were carried out between 1975 and 1986. They began, therefore, before our arrival in government, and it was with precisely this government that they were ended.'[42]

He got a quick and dusty reply from his predecessor, Leopoldo Calvo Sotelo, who claimed that there had been not a single dirty war action during his two years in power.[43] This is not strictly true – there were several attacks, including killings, in Spain and France attributable to the Basque Spanish Battalion up to June 1981. It is true, however, that the death squads were silent, with the exception of an obscure killing in the USA,[44] for the rest of Calvo Sotelo's premiership, and for the first year the PSOE were in power, that is, for a total of twenty-seven months. The Socialist claim that there was unbroken continuity between the Basque Spanish Battalion and the GAL simply does not stand up. Nevertheless, the thesis that the GAL were dismantled, but not created, by the Socialists formed the core of Barrionuevo's and Vera's defence before the Supreme Court in 1998. It can be found in its most polemical form in Eliseo Bayo's 1997 book, *GAL: Punto Final*.[45] The arguments put forward by Barrionuevo and Vera did not convince a majority of their judges.[46]

González's parliamentary performance was not strong enough even to convince all of his own supporters. Ventura Pérez Mariño, the third judge whom he had recruited as an independent candidate in 1993, resigned his seat immediately afterwards, calling on González to stand down and allow a caretaker PSOE Prime Minister to call early elections. Pérez Mariño's speech did considerably more damage to the government than the curiously lacklustre parliamentary response by the leader of the opposition, José María Aznar.

The idea that the scandals, and particularly the GAL hearings, were putting the whole political system in danger became commonplace. 'If we exclude the 23-F,[47] this is the most dangerous moment Spanish democracy has experienced,' a senior member of the Partido Popular, Juan José Lucas, had said in January.[48] Aznar had floated the idea of a pact to preserve the institutions of the state earlier in the month. Yet the Partido Popular kept wobbling between the options of 'statesmanship' and streetwise political abuse, with the latter often proving irresistible. The danger of pushing their advantage against the Socialists too far in this terrain was that the Partido Popular was throwing stones from a glass house. Any sustained focus on the PSOE's relationship with the GAL threw up the question of the UCD's links with the earlier dirty war. The *really* appalling vista for the legitimacy of the Spanish state was the one in which *every* democratic government since 1977 might be revealed as, at the very least, a passive participant in death squads.[49]

General José Antonio Sáenz de Santamaría, who had held top anti-terrorist positions for both the UCD and PSOE,[50] and was now closely identified with the latter, said the attitude of the Right was 'obscene'. 'They are opportunistically taking advantage of a crisis of the State which should be resolved by a constitutional pact.' He made it clear that he believed both governments had used similar methods against terrorism.

When he was asked if he had ever used dirty war tactics, he gave a revealing insight into the Spanish military mind under democracy: 'In the anti-terrorist struggle, there are things which should not be done. If they are done, they should not be spoken about. If they are spoken about, they must be denied. I think that answers your question.'[51]

His implication that the Right was co-responsible for dirty war activities prompted a fierce riposte from the Partido Popular's deputy leader, Francisco Álvarez Cascos. He dismissed Santamaría as a 'well-fed stomach' of the Socialists. He said that González's problem was 'not with the opposition but with the truth and his own conscience'.[52] Socialists as far apart as Benegas, who represented the party apparatus, and Belloch, who represented the most reformist elements, coincided in accusing Álvarez Cascos of having 'crossed the line of what is tolerable in a democracy', and said that he was undermining the basis of the system itself.[53]

The volatility of the situation was demonstrated most clearly by the fact that Santamaría's call for a constitutional pact was defended by the Partido Popular's founding leader, Manuel Fraga. This former Francoist minister not only stood over his notorious declaration that 'the best terrorist is a dead terrorist'.[54] He had consistently warned that the Right must not take party political advantage of the GAL scandal. Too much digging could bring the whole house down, and Fraga is said to have argued privately that King Juan Carlos himself might be toppled unless a bilateral agreement to 'move beyond' the GAL scandal could be reached.[55]

No matter what the politicians decided, however, it was too late now to switch off the judicial machinery. On 20 February, the Supreme Court significantly amplified its earlier decision in favour of the right to investigate reserved funds. 'The secrecy of such [funds] shall in no way be an obstacle to the investigation of a specific crime . . . To hold the opposite opinion would be a severe attack against, if not the abolition of, the rule of law . . . One of the essential purposes of the rule of law is to put an end to the so-called "immunities of power".'[56] This firm statement of the role of the judiciary in a democracy was prompted, ironically enough, by one of Vera's appeals against Garzón.

'DOES LAOS EXIST?' THE EXTRAORDINARY CAPTURE AND STRANGER RETURN OF LUIS ROLDÁN

Even as the political debate on the GAL investigation was raging, another storm broke, though it looked like a ray of sunshine for the PSOE at first sight. On 27 February, a euphoric Belloch informed the media that Luis Roldán, the fugitive former Director General of the Guardia Civil, had been handed over to Spanish police custody in Bangkok, after being extradited from Laos. Of all the scandals to hurt the PSOE, Roldán's flight from Spain had probably cut the deepest. Many people believed that senior Socialists had helped their old comrade to escape to avoid further embarrassment. Roldán knew too much, about everything from financial corruption to the GAL.

There was also well-informed speculation that his life was in danger. Margarita Robles, who was Belloch's secretary of state at the time, says: 'We had suspicions, not to put it any stronger, an intuition that certain sectors had no interest in the reappearance of Roldán . . . and in fact strange movements were detected in Paris, of people who said they belonged to the CESID but did not, looking for Luis Roldán . . . For what? We thought it was not for any good purpose.'[57] If he had had any accidents on his travels, the finger of suspicion, rightly or wrongly, would have pointed straight at the PSOE leadership. Now Belloch was able to demonstrate dramatically that his Ministry of the Interior really had clean hands: it was bringing to book 'the key man in the nervous system of corruption'.[58] A sophisticated and costly international police operation had ended successfully.

Or not. Within twenty-four hours, *El Mundo* was able to publish a Laotian extradition document which plunged Belloch's team from triumph to ridicule. It suggested that his agents had signed a document limiting the crimes for which Roldán could be tried to two, and not the six for which he was being prosecuted.[59] The Socialists appeared to have done Roldán a major favour after all, the price of which was assumed to be his silence. Belloch, who had appeared before the press the day before as a victor, now had to offer himself to the media as a target for anger and ridicule, admitting to having bungled – at least – a central aspect of Roldán's arrest. In mitigation, he was only able to give the opinion that Spanish judges would not have to be bound by the document.

This was all bad enough, but the next day the Laotian authorities dropped a new bombshell: the extradition documents were false; no Laotian police had accompanied Roldán to Bangkok; in fact they had no record of Roldán's entry to, or exit from, their country.[60] The story was taking on shades of absurdist comedy. Columnists were not short of headlines like 'Does Roldán exist? Does *Laos* exist?'

The suspicion now arose that Roldán himself had been involved in the falsification of documents, in order to plead illegal detention and have all the proceedings against him annulled. Once again, it seemed that the Socialists had done a deal with their old crony, in exchange for his discretion on mutually embarrassing matters. Such speculation was reinforced by the reappearance of the shadowy figure of Francisco Paesa in the story. This was the alleged agent of Interior who had pressurised Blanca Balsategui before the Amedo trial.[61] Paesa was now said to have assisted Interior in locating Roldán and preparing 'extradition' documents, but it was also suspected he was a partner in Roldán's financial affairs. Whether he had been aiding Roldán, or betraying him, or both, was characteristically unclear.

Badly damaged, the government retreated behind the legal doctrine of *male captus, bene detentus*: while Roldán might have been 'badly captured' he was now 'well arrested', and would indeed face all the charges against him.[62] Belloch himself kept insisting that Roldán had been quite brilliantly captured, but would not explain how. He had to weather tempestuous parliamentary and media questions on the bizarre background to Roldán's arrest, and stonewalled them all. The liberal judge who had demanded democratic transparency in the administration of government was now, as a minister, hiding behind the opaque shield of 'state secrecy'. He had gained a seat with the PSOE, the Partido Popular mocked him, but he had lost his credibility. He had certainly ceased to be a magistrate involved in politics, and had become irrevocably a politician who happened to have judicial training.[63]

Baltasar Garzón, of course, had taken the same route, and then reversed. As though he had become Belloch's nemesis, he managed to take control of part of the judicial investigation of the 'Laos papers'. He also called Roldán as a witness in the Segundo Marey case, in which he became a suspect for his role in authorising the kidnappers' border crossing.[64] Roldán used these appearances to make good his old threat to let cats out of bags. He made a series of spectacular allegations, obviously self-serving but still very damaging to the PSOE leadership. He accused the deputy Prime Minister, Narcís Serra, and the Minister for Defence, Julián García Vargas, of improperly financing a secret investigation of Mario Conde. And he gave Garzón a wealth of detail about the payment of 'supersalaries' to Ministry of the Interior staff from reserved funds.[65]

Black comedy was the dominant tone of Spanish politics in the first days of March, but as the month progressed the underlying note of tragedy sounded harshly and starkly once again. On 21 March, the Basque newspaper *Deia* broke a quite extraordinary story. A policeman in Alicante, spurred by Amedo's reference to a proposed quicklime burial in the Marey case, had rechecked the identity of human remains found in such a grave ten years earlier. They turned out to be the bodies of Joxean Lasa and Joxi Zabala, the two young *etarras* who had disappeared in Bayonne two months before the GAL publicly launched their campaign. In a context where many Spaniards now believed their government to have backed the GAL, the sudden appearance of these gruesome, shattered skeletons, initially reported to have had their fingernails torn off, was almost theatrical in its timing. Behind all the noisy and confusing judicial argument and political point scoring, there lay the terrible simplicity of the image of these poor bones.[66]

Meanwhile, Garzón continued to pursue other GAL cases. In February he had reopened the files on the Batxoki and Consolation shootings for which Amedo and Domínguez had already been convicted. The Supreme Court's ruling on reserved funds permitted him to investigate whether these crimes had been financed by Interior. An *El País* editorial summarised his task thus:

'In no democratic country, except Spain, has the justice system had to confront such an inordinate and perilous challenge: nothing less than the criminal investigation of the entire state apparatus.' Commenting on the tangled motives of his witnesses, the writer added: 'the judge must make use of extraordinary professional skills to find the judicial truth in such an extraordinarily confused situation'.[67]

In April, Garzón merged the Batxoki/Consolation case with the Segundo Marey investigation, and on the 18th of the month he produced a devastating charge-sheet. 'Some senior Interior figure supported and authorised the GAL,' he said.[68] He accused Vera of financing the GAL, and Damborenea, Sancristóbal, Álvarez and Planchuelo of setting up the organisation. All five were charged with the false imprisonment of Segundo Marey. In all, fourteen former or current Interior bosses and police officers faced charges, including Amedo and Domínguez. The sensational allegations which they had made in *El Mundo* in December were mostly taken on board in the judge's writ, including Amedo's claim that he had successfully opposed Sancristóbal's and Damborenea's plan to kill Marey. Garzón insisted Amedo and Domínguez had 'demonstrated their genuine remorse by their active and intense collaboration with the law'.[69] Even among those who sympathised with Garzón's aims and admired his skill and energy, there was some unease about the extent of the credit that he was extending to his key witnesses.

All the other defendants denied all charges. Garzón released most of the accused on bail, including Damborenea and Álvarez, but he kept Vera, Sancristóbal and Planchuelo in custody. His detractors had a field day with this decision. *Prisión preventiva* is supposed to protect other witnesses and the public from dangerous miscreants, and to prevent suspects from going into hiding pending trial. The judge's critics said he was using this power for the illegitimate and oppressive purpose of forcing confessions.

Meanwhile, local elections in May strengthened González's position within the PSOE. True, the Partido Popular changed the colour of the Spanish municipal map, winning in forty of the fifty Spanish capitals, and in ten out of the thirteen autonomous regions contested. But the PSOE regained a million votes over its dismal performance in the European elections the previous year, and did not slide nearly as much as opinion polls had predicted. The guessing game over whether or not González would lead his party into the next general elections shifted back in the Prime Minister's favour, and he confidently insisted that his besieged government would serve out its term until 1997. Privately, Belloch attributed the PSOE's recuperation of votes to his campaign against corruption. His attacks on Roldán, and all he represented, had gone down well with Socialist supporters on the campaign trail.[70]

Back in the courts, in the Laos papers case, Garzón appeared to be giving the benefit of the doubt to Roldán, exonerating him from responsibility for the falsification of the documents, and attributing the blame to Paesa, whom he had not even been able to question.[71] The judge's critics said he was being soft on the former fugitive in order to gain his collaboration on the GAL cases. Garzón's practice was certainly unconventional, his style buccaneering. Yet, faced with cases of such complexity, and so open to manipulation, was this not precisely the exercise of the 'extraordinary professional skills' which the situation required? Some idea of his workload can be gauged from the fact that at this time he was not only reactivating the Monbar case,[72] but also investigating the complex subterranean links between Herri Batasuna and ETA.[73] Detractors and supporters alike agreed that the judge never slept.

Neither, it seemed, did the journalists at *El Mundo*, who in mid-June produced another dramatic scoop. They revealed that the Spanish military intelligence service (CESID) had been tapping the mobile phone conversations of dozens of prominent Spanish citizens, starting with the King himself. They also revealed some of the contents of those conversations. Once again, scandal rocked the Socialist establishment to its increasingly shaky foundations, but González resisted the ritual calls for his own resignation and – by a hair's breadth – managed to retain the parliamentary support of the Catalan nationalists. He paid a high price, however, having to accept the resignations of his own deputy, Narcís Serra,[74] his Minister for Defence, Julián García Vargas, and the long-time Director of the CESID, General Emilio Alonso Manglano.

The fact that an intelligence service would tap the phones of the very people whose interests it might have been expected to protect was bad enough. The CESID insisted there was no sinister motive: the origin of the surveillance was a technical exercise. A random sweep of the airwaves had accidentally picked up private conversations of establishment figures. But in that case the tapes should have been destroyed immediately. Instead, they had been preserved, and then allegedly stolen, by a very senior CESID officer, Colonel Juan Alberto Perote, prior to his own dismissal.[75] It then emerged that Perote had had a secret meeting with Mario Conde the day after extracts from the tapes had been published. The hypothesis that the disgraced banker was orchestrating and financing a plot to blackmail the Socialists gained another important strand.

If so, where did the final responsibility lie? The editor of *El País*, Jesús Ceberio, told a journalism seminar at this time that 'the democratic system is paying a high price' for the constant refusal of the government to take political responsibility for the scandals which had so persistently erupted under its administration.[76] If the PSOE was the victim of conspiratorial blackmail, it had left plenty of ammunition lying around for its enemies to use.[77]

The web of complex interaction between the various scandals was indicated again when Garzón summonsed Perote as a witness in the GAL cases. Links between the CESID, the Guardia Civil and the GAL were surfacing in evidence given by Amedo and Planchuelo in the Monbar case. Garzón wanted to know if any of the thousands of documents which Perote was believed to have 'extracted' from the intelligence files related to the dirty war.[78] Perote coyly refused to give this information 'for now',[79] but new trails were opening which would become superhighways to information on the GAL in the years to come.

Meanwhile, the most advanced GAL case – Segundo Marey, Batxoki and Consolation – was reaching a climax.[80] On 12 July, Rafael Vera was released by Garzón on bail of 200 million pesetas, paid by the PSOE. In a frank and revealing interview, he gave his word of honour that he had not enriched himself from the reserved funds. When asked whether he had financed the GAL from the same source, he declined to put his honour on the line: 'Why should it be necessary? I simply say that I didn't do it.' He agreed that the dirty war had been ethically wrong and of doubtful efficiency, 'but in terms of popular morale it probably had its [positive] effect on the anti-terrorist struggle'. He attacked the hypocrisy of those politicians and journalists who had actively or passively supported the GAL in the 1980s and now used the scandal to attack the PSOE. He defended the attempted kidnapping of Larretxea as a necessary part of the security policy of 'any country that takes itself seriously'. Asked if he valued the interests of the state above individual rights, he said that he did, 'above all when the State is fragile'.[81]

The fact that Vera's enormous bail was paid by the PSOE may have been the straw which broke the heavily burdened back of at least one of his fellow defendants. Miguel Planchuelo, Amedo's one-time police chief in Bilbao, had had a particularly bad time in custody due to ill-health. He had also lost his job, and the family home which went with it, and felt abandoned by the PSOE establishment.[82] On the weekend of 17 July, he went voluntarily to Garzón's chambers, and sang like a canary. He incriminated himself in the kidnapping of Marey. He claimed that he had participated on the instructions of Sancristóbal, whom he said had told him he had the approval of Vera – and of Barrionuevo.

When Planchuelo withdrew his hand from the dyke, a flood of confessions followed. They bore the hallmarks of a new and co-ordinated defence strategy, of which the centre-piece was the justification of 'obeying orders'. Once again, the world was turning upside down for the Socialist leadership. As the suspects turned yesterday's slanders into today's admissions, the erstwhile heroes of Interior became villains or, at the least, the broken victims of Garzón's oppressive and vengeful investigation, as far as González's circle was concerned.

Sancristóbal and Álvarez, who had seen their positions steadily weakened by a series of damaging financial discoveries by Garzón, caved in the day after Planchuelo. The former Civil Governor of Vizcaya and Director of State Security, who had gone on television to proclaim his innocence and accuse Garzón of being a conspirator against González, became an active collaborator in the judge's investigation. He admitted that he had enriched himself from reserved funds (which he promised to return), and also to his involvement in the Marey kidnapping. He added that the kidnapping had the support of Vera and Barrionuevo, and implied that González was fully informed about, and ultimately responsible for, the GAL.

Álvarez, former head of both the Unified Counter-terrorist Command (MULC) and the Intelligence and Special Operations Committee (GAIOE), had more specific information. He offered a colour code for the different branches of the GAL, some of which passed quickly into common parlance. The 'blue GAL' was drawn from the National Police, the 'green GAL' from the Guardia Civil, and the 'brown GAL' from the CESID and the army; the French GAL, obviously enough, was made up of French police.[83] He implicated Vera, Roldán and Barrionuevo. He confirmed Planchuelo's allegation that it was the former Minister for the Interior who had instructed them to continue with the Marey kidnapping even though they had picked up the wrong man. The different branches of the GAL were co-ordinated, he said, by 'someone superior to Barrionuevo'. The spectre of Señor X was casting a bigger and bigger shadow.

Álvarez also mentioned Lieutenant-Colonel Enrique Rodríguez Galindo, the charismatic commander of the Guardia Civil anti-terrorist units in Intxaurrondo barracks in San Sebastián. Álvarez echoed what the early targets of the GAL had suspected from the first: he said that Galindo, along with two other top Guardia Civil officers, was a key figure in the 'green GAL'.[84]

In just three days, Felipe González's boast that the state apparatus could never be proven to be involved in the GAL had been swept away; his insistence that the government was not involved was also well adrift in this cascade of allegations from insiders. But the biggest wave of this particular storm had still to break.

Two days later, Ricardo García Damborenea, former leader of the Socialist Party in Vizcaya, went to see Garzón, the judge he had described as 'inquisitorial' six months earlier. He then gave a press conference. He proclaimed, indeed he almost boasted, that the responsibility for the GAL belonged squarely to the government. 'We are not dealing with a matter which was born from the imagination or the initiative of two or three policemen; we are dealing with political decisions.' Asked about González's involvement in the GAL, he replied: 'González knew about it because I spoke to him about it, not once but on several occasions.' He went on to suggest that the entire senior PSOE leadership in the Basque Country, including Benegas, had approved the GAL strategy, but that it could not have gone ahead without the specific support of the Prime Minister.[85]

Damborenea corroborated all the points made by the Interior bosses and policemen, adding his authority as a leading politician who had had direct access to González. However, at this stage he brought no proofs other than his own word, which the Prime Minister promptly dismissed as false.[86] Tantalisingly, he did mention having seen a document which had laid down guidelines for the GAL's operations, and promised to try to find a copy for the judge.[87] This so-called 'Founding Memorandum of the GAL' would ultimately become an important element in the dirty war investigations. For the moment, however, without documentary evidence, Damborenea was a bad witness in judicial terms, undermined by his manifest hostility to the PSOE in recent years.[88]

In political terms, however, the short-term impact of his theatrically managed intervention was a particularly big nail in the already well-hammered coffin of González's credibility. And it defined the new strategy of the GAL defendants from Interior.

They confessed to a vague responsibility for the GAL in general, but only acknowledged responsibility for a single specific action, the Marey kidnapping, which was the least serious in legal terms. They constantly attempted to push the real responsibility further up the chain of command, ideally to González himself. They seemed to believe that, if the Prime Minister or a cabinet member could be seriously implicated in the GAL, some formula involving an amnesty or pardon would be forthcoming, which would have to benefit all the defendants. Their precedent was the so-called 'law of the full stop' in Argentina, which had protected those who had participated in death squads under the military dictatorship from legal retribution under democracy. They thought that such a law would be more likely to be introduced by a Partido Popular government, which could plead statesmanship while being innocent of partisan interest, so their weakening of the PSOE had a double motive.[89]

Another feature in this strategy, which might seem to contradict the foregoing, was an insistence that the GAL did not have a unified command structure, but rather comprised a loose series of semi-autonomous groups. The point here was probably not to offer accurate information about the GAL, but to evade personal responsibility for specific killings.[90]

González's response was predictable: he roundly accused Damborenea of lying, said that there would be no pardon for anyone involved in the GAL, and insisted that he would not call elections as a result of the revelations of the previous week. 'The government has committed no illegality whatsoever in the struggle against terrorism,' Felipe González told parliament in a specially convened debate on the issue on 27 July. Damborenea would have to prove his accusations in court. The Prime Minister insisted that his government would 'collaborate with the judicial investigation, respect the decisions of the courts, and support [them] when they convict the guilty'.[91]

On the same day, the news broke that Garzón had handed over the Marey case to the Supreme Court, because his investigation revealed a case against persons protected by parliamentary privilege.[92] Garzón was not only accusing Barrionuevo, according to a leaked report. He had found 'legally sufficient evidence' that the Prime Minister, Felipe González, was himself guilty of membership, as a founder and leader, of a terrorist organisation, the GAL.[93]

The leak turned out to be an exaggeration of Garzón's findings. He had actually said that, while he found the defendants' allegations against González 'credible', they did not constitute 'evidence'. He had no such reservation about the implication of González's former Interior Minister: 'in this [Barrionuevo's] case, the avalanche of data and evidence is much greater'.[94]

The investigation of the GAL had now reached a point of no return. For the second time in seven months, and at a much, much higher level, members of the state apparatus had acknowledged that acts of terrorism had been organised and financed by the servants of democracy. The only real question now was how far the disease had spread, and whether Spain's democratic structures could survive further diagnosis, let alone endure whatever surgery might be necessary to cure the body politic. Meanwhile, revelations in the Lasa and Zabala case were making it clear that things were going to get worse before they got better.

NOTES

1   *El Mundo*, 26 December 1994.

2   Ibid.

3   Conde had at one stage owned at least 4.5 per cent of *El Mundo*, through his bank Banesto, which had also invested heavily in other media. Some observers argued that his holding in *El Mundo* was in fact much larger, perhaps as high as 50 per cent, through front companies and front men. He had been removed from the presidency of Banesto by the intervention of the Bank of Spain in December 1993, and *El Mundo* editorials were presenting him as a victim of Socialist power. His considerable impact on the GAL investigations is dealt with in ch. 20.

4   The interviews were structured in two blockbuster series: 'How the GAL were born' ran from 27 to 30 December 1994, and 'How the GAL were covered up' ran from 9 to 13 January 1995.

5   *El País*, 10 and 11 May 1997.

6 *El País*, 22 December 1994.
7 Ibid.
8 *El País*, 21 December 1994.
9 The fact that Amedo and Domínguez had documents which appeared to incriminate their bosses was critical in the full reopening of the case. However, they had no documentary evidence against Barrionuevo and Vera. But the testimony of convicted criminals, and of defendants who are pleading guilty, can be used under Spanish law if the evidence amounts to a 'coherent account of the facts', even if that testimony is unsupported by documentary or forensic evidence. Garzón himself would later pursue this line in his final recommendation that the Supreme Court should charge Barrionuevo, Vera and even González.
10 *El País*, 20 December 1994.
11 He was supported in this stance by the leader of the PSOE parliamentary group, Joaquín Almunia, who would replace Felipe González as party leader in 1997. The Catalan nationalists also supported him.
12 *El País*, 23 December 1994.
13 *El País*, 22 December 1994.
14 *El País*, 15 January 1995.
15 *El País*, 22 December 1994.
16 *El País*, 24 December 1994.
17 Jaime García Añoveros, in *El País*, 5 January 1995.
18 *El País*, 30 December 1994.
19 See also p. 266, and ch. 20, p. 296.
20 Interview with Javier Pradera, Madrid, November 1997.
21 Ricardo Arques and Melchor Miralles, *Amedo: El Estado contra ETA* (Barcelona: Plaza & Janes/Cambio 16, 1989), pp. 379 and 516. My emphasis.
22 *El País*, 23 December 1994. My emphasis.
23 *El País*, 22 December 1994.
24 *El País*, 10 and 11 January 1995. United Left included the still influential Communist Party. Alcaraz was the first mainstream politician to make this accusation, familiar on the streets from the earliest anti-GAL demonstrations.
25 He specified the summarised version of the television interview published in *El País* on 10 January 1995, which is the version followed here. The more recent interview specified by González as accurately representing his views on the GAL was published by *El País* on 29 June 1997. Since González declined to give an interview for this book, in November 1997, he has in fact had a great deal more to say about the GAL. See chs. 23 and 24.
26 The Spanish Prime Minister is always addressed as 'President'. See ch. 3. n. 11.
27 Several leading Socialists had made statements which tended towards exculpating the GAL on the grounds that the dirty war was an understandable (if mistaken) response to the intensity of ETA's terrorism in the early 1980s. Some went further. A Galician PSOE leader baldly told a radio station that 'the best terrorist is a dead terrorist'. *El País*, 16 January 1995.
28 When Barrionuevo and Vera were themselves 'found guilty by our justice system' – in this case the Supreme Court – three years later, González refused to accept the verdict. He continues to reject political responsibility for the GAL on the basis of their conviction. Consistency has not been his strong suit in arguments about the GAL.
29 The head of police intelligence, Jesús Martínez Torres, had told two different court hearings that the police investigation of the GAL had been limited to collecting press cuttings, and had not been checked with their French or Portuguese colleagues. (*El País*, 29 January 1995.) Other claims that the police had investigated the GAL were made, but not substantiated, as part of Vera and Barrionuevo's defence in the Supreme Court in 1998.

30 The President of the Catalan government, Jordi Pujol, had been particularly helpful to the PSOE on this point, praising the 'maturity' of democracies like West Germany. When a group of Baader-Meinhof leaders were found dead in their prision cells, the Chancellor, Helmut Schmidt, had only to tell the country's newspaper editors that the stability of the country depended on how they treated the story to ensure that these dubious 'suicides' were accepted as such by the German media. *El País*, 20 February 1995.

31 The clarity of this position contrasts sharply with the fuzzy ambiguity of González's own previous statements about the necessity to 'defend democracy in the sewers as well as in the salons'.

32 See ch. 14, pp. 183–4.

33 *El País*, 11 January 1995.

34 *El País*, 15 January 1995.

35 *El País*, 10 January 1995.

36 *El País*, 22 January 1995.

37 *El País*, 21 February 1995.

38 *El País*, 22 July 1995.

39 *El País*, 11 January 1995.

40 See also ch. 19, pp. 283–5. The suffering of ETA members and supporters, the theory ran, should be 'socialised' – as in 'shared equally' – by all sectors of the Basque population. This was achieved by any means to hand: burning cars and telephone boxes, intimidating citizens who carried Madrid newspapers in the street, beating up people who wore the 'blue ribbon' which indicated solidarity with ETA's kidnap victims.

41 ETA chose to present this programme as part of the communiqué which acknowledged responsibility for the killing of two policemen and the attempt on Aznar's life. See *El País*, 27 April 1995, and Antonio Elorza (ed.), *La Historia de ETA* (Madrid: Temas de Hoy, 2000), pp. 404–6.

42 *El País*, 9 February 1995.

43 *El País*, 16 February 1995. Calvo Sotelo was Prime Minister from February 1981 to October 1982.

44 José Ángel Uriagereka was killed in the US on 17 June 1982, in an attack claimed by the Basque Spanish Battalion, but very few details are available. See Arques and Miralles, op. cit., pp. 139–40.

45 It also gets an outing in the Socialist magazine *El Siglo*; see 'El GAL de la UCD', 19 January 1998.

46 For an account of this Supreme Court case, see chs. 23 and 24.

47 The attempted military coup by Tejero on 23 February 1981.

48 *El País*, 23 January 1995.

49 While the UCD was not the direct precursor of the Partido Popular, the latter had inherited a large number of UCD supporters after Suárez's centre party project fell apart. Meanwhile, Aznar had moved the Partido Popular towards the centre, UCD's chosen territory. Moreover, former UCD ministers were linked closely enough to the Partido Popular to cause potential embarrassment. In terms of the fundamental Right–Left fissure in Spanish society, both parties belonged to the same family, and the past history of one could seriously damage the future of the other.

50 He had been the UCD's special representative in the Basque Country in 1980, and Director General of the Guardia Civil for the PSOE until 1986. Because he was believed to have played a key role in the frustration of the 1981 attempted military coup, he was one of the few army men of his generation to be warmly regarded by many Spanish democrats.

51 *El País*, 24 February 1995.

52 *El País*, 26 February 1995.

53   Ibid.
54   Ibid.
55   Fraga's private reference to the King's vulnerability is from a confidential source.
56   *El País*, 21 February 1998.
57   Interview with Margarita Robles, Madrid, November 1997.
58   Fernando López Agudín, *En el Laberinto* (Barcelona: Plaza y Janés, 1996), p. 90.
59   Moreover, there had been a twenty-two-hour delay in making the judge in charge of his case aware of the document. *El Mundo*, 28 February 1995.
60   *El País*, 4 and 5 March 1995.
61   See ch. 15, p. 223, and ch. 16, p. 234. Paesa had finally handed himself over to Spanish justice only after Amedo and Domínguez had been sentenced. In a controversial legal decision, the case against him for pressurising a witness was dropped in April 1992. *El País* and *El Mundo,* 8 April 1992.
62   *El País*, 13 March 1995.
63   See Juan G. Ibañez, 'El Magistrado renuncia su virginidad', *El País*, 8 March 1995.
64   Roldán had been Government Delegate in Navarre at this time.
65   *El País*, 11 June 1995.
66   The Lasa and Zabala case is the subject of ch. 19.
67   *El País*, 17 February 1995.
68   *El País*, 19 April 1995.
69   Ibid.
70   López Agudín, op. cit., pp. 132–3.
71   The legal knot here was almost absurdly convoluted. Another judge was investigating the same case in a different court, and reached the opposite conclusion on the falsification issue. Roldán made Spanish legal history, of a kind, in being the only person ever to be simultaneously considered the victim and perpetrator of the same crime. In the end, a third judge decided that the falsification had no bearing on the charges faced by Roldán in Spain. *El País*, 11 July 1995.
72   He interrogated Amedo and Domínguez as suspects in this case (*El País*, 13 June 1995), but even if convicted of these four murders they would serve the sentence simultaneously with the maximum one they were already 'serving' in their special open regime. Garzón could have returned them to prision because they did not collaborate with the Monbar investigation, but he chose not to. They continued to help with his inquiries in the Segundo Marey case, and continued to sleep at home.
73   *El País*, 8 June 1995.
74   Serra had special responsibility for the CESID.
75   Perote was found not guilty on this particular charge in 1999, though he was found guilty of participating in the illegal tapping of the mobile phones. However, he was found guilty of the theft and revelation of much more significant CESID documents in 1997, as we shall see. See *El País*, 11 July 1997, 1 April 1998 and 27 May 1999.
76   *El País*, 16 June 1995.
77   The role of conspiracies in the unveiling – and shrouding – of the GAL saga will be examined in ch. 20.
78   Estimates of how many files Perote took with him varied. Ernesto Ekaizer, who has followed the subject more clearly than most, gives figures ranging from 3,000 to 5,000, copied onto microfiches. Perote himself, who has been convicted of stealing some documents and cleared of stealing others, admits to 'accidentally' removing 1,245 'pages' of varying importance, copied onto twenty-three microfiches, when he cleared his office. See Ernesto Ekaizer,

Vendetta (Madrid: Plaza y Jamés, 1996) and Juan Alberto Perote, *Confesiones de Perote* (Barcelona: RBA Libros, 1999), p. 207.

79   *El País*, 6 July 1995.
80   The Batxoki and Consolation operations would subsequently be separated out again, and only the Marey investigation would come to court at this stage.
81   *El País*, 15 July 1995.
82   Planchuelo was still in the police force. Belloch's ministry would not keep open the job of a senior officer accused of such serious crimes and suspended him from his position. Once again, Belloch's reforms had inadvertently assisted Garzon's investigation.
83   It is clear that some members of the French security forces collaborated with the GAL, but whether there was any formal network of such collaborators, constituting a 'French GAL', remains unclear.
84   *El País*, 18, 19 and 20 June 1995. See ch. 14, pp. 199–200.
85   *El País*, 21 July 1995.
86   *El País*, 22 July 1995.
87   *El País*, 20 September 1995.
88   While in the PSOE, Damborenea had been famous for his populist, anti-nationalist speeches. He incited the alienated immigrant workers of Bilbao's industrial belt against all aspects of Basque nationalism, and not just against ETA. As for the latter, he had marked himself out as an apologist for 'robust' anti-terrorist policies, and practically identified himself as a theorist of dirty war tactics. In the end, his rhetoric had too rich a mix for many of his comrades, and he was expelled in 1990. His one-time protégé, Julián Sancristóbal, financed his attempt to set up his own organisation, and when that failed Damborenea moved towards the Partido Popular, appearing on an election platform with Aznar in 1993.
89   One lawyer, Jesús Santaella, made specific suggestions about a legal mechanism which would allow for a 'constitutional political acquittal'. (*El País*, 23 July 1995.) Santaella represented the disgraced CESID agent Juan Alberto Perote, and turned out to be involved in a very shady negotiation with the government at this time. See ch. 20.
90   Even on the Marey case, Damborenea was remarkably vague and sometimes demonstrably inaccurate. He said several times that the purpose of this kidnapping was to secure the release of Captain Barrios, who had in fact been killed by ETA(p-m) several weeks before Marey was abducted. The attempted kidnapping of Larretxea was aimed at securing Barrrios's release. One of the secondary motivations for the Marey kidnapping, once the perpetrators realised they were holding an innocent French resident, was to 'persuade' the French authorities to release the Spanish police held for, precisely, the bungled Larretxea operation.
91   *El País*, 28 July 1995.
92   These also included the former deputy Prime Minister, Narcís Serra, and the Basque socialist leader and PSOE 'number three', José Maria ('Txiki') Benegas.
93   *El País*, 28 and 29 July 1998. The speed with which Garzón brought an accusation against González contrasted sharply with his tardiness in charging Barrionuevo. This added to the argument that Garzón had delayed charging Barrionuevo in order to avoid handing over the case to the Supreme Court. Once he was obliged to pass it on, he did not hesitate to add the suggestion, in this case arguably premature and insufficiently substantiated, that the Prime Minister was also legally implicated in the GAL.
94   *El País*, 22 August 1995.

19

Old Bones Tell Their Story:
the 'green GAL' feel the heat

The GAL had become a spectre haunting Spain in 1995. The haunting took its most dramatic form in the bones of Lasa and Zabala. No other image from the dirty war so captured the horrified imagination of the Spanish public, and so poisoned the atmosphere of Spanish public life. No other GAL atrocity would offer, twelve years after it took place, such an explosive propaganda weapon to the supporters of ETA, the organisation to which Lasa and Zabala had belonged.

Two young men had been kidnapped, tortured for days and possibly weeks, then murdered and buried in quicklime. From the moment their remains were tentatively identified, in March 1995, those bare facts cast a grim shadow. The subsequent indictment of two senior Socialist politicians and a Guardia Civil general in the Lasa and Zabala case pointed directly to state responsibility for these crimes. 'Disappearances' in Argentina and Chile were familiar in the Spanish media. Now it seemed that they had also been part – albeit on a much smaller scale – of the security policy of a progressive European democracy. This was certainly, as *El País* put it, 'one of the most macabre stories of the Socialist era'.[1]

It was a story which would switch the focus of the investigation of the GAL back to an institution which had been the prime suspect in 1983 and 1984. Once José Amedo and the National Police were caught in the legal spotlight in 1987, the Guardia Civil's role in the death squads had remained unilluminated. Now the involvement of Spain's other major internal security force in the dirty war came sharply back into the frame. And the trail of the 'green GAL' of the Guardia Civil would lead to the same place to which the 'blue GAL' of the National Police had already brought investigators: the apex of the 1980s Interior Ministry.

This ministry was now, of course, in new hands, and subject to the reforming zeal of Juan Alberto Belloch and Margarita Robles. There was a sharp contrast between Interior's attitude when the Amedo story broke in 1987, and Barrionuevo and Vera were in charge, and the response in 1995 when Lasa's and Zabala's remains were identified.

In 1987, Interior's approach had been to stonewall, with Vera declaring that 'the Ministry is not concerned by this affair'.[2] In March 1995, the new joint Ministry of the Interior and Justice wore its concern on its sleeve: 'Given the evident and horrific data which confirm the kidnapping, torture and murder of Lasa and Zabala, the Ministry expresses its most robust condemnation of practices which are an outrage against the rule of law . . . [It] manifests its most firm intention to collaborate with the judiciary in the complete elucidation of what happened, and bring to justice those responsible for this barbarity.'[3] This would be easier said than done.

The 'macabre story' began, as we have seen in earlier chapters,[4] with the disappearance of Joxean Lasa and Joxi Zabala, two young *etarras*, in Bayonne in October 1983, two months before the GAL first publicly announced their existence. The ETA community in exile, and the victims' families, strongly suspected that the Guardia Civil was responsible. For many years no proof was forthcoming. There was no case to make, because their bodies had not been identified, though they had in fact been found. They were initially discovered, not due to the diligence of the police, but thanks to the curiosity of a dog.

Human bones were disturbed by a hunting dog in arid scrubland near Busot, in the south-eastern province of Alicante, in January 1985. The Guardia Civil was called in, and found a quicklime grave containing skeletal remains, bullets, blindfolds and bandages. It was obvious from the condition of the bones that this was a case involving torture and murder, but the Guardia Civil made only the most cursory attempts to pursue it. A note on the discovery was circulated throughout the force, but there was no cross-checking with archives on missing persons outside the immediate area.[5]

Yet the gruesome find had caused some commotion in Alicante, and a local journalist had wondered in print if the bones might have belonged to 'the two *etarras* who disappeared in the south of France some years ago, [a disappearance] attributed to the GAL'.[6] A local radio station had cause for more than speculation. Almost exactly a year earlier, on 20 January 1984, Radio Alicante had received the following anonymous telephone call: 'We are the GAL . . . At 15.00 hours we executed Lasa and Zabala. They died crying like cowards. They asked for a priest but we refused because they didn't deserve one.'[7]

There was no serious police follow-up, not even when a similar call was received by another radio station after the discovery of the bones in 1985. (As we saw in chapter 5, this call, received by Radio Popular de Alicante, was not broadcast.) An investigating magistrate closed the case, attributing the deaths to a drugs dispute involving unspecified foreigners. The bones would have been consigned to a common grave, and probably lost for ever, but for the professional dedication of a pathologist, who insisted the remains should be properly preserved.

Ten years later, an equally zealous policeman, Jesús García, was doing a periodic update on unsolved cases. Checking the bones, he suddenly linked them with remarks made by José Amedo about the GAL, then being splashed all over the Spanish media.[8] After doing some initial checking of his own, he got in touch with Ignacio Gordillo, a senior prosecutor at the Audiencia National, and told him that he thought he had found Lasa and Zabala. Gordillo contacted their families for photographs and dental records. A photograph of Lasa, laughing, showed a gap in his smile, just where a tooth was missing on one of the jaws found in Alicante.

Gordillo called the families and their lawyer, the Herri Batasuna leader Iñigo Iruin, to Madrid for a meeting. It was a strange encounter. Gordillo had been a prosecutor on the first GAL case, where he had been deeply frustrated by official obstruction. But he had also earned the ire of ETA for prosecuting many of its most feared leaders. Another Audiencia Nacional prosecutor, his close friend Carmen Tagle, had been killed by ETA in 1989, and Gordillo himself was under constant threat of assassination. Nevertheless, he made the families and their lawyer a promise: 'Justice acts equally for everyone: for those who killed your brothers, and for those who may have died through the actions of your brothers.'[9]

Justice, unfortunately, is almost always slow and in this case it was almost incredibly clumsy. For several weeks after the identification of the bodies was made public, Spain reeled in disgust at the revelations. Felipe González assured parliament that the government was determined to 'clear up every last detail' of the killings, which he described as 'execrable . . . and absolutely unjustifiable'.[10] But he simultaneously defended Barrionuevo, who had been Interior Minister when the killings took place, against calls that he should resign his seat in parliament. No doubt relieved, Barrionuevo said that his conscience was clear and that the idea of resignation had never occurred to him. *El País* commented: 'If the person who was the top political authority in the anti-terrorist struggle when Lasa and Zabala were kidnapped, tortured for months[11] and finally murdered, has a quiet conscience, it must be because he has no conscience at all. For either he did not know about it, in which case his incompetence is remarkable, or he did know about it, in which case he would deserve a description which we would prefer not to express.'[12]

The acute concern and anguish in the rest of the country was even more intense in the victims' home region. And in those quarters of the Basque Country where Lasa and Zabala were regarded not only as victims but as martyrs, fury reached fever pitch.

Four days after the Basque nationalist newspaper *Deia* broke the news that the bodies had been identified,[13] new horror was born from the old. A van carrying five members of the Basque autonomous police force, the Ertzaintza, was attacked with petrol bombs in the traditional combat zone of Orereta in Rentería. The flames penetrated the vehicle, which erupted like a fire-ball and went out of control.

It careered towards two young women passers-by, who were both seriously injured. So were two of the *ertzainas*. A third, Jon Ruiz Sagarna, very nearly died. Third-degree burns scarred more than 50 per cent of his body, and practically destroyed his face, leaving him so terribly disfigured that he could hardly face a mirror a year later. The youths who hurled the bombs were subsequently arrested. Herri Batasuna and the youth organisation Jarrai both justified such actions as 'a reflection of the anger and indignation' of the people.[14] The polarisation of Basque society, which was part of Herri Batasuna's new strategy of 'socialising the suffering', *Oldartzen*, was well served by the grim discovery in Alicante.

That strategy was better served again by the crass judicial blunders which led to cruel scenes at Lasa's and Zabala's funerals. The families of the two victims were undoubtedly relieved that the terrible uncertainty of the twelve-year 'disappearance' had come to an end. They had long since ceased to hope that the two young men were alive. Now, they thought, they could at last give them the dignity of a decent burial in their home town of Tolosa.

It would not be that simple. They got an inkling of what was to come when they went to Alicante, immediately after the discovery was announced. The local investigating magistrate would allow only three members of each family to view the remains, a decision which incensed them. Most of the brothers and sisters were not allowed to enter the morgue. When they went to lay flowers on the quicklime grave in Busot, the families found themselves almost outnumbered by members of the Guardia Civil.

The case was then transferred to the Audiencia Nacional in Madrid, where it was to be handled by Judge Carlos Bueren. This caused a further bureaucratic delay in handing over the bodies. Lasa's elder brother, Mikel Mari, remembers an anguished visit to the capital.

'This was all we needed,' he says ironically. 'After twelve years the bodies turn up. The only people allowed to see the coffin in Madrid were my parents and I. We are – we were – nine brothers and sisters. Now we are eight . . . Not to be able to see what was in the coffin . . . we didn't know if they were ashes or bones. We don't know.'[15]

The bodies were finally released for burial in June, but, unbeknownst to the families, Judge Bueren had given the police some odd instructions. The families and Iñigo Iruin had understood they were going to receive the coffins at the little airport in Fuenterrabía, hold a vigil for them overnight in Tolosa, and carry out formal funeral rites the next day. The whole affair started badly before the coffins even arrived, with violent clashes at the airport between police and Herri Batasuna supporters, in which several parliamentarians were injured. When the plane touched down, the coffins were held on the tarmac for over an hour, while Iruin and the Basque autonomous police argued.

'Bueren had issued a rather contradictory order,' Iruin explains. 'He said that the coffins should be handed over to the families in Fuenterrabía, but that at the same time [the police] must guarantee that the seals on the coffins were not broken.'[16] After consulting Bueren on a mobile phone – Iruin was not able to hear what the judge actually said – the police decided that the only way to carry out the second part of the order was to defer compliance with the first part. They told Iruin they would withhold the coffins from the families until they reached the cemetery at Tolosa, and insist on their immediate burial that evening.

So Lasa and Zabala were effectively kidnapped a second time, on this occasion by the police force controlled by the Basque autonomous government. Had someone wanted to set up a scenario to prove Herri

Batasuna's thesis that the Ertzaintza was no improvement on the Guardia Civil, and that autonomy was only a façade behind which an oppressive Madrid still ruled, they could hardly have done it better.

A bad situation turned grotesquely worse when the heavily guarded hearses finally got to the graveyard. The police had occupied the cemetery and allowed only about thirty family members past the gates. Juan Mari Zabala takes up the story: 'When the families finally approached the hearse to take out the coffins, and begin a religious ceremony, the police charged. Uncles, aunts, grandmothers and grandfathers were all knocked to the ground. Our parents wanted to give them a simple religious ceremony, and could not even do this. Even in the chapel the police were there, defiant and leering.'[17]

Mikel Mari Lasa finishes for him: 'The older people said afterwards: "In the [Civil] War there was respect for the dead, at least until they were buried. Here there was not even that."'[18]

Independent journalists present saw the police use tear-gas, batons and rifle butts against the relatives, three of whom were injured inside the cemetery.[19]

There is no doubt that the Ertzaintza was under enormous pressure at this time. As we have seen, Herri Batasuna and the radical youth group Jarrai had unleashed a ferocious offensive in the streets of the Basque Country. The *kale borroka* (street struggle) used the entire repertoire of hooliganism to 'socialise the suffering' experienced by ETA prisoners and ETA supporters. The Ertzaintza was, on a daily basis, dealing with a kind of low-intensity war.

ETA was meanwhile holding a kidnap victim, a Basque businessman with close links to moderate nationalism. Peaceful vigils calling for his release were met by violent mass assaults by radical demonstrators. The language of these rallies was imbued with a terrifying mixture of generalised hatred and intimate personal threats. The Ertzaintza had the thankless job of trying to guarantee the right of peaceful protest. 'You're dressed in black today; tomorrow your family will be in black for you', the radicals would chant at them. 'Orereta, Orereta', Jarrai's teenagers would shout gloatingly, in reference to the place where the young *ertzaina* had had his face burnt off in the first wave of protests after Lasa's and Zabala's bones were identified.[20]

The autonomous police seem to have vented a great deal of pent-up anger in the cemetery in Tolosa. They could not have chosen a worse place to do it. The aborted funerals added appalling insult to the great injuries already suffered by the Lasa and Zabala families. And they represented a major propaganda victory for Herri Batasuna and ETA.

In the 1980s, the GAL taught many young people of the first post-Franco generation in the Basque Country to hate the Spanish security forces. In the 1990s, the poisonous legacy of the GAL initiated another generation in the same hatred, this time extending it to their own local police force. As José Luis Barbería, one of the most seasoned and sober observers of the Basque scene, put it at the time: 'Rage propagated itself yesterday in Tolosa like a blind tide, which threatens to bury all the Basques in civil conflict.'[21]

DBS Arts Library

Nor was the story over yet. The bones of Lasa and Zabala had been buried at home at last, but their case would continue to be investigated for years. Indeed, two months before they were buried, there were already reliable reports that members of the Guardia Civil, from Colonel Enrique Rodríguez Galindo's headquarters at Intxaurrondo, were the main focus of the joint Guardia Civil/police inquiry. The co-ordinator of this inquiry for the police, Superintendent General Enrique de Federico, had to ask for protection for his family because of fears of intimidation by suspects. The Guardia Civil was accused of obstructing his work.[22]

Despite the very damaging evidence against those under his command, and eventually against himself, Galindo was promoted to the rank of general in August.[23] Belloch said he felt he had no right to stop a promotion to which Galindo was entitled by seniority. Others, including Belloch's deputy at Interior, Margarita Robles, wondered what Interior was doing by enhancing the status of a man so heavily under suspicion.[24]

GENERAL ENRIQUE RODRÍGUEZ GALINDO: ANTI-TERRORIST PROFESSIONAL OR DIRTY WARRIOR PAR EXCELLENCE?

Enrique Rodríguez Galindo was a remarkable commander. Short and stocky, with hooded eyes and a cold, impassive face, he nonetheless radiated military charisma. He was loved, indeed idolised, by his men. He seems to have loved them back, to the extent of overlooking their criminal sidelines. He was a hero to the Spanish Right, and the armed forces generally. A posting at Intxaurrondo under his command was regarded as more prestigious than its equivalent at any army barracks. It was the best-known Guardia Civil headquarters in Spain, and had lost ninety men to ETA, more than 10 per cent of all ETA's victims over thirty years.[25]

This was the front line of the anti-terrorist struggle. Galindo's elite units, who seem to have been a law unto themselves, certainly dismantled a record number of ETA *comandos*. But they were widely believed to favour torture as their first and last method of interrogation. Their critics say that their methods created more *comandos* than they broke up.

The commander of Intxaurrondo was a deeply religious man, and liked to talk about the miracles performed under the patronage of the Virgin of Pilar as part of his lunchtime conversation. There is no necessary contradiction here, however. As the writer Manuel Vázquez Montalbán reminded Felipe González, apropos of Galindo's religiosity, Franco's political police force 'was full of torturers who took daily communion'.[26]

Fernando López Agudín, head of public relations for Interior under Belloch and Robles, says Galindo was a true professional. After some initial tensions, he says, the Intxaurrondo commander worked splendidly for the new team. Their instinct, however, was to sack him, given his reputation for tolerating, and perhaps promoting, illegal methods.

'But to sack him was very difficult. He was the maximum expert on ETA, and he was then a person with very great support within the state,' says López Agudín.[27] He adds that Belloch prioritised other difficult reforms, and could not take on the flak sacking Galindo would have created at this time. 'Until the investigation of Lasa and Zabala, Galindo was very loyal and very efficient.'

When that investigation was two months old, López Agudín had an initially amicable dinner with Galindo in Madrid, which marked the final watershed in relations between the new ministry and the commander. Over brandies, he told the officer that men under his command were the prime suspects for the killings. While López Agudín must have known he was being provocative, he says Galindo's response amazed him.

'He is a self-possessed and very intelligent man . . . he is a great expert in this type of situation. His reaction was surprising, it was virtual confusion. He evidently had something to do with the story I was telling him.' Galindo hurriedly made his excuses and left, leaving a full drink on the table.

Relations with the ministry, which was clearly backing de Federico and the police in their line of inquiry, became glacial. Yet Belloch still made Galindo a general in August.

By July 1995, new witnesses had come forward in the investigation. Some of them had an intimate knowledge of the web of bribery, corruption, smuggling and drug dealing that emanated from Intxaurrondo.[28] Just as the names of Amedo and Domínguez had emerged in the public mind as primary GAL suspects from among a miasma of low-lifes and mercenaries in the late 1980s, so the names of two particular *guardia civiles* surfaced from a squalid pool of drug dealers and smugglers in mid-1995.

Sergeant Enrique Dorado Villalobos and Agent Felipe Bayo had deeply chequered records. They had both formed part of one of Galindo's elite anti-terrorist teams at Intxaurrondo. But they had something else in common. They shared convictions for torture and armed robbery. Dorado had also been found guilty of bribing a fellow *guardia civil* to turn a blind eye to his tobacco-smuggling operations.

Despite these black marks on their service sheets, both men had enjoyed great benevolence from their superiors. Bayo was sent on a pilot's course to the US, with all expenses (6 million pesetas) paid. He was then given free treatment in two hospitals for psychiatric problems. He was discharged from the force in 1987, but given a special pension as compensation for his 'loss of psycho-physical abilities'.[29] His parents were also given a donation of 2 million pesetas from the Guardia Civil widows' and orphans' fund. Dorado was only expelled from the Guardia Civil in June 1995, as the Lasa and Zabala case took shape, six years after his first conviction. It was a fairly painless expulsion, as he received a pension equivalent to a colonel's.[30]

Now his erstwhile smuggling partner, Pedro Luis Miguéliz, was telling Judge Bueren that Dorado had boasted of taking part in the kidnapping of Lasa and Zabala.[31] Other *guardia civiles* were also implicating them.[32]

The girlfriend of a *guardia civil* who had committed suicide provided some corroborating evidence. Most seriously of all, a member of the National Police, Angel López Carrillo, claimed to have witnessed several events related to the kidnapping and torture, including an incriminating conversation between Galindo and the Socialist Civil Governor of Guipúzcoa, Julen Elgorriaga. Carrillo also gave details of payments to French police for their collaboration in illegal Spanish operations on French territory.[33]

Carrillo's practice of telling *El Mundo* what he had just told the judge raised now familiar questions about the manipulation of the case by other interested parties.[34] However, both Bueren and the judge who succeeded him on the case held his testimony to be valid and credible. Carrillo's motivation may perhaps be found in his anger that the anti-terrorist struggle had made some people very rich: 'While some of us were risking our lives in the sentry box, others were risking our money in the casino.'[35]

A single sensational theme united all these allegations. Lasa and Zabala had not been held, like Segundo Marey, in some isolated hideout in the mountains. They had been brought directly from Bayonne to San Sebastián. There they were tortured, for days or weeks on end, in the very heart of the city. They were held prisoner by *guardia civiles* from Intxaurrondo in specially prepared cells in La Cumbre, a disused palace assigned to the Civil Governor and the Ministry of the Interior.[36] Carrillo was able to give Bueren some material evidence: he had kept the key to La Cumbre, attached to which was a card handwritten by Elgorriaga's secretary.[37]

VERA'S HYPOTHESIS: THE GUARDIA CIVIL CANNOT BE GUILTY BECAUSE THE GUARDIA CIVIL WOULD NOT GET CAUGHT

None of this evidence impressed Rafael Vera, Director of State Security at the time of Lasa and Zabala's kidnapping. When I spoke to him, more than two years after the investigation had started, Felipe Bayo had already admitted to a role in the kidnapping, and Vera himself had been charged with covering up the crime.

Vera said he was convinced that the Guardia Civil had had no part in these events. Bayo had only confessed, Vera continued, because he had been promised release from custody,[38] because of 'tremendous pressure' on his family and 'because he has received so little political support'.[39] He then advanced a remarkable hypothesis.

'How is it possible that the Guardia Civil, if it is the author of these murders and the subsequent burial, [should leave] the bones for years and years in . . . a mortuary, abandoned on top of a table, with the door unlocked? Knowing that this evidence existed, which could some day be used against them, wouldn't [the Guardia Civil] go to the mortuary, take the bones, throw them out or switch them, make them disappear? Do you believe that the Guardia Civil, given their style of work – they are not stupid, that is obvious – would have permitted the bones to remain where they were? That means that they did not know the bones were those of Lasa and Zabala. If they didn't know, they didn't do it.'

This is a remarkable insight into the *modus operandi* of the Guardia Civil regarding the disposal of damaging evidence, from one of the most powerful men in the Interior Ministry since the death of Franco. It is repeated with an embellishment in Eliseo Bayo's book, *GAL: Punto Final*, which Vera describes as the best book on the subject.[40] The author (who is no relation of Felipe Bayo) suggests that the National Police were responsible for establishing false connections between the bones and the Guardia Civil, because the police were angry at having to take all the blame for the dirty war.[41]

Margarita Robles, who filled Vera's position in Interior when the Lasa and Zabala case was being investigated, dismisses this theory of a byzantine police conspiracy against the Guardia Civil.

'All I can say is that the [police] investigation led by Enrique de Federico was very serious, and in my opinion merits total credibility.'[42] That investigation was itself the object of persistent surveillance and harassment. Many people believe that *guardia civiles* were responsible for a series of incidents, ranging from spying to burglary to the homosexual rape of a witness.[43] Asked if she believed that *guardia civiles* were behind this campaign of harassment, Robles replies: 'I would not dare to say who it was. We could never prove exactly who was behind it. Witnesses were followed, there was counter-surveillance, there was an attempted burglary of Enrique de Federico's house. Who was it? Well, one has to assume that it was the people who were affected by the investigation.'[44]

The problem with Vera, she says, is that after so many years in power, 'he had come to believe he himself was the security of the state. From that position, you can justify many things.'

Despite the accumulation of a solid body of evidence, Judge Bueren seemed to move very slowly in terms of charging people. The prosecution lawyer Iñigo Iruin suggests that Bueren's close relationship with Rafael Vera in the past inhibited his work.[45] Margarita Robles simply says that, on a scale of one to ten, Bueren's diligence in this case scored considerably less than one.[46] Fernando López Agudín has a more sympathetic view, saying he was subject to intolerable pressure from associates of the suspects.[47]

In January 1996, for whatever reasons, Bueren resigned from the judiciary, to take up a lucrative and much less stressful private legal practice. For a few weeks, the Lasa and Zabala case landed in the lap of the rather more energetic Garzón, to the horror of those who thought this judge was already excessively zealous on the GAL cases.

As it happened, the case finally fell to a magistrate who would be at least as controversial. Javier Gómez de Liaño's mere arrival in the Audiencia Nacional was felt to be improper in some quarters.[48] It would bring him into close proximity with the judge who was investigating a case concerning his brother Mariano, who was a lawyer for the disgraced banker Mario Conde. Given that Conde was believed to be using the GAL scandal to blackmail the government, Gómez de Liaño's control of one of the key dirty war cases was bound to cause concern.

The investigation, however, now had an unstoppable momentum of its own. By April 1996, Gómez de Liaño and Garzón were working closely together on the implication of Galindo in various GAL cases, which were now proliferating at a bewildering rate.

Garzón had opened or reopened a battery of investigations in the previous year, including those into the deaths of Juan Carlos García Goena, Ramón Oñederra, Mikel Goikoetxea, Christian Olaskoaga and Rafael Goikoetxea. From his prison cell in Thailand, Ismael Miquel, the alleged GAL organiser wanted for the killing of Robert Caplanne, said that Francisco Álvarez had told him the GAL were working for the government. Secret service (CESID) documents, surfacing through the obscure manoeuvres of Colonel Perote, the former military intelligence commander, were providing new clues to the implication of the army, and of Felipe González, in the GAL.[49] *El Mundo* was publishing transcripts of CESID tapes which appeared to link General Galindo directly to the killing of Lasa and Zabala.[50] In May, Luis Roldán also began to offer the courts information on the GAL which would lead to new charges, and Gómez de Liaño went into top gear.

Garzón had begun to suspect that *guardia civiles*, perhaps the same individuals, were involved in many of the early GAL cases. Giving evidence on the killing of Oñederra, Roldán told Garzón that he had been asked, by Rafael Vera and the Interior lawyer Jorge Argote, to arrange the 'elimination' of Enrique Dorado Villalobos and Felipe Bayo. They had told him that the two *guardia civiles* knew too much about the dirty war, including the Lasa and Zabala episode.[51] Picking up on this allegation, Gómez de Liaño called in Roldán on the Lasa and Zabala case, and the former Director General of the Guardia Civil incriminated himself, Vera, Argote, Dorado and Bayo.[52]

Gómez de Liaño now formally declared Vera and Argote to be suspects in the case. Argote protested furiously because he was the legal representative of several of the other suspects, including Dorado and Bayo[53] and, later in the case, General Galindo. The two judges were now investigating a direct link, through Vera and Argote, between the 'green GAL' of the Guardia Civil and the 'blue GAL' of the National Police.

Meanwhile, in the Oñederra case,[54] Garzón had made an even more dramatic move. He summonsed three of Spain's most eminent anti-terrorist generals as suspects: Andrés Cassinello, former Chief of Staff of the Guardia Civil; José Antonio Sáenz de Santamaría, former Director General of the same force and former Inspector General of the National Police; and Enrique Rodríguez Galindo, former commander of Intxaurrondo barracks. Barrionuevo and Vera moved swiftly to defend their former top brass, but many observers remembered the deeply ambiguous statements which the generals had made about the GAL in the past.[55] Garzón went on to cite Vera, Argote and former Interior Minister José Luis Corcuera as suspects in the same case only days later.[56]

As the inquiry progressed, a new element emerged which must have raised eyebrows in the more conservative circles of the Guardia Civil. Garzón wanted to take evidence from Dorado's 'sentimental companion'. It emerged that this most macho sergeant of a quintessentially macho force was a very active homosexual. His lover, Juan Francisco Cruz, would become a fixture outside the Audiencia Nacional, with a rather makeshift placard reading 'Kike. I believe in you. You are innocent.'[57] The Guardia Civil would never look quite the same again.

Dorado and Bayo were charged with the kidnapping, torture and murder of Lasa and Zabala on 20 May 1996, and remanded in custody.[58] In a very detailed writ, Gómez de Liaño specified that the 'serious pain' they had inflicted was motivated not only by zeal to extract information, but also by vengeance for the crimes of ETA. It was beginning to look as if the two young *etarras* had had an even worse time than had been imagined. Showing signs of mental instability which would become more acute in prison, Bayo responded to the charges by calling the victims' lawyer, Iñigo Iruin, a 'murderer' and hurling a typewriter at him across the judge's chambers.[59]

Three days later, Gómez de Liaño took the momentous step of imprisoning a general of the Guardia Civil, the first officer of this rank to be remanded in custody since the attempted *coup d'état* fifteen years earlier.[60] In a very detailed writ on the events which led to the death of Lasa and Zabala, Gómez de Liaño affirmed: 'It was Enrique Rodríguez Galindo who decided, given the lamentable physical state of the two boys, the result of torture, that Lasa and Zabala should be taken to Alicante, where they would be made disappear.'[61]

Barrionuevo, Vera and Corcuera called a press conference to say they wanted to take Galindo's place in prison. Felipe González expressed his 'sadness and frustration' at Gómez de Liaño's decision. Barrionuevo compared Galindo's fate to that of Hernán Cortés, the conquistador of Mexico who suffered judicial persecution on his return to Spain.[62] Someone in the PSOE leadership had a black sense of humour – they sent Galindo a copy of Gabriel García Marquez's *News of a Kidnapping*.[63]

Three weeks later, Rafael Vera was charged with attempting to cover up the kidnapping, based on Roldán's declaration that Vera and Argote had asked him to have Dorado and Bayo eliminated.

There was much more corroborated evidence in the case of Julen Elgorriaga, former Civil Governor of Guipúzcoa. He was charged and sent to prison on 19 June. In his writ, Gómez de Liaño established to his own satisfaction that Elgorriaga had known about the kidnapping, had visited Lasa and Zabala with Galindo while they were being tortured, and was an accomplice to their murders. 'Despite his authority, he did nothing to prevent the final destiny of the two youths.'[64]

The Lasa and Zabala case has many parallels with the GAL investigation into the kidnapping of Segundo Marey, though it has been, in every sense, even more grotesque. Like the Marey investigation, this case brought into play another set of controversial judicial personalities. The judges and prosecutors who investigated it suffered systematic obstruction. Some of them also became entangled in serious allegations of corruption and conspiracy. Witnesses have been intimidated by agents of the state. And just as a pair of relatively junior policemen were the weak link which led to the breaking of an entire chain of command in the Marey case, so two *guardia civiles* seemed likely to provide the path to those who ordered the kidnapping, torture and murder of Lasa and Zabala.

DBS Arts Library

Amedo and Domínguez only began to reveal some of the truth after six years in prison. Once they had confessed, it took a far shorter time for most of their superiors to admit their guilt. By 1996, there were far fewer reasons for a pawn to keep his mouth shut. After only fifteen months in prison, Felipe Bayo admitted a minor role in the kidnapping of Lasa and Zabala. He implicated General Enrique Rodríguez Galindo and former Socialist Civil Governor Julen Elgorriaga directly in the interrogation of the young men.

The sewers were reaching the salons again, by a different route.

NOTES

1   *El País*, 26 March 1995.

2   *El País*, 2 December 1987. See ch. 15.

3   Quoted in Fernando López Agudín, *En el Laberinto* (Barcelona: Plaza y Janés, 1996), p. 112.

4   See prologue, pp. 8–9, ch. 5, pp. 72–81, ch. 18, pp. 271.

5   *El País*, 23 March 1995.

6   *La Verdad*, 30 January 1985.

7   Quoted in the Preliminary report of the joint committee of Guardia Civil and National Police on the deaths of Lasa and Zabala, Office of the Secretary of State for the Interior Ministry, Madrid, 21 April 1995. This report summarised the first official inquiries after the case resurfaced in March of that year. The call to Radio Alicante was broadcast by the station, but at this stage, of course, no human remains had been found to give it substance.

8   It seems that two comments by Amedo sparked off the association of ideas. He had mentioned the alleged proposal to bury Segundo Marey in quicklime. He had also made an off-the-cuff comment about Lasa and Zabala: 'Those two were a matter for the greens [Guardia Civil] and they are in Alicante.' (*El Mundo*, 27 December 1998.) The source of Amedo's information seems to have been a chance encounter in prison with one of the *guardia civiles* allegedly involved, many years after the event. This suggests the 'green' and 'blue' branches of the GAL may have maintained a considerable degree of mutual secrecy at the time of their operations. This would be consistent with the rivalry between the Guardia Civil and the National Police.

9   *El País*, 26 March 1995.

10 *El País*, 23 March 1995. González would later concede that 'the GAL and the bodies of Lasa and Zabala emboldened ETA'. López Agudín, op. cit., p. 124.

11 The period for which Lasa and Zabala were held has not been firmly established. If the GAL claim to Radio Alicante was accurate in its details, they were held for three months. This seems unlikely, however, and the time frame may have been much smaller, as the Audiencia Nacional indicated in its judgement, 26 April 2000.

12 *El País*, 26 March 1995.

13 *Deia*, 21 March 1995.

14 *El País*, 28 and 29 March 1995.

15 Interview with Mikel Mari Lasa, Tolosa, June 1997.

16 Interview with Iñigo Iruin, San Sebastián, June 1997.

17 Interview with Juan Mari Zabala, Tolosa, June 1997.

18 Interview with Mikel Mari Lasa, Tolosa, June 1997.

19 *El País*, 22 June 1995.

20 Ibid.

21 Ibid.

22 López Augudín, op. cit., pp. 116–17. Judicial obstruction was also suspected when Gordillo was removed as prosecutor from the case and replaced by his

boss, José Aranda, the man who made such a poor job of prosecuting Amedo and Domínguez in 1991. Aranda himself was eventually replaced by Jesús Santos Alonso, who proved a much more zealous prosecutor. See *El País*, 29 April 1995.

23 He had relinquished command of Intxaurrondo some months earlier, officially so that he could concentrate on the formalities required for his promotion.

24 Interview with Margarita Robles, Madrid, November 1997. See also López Agudín, op. cit., p. 159.

25 López Agudín, op. cit., p. 45.

26 Manuel Vázquez Montalbán, *Un Polaco en la Corte del Rey Juan Carlos* (Madrid: Alfaguara, 1996), p. 452.

27 Interview with Fernando López Agudín, Madrid, November 1997.

28 An inquiry by the San Sebastián prosecutor, Luis Navajas, had revealed an extensive network of corruption in Intxaurrondo. Very few prosecutions followed, apparently because those most involved in corruption had also been involved in the dirty war, and could impose a 'law of silence' on their fellow *guardia civiles*. See *El País*, 30 July 1995.

29 *El País*, 2 August 1995.

30 *El Mundo*, 16 May 1996. See also Auto de Procesamiento [Prosecution Writ] contra el General Enrique Rodríguez Galindo y Otros, Sumario 15/95 [Lasa and Zabala], Audiencia Nacional, Madrid, 27 May 1996.

31 Miguéliz, nicknamed Txofo, had also been a business partner of Victor Manuel Navascués, charged and acquitted of the GAL killing of Jean-Pierre Leiba.

32 *La Vanguardia*, 20 July 1995.

33 *El Mundo*, 4 September 1995.

34 See ch. 20 for a detailed account of such manipulation.

35 The defence argued in court that his motivation was very different. He was, they pointed out, the former lover of Barbara Durkhop, widow of the assassinated PSOE leader Enrique Casas. The defence claimed that he was dropped by Durkhop on the advice of Julen Elgorriaga, and that he was motivated by resentment against his former boss over this issue.

36 *El País*, 30 July 1995.

37 López Agudín, op. cit., p. 166.

38 Bayo in fact remained in custody after his confession, though he was moved to rather better conditions in a military prison.

39 Interview with Rafael Vera, Madrid, November 1997.

40 This is not surprising, since this highly polemical book is devoted almost exclusively to defending Vera's position, and that of Galindo and Argote.

41 Eliseo Bayo, *GAL: Punto Final* (Barcelona: Plaza y Janés, 1997), p. 261. See also López Agudín, op. cit., p. 137.

42 Interview with Margarita Robles, Madrid, November 1997.

43 *El País*, 28 October 1995.

44 Interview with Margarita Robles, Madrid, November 1997.

45 Interview with Iñigo Iruin, San Sebastián, June 1997.

46 Interview with Margarita Robles, Madrid, November 1997.

47 Interview with Fernando López Agudín, Madrid, November 1997.

48 He had previously been a member of the General Council of the Judiciary, and his move to the Audiencia Nacional was a voluntary step down the career ladder. *El País*, 14 February 1996.

49 See ch. 21 for a full account of the saga of the CESID papers.

50 *El Mundo*, 9 April 1996.

51 *El Mundo*, 6 May 1996.

52 *El País*, 7 May 1996.

53 *El País*, 9 May 1996.

54 This case now took in the killings of Ramón Oñederra (*Kattu*), Bixente Perurena (*Peru*), Angel Gurmindo (*Stein*) and Christian Olaskoaga.

55 *El País*, 8 May 1996. Cassinello, for example, had described the GAL as 'an imaginative campaign, successfully conducted'. (*El País*, 21 December 1994.) He also told a journalist that he was not the leader of the GAL, 'but if that were true and you had discovered it, your life would be worth only two pesetas'. (*El País*, 22 July 1984.) Santamaría had hinted broadly that in counter-terrorist work it was necessary to operate outside the law. (*El País*, 24 February 1995.) Galindo had said that 'the GAL raised the morale of the part of society most threatened by ETA . . . the GAL stopped ETA committing more murders than it would otherwise have done.' (Bayo, op. cit., p. 26.)

56 *El País*, 10 May 1996.

57 *El Mundo*, 23 May 1996; *El País*, 15 May 1996. 'Kike' was one of Dorado's nicknames, a diminutive of Enrique.

58 *El País*, 21 May 1996.

59 *El País*, 23 May 1996.

60 *El País*, 24 May 1996.

61 Auto de Procesamiento contra el General Enrique Rodríguez Galindo y Otros, Sumario 15/95 [Lasa and Zabala], Audiencia Nacional, Madrid, 27 May 1996. The writ specified that Galindo should be kept in custody because of the risk that he would interfere with witnesses (p. 19).

62 *El País*, 19 June 1996. This was a curious analogy for several reasons, not least in that it suggested that Barrionuevo thought Galindo had *conquered* the Basque Country. The same applies to Galindo's extraordinary comment, made during the oral hearing, that 'with six men like them [Dorado and Bayo] I could have conquered all of Latin America'. *El País*, 16 December 1999.

63 *El País*, 18 June 1996.

64 Auto de Procesamiento contra Julen Elgorriaga y Rafael Vera, Sumario 15/95 [Lasa and Zabala], Audiencia Nacional, Madrid, 19 June 1996.

20

Who's Cheating Who?
bankers, spies and audiotapes

The one class of human being I hold in contempt is that of the blackmailer. The blackmailer never has any limits. Today he gets four, tomorrow he asks for eight, and the day after that sixteen. To think that you have silenced a blackmailer is always an error. We cannot consent to a situation where the state is blackmailed.

Margarita Robles[1]

It has been said that the GAL affair, and a good part of the scandals which stain the government, affect the political past; but now it is becoming evident that in fact they affect the future, and perhaps set conditions for it.

El País[2]

Who guards the guardians? The problems faced by those investigating crimes committed by state security forces are as old and intractable as Plato's conundrum, but in a technologically advanced society they are infinitely more complex. In the hands of intelligence services, 'information technology' often serves strategies of disinformation.

Microchips and mobile phones, like the camera before them, can transmit falsehood as easily as truth, and are easily susceptible to manipulation and distortion. Uncommon common sense was required to unscramble the signals when the GAL investigations became fixated on a series of documents stolen from Spanish military intelligence, and manipulated by obscure interest groups who were not motivated by the pursuit of justice. We will examine these documents in the next chapter. First, to understand the degree to which the GAL scandals poisoned Spanish public life, it is necessary to look at the strange and tortuous way the documents came to light.

The waters of the GAL investigations were never going to run clear, and the guilty parties who had most to lose were most likely to muddy them. There were, however, many other individuals and groups who saw they had a great deal to gain by diverting the investigations to serve their own disparate, and sometimes incompatible, ends.

Opposition parties naturally sought to make political capital out of revelations which linked González's cabinets more and more closely to crimes of kidnapping, torture and murder. Meanwhile, sectors of public opinion, especially in the media, had become deeply concerned, not to say frustrated, that the avalanche of scandals in the early 1990s had failed to dislodge the PSOE from power.

The Socialists were beginning to look – and not only to their rivals – a little like the Mexican Institutional Revolutionary Party (PRI), which held power for seven decades despite massive corruption and widespread human rights violations.[3] The opposition and sections of the media began to make the perfectly reasonable analysis that the election of an alternative government was the first priority of Spanish democrats. Some of them, however, quietly added that this should be achieved 'by any means necessary', which led them into bad company and worse practices.

A tangled web of alliances emerged, in the early 1990s, which forced the GAL investigations into a hall of distorting mirrors. Legitimate questions about state terrorism became powerful weapons in the hands of people who had little interest in democracy, legal accountability, or human rights. This, in turn, offered those Socialists tainted by the GAL scandal a morally spurious but emotionally powerful shield: 'If you are attacking us,' they could say to their democratic opponents (inside and outside the party), 'look at the company you are putting yourself in.'

Santos Juliá, a sympathetic but scrupulous historian of the PSOE, expresses the dilemma of those who tried to persuade the Socialists to clean up their own backyard: 'Those of us here who have tried to maintain some kind of political rationalism have found ourselves under assault from every side, haven't we? They [the Socialists] ask us for total complicity. That is, either you are on their side, or you are with Mario Conde and the anti-democratic conspiracy.'[4]

The GAL campaign had itself been a classic conspiracy, and conspiracies are rapid breeders of more conspiracies, real and imagined.

According to his most extreme critics, Baltasar Garzón, the magistrate who has pursued the GAL investigation most tenaciously, has been either a participant in, or a tool of, a plot to pervert the course of justice and undermine the institutions of the state.[5] These charges have never been substantiated, and are mostly made by those who have been most threatened by his findings. This does not mean, however, that such conspiracies did not exist, nor that the conspirators did not pass through Garzón's chambers, and those of other judges. They usually left sensational material behind them. Sometimes their testimonies were spurious, or of no legal value. On other occasions, they provided crucial substantiation for allegations against the GAL defendants. It seems very likely that Garzón exploited this material ruthlessly. The unsettling fact that bad witnesses were supplying good evidence gives many of the passages in the GAL labyrinth an additional disorienting dimension.

Most of the conspiratorial threads lead back, again and again, to one man: the disgraced banker Mario Conde, the former president of Banesto who was facing fraud charges as a result of an emergency audit of the bank in December 1993.[6] We have already seen that there were curious coincidences between the investigation of Conde's business affairs and the investigation of the GAL in different chambers of the Audiencia Nacional.[7] On the very day Conde was called to give evidence for the first time, 19 December 1994, Garzón imprisoned Sancristóbal and his subordinates on the evidence of Amedo and Domínguez. The judge investigating Banesto, Manuel García Castellón, imprisoned Conde on 23 December. Three days later, *El Mundo* announced the publication of their two blockbuster series of interviews with Amedo and Domínguez, which ran over the next two weeks.

There is no hard evidence that Conde had any control over the two former policemen, but rumours had long circulated that they were being bankrolled by businessmen who had fallen foul of the law, of the Socialists, or of both. It was not unnatural that many observers already drew the conclusion, probably premature, that Conde was sending a message to the Socialists along these lines: 'Whenever the courts put me under pressure, I will release information to damage the government.'

At the time, there was almost certainly more significance in other contacts, not reported till much later, between Francisco Álvarez Cascos, deputy leader of the Partido Popular, Pedro J. Ramírez, editor of *El Mundo*, and Jorge Manrique, lawyer for Amedo and Domínguez. The confluence of interests between the main opposition party, a major newspaper and two convicted criminals has never been fully explained by the participants, but it takes very little imagination to understand it.[8]

An even stranger coincidence followed, which Conde certainly exploited to the full. In prison, he found himself sharing the same recreation area, at Alcalá Meco, as Julián Sancristóbal. A video smuggled out of the jail showed the two men deep in conversation, and images from it were widely publicised.

Though Sancristóbal still appeared to be loyal to the government line on the GAL,[9] and would not admit his participation in the kidnapping of Marey for another seven months, the sight of the former banker and the former security chief taking long strolls together must have sent shivers down the collective spine of Sancristóbal's erstwhile superiors. Conde ostentatiously had a word processor installed in his cell, and let the rumour circulate that he was inputting copious notes after every conversation with Sancristóbal.

One of his former superiors, José Barrionuevo, was a regular visitor to Sancristóbal, as a friend, legal advisor and, one supposes, a very anxious observer of his state of mind. On one such visit in January 1995, he raised the question that everyone in Spain's chattering classes was asking at the time: was Sancristóbal telling Conde 'stuff about the GAL'?

'What would I gain by telling him?' was Sancristóbal's reply. He told Barrionuevo that Conde had assured him that he had not been financing Amedo.

Barrionuevo (and, separately, Sancristóbal) told the *El País* journalist Ernesto Ekaizer about this conversation in March 1996.[10] It raises an interesting point. In January 1995, Sancristóbal, like Barrionuevo and González himself, claimed to have no information about the GAL which was not already in the public domain. Yet this conversation makes clear that they had, indeed, something more to tell.

Amazingly, Sancristóbal was subsequently able to set up a three-way meeting in jail with himself, Barrionuevo and Conde, which enabled him to further reassure the former, and impress the latter, about his continuing influence with government figures.

In fact, Conde had a bone to pick with Sancristóbal, the Crillon report, which had first been tossed into the public arena by another highly conspiratorial figure, Luis Roldán.

CONDE'S FIRST MANOEUVRE: ROLDÁN, SANCRISTÓBAL AND THE CRILLON REPORT

Shortly after he had gone underground in April 1994, Roldán had revealed, courtesy of *El Mundo*, that, as Director General of the Guardia Civil, he had paid 67 million pesetas for an American detective agency, Kroll Associates, to investigate Conde in 1992. He said that the instruction had come from Narcís Serra, González's deputy, and that the payment had been made out of reserved funds. Roldán's intermediary with the agency had been Sancristóbal.[11]

Roldán's point in releasing this information was that the government had used reserved funds to pay for the investigation of a private citizen, who had subsequently been deprived of control of a private bank by state intervention.

When he was removed from Banesto in December 1993, by the intervention of the Bank of Spain, Conde presented himself as a victim of *los beautiful*. This jet set included the bankers and financiers who formed a privileged golden circle around González's Socialist elite. Conde's carefully cultivated and glamorous public image – aquiline features, gelled hair, immaculately cut suits – made him 'the archetype of the new, classless financier'.[12] But he had remained an outsider.

Conde came to epitomise buccaneering opposition to the PSOE's cronyism, and the government repaid his enmity in kind. In the words of one independent commentator, the merger which created the Banco Central Hispanoamericano in 1991 'represented a highly significant step in the government's policy of concentration in the banking world: four of the five largest banks were now in the control of presidents closely connected to the world of *los beautiful*. The one exception was Conde's Banesto, which was thereby excluded from any policy-making influence with the banking sector.'[13]

Conde also asserted that the Socialists had targeted him because they feared he had political ambitions. He was openly hostile to their eager espousal of European monetary union. And Conde's influence in the early 1990s extended well beyond the financial sphere. A survey showed that 42 per cent of Spaniards between the ages of sixteen and twenty-two saw him as their favourite role model.[14] His persuasive charisma is well illustrated by the fact that he was invited to give a lecture on business ethics at the Vatican, despite the fact that he was believed to be a freemason.

He had turned down an opportunity to lead the apparently moribund precursor of the Partido Popular in 1986, and had flirted with the idea of leading a new right-wing party ever since.[15] He also had major investments across a very influential share of the print and electronic media.[16] He was regularly portrayed as a heroic opposition figure by Pedro J. Ramírez in his polemical editorials in *El Mundo*.[17] When he fell from grace, *El Mundo* portrayed him as a target of Felipe González's overweening ambition. The paper continued to do so, long after it had become evident that Conde's Banesto was as corrupt as any of the worst enterprises run by Socialist cronies and appointees.

Roldán hinted that the Kroll investigation, confusingly known as the Crillon report, had been commissioned by the PSOE to smear Conde's private life and cripple his political prospects. The use of public money for such an exercise would be a clear abuse of power by the government.[18]

However, the Bank of Spain had had substantial grounds for its emergency audit of Banesto, in December 1993. The state bank estimated that there was a 'hole' of 503,000 million pesetas in Banesto's accounts, a figure later revised upwards by Price Waterhouse to 605,000 million pesetas.[19] Nor was this simply a case of chronically inefficient management: Conde was ultimately charged with operations involving fraud and misappropriation of funds totalling 7,700 million pesetas.[20] He was found guilty on some of these charges, and acquitted on others, in April 2000.[21]

Nevertheless, Conde had naturally seized on Roldán's information about the Crillon report. He had made the most of it in the months before he went to prison. In May 1994 he already knew that criminal charges were likely to be preferred against him, and grasped at this opportunity to get his retaliation in first. He secured a meeting with Felipe González, which gives some idea of the influence he still had. The Prime Minister denied any involvement in the Crillon report, and ignored Conde's insinuations about the motives for the emergency audit of Banesto. After this meeting, González is alleged to have said of Conde: 'He doesn't have the atomic bomb, but he can do damage.'[22]

In prison eight months later, Conde used all his charm to try to persuade Sancristóbal to give evidence that the deputy Prime Minister, Narcís Serra, had authorised the payment for the report. Sancristóbal was confident that Serra was the source of the money, but could not offer Conde, or the courts, any proof that this was so.[23]

Ekaizer makes the telling point that, even if Serra had authorised the report, he would have considered it within his rights to deny having done so.[24] The culture of 'deniability' was obviously deep-rooted in the Socialist cabinet. The Supreme Court finally decided – without investigating who had commissioned it – that the report had been a legitimate inquiry into suspicious financial practices.[25]

Conde left jail on bail at the end of January 1995 with only a vague promise from Sancristóbal that his lawyer would give him a full copy of the report. He needed to bring much stronger pressures to bear on the government. As it happens, he almost certainly used a friend of Sancristóbal's to do so. Colonel Juan Alberto Perote had met Sancristóbal when he was commanding officer of the AOME (Special Methods Operational Group), the most secretive and powerful unit in the CESID. They were introduced by Francisco Álvarez in the mid-1980s, when Álvarez was one of Sancristóbal's top anti-terrorist officers. When Sancristóbal and Álvarez went into private business, they both remained in close touch with Perote. The latter was quietly dismissed from the CESID in 1991 and, as we have seen in chapter 18, was subsequently accused of taking confidential intelligence documents with him.[26]

Perote was certainly in possession of documents which, if not as explosive as the atomic bomb, could do terminal damage to the González government. Handled carelessly, they could endanger the state itself. The documents, if authentic, appeared to provide devastating evidence that the whole state security apparatus, all the way up to González himself, had planned and executed the dirty war against ETA. The 'CESID papers' would dominate most discussion of the GAL investigations for the next four years.

Whether what happened next was a conspiracy is a matter of interpretation, hotly contested by different interests within the Spanish media and political elites. Most of the known facts, however, suggest that Conde and his advisors had a very carefully prepared and complex strategy, which moved on several fronts simultaneously. Knowing they had a big stick, they walked at first very softly indeed.

Conde had quietly hired a lawyer with excellent media and political contacts, Jesús Santaella, in early January. One of Santaella's first moves had, on the face of it, nothing to do with the Conde case. He was on the editorial council of *El Mundo*, which carried an opinion piece by him on 25 January.

In this article, Santaella argued that, since the GAL was a political case, the proper forum to hear it was the parliament, not the courts. He was essentially calling for the whole dirty war mess to be cleaned up, once and for all, by a kind of impeachment process. This would probably be much less harsh on the defendants than the judicial system would be. His article appeared to be a disinterested contribution to the debate, but it sent out a message to Barrionuevo and company that Conde's team were not necessarily hostile to their interests. It was an article which found some echo among a broad spectrum of judges during the year.

In February, Conde's team tacked, even more discreetly, in the opposite direction. In his 8 February State of the Nation speech Felipe González had essayed a new, aggressive Socialist strategy on the GAL scandal, which reminded his critics that there had also been a dirty war under the UCD.[27] The implied threat to drag a second set of skeletons out of the closet, if the GAL investigations continued, was received with anger and alarm among conservatives, and in the military establishment.

On 20 February, *El Mundo* reported that a senior CESID officer had met *guardia civiles* linked to the GAL, and offered them generous compensation if they would implicate the UCD in the earlier dirty war.

Two days later, Adolfo Suárez, the former Prime Minister, received a visit from the editor of *El Mundo*, Pedro J. Ramírez. He was accompanied by Colonel Perote, who played the former Prime Minister an audio tape. Suárez was amazed, and outraged, to hear himself in conversation with CESID officials in 1978. The tape included phrases like 'They should rub out a couple of guys, that's the sort of thing that will boost the morale of our [security] forces.' Perote explained that this tape had been preserved on the express orders of the Director of the CESID, General Emilio Alonso Manglano. He pointed out that the tape included gaps, which could easily be manipulated to make the contents even more compromising for Suárez. The journalist and the former spy left Suárez a copy of the tape, and *El Mundo* published the story a few days later.[28]

Suárez rang González, and was reassured in turn by Serra and Manglano that there was no plot to incriminate him. Manglano, though, was far from reassured himself. Perote had shown his first card, but Manglano knew that his former subordinate had many more up his sleeve, and that some of them were aces.

Only Manglano and one or two of his officers were aware that, when Perote left the CESID in contested circumstances in 1991, he had 'accidentally' taken with him secret files on microfiches amounting, it was thought, to several thousand documents. He had had plenty of time to copy them before he was asked to return them. Most of the documents, Manglano knew, related to events much more recent than 1978. Realising the stakes were now very high indeed, Manglano told the disturbing news to the Minister for Defence, Julián García Vargas.

Meanwhile, Santaella was applying pressure at another point. He met Barrionuevo twice in February, and set up a meeting between him and Conde. According to Ekaizer, there were hints that, in return for unspecified favours, Conde might exercise some control on *El Mundo*'s publication of further revelations about the GAL.

In the midst of these manoeuvres, Roldán was 'recaptured', and proceeded to make his series of sensational revelations in court. But neither his evidence on the Crillon report nor Sancristóbal's evidence later gave Conde real support in his quest to implicate the Socialist government in illegal activity.

Conde's strongest cards were elsewhere. While he pursued a legal strategy to unseat García Castellón, the judge hearing his case, and replace him with a more benevolent figure,[29] he also began to show his aces.

On 21 March, the banker went to see Suárez and suggested that, in the interests of the state, the former Prime Minister should inform both González and the King that Conde was in possession of information which could do them both great damage.[30]

On 11 April, Santaella had a meeting with the Justice and Interior Minister, Juan Alberto Belloch, in which he touched on three matters affecting his client: the Crillon report, the need to unseat García Castellón, and Conde's demand for 'compensation' for his removal from Banesto. According to a witness, Gerardo Viada, Belloch limited himself to listening to Santaella's arguments.[31]

As the legal battle with García Castellón approached one of its climaxes, Santaella suddenly pushed much harder. On 22 April, according to Ekaizer's account, Santaella went to see Belloch for a second time. On this occasion, Viada was not a witness to the meeting, and Ekaizer gives no details, though he asserts that this was the occasion on which the lawyer dropped his mask and the blackmailer appeared without dissimulation.[32]

The next day, things became rather more explicit. Santaella returned to the parliament and gave Barrionuevo a bundle of documents of uncertain origin. They contained information about the security forces' involvement in a number of GAL operations. Santaella helpfully supplied an appendix, entitled 'Conclusions', also drafted by an anonymous hand. The appendix stated baldly: 'The CESID had first-hand information . . . about what had happened to Lasa and Zabala, as is demonstrated by a tape of the conversation attached to these documents. They were executed in Alicante, each of them shot in the back of the head, after they had been forced to dig their own "holes".'[33]

Arguing that the Socialists' decision to approve the GAL campaign was a quid pro quo for restless army officers who might have otherwise attempted another coup, the appendix continued: 'In any case, the State is informed about the Green GAL and [the GAL] of the Police, and not only does nothing to obstruct them, but collaborates with them through the CESID . . . sending information to . . . Galindo to facilitate attacks and even supplying arms for this purpose.'

Santaella made the rather obvious suggestion that Barrionuevo should give these documents and the appendix to González.

Ekaizer remarks that this was a case of a lawyer going to the president of the parliamentary committee dealing with constitutional issues and showing him evidence that the state was involved in serious crimes. 'But not to expose the facts! He did it to traffic in information!'[34] Ekaizer alleges that Santaella was using the documents to blackmail the government.

This argument cuts both ways. Neither Barrionuevo nor deputy Prime Minister Narcís Serra, to whom he passed on the document, felt any obligation to bring this catalogue of state terrorism to the attention of the courts. Since they had come to identify their own interests with those of the state, they probably saw no reason to do so. And if, as Ekaizer says, the whole affair shows Spanish society's understanding of the rule of law in a very bad light, that society was by 1995, to some extent, the creation of the Socialists themselves.

A poor grasp of the concept of the rule of law was not, however, a weakness exclusive to the Socialists. A similarly 'pragmatic' reading of the concept of criminal responsibility is reflected in Suárez's response to this affair. For Suárez, also, 'reasons of state' clearly prevailed over the rights of the individual to legal protection and justice.

Suárez knew about the documents because Santaella could not be certain they would reach González through Barrionuevo, and, as a belt and braces measure, approached the man for whom he had once worked as an advisor.[35] He gave a copy of the appendix (the 'Conclusions') to Suárez, who promptly communicated it to González and the King. Ekaizer says that González asked Suárez whether he would have granted Conde a meeting if he were still Prime Minister.

'I don't know, Felipe,' said Suárez, 'that depends on the reality of the danger that may lie in this' – he indicated the appendix – 'I don't know if these things are true.'[36] He did, however, go so far as to recommend that González should receive Santaella, whose integrity on matters of state he vouched for, as Conde's representative.[37]

For several more weeks, González kept his counsel, holding his nerve through the municipal elections on 28 May, though he did make a cryptic reference to 'a conspiracy' during the campaign.

On 1 June, General Manglano, Director of the CESID, had to give evidence on the Crillon report. Conde let him know, through three different conduits, that it would be in his interests to implicate Serra in the funding of the report.[38] Manglano told the court that neither his superiors nor he himself knew anything about it. Eight days later, Conde suffered another major blow when the Supreme Court rejected his case against García Castellón.

Just three days after that, on 12 June, *El Mundo* broke a sensational story, and Manglano, Narcís Serra and the Minister for Defence, Julián García Vargas, lost their jobs as a result. Antonio Rubio and Manuel Cerdán revealed, as we have seen in chapter 18, that the CESID had been tapping the mobile phones of the King, politicians and journalists without any legal authorisation.[39]

El Mundo had copious copies of CESID documentation to prove this story. Whether these documents came from Perote, as Ekaizer suggests, or from some other source, as Rubio and Cerdán insist,[40] it is more than plausible to see the hand of Conde moving behind the scenes. Perote was eventually acquitted of leaking the transcriptions to *El Mundo* by a Madrid court, but convicted, with General Manglano and others, of illegally tapping the calls.[41]

The fallout from the phone-tapping scandal was carnage. The loss of two ministers and a military intelligence chief made González look mortally wounded. They revealed an intelligence service either out of control or serving a government which had ridden roughshod over the right to privacy.

Even voices usually sympathetic to the PSOE could not restrain their anger. The former editor and founder of *El País*, Juan Luis Cebrián, who was one of the targets of the tapping, recalled that he had been a victim of the intelligence services under the UCD: 'I once thought that the Socialist government had put this kind of activity out of bounds, but they have long since disillusioned me in this respect,' he commented acidly.[42]

Hardly anyone believed Serra's limp explanation: an experimental sweep of the airwaves by the CESID had 'accidentally' picked up these communications. There was no explanation forthcoming as to why such an accident should have resulted in the meticulous transcription and preservation of hundreds of conversations. It also seemed a remarkable coincidence that all of the phone calls intercepted accidentally should have been between public figures. Nor could he explain why the order to destroy the transcriptions, which had been supposedly issued when the 'accident' took place, had never been carried out.[43]

The story catapulted Colonel Juan Alberto Perote into the public eye, when *El País* reported that he had held a long meeting with Conde and the lawyer/businessman Mariano Gómez de Liaño at the house of Conde's right-hand man, Fernando Garro, the day after the phone-tapping story was published. The conspiracy theory suddenly had names and faces. Perote became an instant media star, appearing on radio talk shows, and, curiously enough, proposing a 'law of the full stop' for the GAL cases.

On 21 June, he was charged by a military court with leaking the tapes. The officer who succeeded him in the CESID, Colonel Fernando López Fernández, was reported as telling the court that, among the microfiches he believed Perote had removed, were documents about the GAL.[44] Perote was remanded in custody in a military prison. The conspiracy theory got a further boost when the former agent chose to be represented by the same lawyer as Mario Conde: Jesús Santaella.

González denounced a conspiracy which was trying to 'blackmail the State' and 'throw down a gauntlet to the State' – that is, threatening not just his government but democratic institutions – at a private meeting of Socialist MPs which was leaked to the press.[45] He caused further confusion, however, when he made no reference to any conspiracy when he addressed an emergency debate on the phone-tapping ten days later.[46]

'BLACKMAIL' AT THE MONCLOA PALACE: THE PRIME MINISTER ENTERTAINS HIS ENEMIES

The Spanish public might have been even more perturbed if they had known then what was only revealed in September. Between those two speeches, Felipe González had received, in the Moncloa Palace, his official residence, and in the presence of his Justice and Interior Minister, Juan Alberto Belloch, the representative of those he claimed were blackmailing his government and imperilling the state itself: Jesús Santaella.

This extraordinary meeting took place on 23 June. Santaella, now doing a double act as the advocate for both Perote and Conde, took the easy part first. He would not, of course, have blackmailed the Prime Minister directly, nor would the Prime Minister have let himself appear to be subject to blackmail. But both men expressed concern at the circulation of certain classified documents. It seems a deal of sorts was done whereby Perote would write a letter incriminating himself, which would not be used as long as he did not leak any CESID documents in the future.[47]

Regarding his other client, Santaella was less modest. He seems to have taken it for granted that the charges against Conde would, one way or another, be dropped. Now he had a bigger fish to fry. He told González that the banker had lost 14,000 million pesetas as a result of his removal from the bank, and he expected compensation. He had already made the helpful suggestion to Belloch that this money could be found, not out of the public purse, but from the Banco Santander, which had bought the restructured Banesto in 1994.[48] He was nothing if not audacious. The meeting reached no conclusion on this point. However, the Prime Minister's dropping of any reference to a conspiracy in his parliamentary address a week later must have been consoling to the lawyer and his clients.

The long, hot summer of 1995 followed, in which the defendants in the Marey case, with the exception of Vera, admitted their involvement in the GAL in a spectacular reversal of evidence to Garzón. The magistrate then made his report to the Supreme Court, in which he presented a powerful case against Barrionuevo, and advised that charges should be considered against José María ('Txiki') Benegas, Narcís Serra and Felipe González. The Supreme Court agreed in principle to take on the case.

This was also the summer in which the Lasa and Zabala investigation heard that the two *etarras* had been imprisoned and tortured in a palace belonging to the Socialist Civil Governor of Guipúzcoa. It was the summer in which ETA came very close to killing the King.[49] July and August were one long nightmare for the Socialists, and must have seemed propitious months for anyone who wished to blackmail them.

In any event, Santaella, sometimes accompanied now by Mariano Gómez de Liaño, continued to meet more junior government representatives over this period. Some concessions appeared to be made, but almost from the beginning there were signs that the deal, if deal there was, was falling apart.

Damborenea, in his sensational evidence to Garzón in late July, had told the judge about a so-called 'Founding Memorandum of the GAL', drawn up by the CESID in 1983. He said that he had once had a copy, but could not find it now. On 7 August, Perote told Garzón he had drafted this document himself, on the direct orders of Manglano, though he could not offer the court a copy. His declaration was leaked to *El Mundo*, as Damborenea's had been earlier.

The reason for Perote's declaration at this time, which would have breached any pact of silence with the government, may have been that the conspirators wished to show González that they were not bluffing. But it seems more likely, as Ekaizer suggests, that Garzón was simply not willing to let the glittering prize of the CESID documents lie unclaimed, and was forcing the pace of the investigation.[50] This strongly indicates that the judge was not in cahoots with Conde, because his investigation was surely moving much too fast and much too openly to serve the banker's conspiratorial interests. Conde and his circle would have needed to allow time for the government to manoeuvre discreetly to deliver the conspirators' shopping list. Instead, Garzón demanded that the CESID release all documents related to the GAL to his investigation. The agency, unsurprisingly, refused on the grounds of state secrecy.

It may also have been that *El Mundo*'s role was less subservient to Conde's interests than the paper's critics and rivals allege, and that Cerdán and Rubio indeed had ways of tracking down the CESID documents without any help from the banker. Chaos theory sometimes seems more appropriate than conspiracy theory as a means of analysing the bizarre events of that summer. There were so many balls in the air that some of them were bound to collide, with unpredictable results.

Either way, by the beginning of September Santaella's contacts had clearly borne no real fruit. He had his last meeting with government representatives on 1 September. On the 5th, the gloves came off as Perote brought González directly into the frame once more. He told Garzón that he had given Manglano a memo in September 1983, advising him that the dirty war was about to begin. He claimed that the general had attached a note to the document annotated 'Me lo quedo, Pte. para el viernes' ('To be retained by me, Pte. for Friday'). Perote claimed 'Pte' was an abbreviation for 'Presidente' (i.e. González, since this is the Prime Minister's title in Spain). Manglano immediately advanced the credible counter-claim that it simply meant 'pendiente' – pending.[51] What was less credible was the idea that any intelligence chief would not immediately have informed his political superiors, including González, of such momentous news.

The very same day, Damborenea told Garzón that he had at last found his missing copy of the so-called 'Founding Memorandum of the GAL'.[52] It appeared verbatim in both *El Mundo* and *ABC* the next morning, and in *El País* the day afterwards. It proved to be a theoretical document on the pros and cons of fighting terrorism with illegal methods. It concluded with a sentence that dovetailed perfectly with the opening of the GAL campaign: 'It is considered that the most advisable form of action is disappearance by kidnapping.'

It was *El País*'s turn to break a story on 19 September. Ernesto Ekaizer chronicled, with a wealth of detail, the contacts between Conde and his representatives, and González, Belloch, Suárez, Barrionuevo and Manglano. It was a devastating exposé, which caused a sensation, even in a Spain punch-drunk with scandal-fatigue. Ekaizer insisted that a clear-cut attempt to blackmail the government had taken place, using material illicitly removed from CESID files.

The Socialist leadership immediately acknowledged that the contacts had taken place, but they held back from publicly endorsing Ekaizer's blunt characterisation of the events as 'blackmail'. Belloch went so far as to deny that any blackmail had taken place. He presented the government as having behaved responsibly throughout a very delicate situation. The executive, he said, 'does not only have the right to recover papers which affect State security, it is also obliged to do so'.[53] The erstwhile advocate of transparency in affairs of state, who had trenchantly defended the release of information on reserved funds requested by Garzón in the 1980s, was now singing from a very different hymn-sheet.

The following day, González said that the 'pressures' brought to bear by Conde backed up his allegations of a conspiracy. However, he said that the government lacked sufficient proof to bring a court case accusing the financier and his circle of blackmail. If Ekaizer's account (which must have used very senior Socialist sources) is accurate, what further proof could they possibly have needed? But then, González was in a cleft stick here. It must have suited him very well to have his conspiracy theory apparently confirmed in the press; but it would have seriously embarrassed him to acknowledge the documents with which the blackmailers were allegedly threatening him.[54]

González also chose this day to make the long-delayed announcement that he was calling early elections, in March 1996. The flood of scandals had finally undermined the support of the Catalan nationalists who had been propping up his minority administration.

In an editorial comment which was supposed to castigate Conde, *El País* declared: 'Blackmail would not cease to exist because the material on which it is based is actually incriminatory.'[55] Yet again, this argument is double-edged. No democrat could defend Conde's actions. But could any democrat defend a government which sought to keep evidence of torture and murder secret?

Santaella responded to the breaking news flamboyantly, by holding a press conference. He accepted that the meetings had occurred, but he tried to turn the tables totally. He said that the government had *initiated* contact with him, in order to acknowledge that the removal of Conde from Banesto had been an error. He added that the government had *offered* compensation of 14,000 million pesetas, without seeking anything in return. He denied that Perote had any documents compromising the CESID. This was too much for the assembled press to swallow, and Santaella conceded that the government (again, at its initiative, not his) had asked for his help to make sure that, 'if it were the case that sensitive documents were out of the government's control, they could be restored to proper custody'.[56] He thanked the government (in advance of any such announcement) for denying that he had blackmailed them.

Santaella's characterisation of the facts was no more credible than González's, and he was eventually sanctioned severely by the General Lawyers' Council (Consejo General de la Abogacía) for this whole affair.[57] His peers described his conduct as 'a serious offence against the dignity of the profession' and 'the ethical rules which govern it'. He had, they said, used documents affecting the security of the state 'supposedly in the power of two of his clients . . . with the aim of obtaining benefits for both of them'.[58]

El Mundo responded to this development by publishing information relating to several GAL killings and other police abuses, allegedly based on CESID documents obtained through sources other than Conde or Perote.[59] The paper demanded that Perote, or whoever had the documents, should present them in court. *El Mundo*'s editor, Ramírez, still stoutly resisted any conspiracy theory which would implicate his journalists, though he recognised that Conde had been involved in 'negotiations' with González. He put a very plausible construction, and a much less noble one than Belloch's, on the government's motivation for this series of meetings: 'What is the connection between the decision of González to receive the lawyer of Conde and Perote in the Moncloa Palace (an action as incriminatory as it is unusual in itself), and the breakdown of negotiations and the invention of the conspiracy theory? The key is the fact that nothing which appears in the documents is sufficiently weighty and specific to change his [González's] prospects of indictment.'[60]

There is more than a little disingenuity in Ramírez's language. Dismissing the conspiracy as an 'invention', and then describing the operations of the conspirators as a 'negotiation', is an exercise in manipulative semantics.[61] Nevertheless, Ramírez's partisan stance and flashy tone should not blind us to the fact that he is raising an absolutely critical point, all too often ignored by his peers in *El País*. Why did González and his closest associates tolerate, over a six-month period,[62] the circulation of material which implicated the security forces in terrorism, unless there was some substance in the documents? And if the documents were genuine, why did they not act immediately against those implicated, unless they themselves had something to hide? Did they fear that Perote had even more damaging evidence, and play out the game to make him reveal his entire hand? Did they consider doing a deal up to the point where it became clear to them that Conde's representatives had nothing which would definitively link González himself, or his closest colleagues, to the death squads, as Ramírez suggests?[63]

We will probably never know the answers to these questions for certain, but they suggest a very credible scenario. Belloch's defence, as we have seen, is that it was the government's duty to act extremely circumspectly when the security of the state was at risk. The CESID is the nexus between the government and foreign intelligence services, and leaks could have seriously damaged relationships with Spain's NATO allies.

These arguments would be a great deal more plausible if the government concerned, or at least some of its members, were not so compromised by the contents of the documents. This, after all, is the administration which had used public funds to pay for Amedo's silence. Belloch, who had cut off these payments, knew that only too well. Why would it not pay off Conde and Perote, if it needed to, and could afford to? Small wonder Belloch felt he had to deny that any blackmail had taken place in this instance. His reputation as the man who was cleaning up Interior would have been in tatters if he had acknowledged what the facts clearly pointed to.

His deputy, Margarita Robles, is reluctant to overtly criticise Belloch, whom she still greatly admires. But when she is asked directly whether or not it was an error, from the point of view of the real reformers in Interior, to entertain Santaella and his proposals, she does not evade the point.

'I support the view that all blackmailers, all of them, should be stopped in their tracks before they get started. So it seems to me that everything which emboldens blackmailers is an error.'[64]

There is no doubt that the unveiling of all these elements of conspiracy and blackmail made the job of these reformers in the PSOE administration much more difficult, if not impossible. They were now under fire from all sides. Fernando López Agudín, who worked on the Belloch/Robles team as press secretary, stresses that 'decent socialists, who are the majority', who were not implicated in any shady dealing and who approved of the reform of Interior in principle, now faced a tough political dilemma: 'The clean-up is helping Conde to blackmail the government, and it is also helping the Partido Popular. So the attitude was that the clean-up is all very well, but it is forcing the Left out of power.'[65]

Faced with a choice between power and principle, most Socialists now opted firmly for the former, and tended to blame those who revealed the crimes of the past more than those who had committed them.

But it was much too late to turn back the clock. As the writer and commentator Manuel Vázquez Montalbán puts it: 'The conspiracy exists. I don't think it is a plot with all the t's crossed and all the i's dotted, but it is an implicit conspiracy, isn't it? So far so good, but what you can't deny is that what has been revealed in *El Mundo*, for example, is true. The facts are the facts, nobody can deny that. And sometimes [the Socialists] have fallen back on the childish formula that because the aims of the conspirators are illegitimate, the facts did not exist. Excuse me, Sir, the facts did exist.'[66]

Among the most prominent of these facts were the CESID papers, which were not going to go away just because they had been manipulated by unscrupulous interests.

NOTES

1 Interview with Margarita Robles, Madrid, November 1997. In this instance she was talking about Amedo, but her words apply with even more force to the events described in this chapter, as she made abundantly clear later in the same interview.

2 *El País*, editorial comment on 20 September 1995, the day after the newspaper broke the story that Mario Conde and his associates appeared to be using information about the GAL to blackmail the government.

3 The PRI was finally voted out of office in 2000. At least some Socialists saw the PRI as a role model from the moment they took power. Guillermo Galeote, MP and head of PSOE finance and administration for many of the González years, declared in 1982: 'We are going to set up the Mexican PRI in Spain; we are going to be in power for 20 years.' Galeote had to resign from parliament over the Filesa funding scandal in 1993. See José Luis Gutiérrez and Amando de Miguel, *La Ambición del César* (Madrid: Temas de Hoy, 1989).

4 Interview with Santos Juliá, Madrid, November 1997.

5 Those are the sort of charges which one would expect to be levelled at anyone bold enough, and bright enough, to take on the challenge of scrutinising the inner workings of the state. As we have seen, there are legitimate questions about Garzón's motivation, given his controversial flirtation with the very Interior Ministry that he was investigating. But such questions are speculative by definition. There is also a widely held view that his investigative methods are flawed, though any fair assessment would conclude that his brilliance outweighs his brashness.

6 Banesto is the trade name for the Banco Español de Credito.

7 See ch. 18, p. 259.

8 See ch. 18, p. 259.

9 It was precisely during the month Conde shared his prison walks that Sancristóbal gave his notorious television interview from jail. He denounced the GAL investigation as a conspiracy to unseat González, masterminded by a 'Señor Z', whom many people took to be Conde himself, though the reference was sufficiently ambiguous to also suggest journalists like *El Mundo's* editor, Pedro J. Ramírez. See ch. 18, p. 266.

10 Ernesto Ekaizer, *Vendetta* (Barcelona: Plaza y Janés, 1996), p. 333. Ekaizer's account of Conde's alleged conspiracy to blackmail the government, which forms part of his book, is a valuable source of information on this aspect of the GAL investigation. Ekaizer also broke the story of Conde's involvement for his newspaper, and published further substantial articles on the subject.

11 *El Mundo*, 11 May 1994; Ekaizer, op. cit., p. 330.

12 John Hooper, *The New Spaniards* (London: Penguin, 1995), p. 59. Conde was the son of a customs official.

13 Paul Heywood, *The Government and Politics of Spain* (London: Macmillan, 1995), pp. 257–8.

14 The survey was carried out for *Cambio 16* in late 1990. Quoted in Heywood, op. cit., p. 293.

15 Some observers suspected him of sympathies with the authoritarian Right. Others thought he might seek to front the kind of centre-Right options favoured by the President of the Catalan autonomous government, Jordi Pujol, and the former Prime Minister, Adolfo Suárez, to whom he had close connections.

16 Through Banesto, he had been a major force behind the successful – and virulently anti-PSOE – private television channel Antena 3, in which Rupert Murdoch was another powerful shareholder. He had many other media interests, some less visible than others, especially, as we saw in ch. 18, in *El Mundo*.

17 For a selection chosen by Ramírez himself, see Pedro J. Ramírez, *David contra Goliat* (Madrid: Temas de Hoy, 1995), pp. 103–33.

18 It would also, Roldán hoped, make his own abuses of public funds look less culpable.

19 The 'hole' represented the cost of writing off Banesto's debts and restructuring the company under new ownership. Ekaizer, op. cit., p. 67.

20 Ibid., p. 549.

21 *El País,* 3 April 2000.

22 Ekaizer, op. cit., p. 28.

23 The reader may wonder why Sancristóbal would have even considered helping Conde at this stage, since he himself was still being courted by Barrionuevo. It is at least plausible that he nevertheless feared that he was about to be scapegoated for the GAL, and was seeking potential allies for that eventuality.

24 Ekaizer, op. cit., p. 330.

25 *El País*, 26 July 1995.

26 Perote has published his own highly coloured version of all these events. See Juan Alberto Perote, *Confesiones de Perote* (Barcelona: RBA Libros, 1999).

27 See ch. 18, pp. 267–8.

28 This is a summary of the account given by Ekaizer, op. cit., p. 343, based on his interview with Suárez. A very different slant on this meeting is given by two of *El Mundo*'s leading investigative journalists, Manuel Cerdán and Antonio Rubio, in their book *El Origen del GAL* (Madrid: Temas de Hoy, 1997), pp. 283–302. They explicitly reject Ekaizer's thesis that the source for their 'exclusives' on this story, on the CESID phone tappings and on the CESID documents was either Conde or Perote. According to Ekaizer, however, Suárez himself identified Perote as the officer present at this meeting.

29 This complex and obscure strategy was, according to Ekaizer, based on the fact that one of Conde's closest associates, Mariano Gómez de Liaño, was the brother of the man who ultimately became the investigating magistrate in the Lasa and Zabala case, Javier Gómez de Liaño. The latter denied any improper dealings with his brother in an interview in Madrid, November 1997. See Ekaizer, op. cit., pp. 123–6, 403–6, 417–19.

30 Ekaizer, op. cit., p. 388.

31 *El País,* 20 September 1995. Gerardo Viada Fernández-Velilla, a lawyer and mutual friend of Santaella's and Belloch's, set up the meeting at the former's request. He was also a legal advisor to *El País*. Naturally, *El Mundo* made much of this connection when *El País* broke the whole story of the conspiracy the following September.

32 Ekaizer, op. cit., p. 397.

33 *El País*, 1 June 1997.

34 Ekaizer, op. cit., p. 404.

35 Santaella had worked for Suárez, in the Ministry of Justice and elsewhere, while he was UCD Prime Minister.

36 Ekaizer, op. cit., p. 408.

37 This is confirmed by Suárez's own statement to the press, published in *El País* on 20 September 1995.

38 These intermediaries were Luis María Ansón, editor of the deeply conservative newspaper *ABC*, a CESID general close to Perote, and Suárez himself, according to Ekaizer, op. cit., p. 416.

39 See ch. 18, p. 273.

40 Cerdán and Rubio, op. cit., p. 299.

41 *El País*, 27 May 1999. This verdict is under appeal at the time of going to print.

42 *El País*, 14 June 1995.

43 Ekaizer, op. cit., p. 427.

44 *El País*, 19 September 1995. Such a declaration would have been dynamite: it would have clearly demonstrated that the CESID had had knowledge of, and possibly involvement in, the dirty war. However, a later report in *El País* (25 September 1995) cited court documents to show that López Fernández had made no specific references to the GAL in his evidence. Perote (op. cit., pp. 305–8) claims that López Fernández inadvertently but accurately implicated the CESID in the GAL, and that his original declaration was then, quite illegally, struck from the record. We are in *Through the Looking Glass* territory here.

45 *El País*, 21 June 1995.

46 *El País*, 30 June 1995.

47 Ekaizer, op. cit., p. 432. Some of the charges against Perote were lifted on 12 July, and he was allowed leave prison under house arrest on 15 July. To suggest this was as a result of a deal with González would be to accept that the Prime Minister was willing, and able, to trespass on the independence of the military judiciary. Whether he did or not, Perote's release would have seemed a reassuring gesture to Santaella and Conde.

48 Ibid., p. 391.

49 Three suspected *etarras* were arrested in Palma de Majorca on 9 August, accused of targeting King Juan Carlos. It appears they literally had the King in their sights on at least one occasion, but did not pull the trigger because they had not worked out an escape route.

50 Ekaizer, op. cit., p. 440.

51 Ibid., p. 453.

52 This was a title given to the document by the media and some of the protagonists, who had their own interests in such a tendentious phrase becoming common currency. Its actual title was, as one might expect from a military intelligence report, rather less revealing: 'Actions in France'.

53 *El País*, 20 September 1995.

54 *El País*, 21 September 1995.

55 *El País*, 20 September 1995.

56 Ibid.

57 Indeed, his facts were shakier than the Prime Minister's. By the following day he had to backtrack on several points, including the assertion that the contacts were at the government's initiative, not least because both Suárez and Luis María Ansón publicly said that they, as intermediaries, knew that the advances had come from his side. (Ansón was editor of *ABC*, and no friend of either the Socialists or *El País*. He was an intermediary between Santaella and Manglano regarding the evidence Manglano was giving on the Crillon report.)

58 *El País*, 29 June 1996.

59 *El Mundo*, 20 September 1995.

60 *El Mundo*, 13 October 1995.

61 Similar euphemisms can be found in other media which had lionised Conde in the past, and whose obsession with bringing down González tended to turn all the Prime Minister's enemies into honourable combatants for liberty. The magazine *Época*, for example, accepted Santaella's explanation that he was only attempting a 'harmonisation of interests' in a 'dialogue in good faith', which would have saved the Spanish establishment from destabilisation. *Época*, 2 October 1995.

62 Some reports suggested that Barrionuevo received a copy of the CESID documents from Santaella as early as February. In any case, Manglano had a clear idea, from Perote's meeting with Suárez on 22 February, that highly sensitive, not to say highly incriminating, material was available to the government's enemies, and González, Serra and the Minister for Defence, García Vargas, were all aware of the situation from then on.

63 The documents turned out to be distinctly vague on that crucial point.

64 Interview with Margarita Robles, Madrid, November 1997.

65 Interview with Fernando López Agundín, Madrid, November 1997.

66 Interview with Manuel Vázquez Montalbán, Madrid, November 1997.

21

The Paper Chase:
state secrecy v. the right to know

JUAN ALBERTO PEROTE: But when they took out Zabala, and . . .
    the other one, which was he?
PEDRO GÓMEZ NIETO: You mean Lasa?
PEROTE: Lasa and the other one . . .
GÓMEZ NIETO: They gave them two shots in the head.
PEROTE: Two shots, and that wasn't with a hood or anything?
GÓMEZ NIETO: No, no, it was two shots.
PEROTE: That is, they killed them, they didn't die on them.
GÓMEZ NIETO: No way, no way, no way, no way! . . . That is, first
    they made them dig two holes. We made them dig two holes.
PEROTE: Fuck it! When you tell me this, my hair stands up on
    end . . .

Readers of *El Mundo*, jaded though they were with sensational scandals, must have felt their own skin start to prickle when they saw this conversation reproduced in the newspaper on the morning of 27 May 1996.[1]

This mass readership was suddenly privy, apparently, to a secret discussion between a CESID commander, Juan Alberto Perote, and a Guardia Civil sergeant, Pedro Gómez Nieto. They seemed to be overhearing a first-hand account of the killing of Lasa and Zabala, followed by a convincingly confused attempt to rationalise the terrible thing that had been done:

GÓMEZ NIETO: Look, don Alberto, I often take a critical look at my own
    actions, in a detached way, and I don't know often how far a person
    can go and I believe that everything must be justified in, I don't
    know, in some ideals, in some aspirations, in some things, obviously
    we are into the end justifying the means.
PEROTE: I would have done it.
GÓMEZ NIETO: I don't know, I say, that is . . . when I did the jobs I did, in
    which I participated, of which I am very proud, and I organised them
    and I prepared them, I think of the 60,000 *guardia civiles* I had
    behind me, who were with me morally, and that gave me a strength,
    knowing what I knew, that we had no support, that if we were caught
    the Guardia Civil were going to expel us, that we didn't have a way

out or anything.[2] And a gold medal does not make up for that. It's clear, no? It's not to compare one thing with another, I believe that there are other ideas, other reasons for living, and so I am burnt out, burnt out, burnt out. And I don't know, to get out of the country, even as the driver in an embassy, eh, no, what I say is sincere, don Alberto. I think I have many options, and no, and moreover I am banging my head against the system, I am banging my head . . .

Of all the 'CESID papers' to emerge over the next few months, this one seemed to penetrate most deeply into the dark, sorry heart of the GAL.[3] However, the CESID has been unable to find the audiotape from which it was allegedly transcribed, so its authenticity remains in doubt.

It was just three weeks since José María Aznar had at last been ratified by parliament as Prime Minister to replace González. In publishing this 'CESID paper', *El Mundo*'s editor, Pedro J. Ramírez, was putting down a big marker that the GAL scandal was not going to go away just because the alleged masters of the dirty war were no longer in power. A year after Jesús Santaella had so thoughtfully brought the CESID papers to the attention of González, the issue of whether or not these documents should be released to the courts remained the hottest potato in Spanish politics. Aznar was finding that it could burn his hands too.

True, the CESID papers, like the GAL investigations themselves, referred only to the period when the Socialists were in power. That was precisely what had made it so very attractive for Aznar to pursue these questions while in opposition. Now that the Partido Popular was assuming the mantle of government, however, things began to look rather different. The seductive logic of statesmanship, and of 'reasons of state', came into play. The ambiguous phrase *pasar página* – 'to turn over the page, to move on' – became part of Aznar's vocabulary whenever the GAL issue arose.

There was another compelling reason why delving deeper into the GAL, and in particular into the CESID papers, was now beginning to seem much less attractive to the Partido Popular. Many of the CESID papers cast Spanish military intelligence and the Guardia Civil in a very bad light. The Partido Popular, and its electorate, had no problem in pursuing Socialist functionaries, and even a few senior police officers, for operating death squads. But it went against every conservative fibre at the Partido Popular's core to raise questions which were likely to bring the Spanish army and the Guardia Civil into serious disrepute.

The idea that the CESID papers could offer crucial evidence on the GAL had entered the public domain nearly a year earlier, when *El Mundo* broke the CESID phone-tapping story in June 1995.[4] *El País* suggested that the likely source was Colonel Juan Alberto Perote, using the documents he had removed from the CESID in 1991.[5] Because the sequence of events is rather complex, we must now revisit some of the ground covered in the last chapter, viewing it from the perspective of the battle to bring these documents out of the shadows and into the courts of law.

This battle was enormously complicated by the nature of the newspaper most intimately associated with their first publication. *El Mundo*, as we have seen, was very closely associated with both the Partido Popular and

Mario Conde. Since it was established in 1989, it had campaigned on a daily basis for the removal of Felipe González and the Socialists from power. Even for many who were critical of the Socialists, the one-note tone of its editorials and supporting chorus of opinion columns, often amplified to rabid hysteria, quickly became distasteful. In its news columns, wild allegations were often presented with the same conviction as revelations of real national importance, making it a most unreliable source. Nevertheless, it repeatedly did break news which other areas of the Spanish media could not, or would not, touch.

Despite understandable allegations from the Socialist camp that *El Mundo* was entirely at the service of the Partido Popular, it would be more accurate to say that it was dedicated to undermining the PSOE. Pedro J. Ramírez seems to have had his own agenda for his newspaper. When it came to the CESID papers, he had no intention of letting the Partido Popular's sensitivities about the honour of the army get in the way of a good story. On 9 April 1996, while Aznar was putting together his new government, *El Mundo* had fired a warning shot across the bows of the Partido Popular by publishing another CESID paper.

A transcribed tape purported to record how Enrique Rodríguez Galindo, the Guardia Civil's icon in the war against ETA, had instructed the same Guardia Civil sergeant, Pedro Gómez Nieto, in the initiation of the whole GAL campaign. Ramírez published an editorial on that day which described the investigation of these events as a 'touchstone' for the new government. He made it clear that the 'declassification' of the CESID papers, so that they could be used in evidence by the courts, was a question he would keep on the front page.

The judicial investigation into Perote's theft of CESID documents, which followed on *El Mundo*'s phone-tapping reports, almost immediately triggered references to the GAL.[6] The continuing leakage of GAL-related CESID material over the summer of 1995 confirmed the impression that Perote, or *El Mundo*'s investigative team, or both, had in their hands the key that would at last unlock the definitive secrets of the death squads.[7]

On 20 July, Ricardo García Damborenea made his sensational declarations to Garzón, and to the press, implicating Felipe González in the GAL. His judicial declaration included references to the so-called 'Founding Memorandum' of the GAL, which he said had been given to him by a CESID agent, Jesús Somontes.[8] Conveniently enough, Somontes could not be questioned because he was no longer alive. Damborenea told Garzón he had lost the document, but promised to hand it over if he found it. The trail to the archives of the military intelligence service was beginning to look very hot.

It got much hotter, fast. On 7 August, Perote told Garzón that he himself had written the 'Founding Memorandum' on behalf of the CESID.[9] Again, he could not supply the court with a copy at this moment. Garzón had already asked the CESID for this document but, unsurprisingly, the intelligence agency insisted that it could not do so because of secrecy laws.[10] Garzón's battle to obtain the CESID papers now assumed the same importance that his struggle to get access to reserved funds records had had in his first GAL investigation.

On 5 September, immediately after Mario Conde's 'negotiation' with the government had finally broken down, Perote told Garzón about another CESID document. It allegedly recorded his meeting with the intelligence supremo, General Emilio Alonso Manglano, to discuss the beginning of the dirty war. He claimed there was an annotation ('Pte') on the document which indicated that Manglano intended to discuss the matter with Felipe González.[11]

The next day, after Manglano and Perote had had a *careo* (face-to-face confrontation) in the judge's chambers, Damborenea returned to the Audiencia Nacional, and handed in a copy of the so-called 'Founding Memorandum'. The following morning, its full text appeared in *El Mundo* and *ABC*, and then, a day later, in *El País*.

It turned out, as we saw in the last chapter, to be not so much a record of the GAL's formation as a position paper. It was a theoretical consideration of the pros and cons of carrying out a dirty war, and how to 'cover up the real origins' of the operations. But it did contain such telling phrases as 'the most advisable form of action is disappearance by kidnapping', which so clearly echoed the fate of Lasa and Zabala. Moreover, the fact that the CESID's head of special operations had drafted such a paper, and discussed it with his colleagues, just three months before the GAL's very non-theoretical dirty war began, was surely likely to be seen as valuable contextual evidence of state participation in the death squads – if the document could be authenticated.[12]

There was now huge public and political concern about what other CESID documents might reveal. The government made a less than convincing move towards transparency in early October, by allowing the six members of the parliamentary Official Secrets Commission to peruse the documents known to have been removed by Perote.

The deputies had brief sight of hundreds of papers. Few of them appeared to relate directly to the GAL.[13] The Defence Minister, Gustavo Suárez Partierra, did put some highly sensitive material on the table, but most of it did not have to do with the dirty war. It concerned intelligence operations with other countries, security arrangements for the King, and the names of informers within ETA.[14] The intention may have been to convince the opposition that everything in the CESID archives should remain classified as state secrets for security reasons.

The Justice and Interior Minister, Juan Alberto Belloch, made a further shift away from his liberal past by insisting, a few days later, that CESID records should be examined 'exclusively in parliament, not in the courts'.[15]

With the screen of state secrecy being erected in this most reformist sector of the cabinet, it was no surprise that Suárez Partierra rejected Garzón's request for the documents, arguing that the judge had no jurisdiction over their declassification. The judge then appealed to the Court of Conflicts of Jurisdiction. The landmark 1995 decision of the Supreme Court on reserved funds, which declared that state secrecy should never be an obstacle to the investigation of a crime, was cited by Garzón as a strong precedent for releasing the papers.[16]

There was amazement in legal circles when the court ruled unequivocally and unanimously in the Defence Minister's favour.[17] The echo of the refusal of Garzon's superiors to allow him to investigate reserved funds in 1988 was grimly audible. The decision was widely regarded by lawyers as 'legitimising the doctrine of "Reasons of State"'.[18] *El País*, which had been so critical of the manner in which these documents had originally come to light, nevertheless warned that this decision left the government with a dangerous 'area of impunity'.[19]

Whenever the courts came close to finding the government with a smoking GAL gun in its hand, it seemed to public opinion that the executive could still rely on senior elements in the judiciary – that same judiciary the government so often accused of being virtually subversive – to build a new legal barrier to protect government interests.

The court left Garzón with just one avenue to the CESID archives open. He could still appeal to the Defence Minister – the very minister who had originally challenged his jurisdiction – to ask the cabinet to declassify the documents. He followed this clearly sterile procedure, and it was no surprise when the government flatly turned down his request in mid-January 1996. Every route to the CESID papers now seemed blocked.

Nevertheless, Garzón himself continued investigating the Monbar and Oñederra cases. In February he made a breakthrough that was so dramatic, not to say melodramatic, that it revived suspicions that he was in some way involved in Conde's conspiracy. On 8 February, the magistrate raided Perote's prison cell, where he seized a number of documents. Lo and behold, they appeared to be copies of the very CESID papers which related most directly to the GAL. Appearances, however, might be deceptive.

Perote insisted to the judge that the papers in his cell were not the papers he had, as he claimed, accidentally removed from the CESID in 1991. He would not even say they were copies of those papers. He said that they had been sent to him by an unknown person, and that he was working on a 'novel' about the dirty war and using them as background.

Perote is one of the most shadowy of the many obscure players in the GAL drama. There may have been some Walter Mitty aspects to his often bizarrely contradictory behaviour. But his general strategy seems to have been to implicate as many senior figures as possible in as many scandals as possible. He apparently hoped that this would enable him, and his varied associates, such as Conde, Sancristóbal and Álvarez, to all ultimately benefit from a 'political solution' to the crisis – that is, some sort of general amnesty.[20]

A different type of political solution seemed to be indicated by a key appointment to Aznar's first cabinet, which finally took office in May. He assigned an enigmatic figure, Eduardo Serra, to the key Ministry of Defence. Serra had been Under-Secretary of State for Defence in the last governments of the UCD from 1981 to 1982, and was kept in this position by their Socialist successors, until he was promoted to Secretary of State for Defence by his unrelated namesake, Narcís Serra, in 1984. A man with the appropriate features of a smaller, neater Henry Kissinger, he stayed in this post until 1987. He had thus been in a unique position to observe and influence the policy of the CESID before, and during, the entire GAL period.

DBS Arts Library

His reappearance in the Defence Minister's chair was praised, predictably, by his PSOE predecessors. But it was greeted with strong protests from those who were seriously interested in investigating the GAL, like Antonio Romero of the Communist-led United Left. 'It is very clear that they are trying to cover up everything connected to the intelligence services, because Serra was the "number two" in Defence when the whole GAL affair got under way. He could be a good blanket to cover everything up,' Romero declared.[21] It was certainly hard to avoid the conclusion that the Spanish establishment was now closing ranks against the continued investigation of the GAL.

It did not take long to discover how assiduous Serra, and his new masters, would be in the defence of state secrecy. On 16 May, Garzón asked the new government to do what the old one had refused to do: release to the courts – and/or declassify as secret – eighteen CESID documents which were relevant to his GAL investigations. He had to follow the same procedure as he had with the Socialists and apply in the first instance to the relevant minister – Eduardo Serra. Javier Gómez de Liaño and another judge[22] made similar applications.

The Partido Popular's deputy leader, Francisco Álvarez Cascos, made the ambiguous comment that the government would respond 'in defence of the rule of law and of the Official Secrets Act'.[23] He did not say how the government would resolve any conflict between these two sets of values.[24]

On 30 June, Serra took advantage of an interview with the conservative and very pro-army newspaper *ABC* to indicate which value he wanted the government to prioritise. He was against handing over the documents to the court, he said, because such an action could result in 'a loss of confidence in our intelligence services . . . there are matters which, we should be aware, are being observed from abroad . . . there is a terrifying ignorance [in Spain] of what our foreign relations [interests] are'. It was a clever appeal for the superior right to state secrecy, under the guise of 'mature' international statesmanship. He also asserted that some of the documents had been invented by Perote, who could well, he added, have doctored the contents of the rest of them.

After several delays, including a consultation with the Council of State,[25] which bounced the ball back to the government, Aznar chose the cabinet meeting on the last Friday before the August holidays to take his most controversial decision since taking office: not a single paper was to be released to the judges. Serra's view had prevailed totally. The argument for state security, and state secrecy, had taken primacy over the duty to collaborate with the courts. Serra's suggestion that the papers might also have been manipulated, and that they could therefore, curiously enough, be simultaneously forged and secret, also figured in the full version of the government decision.[26] The government insisted as well that three of the 'papers' – in fact two audiotapes and a rubber stamp – were not in the CESID archives, and nor was there any record that they had ever been there.[27]

Not himself a Partido Popular member, Serra got the job of presenting to the press a ruling which was a U-turn for the party. 'I feel proud,' he said, 'to belong to a government which takes its obligations seriously and rigorously.'[28] The presentation would undoubtedly have been more embarrassing for many of his colleagues. The press was quick to remind Álvarez Cascos that he had told González only the previous February that the principle of *national* security is being used as a shield to protect the *personal* security of the members of the government'.[29]

In an editorial almost as ferocious as any he had directed against González, Ramírez told Aznar that this decision was 'the first great disappointment of your mandate'. He highlighted the paradox that, in insisting on the secrecy of documents which had (mostly) already been published, the government had effectively authenticated them. Was a plan to launch the GAL pertinent to the security of the state, he asked acerbically, and, if so, what sort of state had Spain become? He answered his own question thus: 'A State whose security is strengthened by making it difficult to punish those who have kidnapped, tortured and murdered two people, finally burying them in quicklime, may be called whatever you like, but it cannot be called a State subject to the rule of law.'[30]

The news that this political decision coincided with a separate judicial decision to release General Galindo from custody created, however inadvertently, a widespread impression that the PSOE and Partido Popular had secretly negotiated a pact similar to the Argentinian 'law of the full stop'. The GAL crimes, however, were not committed under a dictatorship, and Spanish commentators began to look at other European democracies to see how they dealt with this conflict of interest between the security of the state and the rule of law. In Britain, they found, it was the judges rather than the government who decided in each instance whether state secrecy outweighed the right to investigate crimes. In France, however, the government had the final say, and seemed to follow Interior Minister Charles Pasqua's chilling 1988 maxim: 'Democracy ends where the interests of the State begin.'[31] It remained to be seen which route Spain would ultimately follow.

The news that the Partido Popular was concurrently drafting a very controversial revision of the Official Secrets Act, which would have made the state considerably more hermetic than it already was, added to the atmosphere of pessimism which descended on advocates of open democracy and transparency in the summer of 1996. Those who had voted for the Partido Popular in the hope that, while right of centre, Aznar's party would be more honourable and honest than the PSOE, began to feel seriously betrayed. Those who were deeply suspicious of both parties felt confirmed in their antipathy.

Manuel Vázquez Montalbán was among the latter. In a cutting broadside in *El País* he described Eduardo Serra as a 'now-you-see-him, now-you-don't type of person who plunged into the depths in the epoch of the Socialist sewers, and reappears now to facilitate the creation of sewers for Aznar . . . He is going to cover up the shit from the past, and patent his own variety of faeces.'[32]

The paradox that these 'secret' CESID documents were already largely in the public domain was highlighted by their publication, in highly summarised form, in both *El País* and *El Mundo* on the weekend of the government decision that they could not be released.[33] Without official authentication, however, they could not serve as evidence in court. Jesús Santos, the prosecutor in the Lasa and Zabala case, dropped charges against Gómez Nieto in the light of the government decision. The CESID papers, he said, had been the 'nuclear core' of the investigation.[34] The same prosecutor, however, firmly rebuffed a demand from Jorge Argote, who was defending the suspects, that the court should return whatever copies of the documents it had to the CESID.[35]

Some new routes to the papers were now explored by the investigators. One was to subpoena the members of the parliamentary Official Secrets Commission, in the hope that they could authenticate the documents. Some of its members, invariably Communists or Basque nationalists, suggested that they would collaborate with such a move from the courts. This was the route favoured by the judge investigating the Lasa and Zabala case, Javier Gómez de Liaño. He had baldly stated, in a writ releasing one of the suspects from prison, that the government's decision on the CESID papers 'slows down and obstructs – one supposes unintentionally – this investigation'.[36] Gómez de Liaño's efforts to pursue members of the Official Secrets Commission were repeatedly stalled over the next few months.[37]

It turned out that there was another road to the documents, however, which was that taken by Iñigo Iruin, the lawyer representing the Lasa and Zabala families. This was to appeal to a specialist chamber of the Supreme Court[38] for a judicial review of the government's refusal to declassify the papers. His grounds were that the refusal to release the documents violated the rights of his clients to effective legal protection.[39] The appeal was accepted for consideration by the court. The possibility that the Supreme Court might overturn a government decision kept the debate on state secrecy and the right to information alive through the autumn of 1996. Prestigious figures like Margarita Robles, Belloch's former deputy, threw her weight behind the campaign to release the papers.[40]

The progress of this appeal evidently worried Eduardo Serra, who made a blundering effort to get his retaliation in first. Should the Supreme Court uphold the appeal, he said, the government should disobey any judicial instruction to release or authenticate the CESID papers. He based his argument on a law passed under Franco's dictatorship, which most legal opinion held to have been superseded by the democratic constitution.[41] The Communist leader, Julio Anguita, accused Serra of 'subversion of the democratic state'. The leader of the New Left party, Diego López Garrido, whose declarations, unlike Anguita's, were usually models of considered moderation, said Serra was 'in defiance of the rule of law'.

Support for Serra's position came from Felipe González, which was hardly surprising, and from Juan Alberto Belloch, which perhaps still was.[42] Serra's own government colleagues, however, came down very hard on his proposal. 'The government is not going to disobey the highest judicial authority in the land,' said Mariano Rajoy, Minister for Public Works, in a statement which clearly had the support of Aznar, and was remarkably close to the language of Serra's left-wing critics. Despite this, Serra's position in the cabinet was regarded as safe.

The Socialists' hostility to the judiciary became more and more pronounced, with the President of Madrid Autonomous Community, Joaquín Leguina, painting a grossly distorted picture of what was really happening: 'If the judges have the capacity to twist the government's arm, the situation is becoming impossible.'[43]

THE GREAT DEBATE: ARGUING FOR THE DIGNITY OF THE DEMOCRATIC STATE

The debate about the CESID papers revived many of the arguments which had accompanied the GAL investigations of the late 1980s. Fernando Savater, a popular philosopher who had regularly excoriated the crimes of ETA, made a lucid contribution to a debate on the issue in *El País* at the end of October 1996. He pointed out that the Spanish state had never totally committed itself to a terrorist strategy (as had occurred in Videla's Argentina), and that, in most cases, ETA suspects had been granted all the rightful privileges of the due process of law. But he continued:

'Only those who want to cover up [these matters], and those who think that [in the name of the State] "anything goes", can deny that there has also been criminal terrorism organised and carried out by State functionaries, with an outcome of at least 30 deaths . . . Only the most obtuse observers can be oblivious of the fact that these crimes have never been investigated by those who should have done so and, when they were exposed, everything possible has been done to obstruct a full explanation, and when they have been (partially) explained, special privileges have been obtained for those convicted so that they do not expose others, also implicated, of higher rank.'[44]

González, he added, had been trying to muddy the waters in recent weeks by praising the CESID for having prevented 'hypothetical' *coups d'état*. This was irrelevant here: the issue was that the CESID either had participated in state terrorism itself or had failed to investigate it when it was happening under its nose. The dignity of the democratic state, he argued, consisted precisely in not making any exceptions to the rule of law.

Luis Mari Diez-Picazo, a professor of public law, also made an unusually rich and complex contribution to the same debate. There was a real degeneration of democratic sensibility in contemporary Spain, he said. Even the parties which did raise the GAL issue usually only did so to damage their opponents. They did not want to deal with the underlying issue: the illegitimate creation of 'a category of government decisions which, because of their extraordinary importance, should not be subject to judicial control'.[45]

He suggested that the privileges granted to Amedo and Domínguez for turning state's evidence also smelt of a kind of impunity, and that the Conde conspiracy had seriously damaged the legitimacy of the GAL investigations. While he argued that the courts must have the full backing of the state for these investigations, he insisted that legal

> investigation alone was not enough: 'Without interfering in the judicial process, Parliament should take some initiative about the GAL case which would allow two urgent objectives to be achieved: firstly, to give an explanation of what happened to the citizens; secondly, to free Spanish democracy of this burden which weighs it down like a millstone.'
> Spanish parliamentary democracy has not yet taken up this challenge.

Long before the Supreme Court reached its decision, the CESID papers had become the most open official secrets in recent Spanish history, though they were none the less enigmatic for that. On 16 December, *El Mundo* published five of them, and announced that the rest would be published in their entirety over the next few days. The date of publication just happened to coincide with the indictment of Mariano Gómez de Liaño, Mario Conde's associate and brother of Javier Gómez de Liaño, in the Banesto fraud case. Once again, the conspiracy theory raised its head. Many Socialists were convinced that Conde, having failed to blackmail the previous government with the CESID papers, was now releasing similar information, in carefully controlled doses, for the rather lesser end of distracting public attention from the progress of the case against him.[46]

The following day, *El País* published all twenty of the CESID papers requested by the judges, in a pull-out dossier with commentaries which generally cast doubt on either their judicial significance or their authenticity, or both.

This was one of the moments when the daily sniping between these two entrenched newspapers suddenly erupted into heavy artillery fire. *El Mundo* denied *El País*'s allegations that it was the recipient of leaks from Conde or Perote, and claimed that its 'exclusives' were the result of years of brilliant investigative journalism. *El País*, it claimed, had received the CESID papers 'courtesy of a driver from the Defence Ministry'.[47]

In fact, it was clear that both newspapers were drawing largely on the same source for their versions of the CESID papers. They had used the writs requesting the papers prepared by the three judges. These writs included transcriptions of the documents the judges wanted authenticated. *El País* made these sources quite explicit, citing the entire writ including the judicial reasoning behind each request. The texts published by *El Mundo* were identical, and its analysis seemed to draw heavily on the judges' arguments. Moreover, both papers had had access to the writs since at least the previous August when, as we have seen, they both published summaries of the contents of the papers. *El País*'s summary then, it has to be said, was rather more precise than *El Mundo*'s had been.

The writs themselves should, of course, have been secret, but publishing embargoed writs is a frequent practice in all Spanish newspapers, and the court system leaks like a colander.[48]

What this media battle really established, beyond all doubt, was something most people had already surmised. The judges already had the papers, and only needed their authentication.

In publishing the documents in their entirety, in the context of the judges' legal reasoning, *El País* was providing a service to the public interest which contrasted with the sensationalisation – or manipulation – of the issue by *El Mundo*. Yet one must wonder why *El País* did not publish these documents until its competitor had revealed that it was going to do so.

The enmity between the two newspapers now extended well beyond even the usual bloody-mindedness of circulation wars. The polarisation which poisoned Spanish political life in the 1990s was clearly reflected in the media. *El País* saw itself as the Spanish newspaper of record, a claim which *El Mundo* regarded as a cloak for support for the Socialists. *El Mundo* viewed itself as a crusading daily, committed to investigative journalism. *El País* regarded *El Mundo* as a sensationalist organ in the service of right-wing interests, ranging from the Partido Popular to Mario Conde. Such polarisation produced inevitable distortions and partisan editorial decisions in moments of crisis such as this. It could be argued, however, that such ferocious competition contributed to putting so much sensitive information into the public domain.

WHAT IT SAID IN THE PAPERS: 'VIOLENT ACTIONS', 'CLEAN WEAPONS' AND DANGEROUS ABBREVIATIONS

The first three CESID papers requested by Garzón would have disappointed anyone seeking sensational revelations. They were personnel notes which stated that Pedro Gómez Nieto and Felipe Bayo Leal, both investigated in the Oñederra and Lasa and Zabala cases, had been members of the CESID and under the orders of Perote while they were serving with the Guardia Civil in Intxaurrondo.

The fourth was much more dramatic, though it was not as revealing as its media sobriquet, 'Founding Memorandum of the GAL', appeared to promise. Titled 'Actions in France', it was, as we have seen, more a discussion document than a commitment to set up death squads, and never mentions the GAL as such. But it does provide significant contextual evidence of military intelligence involvement in the dirty war.[49] In his writ, Garzón describes it a 'basic document which describes the strategic development of armed actions against ETA and which constitutes the initial seed of the GAL'. The fifth paper was an internal memo which appeared to confirm the participation of Perote's branch of the CESID in drawing up that document and, more seriously, in putting some of its scenarios into action.

The sixth document proposed a pact with mafiosi, in exchange for 'certain services in the anti-terrorist struggle'. While general in tone, this document acquired specific significance in the context of the GAL's use of mercenaries.

The eighth paper, titled 'Subject: South of France', was one of the most significant. It stated that 'it is known from a totally reliable source that violent actions in the south of France are planned for the immediate future'. These operations would be carried out by *guardia civiles* from Intxaurrondo, the document specified, parallel with others carried out by individuals contracted in France. This document was dated 28 September 1983, just three weeks before the disappearance of Lasa and Zabala – allegedly at the hands of *guardia civiles* and mercenaries contracted in France. Garzón suggests that the 'totally reliable source' is Gómez Nieto, reporting from within Intxaurrondo to Perote.

There was an interesting coda to the document: 'It is considered that uncoordinated actions without a long-term aim do not advance the success of the anti-terrorist struggle; on the contrary, they sensitise the territory, and *make other actions, already planned with a more decisive strategy, more difficult*' (my emphasis). The implication appears to be that the CESID had planned its own dirty war, and felt upstaged by the Guardia Civil.

The seventh paper was, on the face of it, only an office note attached to 'Subject: South of France'. Three ambiguous letters, however, made it one of the most controversial items of all. The annotation, in the handwriting of General Manglano, Director of the CESID, simply said: 'To be retained by me, Pte. for Friday.' Perote had argued that 'Pte' was an abbreviation of 'Presidente', and meant that Manglano was going to bring the matter of these 'violent actions' to the attention of Felipe González. Manglano had insisted, in a *careo* with Perote in front of Garzón, that 'Pte' was an abbreviation of 'pendiente' ('pending') and simply meant that he was keeping the attached memo pending his next regular Friday meeting with Perote.[50]

The *El País* journalist Miguel González later pointed out, correctly, that, in similar CESID office documents, Manglano uses the word 'pendiente', and asserts that this supports Manglano's case that this is also the meaning of the abbreviation 'Pte' here.[51] However, he fails to note that, on the document relating to impending violence in France, the abbreviation is spelt with a capital 'P' though it is not at the start of a sentence, which could swing the reading back in favour of Perote's interpretation.[52]

Needless to say, such micro-analysis of three letters would hardly constitute cast-iron proof, positive or negative, of Felipe González's involvement in the GAL.

Nevertheless, the seventh and eighth documents, taken together, clearly suggest some degree of involvement by Manglano and the CESID in the dirty war, at least by culpable omission.[53] They prove conclusively that the head of military intelligence knew about the imminence of violent actions by Spanish security forces on foreign territory. Why, then, did he do nothing about it? Why, when Manglano and Narcís Serra told the Spanish parliament in 1985 that the CESID had investigated the GAL, did they say that the agency did not have 'many facts' at its disposal?[54] Was it credible, or justifiable, that they would *not* have given González such vital information?[55]

The ninth paper was a transcript of an audiotape in which Galindo discussed the operational details of launching the dirty war with Gómez Nieto. The latter had allegedly taped the conversation and passed it on to Perote. If authentic, it would be damning. Gómez Nieto appears to put up quite a strong argument to his commanding officer against the course of action they are about to embark on.

'Let's think this through, *mi comandante*: What [guarantees] do we have that this is really worth doing? That is to say, *mi comandante*, we go there, we take someone out. That is the least of it, you know what we gain from that. You already know that one thing we may achieve is that there will be 10 new members who join ETA as a result of this [action]. Have you thought about the kind of publicity this will get? What kind of cover-up line are we going to give to the media?'

Galindo, apparently, was dismissive of these intelligent and, as it turned out, very prescient doubts.

Gómez Nieto persisted: 'And the people? What will they think?'

'The people can think whatever they like. We won't breathe a word of it.'

Gómez Nieto raised a whole series of further objections. Would such actions not merely mean that ETA in France would go underground, and make surveillance of the terrorists more difficult? On a practical level, was not the Guardia Civil at a great disadvantage operating in the French Basque Country, where ETA felt quite at home? 'We can't organise a support network there *because we are not French, because we are not Basques . . . We might as well be going to Japan*' (my emphasis).

Galindo was unimpressed. 'What I see is that you see too many problems,' he said at one point. Despite such a heavy hint from a tough commanding officer, Gómez Nieto expressed further concerns. Possibly, the sergeant's CESID controller had encouraged him to test out how fully committed Galindo was to the enterprise, and whether it would be possible to dissuade him from carrying out such 'unco-ordinated actions'.

In any case, Galindo continued to insist that it would be possible to 'strike blows against' ETA at irregular intervals, when least expected. The operations should be well researched, and then carried out with dispatch: 'go, hit them, and come back'. He could offer no comfort when Gómez Nieto asked him what support might be on offer from the French police. Surprisingly (again assuming the transcript is authentic), Galindo said that 'we will get no help at all from them'.

The first part of this transcript is dated 26 September 1983, just two days before Perote reported on the 'totally reliable source' who had told him of 'violent actions in the south of France in the immediate future', according to CESID paper No. 8. The next part is dated 29 September, by which time Gómez Nieto seems to have overcome his doubts, as the matters discussed now are strictly operational, and contain several references to places where the GAL later carried out killings.

The tenth and eleventh papers are memos on arms. The first is an inventory of 'legally unregistered arms' in Perote's unit. It includes a reference to a rifle with a telescopic sight. While Garzón does not specify this weapon at this stage, it was later alleged to be the rifle with which the GAL shot Eugenio Gutiérrez Salazar.[56] The second sets out options for purchasing 'clean weapons' through legal but untraceable channels, for example from South Africa, through the 'Director General of State Security'. This position was held at this time by Julián Sancristóbal, though he is not named in the document.

The following two papers relate to a rubber stamp, or stamps, with the phrase 'Grupos Armados de Liberación',[57] which was supposed to have been designed and made by the CESID, so that GAL communiqués could have their own logo, just as ETA's did.

The fourteenth document, dated 16 November 1983, named a number of ETA leaders, including Mikel Lujua. This man was known to have been the original target of the GAL operation which resulted in the kidnapping of the hapless Segundo Marey on 4 December. There is also a reference to 'Kaitu', which is very close to the alias *Kattu* used by Ramón Oñederra, the GAL's first acknowledged mortal victim, who was shot on 19 December.[58] This paper includes a complaint that 'the activities carried out by the other State security forces hindered a full investigation'.

The fifteenth document assesses the state of the Comandos Autónomos, a radical nationalist group which acted independently of ETA, and suggests the moment is right for a 'definitive blow' against them. There is no record of a successful GAL operation against the Comandos Autónomos, but this ETA splinter group had claimed responsibility for the killing of the Socialist leader Enrique Casas in February 1984, which was followed immediately by the GAL's killing of the *etarra* Eugenio Gutiérrez Salazar.[59] This paper was dated two months after Gutiérrez Salazar's killing.

The next two documents refer to the creation of 'special' anti-terrorist groups by the Guardia Civil and the Ministry of the Interior in October 1984. The eighteenth and final document requested by Garzón is a December 1984 CESID surveillance report on *etarras* in France, which speaks of 'physical action against a target still to be designated'.

The document which refers to 'violent actions in the south of France' (No. 8) and the transcript of the conversation between Galindo and Gómez Nieto (No. 9) were also requested by Judge Gómez de Liaño in pursuit of the Lasa and Zabala investigation. Gómez de Liaño also requested the transcript of the graphic conversation between Gómez Nieto and Perote, quoted at the beginning of this chapter. This became known as CESID paper No. 19. Judge Justo Rodríquez, who was investigating the '*tiro en la nuca*' (shoot-to-kill) case, was also seeking a CESID document which indicated that the evidence in this case had been tampered with and manipulated, and alleged that Felipe González, Narcís Serra and Rafael Vera were all aware of this. This became known as CESID paper No. 20.

El País's mode of publication made crystal clear what had been evident for some time: the issue was authentication of the documents, rather than their 'release'. The magistrates already had copies of almost all the texts they required.[60] However, these were useless as evidence unless the state would confirm that they really were official military intelligence records, and not the product of the malicious fantasy of Perote, inspired by the needs of Mario Conde and his associates.

It was now compellingly clear, as Garzón had put it so laconically in his 1989 writ on reserved funds, that the security of the state had been 'confused with the security of certain persons'.[61] But *El País* saw no reason to stress that significant point to its readers. This was not the finest hour of Spain's newspaper of record. The focus of its GAL coverage was shifting from the issue of the state's involvement in a dirty war to the issue of the manipulation of that involvement by media and parties hostile to the PSOE.[62] However, the arguments put forward by some *El País* writers questioning the authenticity of the CESID documents deserve some further attention.

Miguel González wrote: 'Not all the *CESID papers* are papers. Some are stamps or recordings. Many of them do not belong to the intelligence service, or at least that is what the CESID claims. And none of them expressly mentions the GAL. Anyone who hoped to find the definitive proof of the origin of the dirty war [in these papers] will be disappointed. The documents whose declassification must be decided by the Supreme Court are, in reality, transcriptions of transcriptions, copies of dubious authenticity, fragments selected from an anthology whose purpose is not known.'[63]

This was a punchy piece of polemical writing, but it generated more heat than light. The fact that some of the 'papers' were tapes in no way detracted – if they were authentic – from their value as evidence. The CESID's denial of authorship was only to be expected. Only three papers – which is hardly 'many' out of twenty – were not in the CESID archives, according to the government itself.[64] Like the so-called 'Founding Memorandum of the GAL', which both the Defence Minister and the CESID had first disclaimed, and then, as the pressure increased, located in a 'secondary' archive, the tapes and stamp might yet turn up.[65] And while the papers might not mention the GAL in so many letters, as it were, the documents are saturated in references to the GAL's dirty war.

As for whether the CESID papers were definitive proof of the state's involvement in that dirty war, that was indeed for the courts to decide. But paper No. 8, for example, specifically describes the Intxaurrondo Guardia Civil's involvement in 'violent actions in the south of France'. If the courts authenticated this document, it would surely constitute a smoking gun found in the hands of the state apparatus. It is quite true that the papers provide little, if any, specific evidence of the criminal responsibility for the GAL of those Socialist leaders still untouched directly by the investigations, like Felipe González.[66] But their political responsibility for the dirty war was more evident than ever, if the documents were genuine.[67]

Miguel González is quite right in pointing out various serious doubts raised by the papers. He makes a sustained, but not entirely convincing, attempt to show that the whole case against Gómez Nieto collapses if the audiotapes cannot be authenticated. Regarding those documents which were likely to be authenticated, Miguel González argues that no originals were now known to exist. Perote had had the originals copied on microfiche and then, apparently, ordered the originals to be destroyed.[68] He suggests that the microfiches could then have been manipulated by Perote, who had removed them from the CESID archives for several months. Miguel González adds that some of the papers are fragments of longer documents, and are presented in fragmented form in the writs. Paragraphs from a single document are presented as two separate papers. Contextualisation and missing passages might provide very different readings.

Ironically, support for the authenticity of the documents came almost immediately, from a most unlikely but most authoritative source: Eduardo Serra. In a press conference in Brussels on the day *El País*'s supplement was published, Serra amazed journalists by saying that there was a 'substantial correspondence' between the papers published by *El País* and those in the CESID archives. A few hours later he tried to backtrack from this position, not on the grounds that what he had said was inaccurate, but on the grounds that state secrecy prevented him confirming any such comment![69] The following day, Aznar tried to minimise the significance of this gaffe, but commentators recognised it as a hint of declassification to come.

Despite the enormous media pressure and public interest which now existed around the issue, the Supreme Court refused to be rushed. In February 1997, the court decided that all thirty-three members of its Third Chamber would consider the case. They began their deliberations on Wednesday, 19 March, and continued until the following Saturday evening, days which kept the whole country, in the words of one of the magistrates, 'up in the air'. In yet another of the extraordinary coincidences that dogged this case, Mario Conde received his first prison sentence on the second day of their discussions.[70]

Over these four days, the news began to leak that at least some of the papers would be declassified, and on Saturday afternoon the court finally made a brief announcement: thirteen of the papers, including some – but not all – of the most significant, would be declassified. Aznar's government immediately announced that it would accept the decision of the court. Serra's proposal the previous October that the cabinet might defy the judicial decision had sunk without trace.

Rafael Vera, who of course had much to lose by the declassification of the papers, describes the decision as a 'barbarity'. He insists that he is not speaking out of self-interest but out of concern for the democratic system, which he claims was under threat from Conde's conspiracy. The intelligence services, he insists, are the 'third pillar' of democracy: 'It is an element of the defence of the state, and so they undermine the state by way of the GAL, and by way of the CESID papers, with Colonel Perote.'[71]

It was one thing for someone accused in several GAL cases to take such a position, but powerful elements in the PSOE party leadership also defended it, and made a last stand on the issue. Parliament, said Joaquín Almunia, who was shortly to take over leadership of the party from Felipe González, should challenge the decision before the Constitutional Court as a 'conflict of powers'. Otherwise, he declared dramatically, 'the State has no one to defend it'.[72] Not a single other party supported this manoeuvre, and other Socialist leaders were embarrassed by it.

On 10 April, the Supreme Court judges published their decisions on the declassification of the CESID papers. They could not, they argued, declassify the audiotapes (Nos. 9 and 19) or the GAL stamp and the documents related to it (Nos. 12 and 13). This was because the CESID insisted that no record of this highly incriminating material existed, or had ever existed, in its files. Nor would they declassify documents which could affect the security of the state, *where their relevance to the cases under investigation was not absolutely clear.* This ruled out, in their view, the document referring to a deal with the mafia (No. 6), the document relating to the acquisition of arms (No. 11) and a document on the formation of a special anti-terrorist group (No. 17). In contrast, the document on an inventory of the arms in the CESID (No. 10) should be declassified, because one of the weapons mentioned was alleged to have been used in a specific GAL crime.

The other thirteen documents which would be declassified and authenticated included the so-called 'Founding Memorandum of the GAL' (No. 4), the memo on impending violent actions in the south of France by the Guardia Civil (No. 8) plus the covering note with the controversial annotation 'Pte' (No. 7), and the memo which proposed 'physical action on a target still to be designated' (No. 18). All of these could now be used as evidence to prosecute those accused of GAL crimes.

At the core of each of the three Supreme Court judgements was the view that the Official Secrets Act was to preserve state secrecy 'and not that of its authorities or servants who may be personally involved in a penal case'.[73] This was remarkably close to the wording of Garzón's long-standing argument against the creation of a space of impunity in the state apparatus, which went back to his battle for access to information on reserved funds. The security of the state, the judges argued, was ultimately that of its citizens, and evidence of crimes against citizens by the security forces could not be exempt from judicial scrutiny. The judges suggested, and the government agreed, that those papers which were declassified should be released in their entirety.

The practical utility of the CESID papers in the investigation of the GAL has still to be fully tested, though the legal relevance of some of the documents was established in the Segundo Marey Supreme Court case.[74] Though the declassification of the papers was a major victory for the investigators, the inability of the judges to authenticate the audiotapes and the GAL stamp, purely because the CESID itself could not – or would not – verify their existence, indicated a major gap in the judiciary's ability to independently investigate the secret service.

Iñigo Iruin, the lawyer for the Lasa and Zabala families whose appeal led to the Supreme Court's landmark decision, has an acerbic analysis of this aspect of their ruling. 'There was a pact with Perote. The pact with Perote had, let's say, a double content. Firstly, to strip value and credibility from the papers, to say no, these documents are unproven information, they are rumours and so on. And the second promise or pact with Perote was to ensure that the most important documents, which are the tapes, do not appear at all . . . And they are the most important. Why? Because there, in those tapes, they speak of concrete individuals with Christian names and surnames. In the other documents, no names appear, but in the tapes, they do.'[75]

This is the conspiracy theory seen from the other side of the looking glass to the Socialist point of view. It makes some sense: it is certainly conceivable that Perote and Conde had decided to release just enough information to damage the Socialists, but not enough to produce hard evidence which would directly incriminate either Perote himself or his erstwhile friends in the Guardia Civil.

Regarding Iruin's first point, however, which implied that Perote would undermine the value of those documents which could be authenticated, the colonel's own trial put paid to whatever intentions he had in that regard. When Perote was finally convicted of stealing the CESID papers in the summer of 1997, the judges dismissed the widely disseminated theory that he had manipulated the microfiches while they were in his possession.[76] Those papers which the Supreme Court had authenticated were now doubly verified. They might or might not incriminate individuals. But they offer clear and devastating indications of the complicity, by commission or omission, of the high command of Spanish military intelligence in the dirty war. Is it really credible that the CESID then kept its Socialist masters in the dark?

The most important result of the battle for the CESID papers, however, relates to much wider issues than the GAL investigation alone. The principle that the right to investigate crimes by the state took priority over the right of the state to preserve its secrets was a legal landmark. The pursuit of the CESID papers marked a major advance in the primacy of the rule of law in Spain. This was a legacy that those who had ridden roughshod over the law, first by launching a dirty war and then by seeking to prevent the judiciary from investigating their actions, could never have imagined.

NOTES

1   All texts of 'CESID papers' quoted in this chapter are translated from the writs of judges Baltasar Garzón and Javier Gómez de Liaño to the Supreme Court, as reproduced in *El País* on 17 December 1996. See pp. 323–6 for an account of the papers' contents.

2   Gómez Nieto appears to be saying that his rank-and-file comrades in the Guardia Civil would support him, if these dirty war activities came to light, but the institution itself would not.

3   The 'CESID papers' was the colloquial title given to the group of twenty items from the military intelligence agency's archives which Garzón, Gómez de Liaño and another judge sought to have authenticated and/or released between 1995 and 1997. They were not all papers – they included audiotapes and a rubber inking stamp with the GAL logo – and in due course Garzón would seek other documents from the CESID.

4   *El Mundo*, 12 June 1995.

5   *El País*, 14 June 1995.

6   *El País*, 24 June 1995. Perote was investigated and tried by the military judiciary, because he was accused of breaches of military discipline. Garzón had an ongoing dispute with the military judge investigating Perote, Jesús Palomino, over jurisdiction and access to documents.

7   The first documents published by *El Mundo* over the summer of 1995 included documents connected to events related to, but not strictly speaking part of, the GAL's operations. For example, on 17 July 1995, it published details of a CESID cover-up operation after a Guardia Civil 'shoot-to-kill' incident in San

Sebastián in 1987. The *etarra* Lucía Urigoitia had allegedly been despatched by a *tiro en la nuca* – summary execution by a shot to the head. One of the CESID papers indicated that military intelligence had collaborated actively with the Guardia Civil in tampering with evidence which indicated that she had been shot in cold blood. Like the Zabalza case, in which an innocent suspect was allegedly tortured to death in a 'bath tub' in Intxaurrondo, and then 'drowned' in the Bidasoa river, this case was not a GAL operation. But some of the same individual *guardia civiles*, including the ubiquitous Galindo, were allegedly involved. The publication of such documents, rather than those central to the GAL itself, was interpreted by those who saw *El Mundo* as participants in the Conde conspiracy as a warning to the government of what could – and did – follow. The timing of this publication, on the very day on which Julián Sancristóbal and Francisco Álvarez implicated Interior in the GAL to Garzón, was certainly striking. See *El País*, 18 July 1995, as well as Manuel Cerdán and Antonio Rubio, *El Caso Interior* (Madrid: Temas de Hoy, 1995), pp. 91–121.

8   Damborenea's declaration was published by *El Mundo* on 27 July 1995.

9   His 'secret' declaration appeared in the following day's *El Mundo*.

10   Ernesto Ekaizer, *Vendetta* (Barcelona: Plaza y Janés, 1996), p. 444.

11   *El Mundo*, 6 September 1995.

12   The *El País* journalist Miguel González argued that much of the 'Founding Memorandum' had been plagiarised from an earlier CESID text. (*El País*, 10 September 1995.) The theoretical manual, *Lucha Contra el Terrorismo* ('The Struggle against Terrorism'), was, he points out, written four years earlier, when the UCD was in power. In fact, there is nothing surprising about similar points being made in two position papers on the same subject and by the same organisation. Contrary to what Miguel González implies, the tone and much of the content of the 'Founding Memorandum' stress the dangers, from a pragmatic point of view, of embarking on a dirty war, and give the strong impression that such dangers outweigh any possible benefits.

13   See *El País*, 31 August 1996, for a retrospective view of this meeting.

14   *El País*, 3 October 1995. The opposition deputies appear to have been less impressed by the documents themselves than by the state of the CESID revealed by the minister's report. Rodrigo Rato for the Partido Popular: 'If we believe what the government says, the level of inefficiency is worse than we could have ever dreamed of. If we don't believe the government, we have to start again from the ground up.' It seemed inconceivable to many of them that Manglano had waited four years before informing the government that such sensitive documents had been stolen.

15   *El País*, 5 October 1995.

16   *El País*, 2 November 1995. For this Supreme Court decision, see ch. 18, p. 269.

17   See *El País*, 16 December 1995. The court was a heavyweight body, made up of three members of the Supreme Court, including the usually liberal president, Pascal Sala, and three members of the Council of State.

18   Ibid.

19   Ibid. This editorial also pointed out that the court based its decision on Francoist legislation which predated the democratic constitution by ten years.

20   *El País* advanced this argument in an editorial on Luis Roldán on 8 May 1996, quoting Perote's own words from October 1995 on the need to 'reach a political resolution for those who face charges – or who may do so in the future'.

21   *El Mundo*, 3 May 1996.

22   Justo Rodríguez, who was investigating the so-called '*tiro en la nuca*' case. See n. 7 above.

23   *El Mundo*, 17 May 1996.

24 It was common knowledge that there were deep divisions in the cabinet on this issue. Álvarez Cascos himself had shamelessly reversed the position he had held in opposition, though he was said to still be in favour of some selective declassification, as was the Interior Minister, Jaime Mayor Oreja. The Minister for Justice, Margarita Mariscal, and for Agriculture, Loyola de Palacio, were both strongly inclined to hand over all the papers the judges had asked for. Aznar was thought to be undecided, but moving towards Serra's view that no CESID paper should be released. See *El País*, 25 May and 3 August 1996.

25 The supreme consultative body of the Spanish government, whose members include senior military, judicial and cultural figures.

26 This aspect of the decision was not divulged until 27 August. See *El País*, 28 August 1996.

27 *El País*, 3 and 28 August 1996. The Socialists had issued similar denials about the existence of the 'Founding Memorandum of the GAL' and then had had to acknowledge that this document had turned up in a 'secondary archive'. See *El País*, 6 September 1995 and 31 August 1996.

28 *El País*, 3 August 1996.

29 Ibid. Álvarez Cascos had also said that 'The Official Secrets Act serves as a refuge for criminals because they appeal to it to cover up and hide their actions.' And at the Partido Popular conference prior to the 1996 elections, he had thundered: 'We reject appeals to national security to protect documents from democratic investigation, in an unjustifiable manner, when those documents only compromise the personal security of [members of the] government and could be decisive in investigating conduct which is under legal suspicion.' *El Mundo*, 3 August 1996.

30 *El Mundo*, 3 August 1996.

31 *El País*, 4 August 1996.

32 *El País*, 26 August 1996.

33 *El Mundo*, 3 August 1996; *El País*, 4 August 1996.

34 *El País*, 6 August 1996.

35 *El País*, 28 August 1996.

36 *El Mundo*, 29 August 1996.

37 Sometimes on very bureaucratic grounds; see *El País*, 16 October 1996.

38 La Sala Tercera de lo Contencioso-administrativo del Tribunal Supremo (The Third Chamber of the Supreme Court for Judicial Review of the Central Administration).

39 *El País*, 3, 5 and 9 October 1996. See also *El País* supplement on CESID papers, 17 December 1996.

40 *El Mundo*, 12 October 1996.

41 *El País*, 14 October 1996.

42 *El País*, 15 October 1996. Belloch's steadily hardening stance against transparency in affairs of state has been analysed thus by Manuel Vázquez Montalbán: 'Belloch, in the interview I did with him, told me that there had been state terrorism. The problem is that the Socialists, at a certain point, blamed Belloch because he had made their history too transparent. Then he panicked, fearing he would destroy his political career, and began to retreat from these positions; he is talking garbage now, talking rubbish.' (Interview with Manuel Vázquez Montalbán, Madrid, November 1997.) Meanwhile, Felipe González's disregard for the separation of powers between executive, legislature and judiciary had become increasingly evident, and would become more so. See also ch. 25, p. 413–4.

43 *El País*, 16 October 1996. Those Socialists who fostered this hostility to the judiciary were handed easy arguments by an unseemly internecine feud

between the prosecutors at the Audiencia Nacional which provoked calls for this court to be abolished.

44   *El País*, 31 October 1996.

45   Ibid.

46   Some members of the Partido Popular were also now acknowledging publicly that there was an unhealthy connection between revelations in the GAL case and the state of play in the investigation into Conde.

47   *El Mundo Anuario* [Yearbook], 1997, p. 105.

48   High-minded papers like *El País*, which disapproved in principle of the practice, nevertheless did it themselves. Secret details of the investigation into Mario Conde's affairs were published by the paper in December 1994, and, of course, the paper also published the writs relating to the CESID papers.

49   There were sections which read more like a working paper than a purely theoretical document. Under the heading of 'reprisals', for example, the following telling phrase occurs: 'To a degree, it has already been tried and did not achieve positive results.' Under the same heading, there is a reference to carrying out reprisals against 'relatives'. It could be said that the justification for shooting Karmele and Nagore Martínez (see ch. 12) came early. The concluding sentence, already quoted above, that the 'most advisable form of action is disappearance by kidnapping', also had an extraordinary resonance in the GAL context.

50   This *careo* had taken place on 6 September 1995. Perote had not produced these two documents at this stage, but he had described them in detail. He added that Manglano had told him that this matter was so important he had to tell González about it. Perote said that he had always believed that González himself had ordered the drafting of the so-called 'Founding Memorandum of the GAL'. Manglano denied all these allegations, not only in court but in a press release. (See *El País*, 7 September 1995.)

51   *El País*, 24 April 1997.

52   To complicate matters yet further, a document whose authentication was *not* originally requested by Garzón does contain the abbreviation 'pte', where it unequivocally means 'pendiente'. Garzón, some observers implied, might be excluding any evidence which contradicted his thesis that 'Pte' meant 'President'. See *El País,* 12 April 1997, for an article by Miguel González which tends towards this view. However, the same journalist conceded that Garzón was in fact pursuing this additional document on 15 May 1997.

53   Assuming, of course, that they could be authenticated, which they ultimately were.

54   *El País*, 27 April 1985 and 31 August 1996.

55   Curiously, Garzón himself makes no analysis whatsoever of the implication of 'Pte' in the writ published by *El País*.

56   This rifle turned out to be missing when the CESID was asked to produce it. (See *El País*, 26 May 1996.) Another of the weapons on this list is especially appropriate to an intelligence agency: a '.22 calibre biro-pistol'.

57   This variant of 'Grupos Antiterroristas de Liberación' is thought to have been favoured by the 'green GAL' associated with the Guardia Civil.

58   Garzón, however, does not make this connection here, and the alias may well have belonged to another *etarra*. *El Mundo* (16 December 1996) had claimed that this document related to *Kattu*/Oñederra.

59   The Comandos Autónomos had, however, been the target of what appeared to be a 'shoot-to-kill' operation by the security forces in Pasajes de San Pedro in March 1984, in which at least one GAL suspect, Julen Elgorriaga, was involved. See ch. 7, pp. 109–10. According to one account, the Comandos Autónomos also came under GAL surveillance in France. See Ch. 14 pp. 195.

60 There were exceptions: Garzón had neither the GAL stamp itself (No. 12) nor the document relating to its production (No. 13). Crucially, he had no copies of the audiotapes (Nos. 9 and 19), only the unsubstantiated transcripts.

61 See ch. 16, p. 230.

62 The *El País* editorial (17 December 1996) defending its decision to publish the CESID papers devoted itself almost entirely to the question of whether *El Mundo* had used the documents as a weapon in the anti-Socialist conspiracy. It hardly dealt at all with the contents of the documents themselves. An editorial the following February went further, coming close to attacking the Supreme Court for allegedly denying 'governmental autonomy in these matters'. *El País*, 3 February 1997.

63 *El País*, 17 December 1996.

64 See Miguel González's own article, *El País*, 31 August 1996.

65 See *El País*, 6 September 1995 and 31 August 1996.

66 Apart from the possible reference to Felipe González as 'Pte' in CESID paper No. 7, there is a direct reference to him in CESID paper No. 20, relating to the '*tiro en la nuca*' case. Not only is this not a GAL case properly speaking, but the reference itself is weak in that it is clearly based on hearsay.

67 Javier Pradera correctly pointed out that many of those who wanted to see Felipe González in the dock for the dirty war were at the same time trying to exonerate the army and the Guardia Civil from any responsibility. *El País*, 27 December 1996.

68 Perote gave contradictory accounts as to whether he had, in fact, destroyed all the originals.

69 'Do they coincide with each other? It is possible that I said so, and I don't deny that they coincide with the CESID [papers].' (*El País*, 18 December 1996.) Serra, in the same comments, makes much of the possibility that the microfiches in the CESID were not originals, and might have been manipulated by Perote.

70 This was a six-year sentence for illicit appropriation of funds and falsifying business documents in the subsidiary Argentia Trust case, small beer compared to the charges he faced in the Banesto case. Javier Pradera speculated that the severely wounded but still potent Conde would now switch from 'preventive intimidation' to 'reprisal with lethal weapons'. (*El País*, 23 March 1997.) But it seems the former banker had no more lethal ammunition than the CESID papers, and that that arsenal was now empty.

71 Interview with Rafael Vera, Madrid, November 1997.

72 *El País*, 25 March 1997.

73 There were three separate decisions on the writs from Garzón, Gómez de Liaño and Rodríguez. Each was approved by a large majority of the thirty-three judges. The maximum number to vote against a decision to declassify was six. *El País*, 11 April 1997.

74 See ch. 24, pp. 383–4.

75 Interview with Iñigo Iruin, San Sebastián, June 1997.

76 'This is a mere theoretical hypothesis lacking the least proof to sustain it, which has not been demonstrated in any way and which is most improbable given the extreme difficulty of such a practice.' (Judgement of court, quoted in *El País*, 11 July 1997.) Perote was convicted of stealing the CESID papers for 'unmistakable personal interest and personal benefit'. The sentence made no reference to his alleged use of the papers in collaboration with Mario Conde, or with *El Mundo*. He was sentenced to seven years in prison by a military court, which attracted severe criticism for holding the entire trial behind closed doors for security reasons. See *El País*, 11 July 1997.

22

A Divided Democracy:

shockwaves from the GAL scandal fracture Spanish institutions

'I have no experience of the informer's trade.'[1] José Barrionuevo, former police minister turned criminal suspect, helped seal his own fate with these words on 9 June 1998. Many people have been betrayed by informers, but Barrionuevo was betrayed as much by his own use of the word as by the allegations of his renegade comrade, Ricardo García Damborenea.

Standing before eleven Supreme Court judges with his arms folded defensively, Barrionuevo knew he was fighting for what remained of his reputation, and looking at twenty-three years in prison if he lost. Yet he seemed oddly rattled and querulous for a man of his political experience. The *careo* – the face-to-face confrontation between conflicting witnesses, in which the court attempts to assess their credibility – had clearly taken him by surprise.

The point of contention in the *careo* was a phone conversation. Julián Sancristóbal claimed that Barrionuevo had made the call to him in the early hours of 4 December 1984, to authorise the kidnapping of Segundo Marey. Damborenea said he had witnessed the call and could verify its contents. It was a crucial element in their joint allegation that the former Interior Minister, and his deputy Rafael Vera, had been involved in the GAL's first acknowledged action.

It was, however, a question of their word against his, and the court used the controversial option of requiring Barrionuevo to challenge both men's account of the phone call. It was controversial because the *careo* was regarded as a very unreliable means of ascertaining the truth. The presiding judge himself argued that it was a very subjective device, and that the perceived 'winner' was often not the person telling the truth, but 'the most daring, the most skilful, or he who shouts most'.[2] Only the previous day, he had turned down a request for a *careo* from Damborenea's defence lawyer.

A majority of the judges disagreed, however, and Barrionuevo was unexpectedly called from his seat along with Sancristóbal as the trial reopened the following morning. They were invited to 'reach an agreement' on whether or not the conversation had taken place. Not surprisingly, they did the opposite.

Speaking firmly and gesticulating forcefully, Sancristóbal insisted that he had spoken not once but several times that night to Barrionuevo, and had obtained his 'approval and authorisation' to continue with the kidnapping. The former minister, sounding more peevish than confident, retorted stiffly that this was 'totally untrue'.

Then the presiding judge called up Damborenea to challenge Barrionuevo's account, and the former minister let slip the fateful word 'informer'. As one commentator put it the next day: 'One either lies or one informs. Both things are, in their own way, despicable, but lying entails falsehood and informing does not.'[3] Moreover, the word has the same connotation in Spanish as it has in English, being generally applied by members of paramilitary or terrorist groups to their own renegade members.[4] Barrionuevo, in accusing Sancristóbal of 'lying' about the existence of a phone call, and then accusing Damborenea of 'informing' about the same conversation, was hoist between his own insults.

It was three years since Damborenea, Sancristóbal, Francisco Álvarez and Miguel Planchuelo had all changed their innocent pleas to guilty, and implicated Barrionuevo, Vera and Felipe González in the organisation of the GAL. Judge Baltasar Garzón had then handed over the Segundo Marey case to the Supreme Court, along with his findings that there was an 'avalanche of data and evidence' to show that Barrionuevo had participated in the kidnapping.[5] Garzón had also, in a highly contentious move, informed his superiors that while he could not say that the other defendants' allegations against González constituted 'evidence', he did find them 'credible'. He also gave some weight to equally flimsy allegations against the former deputy Prime Minister, Narcís Serra, and the Socialists' 'number three', José María ('Txiki') Benegas. If the PSOE leadership had felt under attack from the judiciary before, it felt under full-scale siege in the summer of 1995.

Rational discussion of the issue was not assisted by the Partido Popular, which began to exploit the GAL case to its electoral advantage more ruthlessly than ever, and sometimes quite recklessly.

The Segundo Marey case had barely landed on the desk of the Supreme Court when Francisco Álvarez Cascos, the Partido Popular's deputy leader and spokesperson on terrorism, made a remarkable statement: 'Public opinion is clearer with every day about the verdict on the GAL case, and therefore, with every passing day, the sentence which the judges hand down is important for the reputation of justice, so that the Spanish justice system gains prestige among its own citizens. Because, insofar as the court's decision, the sentence, does not correspond to the verdict of the citizens in the light of the facts which have been established, it is the justice [system] itself which is going to lose out.'[6]

This outburst confirmed the view of many Socialists that the justice system was being pressurised and manipulated by the Right, and that the GAL investigations were simply a legal lever to remove González from political power. Thus each side fed the conspiracy theory of the other.

In fact, the transfer of the Marey case to the Supreme Court meant that every aspect of Garzón's investigation had to be duplicated by a senior colleague, a strong guarantee, one might have thought, of judicial independence. The job fell to Eduardo Moner, a respected sixty-seven-year-old with a reputation as a meticulous jurist and a defender of individual rights, without political affiliation.[7] Such an appointment might have reassured the Socialists about the independence of the judiciary – under normal circumstances.

These circumstances were not, however, in any way normal, and the Socialists refused to accept that justice was being done. 'I have no faith whatsoever [in our justice system],' Rafael Vera says. 'I respect Moner, he seems to me a serious judge, a good examining magistrate, but I know that he is being pressurised . . . the justice system is being used, like in Italy, not to clean up political life, that is only the excuse, it is being used to seize power.'[8]

Moner started work with an initial report on Garzón's investigation from the Supreme Court's prosecutors, which saw no basis for charges against González, Serra or Benegas, but found that the 'incriminating accusations' against Barrionuevo were 'specific, repeated and concordant'.[9] It was an assessment that Moner would slowly but surely endorse over the months to come.

In October 1995, Moner found that there were sufficient grounds to summons Barrionuevo. By González's own criteria, a GAL case had now reached the cabinet table: one of his ministers was a suspect.[10] Barrionuevo was no longer just the target of media allegations, nor of a judge whom the PSOE regarded as tainted by ulterior motives; he was under suspicion in the eyes of an eminent investigating magistrate of the Supreme Court. One might have expected that the PSOE would begin to honour its promise to collaborate with the justice system, and clarify what had really happened in the Interior Ministry in the 1980s.

The first test came immediately: since Barrionuevo refused to give up the privileges of his parliamentary seat voluntarily, Moner needed the permission of parliament to lift his legal immunity and summons him. Some 200 MPs, a clear majority, voted to remove his privileges, and he was obliged to face Moner. However, to the disgust of many observers, 122 MPs, a considerable majority of the PSOE's 159 deputies, voted against. Even assuming that this was a gesture of solidarity with a party comrade, rather than a direct challenge to the judiciary, it was a clear indication of how the GAL investigation was creating a dangerous rift between the major institutions of Spanish democracy.

Lifting immunity, after all, did not imply taking any position on the charges against Barrionuevo; it simply permitted the courts to carry out their normal duties. By voting against it, the PSOE was sending out a message that it no longer trusted the political impartiality of the legal system – or that the party knew it had something to hide.

Barrionuevo appeared before Moner on 13 December, and denied all charges against him. He did, however, admit on several occasions that he might have telephoned Sancristóbal on the night of the kidnapping, something he would totally deny when the case came to trial. Moner released him 'for the moment' without bail.[11]

Within the week, there was another demonstration of PSOE solidarity with a suspected state terrorist. No fewer than 740 leading party members attended a dinner in solidarity with the former minister. The former deputy Prime Minister, Narcís Serra, the party's parliamentary spokesman and future leader, Joaquín Almunia, the party president, Ramón Rubial, and Felipe González's wife, the MP Carmen Romero, all attended. So did some of the most prominent GAL suspects, including General Enrique Rodríguez Galindo and Julen Elgorriaga, who would later face charges in the Lasa and Zabala case, as well as Barrionuevo's co-accused, Rafael Vera. There were telegrams of support from Javier Solana, the longest-serving González minister who had recently been appointed NATO Secretary General, and from Public Works Minister José Borrell, a future, though short-lived, PSOE leader. Rubial assured Barrionuevo that 'all the Socialists' were behind him.

There was a widely held view at the time that Barrionuevo could be the weak link in the chain of command which led to González. If Barrionuevo felt abandoned by his party, this theory ran, he was much more likely to crack and talk, as his subordinates had done before him, than Rafael Vera was. At the dinner, he made a remarkably revealing speech about his motivation in politics: he was, he said, 'insatiable for the affection and love' of his peers.[12] If Barrionuevo knew more about the GAL than he had told the court, his party was giving him a great deal of love and affection to keep him quiet. In any case, the PSOE was giving another clear signal that it was going to exert the maximum political pressure in his defence. Even some of those who had voted in favour of lifting his immunity attended the dinner. This heavyweight celebration of an alleged criminal was hardly in keeping with Felipe González's exhortation to 'let the judges do their work'.[13] Moreover, his wife's attendance was taken as a sign of his personal approval. In case anyone had any doubts, González himself expressed 'all my solidarity and friendship towards Pepe Barrionuevo' a few days later.[14]

Moner was impervious to these manoeuvres. In early January 1996, having observed Barrionuevo in various *careos* with Damborenea, Sancristóbal and Álvarez, he insisted that he post bail of 15 million pesetas to stay out of prison while the investigation continued. This decision signalled that he would almost certainly be charged with very serious crimes, which Moner confirmed on 24 January. This judge's charge-sheet was even more severe than Garzón's, in that he added accusations of creating and directing an armed gang, a charge which he also applied to Rafael Vera. The general thrust of Garzón's investigation had thus been not only ratified but amplified by an independent senior magistrate.

Meanwhile, the political temperature in Spain was rising towards boiling point, as the general elections called by González for 3 March approached. The Partido Popular's January annual congress gave an early indication of the double standard it would apply to the GAL investigation as the party neared its first taste of government. On the one hand, the party would pursue Felipe González and his party implacably with the charge that they had been politically responsible for the GAL. On the other, party leader José María Aznar in particular would begin to back off endorsing an equally implacable legal pursuit of the GAL, and would begin to make references to *pasar página* – turning over the page – wherever the GAL might affect the security of the state.[15]

Thus Álvarez Cascos, the Partido Popular's pugnacious deputy leader, declared that the party was 'firmly convinced that the actions of the GAL entail the gravest responsibilities for the government and for [the Prime Minister], without whose consent the actions of these groups could never have been initiated, nor been prolonged over four years, nor made to disband.'[16] Yet Aznar could start talking like a statesman about how the need to modernise Spain was more important than becoming entangled in an investigation of the GAL scandal.

Critics on the Left began to suspect that Aznar would use the scandal to help force González out of government, and then seek a way of discreetly imposing an Argentinian-style 'law of the full stop' on the whole question of the dirty war, in case the Right's own skeletons fell out of the cupboard. Pilar Rahola, of the Republican Left of Catalonia (Esquerra Republicana de Catalunya), had this to say: 'the Partido Popular did not want to investigate the GAL case . . . because, if it did, it would probably find its own shadow in the sewers of the State'.[17]

The question now arose as to whether Barrionuevo should run as a candidate for the party in the upcoming March elections. In favour of his inclusion in the PSOE lists, it could be said that a withdrawal might appear to be an admission of guilt. But it was hardly healthy for the party, desperately fighting to present a clean image to the electorate, to put forward someone who had been charged with membership of an armed gang, abuse of public funds and kidnapping.

The Socialists in general, however, and González in particular, were in no mood to take such niceties into consideration. At an extraordinary meeting of the PSOE's federal committee, just three days after Barrionuevo had been charged, he was selected by acclamation as a candidate on the list for Madrid. During the meeting, González melodramatically insisted that the right of the party to choose its own candidates was at stake: 'if we do not take this decision [to include Barrionuevo on the PSOE electoral lists] we will lose our autonomy for ever'. He went even further: 'We are speaking about the defence of the State.'[18] And he complained bitterly that the Supreme Court should not have taken a decision affecting Barrionuevo at election time. All shades of judicial opinion were outraged at his remarks, described by one judge as bordering on 'contempt'.[19] Opposition leaders said his comments were an attack on the rule of law itself.[20] The fissure between the Socialists and the judiciary was becoming a chasm, long before the Marey trial even started.

The judiciary came under a different sort of attack on 15 February, when ETA killed Francisco Tomás y Valiente, a highly respected and well-loved former president of the Constitutional Court, as he sat in his university office in Madrid. He was also a personal friend of González's. ETA was repeating its old strategy of spectacular assassinations during election periods. A week earlier, they had killed a socialist lawyer, Fernando Múgica, brother of a former Justice Minister, in San Sebastián. Tomás y Valiente's death, in particular, appalled Spanish public opinion, and there were very big anti-ETA demonstrations, precursors of the huge mobilisation which would follow the killing of Miguel Ángel Blanco in the summer of 1997.

After a brief show of democratic solidarity against terrorism between the Partido Popular and the PSOE, the election campaign resumed its acrimonious tone. José María Aznar's Partido Popular emerged as the victor, though still twenty seats short of an absolute majority, as we have seen. Despite the bitterness of the campaign, power passed peacefully from Left to Right for the first time in Spain since the 1930s, and the PSOE found itself in opposition for the first time in thirteen years. However, large sections of the Spanish public certainly did not seem to share the concerns of the opposition parties, the judiciary and the media about the PSOE's fitness for office, despite all that the scandals had revealed. Its share of the vote only dropped by just over 1 per cent, and its absolute vote actually rose by more than 200,000. The Socialists called the result, with some justification, a 'sweet defeat'.

The fact that the Socialists performed so much better than expected no doubt contributed to the defiant attitude they would take towards the continuing GAL investigations. Nor was there much feeling within the party that the GAL scandal was to blame for their defeat. When the party leadership handed out thousands of new membership cards at a rally in the Casa del Campo in Madrid in June, Barrionuevo, who had been re-elected to parliament, got more standing ovations than Felipe González.[21]

PSOE morale was also boosted by a series of contradictory declarations made by Amedo and Domínguez during this period, which seemed to undermine some of the case against Barrionuevo and Vera.[22]

The Socialists were delighted when Moner decided not to summons Felipe González because his investigation had uncovered nothing which implicated him, beyond the unsubstantiated allegations of Damborenea and an inference of Sancristóbal's. Damborenea's allegations, the magistrate declared, were neither 'well-founded nor credible'.[23] Joaquín Almunia, the PSOE leader who had apparently impugned Moner for deciding to accuse Barrionuevo during the election campaign, now responded in a very different tone when this news first appeared in the media: 'Justice, when it is authentic justice, acts without taking any outside influence into account, and the Supreme Court, and particularly Judge Moner, take decisions according to the law and without regard to the political calendar.'[24]

It was a generous statement from a critic; one can only wonder if the same generosity would have been displayed if Moner's decision had gone the other way. When it came to legal decisions, sauce for the goose was rarely sauce for the gander. When the PSOE praised 'authentic justice', the Partido Popular and the United Left were likely to cry 'whitewash'. When the Partido Popular praised 'authentic justice', the PSOE would shout 'witch-hunt'.

There was rather less welcome news for the Socialists in late June, when a tape-recording surfaced of a conversation between Barrionuevo and Sancristóbal. It had been made during the first half of 1995, while the latter was already in prison on Marey charges but before he had admitted his participation. According to the tape, Barrionuevo had encouraged Sancristóbal to believe that the government had a strategy which would get him and his colleagues out of jail. This seemed to involve the former minister accepting some vaguely defined political responsibility for the GAL. Exchanges from the alleged conversations appeared on the front page of *El Mundo* on 24 June.

Barrionuevo claimed the tapes were cut and manipulated, but did acknowledge that he had had conversations along these lines with Sancristóbal. While he denied that he had been involved in any criminal activity, he reaffirmed, not very convincingly, his willingness to take political responsibility for the actions of his subordinates. Sancristóbal, in turn, denied taping the conversation or supplying it to the newspaper.[25]

Just as the Supreme Court was rejecting some of Barrionuevo's and Vera's appeals against hearing the charges against them, another Supreme Court case concerning a different armed gang was getting under way. During the 1996 elections, Herri Batasuna had publicly screened a video in which hooded and armed members of ETA presented their 'Democratic Alternative' programme. Now the twenty-three members of the radicals' national committee found themselves charged with collaboration with terrorism.[26] This case came to be seen, by those who doubted the independence of the Spanish judiciary, as a sort of quid pro quo for the Marey trial: the jailing of Socialist leaders for state terrorism would be balanced by imprisoning Basque radicals for revolutionary terrorism.

In its inner circles, the PSOE began to debate the lessons of its electoral defeat. There was a characteristically extreme proposal from the Estremaduran leader, Juan Carlos Rodríguez Ibarra, that the entire executive should resign in order for the party to renew itself. Others, like the former Minister for Public Works, José Borrell, believed that removal from office meant that the PSOE had paid its political debt to society already. 'We Socialists already paid our political debts on 3 March,' he told the federal committee in late July, and added, significantly: 'the judicial account will be settled in the courts'. González, however, continued to talk of a sinister Partido Popular strategy to 'destroy the legitimacy' of the PSOE, and echoed the controversy over his alleged attack on the judiciary in January when he said that the Partido Popular could count on 'the invaluable help of the judicial Right' in order to do so.[27]

'TERRORISM OF THE WINE CELLAR': GONZÁLEZ, ÁLVAREZ CASCOS AND THE MEANING OF STATE TERRORISM

González did not resign from the party leadership, given the 'sweetness' of the March defeat. During the summer and autumn of 1996, while an appeal by prosecution lawyers against Moner's decision not to summons the former Prime Minister tied up the investigation, he continued to air his views on the GAL. Sometimes he poured oil on troubled waters, insisting to journalists that 'everything the Supreme Court does is well done.'[28] At other times he seemed recklessly intent on adding fuel to the fire. A radio interview in late September produced another entry for his catechism of ambiguity on the theme of the dirty war.

Asked if there had been state terrorism in Spain, he replied roundly: 'Evidently not . . . had there been state terrorism there would not be 900 victims in the security forces and in the civilian population, and 28 victims, plus those from before,[29] among alleged terrorists. Where there has been state terrorism, the balance between the numbers of victims on either side has been the reverse.'

And he continued: 'Incidents like those which have taken place in Spain have happened in all countries where terrorism has attacked democracy . . . but the whole world applauds Clinton and Bush, when there is a terrorist attack, people say "Let's go after them wherever they are hiding." Applause all round. "There is a president capable of fighting terrorism."'[30]

Both González's language and his arguments are worth close analysis here. He describes the victims of the GAL as 'alleged terrorists', when at least one-third of them were demonstrably innocent of any terrorist association. He refers to their killings as 'incidents', the kind of debased abstraction used by ETA supporters when they describe a killing as 'an operation'.

His theory that state terrorism is defined, not by the level of involvement of the state apparatus in terrorist actions, but by the number of victims it claims, would be simply risible, were it not made by a former Prime Minister awaiting a final Supreme Court decision on his own implication in such crimes. His insistence that 'other democratic countries do it', a constant refrain of PSOE apologists at this time, is seriously flawed in factual terms, as we will see in the final chapter. Even where it is true, it hardly represents a moral justification; rather the contrary.[31]

Even more significantly, the argument carries his usual double edge: is he saying that he, as Prime Minister, had also been 'capable of fighting terrorism', willing to pursue terrorists 'wherever they are hiding'? Yet again, González is attempting the double act of denying involvement with the GAL, while appealing to the populist sentiment that the dirty war was not really such a bad thing, after all.

Perhaps the greatest indicator of the decay of debate inside the PSOE on this issue was the fact that Juan Alberto Belloch, erstwhile democratic defender of individual rights against the state, leapt to his leader's defence. He argued that while there were 'members of the State security forces implicated in terrorist acts', this did not constitute state terrorism.[32] As the man who had stopped the state funding of two men accused of terrorist crimes, his reasoning had become remarkably Jesuitical.

Never one for complex reasoning, the Partido Popular deputy leader, Francisco Álvarez Cascos, hit back hard. If there was no state terrorism, that was because most of the powers of the state were not involved in the GAL, he told a rally in Mérida. The GAL, however, had been 'organised' by the Prime Minister and his coterie: 'It was something orchestrated by Felipe González and people in his inner circle . . . the GAL was simply terrorism of the wine cellar.'[33] The wine cellar he referred to was the well-known private bar in the Moncloa Palace where González used to entertain his intimate collaborators. A

PSOE spokesman, Luis Yañez, responded by describing Álvarez Cascos's speech as reminiscent of 'the worst times of fascist bully-boy tactics in the 1940s'.[34]

The polarisation which the March elections had been supposed to dissipate was poisoning political discourse more acutely than ever.

González had a narrow escape in the early hours of 5 November 1996, when the Supreme Court finally rejected the prosecution appeals that he should be among the accused in the Marey case. The court, deeply split, decided on the issue by a six–four margin after debating until well past midnight. The four dissidents who wanted to charge him were classified by the press as two conservatives, one moderate and one left-winger.[35] The court left open the possibility that he could be called as a witness in the trial itself.

There was some further relief for the Socialist leadership in January 1997, when *Diario 16* published a document, apparently in Amedo's handwriting, which accused Garzón, and the editor of *El Mundo*, Pedro J. Ramírez, of pressurising him to make allegations against his superiors in 1994. Slippery as ever, Amedo acknowledged the document as his, but refused to confirm whether its contents were fact or fiction.[36]

The first half of the year was characterised by further ferocious hostility between the PSOE and the Partido Popular. There were two main poles of tension, the media and the judiciary. A battle over digital television rights, in which the new government blatantly bent the rules to favour an option which would exclude opposition voices, raised fears that the Partido Popular really did want to limit freedom of expression. The target here was the digital television company Sogecable, an offshoot of the multi-media PRISA group, which includes *El País* and Canal Plus TV. The appointment of right-wingers with dubious democratic credentials to the key positions of Attorney General (Jesús Cardinal) and chief prosecutor at the Audiencia Nacional (Eduardo Fungairiño) fed the Socialist obsession that the courts were becoming an instrument of conservative power.[37]

The digital television war got very dirty. Sogecable was subjected to judicial investigation, on dubious grounds, by government supporters. The owner and the founding editor of *El País*, the power-brokers in PRISA, were forbidden to leave the country without the permission of Judge Javier Gómez de Liaño, who had been allegedly linked to the anti-Socialist conspiracy of Mario Conde.[38] It became impossible to avoid the conclusion that the Partido Popular was engaging in the harassment of a media group it regarded as a political enemy. 'Judicial security is in serious doubt, the rule of law is threatened, freedom of expression and of the press is in danger,' an *El País* editorial thundered in early April.[39]

While the newspaper was clearly not a neutral observer of the situation, and its rhetoric was somewhat overblown, it was an accurate reflection of the fears of many Spaniards who had not voted for the Partido Popular, and probably also of some who had. The vague nightmare that, behind the democratic façade of Aznar, there still lurked the Rottweiler of authoritarianism, which had haunted the election campaign a year earlier, was taking a more definite shape. *El País* won the support of prestigious foreign papers like the *New York Times, Le Monde, La Repubblica* and *Der Spiegel* for its case. The courts eventually found that there was no case whatsoever against Sogecable.[40]

In this volatile political climate, the investigation of the Marey case was completed by Judge Moner without further surprises, confirming the charges of kidnapping, abuse of public funds and leadership of an armed gang against Barrionuevo and Vera. No sooner had the magistrate handed over his findings to his colleagues, who would hear the case in open court, than new evidence seemed to emerge from, of all people, Felipe González.

In early May, Álvarez Cascos had taken advantage of a comment by González about 'brainless judges' to make a punning reference to the former Prime Minister as 'the brain of the GAL'.[41] González fired back an accusation that Álvarez Cascos 'plotted and promised things' to Amedo and Domínguez prior to their 1994 declarations to Garzón and *El Mundo*. Socialist sources told *El País* that they had sound tapes which proved that Álvarez Cascos had met the policemen's lawyer, Jorge Manrique, in the offices of *El Mundo* and in the presence of the editor, Pedro J. Ramírez, at that critical moment for the reopening of the GAL case.[42]

González further challenged Álvarez Cascos as to whether he had offered to facilitate a pardon for the two defendants, once the Partido Popular came to power, if they would implicate the Socialist leadership in the GAL. Álvarez Cascos first issued robust denials, but his increasingly evasive responses left the murky waters of the conspiracy theory on the GAL investigation still more opaque.[43] The issue would only be partially clarified when the case came to trial.

González and his wife Carmen Romero both offered effusive solidarity to Barrionuevo within days of each other in early June. The occasion for the former Prime Minister's demonstration of loyalty was the publication of Barrionuevo's memoir, *2,001 Días en Interior*. In a short foreword, presented at the book launch, González said of his party colleague: 'I feel that . . . he is not the main quarry in this hunt into which some people have converted politics. When some people (from the hunting pack or those who direct it) insist that they want to see me charged, or at least as a witness – *the photo*[44] – I want to say that I am ready and willing. In the service of friendship and justice, or, if they prefer, in the service of justice and friendship.'[45]

Some observers felt that this offer came rather late in the day, when the investigative phase of the Marey case, which had lasted more than two years, was already closed. The foreword itself also seemed to be a bit of an afterthought. It was delivered too late to be bound with the first edition, and was attached to it like a pamphlet.[46]

Such details fed the rumour that Barrionuevo, though not remanded in custody, was feeling abandoned to the mercy of the courts, and was on the point of 'doing a Sancristóbal', as it were, and implicating his former boss. González's obviously rushed foreword was seen as a hasty attempt to keep his lips sealed.

On 4 June, Carmen Romero made a striking contribution to the GAL debate. Asked on radio whether the GAL scandal had caused the Socialists any qualms of conscience, she replied: 'Why should we lose sleep because of a phenomenon which has happened in Spain like it happened in France, in Germany, in all democratic countries? Phenomena of dirty tricks, settling of accounts, are normal in very many countries.'[47] This airy dismissal of the GAL's shootings, bombings and torturing as normal 'phenomena' in a democracy was perhaps the most shocking of all the PSOE's declarations on the dirty war, especially as it came from the former Prime Minister's wife, a parliamentary deputy and a respected advocate of feminism and democracy in her own right. She concluded: 'Pepe Barrionuevo has the support of all socialists at this time. Of course he does . . .'

Whatever the motive of such declarations, Barrionuevo remained firm in his protestations of innocence, and in his refusal to implicate González.

González shocked his own party at the end of June 1997. He abruptly announced that he was standing down as general secretary and party leader, after twenty-three years, on the first day of the PSOE's 34th Congress. The speed and timing of his exit curtailed debate on his successor, and the party chose a safe pair of hands, Joaquín Almunia. He had been a member of González's cabinets from 1982 (when he was the youngest of a very young team) to 1991, and party spokesperson since 1994. He had clashed with the trade unions as Minister for Labour, but he had never been associated either with the dirty war or with financial scandal. Politically, however, Almunia would represent no radical break with the González years. González himself, despite his retirement, continued to cast a giant shadow within the party.

Meanwhile ETA, which had been more violently active than in any year since 1992, suffered a severe blow. For 532 days it had been holding a prison officer, José Antonio Ortega Lara, in miserable conditions, cooped up in a *zulo* not much bigger than a coffin. ETA's condition for his release was the return of its prisoners to jails in the Basque Country.[48] ETA had also been holding a Basque businessman, Cosme Delclaux, in rather better but still grim conditions for 232 days, for ransom.

In a single, extraordinarily dramatic day, all that changed.

At 1.30 a.m. on 1 July, Delclaux was released voluntarily by ETA, after most of his ransom had been paid. Just six hours later, a spectacular and bloodless Guardia Civil operation liberated Ortega Lara, and detained the *etarras* who had been holding him captive. On television that night, he looked as disorientated and cadaverous as a concentration camp victim. These images made a huge impression on the Spanish public.

ETA was angry and frustrated. It had lost a valuable hostage and a key *comando* on the day it should have been celebrating Delclaux's ransom payment. Perhaps 'desperate' would be a more appropriate adjective. An indication of the total disjuncture between the Basque radical's world-view and that of the average citizen was given in the headline which the pro-ETA newspaper *Egin* ran on the day of Ortega Lara's liberation: 'Ortega Lara goes back to prison'. This was not only a cruelly 'humorous' reference to his work as a prison officer – it demonstrated the almost unbridgeable gap between those for whom ETA members were terrorists and kidnappers, and those for whom they were a legitimate 'army of the people'. Nine days later, ETA undertook an operation that changed the nature of the Basque conflict.

DBS Arts Library

Miguel Ángel Blanco was a Partido Popular local councillor in the Basque town of Ermua.[49] He was twenty-nine years old, political small fry but popular in his home town as a football supporter and amateur rock musician. ETA kidnapped him on his way to work on the afternoon of 10 July, and issued an ultimatum: if the government did not return all ETA prisoners to the Basque Country within forty-eight hours, Miguel Ángel Blanco would be shot.

It was a gratuitously cruel demand, because even if the government had found it democratically acceptable to concede, the logistics and time-scale of such an operation were virtually impossible. The response of the Spanish people – particularly of the Basques – was unprecedented. As the deadline approached, 100,000 people demonstrated in Bilbao alone, begging ETA not to carry out its threat.

An hour after the deadline expired, Blanco's body was found in a Guipuzcoan wood, with his hands tied and two bullets in the back of his head. He died some hours later.

During the week that followed, several million Spaniards took to the streets to demonstrate their revulsion at his murder. Bilbao saw protests which were almost certainly bigger than those which had greeted the killing of Santiago Brouard. In the Basque Country as a whole, Herri Batasuna members found themselves facing social isolation, and occasional physical attacks. The dynamic of their 'street struggle' was abruptly reversed. Now it was the radicals who had to walk in fear, and they suffered the humiliation of seeing their premises protected by the *ertzainas* they so often had mocked and attacked. The government, and especially the regional and municipal authorities, were scrupulous in ensuring that an angry people did not take the law into their own hands.

A former leader of the long-dissolved politico-military wing of ETA, Fernando López Castillo, was asked why earlier, though much smaller, popular mobilisations had not led to the dissolution of ETA's military wing in the 1980s. He replied that ETA had maintained popular support in the Basque Country because of 'the GAL's dirty war, ended in 1987, but with social consequences which are still catching up with us today'.[50]

Given its long history of ambiguity about the GAL, one could not expect the Socialist leadership to take such a point of view on board, but one might have expected a modicum of sensitivity on the issue at this time. Yet Felipe González waited only one day after the burial of Miguel Ángel Blanco to raise the GAL issue again in the public mind.

At a second launch for Barrionuevo's book, on 15 July, he addressed the gentlemen on the platform thus: 'Pepe [Barrionuevo], Rafa [Vera], Generals, thank you for what you did for Spain. Today it is my duty to say clearly that I am here to take public responsibility [for your actions], and I want to do this because the burden should not fall on you, you don't deserve that.'[51] The generals he was addressing were Galindo, Sáenz de Santamaría and Manglano. Like Barrionuevo and Vera, they were all embroiled in GAL court cases at the time, though only Galindo would be convicted.

The autumn and winter of 1997 saw further indications of the judicialisation of Spanish politics, and the apparent politicisation of the judiciary. The Supreme Court prosecutor in the Marey case, José María Luzón, took on board every aspect of Moner's investigation, and called for twenty-three-year prison sentences for Barrionuevo and Vera. 'I already knew that this was a political trial, and that the sentence, naturally condemnatory, is already handed down,' was Vera's response. Felipe González said Luzón's timing was linked to the imminent elections in Galicia. He described the case as a 'corrupt set-up' and, in a move that set a lot of alarm bells ringing, threatened to reveal links between the Partido Popular and various coup attempts in the 1980s.[52]

In late October, a number of prominent Socialists received prison sentences from the Supreme Court for the Filesa scandal, in which bogus 'consultancy commissions' had been paid by businesses to illegally finance the party. The new Socialist leader, Joaquín Almunia, immediately complained that similar frauds attributed to the Partido Popular had not been treated so harshly, though he did have the grace to apologise to citizens and voters who might feel that the party had betrayed their confidence.[53] This verdict followed hard on a sharp drop in the Socialist vote in elections to the Galician regional parliament, further denting the party's battered morale.[54]

Other Socialists were not so gracious as Almunia. Alfonso Guerra and José María ('Txiki') Benegas, numbers two and three respectively in the party hierarchy when the Filesa fraud was netting 1,000 million pesetas for the PSOE coffers, dismissed the evidence with the ominous phrase that it had been a 'political trial'.

Javier Pradera, who had so often gone out on a limb in support of unpopular Socialist *policies* in the past, maintained his principled opposition to illegal Socialist *practices*. He concluded a lucid column on the case with this acid comment: 'Some socialists are as incapable of learning from history as the Bourbons were after the French Revolution.'[55] It was a remarkably damaging, and perceptive, analogy from a friend of the party. The dual response that 'others did it too' and 'the PSOE is suffering judicial persecution' would become the twin pillars of the PSOE leadership's reaction to the Marey verdict, as we shall see.

Meanwhile, another – and very different – party was also still being hauled through the courts in late 1997. In December, all twenty-three members of the national committee of Herri Batasuna were sentenced to seven years in prison, again by the Supreme Court, for 'collaboration with terrorism'. This seemed a very severe sentence for the screening of a video in which political proposals were put forward, albeit by armed and hooded men. It was widely interpreted as a punishment to the coalition for its refusal to condemn ETA's killing of Miguel Ángel Blanco, and for the persistent street violence which Herri Batasuna often appeared to encourage. Others interpreted the harshness of the sentence as a prelude to equal severity in the Marey case, in which a degree of political responsibility for terrorism would also be at issue. No one could now accuse the court of being soft on revolutionary terrorism and harsh on state terrorism. However one read the judgement, the jailing of the entire leadership of a legal political party could hardly be treated as a triumph for democracy.[56]

CAUGHT WITH HIS PANTS DOWN: THE SEX VIDEO WHICH PEDRO J. RAMÍREZ ATTRIBUTED TO THE GAL

It was another video, however, which really titillated the jaded Spanish palate for scandal in late 1997. The generic scenes on this tape could be purchased in any Madrid sex shop. A white man, dressed as a woman, murmurs adoringly to a black woman, dressed as a dominatrix: 'Oh, you're going to pee on me, what a thrill!'

The visual and aural quality, though, would have been much better in professional pornography, and the actors would have been familiar only to a small circle of 'specialists'. In this case, the quality was fuzzy and the male protagonist was well known to the general public. Over the summer of 1997, this video went into circulation, very discreetly at first. By the autumn, the video began to arrive, unsolicited, with the regular mail of influential people in the Spanish media and politics. And in case the focus on the face of the male lead was not sharp enough, the video was accompanied by a helpful note from the dominatrix.

This woman, Exuperancia Rapú, assured recipients of the tape that her partner was none other than Pedro J. Ramírez, editor of *El Mundo*. It was not an image that flattered a man who liked to pose at Holy Week processions with the very Catholic leader of the Partido Popular and his equally devout first lady. One Socialist leader, Joaquín Leguina, could not resist gloating publicly on this topic from the pages of *El País*.[57]

At first the video was thought to be a particularly nasty piece of blackmail, or simply vengeful character assassination. Ramírez, often known simply as 'Pedro J.', had plenty of enemies. Many of them were in the Socialist Party. They reminded him, every time they formally condemned the intrusion into his privacy, that he had himself been guilty of intruding into the privacy of others.[58]

However, his real sin, as far as these Socialists were concerned, was to have investigated Socialist corruption and the dirty war. Leguina himself made this quite explicit when he compared the publication of the editor's erotic predilections with *El Mundo*'s publication of the CESID papers. As had become characteristic in such matters, the Socialists had their categories hopelessly confused here. Pedro J.'s sex life was of no public interest; documents which linked military intelligence with the death squads certainly were.

Ramírez decided that the best means of defence was attack. He is probably the first national newspaper editor to run a front-page story in which the central element was his own extracurricular amours.

The day after Leguina's article appeared, an *El Mundo* headline described the filming and diffusion of the video as 'The latest attack of the GAL'. It was all a grotesque plot, said the newspaper's investigative journalists Manuel Cerdán and Antonio Rubio, set up by Rafael Vera to damage the man who had done so much to bring the GAL to light.

Ramírez had already had Rapú locked up on charges of invasion of privacy. (She had allowed an accomplice to film them from inside a wardrobe.) He now managed to get Judge Javier Gómez de Liaño to take up the case, on the grounds that it was related to the dirty war.

This gave the investigation a very high national profile at the Audiencia Nacional. Rapú began to name names, which appeared to reveal a network of conspirators including Rafael Vera, José Ramón Goñi Tirapu (a Socialist leader very publicly supportive of GAL suspects) and two former government advisors. Initially, Rapú endorsed *El Mundo*'s interpretation of events. Within a month, however, the case had been returned to a local Madrid jurisdiction, where Vera's involvement is still under investigation.[59]

Meanwhile, the Socialists enjoyed a fiesta of *schadenfreude* with this story. Even González made sly references to journalists about 'golden showers'. The polarisation of Spanish society was coarsening public debate into crude and vicious abuse.

Dirty wars much bloodier than the GAL's were meanwhile coming to the attention of the Spanish courts, in developments which would have major national and international repercussions. Relatives of the thousands of victims of torture and 'disappearances' under the Chilean and Argentinian dictatorships had approached Spanish investigating magistrates to see whether these crimes could be tried under Spanish jurisdiction. Some judges, among them Baltasar Garzón, thought they could be, both under international laws against torture, war crimes and genocide, and on the grounds that some of the victims had been Spanish citizens.

The Partido Popular-appointed chief prosecutor at the Audiencía Nacional, Eduardo Fungairiño, disagreed, as did the Attorney General, Jesús Cardenal. A single paragraph from Fungairiño's December 1997 report on the subject, backed by Cardenal, sparked a controversy which resulted in a parliamentary row that revealed how deep and complex the fractures in Spanish society had become.

Fungairiño argued that the Argentinian military, in seizing power illegally, had 'only sought the temporary substitution of the established constitutional order through an institutional intervention which aimed . . . to remedy the inadequacies of that constitutional order and maintain the public peace'. On the face of it, this was nothing less than a legal defence of military dictatorship in defence of public order.[60] Such a statement, from such an authority, would have provoked a furore in any democracy. In Spain, where the Partido Popular and the PSOE had diametrically opposed views on Franco's military rebellion against the Republic, it was bound to reopen raw wounds.[61]

In January 1998, the Socialists led the charge against Fungairiño and Cardenal in parliament, supported by the United Left. The Partido Popular supported its appointees, with some reservations. That much could have been expected. The surprise came from the moderate Basque Nationalist Party, which could hardly be accused of any nostalgia for fascism. It voted with the government to block the PSOE protest. The party argued that it could not accept any lessons on democracy and dirty wars abroad from the Socialists, as long as that party was defending a leader accused of masterminding death squads in the Basque Country.

The Basque Nationalist Party's Joxe Juan González de Txabarri challenged the PSOE thus: 'Now that you are so worried about dirty wars, I think you should look at comparative law. How do you make an Interior Minister, later made Transport Minister, now a member of this permanent parliamentary committee, into a senator for life?'[62] This was a direct comparison of Barrionuevo, whom the PSOE had consistently maintained in legally privileged parliamentary positions since the GAL investigations had begun, with Chile's General Augusto Pinochet, who had just organised for himself the legally privileged position of lifelong senator. The degree to which the GAL controversy had sent fissures through Spanish democracy had rarely been more dramatically illustrated.

The Socialists seemed to be losing their natural allies, but they found an unnatural one in February. Luis María Ansón had edited *ABC* from shortly after the PSOE came to power in 1982 until shortly after its 1996 exit, and had made the conservative newspaper a bastion of 'antifelipismo'. He had been repeatedly identified by the PSOE as one of the prime movers of the media–judicial–political grouping which it alleged had conspired undemocratically to undermine González.

Now, in a magazine interview, he said it was all true.[63] A cabal of print and radio journalists, including Ansón and the ubiquitous Pedro J. Ramírez, decided, after González's fourth (and unexpected) election victory in 1993, that exceptional means were necessary to ensure that the opposition had a chance to exercise power. The method chosen was to ruthlessly publicise the PSOE's corruption and dirty war scandals, and thus to polarise public opinion until González was no longer an acceptable leader to a majority of Spaniards. Crucially, from the Socialist point of view, he accepted in the interview that there were aspects of this strategy which 'affected the stability of the State'.

Meanwhile, *El País* published, not once but twice, a much more embellished account of the conspiracy by Ansón.[64] According to the paper, he had given this version ten months previously, over lunch, to the three Socialist leaders Barrionuevo, Vera and José Luis Corcuera. *El País* did not explain why these men, who apparently claimed to have taped the conversation, had not published it immediately, since it put the banker Mario Conde at the head of the conspiracy. Moreover, Ansón allegedly told the Socialists that Conde's aim was to eliminate the party political system in Spain, using the judiciary and the media as his tools. Were this version accurate, the conspiracy had a much more threatening aspect for Spanish democracy than a huddle of anti-González journalists, however influential they might be.

Conde immediately denied the allegations, though, with an ambiguity worthy of González, he added: 'If I had had the historic opportunity to do it, I would have done it.' But he made a sharp point against PSOE claims that the Socialists had lost the election because of the conspiracy. 'Shut up, for fuck's sake, they [the people] didn't vote for you. Don't come along now telling us a story that they didn't vote for you because five gentlemen decided that they shouldn't. Because, if that story is true, you look pretty small in the world.'[65]

That, however, was exactly what the Socialists argued. Even José Borrell, the shining white hope of many PSOE reformers, made this case. He warned that Spanish democracy 'is undermined by very powerful forces prepared to do anything they think necessary, and these forces brought the Partido Popular to power'.[66]

This was surely to stand things on their head. If the PSOE leadership had either tolerated or directed state terrorism, and if many of its most senior appointees had pocketed huge sums of public money, the Socialists had delegitimised themselves from governing, without any help from the media, the judiciary, disgruntled bankers or the opposition. A further PSOE argument was more topsy-turvy still. Some leaders suggested that the media 'plot' to bring down González cast doubt on the validity of the Partido Popular's subsequent election victory. This was an extraordinary distortion of the facts, and itself a potential threat to democracy.[67]

The controversy led to an interesting exchange on radio between Ansón and Ramírez on whether or not revelations on PSOE scandals had put the state itself at risk. Ansón argued that when 'journalists hold a mirror up to these State crimes, they not only tarnish the image of the person who allegedly committed them, they also damage the State'. Ramírez countered: 'It seems to me that the opposite is true: by showing the seriousness of these crimes in the mirror [of the press], we contribute to strengthening and giving democratic authenticity to that State. Neither criticism nor the revelation of the truth can ever be considered as an attack on the State.'[68]

Leaving aside the issue of whether Ramírez had sensationalised or even falsified his paper's presentation of some of the scandals in question, the argument between the two men is a prime example of the incompatibility of two ancient legal proverbs: *Let the welfare of the people be the supreme law*,[69] represented by Ansón, and *Let justice be done though the heavens should fall*,[70] articulated by Ramírez.

Meanwhile, regardless of the pundits and the politicians, the law was now inexorably taking its course in the Marey case. In March, the Supreme Court, as expected, set aside the defendants' appeals that the statute of limitations for the crimes they were accused of had expired. It left open the possibility, however, that this argument could be considered again during the final phase of the oral hearing, scheduled for early summer. This meant that the court would determine responsibility for the crimes, though the judges might still accept, if guilt was established, that too much time had elapsed to punish those responsible.

The other outstanding questions were whether Felipe González should be called as a witness to the oral hearing, as demanded by the prosecution, and whether Álvarez Cascos, and even Aznar, should also be called, as demanded by the defence.

González and the Socialists had kept Álvarez Cascos's contacts with Amedo, Domínguez and Ramírez in the public eye, and had drip-fed the press with fragments of manuscripts and tape transcripts of alleged conversations between them about a pardon. Though these 'documents' do not establish that Álvarez Cascos ever suggested that Amedo and Domínguez should invent accusations about the PSOE in exchange for benevolent penal treatment, Barrionuevo and Vera argued that he, and Aznar, should be questioned about the anti-Socialist 'conspiracy' at the trial.[71]

On 21 April, both sides got their answer. González and Álvarez Cascos would both be called as witnesses, but Aznar would not.

Just two days later, González returned to the attack against Álvarez Cascos. The occasion he chose was a meeting during the internal 'primary' campaign to choose the new prime ministerial candidate of the Socialist Party.[72] This was an innovative idea for the PSOE, based on the primary system in US presidential elections. The two candidates were Joaquín Almunia, backed by González, and José Borrell. Many who had lost their faith in the party hoped that Borrell, though a former minister of González's, would point the party towards renewal and the future, a month before the Marey trial was likely to drag them back towards the unsavoury past.

Certainly, González's speech at Almunia's final rally was still obsessed with settling old scores. Claiming that Álvarez Cascos had had at least one further meeting with Amedo's lawyer *after* he had become deputy Prime Minister, González accused him baldly of 'lying' to parliament on the issue. In a series of obscure but vitriolic threats and innuendoes, the former Prime Minister continued: 'that rabid dog [Álvarez Cascos] knows everything about the secret services, and he knows what I know, and I can say that he lied yesterday, but it is going to cost him dearly if he continues lying'.

This might have seemed like the last throw of yesterday's man, but Almunia chose to echo him. 'The Socialist government has been persecuted savagely by a gang who only know how to live by lying,' he told his supporters.[73]

Perhaps the Socialists' more rational supporters could take some comfort from the fact that, against the odds, and against the wishes of the party's grandees[74] and González loyalists, Borrell won the election and became the party's prime ministerial candidate. Almunia, however, remained general secretary, and therefore retained control of the party's formidable bureaucracy. This 'two-headed' leadership arrangement made it difficult for Borrell to implement any decisive changes. In any case, the upcoming Marey trial and its aftermath would show that the more things changed in the Socialist Party, the more they would remain the same.

NOTES

1   Author's court notes, 9 June 1998.
2   José Jiménez Villarejo, in his dissenting opinion on the Segundo Marey verdict, with Gregorio García Ancos, Voto Particular de D José Jiménez Villarejo y D Gregorio García Ancos, Causa Especial No. 2530/95 [Segundo Marey], Supreme Court, Madrid, 29 July 1998, p. 15.
3   José María Brunet, in *La Vanguardia,* 10 June 1998.
4   The title of Liam O'Flaherty's classic novel of betrayal in the IRA, *The Informer,* in Spanish is *El Delator*, the word used in court by Barrionuevo.
5   As we saw in ch. 18, the case had to be transferred to the higher court as soon as a member of parliament was directly implicated.
6   *El País,* 11 September 1995.
7   *El País,* 17 September 1995.
8   Interview with Rafael Vera, Madrid, November 1997.

9   *El País*, 8 September 1995. They found that the unsubstantiated allegations of Damborenea against González, unsupported by any other proof barring a 'vague allusion' of Sancristóbal's, were insufficient to warrant charges. They made a similar point about the accusations against Serra and Benegas.

10 See González interview with Iñaki Gabilondo, RTVE, 9 January 1995, quoted in ch. 18, pp. 263–6. González had accepted that the government was implicated in the actions of its ministers, though he of course insisted that Barrionuevo was innocent.

11 *El País*, 14 December 1995.

12 *El País*, 19 December 1995.

13 This point was forcibly made in an *El País* editorial, 'Tribal dinner', on 20 December 1995.

14 *El País*, 21 December 1995. The occasion was a press conference with the President of Brazil, Fernando Henrique Cardoso.

15 We have already seen, in ch. 21, how the Partido Popular spoke with this second voice, once in power, in the debate as to whether the CESID papers should be released.

16 *El País*, 20 January 1996.

17 *El País*, 27 January 1996.

18 *El País*, 28 January 1996.

19 *'Desacato'*, contempt or disrespect for a duly constituted authority, is an offence under Spanish law.

20 *El País*, 29 January 1996. González later denied that he had made this comment on the Supreme Court, though his words had been transmitted to the press by official party spokespersons. The comment, González claimed, had been made by Joaquín Almunia, and he had intervened to ask for respect for the judiciary. Even before the PSOE attacked him, Moner had, in any case, put his investigation more or less on hold until after the March elections.

21 *El País*, 3 June 1996.

22 Amedo told Moner that he had been funded by Basque businessmen, and not by reserved funds, though Domínguez stuck to his original version of events (*El País*, 22 and 23 March 1996); then Domínguez said he had had unofficial meetings with Garzón prior to making his December 1994 statements, and that he suffered terrible, though unspecified, pressure to make those statements. *El País*, 31 May 1996.

23 *El País*, 1 May 1996.

24 *El País*, 26 April 1996.

25 *El Mundo*, 27 June 1996. Showing remarkable faith in his fellow man, Barrionuevo chose just this moment to offer his services as a personal lawyer to Julen Elgorriaga, imprisoned for the Lasa and Zabala case. He claimed to have been offering similar services to Sancristóbal at the time the phone conversation was taped, though Sancristóbal had always insisted that their relationship was purely that of friends and former colleagues, and not that of lawyer and client.

26 *El País*, 20 July 1996.

27 *El Mundo*, 29 July 1996.

28 *El País*, 6 June 1996.

29 A reference to the victims of pre-GAL death squads.

30 *El País*, 27 September 1996.

31 Nor, of course, was it true that democrats had universally applauded Bush and Clinton for their 'anti-terrorist' bombings of Libya and Iraq.

32 *El País*, 27 September 1996.

33 *El País*, 30 September 1996.

34 Ibid.

35 *El País*, 5 and 6 November 1996.

36 *El País*, 10 January 1997.

37 Both were appointed in May 1997. These moves were accompanied by the government's toleration of acts of 'indiscipline' by a group of Audiencia Nacional prosecutors considered close to the Partido Popular.

38 See ch. 20, p. 310, n. 29.

39 *El País*, 5 April 1997.

40 *El País,* 18 June 1998. Javier Gómez de Liaño was heavily sanctioned by his peers for his conduct in this case.

41 *El País*, 8 May 1997.

42 *El País*, 10 May 1997.

43 *El País*, 11 May 1997.

44 González's emphasis. He sometimes described attempts to implicate him in the GAL as a sort of negative photo-opportunity for the PSOE, and used the phrase again when he was photographed at the gates of Guadalajara prison in September 1998 as Barrionuevo was going to jail. See ch. 24, p. 399.

45 *El Mundo*, 4 June 1997.

46 The foreword was included in reprints of the book.

47 *El País*, 5 June 1997.

48 The government was maintaining the policy, well established by the Socialists, of 'dispersing' ETA prisoners to many jails across Spain. The policy was supposed to weaken the capacity of the prisoners to organise politically and encourage individuals to renounce their militancy. Its objective result was a great deal of hardship for their families and friends, who had to make punishing round trips of up to 2,000 km to visit them.

49 The same town where Julián Sancristóbal had been mayor in 1979.

50 *El País*, 14 July 1997.

51 *El Mundo*, 16 July 1997.

52 *El País*, 17 October 1997.

53 See *El País* and *El Mundo*, 28 and 29 October 1997. The issue of the funding of political parties has been a central cause of corruption in many countries where there is no agreed method of adequately financing political activity. In Spain, the Partido Popular, PSOE, PNV and Catalan nationalists were all mired in funding scandals – and the Communist Party was alleged to be in receipt of 'Moscow gold'. Almunia has a point, in that the Partido Popular got off on a technicality in the most serious case affecting it. But his attitude smacks of a refusal to fully accept legitimate judicial decisions.

54 The PSOE could take some comfort from the fact that the Partido Popular also slipped a little. The real winners were the left-wing nationalists of the Bloque Nacional Galego. See *El País*, 20 October 1996.

55 *El País*, 2 November 1997.

56 It also seemed to indicate that the Spanish authorities, political and judicial, were moving in the opposite direction to the peace process in Northern Ireland, where Sinn Féin was being encouraged to participate in the institutions of state.

57 *El País*, 15 November 1997.

58 The Supreme Court had found Ramírez guilty in 1993 of 'violating the intimacy' of the businessman José María Ruiz-Mateos and the wife of a business partner, when his former newspaper, *Diario 16*, had falsely reported they were having an affair. See *El País*, 20 November 1997.

59 In April 2000, the state prosecutor dropped all charges against Vera in this case. But the private prosecutor (representing Ramírez) was still calling for his indictment at the time of writing.

60 *El País*, 17 December 1997. As Cardenal pointed out in Fungairiño's defence, there were other points in the report in which he made his revulsion at the

army's actual behaviour, once in power, very clear. Nonetheless, the central argument could hardly be sustained by any democratic jurist.

61 As recently as August 1999, the Partido Popular could not bring itself to condemn Franco's uprising when the PSOE and the United Left presented a motion in parliament.

62 *El País*, 21 January 1998.

63 *Tiempo*, 16 February 1998.

64 *El País*, 15 and 22 February 1998. According to *El País*'s version of events, Ansón claimed he had participated in the conspiracy only to control it from within and prevent it from taking an undemocratic form.

65 *El País*, 20 and 21 February 1998.

66 *El País*, 21 February 1998.

67 This very dangerous argument, that the Partido Popular government's democratic legitimacy was somehow undermined by Ansón's revelations, was made in some surprising quarters, including a column by the usually sober and deeply critical historian of the PSOE, Santos Juliá. The new PSOE leader, Joaquín Almunia, and José Borrell argued that they were not actually challenging the 1996 election result, but many of their followers were not so discriminating. See *El País*, 22 February 1998.

68 *El País*, 17 February 1998.

69 *Salus populi suprema est lex*, Cicero, *De Legibus,* III, iii.

70 *Fiat justitia, ruat caelum.*

71 In a further twist to the conspiracy theory, the United Left accused both the Partido Popular and PSOE of having made a pact, behind the smokescreen of belligerent hostility, to ultimately cover up all the events of the dirty war, to their mutual advantage. See *El País*, 23 April 1998.

72 Joaquín Almunia had replaced González as PSOE general secretary, but many party members doubted whether he was up to the job of parliamentary opposition leader and prime ministerial candidate in the next elections. The general secretaryship did not automatically confer these other roles.

73 *El País*, 24 April 1998.

74 The party's 'barons' were in fact divided between those who supported González and his protégé Almunia, and those who backed the more radical rhetoric of González's disillusioned former deputy, Alfonso Guerra. Both groups, however, closed ranks firmly against demands for a transparent approach to the party's history in government. So, as we shall see, did José Borrell.

23

A Minister in the Dock:
justice for Segundo Marey?

*Don't tell my mother that I'm the Interior Minister: she thinks
I work as a piano player in a brothel.*
> Rosa Montero, columnist and novelist, July 1996[1]

I, too, am Barrionuevo.
> Solidarity badge adopted by Socialist MPs before the trial.

I, too, am Marey.
> Badge adopted in response by Communist deputies

*Everything that is happening is a dirty settling of political
scores disguised as a judicial process.*
> José Barrionuevo, 23 May 1998[2]

*I am convinced of the innocence of Barrionuevo. And I always
will be, whatever happens.*
> Manuel Chaves, 23 May 1998[3]

*If the judges establish responsibility at whatever level, I will
take the responsibility which corresponds to me.*
> Felipe González, 9 January 1995[4]

*[I regret that] they have put the Supreme Court in a situation
whose origin is a political operation . . . this is a tactic to gain
spurious power, whose beneficiary is ETA, because [the trial]
gives ETA legitimacy. The country, and the government which
has allowed this to happen, will pay for it.*
> Felipe González, 21 May 1998[5]

*The trial has connotations which are not strictly related to
crime, [but I reaffirm] my confidence in justice, and in the
innocence of José Barrionuevo.*
> José Borrell, 24 May 1996[6]

The primary reality is that an armed group, linked to the State apparatus, kidnapped and tortured Segundo Marey. All attempts, therefore, to continue politicising the trial should be rejected.

El País, editorial, 25 May 1996

The investigation of the Segundo Marey case has been accompanied from the start by notorious interferences by four well-known personalities: Mario Conde, Juan Alberto Perote, Pedro J. Ramírez and Francisco Álvarez Cascos. We maintain our absolute confidence in the innocence of José Barrionuevo and Rafael Vera and we base that confidence on their personal and political records. We offer them our solidarity, hoping that our belief in their innocence will be corroborated by the Supreme Court.

Statement by PSOE executive, 25 May 1996[7]

I don't make any comments on decisions which are the prerogative of the courts; I have never done so and I am not going to do so now.

Francisco Álvarez Cascos, 23 May 1998[8]

Public opinion is clearer with every day about the verdict on the GAL case, and therefore, with every passing day, the sentence which the judges hand down is important for the reputation of justice, so that the Spanish justice system gains prestige among its own citizens. Because, insofar as the court's decision, the sentence, does not correspond to the verdict of the citizens in the light of the facts which have been established, it is the justice [system] itself which is going to lose out.

Francisco Álvarez Cascos, September 1995[9]

An insinuating hand grasped my elbow as I passed through the enormous green-and-gold double doors of the Second Chamber of the Supreme Court for the first time. I turned to find José Amedo grinning wolfishly, obviously in his element.

'Enjoy yourself in there!' he said in a stage whisper, and moved on. He was accused of kidnapping an innocent man and organising a death squad, but he was treating his trial as public entertainment.

His greeting was characteristically cynical, but not entirely inappropriate. There is, of course, something highly theatrical about all courtrooms and all trials, though the ritual element in the Spanish Supreme Court is surprisingly low key. The judges do not wear wigs, and their robes are simple, with only their elaborate lace cuffs lending a sense of archaic formality to the scene. The defendants sit in chairs with tall backs, upholstered in red leather, rather as if they were attending an academic conference in a somewhat fusty university.

There is something collegiate, too, about the atmosphere in the great halls which lead to the court chamber. I had arrived early on my first morning at the trial, so early that I was the first journalist upstairs. We reached the upper halls via a lift, but the main players, including the defendants, had the option of proceeding up the great double staircase, with its gleaming bronze banisters, from the main entrance. Huge murals of busty peasant women wielding sickles, and muscular workers in smokestack landscapes, give an incongruously 'socialist realist' touch to the cupola above the stairs.

The court chambers are built around a spacious garden courtyard, where a fountain and roses manage to suggest a tranquillity that is unlikely to be reflected inside the walls. The halls gleam with deep red and blindingly white marble in the morning sunlight, peopled at this early stage by only a few policemen and court officials.

Gradually, the protagonists begin to gather. Ricardo García Damborenea, lean and solitary, his long face permanently crumpled in a wry, gruff grin, strides into view, a mobile phone glued to his ear as he paces the corridors. Rafael Vera, fit, suave and debonair as ever, contrasts sharply with his lawyer, Manuel Cobo del Rosal, whose fat, slack-skinned face looks yellowish under his thick and wavy mane of white hair. Damborenea lopes within a yard of them, but there is no hint of recognition. It was the seventh day of the trial, and deadly enemies, perhaps especially those who had once been close friends, had become expert in gracefully dancing around each other. The Herri Batasuna lawyer Kepa Landa, representing the people's prosecution in the interests of GAL victims, has small, intense, glittering eyes, but they never make contact with those of the men accused of setting up the death squads.

Two anonymous-looking men in dark suits move unobtrusively down the corridor with a taller, more forceful-looking figure with a salt-and-pepper beard between them. This is Francisco Álvarez, chief of police in Bilbao at the time of the kidnapping, and self-confessed expert on the different branches of the GAL. I suddenly realise that the slimmer and neater of the two men beside him is Julián Sancristóbal, whom I have not seen in the flesh for nearly twenty years. I raise a hand in diffident greeting, and he disengages himself from his comrades and greets me warmly, like the friend he once was. In this bizarre context, we both may have instinctively realised that a neutral handshake is more appropriate than a traditional Spanish embrace.

We chat easily, using irony about changed times and greying hair to pass over a situation where one of us is accused of state terrorism and the other is writing about it. He promises, as he will several times over the next few days, to talk about more substantial matters when the trial is over, and excuses himself to rejoin Álvarez. I now recognise the third man in his party as Miguel Planchuelo, the police officer who replaced Álvarez in Bilbao police headquarters. At the time of the Marey kidnapping, Planchuelo had been directing regional anti-terrorist intelligence in the Basque Country. When Sancristóbal was appointed Director of State Security early the following year, Álvarez had followed him to Madrid to run the Intelligence and Special Operations

Committee (GAIOE), just as the GAL were really getting into their stride in early 1984. Planchuelo had then replaced Álvarez as police chief in Bilbao. It is tempting to suggest an aura of evil about these men. But they do not look monstrous at all, unless it is monstrous to look banal. They look like discreetly successful entrepreneurs at a convention, with serious business to discuss.

The halls have now filled up considerably, with lawyers, journalists and police. Everyone seems to be smoking, chewing gum or using mobile phones. Most of the men wear dark suits. A lot of them have the unnerving habit of wearing very dark sunglasses indoors. Many of the women wear light summer clothes, and some casually fix each other's hair, oblivious to their austere surroundings. There is a subdued but unmistakable whiff of sex and blood in the air, like before a bullfight.

The arrival of Olga Tubau, Segundo Marey's severely dressed French Basque barrister, is a reminder that, if this is an entertainment, kidnapping and something tantamount to torture are on the programme. Nearby, a man who bears a striking resemblance to the Ringo Starr of the post–Beatles period, with long, slicked-down rocker's hair, a beard and impenetrable shades, hovers uncertainly. He is Luis Hens, one of the police inspectors who guarded Marey in the cabin where he was held captive. The following week, he will make one of the few gracious and humane gestures of this whole wretched trial, along with his colleague José Ramón Corujo, by voluntarily apologising to Marey face to face.

Nearby, Amedo's former sidekick, Michel Domínguez, looks younger than I had expected, and good-looking in a vacuous sort of way. Unlike his mentor, he shuns publicity, and wears a motor-cycle helmet as he comes into the building, each morning, to foil photographers.

José Barrionuevo, tanned but tense, has joined Vera and Cobo del Rosal. There is *bonhomie* in their banter, but, unsurprisingly, it looks forced. Across the great stairwell balcony, I catch a glimpse of a vaguely familiar figure scrutinising the assembly, taking it all in. His back is to the sunniest window, the position a policeman, or a terrorist, would instinctively choose, so that it is impossible to make out his features. Only when a cloud briefly obscures the sun does the figure reveal itself as José Amedo, waiting for the curtain to rise on another episode of the drama he has done so much to make his own.

Suddenly, from chambers somewhere up the corridor, the eleven magistrates hearing the case sweep through, including a John Thaw lookalike I later identify as Enrique Bacigalupo Zapater. The double doors open briefly, offering a glimpse of the red velvet finery inside. A few moments later they open again and the rest of us flow in together. Defendants, witnesses, lawyers, journalists and public are briefly all one body which, just as suddenly, divides again into its clearly defined component parts.

In the last chapter we looked at one of the more dramatic exchanges of this third week of the trial, the *careos* between Barrionuevo, Sancristóbal and Damborenea, when the former Interior Minister let the fatal word *informer* fall on the courtroom floor. It will be easiest to grasp the narrative of the whole trial if at this point we return to the beginning, treating the courtroom drama as a series of weekly acts, with daily scenes.[10]

WEEK ONE
Day One: Monday, 25 May
Domínguez's pardon, Amedo's shoes

Amedo and Domínguez opened the proceedings by ratifying the evidence they had already given to judges Baltasar Garzón and Eduardo Moner, though Domínguez repeated his allegation that Garzón had 'pressurised' and threatened him. At one point he said that a prosecutor had said to Garzón, in front of him, '[if Amedo and Dominguez don't] finish off the Socialist government, they are going to be really hammered'.[11] However, he then qualified this revelation by adding 'but I don't say that they threatened me to give any evidence which was not true'. He also confirmed contacts between himself, his lawyer Jorge Manrique, *El Mundo* editor Pedro J. Ramírez and Partido Popular deputy leader Francisco Álvarez Cascos, which he claimed had resulted in Álvarez Cascos's promising that the Partido Popular would 'study the question' of a pardon for them if the party won the 1996 election. Given that the PSOE had already publicly considered pardoning them on several occasions, this hardly amounted to an improper offer, since Domínguez did not say that Álvarez Cascos linked it to the incrimination of the PSOE leadership.

Amedo gave his usual polished and slithery courtroom performance. Questioned about the manuscript in which he had allegedly made similar allegations to Domínguez's about manipulation of their evidence by Garzón, he said: 'Obviously it looks like my writing, but I don't know if it is authentic.'[12] He denied ever having met Álvarez Cascos, but added 'I know that my lawyer has had meetings with many people.'[13]

He could recall, however, a phone conversation with Barrionuevo in 1987, when he and Domínguez were first coming under pressure about GAL allegations. The minister told him, he claimed, 'that I shouldn't worry, that we were all in this together. That he was supported by the President of the government [Felipe González] and that we were going to win this war.'[14] He attributed every aspect of the Marey kidnapping, no matter how insignificant, to 'the top brass in the Interior Ministry', to a point of absurdity where he appeared to be parodying his own evidence. Perhaps his true character showed most sharply when he was asked why he had never gone down the rough mountain path to the cabin where Marey was being held, though he had met the men guarding Marey on the road nearby every day throughout the kidnapping. 'I didn't want to spoil my shoes,' he told the prosecution lawyers.[15]

Day Two: Tuesday, 26 May
High-quality beans and a crime as big as a castle

Julio Hierro, one of the other police superintendents who admitted taking part in the kidnap, told the court that Francisco Álvarez had told him that Marey was 'a very important ETA prisoner' and that his 'very special method of imprisonment' was a 'question of State'. His colleague Francisco Saiz Oceja tried to implicate Marey more directly with ETA, claiming that he worked in the Sokoa co-operative, where 'he who was not a member of ETA was a sympathiser'. This attempt to make the victim of the kidnapping into some sort of legitimate target would become a familiar defence tactic during the hearing.

Luis Hens and José Ramón Corujo, more junior officers involved in actually guarding Marey in the cabin, were more sympathetic towards their erstwhile captive. But they became ludicrous in their attempts to make out that the miserable cabin was a kind of penal Hilton, citing the provision of high-quality canned beans, even though Marey had been too frightened to eat for the ten days he was held.[16] Asked if he would have agreed to detain Marey for a longer period than that permitted by the (extremely broad) provisions of the anti-terrorist legislation, Corujo affected to be horrified by the very suggestion: 'My goodness, that would have been a crime as big as a castle, and I would never have done it.'[17]

Day Three: Wednesday, 27 May
The informer's bargain and González's helping hand
The next defendant called, moving up the chain of command, was Miguel Planchuelo, the first of the senior officers to have confessed to Garzón. His evidence of the phone calls from Vera and Barrionuevo to Sancristóbal on the night of the kidnapping was clumsy and contradictory. He was more lucid about a more recent conversation with Barrionuevo. He claimed that, on one of the former minister's regular visits to him while he was remanded in custody before he had admitted his involvement in the GAL, he had made him a promise: 'The minister told me that he was ready to take responsibility [for the kidnapping] at a press conference. He said that Señor Vera would do the same, and that Señor Sancristóbal would speak out in third place. Moreover, he added: "Well, if Felipe [González] wants to give us a helping hand, so much the better."'[18]

Planchuelo's evidence probably did more damage to the image of anti-terrorist police methods than it did to the former Prime Minister. He described how he, as head of intelligence for anti-terrorist activities in Bilbao, took up an offer from Pedro Sánchez to kidnap a man the mercenary claimed was 'important', but could not even name. When Planchuelo had demurred, Sánchez had threatened to offer the same potential victim to 'other [security] services'.[19] Planchuelo then showed him some photographs of suspects. Purely on the basis that Sánchez thought he could identify his potential target as the senior *etarra* Mikel Lujua, Planchuelo gave the go-ahead for the kidnap.

Someone in Barrionuevo's entourage was heard to say, as they left the court: 'What we deserve is a life sentence for having chosen officers like these to help us.'[20]

INTERLUDE
While the court was in recess over the next few days, Barrionuevo made another offer to incriminate himself, if it would exonerate the other defendants. This time, Felipe González offered to do the same: 'If it were possible to resolve situations as absurd as the one that has been set up here, well, I would also do it, of course.'[21] For many observers it was his offer, rhetorically generous but legally meaningless, which was absurd, and not the trial.

WEEK TWO
Day Four: Monday, 1 June
Obvious even to a child: the theory of the dirty war

'The brilliant idea that if the terrorists, those upright citizens, are in France, then you have to go there and catch them before they continue killing innocent people in Spain, that would occur even to a child . . . the President of the government could also work that out all on his own.'[22]

Ricardo García Damborenea, the ex-Socialist leader who had once said that he would be 'honoured' to be considered the ideologue of the dirty war,[23] had his day in court accusing Felipe González of supporting the GAL. But his evidence was no more specific than his previous declarations, which was precisely the testimony that had failed to convince the Supreme Court to bring charges against the former Prime Minister. His account of Barrionuevo's phone call to Sancristóbal, while more immediate, was based on what he had overheard and deduced from Sancristóbal's comments.

He admitted drafting one of the GAL's communiqués, but strongly denied any part in the one sent to the Red Cross, which offered to liberate Marey in exchange for the release of the Spanish police in prison in France for the José María Larretxea kidnapping. There was a strong legal argument for his stance: illegal detention carried only a ten-year sentence; kidnapping (illegal detention plus setting conditions for the detainee's release) carried fifteen. More important still, the statute of limitations on illegal detention had expired, so that even if found guilty, Damborenea would not have to go to jail. A conviction for kidnapping, however, would still put him inside.

Like Damborenea and Planchuelo, former police chief Francisco Álvarez told the court of overhearing the phone call Barrionuevo made to Sancristóbal the night of the kidnapping. Like Planchuelo, while admitting his own responsibility for Marey's 'detention',[24] he insisted that he, and his subordinates, had thought they were acting within the law. 'We acted as police, rightly or wrongly; that will be decided by this court. But we never formed part of anything, of any group or organisation.'[25]

This was a different Álvarez to the man who had told Judge Garzón about the organisational structure of the GAL, complete with colour codes.[26] But Álvarez did not want a conviction for membership of an armed gang. For a similar reason, he denied drafting the GAL's communiqués. The defendants' 'collaboration with the justice system' was clearly limited by both what that justice system could prove against them and what penalties they faced on conviction. These were not repentant men committed to clarifying their crimes. This made the judges' task of sifting the whole truth from self-interested half-truth very difficult indeed.

Day Five: Tuesday, 2 June
Where politics meets the police: cash in a briefcase and a resonant name for the operation

As Civil Governor of Vizcaya, Julián Sancristóbal was both a political appointee and the highest link in the chain of command between the Bilbao police and the Interior Ministry in Madrid. In his evidence, which was strong on first-hand detail, he set up a clear parallel between the attempted kidnapping of José María Larretxea, for which Barrionuevo had accepted responsibility, and the kidnapping of Segundo Marey. In both cases, he insisted, Barrionuevo and Vera 'were kept regularly informed by me . . . [W]ithout the support of Interior, it would have been absolutely impossible to have carried out [these operations].'[27]

Sancristóbal said that, after the failure of the Larretxea operation, he had gone to Madrid to discuss the kidnapping of 'a leader of ETA-militar' with Vera and Barrionuevo. He got their 'support and authorisation', but they had advised him to use mercenaries rather than police on the French side of the border on this occasion.[28] He said that Vera had advanced him a million francs (in cash, in a briefcase) from reserved funds for the operation.

He ratified his first-hand account of phone calls from both Vera and Barrionuevo on the night of the kidnapping. He admitted that it was he who had chosen the name GAL from several suggestions 'because it was the most resonant'. However, like his colleagues, he denied any part in the GAL communiqué to the Red Cross demanding the release of the Spanish police in France as a condition for freeing Marey. This contradicted his own testimony earlier in the investigation.

The ten defendants who admitted the facts charged against them, ranging from junior policemen to the anti-terrorist top brass, had now given evidence.[29] They had all, with varying degrees of precision and conviction, accused their superiors, Vera and Barrionuevo, of approving the operation. They had failed to provide any material evidence to support this allegation. But they had certainly given the court a 'coherent account of the facts' – a necessary but not sufficient requirement of proof under Spanish law – regarding the kidnapping of Marey. It remained for Vera and Barrionuevo to give their versions.

Day Six: Wednesday, 3 June
Within the limits of legality: abduction, interrogation and lying to the courts
Rafael Vera denied any hand, act or part in the kidnapping of Marey, but he was surprisingly expansive on his role in the kidnapping of Larretxea. His instructions in this case had been, he said, 'Go ahead, as long as you respect the limits of the law insofar as possible.'[30]

He freely admitted giving an order to kidnap a suspect on foreign territory, bring him to the jurisdiction, and obtain information from him (by unspecified means). The suspect was then to be handed over to the courts with a false account of how he had been arrested. Since every one of these acts lies totally outside the law, Vera's injunction to respect legality 'insofar as possible' was a piece of pious claptrap. Indeed, he approved an 'award' of 200,000 pesetas to each of the policemen involved in the kidnapping after the event. This was while they were on French bail, which he did not require them to honour.

Vera said that Interior had been 'taught a lesson' by the Larretxea operation. It had been a double failure: the kidnapping was foiled and Martin Barrios's life was not saved. From then on, he claimed, Interior's only anti-terrorist actions in France were conducted 'on a political and diplomatic level within the strictest legality'.[31] This hardly fitted with the facts: three years of intensive GAL operations in France followed, with the proven participation of some of the same police officers from the Larretxea and Marey cases, and without any effective investigation of these events by his ministry.

For a man who prided himself on being superbly well informed, Vera's knowledge of the GAL seemed incredibly sparse. Asked by a prosecution lawyer how he found out about the GAL's attacks, he replied laconically: 'The same way as you did, if you read the newspapers.'[32] He did claim that, at the urging of the French, a joint group had been set up to investigate the GAL, but he was not aware if it had produced any results.[33]

Vera's evidence was almost totally at variance with that of his nine former subordinates and Damborenea. He did, however, admit that he had made one phone call to Sancristóbal on the night Marey was kidnapped. The purpose of the call, he claimed, was not to discuss the operation, of which he had no knowledge. It was simply to inform Sancristóbal that the French superintendent Joel Cathalá had contacted him about the abduction of Marey, and the possibility that he had been taken to Spain.

He denied providing any funds for the kidnapping. The court instructed financial specialists to determine whether a sum of one million francs had been withdrawn from Interior's Bank of Spain account at this time.

Asked about his relationship with Amedo and Domínguez after they were convicted in 1991, Vera said that he had always supported pardoning them, on the same basis on which members of ETA(p-m) had been effectively pardoned in the early 1980s. He also admitted having given money to their wives, 'for humanitarian motives', but he denied that there had been any regular arrangement.[34]

INTERLUDE

Six legal experts analysed questions raised by the trial for the Sunday edition of *El País*.[35] The most significant issue, given the balance of evidence in the case, was whether the verbal testimony of a co-accused could be decisive in finding another defendant guilty. The experts all agreed that such testimony was perfectly admissible, but they also considered that it had to be weighed against three more elements: the other evidence available, the motivation of the witness, and whether the declarations formed 'a coherent account of the facts'. These would all become key points of contention when the sentence was announced. So far, other evidence was scant on the ground, and the co-accused witnesses had a wide range of ulterior motives for declaring against Barrionuevo and Vera. Despite minor contradictions, however, all ten other defendants had given the court a remarkably coherent account of the facts.

WEEK THREE
Day Seven: Monday, 8 June
Pure invention and a dirty settling of scores
'We put an end to the GAL. What more do you want?' Vera's tone had been assured and ironic; Barrionuevo's shifted unsettlingly from bombast to petulance. Towards the end of a long hearing, in which he had repeated the phrases 'I don't remember' and 'pure invention' like twin mantras, the

Dirty War, Clean Hands

former minister's thin patience seemed stretched to breaking point. A prosecution lawyer had been asking him if Interior had ever investigated the GAL. His voice rose sharply, and he fell back on a line of defence first sketched by Felipe González in 1995. The GAL stopped operating in 1986. The PSOE was in power in 1986. Therefore the PSOE put an end to the GAL. He was not pursued on the double implications of this argument.[36]

Barrionuevo's defence was more confused than Vera's, mainly because he attempted to make a case for the innocence of his co-defendants. This was unsustainable because of the material evidence against them, which underpinned – and had almost certainly prompted – their own admissions of guilt. Sancristóbal's record, he said, was 'competent and worthy of respect'. And while he insisted the PSOE had never gone outside the law in the war against terrorism, he said that he 'admired Damborenea for his position in the anti-terrorist struggle'.[37] As we have seen, Damborenea was the Socialist leader most publicly identified with the ideological defence of a dirty war strategy. Once again, Barrionuevo seemed caught out in the open as he zigzagged between two contradictory defences: every time he denied his participation in the death squads in practice, he could not resist attempting to justify them, however obliquely, in principle; and in denying what was evidently true, he cast doubt on his denials of the less easily sustained charges made by the prosecution.[38]

He insisted that the CESID document which noted that a dirty war was about to start in France was 'a document expressly fabricated for this trial' and made the same claim about the so-called 'Founding Memorandum of the GAL'. The whole case against him, he said, once again, was 'a dirty settling of political scores'.[39]

He chose to repeat in court his melodramatic offer to become the scapegoat for the GAL, while denying the charges, if the other defendants were exonerated. 'If it would help all the others, I would take the blame. I always defend the doctrine of the lesser evil,' he volunteered to the state prosecutor, who replied that this proposal could not be considered by the court.

Day Eight: Tuesday, 9 June
'I have no experience of the informer's trade.'
We saw, at the opening of the last chapter, how the dramatic and unexpected *careos* between Barrionuevo, Sancristóbal and Damborenea were a turning-point in the trial. The use of the treacherous word 'informer' by Barrionuevo was a costly slip-up, and his performance probably influenced the judges in their final decision. Knowing he had his opponent fatally exposed, Damborenea, the street-fighting orator from Bilbao's industrial belt, hammered home his *coup de grâce*: 'In the dock, there are a number of people who have left a trail of evidence, and cannot deny the facts from a certain point onwards. There are two other people who were lucky enough not to leave any trail, and they are evading their responsibility.'[40]

The *careos* were over, and Barrionuevo was at a disadvantage for the rest of the trial.

It was now the turn of a series of defence and prosecution witnesses to take the stand. First up was the disgraced CESID colonel, Juan Alberto Perote. His cold reptilian features gave away little; mostly his answers gave away less. He acknowledged the documents relating to the dirty war as authentic, but insisted that the CESID had not been involved in the GAL; it had merely produced theoretical studies, or reported on the activities of other security forces. However, he agreed that on one occasion the intelligence service had supplied the Guardia Civil with a rifle, which had been used in illegal activities.[41]

He insisted that he had informed General Emilio Alonso Manglano about the start of GAL activities, and asserted without proof that Manglano must have then informed González. Asked if the CESID had subsequently investigated the GAL, he replied: 'It would be more accurate to say the opposite.' This meant, he explained, that they had investigated not the GAL but the *investigators* of the GAL, the journalists and judges, to find out how much they knew.[42]

Strangely enough, no one, not even the lawyers for Barrionuevo and Vera, asked him about his relationship with Mario Conde, or why he had removed sensitive documents from the CESID in the first place.

After such an ambivalent witness, it was a relief to hear a straightforward account of the night of the kidnapping from the policeman who had been in charge of the frontier post at Dantxarinea. Jesús Rodríguez Velasco confirmed that a procession of strange characters, ranging from the mercenary Mohand Talbi to the flamboyant superintendent Amedo, passed through his hands that night.

He had phoned his commanding officer in Pamplona for instructions, and had been told: 'This is an operation from Bilbao. You keep clear of it.'[43] This man then clarified one small but important point. During the ten days Marey was detained, the French had never sealed his section of the border. This gave the lie to one excuse given by Sancristóbal and company for holding Marey for so long – that they had been unable to get him back across the border undetected. The court therefore inclined towards accepting the other, and penally more serious, possibility: they were waiting for the prior release of Larretxea's kidnappers in France.

Day Nine: Wednesday, 10 June
'I have the bad habit of signing without reading.'
After Perote, Luis Roldán. The trial was becoming a gallery of the black sheep of the Socialist regime. But this Roldán was a much more chastened man than the protagonist of previous court cases. His own repeated legal defeats, and isolation in prison, had taken their toll.[44] He made the usual allegations about the GAL, González and the Interior Ministry, but could not substantiate them.

The real drama on this day came earlier, when the former chief of police in Pamplona, Eduardo Couto, abruptly reversed his written evidence. He now gave an account which favoured Rafael Vera. In his original statement to Garzón, Couto had said that the frontier police had told him that Segundo Marey was being held at the border, and that he had passed this news on to Roldán.[45] Roldán claimed he had told Vera, who replied with an order to 'leave it to Bilbao'. This would, of course, independently confirm Roldán's assertion that Vera knew that Marey was in Spanish custody from the outset. Now Couto said that nobody had ever mentioned

Marey on the night in question. As for his written statement to the contrary, he explained lamely: 'I have the bad habit of signing without reading.'[46] He gave a confused and doddery impression in court, but left with an enigmatic smile on his face.

Two of Spain's most senior police officers in the GAL period then gave evidence. Rafael del Rio Sendino had been Director General of the National Police, and Jesús Martínez Torres head of police intelligence. Neither of them, it seemed, had ever felt moved to seriously investigate any aspect of the GAL. They knew very little about the whole issue.[47] However, Martínez Torres, who had airily disclaimed any responsibility for the GAL because they operated in France,[48] claimed a remarkable degree of knowledge about ETA's operations in the same territory. *Everyone* who worked in Sokoa, he said, was either a member of or sympathiser with the Basque terrorist organisation. Marey, who was supposed to be the victim at this trial, was being tarred, again, with guilt by association.

The last witness of the week was General Manglano, Perote's boss in the CESID. He categorically denied Perote's allegation that 'Pte' on a CESID document meant that he had discussed it with Felipe González. Asked if he had ever spoken to González about any form of terrorism, he was equally firm: 'Never, never, never.'[49] While this denial kept González in the clear, it was an extraordinary admission in itself. The head of Spanish military intelligence was admitting that he had failed to tell the government about a violent campaign about to be launched across its borders by elements of its own security forces, though he had been informed of it in writing more than two weeks before it began.

He did acknowledge, however, that the so-called 'Founding Memorandum of the GAL' was a theoretical study by Perote's unit, which threw some very cold water on Barrionuevo's claim that it had been 'fabricated for this trial'. Like Martínez Torres and del Rio Sendino, however, he claimed to have had no hard information on the GAL while they were operating. The bizarre picture of security forces without the least interest in the activities of a terrorist group which was destabilising the Basque Country and causing serious tensions with Spain's most important neighbour was being painted again.

INTERLUDE

By a strange coincidence, another kidnapping case was being heard around the corner from the Supreme Court, in the Audiencia Nacional. Four members of ETA admitted holding José Antonio Ortega Lara in a tiny *zulo* for 532 days. As though echoing the policemen who had guarded Marey, they insisted that their prisoner had received 'good and correct treatment, as far as the seriousness of the situation allowed'. Asked if they had not noticed his emaciated appearance and drastic weight loss, one *etarra* replied: 'I am not a doctor, nor do I know how he was feeling inside. But as for eating, he ate, and the food was good, better than I am getting now in prison.'[50]

In the broader political world, PSOE leaders began to set the tone for their response to a guilty verdict for Barrionuevo. Juan Carlos Rodríguez Ibarra, senior party 'baron' and President of the Estremaduran regional government, launched a double-barrelled salvo. If Barrionuevo had to 'explain' the dirty war under his ministry, then so must his predecessors from the transition, Manuel Fraga and Martín Villa. Then he went further: 'If Vera began to talk, our democracy would suffer very much. If Vera began to talk about the utilisation of the "reserved funds", the fuses of the justice system would blow.'[51] Once again, in protesting their innocence, Socialist leaders did not seem to be able to help implying their guilt.

Nevertheless, González still enjoyed enormous international prestige, and was considered the leading candidate for the presidency of the European Commission, as successor to Jacques Santer. But this bright prospect was being overshadowed by the Marey trial, as the international media increasingly recognised. 'If Barrionuevo is sent to prison, González will have to pay for it in the European Commission,' one influential newspaper commented.[52]

In Argentina, the former dictator General Jorge Videla was arrested on charges of kidnapping five children from mothers of the 'disappeared', despite a 1990 pardon for dirty war crimes and the Argentinian 'law of the full stop'. The Spanish Minister for Foreign Affairs, Abel Matutes, commented: 'The arm of justice is very long, and even though years may pass, he who does wrong pays for it.'[53]

WEEK FOUR
Day Ten: Tuesday, 16 June
Benny Hill, coloured snakes, torture and obeying orders

At last, the victim. Segundo Marey, now sixty-six years old and still visibly marked by his ordeal fifteen years earlier, made a long pause as he walked up towards his seat to give evidence. For perhaps ten seconds, he scrutinised José Ramón Corujo and Luis Hens, the two men who had held him captive in a freezing cabin for ten days but whom, because of his blindfold, he had never seen face to face. Then he took the stand.

He gave the court a blow-by-blow account of his experience as a guest of the Spanish nation. He remembered it beginning like many another banal domestic evening. 'At ten to eight in the evening, my wife and I had finished dinner. We were going to watch a Benny Hill film, because we wanted to laugh.'[54]

There was no laughter for a long time after that. Seized on his doorstep, blindfolded, and half-choked, Marey was dragged shoeless across border country till his feet bled. His captors took him to a cabin without running water or electric light, never told him they were police, and never interrogated him beyond occasional accusations that he was an *etarra* involved in Sokoa.

He felt under constant threat of execution 'and at times I wanted it . . . I felt like an animal when it's caught . . . the psychological torture was horrible.' Then he told the court something which he had never revealed before 'because I was afraid': he believed he had been drugged, though he could not say how. 'I saw snakes on the floor, coloured snakes, hairy ones.'

When he asked his guardians, again and again, 'Why me?' he was told: 'Because we wanted a shit like you.'

On the day of his release, one of his captors told him: 'Segundo, today we're going to let you go.' But another said: 'We should kill him.' The first told him wryly: 'As you see, we also have bloodthirsty comrades.'

Just before his release, although he had eaten pitifully little, they advised him to do exercises. He found to his amazement that his body still functioned normally: 'The body is incredible, an extraordinary thing which can withstand any experience!' he told the court.

Fifteen years later, Segundo Marey's suffering was not quite over. Two defence lawyers, Sancristóbal's and Planchuelo's, aggressively questioned him about his relationship with Sokoa, trying to link him with ETA. Given that their clients had admitted that Marey had been mistaken for the *etarra* Mikel Lujua, this seemed a particularly gratuitous piece of cruelty, an attempt to do in the courtroom what his captors had failed to do in the cabin. After protests from his lawyer, the presiding judge finally cut them off.

To Álvarez's credit, his lawyer apologised to Marey on his client's behalf, and passed up his right to ask any questions. Afterwards, in a small moment of grace, Hens and Corujo approached Marey outside the courtroom, and asked for his pardon. Marey accepted their outstretched hands, and wished them both 'Good health!' He told the watching journalists: 'I felt, well, yes . . . that you have to forgive; because, if you can't, it's a bad business.'

Two other former security officers were called to give evidence on this day. They were Jesús Gutiérrez Argüelles and Francisco Javier López, the men who had attempted to kidnap José María Larretxea. They both acknowledged that, while in prison in France, they had learned (through the media) of the GAL communiqué to the Red Cross demanding their release in exchange for Marey's life. But they insisted that the communiqué only made their situation worse, and therefore would hardly have been issued by their commanding officers. Argüelles added an interesting detail: on their return to Spain, where they broke their bail, they received telegrams of congratulations from a Supreme Court judge and from the royal family. One of the prosecution lawyers asked López if he had understood that the whole operation was illegal. He replied: 'I was aware that it was an operation . . . in line with our objectives . . . if my government gives an order, and has weighed up the consequences, I accept it.'

Day Eleven: Wednesday, 17 June
'The purpose of our activities justified a degree of illegality.'
Like López, indeed like Vera himself, General Sáenz de Santamaría justified the attempted kidnapping of Larretxea on the grounds that it might have provided information which would have led to saving the life of Captain Martín Barrios. It is hard to understand why no one pursued him, or Vera, harder on this argument. The kidnapping of Barrios certainly created a crisis, but it was one of many crises provoked by terrorism in these years. If Interior approved a dirty war action in this case, why should we not assume that it would have done so in others?

This veteran general of the anti-terrorist high command gave the court his usual line: there had been dirty war operations before, during and after the transition, 'although those which provoked most commotion were the operations in 1983'.[55] Yet he insisted that, with the exception of the Larretxea action, Interior had had nothing to do with them. If anyone expected this general, who had allegedly threatened to spill the beans on the dirty war under the UCD if the senate questioned him about the GAL, to spill anything substantial on this occasion, they were disappointed. He resisted prosecution attempts to draw him out on this issue.

Instead, he gave an analysis which favoured Vera's case: in Interior in the mid-1980s, he said, 'there was one political line which was more violent, impulsive and visceral, that was Sancristóbal's; and there was a colder, more pragmatic line, which was Vera's'. He was in agreement with the latter: 'You won't finish off terrorism by killing the last terrorist,' he told the court.

INTERLUDE

Some of the Marey defendants had other dates with the courts during this week. One of the most tangled GAL cases of all, the investigation of the murder of Santiago Brouard, had reopened with fresh evidence against the Interior Ministry, and would haunt a number of its senior ex-employees long after the Marey trial was finished. On 19 June, Amedo travelled to a Bilbao hearing where he admitted attending a meeting in 1983 with Francisco Álvarez and Miguel Planchuelo to pay two mercenaries for their part in the Marey kidnapping. But he denied participating in a further meeting at which the killing of Brouard had allegedly been planned. The judge then initiated a process of indictment against him. The magistrate also heard evidence from Rafael Vera, who admitted sending a *guardia civil* colonel implicated in the case on a long mission to Bolivia, shortly after Brouard was shot.

WEEK FIVE
Day Twelve: Monday, 22 June
The rabid dog bites back

The deputy Prime Minister, Francisco Álvarez Cascos, was greeted at the doors of the Supreme Court by a small group of Socialist demonstrators carrying placards of a Doberman, in reference to Felipe González's description of him as a 'rabid dog'.[56]

In evidence, he admitted having met Amedo's lawyer in December 1994, in the office and in the presence of the editor of *El Mundo*, Pedro J. Ramírez. He insisted, however, that he had simply been gathering information, as part of his job as a parliamentarian, on the crisis in the Interior Ministry following the withdrawal of payments to Amedo and Domínguez. He categorically denied having offered to negotiate a pardon for the defendants if they incriminated the PSOE leadership.

He then turned the tables on Barrionuevo's and Vera's lawyers, who had subjected him to a tough cross-examination, by revealing that he had had other meetings about the case the following month – with Barrionuevo and Vera themselves. He claimed that Barrionuevo had asked him for help with 'the situation regarding his trial'.[57]

Outside the court, Barrionuevo told journalists that the deputy Prime Minister had lied under oath about the content and date of the meeting.

He said that they had met in February, and that he had sought Álvarez Cascos's help, not with his own situation, but to negotiate the release on bail of Damborenea. It did not seem to strike Barrionuevo that this would itself have constituted an interference in the course of justice. Perhaps he had come to take such things for granted.

Álvarez Cascos also told the court that, as a parliamentarian, he attributed to Felipe González all the political responsibility for 'the conception, birth, organisation, financing and termination of the terrorist activities of the GAL'. González would get a chance to reply to these charges, in court, the following day.

Day Thirteen: Tuesday, 23 June
Something new from González

The appearance of Felipe González was bound to be the media climax of the trial. In fact, of course, the former Prime Minister was appearing as a witness, not as a defendant, but he voluntarily brought some new material to the case.

González predictably denied that he had ever ordered a dirty war in France, and insisted that Barrionuevo 'never, ever put forward to me anything of that nature. Neither he nor anyone else.'[58] Despite Manglano's evidence that the so-called 'Founding Memorandum of the GAL' had been drawn up within the CESID, González repeated Barrionuevo's claim that it had been forged for the purposes of the trial.[59] Above all, he argued forcefully that the actions of the GAL, far from persuading the French to collaborate against ETA, actively obstructed collaborative measures which had already been secretly agreed.

His position was based on a written statement, which the court did not permit him to read. This was in turn based on two documents, both of which were published by *El País* the day after González's court appearance.

One was a writ from the French prosecutor in the Larretxea case, dated 18 November 1983. This showed that France was, in principle, already willing to release the Spanish police on bail, two weeks before Marey was even kidnapped. There would therefore have been no point, González argued, in attempting to pressurise the French authorities to release them by threatening to kill Marey.

The second document was a telex from González to his ministers, dated the following day, which summarised a phone conversation he had had with President François Mitterrand. According to González's account, the French government itself had attempted to stop the Larretxea case coming to trial at all, and was still trying to play down the case, but the judge involved was resisting its pressure. The telex continued: 'It is clear that [Mitterrand] has changed his attitude regarding terrorism, which opens up much more efficient methods of co-operation. These range from the denial of residence permits up to the expulsion from France of ETA leaders. He does not want any publicity, and repeats that he is saying all this to me as a friend, but that he wants me to know his attitude.'

González's reading of the documents on both issues can easily be reversed. In the first instance, Mitterrand is baldly admitting that the French executive was willing to collaborate with the Spanish government to pressurise his judiciary not to prosecute Spanish police involved in a dirty war crime on his territory. This admission could shed a lot of light on the impunity with which the GAL continued to operate in France over the next three years.

In the second, Mitterrand says he is willing to collaborate against ETA's terrorism, but adds that he does not want the French public to know he is doing so. Those who argued that the GAL were attempting to change the position of the French leader may well have been wrong, as González contended. But this does not rule out the thesis that the GAL's real role may have been to change French public opinion, especially within Mitterrand's own party in the French Basque Country. According to this view, the GAL 'dirtied the French doorstep' with terrorist actions until French citizens decided that the price of ETA's sanctuary was too high for them to pay. At that point, Mitterrand could afford to give his secret change of heart on terrorism the full glare of publicity.

These counter-arguments were not presented in court, and González stepped down from three hours' testimony relatively unscathed. His great skills in measured political debate, and his own experience as a lawyer, served him well, and he managed to score a few points of his own. He reintroduced the conspiracy theory: 'it is evident that there has been a common purpose between certain individuals to set up this whole affair'.[60] He claimed that Garzón himself had asked for a pardon for Amedo during his brief passage through politics.[61] And while he admitted having had two individual meetings with Damborenea in 1984, he said that they had not discussed anti-terrorist strategy, because 'I did not trust him'.[62]

The first of these meetings had taken place on 15 March, two weeks after the GAL killed Jean-Pierre Leiba and a few days before the death in action of the GAL leader Jean-Pierre Cherid and the GAL's killing of the ETA leader Xabier Pérez de Arenaza. The second took place on 22 May, three weeks after the GAL killed Rafael Goikoetxea and three weeks before they mortally wounded Tomás Pérez Revilla. ETA was also extremely active during this period. But none of these details, apparently, had concerned the then Prime Minister and one of his top party bosses in the zone of conflict – a man who, it could fairly be said, was obsessed with the subject of terrorism. One wonders what they did talk about.

In the afternoon, Narcís Serra and José María ('Txiki') Benegas, formerly González's number two and number three respectively, gave evidence which was equally oblivious of the GAL's operations. Serra gave the conspiracy theory another airing. Benegas insisted that 'never, never, never' had the Socialists in the Basque Country even considered the idea of engaging in a dirty war.

Several commentators noted that the senior Socialist witnesses spoke as though there was no victim; the kidnapping of Segundo Marey did not appear to have made the least impression on them. Indeed, they spoke almost as though there had been no GAL. A book could be written with what they don't know, as Antonio Muñoz Molina put it, quoting Tobias Wolff.[63]

WEEKS FIVE AND SIX
Days Fourteen to Seventeen: Wednesday, 24 June; Monday, 29 June; Tuesday, 30 June; Wednesday, 1 July
The defendants, the victim and the heavyweight witnesses had now all spoken, all been questioned, and all answered after their fashion. With a few minor witnesses to go, the trial was winding down before the summing up and the verdict.

The remaining witnesses were predictable: the Socialist leader Juan Carlos Rodríguez Ibarra came to court as a defence witness to accuse Garzón of acting out of frustrated ambition; Vera's former private secretary, Juan de Justo, gave a hair-raising account of being interrogated, and allegedly threatened, by the same judge. But neither he nor his lawyer could explain why they had not lodged a protest against Garzón at the time.

Then it was the hour of the technical experts. Calligraphers ratified that the handwriting on various GAL documents belonged to Damborenea, Sancristóbal, Planchuelo and Saiz Oceja respectively. Financial specialists could find no precise equivalent of the million francs allegedly withdrawn by Vera to finance the operation, but said that the bank notes could easily have been bought with some of the untraceable 462 million pesetas withdrawn *in cash* from Interior's reserved funds in 1983. The state solicitor supported their argument. Two doctors quantified the price of Marey's mental and physical suffering at 39 million pesetas. Another two handwriting experts confirmed that Amedo had written the document in which he appeared to allege malpractice by Garzón. Whether the contents of this document reflected what had actually happened, or were simply yet another red herring introduced by Amedo, was still an open question.

INTERLUDE
A reminder that the Lasa and Zabala case was still ticking away like a time bomb came with the release on bail of 25 million pesetas of General Enrique Rodríguez Galindo. His lawyer denied that the PSOE had put up the money.[64]

Sancristóbal and Damborenea had to travel to Bilbao to deny their participation in the murder of Santiago Brouard. They described the killing as 'abhorrent' and 'irrational' because 'the consequences benefited nobody'.[65]

As an *El País* editorial put it later in the month, the Marey case was 'only the first of the judicial Stations of the Cross of the Calvary of the GAL'.[66]

In Rome, the international community was attempting to negotiate the creation of an international court which could judge crimes against humanity and human rights.

WEEKS SEVEN AND EIGHT
Day Eighteen: Monday, 6 July
It remained for the main players to sum up their case, starting with Marey's lawyer, Olga Tubau. She targeted the defendants' best argument, whether they admitted or denied involvement: that the statute of limitations on the crimes committed had expired, and they could no

DBS Arts Library

longer be punished for them. The phone call to the Red Cross setting conditions for Marey's release was critical here. If conditions had been set, the statute expired in fifteen years, and the guilty must go to jail. If no conditions had been set, it expired in ten, and they could walk free. But there was no documentary evidence to link them to the call, and the best she could do was point out that the caller knew Marey's age and place of birth, data which 'were not available to just anyone'.[67] She was perhaps on stronger ground, morally if not legally, when she argued that no statute of limitations should apply in any case, since the leading defendants had done everything in their power to delay the case from coming to trial.

The state prosecutor, José María Luzón, followed suit, reaffirming every single one of the charges he had already made, and dismissing out of hand the arguments that either Garzón's controversial investigation methods or the manipulation of evidence by the conspirators could be grounds for the annulment of the trial. He confirmed his call for twenty-three years in prison for Barrionuevo and Vera, without whose assent, he said, the dirty war against ETA would not have been possible: 'The declarations of the other defendants are consistent, but Vera and Barrionuevo obstinately deny them . . . Barrionuevo makes an empty gesture, unworthy of a barrister, to accept responsibility in exchange for some unspecified pact with this prosecutor.'[68]

His rhetoric was strong, but could not quite disguise the fact that he had no incontrovertible material evidence against these two defendants. The lawyers for the people's prosecution were equally eloquent in general terms about the background to the GAL, but still could not quite insert a smoking gun into the hand of Barrionuevo or Vera. Everything now depended on whether the judges would accept that the weight and coherence of the evidence from the ten other defendants, plus the context which other witnesses had provided for the existence of a state-sponsored dirty war, would be sufficient to convict a former minister and deputy minister.

Days Nineteen to Twenty-two: Tuesday, 7 July; Wednesday, 8 July; Monday, 13 July; Tuesday, 14 July

The defence lawyers, and the defendants themselves if they wanted it, had the final say. The fissures among the ten defendants who admitted involvement now became more apparent. Amedo's and Domínguez's lawyer asked for a total pardon for both men, though he also argued that the case against Domínguez should be annulled because of Garzón's allegedly coercive tactics. He also claimed that the statute of limitations for their crimes had, in any case, expired.[69]

Hens and Corujo, the two most junior policemen, had been only obeying orders which they understood to be legal, according to their lawyer. Playing a dirtier game, the lawyer for two of the more senior officers, Hierro and Saiz Oceja, and for Planchuelo, claimed that Marey was either an ETA member or sympathiser, and that therefore his detention had been legal. Álvarez's lawyer made no such allegations against Marey, but argued that, if the Larretxea seizure had been accepted by Interior as legal and justified, it was perfectly reasonable that he should have taken the same approach to a second kidnapping. Damborenea's defence tried to limit his involvement to that of a responsible politician who had simply gone to police headquarters to give his opinion on a sensitive issue.[70]

Sancristóbal's lawyer showed an extraordinary lack of sensitivity to the plight of Marey, describing his kidnapping as 'a relatively trivial and banal event'.[71] Despite the fact that it was Sancristóbal himself who had admitted spending Vera's million francs on the kidnapping, and therefore misusing public funds, his lawyer said that nobody had proved this point in the trial. He also argued that the statute of limitations protected his client.

The real interest, of course, focused on the defence of Barrionuevo and Vera. The latter's lawyer made an impassioned attack on the prosecution's reliance on the verbal evidence of the ten co-accused. These 'late disciples of the inquisition' were turning confession into 'the queen of proofs'. Regarding the thesis that the GAL had been trying to pressurise the French government, he made the inadvertently revealing comment that Mitterrand and his colleagues 'couldn't have cared less if they had killed Señor Marey'.[72]

The main focus of Barrionuevo's defence was the allegedly extreme irregularity of Garzón's investigation. This lawyer also stressed the fact that the court had not demanded any material evidence from the Red Cross of the crucial phone call setting conditions for Marey's release, though it had been widely reported in the press, and acknowledged by the Spanish policemen who had been in jail in France.

At last, on the twenty-second day of the trial, it was the turn of the defendants themselves to have a last word before the judges retired to consider their verdict.

'Neither by action nor by deliberate negligence have I caused any harm to Señor Marey,' proclaimed Barrionuevo. That said, he concluded by focusing on 'the parallel and premature trial in which the sentences have already been dictated. One sentence has been handed down by political adversaries; another by enemies with power in the media. Now it remains for justice to speak. In justice we trust, your lordships.'[73]

Vera also asserted his innocence. Most of the other defendants repeated that they had only been obeying orders. Once again, the most gracious comments came from the most junior policemen: Luis Hens said that his admission had been, for him, something which had freed him 'from a very heavy load', although he had not realised at the time that he was breaking the law. He concluded that he 'regretted profoundly having contributed to the suffering' of the man who had been forgotten so often during this trial: the victim, Segundo Marey, a commercial traveller who had been in the wrong place at the wrong time.

INTERLUDE

On the same day, in Argentina, General Jorge Videla was formally charged with the theft of four children of the 'disappeared' during Argentina's dirty war. All over the world, the space of impunity for crimes committed by the state was shrinking. In September, General Augusto Pinochet, former dictator of Chile and lifelong senator immune from prosecution, would be arrested in London on a writ from a Spanish judge, Baltasar Garzón.

NOTES

1 In this column, Montero also awarded the Spanish Interior Ministry 'the gold medal for horror, betrayal and darkness'. *El País*, 29 July 1996.

2 *El País*, 24 May 1998.

3 Ibid. Chaves was previously PSOE minister and President of the Andalusian regional government.

4 In a television interview with Iñaki Gabilondo, after José Amedo implicated his superiors in the Segundo Marey kidnapping. *El País*, 10 January 1995. See also ch. 18, pp. 263–6.

5 *El País*, 22 May 1998. This quote could be read as applying, not to the Partido Popular and the 'conspiracy', as González intends, but to the PSOE and the GAL.

6 *El País*, 25 May 1998.

7 *El País,* 26 May 1998. The PSOE statement makes no reference to the numerous interferences in the GAL investigations by the González government. See ch. 15.

8 *El País*, 24 May 1998.

9 *El País*, 11 September 1995. See also ch. 22, p. 336.

10 The trial opened on Monday, 25 May 1998, and ran from Monday to Wednesday inclusive for eight weeks, with the exception of Monday, 15 June, until it ended on Tuesday, 14 July.

11 *El País*, 26 May 1998.

12 See ch. 22, p. 343.

13 *El País*, 26 May 1998.

14 *El Mundo*, 26 May 1998.

15 *El País*, 26 May 1998.

16 *El Mundo*, 27 May 1998. Hens described the food they offered Marey as 'tinned food, but quality tinned food, like Litoral beans, a well-known brand and very good one'.

17 *El País*, 27 May 1998.

18 *El Mundo*, 28 May 1998.

19 These were, presumably, the Guardia Civil. This was an implicit admission by Planchuelo that the two forces were in direct competition for terrorist 'trophies'.

20 *El País*, 28 May 1998.

21 *El País*, 30 May 1998.

22 *El País*, 2 June 1998.

23 See ch. 18, p. 261.

24 Many defendants used the word 'detention' rather than 'kidnapping', indicating that even those who accepted the facts proved against them still considered they had been acting under orders they had considered legitimate at the time.

25 *El País*, 2 June 1998.

26 See ch. 18, p. 274.

27 *El País*, 3 June 1998.

28 Sancristóbal specifically said that they advised him to use 'the team of Superintendent Guy Metge'. This French police superintendent was allegedly a key contact for Amedo and other GAL organisers in the French Basque Country. Metge was in no position to give evidence, because he had died in the meantime.

29 They did not necessarily plead guilty to any or all of the charges which the prosecution based on these facts, and attempted to deny those facts which could result in heavier sentences.

30 *El País*, 4 June 1998.

31 Ibid.

32 This comment so clearly echoes notorious previous comments by the former chief of police intelligence, Jesús Martínez Torres, and by Felipe González that many observers read it as open defiance of the court.

33 *El Mundo*, 4 June 1998. The superintendent in charge of this group, according to Vera, was Alberto Elias. He was unable to give evidence at the trial because he was dead. No report from this group was produced in evidence.

34 *El País*, 4 June 1998.

35 *El País*, 7 June 1998.

36 The Socialists could hardly have put an end to the GAL, without any significant investigation and without arresting any key figures, unless they were running the organisation themselves. At one point Barrionuevo said that the GAL 'terminated their activities because of police activities on both sides of the border', and again, 'we were so efficient against the GAL that we stopped them'. The consistent refusal of the Spanish authorities to collaborate with even the most basic French judicial requests on the GAL issue tells a very different story. Barrionuevo specifically claimed in court that he 'could not remember' his own cabinet's refusal to extradite Georges Mendaille. See *El Mundo*, 9 June 1998.

37 Author's court notes, 8 June 1998.

38 For an excellent analysis of the differences between Barrionuevo's and Vera's defence strategies, see Enrique Gil Calvo's article, 'Marey', in *El País*, 15 June 1998.

39 *El País*, 9 June 1998.

40 *El Mundo*, 10 June 1998.

41 This weapon, allegedly, was the one used to kill Eugenio Gutiérrez Salazar in February 1984, though Perote did not specify this in court.

42 Author's court notes, 9 June 1998; *El Mundo*, 10 June 1998.

43 *El País*, 10 June 1998.

44 Even on this occasion, however, Roldán managed to create a minor scandal by breaking court rules and talking to his former lawyer during a recess. The lawyer, it turned out, was trying to get him to pay an overdue bill!

45 At this point, Roldán was the Government Delegate in Navarre. The Government Delegate was Madrid's representative to autonomous regions. In cases like Navarre, where the autonomous region coincided with a single province, his duties were similar to those of the Civil Governor at provincial level, the position Julián Sancristóbal and Julen Elgorriaga had held in Vizcaya and Guipúzcoa, respectively. See Paul Heywood, *The Government and Politics of Spain* (London: Macmillan, 1995). Roldán did not become Director General of the Guardia Civil until 1986.

46 Author's court notes, 10 June 1998.

47 Martínez Torres did, however, repeat Vera's claim that a joint French–Spanish team had investigated the GAL. Martínez Torres had mentioned this investigation to Moner (see *El País*, 3 November 1995), but produced no material evidence of its activities.

48 See ch. 14, p. 191. Martínez Torres was the officer who had produced a dossier of press clippings in court when asked what information he had on the GAL in 1985. See *El País*, 2 November 1995.

49 Author's court notes, 10 June 1998; *El País*, 12 June 1998.

50 *El Mundo*, 11 June 1998.

51 *El País*, 10 June 1998.

52 *The European,* quoted in *El Mundo*, 12 June 1998.

53 *El Mundo*, 11 June 1998.

54 *El Mundo*, 17 June 1998.

55 *El País*, 18 June 1998.

56 The PSOE had also used images of a Doberman intercut with footage of Partido Popular leaders, in a notorious 1996 election video which was withdrawn after protests, some from within the party.

57 *El País*, 23 June 1998. When Vera's lawyer pointed out that Barrionuevo had not been charged at that stage, Álvarez Cascos withdrew the phrase, but pointed out that the former minister had demanded the right to be heard at Garzón's investigation, and said that it was with this appeal that Barrionuevo had sought his help.

58 *El País*, 24 June 1998.

59 Manglano did not, of course, accept the interpretation that the prosecution put on this document, but he did agree that it had been produced, purely as a theoretical exercise, by his agents. González, in claiming that the document had been forged, was undermining his own credibility by contradicting the expert evidence of another defence witness.

60 EFE/Reuter, 23 June 1998.

61 Garzón denied this the following day, and was able to show that he had taken a public stance against a pardon for Amedo and Domínguez while in office with the Socialists, and had in fact suggested that he would resign if such a pardon was granted. *El País*, 25 June 1998.

62 *El País*, 24 June 1998.

63 Ibid.

64 *El País*, 27 June 1998.

65 *El País*, 4 July 1998.

66 *El País*, 15 July 1998.

67 *El País*, 7 July 1998.

68 Ibid.

69 *El País*, 8 July 1998.

70 *El País*, 9 July 1998.

71 *El País*, 14 July 1998.

72 Ibid.

73 *El País*, 15 July 1998.

24

Judgement and Response:

Barrionuevo in jail,
Socialists in denial

The guarantees of the criminal trial are an essential part of the rule of law, and the rule of law cannot be restored by abandoning such guarantees. The opposite way of thinking is, very probably, the one which found expression in such reprobate acts as the ones which are before the court.
Judge Enrique Bacigalupo Zapater, in his dissenting opinion
on the Segundo Marey judgement[1]

The government is clear as to what its conduct should be: to collaborate with the judicial investigation, respect the decisions of the courts, and support the punishment of the guilty.
Felipe González, during a parliamentary debate on the GAL,
27 July 1995[2]

It was high summer; most of Spain waited for the Marey verdict in the dead heat of late July. Speculation was rife, and various. Would the magistrates find Barrionuevo and Vera guilty, despite the lack of material evidence to corroborate the testimony of the other ten defendants? Could they find them innocent, given the 'coherence' of that testimony, and the strong circumstantial evidence that the Socialists had decided to embark on a dirty war in the autumn of 1983?

If they found them guilty, would the judges take what was seen as the easiest route, and rule that the statute of limitations on the crimes they had committed had elapsed, so that they would not have to go to prison? That decision hung on the issue of whether the defendants had made the call to the Red Cross, setting conditions for Marey's release. The evidence in this matter was fragile enough to leave the statute of limitations route wide open.

Might they take another relatively easy exit, and annul the whole proceedings on the basis of alleged flaws in Baltasar Garzón's investigation?[3] Or would they take the most 'political' route, and find the two senior defendants guilty, but recommend that they be pardoned because of the special circumstances in which the crimes were committed? Lastly, would they take a decision which would send, for the first time since Spanish democracy had been re-established, a former minister to jail?

The judges must have known that they would be damned by a large section of public opinion if they found Barrionuevo and Vera guilty, and damned by another powerful sector if they didn't. If they were to have a chance of presenting a verdict which would be accepted as independent, it was critical that they should be able to deliberate without pressure from politicians or the media. Two incidents illustrate how difficult this was going to be.

On the day after the Marey trial concluded, the indefatigable Judge Garzón took yet another controversial decision. He ordered the closure of the radical Basque newspaper *Egin* and its sister radio station, on the grounds that they formed an intrinsic part of the criminal activities of ETA. A judge with his record on human rights was not likely to take such a decision lightly. He was sensitive to the potential accusation that his action was a direct assault on freedom of expression. His writ painstakingly makes a case which is not based on the views expressed in these media, but on evidence that ETA was directly involved in appointing senior members of *Egin*'s staff. He also produced evidence that the paper's finances were an essential link in ETA's fund-raising operations.[4]

So far, so good. The following week, the Prime Minister, José María Aznar, tried to take full political credit for this purely judicial action. At a press conference in Turkey, he implicitly criticised the Socialists for not closing down *Egin* previously, and then commented: 'Well, now, [*Egin*] has been closed down. Did someone think we weren't going to dare to do it?'[5] This piece of government bravado not only handed a massive propaganda weapon to ETA supporters, but also suggested a very shaky grasp on the relationship between executive and judiciary on the part of the Prime Minister.

It is only fair to point out here that the Partido Popular was itself under great pressure to be seen to be 'tough' on terrorism at this time, given the continuing ETA offensive against its local councillors, which had claimed six lives since the killing of Miguel Ángel Blanco a year earlier. This was the most sustained series of attacks on politicians of one party in the history of ETA, with the possible exception of a campaign against the UCD in 1979 and 1980.[6] Nevertheless, at a most sensitive moment for the relationship between executive and judiciary in Spain, the Prime Minister had implied that the government habitually intervened in the decisions of the courts. No amount of subsequent 'contextualising' by his spin doctors could erase that impression from the public mind, just as the Marey verdict made the headlines.[7]

Those headlines were themselves the other great pressure on the judges: they were the result of a leak of their provisional conclusions to *El País*. Notoriously porous as the Spanish legal system is, this was one discussion which it should have been possible to keep behind closed doors. Somehow, however, the newspaper closest to the Socialists seemed to be privy to almost every detail of the eleven magistrates' private deliberations.

The Supreme Court, the paper announced on 23 July, had found Barrionuevo and Vera guilty of false imprisonment with conditions. It had ruled that the statute of limitations did not therefore apply. It had also found them guilty of misappropriation of public funds. They were sentenced to thirteen years in prison. But the judges had absolved them of the charge of membership of an armed gang. All decisions regarding Vera and Barrionuevo had been adopted by a split vote of seven to four. The dissenting judges – who including the presiding judge – could publish their individual arguments. The eleven magistrates had unanimously found the other defendants guilty as charged, with the exception of the 'armed gang' issue, and sentenced them all to long prison terms.

The leak, which was rapidly picked up by other media, was initially treated with a considerable degree of caution by most parties concerned. 'Judgements are handed down by judges, not by journalists,' was the only comment from the Socialist general secretary, Joaquín Almunia, and the party limited itself to a brief statement reiterating its belief in the innocence of Barrionuevo and Vera.[8] There was serious concern that such an important judgement, from such a senior court, had leaked at all, let alone with such a wealth of details. The Supreme Court magistrates had to submit to the indignity of an (inconclusive) internal investigation.

El País produced more details over the next few days; the paper reported that the *careos* had been decisive in sealing Barrionuevo's fate, and that Marey's eloquence and the defence's attempts to criminalise the victim had also counted heavily.[9] The paper also conceded, however, that the presiding judge was insisting that the sentences had not been finally decided. This led to some suspicion that the leak could have come from a source sympathetic to the PSOE leadership, in order to arouse public sympathy for Barrionuevo and Vera, and pressurise the judges to reduce the penalties.[10]

An *El Mundo* editorial called for Felipe González to honour his promises to accept political responsibility for the GAL if any member of his cabinet was convicted, although the decision was still not official.[11] The new government spokesman, Josep Piqué, echoed this call, and the gloves were off.

González gave an aggressive press conference, calling for the 'pack of hounds' to stop attacking his supporters and attack him directly instead. As for accepting responsibilities, he said cryptically that 'I accept them absolutely and fully, but probably in the opposite sense to the [sense meant by] the criminal syndicate.'[12] The meaning of this circumlocution would become clearer over the coming weeks.

The previous day, Almunia had given another indication of what the final Socialist response to a guilty verdict might be: 'Every effort is being made to condemn two men who have defended Spain and fought against terrorism . . . The Right have tried to drive the PSOE out of political life on many occasions, and unhappily they have done so many times by force. But they are not going to drive us out, and still less are they going to drive out Felipe González if he doesn't want to go.'[13] The PSOE appeared to be losing its grip on its commitment to accepting the judges' decision. Moreover, its leaders were beginning to call up the ghosts, banished from mainstream Spanish political debate since the transition, of the Spanish Civil War.

Always the most radical in these matters, Juan Carlos Rodríguez Ibarra, party 'baron' and President of the Estremaduran regional government, called for 'institutional resistance', an end to all normal co-operation with the Partido Popular for the rest of the parliament.[14] His neighbouring party boss in Southern Castile, José Bono, said that Partido Popular politicians like the deputy Prime Minister, Francisco Álvarez Cascos, 'want to finish off the former president of the government, and I don't know if it goes further than that; from a political point of view they want to finish him off physically'.[15] Such people, he said, hated González more than they hated ETA.

Thus the PSOE, even before the verdict was officially announced, was adopting a more and more polarised discourse, which seemed to negate the purpose of the election of José Borrell as its new prime ministerial candidate. *El País* warned that the Socialists had to bite the bullet, and that they could not move forward while reopening the wounds of the past: 'It would be a huge blunder if, in the heat of the moment, [the PSOE] lost its sense of reality and some of its members let themselves be carried away by plans for revenge and a return to a total polarisation of politics. To retreat to a bunker now . . . would only serve to prevent the recovery of the party. The Socialists need a strong and responsible leadership which looks more to the future than to the past, however difficult that may be for party activists at this moment.'[16]

It would soon become apparent that no such leadership was in place. No doubt aware of this, the Partido Popular was moving quite skilfully towards the political centre and shedding much of its right-wing stridency. Aznar was steadily marginalising the bellicose Álvarez Cascos from the leadership, and had replaced a notoriously acerbic government spokesman with a much milder figure.[17] To the fury of the Socialists, Aznar was developing warm relationships with some of their own natural allies in Europe, especially Britain's Tony Blair. The Partido Popular was beginning to sound like a natural party of democratic government, the PSOE like a slightly hysterical party of demagogic opposition.

Six days after it had been leaked by *El País*, the judges finally published their decision. The first page of the judgement was very simple – 'Marey Case: Acquittal on armed gang and guilty on misappropriation of public funds and illegal detention or kidnapping. To be treated jointly. No statute of limitation applies to the crime.'

Nothing else was simple, however. The fact that the judges had agreed that all the offences could be treated jointly meant that the top sentences – for Barrionuevo, Vera and Sancristóbal – were rather more lenient than those reported in *El País*, ten years instead of thirteen. Those who believed that the original sentences had been leaked to influence the magistrates to reduce them claimed vindication, though there is no hard evidence that this occurred.

Otherwise, however, the decision ran very much along the lines drawn by the newspaper. Those convicted were also barred from holding public office (for twelve years in the cases of Barrionuevo and Vera). Fines were also imposed for misappropriation of public funds, and a total of 30 million pesetas in damages was levied against the defendants, in varying proportions, to compensate Marey.

This judgement reflected the opinion of seven of the eleven magistrates, as *El País*'s story had reported. The greatest novelty lay not in the majority judgement, however, but in the detail of the closely argued dissenting opinions presented by the four remaining magistrates, including the presiding judge, José Jiménez Villarejo. Before we can consider the arguments put by the minority, we must first give detailed attention to the majority position.[18]

The judgement recognises that there were two central points at issue:

- whether Barrionuevo and Vera participated in the kidnapping
- whether any or all of the defendants were responsible for the telephone call to the Red Cross which set conditions for Marey's release.[19]

Every other major point, after all, had already been resolved by the self-incriminating evidence of Sancristóbal and the other nine defendants.[20]

On the basis of that evidence, the judges set out the 'proven facts' of Segundo Marey's abduction, detention and release in great detail. Firstly, they establish the context in which the crime was committed. ETA's terrorism 'constituted a political and social problem of the first order . . . particularly aggravated because the French Authorities did not collaborate with their Spanish counterparts, so that the south of France had been converted into a sanctuary for *etarras*'. The response to this phenomenon, the judges note, was that 'in various sections of society, the idea was gaining ground that to win the anti-terrorist struggle it was necessary to intervene on French territory, in order to persuade those responsible in the neighbouring country to collaborate with the Spanish police'.[21]

The main – indeed the only – concrete instance which the judgement gives of this clamour for intervention in France is provided by the CESID papers – thus conferring upon these much-contested documents a further stamp of legal authentication. The court quotes the theoretical document entitled 'Actions in France',[22] with its suggestive conclusion: 'It is considered that the most advisable form of action is disappearance by kidnapping.' It also quotes the document in which Perote informed Manglano of the imminence of 'violent actions in the south of France'.[23]

From here the judges shift to the kidnapping of Larretxea, accepting Sancristóbal's version that not only Vera but also Barrionuevo had fully approved the operation in advance.

This is followed by an account of the Marey kidnapping itself, in which the evidence of Sancristóbal and his subordinates against Vera and Barrionuevo is fully accepted by the court. Their assertions that they had no part in the crucial phone call to the Red Cross, however, are rejected by the judges.

The court's analysis of these 'proven facts' proved deeply divisive, as we shall see from the dissenting opinions of the minority. The majority argue that the facts regarding the participation of Barrionuevo and Vera in the kidnapping are proven by:

- the declarations of the ten defendants who pleaded guilty
- the evidence of several witnesses, especially the victim, Segundo Marey

- the CESID documents
- expert medical, economic, accountancy and handwriting testimony
- the context provided by the Larretxea kidnapping
- Interior's failure to investigate the affair
- a series of deductions based on the principle that Interior operated on a strictly hierarchal basis.

It is clear, however, that only the defendants' evidence bears directly on Barrionuevo and Vera, though the CESID documents, the Larretxea kidnapping and the testimony on reserved funds could be seen to corroborate their involvement indirectly. The court, says the judgement, 'has no doubt whatsoever' that the version given by Sancristóbal and company corresponds to the truth.[24]

The majority find no trace of ulterior motive in the evidence of these ten defendants, no hint of 'enmity, vengeance, hatred, desire to exonerate themselves or *to obtain some legal advantage,* because they had first admitted their own participation in the events, with full and complete details'.[25] It seems extraordinary that the court does not consider that declaring that a cabinet minister and his deputy had authorised their crimes was a considerable 'legal advantage' to these defendants. The accused, against whom there was damning material evidence, might have been seeking to avail of an amnesty, or at least of leniency on the basis of obeying the direct instructions of the government. The judges' failure to entertain this scenario is one of the elements which casts a shadow on the objectivity of the judgement.

More credibly, the judges go on to cite the Larretxea kidnapping and the CESID documents as indications, additional to and independent of the evidence of the other defendants, that Barrionuevo and Vera authorised the Marey kidnapping. Interior's failure to effectively investigate the Marey affair is also, again credibly enough, cited as corroborative evidence.

The judges move back to shakier ground when they speculate as to whether an operation like the Marey kidnapping *could* have been carried out by such senior figures as Sancristóbal, Damborenea and Álvarez without the authorisation of Madrid. Rather limply, the judges conclude: 'It does not seem credible to us that such senior officers in Vizcaya could act without the knowledge and approval of the senior authorities in the Interior Ministry.'[26] While the approval of Interior would have obviously made the kidnapping much easier, it was hardly impossible for Sancristóbal and company to carry it out without such backing. Unlikely, maybe, and hard to swallow certainly, but hardly 'incredible' in legal terms, or even in terms of common sense.

The court makes two other points based on the premise that Sancristóbal was 'necessarily' acting on the instructions of his superiors. Again, the common-sense response must surely be: 'Probably yes, "necessarily" no.' By the same principle of hierarchy, the court could conceivably have convicted González, and even the King. By slipping into this sort of legal speculation, the judges were risking being accused of paying more attention to the 'popular verdict' cited by Álvarez Cascos than to the legal guarantee of presumption of innocence.

They make a similar leap beyond logic when they argue that the money for the kidnapping could 'only' have come from reserved funds. It was surely quite 'credible', to use their own word, that the funding could have come from some of the many businessmen opposed to ETA.

In conclusion, they return to the 'direct proof' of the testimony of the ten other defendants against Barrionuevo and Vera, 'greatly strengthened', they note, by the *careos* which [Sancristóbal and Damborenea] had with Barrionuevo before this court'.[27] That little word 'informer' had evidently cost the former minister dearly.

What is so strange about this assemblage of arguments is that the strong ones could have stood alone without the weak ones. A conviction against Barrionuevo and Vera could have been clinched by the testimony of their co-accused and other witnesses, plus the corroborating elements of the CESID documents, the Larretxea kidnapping, the failure to investigate the Marey affair, and the *careos*. By ladling on arguments as flawed and flimsy as the others cited above, and by giving them such weight, the majority cast a serious doubt over the whole proceedings. In a word, they seemed to be protesting too much. Phrases such as 'it does not seem credible' and 'it does not seem logical' all too easily suggested their own opposites.

Regarding the second crucial point, the phone call to the Red Cross, the judges were able to demonstrate that, while all the defendants except Amedo denied all knowledge of it during the oral hearing, some of them had admitted collaborating in it during the investigation of the case. Sancristóbal, for example, had told Garzón that 'we issued other communiqués, like the one which declared that "if in the space of 48 hours the four Spanish police are not freed, Segundo Marey, 51 years old, from Irún, will be executed". Obviously we had no intention of carrying out this threat, we were just trying to influence the French authorities.'[28]

The judges recognise that the defendants were almost certainly aware that the Spanish police were about to be released in any case. They suggest that the real purpose of the call was to make the Marey kidnapping débâcle look as if it had some real purpose: 'It was a way of putting a positive spin, from the point of view of the organisers of the kidnapping, on an operation which had been a fiasco.'[29]

Having established that Sancristóbal, at least, had known about the phone call, the judges again appear to gild the lily of their judgement by making a most unconvincing analysis of the GAL communiqué which had been left in Segundo Marey's pocket.[30]

The magistrates then conclude, in an extraordinarily woolly fashion, that 'We consider that it can be justifiably affirmed, as a proven fact, that *one or more* of the organisers . . . with the consent of the rest . . . agreed to issue the communiqué in question to the Red Cross. *The proof of the exact identity of the person who thought up the idea, and of the person who actually made the telephone call to issue the communiqué, is irrelevant.* What is important is that the communiqué existed, imposing a condition for the freedom of the kidnapped man, Segundo Marey, and that that communiqué originated from the group who organised the kidnapping.'[31] Once again, when a clearer and narrower focus would still have established guilt, the judges seem unable to resist a scattershot approach.

The judgement is more focused and effective in dismissing the many appeals made by various defendants, especially Vera, against Garzón's investigation of the case. The judges argue robustly that this magistrate neither was biased nor abused his powers. Vera's appeals in particular, the judgement declares, 'confuse his [Garzón's] supposed partiality with his tenacity in the investigation, in fulfilment of his duty'.[32] Again, however, an acknowledgement that some aspects of Garzón's investigation were at least legitimately questionable would have made for a more convincing verdict.

Contrary to the decidedly loose interpretation of the evidence in the foregoing, the judges were highly restrictive in their reading of the charge of 'membership of or collaboration with an armed gang'. They recognise that four criteria must be met for this charge to stick: (1) the group concerned must involve 'a certain duration or stability in time'; (2) its use of arms must be sufficient to cause 'alarm in the population and disturbance of the public peace'; (3) the purpose of its actions must be to produce 'the alarm or fear specific to terrorism'; (4) the gang must have a subjective intention of creating such alarm and fear.[33]

We have seen that the 1991 judgement against Amedo and Domínguez had, notoriously, found them not guilty of belonging to an armed gang, or of terrorism. In that case, the court found that their motivation was not to destroy democracy, but to defend it, 'although they used judicially reprehensible methods'.[34] Interestingly, the judges in the Marey case leave this door open: 'Armed gangs are both those who aim to change the established order . . . and those others who, with the ultimate aim of preserving our democracy by fighting those who want to overthrow it, have as a short-term aim the aforesaid serious disturbance of the public peace through the use of the arms in their possession.'[35]

Being an activist of the GAL, one might have thought, fitted perfectly into this definition. Nevertheless, the court points out that in this case it can only consider a single action, the kidnapping of Segundo Marey. In this action, the judges argue, the GAL had no 'stable character', since it was their first operation. Neither did the group use weaponry to produce general alarm or terror in society. Finally, 'the isolated act of the kidnapping [did not bring about] a disturbance of the public peace through producing the alarm or fear specific to terrorism'.[36]

Within these restrictive terms, then, the defendants were absolved of membership of an armed gang. But it is a ruling which leaves open intriguing possibilities for judgements in future GAL cases, where the 'stable character' of the group becomes much more evident (and some of the same individuals are indicted); where the armaments used certainly produced fear among citizens; and where the aim of operations was clearly to disturb the public peace.

Regarding the thorny and highly technical issue of whether those convicted were exempt from punishment because the statute of limitations which applied to their crimes had expired, the majority of the judges took a quite radical stance. They argued that the crimes had been committed by a 'collective', not an individual or individuals. Therefore, even though most of the defendants had not been named in the investigation until 1994, the fact that they were linked by a strict hierarchy meant that, once the junior members had been investigated, the senior members should also be considered under investigation. Even if this interpretation was rejected, the judges continued, the statute of limitations for kidnapping with conditions was fifteen years, less than the period which had elapsed between the crime and the first naming of the senior defendants in the investigation. They further argued that, although the statute of limitations on misappropriation of public funds was only ten years, the fact that those funds were a necessary condition for the kidnapping made this offence subject to the same fifteen-year statute as the kidnapping.[37]

The concept of 'treating the crimes jointly' – considering that the two crimes of misappropriation of public funds and kidnapping were essentially interrelated offences – actually benefited the senior defendants. As we have seen, their sentences were reduced from an aggregate of thirteen years to a concurrent sentence of ten years. This applied to Barrionuevo, Vera and Sancristóbal. Álvarez, Planchuelo and Amedo each got nine years and six months. Damborenea got only seven years, because the aggravating factor of membership of the security forces did not apply to him. Hierro and Oceja got five years and six months, and Hens and Corujo five years. Domínguez, whose participation had come very late in the kidnapping, got off lightest, with only two years and four months.[38] All the sentences, however, were heavy, and there was no sign that the ten who had pleaded guilty and incriminated Vera and Barrionuevo had received lenient treatment because of their 'collaboration with justice'.

Some of the defendants had asked the judges to include a proposal for a government pardon in the judgement. The court was curt and categorical in its dismissal of this plea: 'There is no argument whatsoever on which such a proposition can be based.'[39]

The seven–four majority on the bench gave the judgement the full force and legitimacy of the law. But the minority had disagreed strongly and fundamentally with their colleagues, and published, as was their right, their dissenting opinions. The gulf between the majority and minority views was so large that, reading them in sequence, it is sometimes hard to believe that they had been formulated within the same legal system, let alone within the same court of colleagues.

Two of the judges, José Jiménez Villarejo and Gregorio García Ancos, produced a joint document which, despite the respectful language in which it was couched, constituted a broadside at the majority.

The politicisation of the case is immediately apparent in their opening comments: 'It should have been said in the declaration of proofs that it has not been confirmed . . . that the idea of carrying out actions against ETA outside the law was ever taken up by the Government of the Nation in 1983.'[40] There are points, such as these, when it seems as though these two judges were motivated as much by a desire to defend the record of the PSOE government against charges implicit in the majority decision as by their conviction that Barrionuevo and Vera had not been proved guilty of the explicit charges against them as individuals.[41]

Then they cut to the chase. They do not consider that the evidence heard in court proves that either Barrionuevo or Vera participated in any way in the kidnapping of Segundo Marey; nor do they consider it proven that *any* of the defendants made the phone call to the Red Cross imposing conditions for his release. They are therefore totally at loggerheads with their fellow magistrates on the questions identified in the majority judgement as the only seriously contentious issues in the case. Why?

Villarejo and Ancos argue that their colleagues failed to distinguish between political responsibility and penal responsibility. They point out that it is no secret that the Marey case 'was used profusely by some parties to attack the government to which Mr Barrionuevo belonged'.[42] Those judging the case, they say, should therefore have exercised great prudence 'to prevent political responsibility being demanded, surreptitiously, through the criminal courts', turning the judges themselves 'almost into instruments of political struggle, and seriously affecting the delicate balance which the powers of the democratic State must maintain between themselves'.[43]

The 'blurring' of the line between political responsibility and penal responsibility leads, they say, to an inversion of the 'presumption of innocence' into its opposite, a 'presumption of "no confidence"'.[44] The latter is perfectly appropriate for the political world, they argue, but has no place in court.

After this general preamble they move to specifics. They find a 'shadow of irregularity' hanging over Garzón's investigations, which 'requires us to be very cautious in considering [the results of these investigations] as authentic proofs'. They partially endorse several of Vera's and Barrionuevo's complaints against the investigation, and while they reject the defendants' argument that these flaws are enough to annul the case, the two judges warn that his work does not offer 'a legally secure profile, so that we should be on our guard against the reproduction of these proofs in the oral proceedings'.[45] They do not believe that Judge Eduardo Moner's investigation was sufficient to cleanse these alleged irregularities in Garzón's work.

This leaves them with the evidence actually produced before them at the oral hearing, and they dismiss most of that as well. They deny that the CESID documents establish that the Spanish authorities took a decision to intervene illegally in French territory in 1983. (The majority judgement does not specify this, but Villarejo and Ancos are concerned that it leaves this interpretation open.) However, they are not themselves immune to running beyond the facts with their interpretations, in the opposite direction to their colleagues. They attempt to discredit the CESID documents altogether, saying that Perote could have doctored them. This theory not only had been quashed by the Supreme Court's own authentication of the documents in 1997, but had been ruled out in the strongest terms by the military court which convicted Perote for stealing them.[46]

Their judgement is particularly severe on the (unstated) linchpin of the majority verdict: the evidence of Sancristóbal. 'Does Señor Sancristóbal merit so much credibility that we can allow the most important part of our belief in the guilt of Señor Barrionuevo and Señor Vera to rest on his quasi-testimony? Clearly, we think not.'[47] They cast serious – and credible

– aspersions on the character and motivation of other witnesses, and, as we saw earlier, they make a scathing attack on the subjective nature of the *careo*, in which the 'winner' is often simply 'he who shouts most'.[48]

They also argue strongly against the deduction that Sancristóbal and his subordinates 'necessarily' must have sought authorisation from Barrionuevo and Vera, pointing out that there was a strong tradition in the security forces, deriving from the Franco period, of acting autonomously (and illegally) against terrorism. Once again, however, they themselves go further than their own logic permits. Rather than simply show that the 'hierarchy' argument is insufficient to prove Barrionuevo's and Vera's guilt, they effectively try to reverse it and show that it proves their innocence.[49]

Villarejo and Ancos argue that the attempted kidnapping of Larretxea is *completely* unrelated to the kidnapping of Marey. They concede that Barrionuevo received 'almost unanimous support . . . of virtually the whole political spectrum' in parliament when he took responsibility for the attempted kidnapping of Larretxea.[50] They insist that this was because information from Larretxea might have saved the life of the army officer kidnapped by ETA(p-m), Captain Martín Barrios. Why, then, is it so unlikely that Barrionuevo would have authorised the kidnapping of Mikel Lujua (the intended target of the Marey kidnapping), who had information that might have saved many other lives? Might not the remarkable support the minister received from the opposition for one illegal action have propelled him to assume he could authorise another with equal impunity?

Neither are they convincing when they imply that only Basque members of the PSOE advocated illegal action against ETA.[51] There is good reason to believe that this option was widely supported across the country at the time, and not only within the PSOE, as the majority judgement correctly asserts.[52] Villarejo and Ancos are right when they describe Damborenea as 'by his own admission an advocate of responding to ETA, even outside the national territory, with violent actions'.[53] But they are wrong to suggest that there was some kind of cordon sanitaire between Bilbao and Madrid which prevented such passions from infecting Barrionuevo. For this we have the former minister's own word, as recently as 1997, when he warmly praised a book in which Damborenea had set out his ideology during the GAL period.[54]

Despite the formal respect in which Villarejo and Ancos couch their dissenting opinion, the radical discrepancy between their views and those of their peers keeps showing. They dismiss points made by the majority in support of the 'hierarchy' argument with something very close to contempt: '[This argument] cannot stand the weight of the lightest criticism.'[55] Their own case is very fragile, however, when they attempt to argue that Interior made serious efforts to investigate the Marey kidnapping.[56] Once again, they seem to be defending the PSOE leadership rather than judging the facts.

They are scathing about their colleagues' thesis that the precise identity of the person or persons who wrote the communiqué and made the phone call to the Red Cross is 'irrelevant': 'Criminal responsibility is personal, and cannot be made collective when the person responsible cannot be identified', they thunder. In this respect, they continue, the majority judgement is clearly working on the basis of 'presumption of guilt'.[57] In this instance, one can only wonder how the majority credibly defended its position in discussion against them.

They are equally devastating about their colleagues' assumption that the Marey kidnapping must have been financed directly by Madrid. They unpick key elements of the financial transactions allegedly involved with a precise attention to detail that is singularly lacking in the majority judgement.

On the technical question of the application of a statute of limitations, they take precisely the opposite point of view to their colleagues, with the remarkable result that only two of the defendants should, in their view, be sent to prison. These are those *bêtes noires* of the Socialist Party, and long-time scapegoats for the GAL, Amedo and Domínguez.

The majority judgement had certainly left itself wide open to a number of these dissenting views. Villarejo and Ancos exposed some of its vulnerable aspects. However, their own tendency to take diametrically opposite positions to their colleagues leaves their conclusions vulnerable in their turn. In attempting to demolish all hypotheses which implicate the former government in the GAL, they appear more as advocates of the Socialist Party and its good name than as judges of Barrionuevo and Vera. The judiciary had evidently not been immune to the polarisation of the political world, and legal reasoning *on all sides* was undermined as a result.

The dissenting opinion of one of the other judges, Enrique Bacigalupo Zapater, represents a significantly graver indictment of the majority view. This is because it is presented in much cooler, more temperate language, and does not attempt to rule out hypotheses which implicate the González government in the GAL. Nor does this magistrate make a partisan critique of the investigation of Garzón and Moner. Bacigalupo simply argues that, because equally credible alternative hypotheses present themselves, the circumstantial evidence is manifestly insufficient to convict Barrionuevo and Vera.

He opens with a statement of respect for the majority decision 'which I consider worthy of all the legitimacy which is accorded by the Constitution to a judicial judgement as the product of the conscientious conviction of the judges'. His intention, he says, is in no way to 'undermine the majority judgement'. (This was, perhaps inevitably, the use to which the Socialists would put his work.) His arguments, he insists, should not be taken as 'a justification of the acts which are attributed to certain persons, which in this case are certainly very serious and which do not deserve any tolerance whatsoever'.[58]

However, he also enters a caveat, quoted at the start of this chapter: 'The guarantees of the criminal trial are an essential part of the rule of law, and the rule of law cannot be restored by abandoning such guarantees. The opposite way of thinking is, very probably, the one which found expression in such reprobate acts as the ones which are before the court.' It is discreetly put, but a clear warning nonetheless: the law must never be bent, even to obtain a conviction against those who may have bent the law themselves. The same principle which abhors state terrorism abhors convicting alleged state terrorists without adequate proof.

Like Villarejo/Ancos, his fundamental disagreement with his colleagues concerns the guilt of Barrionuevo and Vera. He stresses that the majority judgement rests on the testimony of Sancristóbal and their other co-defendants, corroborated by circumstantial evidence. He points out that such testimony should always be considered dubious, and must always be treated with 'extreme caution'. In stark contrast to the majority judgement, he sees no virtue in the fact that the co-accused also incriminated themselves, since there was already compelling material evidence against them. The incrimination of their superiors, in pursuit of a pardon, or at least of leniency on the grounds that they were obeying government orders, was thus clearly in their interests.[59] That element of self-interest casts a reasonable doubt on everything Sancristóbal and company said. (It should be pointed out, however, that these defendants did not benefit in any obvious way from their testimony: their defence that they were 'obeying orders' was explicitly rejected in the judgement, and the penalties they suffered were severe. And, as we have seen, the judgement explicitly rejected the petition of some defendants that the court should recommend a government pardon.[60])

Bacigalupo then proceeds to fillet the circumstantial evidence which the majority adduce to support this testimony of co-defendants. In each case, he says, there is an '[obvious] clash with the rules of proof'. Regarding the Larretxea case, he says, 'the proof of one fact does not permit the deduction of another and distinct fact'.[61] Unlike Villarejo/Ancos, he does not argue the case against the authenticity of the CESID documents. He simply points out that, if authentic, they were elaborated by an agency outside the control of the Interior Ministry, and that there is no evidence that Barrionuevo and Vera ever saw them.[62]

He neatly dismantles the principle of hierarchy, which the majority said made it 'incredible' that Sancristóbal and his subordinates could have acted without Barrionuevo's and Vera's authorisation. He raises the obvious alternative hypothesis that differing strategies could have been espoused by different members of the same hierarchy. And he develops this point to suggest that Interior's failure to investigate the Marey kidnapping does not necessarily imply that Barrionuevo and Vera authorised it, but simply that they did not want to dig too deeply into a divisive and contentious matter at a critical moment in the war against ETA.[63] (He does not, however, examine a consequence of this hypothesis: such reluctance to investigate a crime, however motivated, would surely have made Barrionuevo and Vera criminally as well as politically complicit in the kidnapping, albeit after the fact.)

His central point is that each point of circumstantial evidence is 'ambiguous': that is, it permits an alternative explanation more favourable to Barrionuevo and Vera than that given in the co-defendants' testimony. He therefore considers that Barrionuevo and Vera have been treated in a manner 'incompatible with a trial with full guarantees'.[64] Regarding the 'collective' way in which his majority colleagues have interpreted the law on the statute of limitations, he goes even further: the central legal principles of 'legality' and 'guilt' have been 'violated' in the trial.[65]

The fourth dissenting opinion, from Joaquín Martín Canivell, reached the same conclusions as Villarejo/Ancos and Bacigalupo, by broadly similar if less precisely argued routes. He concluded that the testimony of the ten co-defendants was rendered unreliable by their self-interest, and that the circumstantial evidence did not provide sufficiently secure grounds to corroborate it. Barrionuevo and Vera had therefore not been proven guilty within the requirements of the law.[66]

Four Supreme Court magistrates had now expressed opinions which differed drastically and substantially from their peers on basic points of law. The deep fissures which the GAL scandal had driven through the Spanish institutions were now more clearly visible than ever. It was unfortunate that the division could, to a degree, be read along the fault lines of the political sympathies of the judges. Five members of the majority were thought to be close to the Partido Popular, and the other two were also believed to be hostile to the PSOE, though from left-wing positions. The four dissenting judges all had links, closer in some cases than others, to the Socialists.[67]

One must assume that each judge left his personal sympathies aside when he came to consider the case, but the citizen in the street was hardly likely to share this assumption. The political parties themselves, from their opposed perspectives, shamelessly attributed partisanship to those judges who appeared to have opposed their 'line' on the GAL, and objectivity to those who appeared to have defended it. The senior judiciary, far from healing the wounds which the GAL scandal had inflicted on the body politic, seemed to be almost as traumatised by the GAL phenomenon as the politicians themselves.

The politicians and their supporters were not slow to react.

STANDING UP FOR BARRIONUEVO: THE SMALL BEGINNINGS OF A SOLIDARITY CAMPAIGN

'Look at how much Barrionuevo and Vera have done for Spain. And look what Spain is doing to them now.' María Silverio Velez, elderly, working class and feisty, could hardly contain her indignation. Waiting outside the Supreme Court on 30 July, the day Barrionuevo and Vera came to receive their sentences,[68] she fanned herself angrily against the midday heat, and against a world which had done down her heroes.

She had joined a few dozen Socialist supporters, outnumbered by journalists, to show solidarity with the two defendants. José Acosta, former president of the Madrid federation of the PSOE, was one of the few semi-prominent party members to show up. 'I feel a sense of clear indignation,' he told me, 'a sense of injustice. There should be protests through the institutions of the state, and protests in the street.'

All through the morning, the other defendants had been arriving to receive their sentences. 'Sancristóbal and Damborenea set up the GAL without higher authorisation,' one Socialist shouted. 'Pig! *Pistolero!*' another yelled at Damborenea.

Dirty War, Clean Hands

When Vera and Barrionuevo finally arrived, they gave an impromptu rally to their supporters from the steps of the court. Vera looked a little haggard, but otherwise seemed as suave and ironically amused as ever. Barrionuevo looked crumpled and wounded, his voice cracking: 'We have paid very dearly for our defence of democratic values,' he declared. 'The rule of law has been violated. We had a right to a fair trial. The magistrates have not respected our lives.' While Vera kept his counsel, the former minister sank into a morass of self-pity, in which the victim of the kidnapping became, once again, a kind of target: 'Does our work, our political record, deserve ten years in prison? Do we deserve to be left without the means to support our families, or to see the meagre patrimony we have inherited end up in the hands of Señor Marey?'[69]

Vera had said the previous day that he would appeal the sentence to the Constitutional Court, 'although I'm not very hopeful', and if that failed he would appeal to the European Court of Human Rights in Strasbourg, 'where my hopes are very high'. Spanish justice, he said, had been politicised to a point where it lacked any objectivity: 'A trial like the one we have had is unthinkable in any democracy that takes itself seriously.'[70]

He made the (by now) standard comment that there had been dirty war episodes under previous administrations, but that this was not the moment for him to 'tell my truth'. Of previous ministers, he said: 'each one did what he had to do, but I am not going to open Pandora's box now'.[71] Yet again, Vera seemed unable to assert his innocence without, almost in the same breath, justifying the kind of crimes of which he was accused on the grounds of unaccountable 'reasons of state'.[72]

The demonstration in support of Barrionuevo and Vera at court was small and poorly organised; supported by no figures of national prominence, it had an air of angry resignation about it. Perhaps the party leadership, under the still-fresh prime ministerial candidacy of José Borrell, was going to avoid a descent to entrenched positions from which it would be difficult to move forward as an effective opposition? Perhaps it might recognise some measure of responsibility for the events which had led to the judgement, and move forward with grace and renewal?

Or perhaps not. The party leaders had been behind closed doors, drafting their considered response, and Felipe González, though he no longer held any official leadership position, was with them.[73]

Their friends had warned them of the dangers of rejecting the judgement. Under the headline 'Risk of a fracture', an *El País* editorial on 30 July said that the opinions of the dissenting magistrates, while very well argued, did not constitute 'a kind of "alternative" judgement' which acquitted Barrionuevo and Vera. The paper added that 'the split among the judges reflects fairly accurately the fracture which this affair has created in Spanish society'.

The editorial nonetheless accorded significant space to these dissenting arguments, and to the sense of grievance felt in the PSOE because the Partido Popular had never had to account for previous dirty war operations under conservative administrations. But the paper appealed to the Socialists to have sufficient maturity not to further deepen divisions in Spanish society over the issue. It also appealed to the Partido Popular not to use the judgement to criminalise the whole González era. 'Now more than ever it is necessary that the Partido Popular and the PSOE should remake a basic consensus to give a firm structure[74] to a society built on citizenship, and eradicate terrorism. Anything else would be suicide.'[75]

'Anything else' was what the Socialists chose to do. The deliberations of the party bosses and González produced a ten-point statement which, while not as extreme as the wilder men in the party would have liked, nonetheless showed that the party was still digging a hole for itself, and that that hole was looking increasingly like a bunker.

'We respect and abide by the judgement,' was the first line of the declaration. Almost every line which followed suggested the contrary. 'But we disagree radically with it, because we believe that the trial has not shown any proof that José Barrionuevo and Rafael Vera are guilty.' The PSOE promised to continue to support the convicted men and their families: 'They will count on our collaboration to persevere in defence of their innocence and their rights before the courts, and to re-establish their good name before Spanish society.'

The Partido Popular, United Left and other parties, said the PSOE, had set up the trial as a political operation to remove the Socialists from power. 'The intolerable political and media pressure which has been exercised on the court with the aim of destroying its independence and, therefore, its impartiality *has contaminated the trial politically and nullified its development*' (my emphasis). How this position was consistent with 'respecting and abiding by the judgement' the Socialists did not explain.

The Partido Popular and other parties 'have sought to make the justice system an instrument of power rather than a power of the State,' the statement continued. 'They have tried to criminalise a government and remove legitimacy from the PSOE and Felipe González. His annihilation, to put an end to an epoch of progress, is the object of the operation which we are exposing.'

Many citizens, the Socialists said, were scandalised that the dirty war, which had begun before they took office and ended during their time in government, should be attributed to the PSOE. There followed a reminder of the sins of other governments, in the form of a promise not to reveal them. It was a familiar theme from previous statements by González, Barrionuevo and Vera. 'We have decided not to avenge the past out of respect for peace, progress and the future. We do not want to put in question the transition to democracy, which would deny the Spanish people a part of their collective history of which they feel proud.'

Many citizens, it might be said, were much more scandalised by the fact that the Socialists, in this extraordinary statement, were implying that the transition would in some way be negated if the PSOE told its full history. It was hard to see how the integrity of a great political achievement could best be defended by concealing its negative aspects.

They concluded in grandiose and self-congratulatory terms by describing the fourteen years of Socialist government as 'the most brilliant period of our contemporary history'. The Socialists appealed to the public to give them majority support at the polls once more, to 're-establish the rules of the game, defend the liberty and dignity of innocent people, as well as the stability and strength of our democracy'.[76]

The statement is remarkable for its refusal to acknowledge any *political* responsibility, or even any humanitarian concern, for the fate of Segundo Marey and the GAL's other victims. Leaving aside the question of the active involvement of Barrionuevo and Vera, a very dirty war *had* taken place while the Socialists were in power, and that government's own anti-terrorist high command, including very senior Socialists, had confessed to participating in it. If this was cause for self-congratulation on 'a brilliant period', one wonders how a Socialist government going through a bad period would have run the country.

ONE CHEER FOR DEMOCRACY: THE SOCIALISTS CONDEMN THE DIRTY WAR

The morning after this statement was issued, I phoned a supporter of Borrell's, a veteran Socialist who had previously expressed to me his revulsion at his own party's behaviour regarding the GAL and corruption.[77] I suggested that the PSOE had completely failed to confront legitimate democratic concerns about its record in this statement, and had become trapped in a wilfully blind defence of the González era. I fully expected him to share at least some of my criteria on the basis of past conversations.

To my amazement, he told me that I was being 'ingenuous', and that the statement was a triumph for Borrell over Socialist barons like Rodríguez Ibarra, who had wanted to use much stronger language, reject the judgement explicitly, and make the liberation of Barrionuevo and Vera from prison the first plank in a new Socialist election platform.

The language might be more moderate than Rodríguez Ibarra's, I conceded, but where was the positive input of Borrell and his team into the statement?

I was missing something very important, he told me: 'The condemnation of the dirty war was introduced by Borrell, and is a significant element in the document.'

It is quite true that the statement does contain a condemnation of dirty war tactics, in point number four, in the following terms: 'The barbarity which has led to the murder by ETA of more than 800 Spanish people cannot justify the imitation of ETA's practices nor the abandonment of the law. We want, especially today, to condemn anew any form of illegal struggle against terrorism. We did so in the 1970s. We did so until it [the dirty war] disappeared. And we continue doing it today.'

It is also true that these terms are untainted by the ambiguity of so many earlier PSOE comments on the dirty war, where the explicit condemnation was almost invariably twinned with an implicit justification. Nor does the statement repeat the claim – certainly an 'ingenuous' one – that the PSOE had actively combated the dirty war, as González, Barrionuevo and Vera had said in the past. The GAL had simply 'disappeared'. Something, indeed, had been learned, at this very late stage.

But I still found it shocking that I was being asked, by a man with impeccable democratic credentials, to appreciate that it was a momentous step for a democratic party to condemn state terrorism. It spoke volumes that such a condemnation was regarded as a major advance by the post-González leadership.[78]

It was bad enough that the PSOE was trying to write off the judgement as the result of the machinations of its enemies. But things were worse than that. Despite the (relatively) moderate language of the statement, the PSOE leadership was gearing up for a dramatic campaign that cannot have disappointed even Rodríquez Ibarra too much.

El País was relieved that the Socialists had not called for 'a general indictment of the transition, which would lead at a minimum to the reinvestigation of the behaviour of Barrionuevo's predecessors in Interior'. However, it turned out that some Socialists wanted to go back even further in time to find a historical parallel with what the paper described as 'one of the most bitter moments in its history'.[79]

Meanwhile, the Partido Popular was maintaining a relatively restrained response, consistent with its shift to a less strident and more centrist position. Aznar indicated that he was willing to study the feasibility of granting Barrionuevo and Vera a pardon, regardless of whether they asked for one.[80] However, the Prime Minister's comment that 'after this judegement, the whole political situation is going to change' undoubtedly infuriated the PSOE.[81] The Socialists read it as a coded call for González to resign his parliamentary seat, a demand being made explicitly, and very stridently, by *El Mundo*.

On the Friday following the verdict, González broke his short silence in an interview with Europa Press, and it was obvious that resigning was the last thing on his mind.

Far from accepting the slightest responsibility for the events which had put his subordinates in the dock, he made it clear that he intended to pursue a polarised political war with the Partido Popular. Though he said that he would not be 'as wretched towards them as they are being towards us', he accused Aznar's government of pressurising the Supreme Court, and breaking with 'the values of the transition'.

Far from showing respect to the court, he said that it was 'evident' that it had been subjected to political pressures, described the judgement as 'radically unjust', and said he was sure it would be annulled.[82] In an inversion of Álvarez Cascos' notorious pronouncement that the judges had to confirm the verdict of popular opinion, González said that if the Constitutional Court did not resolve the matter in accordance with his views, 'the functioning of our judicial system would come under question'.[83]

He compared himself to a star footballer who could no longer score goals, not because of the skill of the opposition, but because they had broken his legs. On the same day, his party paper *El Socialista* conjured up the ghosts of the Civil War. It compared González to a great President of the 1930s Republic, Manuel Azaña. He had been attacked by both the far Left and the Right when *guardia civiles*, apparently acting on their own authority, massacred anarchist villagers in the Andalusian village of Casas Viejas. The same day, Borrell took it upon himself to remind the Spanish people ('it is good that they should know') about the victims of the dirty war under the UCD, while simultaneously promising not 'to poke about in the past'.[84]

The party's general secretary, Joaquín Almunia, complained that the whole PSOE had been 'criminalised', and went further still into the past, albeit ironically: 'They hold us responsible for everything which has happened since Charles V!' he told *Le Monde*. 'We never put the transition on trial, and everyone knows what happened before and during the transition. It is irresponsible to say today that everything which came from the Socialist period is bad. We don't want to pay the bill for everyone, we want everyone to pay their share.'[85]

The media in other democracies took an active interest in the issues raised. *Le Monde* argued that the judgement was neither a triumph for democracy against state terrorism nor the outcome of a low political conspiracy against the PSOE. In true editorial fashion it concluded that the verdict was 'without doubt half-way between these two affirmations'. But it warned the Socialists that it was unwise 'to challenge the highest court in the land on an issue which is scarcely to their advantage'.[86]

Both the *International Herald Tribune* and the *New York Times* said the judgement reopened the debate on what González knew about the dirty war. *Libération* asked if anyone could really believe he had not been informed about it. His candidature for the presidency of the European Commission, where he had been hotly tipped to succeed Jacques Santer, now seemed 'frankly grotesque' in the opinion of *Corriere della Sera*, a view echoed by *The European*.

If González could hardly now seek a new career in Europe, there was an option, known only to his immediate circle, that he could go back to his old career as a lawyer. He had said he would defend Barrionuevo and Vera 'to the end', but few had thought he meant this literally. It emerged over the weekend that he had offered to join their legal team, and personally present their appeals to the Constitutional Court and, if necessary, in Strasbourg.[87] The spectacle of a former Prime Minister defending his former minister in open court may have been reassuring to the appellants and their supporters – Vera went so far as to describe González as 'the most important Spanish politician of this century, and probably the most important European one'.[88] To the rest of the world, however, it simply looked like desperation.

'The lawyer González is going to defend the governments of González before a court chosen by González,' mocked Pablo Castellano of the United Left.[89] Other commentators, more sympathetic to the PSOE, pointed out that what is possible and legal is not necessarily desirable, and that González's direct and dramatic role in the case could only increase the politicisation of the justice system which he claimed to lament.[90] This was a position which Borrell himself would discreetly endorse, but it was

DBS Arts Library

becoming clear that the nominal prime ministerial candidate had little weight in the party hierarchy compared to the former Prime Minister.[91] The *Financial Times* reported that González's decision 'has aborted speculation that Mr Aznar would consider a general pardon for Mr Barrionuevo and 11 other co-defendants', and concluded: 'Others [outside the PSOE] say that Mr González has thrown himself into Mr Barrionuevo's defence to prevent responsibility for the "dirty war" reaching further up the political ladder and directly affecting him.'[92]

August was, as we have said, a holiday month for the courts, but it did not prove to be a cooling-off period. By early September, even more provocative statements were being made by PSOE leaders than those which had initially greeted the verdict.

González told his comrades at a PSOE summer school that Barrionuevo and Vera were 'found guilty because they belonged to a left-wing government'. The future of the Socialists and Spain could not be built, he said, on the 'iniquity' of the verdict. 'What is unjust is unjust, it seems to me. The people least responsible for this situation are the Supreme Court judges, who are the victims of a [political] operation to which they should never have been subjected.'[93] The PSOE had come a long way from 'respecting and abiding by' the judgement to portraying the judges who delivered it as creatures so weak as not to be responsible for their own actions.[94]

Extremist as ever, Rodríguez Ibarra upped the ante still further at the same gathering. He called for the Attorney General to investigate the dirty war prior to 1982, and continued: 'If this party makes an effort to save Barrionuevo and Vera from going to prison, they will not have to go.' He told a most appreciative audience that he could not say more in front of the media, but hinted that thirty thousand people should demonstrate outside the prison where Barrionuevo and Vera were shortly to be locked up.[95]

Rodríguez Ibarra's words turned out to be hot air, though they made their sad contribution to souring the PSOE's relationship with the institutions of democracy. In the event, only seven thousand people turned up at the gates of Guadalajara jail on the evening of Thursday, 10 September, when Barrionuevo and Vera were finally required to comply with the sentence and enter prison.

What these hard-core Barrionuevo supporters lacked in numbers they made up in militancy. From their slogans, they seemed to be in a time warp. 'Vosotros, fascistas, soís los terroristas' ('You fascists are the real terrorists'), they shouted angrily, an old anti-Franco slogan that the PSOE had never previously used against the parliamentary Right, and certainly never against the judiciary, since the transition. 'They are putting us in prison like they did before,' they roared, forgetting that the condemned men had enjoyed all the guarantees of due process which had been systematically denied to the victims of fascism – and to the victims of the GAL.

What the demonstrators lacked in numbers they made up in seniority. Most of the leading Socialists of the González era were present. The president of the party, the elderly Basque Ramón Rubial, who had given Julián Sancristóbal his first paid party position, was there. So were Alfonso Guerra and José María ('Txiki') Benegas, González's first and second lieutenants in the GAL period. So were the party barons, Juan Carlos Rodríguez Ibarra from Estremadura, José Bono from southern Castile, Manuel Chaves from Andalusia. So were Joaquín Almunia and José Borrell, the 'double-headed' new leadership of the party. So was the man who still totally dominated the party, Felipe González. So, of course, were the two condemned men, José Barrionuevo and Rafael Vera.[96]

'In a moment, Rafael and I are going to submit, as is our duty, to a legal but unjust decision,' Barrionuevo told his well-wishers from the platform he shared with the PSOE hierarchy. It was curious that he had used the same phrase, 'legal but unjust', of the verdict on José Amedo seven years earlier.[97] 'We are innocent,' he continued, 'but we are going to do our duty, as we have throughout our political lives.' He appealed to their supporters 'not to resign themselves to accepting this injustice'.[98] By the time he wished them 'Hasta Siempre!' there was not a dry eye on the platform.

The two men then walked the hundred metres uphill to the prison gates, accompanied by their families and by Felipe González, while the crowd chanted 'Inocentes! Inocentes!'

After Barrionuevo and Vera had stepped through the small door in the large green gates and vanished from view, González remained standing alone outside the entrance. After he was photographed many times, he told a radio station that his enemies 'wanted an image; there they have it.[99] They don't have a picture of two men, they have one of three. It is true that one stayed in front of the outer door, though they would have liked to have had him go inside. Those who are inside are the victims of a hunt of which I am the quarry.'[100]

To almost hysterical cries of 'Felipe, get them out of there!' the man many people still believed to be the 'Señor X' of the GAL, and others regarded as the best Spanish politician of the century, walked away from prison.

NOTES

1   Voto Particular que formula el Excmo Sr D Enrique Bacigalupo Zapater, Causa Especial No. 2530/95 [Segundo Marey], Supreme Court, Madrid, 29 July 1998 [hereafter 'Bacigalupo'], p. 1.
2   El País, 28 July 1995.
3   The fact that their colleague Eduardo Moner had corroborated Garzón's investigation would, of course, have cast a shadow on the credibility of this option.
4   El País, 16 July 1998.
5   El País, 23 July 1998.
6   See Robert P. Clark, 'Patterns of ETA Violence: 1968–1980', in Peter Merkl (ed.), Political Violence and Terror (Berkeley: University of California Press, 1986), p. 139.
7   The connection was spelt out by the PSOE leader in Andalusia, Manuel Chaves: 'Many citizens will think that if the Prime Minister can close a newspaper, then he can also use the same power to influence the justice system in the second chamber of the Supreme Court, as to what decision they should reach [in the Marey case].' El País, 25 July 1998.
8   El País, 24 July 1998.
9   El País, 26 July 1998.
10 The newspaper itself claimed that there was no single leaked document, and that its account came from the meticulous reconstruction of information from a variety of court sources.

11 *El Mundo*, 24 July 1998.

12 *El País*, 26 July 1998. The *'sindicato de crimen'* was the PSOE term, popularised by González, for hostile media like *El Mundo*, *ABC* and the COPE radio network, and their dominant personalities such as Pedro J. Ramírez, Luis María Ansón and Luis del Olmo.

13 *El País*, 25 July 1998. Another example of this kind of 1930s rhetoric – almost Stalinist in tone – was provided by the general secretary of the Madrid Socialist Federation, Jaime Lissavetzky: 'Barrionuevo is an innocent person, *a worker incapable of carrying out any criminal action whatsoever. El País*, 26 July 1998. My emphasis.

14 *El País*, 27 July 1998.

15 Ibid.

16 *El País*, 26 July 1998.

17 Miguel Ángel Rodríquez was replaced by Josep Piqué. However, the latter, as we have seen, had not been able to resist goading González as soon as the decision was leaked. But in general the Partido Popular did not gloat too publicly at the PSOE's discomfiture.

18 While the decision was not unanimous, the dissenting magistrates also formally subscribed to the court's judgement.

19 Sentencia No. 2/1998, Tribunal Supremo, Sala de lo Penal, Causa Especial No. 2530/95 [Segundo Marey], Supreme Court, Madrid, 29 July 1998 [hereafter 'Judgement'], p. 45.

20 Every major point, that is, except armed gang membership, though the judges did not draw attention to that issue in this part of the judgement.

21 Judgement, p. 30.

22 The so-called 'Founding Memorandum of the GAL', though the judgement does not so describe it.

23 Judgement, pp. 30–1.

24 Ibid., p. 46.

25 Ibid. My emphasis.

26 Ibid., p. 48.

27 Ibid., p. 50.

28 Ibid., p. 51.

29 Ibid., p. 52.

30 They argue (ibid.) that the 'gesture on the part of the French Government' referred to in the first written GAL communiqué relates to the release of the Spanish police. In fact, it is much more likely that the word 'gesture' refers to the liberation of Marey himself by the kidnappers. The full sentence in the GAL communiqué read: 'As a sign of goodwill and convinced of the proper evaluation of the gesture on the part of the French Government, we are freeing Segundo Marey, arrested by our organisation as a consequence of his collaboration with the terrorists of ETA.' In a more detailed consideration of this evidence later in the judgement (p. 95) they repeat this reading of the communiqué even more categorically, without supplying any additional grounds for their interpretation. It is hard to see why, if the 'gesture' had indeed referred to the release of the Spanish police, the kidnappers would not have mentioned the GEOs specifically, if they were trying to put a good face on their botched enterprise.

31 Ibid., pp. 51–3. My emphasis.

32 Ibid., p. 68.

33 Ibid., pp. 77–9.

34 See ch. 16, p. 241.

35 Judgement, p. 78.

36 Ibid., p. 79. The citizens of Hendaye, at least, might have legitimately claimed that Marey's kidnapping did produce fear and alarm. One could also argue

that the communiqué left with Segundo Marey, with its list of future threats of armed action and sabotage, constitutes the very manifesto of an 'armed gang' committed to spreading alarm.

37 Ibid., pp. 105–11.

38 All of the defendants received corresponding penalties of disbarment from public office, and from any privileges they derived from previously held public offices. See ibid., pp. 116–18.

39 Ibid., p. 115. Barrionuevo and Vera, of course, did not ask for pardon because such a petition would have implied acceptance of their guilt.

40 Voto Particular de D José Jiménez Villarejo y D Gregorio García Ancos, Causa Especial No. 2530/95 [Segundo Marey], Supreme Court, Madrid, 29 July 1998 [hereafter Villarejo/Ancos], p. 0.

41 See also ibid., p. 11: 'It must be said, to eliminate any ambiguity or suspicion whatsoever, that it has not been proved that that idea [dirty war against ETA] was taken on board by the Spanish Government.' And they go further, in reference to the CESID documents: 'Not a single one of them . . . can serve *minimally* to attribute to the Government of the Nation the decision to carry out violent and illegal actions in its struggle against the terrorism of ETA' (p. 12, my emphasis). To most reasonable people these documents would, in the context, at the very least *minimally* serve to make just such an attribution.

42 Ibid., p. 3.

43 Ibid.

44 The Spanish word *desconfianza* means 'distrust' in general terms, but in the political field it corresponds to the concept of 'no confidence', as in a 'vote of no confidence in the government'.

45 Villarejo/Ancos, pp. 7 and 10.

46 See p. 334, n. 76. It is particularly puzzling that these two judges ignore this ruling, because they cite other aspects of the Perote judgement in their opinion.

47 Villarejo/Ancos, p. 14.

48 Ibid., p. 15. See ch. 22, p. 335.

49 This is ironic because it is precisely these judges who make the point very powerfully that under Spanish law 'there is no obligation on the part of the accused to prove his innocence'. Ibid., pp. 5–6.

50 Ibid., p. 16.

51 Ibid.

52 See, however, ch. 12, n. 1, for a qualifying view.

53 Villarejo/Ancos, p. 17.

54 See ch. 14, p. 187.

55 Villarejo/Ancos, p. 18.

56 Ibid., p. 19.

57 Ibid., p. 23.

58 Bacigalupo, p. 1.

59 'They had no other defence than that of having undertaken an operation approved by the State' (ibid., p. 6). He cites the Italian judicial campaign against the Mafia as a paradigm where the 'criminal informer' has been, of necessity, a key figure, and such 'extreme cautions' are nevertheless exercised rigorously. He also suggests that the evidence of Amedo and Domínguez could, in this context, be considered as 'bought'. Their release from prison by Garzón, he says, amounts to 'a pardon with state protection' (p. 7).

60 Judgement, p. 115. See also *El País*, 30 July 1998.

61 Bacigalupo, p. 8.

62 Ibid., pp. 9 and 10.

63 Unlike Villarejo/Ancos, Bacigalupo does not attempt to challenge the majority view that no serious investigation actually took place.

64 Bacigalupo, p. 14: 'Our analysis demonstrates that the data on which the majority of the chamber have based their acceptance of the credibility of the declarations of the co-defendants . . . are, individually considered, ambiguous. That is to say, they do not exclude other equally plausible and feasible hypotheses. It is clear that, with ambiguous data, *although they may be plentiful,* it is not possible to consider that the demands which jurisprudence imposes . . . on the declarations of co-defendants have been satisfied.' My emphasis.

65 Ibid., p. 22.

66 Voto Particular que formula el Magistrado Joaquín Martín Canivell, Causa Especial No. 2530/95 [Segundo Marey], Supreme Court, Madrid, 29 July 1998, pp. 1–14. Like his dissenting colleagues, Canivell also argues against the 'collective' interpretation of the statute of limitations in the judgement, which leads him, albeit reluctantly, to conclude also that only Amedo and Domínguez can legitimately be sent to jail.

67 *El País*, 30 July 1998, described the make-up of the Supreme Court as a small-scale map of the political composition of the country.

68 This is a formality, where the defendants are required to call into the court offices to pick up their sentences in writing. The judges had publicly announced their verdict the previous day. None of the defendants had to enter prison at this stage: a simple appeal for clarification of the sentence, coupled with the judicial holidays which fell in August, meant that the execution of the sentence would be postponed for several weeks.

69 Writer's notes, 30 July 1998.

70 *La Vanguardia*, 30 July 1998.

71 Ibid.

72 Regarding dirty wars conducted under previous Interior ministries, Vera told *El País*: 'I could give an infinity of facts and names' because after thirteen years in Interior he had a lot of information. 'We ourselves could have done an exercise of recuperation of memory, but that seems to me to be a despicable thing to do.' (*El País*, 30 July 1998.) A PSOE 'baron', José Bono, came up with the definitive formula in this respect: 'All the Interior Ministers since 1977 are innocent of the crimes which may have been committed in the struggle against ETA.' *El Mundo*, 30 July 1998.

73 González officially played no part in the final drafting of the party's first formal response to the judgement. Yet he had sat in on his colleagues' deliberations for many hours, and undoubtedly had an input into the document they finally produced. Over the next few days, any pretence that González was playing a hands-off role would be abandoned.

74 The writer used the evocative verb *vertebrar,* which for any politically literate Spaniard recalls Ortega y Gasset's key essay 'España invertebrada' ('Spain without a backbone'), first published in 1921.

75 *El País*, 30 July 1998. Javier Pradera expanded on these points with some illuminating qualifications. (*El País,* 31 July 1998.) He made the very sensible point that, while the GAL scandal could not cancel out all the achievements of the Socialist years in government, those achievements could not cancel out the manifest flaws of that period. *El Mundo* also published an editorial on 30 July, which welcomed the court's decision as a 'triumph of democracy' and 'an impeccable judgement which reconciles common sense with the rule of law'. Strangely, it highlighted some of the weakest arguments of the judgement as its greatest strengths. And it dismissed, in a few poorly argued lines, the legitimate doubts raised by the dissenting magistrates. The 'fracture' in the media was as evident as ever.

76 *El País*, 31 July 1998.

77 This source was speaking off the record, and does not want to be identified, which perhaps tells its own story.

78 There was some dissent within the PSOE about the party's response to the judgement. The Socialist mayor of San Sebastián, Odón Elorza, described it as 'pathetic . . . playing the role of the victim excessively'. (*El País*, 12 August 1998.) A leader of a leftist sector of the party, Antonio García Santesmases, declared that 'criminal activity emanating from the State apparatus should be condemned politically and morally'. (*El Mundo*, 11 August 1998.) Both men also accused the Partido Popular of hypocrisy on the issue. Neither had any serious influence in the PSOE leadership.

79 *El País*, 31 July 1998.

80 This offer brought the following incendiary response from the irredentist Rodríguez Ibarra: 'They should not be pardoned by the executioner of the day, which has been José María Aznar.' *El País*, 3 August 1998.

81 *Le Monde*, 1 August 1998.

82 Two of the Supreme Court judges whose dissenting opinions were seized upon by Barrionuevo's and Vera's defence teams denied that they had suffered any pressure whatsoever in the exercise of their duties. These were Bacigalupo and Canivell. See *El País,* 4 August 1998.

83 *El País* and *El Mundo*, 1 August 1998.

84 *El País*, 1 August 1998.

85 *Le Monde,* 1 August 1998.

86 Ibid.

87 *El País*, 2 August 1998.

88 Ibid.

89 *El País*, 4 August 1998. The Constitutional Court's twelve members were in fact selected by the Congress (4), the Senate (4), the government (2) and the General Council of the Judiciary (2). González would certainly have been influential in several of these appointments.

90 See *El País* editorial, 4 August 1998.

91 Apart from expressing mild dissent at González's entry into the legal fray, Borrell never shifted a millimetre from the increasingly polarised position of the rest of the Socialist leadership over the summer. He told a large meeting of miners in León in late August that it was 'lamentable that a democratic minister should go into prison because of an unjust verdict and others, under whose authority the same things happened, should pass for democrats'. (*El País*, 22 August 1998.) Since this remark won him the biggest ovation of the meeting, the leadership was probably not out of step with the sentiment of the rank and file of the party.

92 *Financial Times*, 5 August 1998.

93 *El País*, 7 September 1998.

94 The president of the Supreme Court, and of the General Council of the Judiciary, Javier Delgado Barrio, felt moved to issue an unprecedented personal statement in defence of the independence of the courts. He pointedly asserted that the Constitutional Court would hear the Marey appeal on the basis of the facts, and not on the basis of what lawyer was making the case for it. (*El País*, 7 September 1998.) His statement led to further bitter exchanges between the PSOE and the judiciary.

95 *El País*, 6 September 1998.

96 The signal exception was the former Interior and Justice Minister, and then justice spokesman, Juan Alberto Belloch. When questioned by the media about his absence, Belloch said he felt 'represented' by the other leaders present.

97 See ch. 16, p. 235.

98 *El País*, 11 September 1998.

DBS Arts Library

99 This was 'the photo' which, he had repeatedly said in the past, his enemies desired to see on the front pages of the newspapers.
100 *El País,* 11 September 1998.

PART IV

Conclusions:

Cleaning Up After a Dirty War

PART IX

25

Waking from the Nightmare:
what the GAL tells us about Spanish democracy

Terrorism, although it can cause great evil, is not generally capable of threatening the existence of a democratic State; but an illegal anti-terrorist policy, maintained over a sufficient period of time, brings about the certain liquidation of democratic liberties and institutions. The question is, therefore, what can the democratic State do to combat terrorism without itself ceasing to be democratic?

Patxo Unzueta, political commentator and author[1]

Someone had to type my name on the manilla envelope; somebody made the bomb. I often ask the question: 'What did these people tell their children they did that day?' . . . However, the fact that such a sophisticated bomb found its way through the post to me . . . I lay sole responsibility for that with [South African President] F.W. de Klerk . . . de Klerk knew about the hit squads . . . but de Klerk chose to do nothing about it.

Father Michael Lapsley, ANC activist and chaplain[2]

People do not want to understand that we inherited a State apparatus, in its entirety, from the dictatorship.

Felipe González[3]

I have dirty hands. Right up to the elbows. I've plunged them in filth and blood. But what do you hope? Do you think you can govern innocently?

The communist leader Hœder in Jean-Paul Sartre's play
Les Mains Sales[4]

There is no horror, no cruelty, sacrilege, or perjury, no imposture, no infamous transaction, no cynical robbery, no bold plunder or shabby betrayal that has not been or is not daily being perpetrated . . . under those elastic words, so convenient and yet so terrible: 'for reasons of state'.

Mikhail Bakunin, nineteenth-century Russian anarchist[5]

The GAL phenomenon achieved what ETA sought but could not accomplish alone: it inserted a corrosive question mark into the widely accepted success story of the Spanish transition to democracy. This is especially true if we consider the GAL not just as the organisation which carried out a dirty war against ETA in the mid-1980s, but as the persistent obstruction, by the Socialist Party leadership, of every investigation into that dirty war ever since. This obstruction has been repeatedly accompanied by a tendency, sometimes almost subliminal and sometimes blatant, to justify the kind of state terrorism which the Socialists denied had existed under the González governments in the first place.

'The overriding importance of the GAL, in my opinion,' says Javier Pradera, elaborating on one of his central arguments on the subject, 'did not lie in its operations in themselves. Of course, they were disgusting operations, dirty, as those of any dirty war always are.' He argues that the Socialists could have believed, wrongly but in good faith, that a dirty war was morally justified if it ultimately saved lives. Their refusal to accept responsibility for that war, however, has no moral justification, he says, and did the worst damage to democratic institutions.

'I believe that the real rupture with the rule of law was produced when the Socialist government began to obstruct and impede the investigation of the GAL. But do you know what makes them [the Socialist leadership] repulsive in this respect? They want to give the message that they didn't do it [organise the GAL]. But later they want to say that what they did was heroic, and that they deserve the gratitude of the people. It's a little bit like the syndrome of Oliver North [in the Iran–Contra case]. This is evident in the attitude of Vera and Barrionuevo. "Instead of decorating us, they persecute us."'[6]

The GAL scandal started with members of an immature government resorting to state terrorism under extreme pressure from ETA's ferocious terrorist campaign. The Socialists had expected, reasonably enough, that the Basque radicals would recognise their democratic credentials and give them some sort of respite when they won the 1982 election. Instead, they found themselves under immediate assault. They had not even taken office when ETA killed General Victor Lago Román, commander of the Brunete armoured division, an emblem of the prestige of the Spanish army.

The Socialists, in their first year in power, felt caught between the threat of a military coup and the terrible haemorrhage of the security forces under ETA attacks, which made such a coup more likely. They were desperately anxious to avoid what they saw, again not unreasonably, as the great error the Left had made the last time it had governed Spain, in the 1930s: the disintegration of public order. And, as Felipe González says, they had inherited a security apparatus intact from the dictatorship. However, their failure to purge that apparatus of its anti-democratic officers, torturers and dirty warriors was a cardinal error in itself, though the task would undoubtedly have been a daunting one. Instead, the new Minister for the Interior, and his political staff, acted as though *they* had to prove their security credentials to the police commanders. This inverted the principle involved: the police officers should have been obliged to prove their democratic credentials to the new administration.

Javier Pradera says that the young PSOE leadership were deeply influenced by 'Leftist' ideas. He cites especially Jean-Paul Sartre's insistence, in *Les Mains Sales*, that only naive idealists imagine they can exercise political power without getting their hands dirty.[7] Paradoxically, some of them seem to have applied this principle to embrace active collaboration with a group of security officers whose ideology was drawn from the Right.

Pradera's hypothesis about the PSOE's involvement with the dirty war is based on the metaphor of supply and demand. The 'supply' came from the security forces, and was permanently on offer from the mid-1970s. His conjecture – and he insists it is just that – is that under the UCD dirty war operations were tolerated, within limits, by senior politicians. 'They kept the *incontrolados* under control.'

Once the Socialists come to power, however, 'that "supply" finally meets its "demand" . . . someone in the state apparatus, we don't know who, accepts the offer from these groups who say: "Give us money and cover, and we will clean up things for you. If you give us a free hand, we will finish off ETA in a very short space of time. We don't want to do it in an amateur way, like it was done until now, and under the fear that we would be reprimanded for doing it. We want to do it with the security of having the political support of a left-wing and democratic party." Well, knowing them [the PSOE leadership] as I knew them at that time, I think they could have fallen into that trap.'

He adds that in his conversations with them, they 'never recognised their participation, and so I could never testify before a court, but there is non-verbal communication, and from their non-verbal communication I don't have the slightest doubt . . .'[8]

Under all these conditions, the decision by some senior Socialists to accept this Faustian bargain and undertake dirty war operations, and of others to turn a blind eye to their participation in the GAL, was perhaps not so surprising, though hardly excusable either. At the time, few members of the opposition, and few people in the media, actively opposed the use of death squads. Some applauded the GAL's campaign, and public opinion was also generally passive when not actually supportive. A Socialist MP, who did not support the GAL, has described how he was shocked by the way his constituents used to congratulate him every time the death squads claimed a victim. They took his curt denials of responsibility as a kind of nudge-and-wink complicity.[9] Those who opposed the GAL between 1983 and 1986, says Pradera, 'were absolutely alone'.

To what extent was this lack of an active commitment to the democratic rule of law specific to Spanish political culture – a hangover from Francoism, perhaps? To what extent is it typical of any democratic country under attack from terrorism?

'I do not think that [this lack of commitment] reflects some congenital defect in the Socialists or in the Spanish public,' says Patxo Unzueta. 'They acted like their Israeli, French, English or German equivalents in more or less comparable circumstances.'[10]

This answer, of course, begs the question as to whether the circumstances in any of these countries really were comparable to those under which the GAL waged their campaign. It has become a cliché of the

Socialists' defence of their conduct to say that 'other countries do it too'. Or, as Carmen Romero put it, 'phenomena of dirty tricks, settling of accounts, are normal in very many countries.'[11] So, of course, are torture and corruption, but such terrifying normality hardly provides a justification for democrats to engage in such pursuits.

More specifically, the kind of dirty war fought by the GAL is, in fact, quite unusual in other developed democracies. Israel is a special case. The Israeli security forces have certainly carried out dirty war operations over long periods, and in many countries, with considerable support from Israeli public opinion, though also with significant democratic opposition. But the fact that Israel has spent most of its existence in a state of virtual or actual warfare with most of its neighbours, which are themselves largely dictatorships, makes it a poor yardstick to apply to 1980s Europe.

The German authorities' treatment of Baader-Meinhof militants is often used as an analogy by Socialist apologists. The Germans certainly took a 'tough' line on terrorism, and there are unanswered questions about a number of Red Army Faction deaths, in and out of prison. But this record pales beside the GAL's sustained campaign of terror, over three years, mostly on foreign soil and with some sixty victims, including many 'civilians' and some children.[12]

The closest parallel would appear to be with the British security forces, who have frequently been accused of dirty war tactics in Northern Ireland. In the early and mid-1970s, senior officers such as General Frank Kitson put into practice his theory of 'low intensity operations'.[13] There were a number of republican, loyalist and 'civilian' victims of these tactics, which caused widespread outrage, and such actions seem to have been largely abandoned by the 1980s. However, the British forces continued to periodically implement a 'shoot-to-kill' tactic in dealing with known terrorists, which led to inquiries, which were often actively obstructed by the authorities. Allegations made in recent years of collusion between senior unionist politicians, the security forces and loyalist death squads also certainly deserve further investigation. To find a British analogy for the GAL, however, we would have to imagine a dirty war campaign run by London against IRA members, their families and ordinary civilians in the Republic of Ireland, in towns like Letterkenny, Monaghan and Dundalk, over a span of several years.[14]

France is perhaps the European Union democracy where the security forces are least subject to democratic scrutiny, and where the ideology which holds that 'reasons of state' override democratic rights is most deeply rooted.[15] Charles de Gaulle's ruthless repression of the OAS is well known. Much more recently, François Mitterrand's support for the French secret service bombing operation in New Zealand against Greenpeace's *Rainbow Warrior*, which cost the life of an ecologist, has received widespread publicity.[16]

Felipe González himself has invoked Mitterrand's 'understanding' of the GAL campaign, quoting the French President as saying that, if French police were being shot at the rate Spanish police were being shot by ETA, the gendarmes would take the law into their own hands and no one would stop them.[17] One of Mitterrand's Interior ministers, Charles Pasqua, stated openly that 'democracy ends where the interests of the State begin'.[18] Such 'comprehension' from the French authorities, therefore, provides no democratic justification for the GAL. And it raises another question. To what extent did the French collaborate in Spain's dirty war?

From the very first GAL operations, there were allegations from the Basque refugees and their French support network that French police were either actively assisting the death squads or turning a blind eye to their comings and goings. There is considerable circumstantial evidence that the French authorities, on numerous occasions, were less than diligent in their pursuit of the GAL. Checkpoints were set up after attacks, but rarely between the crime scene and the Spanish border, despite abundant indicators that this was where the perpetrators habitually fled. Several of the major GAL detentions in France were made by ordinary citizens, and did not appear to be welcomed by the local gendarmes.

On the other hand, some French officers, like Roger Boslé, were energetic and effective in pursuit of the GAL, and brought many mercenaries to justice. Boslé, and several members of the French judiciary, explicitly linked the GAL to the Spanish security forces. The justice system, however, also sent out contradictory signals, and we have seen how Judge Michel Svahn allowed a number of GAL suspects, including the notorious Jean-Philippe Labade, generous bail terms which enabled them to abscond with ease.

Evidence has now been accepted by the Spanish Supreme Court that there was French co-operation with José Amedo at the level of a particular police inspector, Guy Metge, conveniently deceased. Several GAL mercenaries have spoken about being guided to their targets by a French police officer called 'Jean' or 'Jean-Louis'. But attempts to establish GAL links with more senior French officers have failed in the courts.

The most likely explanation is that the French authorities had a broadly *laissez-faire* attitude to the GAL at a senior level. On the ground, a few officers took initiatives in investigating the dirty war, others acted against the GAL only when circumstances forced them to, and a few were bribed by the Spanish to actually help the death squads.

Such a *laissez-faire* attitude at the top would fit well with Mitterrand's apparent 'comprehension', at several levels.

It was frequently argued that the real purpose of the GAL campaign was to 'persuade' the French to change their relatively benevolent policy towards the Basque refugees, break up ETA's 'French sanctuary', and extradite terrorist suspects to Spain. Yet González, and the French ambassador to Madrid at the time, Pierre Guidoni, have both contended that the GAL campaign damaged relations with France, just as agreements to collaborate more actively against terrorism were being reached.

It is very likely that Mitterrand was willing, almost from the beginning, to help his Spanish Socialist colleagues in their fight against ETA. The document which González brought to the Marey trial seems to confirm that. But that document also makes it clear that Mitterrand did not want to go public on the issue.[19] His hands were tied by the sympathy the Basque refugees enjoyed among his own voters in the French Basque Country.

The GAL campaign, by carrying the grim reality of terrorism to the French Basque doorstep, undoubtedly contributed to a shift in local French attitudes against ETA and the refugees. Javier Pradera agrees: 'You could conclude that [the GAL] did not suit the French badly, that the French said "Well, this protects us in terms of our public opinion."'[20] So it suited Mitterrand to adopt a 'hands-off' policy towards the death squads, and that policy did his friends in Madrid a favour as well. The killing of French civilians by the GAL seems to have been a price both sides were willing to pay, brutally cynical though that seems. However, the 'accidental' killing of the elderly Christophe Matxikotte and the teenage Catherine Brion in February 1986 was probably seen, by both the French and the Spanish, as pushing that price too high. By that time, in any case, French public opinion had shifted against ETA. The GAL abruptly stopped their campaign,[21] and expulsions of terrorist suspects to Spain became the norm. In this sense, as Rafael Vera himself has conceded, the GAL campaign can be considered a 'success'.

In the Spanish Basque Country, however, the GAL campaign was a disaster for the interests of Spanish, and Basque, democracy.

Patxo Unzueta points out that, if one of the aims of the GAL was to force ETA to negotiate its own dissolution, it was 'a total failure'.[22] Far from being forced to surrender, ETA emerged from the GAL period stronger as a terrorist force, and probably much stronger politically, than before.

In 'military' terms, ETA killed forty-four people in 1982, before the GAL started to operate, and maintained a rate of about forty killings a year during the GAL period. In 1987, with the GAL campaign over, ETA claimed fifty-four victims. The rise in casualties can be attributed to ETA's increased use of indiscriminate bombings with civilian victims in these years. This may point to a grim kind of 'success' by the GAL: ETA's shift to a bombing campaign may have reflected the increased difficulty in mounting effective 'military' operations from the virtually dismantled 'French sanctuary'. That was hardly the success that the GAL were seeking.

Politically, the impact of the GAL on Basque society, and particularly on a generation which had never known Francoism, was enormous. The dirty war under the Socialists provided a crucial argument for the thesis of the Basque radicals that nothing much had changed since Franco, that Spanish democracy was a cosmetic façade which covered up a murderous fascist machine. That thesis is a gross distortion of what actually happened during the transition. But the GAL's campaign of bombings and shootings, coupled with the torture of Lasa and Zabala, gave that view sufficient substance to attract the support of a significant sector of the first generation of Basques to grow up under a modern democracy.

'The activity of the GAL,' writes Patxo Unzueta, 'was utilised by the propagandists of ETA as the proof of its theory of two symmetrical violences. The image is false, because it is evident that ETA has continued in action after the disappearance of the dirty war. But it is also evident that that error from the middle of the 80s – as well as its judicial resurrection and media exploitation in the 90s – has been decisive for the generational reproduction of nationalist violence in the Basque Country . . . That exploitation, which was supported, from a given moment, by the party which then led the opposition [Partido Popular], would end up provoking . . . the climate of instability which ETA had not succeeded in provoking 10 years earlier.

'That is the paradox of terrorism. By itself, it is impotent to overthrow the democratic State. But a mistaken response by that same State can seriously destabilise the system . . .

'Even conceding that the GAL were efficient in convincing the French authorities that they had to take seriously the need to dismantle the ETA sanctuary installed in their territory, the GAL were much more efficient as a destabilising factor in the democratic system and as a catalyst for a new flow of members to ETA, prolonging the problem for at least a generation.'[23]

The ETA ceasefire of September 1998 suggested, on an optimistic reading, that that generation might at last have spent its fire, and come to recognise the legitimacy of a democratic rather than an armed struggle for Basque independence. The suspension of that ceasefire in late 1999, and the resumption of full-scale terrorism in 2000, shows that such optimism was sadly misplaced.

The GAL scandal also continues to poison other aspects of Spanish democracy. The Spanish judiciary has undoubtedly not been immune to the corrosive polarisation of Spanish political culture in the late 1990s. Some of its members have offered damaging ammunition to those Socialist demagogues who portray the Audiencia Nacional as a hothouse of right-wing conspiracies. But no unblinkered observer can deny that the tireless and fearless work of Baltasar Garzón and Jesús Santos, to give just two examples, has been of great service in bringing well-protected criminals to justice, and in checking abuses of power by an executive which seemed to think its record should not be open to public scrutiny.

The judicial investigation of the GAL, which may last well into this decade, has revealed not only Socialist complicity with death squads in the 1980s but also the incapacity of the PSOE to come to terms with the independence of the courts in the 1990s. Felipe González launched a deeply disturbing attack on the role of the judiciary in a long and complex interview after his resignation as party leader in 1997.[24] He argued that a historically rooted fear of authoritarian governments had displaced a disproportionate degree of power to the judiciary, and that this trend needed to be reversed. Because judges were not elected, he said, their power was 'fixed, unchangeable and irresponsible'. This was an extraordinary argument for a former lawyer, and a former Prime Minister, to advance. It indicated a very weak grasp of the fundamental democratic principle of the separation of powers.

In a response ironically entitled 'Montesquieu is dead. Long live Hobbes!', Gurutz Jáuregui Bereciartu reminded González that the reverse was true: as masters of an absolute majority, the first PSOE governments had exercised an exceptional degree of power, free of parliamentary checks and balances. As Jáuregui points out, 'the judiciary, happily, did carry out this function [of exercising a restraining control on government]. And it did so clearly within the limits of the role the Constitution confers upon it, that of the safeguard of fundamental rights and liberties.'[25]

González was rejecting the principle of separation of powers in theory, and Spain's biggest democratic party proved unwilling to accept the rulings of the judiciary in practice, when its members were convicted of dirty war crimes. This insistence on refusing to accept what the courts find evident is linked to the party's incapacity to acknowledge its own recent history. But that history remains wrapped around its neck, and will not, unacknowledged, allow the PSOE to move forward and make the contribution Spanish society requires of it.

This constitutes a failure to fully embrace the pluralism and checks and balances of democracy itself, and condemns the party to a sterile, demagogic style of opposition. Its political strategy after losing power sometimes seemed reduced to attempting to expose the Partido Popular's alleged links to the dirty war during the transition to democracy.

The Socialists often proposed a bargain: they demanded that, if they had to take the blame for the GAL, the Partido Popular must take equivalent responsibility for the first dirty war.[26] This position was flawed, on several grounds.

Firstly, the Socialist accession to power in 1982 was supposed to mark the *completion* of the transition from dictatorship to democracy. Conservative ministers with a Francoist past might have some poor excuse for allowing the police to get up to dirty tricks; no such parole should apply to democrats who came to power precisely because their hands were clean.

Secondly, the long gap between the end of the first dirty war and the start of the GAL campaign indicates that the Socialists were not the unwilling inheritors of an active group of death squads. While the GAL initially drew on much of the 'expertise' of the earlier dirty war, their creation, maintenance and dissolution were all matters for which the Socialist administration must answer alone.

Thirdly, while there can be no doubt that conservative ministers had a *laissez-faire* attitude to the first dirty war, and protected senior police involved in it, the kind of hard evidence which links the Socialist administration to the GAL has never been produced in relation to the earlier period. Moreover, none of these former ministers, with the significant exception of Manuel Fraga, currently President of the Galician regional government, now plays a front-rank role in the contemporary Partido Popular.

Javier Pradera dismisses the PSOE's attempt to shift the blame to the UCD in a couple of sentences: 'It's absurd. It's as though you stole my wallet, and then said "No, I want to be acquitted because other people steal wallets and they haven't been caught."'[27]

Nevertheless, the legacy of both dirty wars still presents serious questions about the role of the Partido Popular. In opposition, it had used the GAL scandal to damage González. The party almost certainly participated actively in, and certainly benefited from, a conspiracy to use state papers to blackmail a democratically elected government.[28] When it was defeated in the 1993 elections, the Partido Popular seemed to have real difficulty in accepting that the rules of democracy continue to apply, even when you are beaten several times in a row. The Partido Popular's efforts to expose the PSOE's involvement in the GAL were motivated less by a high-minded desire to see state terrorists face justice than by an almost hysterical determination to dislodge the PSOE from office by any means to hand.

There is a second dilemma for the Partido Popular. The GAL trials are continuing into Aznar's second administration, and are implicating higher and higher levels of the military hierarchy. The Partido Popular does not want – and perhaps cannot afford – to see the army and Guardia Civil top brass repeatedly tarnished by dirty war revelations. A leading anti-terrorist general has already hinted that, if he has to testify on the GAL, he will recall the conservatives' involvement in earlier death squad operations. An appalling vista opens up: that the entire Spanish democratic establishment has had some involvement in state terrorism.

However, there has been one very positive outcome from the Partido Popular's involvement in exposing the GAL scandal. Having criticised the Socialists so bitterly and so long for using undemocratic methods against ETA, Aznar's party has so far been immune to the temptation of getting its own hands dirty in the fight against terrorism. It would face a massive public outcry if it did. It is to be hoped that the repeated provocations offered by ETA's new campaign will not succeed in making this temptation more attractive, or shift public opinion back towards ambiguity on state terrorism.[29]

The GAL engendered a nightmare from which Spain has not yet awakened, with half a dozen murder cases still before the courts. Felipe González, one of the outstanding statesmen of the European Union, has been virtually disqualified from high office in Brussels, and might yet face terrorist charges himself.

It is easy to argue that all this adds up to an indictment of Spain as a dangerously immature democracy. However, the opposite may just as well be true: the most remarkable aspect of the GAL affair is probably the fact that the Spanish judicial system, the media and civil society itself have proved capable of investigating the dark side of the state. There have been flaws in the behaviour of certain journalists, and some of the judicial decisions relating to the GAL are questionable, but on balance the commitment of the Spanish media and the Spanish judiciary to democratic values has been impressive. Western Europe's youngest democracy may actually be more mature in this respect than France, Germany or Britain. Justice has been done, to a degree at least, and the heavens have not fallen. The GAL investigations have proved an inspiration for the use of international law in the defence of human rights, directly so in the case brought against former Chilean dictator General Augusto Pinochet and former dictators in Argentina and Guatemala.

Jesús Santos, a prosecutor with no radical leanings whatsoever, has pursued the Lasa and Zabala case under extraordinarily difficult conditions. He says that it is 'the strength and pride of Spanish democracy that it has taken up the challenge of investigating the GAL'.[30]

Before the Lasa and Zabala case concluded, I asked Santos Juliá, historian of the PSOE and professor of political science and sociology at the Universidad Nacional de Educación a Distancia, whether Spanish democracy could take the shock of seeing a general of the Guardia Civil, and a 'hero' of the war against ETA, sent to jail for torture, murder and state terrorism.

'I have no doubt that the system can take the strain,' he told me. 'That is not the question. The question is whether Spanish democracy could survive intact and healthy if a general of the Guardia Civil, who was guilty of such crimes, could *not* be sent to jail.'[31]

Events appear to have proved him right. In April 2000, General Enrique Rodríguez Galindo, along with the former PSOE Civil Governor Julen Elgorriaga, was sentenced to sixty years in prison for the murder of Joxean Lasa and Joxi Zabala.[32] Spanish democracy not only has survived, but is undoubtedly healthier for the fact that this particularly horrific act of state terrorism has been so thoroughly investigated.

The wounds opened by the GAL, like the far more numerous wounds inflicted by ETA, can never be completely healed, for the victims and their families. In the many cases where no specific judicial responsibility has been established, those wounds will remain especially raw.

The wounds inflicted by the GAL on Spanish society generally also remain painful. It can appear that each new investigation into an individual GAL crime prevents those wounds from closing. Yet who could argue that the families of Santiago Brouard or Juan Carlos García Goena or any of the other GAL victims deserve any less justice than Segundo Marey, or the families of Lasa and Zabala?

In any case, it is not the investigations in themselves which keep the GAL scandal festering. The poison rises, not from the surgical exploration of the past, but from the continued denial of responsibility for what that exploration clearly reveals. Senior Socialists, whether convicted, like Barrionuevo and Vera, or still under suspicion in the court of public opinion, like González, continue to deny all responsibility for the GAL, and still present themselves as the victims of a political, media and judicial conspiracy. Some sections of the PSOE give this position vocal support. Most of the party acquiesces in embarrassed silence.

Sooner or later, the PSOE will have to recognise that the denial of what is evident radically delegitimises its democratic credentials. While the party's response to the Lasa and Zabala verdict was much more measured than its response to the Marey judgement, it still failed to seize an opportunity, once and for all, to tell Spanish society 'We did it. We were wrong. We apologise.'

Just as individuals 'in denial' have a genuine difficulty in recognising that which they deny, so it often seems that those members of the PSOE most closely associated with the GAL actually cannot bring themselves to face the most obvious realities.

While interviewing Rafael Vera for this book, I asked him why he had protected Amedo and Domínguez, when he must have known they were guilty, if he himself had had no involvement in the GAL. There was one curious moment in the course of his detailed response. Amedo and Domínguez, he insisted, were not terrorists, but people who had fought against terrorism, 'by means *which may or may not have been mistaken,* but without doubt they did it in good faith'.[33]

I asked him if he would mind if I recounted to him the story of the attack on the Bar Batxoki, as established in French and Spanish courts. I reminded him that the mercenaries sent by Amedo to shoot *etarras* in

Bayonne had called off their first action, because even they balked at killing innocent women and children in crowded taverns. I reminded him that Amedo sent them back, with specific instructions not to be so squeamish. I recalled for him how one of the mercenaries had stood with his comrades outside the Batxoki's glass frontage and encouraged them to open fire on the young children playing inside, because 'ETA would not worry about something like that'. I reminded him that two little girls, aged three and five, were among the victims of this operation.[34]

To my surprise, he heard me out, almost as though he was hearing the whole story, which he surely knew very well, for the first time. I was more surprised still when he responded to my conclusion that the Batxoki attack was a terrorist action with the words: 'Yes, it is. You are right. It's terrorism.'

Didn't the Segundo Marey kidnapping also fall into the same category, I asked.

'Yes, that is terrorism without any doubt whatsoever.'

This was a remarkable statement from a man who would be convicted of this very kidnapping nine months later. As we have seen, he made no such acknowledgement in court, and still denies his participation in the crime.

There has been much talk, from many quarters, of Spain's need to 'turn over the page' of the GAL. Unless those responsible for the dirty war acknowledge what is so clearly written on that page, however, their indictment for undermining Spanish democracy will remain open.

NOTES

1   *El País*, 24 December 1994. Unzueta is paraphrasing an argument put forward by Grant Wardlaw, author of *Political Terrorism* (Cambridge: Cambridge University Press, 1989).

2   Quoted in Jillian Edelstein, 'The Truth Commission', *Granta* magazine, No. 66 (Summer 1999), p. 124. Fr Lapsley lost both his hands in a letter bomb organised by the South African security forces.

3   *El País*, 29 June 1997.

4   Jean-Paul Sartre, *No Exit and Three Other Plays* (New York: Vintage International, 1989), p. 218.

5   Quoted in Noam Chomsky, *For Reasons of State* (London: Fontana, 1973), p. 7.

6   Interview with Javier Pradera, Madrid, November 1997. As already stated, Pradera's track record as a defender of some of Felipe González's unpopular political decisions in other fields gives his views on the GAL particular credibility.

    Lieutenant-Colonel Oliver North, former US marine, was convicted in 1989 for his part in a secret scheme to raise funds for the Nicaraguan Contras. The scheme was believed to have had the support of President Ronald Reagan.

7   Ibid.

8   Ibid.

9   There were, as we have seen, significant exceptions to this complicity with state terrorism. But such courageous opposition did not succeed in making the GAL a really live issue in Spanish politics until after the death squads had hung up their guns.

10   Written response to questions from this writer, August 1998.

11   See chapter 22, p. 351. Carmen Romero is a Socialist MP, feminist and wife of Felipe González.

12   The GAL killed twenty-seven people and wounded more than thirty others.

13 See Roger Faligot, *Britain's Military Strategy in Ireland* (Dingle and London: Brandon and Zed, 1983), a book with a wealth of detail which needs, however, to be treated with some caution.

14 When I made this point in an article in *The Irish Times*, a reader wrote to remind me of the Dublin and Monaghan bombings of 1974, in which thirty-three people were killed. There are, indeed, indications that these loyalist bombings were assisted by some elements in British intelligence. No one has yet made a convincing case, however, that these elements were authorised to do so by a cabinet minister.

15 See Emile Muley's laconic pun, 'Affaire d'État, rien à faire' ('It's a question of state, nothing can be done about it'), in ch. 3, p. 57. This was Muley's response to a question about the failure by the French government to take up the issue of Spanish involvement in the 1980 Bar Hendayais shooting, of which he was a victim.

16 See ch. 7, p. 239.

17 *El País*, 27 January 1996.

18 *El País*, 4 August 1996.

19 See ch. 23, p. 114 n. 6.

20 Interview with Javier Pradera, Madrid, November 1997.

21 The killing of Juan Carlos García Goena, almost eighteen months later, was, as we have seen, an aberration, almost certainly designed purely for the personal advantage of disgruntled GAL members.

22 This 'plausible hypothesis' is based on a conversation the journalist Pedro J. Ramírez claims to have had with Felipe González in 1987. He reports González as saying: 'the only thing we have to negotiate with ETA is that, if they stop killing us, we will stop killing them'. For a development of this argument, see Patxo Unzueta, *El Terrorismo: ¿Qué era? ¿Qué es?* (Barcelona: Ediciones Destino, 1997), p. 41.

23 Unzueta, op. cit., pp. 43–5.

24 *El País*, interview with Felipe González by the editor, Jesús Ceberio, 29 June 1997. This is one of the two interviews which González's office recommended to this writer as faithfully reflecting González's views on the GAL and related issues.

25 *El País*, 2 July 1997.

26 The Partido Popular is not, of course, the direct inheritor of the UCD conservative governments of the transition, and is more directly descended from the more right-wing Alianza Popular. But Aznar's reinvention of the Spanish centre-Right has absorbed many former UCD leaders and supporters. It also inherited, through Alianza Popular, former Francoist ministers like Manuel Fraga.

27 Interview with Javier Pradera, Madrid, November 1997.

28 The Conde/Perote conspiracy, dealt with in ch. 20, is another of the Socialist Party's stock excuses for not taking responsibility for the GAL. Naturally, the rule applies that the exploitation of a crime by a blackmailer does not exonerate the person who committed the crime in the first place.

29 There have been some disturbing incidents which suggest that sporadic extra-judicial actions against ETA have taken place under the Aznar administrations, but nothing which amounts to a sustained dirty war campaign.

30 Interview with Jesús Santos, Madrid, November 1997.

31 Interview with Santos Juliá, Madrid, November 1997.

32 See epilogue.

33 Interview with Rafael Vera, Madrid, November 1997. My emphasis.

34 See ch. 12 pp. 167–9.

Epilogue

less than the whole truth

*The judgement in the Lasa and Zabala case leaves the great
central question unresolved.*

Jesús Santos, state prosecutor[1]

*Will there be further advances in the GAL investigations? Who
knows? Who would have thought, in 1993, that Amedo would
implicate the Interior Ministry in 1994? These breakthroughs
have always come through strokes of luck.*

José Yoldi, *El País* journalist[2]

WE left the narrative of the GAL with Felipe González outside the
gates of Guadalajara prison, and José Barrionuevo and Rafael
Vera inside, on 10 September 1998. This remains the moment
when the investigation into the dirty war under the Socialists reached its
climax, but the story did not end there, nor has it ended in February 2001,
as this book goes to press.

The 'Circus of Guadalajara', as the weekly PSOE pilgrimage to the prison
was christened by its critics, continued through the autumn and early winter
of 1998. The PSOE leadership, including those who claimed to be committed
to reform, maintained constant pressure on the government to grant the two
prisoners a quick pardon. They still insisted that the Marey case had been
as much a Partido Popular plot as a criminal trial, and that the presence in
jail of Barrionuevo and Vera made normal democratic discourse almost
impossible. 'It sometimes seems', wrote the Catalan historian Joan B. Culla
y Clarà, 'that the ancient prison contains not only an ex-minister and a
former secretary of state, but also the bad conscience of an entire party.'[3]

As we have seen, Barrionuevo and Vera had entered no plea for a
pardon during or after their trial – such a plea would have implied
admission of guilt.[4] They did, however, permit a group of PSOE members
to enter a plea on their behalf after they were convicted. While the
granting of a pardon was the government's exclusive prerogative, the first
step was a petition to the Supreme Court, whose view would carry
considerable weight with the cabinet.[5]

The court prosecutor argued strongly against accepting this petition, but
the magistrates who had tried the case proved more flexible. In contrast to
their sharp divisions over the judgement itself, they reached a quick and

unanimous decision when they met on 18 December. They did not recommend a full pardon, because of the seriousness of the crimes committed and of the fact that they had been committed by people whose duty it was to protect the liberty of the public. But they now accepted that there were a number of reasons to grant a partial pardon: the GAL campaign had ended more than a decade before, and the release of the prisoners would cause no public alarm; there was no likelihood that the convicts would carry out similar offences in the future; and the crimes had not been committed for any personal gain.[6] They therefore recommended that all the sentences should be reduced by two-thirds. Barrionuevo and Vera would now have to serve only three years and four months instead of ten years. Taking into account good behaviour and time already served, they would quickly be eligible for 'third grade' (open regime) status if the government accepted the recommendation.[7]

Government pardons are not based on judicial criteria alone, but on a political assessment of the public good. José María Aznar's Partido Popular government had two strong motives for accepting the court's analysis. Firstly, the ceasefire declared by ETA the previous September meant that the issue of measures of grace for its prisoners was on the table. Many sectors of Spanish society, including some Partido Popular supporters, might find it hard to swallow the idea of early releases for Basque terrorists, if Barrionuevo and Vera remained in jail.[8] Secondly, the government's relationship with the PSOE was poisoned by their continued imprisonment, at a time when a bipartisan stance on the Basque question was urgently required. One Socialist leader openly threatened to obstruct the Basque peace process if the cabinet did not grant a pardon.[9]

It was no great surprise, then, when the government decided, apparently against the wishes of its own Minister for Justice, to rapidly endorse the court's position, just two days before Christmas. This partial pardon had a further judicial consequence. Taking the two-thirds reduction of sentence into account, the Constitutional Court moved quickly to permit the immediate release of the prisoners, pending the hearing of their appeals, which had still not been heard by February 2001.[10] (Very little more has been heard of Felipe González's proposed participation in this deferred courtroom drama.)

So, after serving just 105 nights in prison, the convicted kidnappers of Segundo Marey were, at least for the time being, free men. They are unlikely to have to return to a full prison regime even if their appeals are unsuccessful. The Constitutional Court's decison provoked an inevitable public perception that former ministers merited much gentler treatment than ETA convicts – or, indeed, than the foot-soldiers of the GAL.[11]

There were strong protests from civil liberties and human rights groups. Amnesty International warned against 'measures which have the effect of preventing [the emergence of] the truth and subsequent accountability before the law'.[12] Among the political parties, United Left and the Basque Nationalist Party said that the pardon undermined Spain's status as an *Estado de Derecho*. The United Left leader, Julio Anguita, alleged, without any hard evidence, that Aznar and González had done a deal to cover up everything related to the GAL in 1996, at the royal palace at Marivent, 'under the vigilant gaze of the Crown'. The partial pardons, he said, demonstrated the existence of a state 'where murder is seen as a lesser evil'.[13] His allegations betray a belief that the highest courts in Spain are subject to political diktats, which is, ironically enough, the mirror image of the Socialist assertion that the Marey trial had been a Partido Popular plot.

The possibility that Barrionuevo might, under the pressure of prolonged imprisonment, have finally revealed new evidence about the GAL had now evaporated. Nevertheless, there were still people within the Spanish justice system who were seeking the missing links in the dirty war story. One of the most promising routes still open was the Lasa and Zabala case, which finally came to trial in December 1999. Earlier in the year, two other trials gave grounds for optimism that the courts were not just tying up loose ends, but were willing to investigate the relationship of the command structure of the GAL to the state apparatus. It was no coincidence that the prosecutor in all three cases was the assiduous Jesús Santos.

In February, Ismael Miquel Gutiérrez at last faced trial for recruiting the GAL *comando* which fatally wounded Robert Caplanne in December 1985. Miquel was the police informer who had fled to Thailand when the rest of his GAL comrades had been arrested the following year.[14] He was extradited to Spain in 1997, and initially promised to reveal 'many things' about the GAL chain of command. He withdrew the offer when his demand for release from prison was not met.[15]

Santos told the Audiencia Nacional that Miquel had organised the Caplanne killing under instructions 'from authorities in the Interior Ministry at that time, whom, regrettably, it has not been possible to identify in this trial'.[16] The court agreed with the prosecutor, stating explicitly in its judgement that Miquel's access to police data and false documentation could only have come from 'unidentified' personnel in Interior, who formed the 'armed gang' of which Miquel was the 'last link in the chain of command'.[17] The court sentenced him to forty-five years in prison, not only for murder but also for membership of that armed gang, and echoed Santos's regret that the case had not been able to identify Miquel's superiors in this organisation. This was the first conviction on the latter charge in a GAL case since Daniel Fernández Aceña and Mariano Moraleda, the killers of Jean-Pierre Leiba, were sentenced in the first GAL trial to take place in Spain, in 1985. In all dirty war cases since then, as we have seen, the courts had been extraordinarily reluctant to describe the GAL as an armed gang or terrorist organisation.

Almost simultaneously with Miquel's trial, Santos was prosecuting Miguel Brescia for killing the elderly farmer Christophe Matxikotte and his niece Catherine Brion in 1986.[18] Santos accused Brescia of being one of the 'material authors' of the shooting, but added that 'the intellectual authors still enjoy impunity'.[19] In sentencing Brescia to sixty-eight years in prison, the Audiencia Nacional judges again endorsed Santos's analysis. While they held that Brescia himself was a mercenary rather than a member of an armed gang, they again accepted that such an armed gang existed. Moreover, they gave instructions that documents and testimony from the trial should be further investigated by another examining magistrate, in order to clarify any role played by the Interior Ministry and the police in the killing. They specifically mentioned Rafael Vera, Julián Sancristóbal and

José Amedo, among others, in this regard.[20] However, no further progress appears to have been made in this investigation.

The Lasa and Zabala case, on the face of it, offered Santos much more substantial evidence of the GAL's chain of command than either the Caplanne or the Matxikotte and Brion investigations. The main defendants here were General Enrique Rodríguez Galindo of the Guardia Civil, and the former Socialist Civil Governor of Guipúzcoa, Julen Elgorriaga. They were charged with jointly organising the kidnapping and murder of the two young *etarras*, allegedly carried out under the supervision of Lieutenant-Colonel Ángel Vaquero by the former *guardia civiles* Felipe Bayo and Enrique Dorado Villalobos.[21] (Charges against another *guardia civil*, Pedro Gómez Nieto, had been dropped when the CESID failed to authenticate the papers in which he was mentioned.) A military hierarchy, linked directly to the Socialist administration through Elgorriaga, could be clearly discerned here. Coupled with references in the CESID documents to *guardia civiles* in Galindo's barracks at Intxaurrondo, it seemed to give a firm basis for Santos to argue that these men were members of an armed gang which existed over a period of time. Such a proposition, if accepted by the court, could assist other GAL investigations to advance towards the still obscure heart of the whole matter. He also hoped to convict Rafael Vera and Jorge Argote for an alleged attempt to cover up the crimes. The evidence here, however, looked rather less substantial.

The trial, in the Audiencia Nacional, was dramatic from the outset. Bayo turned up to the first session wearing only a vest and underpants, and so heavily sedated he could hardly stand. The court, suspecting that he had been deliberately drugged to delay the trial, had him transferred from military to civil jurisdiction. Bayo, who had given crucial evidence incriminating himself and the other main defendants, had withdrawn it long before the trial opened. However, he had also spoken of being 'pressurised' to recant. And his confession had dovetailed so closely with the known facts of the case, for which there was solid material evidence, that it was reasonable to expect that the judges would consider that the withdrawn testimony was closer to the truth than his retraction.

Bayo was not alone in suffering from sudden bouts of reversed recollection – four other witnesses retracted statements during the trial. It was not hard to imagine why this might be. The court heard disturbing evidence about intimidation of witnesses from such impeccable Socialist sources as Margarita Robles, Juan Alberto Belloch's former deputy at Interior, and from a successor of Elgorriaga's in Guipúzcoa, Juan María Jáuregi.[22] Elements within the Guardia Civil, it appeared, continued to look after their own.

No one has had a higher public profile in the post-Franco Guardia Civil than General Galindo. He revealed more than he may have intended about the real nature of the institution in a bravura court performance, which was widely compared to Jack Nicholson's screen portrayal of a senior US marine in *A Few Good Men*. He swore 'by God and his honour' that he had had nothing to do with the murders. He then became so carried away by his own rhetoric that he described Bayo and Dorado as 'two of the best men I have ever had in the anti-terrorist campaign'. That was bad enough: these men, after all, were already convicted torturers and armed robbers. 'With six men like them', he blundered on, 'we could have conquered the whole of South America.'[23] It was a telling phrase from the man Barrionuevo had compared to a *conquistador*. Unconsciously, the senior figures related to the GAL seemed to be endorsing ETA's view that the Basque Country was in a colonial relationship to Spain, and that those who served there could behave like buccaneers.

Another spectacular moment occurred when the former CESID special operations commander Juan Alberto Perote was called as a witness. Without any advance warning, he produced from his pocket original copies of three of the CESID papers. One was his own note to General Emilio Alonso Manglano, informing him of 'violent actions' by the Guardia Civil in France. The second was Manglano's annotation with 'Pte', allegedly a reference to Felipe González. The third was an original transcript of what purported to be Pedro Gómez Nieto's taped conversation with Galindo about setting up death squads. (This was one of the documents which the Supreme Court could not release to the Lasa and Zabala investigation, because the CESID claimed it did not have the tape on which it was based.) Perote said he had brought these documents to light because he wanted to show that, if Bayo and Dorado had acted illegally, they had been acting under orders. Extraordinarily, not one of the defence lawyers chose to cross-examine Perote. Nor did any of them challenge the authenticity of these very damaging documents.[24]

The trial also yielded one moment of great poignancy. Jesús García, the policeman who had made the vital connection between the unidentified bones in the Alicante morgue and the Lasa and Zabala inquiry, died of a heart attack in the act of giving evidence. For a few moments, all parties to this murder trial visibly shared a sense of shock in the presence of a natural death.

There was also a curious personal incident at the end of one court session for this writer. Vera's lawyer, Manuel Cobo del Rosal, who had set up my 1997 interview with his client, came over to the press seats to say that he had received a fax from me, sent in error, seeking an interview with Julián Sancristóbal. Repeated efforts to contact my former flatmate after the Segundo Marey trial had yielded nothing but silence. From Cobo del Rosal's account, I had indeed sent one such fax to the wrong lawyer's office. He mentioned it in a good-humoured way, but continued: 'You should know that Sancristóbal is no friend of ours. He is the one most to blame for all this trouble. He is trying to implicate everyone in the GAL. Be careful he does not implicate you!'

Rather more seriously, Cobo del Rosal indicated that he knew the trial was going against Galindo and Elgorriaga, though he was optimistic for Vera. Naturally, he insisted that the entire prosecution case was a fabrication, but it did not look like that from where I sat. Despite the retractions of evidence by prosecution witnesses, the two main defendants seemed in bad trouble, as their alibis crumbled before the surgical precision of the cases presented by Santos (for the state) and Iñigo Iruin (for the private prosecution). It was also clear that the defendants were losing a battle outside the courtroom. In contrast to the Marey trial, Socialist solidarity rarely reached a lukewarm temperature, and the usually phlegmatic Vera indicated that he thought even González, who did offer verbal solidarity, could do better.[25] General

Andrés Cassinello, who had made such ambiguous statements about the GAL,[26] was the only significant figure to regularly attend the trial.

Santos's closing arguments for the prosecution were devastatingly effective. Galindo and Elgorriaga were already in deep trouble on the murder charges, but it was on the charge of membership of an armed gang, and a general indictment of 'reasons of state' and state terrorism, that Santos made the most telling case. The evidence showed, he argued, that all the main defendants met all the criteria for constituting an armed group, called the GAL. The GAL's operations from 1983 to 1986, he said, had dragged Spanish society back to the machiavellian principles of the sixteenth century, and were morally 'at the same level or worse' than those of ETA, giving additional arguments to the 'obscene justifications of the terrorists' own dialectic'.[27]

This was a path down which, however, the judges were not prepared to go. Their judgement, on 26 April 2000, was certainly very significant, in that it sentenced Galindo, the figurehead of Spain's battle against terrorism, to seventy-one years in prison for the kidnapping and murder of terrorist suspects.[28] As we saw in chapter 25, this sentence can be taken to demonstrate the remarkable maturity and stability of Spain's young democracy. However, the judges decided to acquit the defendants of membership of an armed gang, and not to recommend any further investigation of the new evidence supplied by Perote, though they did accept the authenticity of the documents he had brought to court and valued them as circumstantial evidence.[29] Given the strong arguments made by Santos and Iruin, this part of the judgement was a bitter disappointment to those who wanted to uncover the full extent of the relationship between the GAL and the state apparatus. The PSOE was quick to assert that the judgement failed to establish any connection whatsoever between the GAL and the governments of Felipe González.[30]

However, the judgement has been appealed to the Supreme Court, both by all the convicted men and by the people's prosecution and the private prosecution.[31] Much hangs on the outcome of these appeals, which should be heard during 2001. If the defence succeeds in overturning the convictions – which informed Spanish legal opinion believes is unlikely – a major strand in the whole GAL investigation will have unravelled. If, on the other hand, the Supreme Court takes on board the prosecution case for armed gang membership, serious prospects emerge for pursuing the investigation further up the chain of command.

The failure of the Audiencia Nacional judgement to open up this crucial line of inquiry was the second blow in six months to the work of Baltasar Garzón, who continued to pursue the elusive 'Señor X' with his usual tenacity. Of the half-dozen GAL investigations still on his books, the Oñederra case had seemed his last best chance to get to the core of the GAL.[32] Firstly, it was the biggest case still pending, in that it covered four killings over three attacks – those of Ramón Oñederra (*Kattu*), Ángel Gurmindo (*Escopetas*), Bixente Perurena (*Peru*) and Christian Olaskoaga. Garzón was investigating a wide range of suspects, including three of the same *guardia civiles* from Intxaurrondo found guilty in the Lasa and Zabala case: Galindo, Bayo and Dorado. Even more significantly, the case was specifically mandated to investigate the origins and structure of the GAL.

In November 1999, Garzón made what many regarded as a botched attempt to draw Felipe González into the frame in the context of the Oñederra case. He sent a highly controversial report to the Supreme Court, in which he sought guidance as to whether 'new' evidence changed the court's view on the possible implication of González. He acknowledged that the Supreme Court had dismissed the tentative evidence he had suggested existed against González in his report on the Segundo Marey case in 1995. That evidence had been based solely on verbal allegations by Ricardo García Damborenea and speculation by Sancristóbal.[33] But Garzón pointed out that at that time he did not have access to the CESID papers, and suggested that the possible references to González in some of these could now be taken to corroborate the statements by Damborenea and Sancristóbal.[34] He argued that he could not advance the case any further against some of the other senior suspects unless he had the Supreme Court's view on the matter. He stressed that he could not evaluate this question himself, because González's parliamentary privilege meant that only the Supreme Court could decide whether the former Prime Minister should be considered a suspect, or whether, on the other hand, 'he had nothing whatsoever to do with the whole criminal plot which was set in motion between July and September 1983 from the nerve centres of the State's institutions'.[35]

He may have thought that, expressed in this way, the superior court would be reluctant to rule out entirely any possibility of González's involvement in the GAL. But this was one of the points where Garzón got so far ahead of the posse that he left himself very exposed. There were the inevitable expressions of outrage from the Socialists, but this time they would have no cause to complain about the reaction of the judicial system.

The Supreme Court responded with unprecedented speed. Within four days of receiving the report, thirteen magistrates unanimously rejected Garzón's suggestion that the CESID papers constituted new evidence against González. Six of the seven judges who had voted to send Barrionuevo and Vera to jail in the Marey trial participated in this debate. They pointed out that, while the intelligence documents had indeed not been available at the time Garzón had submitted his report on the Marey case, the papers *had* been considered by the Supreme Court when that case had come to trial before its magistrates. Since the court had proposed no further investigation on the basis of these documents at that time, there was no need for it to reconsider the matter now. Moreover, the judges strongly reprimanded Garzón for what they described as breaches of judicial procedure in the form and content of his report.[36]

Garzón was also facing opposition from the state prosecutor in the Oñederra case, Pedro Rubira, who argued that there was insufficient evidence against any of the suspects, let alone González, and that the whole investigation should be formally shelved.[37] Up to the time of writing, Garzón has resisted this pressure and is waiting for the outcome of the Lasa and Zabala appeals to see if their outcome offers any openings for pursuing his inquiries further. Just as this book was going to press, a most unexpected source appeared to offer Garzón an additional avenue of investigation. On 3 November 1999, the GAL mercenary recruiter Jean-Phillipe Labade had made the extraordinary mistake of crossing the

Portuguese-Spanish border, and found himself back in jail. He had served his sentence in Portugal, but was still due to serve a life sentence in France for the murders of Xabier Pérez de Arenaza and Tomás Pérez Revilla. (Because a life sentence in France is unlimited Portugal does not usually extradite to Paris, but Spain does.) Labade kept silent, as had been his practice in earlier investigations. Then, just before he was due to be extradited from Madrid, in February 2001, he implicated the familiar names of Francisco Álvarez, Miguel Planchuelo, José Amedo and Michel Domínguez in these murders. Called in for *careos* with Labade in Garzón's chambers, they rejected his version of events. But Labade undoubtedly knows a great deal about the GAL. Whether his new evidence represents the kind of 'stroke of luck' which José Yoldi refers to at the beginning of this chapter remains an open question.

During 1999, and right through 2000, one other case repeatedly promised to shed new light on the GAL, but each apparent breakthrough left matters even murkier than before. This was the ill-fated investigation into the killing of Santiago Brouard in 1984, which has passed through the hands of no fewer than nine investigating magistrates over the years. A conviction was obtained against one of the material authors of the crime, Rafael Ángel López Ocaña, in 1993, but the man who had allegedly recruited him, Luis Morcillo Pinillo, had absconded to Ecuador, and charges had been withdrawn against Lieutenant-Colonel Rafael Masa of the Guardia Civil.[38] The arrest of Morcillo on a drugs charge in Spain in 1997 reopened the case, and the new judge, José Luis Rodríguez Armengol, seemed to make spectacular progress up the chain of command. By October 1999, he concluded a report which named Julián Sancristóbal as the 'brain' behind the crime. He also laid charges against many familiar police figures from this and other GAL cases – José Amedo, Michel Domínguez, Francisco Álvarez, Miguel Planchuelo and Jesús Martínez Torres – as well as against Masa and Morcillo.[39]

But there were most peculiar anomalies in the judge's investigation, which disturbed the prosecution lawyers almost as much as the defence. In December, his superiors in the Bilbao court instructed him to withdraw charges against everyone except Morcillo and repeat the entire investigation. In March 2000, he again brought charges against the same nine men, but in July the charges were again revoked by a senior court, with the exception of those against Masa and Morcillo.[40] This time it was Masa who absconded, but he was picked up in December 2000 during an anti-drugs operation by his own former colleagues in the Guardia Civil. It remains to be seen whether anything can be salvaged from this shambolic case.

Ironically, some confirmation that each GAL action should be considered the work of a terrorist armed gang has come not from the courts but from the Spanish parliament. The Law for the Victims of Terrorism, approved in December 1999 by all parties,[41] provides for financial compensation for the survivors of terrorist attacks and for the families of those who did not survive. While this bill was debated in the relatively relaxed climate created by the ETA ceasefire, it raised old ghosts from the transition to democracy, and before. There were, of course, differing views on what constituted terrorism. For example, United Left proposed that victims of police repression in the late Franco period should be included. Since this would have implied that the Spanish security forces under the dictatorship were an armed gang, it stood little chance of prospering. In the interests of unanimity, it was finally agreed that all acts of violence carried out by *illegal* groups since 1968 should be considered terrorist. This included ETA, the extreme Right, the extreme Left – and the GAL.[42] The proposal was accepted without dissent by all sides, including the PSOE.

One other major question remains in the air at the time of writing. If the Supreme Court confirms Galindo's sentence in the Lasa and Zabala case, there will be great pressure on the government to pardon him, especially in the polarised atmosphere created by ETA's current ferocious campaign of terrorism. That would, it seems to this writer, be an error of tragic proportions.

In January 2001, I interviewed one of the new generation of Basque radicals. Egoitz Urrutikoetxea is the twenty-nine-year-old son of the 1980s ETA leader José Antonio Urrutikoetxea (*Josu Ternera*). His first experience of violence was at the age of four, during the first dirty war, when a death squad tried to blow up the car in which he and his father were travelling.[43] Today, he is a leader of Abertzaleen Batasuna, the party close to the thinking of ETA in the French Basque Country. Against all the evidence I could offer him, he flatly refused to accept that either democracy or the rule of law applies in his homeland.

I put to him the argument that the imprisonment of Galindo had shown that the opposite was true: democracy and the rule of law were remarkably well established in Spain's post-Franco institutions. 'But that is just for show,' he said. 'They will pardon Galindo in no time.'[44] No democrat could wish to see him proved right.

NOTES
1   Interview with Jesús Santos, April 2000.
2   Interview with José Yoldi, February 2001.
3   *El País*, 11 December 1998.
4   Some of the other defendants had asked for a pardon, but the Supreme Court had found that there was 'no argument whatsoever' to grant them one. Sentencia No. 2/1998, Tribunal Supremo, Sala de lo Penal, Causa Especial No. 2530/95 [Segundo Marey], Supreme Court, Madrid, 29 July 1998, p. 115.
5   In formal terms, a pardon is in fact the prerogative of the monarch, but he acts on the government's recommendation.
6   While it was true that personal gain was probably not the primary motivation of any of those involved, the liberal personal use of 'reserved funds' by at least some of the Marey kidnappers tends to undermine this last argument.
7   *El País*, 19 December 1998. See also ch. 17, p. 259.
8   In the event, Aznar finally proved very reluctant to make significant concessions in this area, though ETA prisoners were gradually brought closer to the Basque Country during the ceasefire.
9   This extraordinarily irresponsible proposal was made by Juan Carlos Rodríguez Ibarra, always the most extreme defender of Barrionuevo and Vera. But it was made in the presence of José Borrell, who did not demur from it. *El País*, 22 December 1998.
10   This was a reversal of a ruling by the same court a month earlier. In November, the Constitutional Court had permitted the release pending appeal of the four most junior policemen convicted for the Marey kidnapping, but

ruled that Barrionuevo, Vera, Sancristóbal, Damborenea, Álvarez and Planchuelo should remain in detention because of the gravity of their crimes and the length of their sentences. Amedo and Domínguez had already been released, under a complex and controversial ruling related to the sentences they had already served. *El País*, 27 November 1998 and 31 October 1998.

11 Comparisons were also inevitable with the very different treatment of the national executive of Herri Batasuna, in prison over the screening of ETA's 'Democratic Alternative' video. Though they were serving shorter sentences, the Constitutional Court had refused to release them while their appeal was pending. Eventually, in July 1999, after exceptionally long deliberations, the Constitutional Court annulled the Supreme Court judgement which had sent them to prison for seven years on the charge of collaboration with an armed gang. The court ruled that the penalty was disproportionate to the offence. Some observers expressed concern that this decision might be seen by the public as a quid pro quo for the Marey case pardons, in the context of ETA's ceasefire. *El País,* 22 July 1999.

12 Amnesty International does not take a position on post-conviction pardons 'once the truth is known', but saw fit to repeat this 1991 warning in a briefing issued in June 1999, in specific reference to the Barrionuevo/Vera pardon. The organisation also drew attention to 'the long delays in the judicial process affecting suspected members of the GAL involved in the dirty war'. See *Spain: A Briefing on Human Rights Concerns in Relation to the Basque Peace Process,* 24 June 1999, Amnesty International Index EUR 41/01/1999. Amnesty International is even-handed in stating also that 'the human rights abuses' committed by ETA 'flout the principles of international humanitarian law and the dictates of public conscience'. See *Spain: ETA's New Killing Campaign Must End,* 12 June 2000, Amnesty International Index EUR 41/007/2000.

13 *El País*, 31 December 1998.

14 In the early 1980s Miquel had been in the pay of a Barcelona police unit commanded by Francisco Álvarez, later convicted for the Marey kidnapping. This was prior to Álvarez's promotion to police chief in Bilbao, and then to the Interior Ministry's Intelligence and Special Operations Committee (GAIOE) during the GAL period. In Miquel's trial, Álvarez acknowledged that he had had a meeting with him in his GAIOE role, but denied that he had known of his involvement in the GAL. *El País*, 17 February 1999.

15 *El País*, 16 February 1999.

16 *El País*, 23 March 1999.

17 *El País*, 29 March 1999.

18 Brescia, the only person to be convicted for this crime, had been foolish enough to tell his story, on tape, to a journalist.

19 *El País*, 7 May 1999.

20 *El País*, 5 June 1999.

21 For technical reasons, Santos dropped the charge of torture, though he made the case that Lasa and Zabala had been severely ill-treated.

22 Jáuregi, who was one of the only leading Socialists to challenge the Guardia Civil on the GAL issue, was killed by ETA just a few months later, an indication of the ruthless polarisation evident in ETA's post-ceasefire killings.

23 *El País*, 16 December 1999.

24 *El País*, 17 February 2000.

25 González had made a strong statement in support of Vera's track record in Interior. But Vera said that he still felt 'abandoned' by the Socialist leadership. Rather cryptically, he added that he would have preferred 'a solemn declaration from Felipe González on his anti-terrorist policy at the time of the Lasa and Zabala kidnapping', the closest Vera has come to implying that

González may know more about the GAL than he has revealed so far. *El País*, 13 December 1999.

26　See ch. 19, p. 300 n. 55.

27　Author's court notes, 23 March 2000. The unreconstructed republican writer Eduardo Haro Teclen took Santos to task for reaching back to the sixteenth century, when the human rights abuses of the much more recent Franco period offered equally valid points of comparison with the GAL. *El País*, 25 March 2000.

28　Elgorriaga, Vaquero, Dorado and Bayo all received slightly shorter sentences. Vera and Argote were absolved on the cover-up charges, where the evidence was felt to be largely circumstantial.

29　They made no specific reference, however, to the document which purports to transcribe the incriminating conversation between Pedro Gómez Nieto and Galindo, which seemed to cry out for further investigation. Sentencia, Sumario No. 15/95 [Lasa and Zabala], Juzgado Central de Instrucción No. 1, Audiencia Nacional, Madrid, 26 April 2000, p. 45.

30　*El País*, 28 April 2000.

31　Jesús Santos did not appeal the judgement on armed gang membership for purely technical reasons.

32　Other significant cases still under investigation by Garzón include the Hotel Monbar attack and the killings of Mikel Goikoetxea (*Txapela*), Rafael Goikoetxea, Xabier Pérez de Arenaza, Tomás Pérez Revilla and Juan Carlos García Goena. 33 See ch 18, p. 280–3.

34　One of the CESID documents he referred to was the so-called 'Founding Memorandum of the GAL', with its reference to the need for approval from the person 'who is ultimately responsible for anti-terrorist strategy'. The others were the report in which Perote warned Manglano of the imminence of 'violent actions in the south of France', and the attached annotation referring to 'Pte', which Perote interpreted as an abbreviation for 'Presidente'. See ch. 21, p. 330.

35　*El País*, 20 November 1999.

36　*El País*, 23 and 26 November 1999.

37　*El País*, 10 December 1999.

38　See ch. 9, p. 137.

39　*El País*, 22 October 1999.

40　*El País*, 20 July 2000.

41　Herri Batasuna (currently renamed Euskal Herritarrok) does not attend the Madrid parliament.

42　The implementation of this law has proved highly controversial. José María Aznar's government entered the qualification, after the law was passed, that members of ETA wounded by the GAL could not benefit, though the families of ETA members killed by the GAL could. Thus, for example, the family of Mikel Goikoetxea has been paid compensation, but surviving victims allegedly linked to ETA, like Ramón Basáñez, have not. This decision was taken in the context of ETA's renewed terrorist campaign. (Victims of the GAL are still denied other government benefits, because the attacks did not take place on Spanish territory.) The anger that the Partido Popular's interpretation of the law caused among Basque nationalists extended to the entire Left, including the PSOE, when the government granted compensation to the family of Melitón Manzanas, the notorious police torturer who was ETA's first selected victim in 1968, and announced that Manzanas himself would receive a posthumous medal, the Great Cross of the Royal Order of Civil Recognition of the Victims of Terrorism, under the terms of the same law. See *El País,* 22 June 2000 and 20 January 2001.

43　See ch. 3, p. 49.

44　Interview with Egoitz Urrutikoetxea, Bayonne, January 2001.

Chronology of GAL Attacks

Names in brackets and italics are the *noms de guerre*
of ETA militants.

1983
16 October

Joxean Lasa and Joxi Zabala disappear in Bayonne.
Their bodies, found in a quicklime grave in Alicante in
1985, are not identified until 1995. Now recognised as
the first operation of the GAL.

18 October

José María Larretxea escapes kidnapping attempt by
Spanish police in Hendaye.

4 December

Segundo Marey kidnapped in Hendaye. Released 14
December. First operation claimed by the GAL.

19 December

Ramón Oñederra Cacho (*Kattu*) shot dead in Bayonne.

28 December

Mikel Goikoetxea Elorriaga (*Txapela*) shot in St-Jean-
de-Luz. Dies 1 January 1984.

1984
8 February

Angel Gurmindo Izarraga (*Escopetas/Stein*) and
Bixente Perurena Telletxea (*Peru*) both shot dead in
Hendaye.

25 February

Eugenio Gutiérrez Salazar (*Tigre*) shot dead outside farmhouse in Ideaux-Mendy.

1 March

Jean-Pierre Leiba shot dead in Hendaye railway station.

19 March

Jean-Pierre Cherid killed while planting GAL bomb in Biarritz.

23 March

Xabier Pérez de Arenaza shot dead in a Biarritz petrol station.

3 May

Rafael Goikoetxa killed and Jesús Zugarramurdi (*Kixkur*) wounded in motor-bike shooting on road between St-Martin-d'Arossa and St-Etienne-de-Baigorry.

15 June

Tomás Pérez Revilla and Ramán Orbe Etxeberria seriously injured by bomb outside Café du Haou in Biarritz. Revilla dies on 28 July.

10 July

First of two GAL attacks on Bar La Consolation, St-Jean-de-Luz; several clients suffer minor injuries from bomb hurled from motorbike.

5 August

Denek factory at St-Martin-d'Arossa burned.

23 August

Etxabe family bar in Bayonne machine-gunned. No serious casualties.

21 September

GAL mercenaries Jean-Pierre Daury and Ángel Vicente García arrested when about to attack bar in Biarritz.

18 November

Christian Olaskoaga shot dead in car park at Biriatou; his brother Claude wounded.

20 November

Santiago Brouard shot dead in his surgery in Bilbao. Only GAL attack in Spain.

11 December

José Ramón López de Abetxuko escapes bomb attack in Hendaye.

1985

1 February

Xabier Manterola injured when his car is booby-trapped in Bayonne.

5 February

Christian Casteigts seriously injured by similarly booby-trapped car, also in Bayonne. (Both February 1985 attacks were attributed to the GAL by Basque Radicals, but French police blamed internecine feuding.)

4 March

Gotzón (Ángel) Zabaleta and Josu Amantes seriously wounded in attack at Bar Lagunekin in Bayonne.

13 March

Three people injured in attack on bar in Guethary.

26 March

Ramón Basáñez and José Luis Calderón seriously injured in shooting and grenade attack on Bar Bittor, Ciboure. (Basáñez also injured in second attack on Bar La Consolation, see 13 February 1986.)

29 March

Benoit Pecastaing killed, Kepa (Pedro) Pikabea seriously hurt and two others less seriously wounded in shooting in Café des Pyrénées, Bayonne.

30 March

Javier Galdeano Arana shot dead in St-Jean-de-Luz.

14 June

Emile Weiss and Claude Doerr, gypsies, shot dead in Bar Trinquet Txiki, Ciboure.

27 June

Santos Blanco González shot dead outside Bar Victor Hugo, Bayonne.

8 July

Second attack on Bar Bittor in Ciboure; Juan Carlos Lezartua injured.

16 July

Fernando Egileor finds bomb under his car in Anglet.

2 August

Juan Mari Otegi Elizegi (*Txato*) fatally wounded on Ascarat road to St-Jean-Pied-de-Port.

31 August

Dominique Labeyrie injured in shooting in St-Jean-de-Luz.

4 September

Failed car-bomb attack on Joseph Arraztoa in St-Jean-de-Luz.

25 September

Joxe Mari Etxaniz (*Potros*), Inaxio Asteasuinzarra (*Beltza*), Agustín Irazustabarrena (*Legra*) and Xabin Etxaide (*Eskumotz*) all shot dead in Hotel Monbar, Bayonne.

4 December

Fernando Biurrun escapes bomb attack in Heleta.

24 December

Robert Caplanne shot in Biarritz. Dies 6 January 1986.

1986

8 February

Karmele Martínez Otegi and daughter Nagore (3), Juan Luis Zabaleta and daughter Ainitze (5), and Frédéric Haramboure all wounded in attack on Bar Batxoki, Bayonne.

13 February

Ramón Basáñez injured (for second time; see 26 March 1985) in attack on Bar La Consolation, St-Jean-de-Luz. (This was also the second attack on Bar La Consolation; see 10 July 1984.)

17 February

Christophe Matxikotte (60) and Catherine Brion (16) shot dead near Bidarray.

1987

24 July

Juan Carlos García Goena dies in booby-trapped car in Hendaye.

Chronology of Investigations

Segundo Marey, Batxoki/Consolation and Lasa/Zabala investigations

1983

December

A mercenary, Pedro Sánchez, is arrested in France for Segundo Marey kidnapping, in possession of Spanish police information. Dies in prison before case comes to trial.

1986

February

A Portuguese mercenary, Paulo Fontes Figueiredo, is arrested in St-Jean-de-Luz after shooting Ramón Basañez in the Bar La Consolation. Figueiredo is tried and eventually convicted in France, and his evidence is the first to directly implicate the Spanish police superintendent José Amedo.

1987

November

Amedo is summonsed to a French rogatory commission investigating GAL crimes in Madrid. As journalistic allegations against Amedo and his deputy, Inspector Michel Domínguez, become front-page news, the Audiencia Nacional initiates its own investigations into the two policemen's activities. The French issue an international arrest warrant for Amedo in connection with the attack on the Bar Batxoki.

Deember

Jean-Pierre Echalier and Mohand Talbi, both French mercenaries, are convicted in France for their part in the kidnapping of Segundo Marey. They give contradictory versions of events, but both say that their recruiter was a Spanish policeman called 'Pepe', a nickname for José.

1988
February / July / October

Judge Baltasar Garzón takes over the investigation of Amedo and Domínguez in February; he remands them in custody in July; in October, the Audiencia Nacional accepts Garzón's case for charging them with organising the attacks on the Bar Batxoki and Bar La Consolation in 1986.

1989
April

The Audiencia Nacional turns down Garzón's proposal to investigate the 'reserved funds' from the Interior Ministry which allegedly financed the GAL.

June

Garzón calls for trial of Amedo and Domínguez for the murder of Juan Carlos García Goena.

July

Audiencia Nacional agrees to bring Amedo and Domínguez to trial for this murder, but refuses to pursue any charges against their senior officers.

1991
February

The Prime Minister, Felipe González, former Interior Minister José Barrionuevo and current Interior Minister José Luis Corcuera notified that they must give evidence as witnesses in Marey case.

June

Trial of Amedo and Domínguez on charges relating to Bar Batxoki, Bar La Consolation, and García Goena cases opens.

September

Amedo and Domínguez sentenced to 108 years in prison for organising the Bar Batxoki and Bar La Consolation attacks. They are acquitted of the murder of García Goena, and of charges of terrorism and membership of the GAL.

1993

April

Garzón has a meeting with Domínguez, at which the possibility of a pardon is apparently discussed.

April/May/June

Garzón takes a sabbatical from the judiciary and runs as a general election candidate for the PSOE at Felipe González's request; he is successful and put in charge of anti-drugs policy, but is not made a minister.

1994

May

Garzón resigns from parliament and returns to judiciary, rapidly re-opening GAL cases.

December

With new evidence from Amedo and Domínguez, Garzón remands five of their superiors in custody. They include Julián Sancristóbal (former Director of State Security), Francisco Álvarez (former Chief of Police in Bilbao and former head of Sancristóbal's anti-terrorist special operations and intelligence unit in Madrid) and Miguel Planchuelo (another former Bilbao police chief). They are investigated for organising the kidnapping of Segundo Marey.

1995

February

Garzón remands in custody Rafael Vera (former deputy Interior Minister) and Ricardo García Damborenea (former General Secretary of the PSOE in the Basque Country) in connection with the Marey kidnapping.

March

The bones of Joxean Lasa and Joxi Zabala are identified in Alicante. The investigation of their murders is reopened, and passes to the Audiencia Nacional.

April

Garzón indicts Vera for financing the GAL

Preliminary investigations by the Interior Ministry in the Lasa and Zabala case point to the Guardia Civil barracks at Intxaurrondo, San Sebastián. Judge Carlos Bueren takes up the case for the Audiencia Nacional.

Planchuelo, Álvarez, Sancristóbal, and Damborenea all reverse their evidence and admit their involvement in the Marey kidnapping, implicating Vera and José Barrionuevo (former Interior Minister). Damborenea claims Felipe González personally approved the GAL strategy.

August

Garzón concludes his investigation into the Marey kidnapping, and sends his report to the Supreme Court so that the process of indicting Barrionuevo, hitherto protected by parliamentary privilege, can begin. He also calls for the indictment of Vera, Sancristóbal, Damborenea, Álvarez, Planchuelo, and six other police officers, including Amedo and Domínguez. Controversially, he adds his view that allegations that Felipe González was implicated in the dirty war are 'credible'.

September

Supreme Court judge Eduardo Moner commences his assessment of Garzon's investigation of the Marey case.

Lasa and Zabala investigation points to involvement of Guardia Civil General Enrique Rodríguez Galindo and Julén Elgorriaga (former PSOE Civil Governor of Guipúzcoa) in kidnapping, torture and murder.

The authenticity (or otherwise) of the 'CESID papers', allegedly leaked during the summer by former head of military intelligence operations, Col Juan Alberto Perote, becomes a major issue in GAL cases. The government insists the papers, if authentic, are official secrets which cannot be presented in court. Allegations come to light that the papers are being used by the disgraced banker, Mario Conde, to blackmail the government, adding a whole new layer of complication to the investigations.

November

Parliament votes to lift Barrionuevo's immunity, so that Moner can summons him as a suspect.

1996

January

Government refuses to declassify CESID papers. Moner formally indicts Barrionuevo for the kidnapping of Marey.

General elections: González's Socialists finally dislodged from power by José María Aznar's Partido Popular.

April

Judge Javier Gómez de Liaño, who has taken over the investigation of the Lasa and Zabala case, and Garzón, who is investigating the killing of Ramón Oñederra among other GAL cases, co-ordinate their examination of the alleged role of Galindo in the GAL.

May

Moner decides not to charge Felipe González in Marey case, but leaves open possibility he may be called as witness.

Gómez de Liaño remands in custody two former *guardia civiles*, Enrique Dorado Villalobos and Felipe Bayo, on suspicion that they are the material authors of the murders of Lasa and Zabala. Their former commanding officer, Galindo, is also remanded on suspicion of organising the murders. Also formally under suspicion in this case are Elgorriaga, Vera, the former Interior lawyer, Jorge Argote, the former Director General of the Guardia Civil, Luis Roldán, and a Guardia Civil lieutenant, Pedro Gómez Nieto.

June

Elgorriaga remanded in custody in Lasa and Zabala case.

August

General Galindo released on bail. Partido Popular government refuses to release CESID papers on grounds of state secrecy.

October

Elgorriaga released on bail, charges dropped against Gómez de Nieto in Lasa and Zabala case.

November

Supreme Court takes definitive decision not to charge González in Marey case, but he may still be called as a witness.

December

Complete texts of 'CESID papers' published in Madrid newspapers; Defence Minister Eduardo Serra appears to inadvertently authenticate them.

1997

March

Supreme Court declassifies most of the 'CESID papers' requested by judges.

June

Perote convicted of stealing CESID documents for his personal benefit and sentenced to seven years and expelled from the army.

August

Bayo reverses his evidence and confirms he saw Galindo and Elgorriaga visit Lasa and Zabala during interrogation sessions.

1998

May

The oral hearing of the Marey case opens in the Supreme Court.

July

The Supreme Court, by a majority decision, finds all the defendants guilty of kidnapping Segundo Marey, of imposing a condition for his release, and of misuse of public funds. They are found not guilty of membership of an armed gang. Barrionuevo, Vera and Sancristóbal are sentenced to ten years in prison, Álvarez and Planchuelo and Amedo to nine, Damborenea to seven, Domínguez to two, and four other officers to five years each. Four of the 11 judges publish dissenting opinions, which argue that there was insufficient evidence to securely convict Barrionuevo and Vera.

Verdict appealed to Constitutional Court. Appeal still pending March 2001.

September

José Barrionuevo becomes the first former minister of the González era to go to jail.

December

Supreme Court recommends partial pardon, granted by government, and both Barrionuevo and Vera are released pending their appeal hearing.

DBS Arts Library

1999

December

The oral hearing of the Lasa and Zabala case opens.

2000

April

Galindo, Elgorriaga, Bayo, Dorado and Guardia Civil Colonel Ángel Vaquero are found guilty of the kidnapping and murder of Lasa and Zabala. They are absolved of membership of an armed gang and of torture charges. Galindo and Elgorriaga are sentenced to more than 60 years in prison. Vera and Argote are absolved of covering up the crimes.

Verdict appealed to Supreme Court, appeal hearing still pending March 2001.

Some Notes
on the Spanish Constitution,
Judiciary and Legal System

To follow the investigation of the GAL's dirty war in the Spanish courts, which occupies much of Part III of this book, a little background on the Spanish constitution, judiciary and criminal law procedures may be helpful. It is hoped that these notes will provide some easily accessible guidance for readers in these areas.

THE CONSTITUTION AND THE *ESTADO DE DERECHO*

Unlike Anglo-Saxon law, which is largely based on convention and precedent developed in common law, the Spanish legal system falls within the continental European tradition of codified legality, based on Roman law.[1] The democratic Constitution approved by referendum in 1978 is the fundamental law of the Spanish state. This Constitution is based on the principles derived from the concept of the *Estado de Derecho*, literally the 'state of law'. In fact, the *Estado de Derecho* is cited in the first clause of the first article of the constitution.

The *Estado de Derecho* is often translated loosely as 'the rule of law', expressed by the popular will represented in parliament. But, as the historian Paul Heywood points out, it includes three other key characteristics:

- the separation of powers between the executive, legislature and judiciary;
- administrative legality, ensured through judicial control of governmental and parliamentary decisions;
- the guarantee of fundamental rights and freedoms.[2]

DBS Arts Library

THE ROLE OF THE JUDICIARY

The 1978 Constitution treats the judiciary as a co-equal power of the state, along with the executive (Prime Minister and cabinet) and the legislature (parliament).[3] The GAL's dirty war, and other scandals, have led to serious conflicts between the executive and the judiciary, in which key elements of the *Estado de Derecho*, such as the separation of powers and administrative legality, have been severely tested. The weakness of the Spanish legislature *vis-à-vis* the executive in contemporary Spanish democracy has often been noted. This was particularly true as the executive's power expanded during the long years of the absolute majorities enjoyed by the Socialist Party in the 1980s. These circumstances led to the judiciary acquiring an unusually high profile in Spanish public life.

Some observers saw the judges as the last line of defence for the *Estado de Derecho* against a corrupt and excessively powerful government. Others argued that the judiciary was allowing itself to be manipulated as a partisan ally of the opposition parties. The power of the judiciary is therefore regarded with distrust by some Spanish politicians. The apparently political role of some judges became highly contentious as the judicial investigation of GAL and corruption scandals undermined the Socialist Party's credibility in the 1990s.

SPANISH CRIMINAL LAW PROCEDURES

Prosecution under Spanish criminal law always involves two distinct phases: judicial investigation (*instrucción*) and trial in open court (*juicio oral*). It is 'inquisitorial' in the first phase, which requires the investigation of the case under the supervision of an examining or investigating magistrate or judge (*juez de instrucción*).[4] This investigation must precede any trial hearing in open court. The 'trigger' for the opening of an investigation may be an accusation (*denuncia*) about an alleged offence by the police, or by an injured party or witness, to the judicial authorities. An investigation may also be triggered by a complaint (*querella*) from an uninvolved citizen or citizens, in instances of alleged offences against public order or the public interest.

The investigating judge, along with a state prosecutor (*fiscal del estado*), and, depending on the circumstances, lawyers acting on behalf of the victim or his/her family (*acción particular*) and the general public (*acción popular*), examine the evidence against the suspect/s. These lawyers are referred to in this book as the 'private prosecution' and the 'people's prosecution' respectively.

The suspect/s may be represented from the outset by defence lawyers, and must be so represented if they are indicted (*procesado*). The investigating judge is supposed to balance all the evidence for and against a suspect, but these judges are sometimes accused of playing a role closer to that of a prosecutor in other systems than of an impartial 'examiner'. Tensions are often evident regarding the balance of responsibilites between the judge and the state prosecutor. This has led to proposals to strengthen the role of the state prosecutor in this process. The state prosecutors fall under the authority of the Attorney General (*Fiscal General del Estado*), who is a political appointee. Attorneys general have been accused of using their powers over prosecutors to obstruct GAL investigations.

The investigating judge has powers to seek further information from the police and from other civil authorities. The right of judges to seek sensitive information from state and financial agencies has been contested throughout the GAL investigations.

Investigations are usually conducted in the judge's chambers, though there may also be visits to crime scenes where witnesses and suspects may be questioned on the spot. The judge also has the power to declare all or part of the investigation secret, withholding information from the defence for specified periods and embargoing press coverage (though the system is notorious for its 'leaks'). The judge has to provide a legal justification for each step he/she takes, however, and each step can be appealed by any of the other parties.

During the course of an investigation, the judge will decide whether any person should be indicted, at which point defence representation becomes mandatory. Once indicted, a suspect enjoys rights enshrined in the Constitution, such as the presumption of innocence, the right to silence and the right not to give evidence against him/herself.[5] The last-mentioned is popularly, and not quite accurately, known as the 'right to lie', but it is more than a simple right to silence: an indicted person cannot be charged with perjury if it emerges that he/she has lied to the investigating magistrate. Had he/she lied before indictment, he/she could be so charged.[6]

Most of the GAL cases have been both investigated and tried in the Audiencia Nacional, a special national court set up in 1977 to deal with serious offences involving terrorism, drugs and fraud. This court is sometimes described as the 'High Court' in English, but its Spanish title is used in this book. Because there has been much legal argument as to whether or not the GAL constituted a terrorist organisation, some cases have been – or are being – investigated and tried in provincial courts (the Audiencia de Bilbao for the still current Santiago Brouard case, for example).

If a suspect is a public representative, it may be necessary to transfer the investigation to a higher court. For example, a sitting MP may be indicted only if parliament agrees to waive his/her privileges, and the case must then be investigated and heard by the Supreme Court. So it was the Supreme Court which tried the Segundo Marey case, because an MP and former minister, José Barrionuevo, was indicted. But that case was investigated in the Audiencia Nacional until his indictment. The entire investigation then had to be repeated by a Supreme Court investigating magistrate before a final decision could be taken as to whether to bring the case to trial.

An indicted suspect may be required to raise bail or may be remanded in custody (*prisión preventiva*) for up to four years while an investigation is in progress. The latter measure should be used, according to most authorities, only where there are well-grounded fears that the suspect might repeat the alleged offence, flee the jurisdiction or interfere with witnesses or evidence. Some jurists argue that it can also be used where the crime committed has created 'public alarm', and the suspect's liberty could be held to exacerbate such alarm. Others argue that this ground for imprisonment conflicts directly with the principle of presumption of innocence.[7] Custodial powers should never be used to pressurise a suspect into confession. Judges in the GAL cases were often accused of abusing this measure for this purpose.

The investigating judge has no powers to pronounce a sentence, and is obliged to uphold equally the rights of all parties, including those of the defendants. His/her final function is to present an impartial and objective report (*auto de conclusión*) to a panel of more senior judges, who will then independently decide whether or not to proceed to trial in open court (*juicio oral*), or shelve the case for lack of evidence. They may also send the case back to the investigating judge for further examination of evidence or witnesses, and a further report.

The investigating judge, therefore, has no role whatsoever in the actual trial of the accused. However, the power to decide the course of the investigation and to formulate the report is inevitably influential and sometimes attracts charges of bias, as we have seen above. Some investigating judges, especially but not only Judge Baltasar Garzón, have become high-profile figures in Spanish public life. They are lionised as 'superjudges' crusading against corruption by some observers, or vilified as publicity-seekers and witchfinders-general by others.

If the panel of senior judges decides on an oral hearing in open court, a judge or judges with no previous contact with the case will again examine the evidence, witnesses and suspect/s. There is, then, a substantial element of duplication in Spanish criminal law procedure, which is considered a failsafe against miscarriages of justice.

The presiding judge/s decide the judgement, verdict and sentence. (It should be noted that, while the jury system is currently being introduced gradually in Spain, no GAL cases have been heard before a jury.) The defendant/s may appeal the decision of the judge/s to a higher court.

In the case of the Supreme Court, appeals can be made only to the Constitutional Court. Theoretically, at least, this tribunal stands above the judiciary itself and the other 'powers' of the state, and 'acts as the ultimate arbiter of constitutional propriety in Spain'.[8] Inevitably, however, there are allegations that its members, who are mostly political appointees, retain some loyalty to the party which promoted them. The judiciary itself is 'policed' by the General Council of the Judiciary (Consejo General del Poder Judicial), a body whose own political independence has also been questioned.

One other characteristic aspect of the Spanish system must also be mentioned. In both the investigative phase and the trial in open court, judges may subject witnesses and suspects whose evidence is in conflict to a *careo*. This is a face-to-face confrontation between those giving conflicting evidence, to assess their relative credibility. The *careo* is a highly dramatic device, but its judicial value is frequently disputed. *Careos* played an important part in the GAL investigations and trials.[9]

1   See Paul Heywood, *The Government and Politics of Spain* (London: Macmillan, 1995), pp. 103–20.
2   Ibid., p. 104.
3   Ibid., pp. 104–5 and pp. 117–20.
4   In the vernacular, the terms judge (*juez*) and magistrate (*magistrado*) are used interchangeably to describe both the person in charge of the investigative phase and the person who hears the actual trial.
5   Constitución Española, 1978, Article 24.2.
6   See Vicente Gimeno Sendra et al., *Derecho Procesal Penal*, 3rd edn (Madrid: Editorial Colex, 1999), p. 392.
7   Ibid., p. 526.
8   Heywood, op. cit., pp. 104–5.
9   For a highly critical view of the *careo*, see José Jiménez Villarejo, in his dissenting opinion on the Segundo Marey verdict, with Gregorio García Ancos. Voto Particular de D José Jiménez Villarejo y D Gregorio García Ancos, Causa Especial No 2530/95 [Segundo Marey], Supreme Court, Madrid, 29 July 1998, p. 15.

Glossary

INTRODUCTORY NOTE

This glossary has been compiled with accessibility and simplicity as the priorities. Entries can be found under three headings: Individuals, Organisations, and Spanish and Basque Terms.

Individuals included usually occur at several different points in the text. Individuals who occur only within a single chapter, where it should always be easy to identify them, are usually excluded. Victims of the GAL, who can be found in the chronology of GAL attacks, are also not listed here. Where an individual is known by both Spanish surnames, but the second alone is more commonly used, the main entry is under the first surname, with a cross-reference from the second surname to the main entry. Thus General Manglano has his main entry under 'Alonso Manglano, Emilio'.

Organisations are listed under the titles most commonly used in the main text, with cross-references where acronyms are also commonly used. Thus the main entry for the Partido Socialista Obrero Español is under 'Socialist Party', with the acronym PSOE cross-referring to this entry. The full name in Spanish and English is then spelt out after the commonly used title.

References to 'the GAL period' in this glossary are to the years of the GAL's violent campaign, 1983–7, and not to the period of the GAL investigations.

INDIVIDUALS

Aceña, Daniel Fernández   GAL mercenary and ultra-Right activist convicted in 1985 for murder of Jean-Pierre Leiba. Has offered conflicting and sometimes fantastic versions of other GAL operations in prison interviews.

Almunia, Joaquín   Minister in several PSOE governments led by Felipe González, whom he succeeded as party general secretary in 1997. Resigned after leading PSOE to crushing defeat by Partido Popular in 2000 general elections.

Alonso Manglano, Emilio Army general; Director General of the CESID under the PSOE. Investigated in one GAL case (Hotel Monbar) and called as witness in several others. Convicted for illegal phone-tapping in 1999.

Álvarez, Francisco Police chief in Bilbao, 1982–4, and subsequently chief of the Interior Ministry's Intelligence and Special Operations Committee. Convicted for Segundo Marey kidnapping in 1998.

Álvarez Cascos, Francisco Partido Popular politician. First deputy Prime Minister to Aznar, 1996–2000.

Amedo Fouce, José Police superintendent stationed in Bilbao in 1970s and 1980s. Convicted in 1991 for GAL shootings in Bar La Consolation (1986) and Bar Batxoki. Acquitted of murder of Juan Carlos García Goena in the same trial. Convicted for kidnapping of Segundo Marey in 1998.

Anguita, Julio Leader of United Left coalition, 1989–2000, and secretary general of Spanish Communist Party since 1988. Pursued González relentlessly on GAL issue.

Argote, Jorge Lawyer retained by Interior Ministry to defend security force members against allegations of human rights abuses. Defended a number of GAL suspects at various stages, including Amedo, Domínguez and General Galindo. Indicted but absolved of cover-up in Lasa and Zabala case, April 2000.

Arzalluz, Xabier President of executive committee of Basque Nationalist Party since 1980.

Aznar, José María Partido Popular leader who led his party to victory over the PSOE in 1996, and again in 2000. Prime Minister.

Ballesteros, Manuel Senior police intelligence officer under Franco, UCD and PSOE. Refused to reveal identity of alleged Bar Hendayais killers.

Barrionuevo, José Interior Minister, 1982–8; Transport Minister, 1988–91. Convicted for Segundo Marey kidnapping in 1998.

Bayo, Felipe Guardia Civil agent. Convicted for the murder of Lasa and Zabala in 2000.

Belloch, Juan Alberto Judge with strong human rights record. Became Justice Minister in González's 'reformed' 1993 administration, and Justice and Interior Minister from 1994 to 1996. His decision to cease payments to families of Amedo and Domínguez probably triggered their GAL revelations in 1994.

Beñarán Ordeñana, José Miguel (Argala) Leading ideologue of ETA from early 1970s until his death in a bombing in Anglet during the first dirty war in 1978.

Benegas, José María ('Txiki') Basque PSOE leader, and 'number three' after González and Guerra in party apparatus from 1984 to 1994.

Borrell, José Catalan PSOE leader, and Minister of Public Works from 1991 to 1996. Briefly co-led party with Almunia as pro-reform prime-ministerial candidate in late 1990s, but resigned over minor scandal before he could be tested in elections.

Bueren, Carlos Investigating judge at Audiencia Nacional from 1986, kept Segundo Marey case active while Garzón was in politics, and took on Lasa and Zabala case after identification of their bodies in 1995. Resigned under somewhat contentious circumstances in 1996.

Cassinello, Andrés Army general; Chief of Staff of the Guardia Civil, 1984–6. Described the GAL campaign as 'imaginative'. Investigated in Oñederra case but never convicted of any GAL-related offence.

Cherid, Jean-Pierre Senior mercenary in both Basque Spanish Battalion and GAL dirty wars. Former French paratrooper. Killed while activating a GAL bomb in Biarritz in 1984.

Conde, Mario Banker with political ambitions. President of Banesto from 1987 to 1993, when an emergency audit by the Bank of Spain revealed fraudulent practices. Allegedly a principal figure in the conspiracy to use GAL-related information to blackmail the PSOE government.

Corcuera, José Luis Interior Minister for González, 1988–93. Highly critical of judiciary, defended priniciple of state secrecy over right to investigate. Resigned when his anti-crime legislation was found to be unconstitutional.

Damborenea, Ricardo García See García Damborenea, Ricardo.

Domínguez, Michel Police inspector and José Amedo's deputy in Bilbao during GAL period. Convicted for same crimes as Amedo.

Dorado Villalobos, Enrique Guardia Civil sergeant. Convicted for the murder of Lasa and Zabala in 2000.

Elgorriaga, Julen PSOE Civil Governor of Guipúzcoa in the GAL period, and subsequently Government Delegate to the Basque Autonomous Community. Convicted for the murder of Lasa and Zabala in 2000.

Escusol, Eladio State prosecutor in 1991 trial of Amedo and Domínguez. Accused by critics of playing role closer to that of defence lawyer.

Fontes Figueiredo, Paulo Portuguese GAL mercenary. Convicted in France for attacks on Bar La Consolation (1986) and Bar Batxoki. His testimony was crucial in revealing Amedo's role in the GAL.

Fraga, Manuel Minister in General Franco's governments, 1962–9, and hardline Interior Minister in first post-Franco government, 1975–6. Founding leader of right-wing Alianza Popular, later Coalición Popular, the main precursor of the Partido Popular, of which he was briefly leader. Supported José María Aznar as his successor in 1989. President of the Galician autonomous goverment since that year.

Galindo, Enrique Rodríguez See Rodríguez Galindo, Enrique.

García Damborenea, Ricardo General secretary of the PSOE in Vizcaya from 1979, and ideologue of belligerent confrontation with Basque nationalism. Parted company with PSOE in 1990. Convicted for Segundo Marey kidnapping in 1998.

Garzón, Baltasar Investigating magistrate at the Audiencia Nacional. Investigated Bar La Consolation, Bar Batxoki, Juan Carlos García Goena, Segundo Marey and other GAL cases. PSOE MP and Secretary of State, 1993–4. His sudden return to the judiciary in 1994 controversially coincided with reopening of GAL investigations. Best known internationally for drawing up warrant to extradite General Augusto Pinochet from Britain to Spain in 1998.

Gómez de Liaño, Javier Investigating magistrate in Lasa and Zabala case.

Gómez de Liaño, Mariano Brother of Javier, a lawyer and associate of Mario Conde.

González, Felipe General secretary of the PSOE, 1974–97, and Prime Minister, 1982–96.

Guerra, Alfonso Deputy Prime Minister and alter ego to González, 1982–91. Waspish scourge of party's enemies, forced to resign when his brother was implicated in corruption scandal. Became leader of 'Guerrist' faction, defending entrenched PSOE apparatus against reformists with a torrent of 'leftist' rhetoric.

Iruin, Iñigo Radical Basque lawyer and influential figure in Herri Batasuna. His defence of ETA prisoners and his prosecution of GAL suspects, especially in the Lasa and Zabala case, are regarded as technically brilliant even by his severest political critics.

Iturbe Abásolo, Domingo (Txomin) Top ETA leader from late 1970s to 1986, when he was expelled from France to Algeria, where he met an accidental death the following year.

Labade, Jean-Philippe Replaced Cherid as main organiser of GAL mercenary commanders in 1984. Implicated in GAL killings in May–June 1984. Absconded while on bail from France to Portugal where he recruited the *comando* responsible for 1986 attacks on Bar La Consolation and Bar Batxoki. Convicted for GAL membership in Portugal, and killings of Xabier Pérez de Arenaza and Tomás Pérez Revilla in France.

López Agudín, Fernando Journalist; head of public relations for Justice and Interior Ministry under Belloch, 1994–6.

Manglano, Emilio Alonso See Alonso Manglano, Emilio.

Martínez Torres, Jesús Chief of police intelligence under PSOE, 1982–94. Senior anti-terrorist officer with unsavoury reputation as interrogator under Francoism, and remarkably poor record in investigating anti-ETA death squads of both Basque Spanish Battalion and GAL.

Masa, Rafael Guardia Civil colonel. Implicated in Santiago Brouard case.

Mendaille, Georges Recruiter of mercenaries for the GAL. The Spanish authorities repeatedly failed to extradite him, despite numerous French judicial demands dating back to 1985. Finally handed over in 1994, he was convicted in 1997 of attacks on Fernando Egileor and Joseph Arraztoa.

Moner, Eduardo Investigating magistrate at Supreme Court. Repeated and confirmed Garzón's investigation of Segundo Marey case in 1995–6.

Paesa, Francisco Businessman whose obscure services to the Interior Ministry are said to include the pressurising of a witness in a GAL investigation and the capture of Luis Roldán.

Pagoaga Gallastegui, José Manuel (Peixoto) Veteran ETA leader, wounded in the first dirty war in St-Jean-de-Luz in 1978, and a senior spokesman for the radical refugee community in France during the GAL period.

Perote, Juan Alberto Colonel in charge of the special operations group in the CESID, 1982–91. Convicted for stealing intelligence documents, the 'CESID papers', in 1997.

Planchuelo, Miguel Head of police anti-terrorist intelligence in the Basque Country, 1981–4. Police chief in Bilbao from 1984. Convicted for kidnapping of Segundo Marey in 1998.

Ramírez, Pedro J. Journalist. Editor of *Diario 16*, 1980–9; founding editor of *El Mundo* since 1989. Backed major investigative work on the GAL. Visceral opponent of Felipe González and PSOE, has been close to José María Aznar and Partido Popular.

Río, Rafael del Director General of the National Police Force, 1982–6.

Robles, Margarita Secretary of State at Interior Ministry under Belloch, 1984–6. Staunchly defended investigation of Lasa and Zabala case.

Rodríguez Galindo, Enrique Guardia Civil commander at Intxaurrondo barracks in San Sebastián during GAL period. Pre-eminent counter-terrorist officer in late 1980s and early 1990s. Promoted to general in 1995. Convicted for murder of Lasa and Zabala in 2000.

Roldán, Luis PSOE Government Delegate to Navarre, 1982–6, and the first civilian Director General of the Guardia Civil, 1986–93. Investigated for corruption, fled the country in 1994 and was mysteriously recaptured abroad in 1995.

Sáenz de Santamaría, José Antonio Army general; Director General of the Guardia Civil, 1983–6. During the 1990s GAL investigations, he repeatedly made ambiguous statements alleging that the UCD's relationship to the first dirty war was identical to that of the PSOE to the GAL. Implicated in the Oñederra case, but never convicted.

Sánchez, Pedro GAL mercenary. Arrested in France shortly after kidnapping of Segundo Marey, in possession of police files and phone number of Francisco Álvarez. Died in prison before trial, allegedly poisoned.

Sancristóbal, Julián Civil Governor of Vizcaya, 1982–4; Director of State Security, 1984–6. Convicted for kidnapping of Segundo Marey in 1998.

Santaella, Jesús Lawyer who represented interests of Mario Conde and Juan Alberto Perote in alleged blackmail operation using GAL information against PSOE government in 1996.

Santos, Jesús State prosecutor in Lasa and Zabala case.

Serra, Narcís Minister for Defence in all González governments until 1991, then deputy Prime Minister until 1995, when he was forced to resign over the CESID phone-tapping scandal.

Suárez, Adolfo Prime Minister appointed by King Juan Carlos in 1976, formed UCD, and oversaw the Spanish transition to democracy. Resigned in 1981, marginalised from active politics, but remains influential.

Svahn, Michel French judge who readily granted generous bail conditions to GAL suspects.

Vera, Rafael Director of State Security, 1982–4; deputy Interior Minister, as Secretary of State for Security, until 1994. Convicted for kidnapping for Segundo Marey in 1998.

ORGANISATIONS

Alianza Popular (People's Alliance). Right-wing party founded by Manuel Fraga in 1977; one of the precursors of the Partido Popular.

Audiencia Nacional Special national court hearing terrorism- and drug-related cases, based in Madrid. See also 'Some Notes on the Spanish Constitution, Judiciary and Legal System'.

Basque Nationalist Party (Partido Nacionalista Vasco – PNV). Dominant nationalist party in Basque Country; has presided over Basque regional autonomous government solely or in coalition since 1980.

Basque Spanish Battalion (Batalión Vasco Español – BVE). Main protagonists of first dirty war against ETA, 1975–81.

BVE See Basque Spanish Battalion.

CESID Centro Superior de Información de la Defensa (Higher Information Centre for Defence). Spanish military intelligence service.

Comandos Autónomos (Autonomous Commandos). Far Left Basque separatist organisation which operated independently of ETA in the early to mid-1980s.

Ertzaintza Police force controlled by the Basque autonomous government. Individual members of the force referred to as *ertzainas*.

ETA Euskadi Ta Askatasuna (Basque Homeland and Liberty). Radical group campaigning for Basque independence since 1959. Espoused 'armed struggle' in the 1960s, and escalated its use of terrorist violence during and after the transition to democracy. Most significant of many splits occurred in 1974, when the 'political-military' faction, *ETA(p-m)*, advocated participation in emerging democratic institutions, while the 'military' faction, *ETA(m)*, insisted on the primacy of armed action. ETA(m) ultimately absorbed most of those members of ETA(p-m) who did not accept their leadership's final espousal of a purely political strategy. From the mid-1980s, ETA(m) is synonymous with ETA. The group went on ceasefire in September 1998, and endorsed a strategy of drawing the moderate Basque nationalist parties into a pro-independence front. Dissatisfied with the results of this new departure, ETA announced the resumption of terrorist operations in November 1999.

Euskadiko Ezkerra (Basque Left). Political coalition formed mainly by supporters of ETA(p-m) and former communists. Dissolved in late 1990s, with some senior members joining the Basque section of the PSOE and others moving to moderate nationalist parties such as the PNV.

GAIOE See Intelligence and Special Operations Committee.

GAL Grupos Antiterroristas de Liberación (Anti-terrorist Liberation Groups). Protagonists of second dirty war against ETA, 1983–7.

General Council of the Judiciary (Consejo General del Poder Judicial). The legal profession's watchdog body. See also 'Some Notes on the Spanish Constitution, Judiciary and Legal System'.

GEO Grupos Especiales de Operaciones (Special Operations Groups). Elite anti-terrorist units within the police. Individual members referred to as GEOs.

Guardia Civil Formed in 1844, and famous for its tri-cornered hats, this hybrid security force is regulated by military discipline but has a major police function, particularly in counter-terrorism. Individual members of the force referred to as *guardia civiles*. Its officers are drawn from the army, and its Chief of Staff is a soldier. The Director General, now usually a civilian, reports to the Interior Minister in peace time, and to the Defence Minister in time of war.

HASI (Herriko Alderdi Sozializta Iraultzailea – Revolutionary Socialist People's Party). Small Marxist party close to ETA(m) and one of the founding parties of the Herri Batasuna coalition. Santiago Brouard was president until his death in 1984. Dissolved in 1992.

Herri Batasuna (Popular Unity). Political coalition which supports aims of ETA(m). Since 1998, uses electoral name of Euskal Herritarrok (roughly 'Basque Citizens').

Intelligence and Special Operations Committee (Gabinete de Información y Operaciones Especiales – GAIOE). Counter-terrorist intelligence unit set up by Director of State Security; under leadership of Francisco Álvarez, 1984–6.

Iparretarrak French Basque separatist group which has carried out several sporadic terrorist campaigns, and has had an uneasy relationship with ETA.

MULC See Unified Counter-terrorist Command.

National Police Force Generally referred to as 'the police' in this book, this is the Cuerpo Nacional de Policía, whose Director General reports to the Interior Minister.

Partido Popular (People's Party). Spain's dominant centre-Right party. In government under José María Aznar's leadership from 1996, re-elected with absolute majority in March 2000.

PNV See Basque Nationalist Party.

PSOE See Socialist Party.

Socialist Party (Partido Socialista Obrero Español/Spanish Socialist Workers' Party – PSOE). Spain's dominant centre-Left party. In government under Felipe González's leadership from 1982 to 1996.

UCD Unión del Centro Democrático (Union of the Democratic Centre). Alliance of former Francoists and Christian Democrats. Political vehicle through which Adolfo Suárez steered the transition to democracy, winning elections in 1977 and 1979, collapsing after PSOE victory in 1982.

Unified Counter-terrorist Command (Mando Único para la Lucha Contraterrorista – MULC). Co-ordinating body for the various security services involved in counter-terrorism.

United Left (Izquierda Unida – *IU*). Coalition dominated by the Communist Party of Spain. Declining in influence.

SPANISH AND BASQUE TERMS

abertzale Basque nationalist (from the Basque-language word for 'patriot').

barrio district or quarter of a town.

bertsolari Basque-language poet who improvises verses in public, often alternating stanzas with one or more colleagues.

careo face-to-face confrontation between witnesses whose evidence is mutually contradictory. See also 'Some Notes on the Spanish Constitution, Judiciary and Legal System'.

comando an ETA *comando* is roughly the equivalent of an 'active service unit' in the IRA or a 'cell' in the Baader Meinhof Group. While the word may seem to confer some military legitimacy on the organisation in English, it is used as an everyday term in Spanish, and cited in police and Interior Ministry communiqués. *Comandos* are made up of small groups of militants, who may be known only to their senior officers. The term is also applied to GAL units, and in this book is used in relation to both organisations.

cuadrilla the tightly-knit group with whom many young Basques spend their adolescence; often the source of life-long bonds in Basque society, despite geographical (and political) distances which may develop later.

españolista pejorative term for Basques whose primary loyalty/ identification is to Spain rather than the Basque Country. Applied in particular to political parties and trade unions whose headquarters are in Madrid.

etarra member of ETA.

frontón the court used for the Basque sport of pelota. The *frontón* is often used for political rallies, and for ritualised tributes to *etarras* killed in action.

fuero a medieval charter of special rights, usually granted by the monarch, to villages, cities, provinces and regions. Many Basque nationalists regard the *fueros* long enjoyed by the region as recognition of its sovereignty. The final abolition of the Basque *fueros* in 1876, after the second Carlist war, is thus read as the destruction of Basque independence.

gudari Basque soldier, used to refer mainly to the Basques who fought for the Spanish Republic against Franco's uprising, now commonly used in the radical nationalist community to refer to *etarras*.

ikurriña the green, white and red Basque national flag, created by Sabino Arana on the model of the British Union flag.

incontrolado (literally 'uncontrolled'). Refers to ultra-Right elements, inside and outside the security forces, who carried out terrorist acts against democrats and regional nationalists during the late Franco period and the transition to democracy, without the authorisation of the state.

kale borroka (literally 'street struggle'). Part of a strategy adopted by ETA supporters from the late 1980s. Teenagers were encouraged to conduct a permanent campaign of political vandalism, burning buses, phone boxes, ATMs and rival political offices, attacking any *ertzainas* who intervened. The *kale borroka* has created an almost unbearable level of social tension in the Basque Country, and has been a fertile recruiting ground for ETA.

mugalari members of ETA unit responsible for guiding activists across French–Spanish border.

prisión preventiva the remanding in custody of unconvicted suspects during a judicial investigation, on the grounds that they might repeat the

crime, abscond, intimidate witnesses or interfere with evidence. See also
'Some Notes on the Spanish Constitution, Judiciary and Legal System'.

zulo a confined hiding place used either for arms or for kidnap victims.

Exchange rate: All sums of money cited in this book are quoted in pesetas. While the rate fluctuated during the period in question, one million pesetas can be taken as roughly equivalent to IR£5,000, Stg£4,000, or $6,000.

Bibliography

BOOKS

Amigo, Angel, *Pertur: ETA 71–76* (San Sebastián: Hordago, 1978)

Arques, Ricardo, and Melchor Miralles, *Amedo: El Estado contra ETA* (Barcelona: Plaza y Janés/Cambio 16, 1989)

Azurmendi, Mikel, *La Herida Patriótica* (Madrid: Taurus, 1998)

Barrionuevo, José, *2,001 Días en Interior* (Barcelona: Ediciones B, 1997)

Bayo, Eliseo, *GAL: Punto Final* (Barcelona: Plaza y Janés, 1997)

Burns Marañón, Tom, *Conversaciones sobre el Socialismo* (Barcelona: Plaza y Janés, 1996)

Calleja, José María, *Contra la Barbarie* (Madrid: Temas de Hoy, 1997)

Carr, Raymond, *Spain 1808–1975*, 2nd edn (Oxford: Clarendon Press, 1982)

Cerdán, Manuel, and Antonio Rubio, *El Caso Interior* (Madrid: Temas de Hoy, 1995)

Cerdán, Manuel, and Antonio Rubio, *El Origen del GAL* (Madrid: Temas de Hoy, 1997)

Cernuda, Pilar, *El Presidente* (Madrid: Temas de Hoy, 1994)

Chomsky, Noam, *For Reasons of State* (London: Fontana, 1973)

Clark, Robert P., *The Basques: The Franco Years and Beyond* (Reno: University of Nevada Press, 1979)

Collins, Roger, *The Basques*, 2nd edn (Oxford: Blackwell, 1990)

De Ugalde, Martín, *Síntesis de la Historia del País Vasco*, 4th edn (Barcelona: Ediciones Vascas, 1977)

Ekaizer, Ernesto, *Vendetta* (Barcelona: Plaza y Janés, 1996)

Elorza, Antonio (ed.), *La Historia de ETA* (Madrid: Temas de Hoy, 2000)

Escrivá, María Ángeles, *El Camino de Vuelta* (Madrid: El País–Aguilar, 1998)

Faligot, Roger, *Britain's Military Strategy in Ireland* (Dingle and London: Brandon and Zed, 1983)

Gallop, Rodney A., *A Book of the Basques* (London: Macmillan, 1930)

García, Javier, *Los GAL al Descubierto* (Madrid: El País–Aguilar, 1988)

Garmendia, José María, *Historia de ETA* (San Sebastián: R&B Ediciones, 1995)

Gilmour, David, *The Transformation of Spain* (London: Quartet Books, 1986)

Gimeno Sendra, Vicente, et al., *Derecho Procesal Penal*, 3rd edn (Madrid: Editorial Colex, 1999)

Gutiérrez, José Luis, and Amando de Miguel, *La Ambición del César* (Madrid: Temas de Hoy, 1989)

Heiberg, Marianne, *The Making of the Basque Nation* (Cambridge: Cambridge University Press, 1989)

Heywood, Paul, *The Government and Politics of Spain* (London: Macmillan, 1995)

Hobsbawm, E.J., *Nations and Nationalism since 1780*, 2nd edn (Cambridge: Canto, 1992)

Hooper, John, *The New Spaniards* (London: Penguin, 1995)

Jáuregui Bereciartu, Gurutz, *Ideología y Estrategia Política de ETA*, 2nd edn (Madrid: Siglo XXI de España, 1985)

Juaristi, Jon, *El Bucle Melancólico* (Madrid: Espasa-Calpe, 1997)

Juliá, Santos, Javier Pradera and Joaquín Prieto (eds.), *Memoria de la Transición* (Madrid: Taurus, 1996)

Letamendía, Francisco, *Historia del Nacionalismo Vasco y de ETA*, 3 vols. (San Sebastián: R&B Ediciones, 1994)

Linz, Juan J., *Conflicto en Euskadi* (Madrid: Espasa-Calpe, 1986)

López Agudín, Fernando, *En el Laberinto* (Barcelona: Plaza y Janés, 1996)

Merkl, Peter (ed.), *Political Violence and Terror* (Berkeley: University of California Press, 1986)

Morán, Sagrario, *ETA entre España y Francia* (Madrid: Editorial Complutense, 1997)

Onaindia, Mario, *La Lucha de Clases en Euskadi* (San Sebastián: Hordago, 1979)

Onaindia, Mario, *Guía para Orientarse en el Laberinto Vasco* (Madrid: Temas de Hoy, 2000)

Payne, Stanley, *El Nacionalismo Vasco: De sus Orígines a ETA* (Barcelona: Dopesa, 1974)

Perote, Juan Alberto, *Confesiones de Perote* (Barcelona: RBA Libros, 1999)

Preston, Paul, *Franco* (London: Fontana Press, 1995)

Ramírez, Pedro J., *David contra Goliat* (Madrid: Temas de Hoy, 1995)

Rei, Pepe, and Edurne San Martín, *Alcalá 20-N* (San Sebastián: Egin/Txalaparta, 1996)

Sánchez, Ángel, *Quién es Quién en la Democracia Española* (Barcelona: Flor del Viento Ediciones, 1995)

Sarrailh de Ihartza, Federico (under the pseudonym Federico Krutwig), *Vasconia* (Buenos Aires: Norbait, 1962)

Sartre, Jean-Paul, *No Exit and Three Other Plays* (New York: Vintage International, 1989)

Sparks, Allister, *Tomorrow is Another Country* (Sandton, South Africa: Struik Book Distributors, 1994)

Sullivan, John, *ETA and Basque Nationalism* (London: Routledge, 1988)

Unzueta, Patxo, *El Terrorismo: ¿Qué era? ¿Qué es?* (Barcelona: Ediciones Destino, 1997)

Vázquez Montalbán, Manuel, *Un Polaco en la Corte del Rey Juan Carlos* (Madrid: Alfaguara, 1996)

Wardlaw, Grant, *Political Terrorism*, 2nd edn (Cambridge: Cambridge University Press, 1989)

Zulaika, Joseba, *Basque Violence, Metaphor and Sacrament* (Reno, Nev.: University of Nevada Press, 1988)

Zulaika, Joseba, and William A. Douglass, *Terror and Taboo* (London: Routledge, 1996)

INTERVIEWS

José Acosta, José Amedo, Xabier Arzalluz, Joseba Azcarraga, Juan Mari Bandrés, José Luis Barbería, Ramón Basañez, Edurne Brouard, Cristina Cuesta, Txetx Echeverry, Karmen Galdeano, Iñigo Goioaga, Javier Gómez de Liaño, Jean-Louis Humbert, Iñigo Iruin, Santos Juliá, Mikel Mari Lasa, Fernando López Agudín, Laura Martín, Karmele Martínez Otegi, Emile Muley, Mario Onaindia, Javier Pradera, Pepe Rei, Izaskun Rekalde, Margarita Robles, Jesús Santos, Izaskun Ugarte, Patxo Unzueta, Manuel Vázquez Montalbán, María Silverio Velez, Rafael Vera, José Yoldi, Juan Mari Zabala

LEGAL DOCUMENTS AND POLICE REPORTS

Judgement in Segundo Marey case
Sentencia No. 2/1998, Tribunal Supremo, Sala de lo Penal, Causa Especial No. 2530/95 [Segundo Marey], Supreme Court, Madrid, 29 July 1998

Dissenting opinions in Segundo Marey case
Voto Particular de D José Jiménez Villarejo y D Gregorio García Ancos, Causa Especial No. 2530/95 [Segundo Marey], Supreme Court, Madrid, 29 July 1998

Voto Particular que formula el Excmo Sr D Enrique Bacigalupo Zapater, Causa Especial No. 2530/95 [Segundo Marey], Supreme Court, Madrid, 29 July 1998

Voto Particular que formula el Magistrado Joaquín Martín Canivell, Causa Especial No. 2530/95 [Segundo Marey], Supreme Court, Madrid, 29 July 1998

Prosecution writs in Lasa and Zabala case
Auto de Procesamiento contra el General Enrique Rodríguez Galindo y Otros, Sumario 15/95 [Lasa and Zabala], Audiencia Nacional, Madrid, 27 May 1996

Auto de Procesamiento contra Julen Elgorriaga y Rafael Vera, Sumario 15/95 [Lasa and Zabala], Audiencia Nacional, Madrid, 19 June 1996

Judgement in Lasa and Zabala case
Sentencia, Sumario 15/95 [Lasa and Zabala], Juzgado Central de Instrucción No. 1, Audiencia Nacional, Madrid, 26 April 2000

Police reports
Preliminary report of the joint committee of Guardia Civil and National Police on the deaths of Lasa and Zabala, Office of the Secretary of State for the Interior Ministry, Madrid, 21 April 1995

NEWSPAPERS

Spain
El Correo Español, Bilbao
Deia, Bilbao
Diario 16, Madrid
Egin, Hernani*
El Independiente, Madrid
El Mundo, Madrid
El País, Madrid
El Sol, Madrid
La Vanguardia, Barcelona
La Verdad, Alicante

France
Le Monde, Paris
Libération, Paris
Sud-Ouest, Bordeaux

Other
The European
Financial Times, London
The Irish Times, Dublin

PERIODICALS

Cambio 16, Madrid
Época, Madrid
Granta, London
Interviú, Madrid
Punto y Hora de Euskal Herria, San Sebastián
El Siglo, Madrid
Tiempo, Madrid

* See especially *Egin,* 'Guerra Sucia' series of supplements, January/February 1995.

Index

Matxikotte investigation, 421
Ortega Lara kidnapping case, 367
Ramírez/Rapú case, 348–9
and 'reserved funds', 224, 230, 231, 234, 255
Rovira trial, 209–10
autonomous system of government, 19–20, 28–30, 52–3, 54, 63, 64, 105, 107, 120, 129, 130
see also Statute of Autonomy
Avanguardia Nazionale (National Vanguard), 47
Azaña, Manuel, 397
Azcarraga, Joseba, 171, 225n
Azcoitia, 88–9
Aznar, José María, 246, 248, 263, 267, 268, 280n, 328, 332n, 339, 343, 351, 396, 398, 415, 420, 447, 448, 450, 452
on Egin closure, 380
forms new government, 314, 315, 317–18, 340
refusal to hand over 'CESID papers', 318–20
relationship with European allies, 382

Baader-Meinhof group, 410
Bacigalupo Zapater, Enrique, 359, 379
dissenting document on Marey verdict, 390–1, 392, 401n, 402n, 403n
Badinter, Robert, 93, 123n
Bakunin, Mikhail, 407
Baldés, Pierre, 144, 192
Ballesteros, Manuel, 45, 54–6, 66–7, 178, 447
Balsategui, Blanca, 222–3, 230, 232, 234, 236–7, 241, 270
retractions, 238–9
Banco Central Hispanoamericano, 298
Banco Santander, 304
Banesto bank, 251, 296, 297, 298, 299, 301, 310n, 334n, 448
Banks Council, 212, 214, 217
Barbería, José Luis, 179, 285
Barcelona Olympics, 246
Barrio, Javier Delgado, 403n
Barrionuevo, José, 55, 66–9, 82–3, 96, 116–17, 119, 137n, 139, 159–60, 161, 171, 179, 181, 183–4, 185, 186–7, 190, 192, 193, 194, 203, 206, 207, 216, 220, 226n, 231, 245, 248, 256, 264, 265, 350, 352, 356, 357, 416,
appointed Interior Minister, 186
collaboration with Sancristóbal, 260–1, 274, 297–8, 310n, 362
and Conde affair, 300, 301, 302, 306, 312n
in general election of 1996, 339, 340
and Lasa and Zabala case, 281, 283, 290, 291, 294n, 423
moved in cabinet reshuffle, 216
offers to be lawyer to Elgorriaga and Sancristóbal, 353n
and 'reserved funds', 213–14, 215, 227n, 237, 363
Supreme Court trial, 268, 274, 276, 277n,

280n, 305, 335–8, 339, 340, 341, 344, 345, 346, 359, 360, 361–2, 363, 364–5, 366, 367–8, 370–1, 374–5, 377n, 378n, 379–80, 396, 443, 447
appeal, 397, 402n, 403n, 420
careos with Damborenea and Sancristóbal, 335–6, 338, 359, 365, 381, 385
imprisoned, 354n, 399, 419
judgement and dissenting opinions, 347, 374, 380–1, 382–92
partial pardon granted, 419–20
solidarity campaign for, 392–3, 394–5, 397–9
taped conversation with Sancristóbal, 340–1
witness at Amedo trial, 235, 237–8
2,001 Días en Interior, 344, 346
Barrios, Captain Alberto Martín, 69, 76–7, 183, 280n, 363, 369, 389
Basáñez, Ramón, 140–2, 165, 429n, 432, 433
Basauri prison escape, 148
Basque Human Rights Association, 247
Basque Nationalist Party (Partido Nacionalista Vasco – PNV), 26–30, 53, 96, 119, 126, 134, 151, 158, 226n, 447, 451
on Barrionuevo pardon, 420
block PSOE protest against Partido Popular, 349–50
call 1947 general strike, 35
and Constitution (1978), 51, 52, 59n, 59n
funding scandals, 354n
in general election of 1977, 50
in general election of 1979, 129
implicated in terrorism, 161
premises attacked by activists, 267
racism, 42n
split, 35
and Western allies, 33–4
Basques
'Basqueness' defined, 34–5, 36–7
Catholicism of, 27, 37
culture of, 27, 35
geography of territory, 20–1
lack of Roman fortification, 23
language see Euskera
nationalism of, 19–20, 21–3, 26–9, 34, 35, 51–3
origins, 17–18
physical appearance, 26–7
racism, 26–7, 36
Basque Spanish Battalion (Batalión Vasco Español – BVE), 48, 67, 101, 111, 128, 178, 198n, 216, 268, 448, 449, 451
1980 campaign, 54
Batalión Vasco Español (BVE) see Basque Spanish Battalion
Batxoki bar attack, 162–4, 166, 192, 201, 203, 210, 213, 215, 216, 234, 238, 241, 255, 271–2, 273, 416–17, 433, 447, 448, 449
Bayo, Eliseo, 187
GAL: Punto Final, 268, 289
Bayo Leal, Felipe, 287, 288, 290, 291, 292,

Orly hotel, 203, 207
Ortega Lara, José Antonio, 345
Otaegui, Ángel, 48, 159
Otegi Elizegi, Juan Mari (*Txato*), 150–2, 226n, 433

Paesa, Francisco, 223, 230, 234–5, 239, 241, 270, 272, 279n, 449
Pagoaga Gallastegi, José Manuel (*Peixoto*), 53, 91, 98, 127
Palomino, Jesús, 330n
Pandraud, Robert, 182, 197n
Pardines, José, 33, 38
Paredes Manot, Juan (*Txiki*), 48, 159
Parmentier, Alain, 154n
Partido Nacionalista Vasco (PNV) *see* Basque Nationalist Party
Partido Popular, 11, 13n, 30n, 153n, 198n, 242n, 246, 247, 248, 252, 256, 259, 263, 267, 268, 271, 272, 275, 278n, 297, 299, 308, 323, 333n, 336, 341, 342, 346, 347, 348, 349, 351, 380, 381, 392, 414–15, 420, 447, 448, 450, 452
    aftermath of Marey verdict, 393–4, 396–9, 419
    annual congress of 1996, 338–9
    defeated in 1993 elections, 414
    digital television rights battle, 343–4
    elections
        1996, 339–40, 360
        2000, 446, 452
    forms new government, 314, 315, 317–18
    funding scandals, 354n
    moves towards centre, 382
    refusal to condemn Franco, 355n
    relationship with *El Mundo*, 314–15, 319, 450
    revising Official Secrets Act, 319
    success in local elections of 1995, 272
Partido Socialista Obrero Español (PSOE) *see* Socialist Party
Pasajes massacre, 109–10
Pasqua, Charles, 167–8, 182, 194, 319, 410–11
Patriotic Socialist Co-ordinating Body *see* Koordinadora Abertzale Sozialista
Pearse, Patrick, 26
Pecastaing, Benoit, 143–4, 153n, 192, 432
'Pedro' ('deep throat'), 207–9
Pérez de Arenaza, Xabier, 110, 118, 203, 211, 212, 372, 429n, 431, 449
Pérez Mariño, Ventura, 256n, 268
Pérez Revilla, Tomás, 48, 116, 117, 188, 191, 201, 203, 211, 212, 224, 372, 429n, 431, 449
Perote, Colonel Juan Alberto, 273–4, 279n, 280n, 290, 300, 301, 303–4, 305–6, 307, 310n, 311n, 313–14, 315–16, 317, 323, 324, 325, 326, 329–30, 331n, 333n, 357, 367, 429n, 449, 450
    accused of manipulating or inventing of 'CESID papers', 318, 327, 328, 330, 388

convicted of stealing 'CESID papers', 330, 334n, 449
    Marey trial, 365–6, 383
    Matxikotte trial, 423, 424
Perret, Clement, 84n
Perret, Gilbert, 84n
Perurena, Miren Argi, 104
Perurena Telletxea, Bixente (*Peru*), 104, 122, 294n, 425, 430
'pieds noirs', 57n
Pikabea, Kepa (Pedro), 143, 432
Piñar, Blas, 46
Pinar, Jacky, 154n
Pinochet, General Augusto, 350, 375, 415, 448
Piqué, Josep, 381, 400n
Pironneau, Patrick, 224
Planchuelo, Miguel, 222, 224, 229n, 232, 256, 260, 272, 273, 336, 370, 426, 449
    confesses to Garzón, 274, 361
    Marey trial, 358–9, 361, 362, 369, 373, 374, 376n, 387
'Plan ZEN' (Zona Especial Norte), 68, 134
Plaza de la República Dominicana (Madrid) bombing, 199n
PNV *see* Basque Nationalist Party
Pope Paul VI, 39
Popular Unity *see* Herri Batasuna
Portell, José María, 53
Portugal, 183, 188, 211
    GAL mercenaries recruited from, 212, 213, 235, 236
    investigation of GAL in, 201–2, 203, 206, 209, 210, 212, 220, 232, 449
Pradera, Javier, 185, 215, 218, 262, 334n, 347, 402n, 408, 409, 414
Price Waterhouse, 299
Primo de Rivera, Miguel, 28, 35
PRISA multimedia group, 343
PSOE *see* Socialist Party
Pujol, Jordi, 278n, 309n
Punto y Hora, 121

Quintana Lacaci, Lieutenant General Guillermo, 103
Quotidien de Paris, Le, 104

racism
    of Basques, 26–7, 36
    of PNV, 42n
Radio Popular de Alicante, 75, 282, 292n
Rahola, Pilar, 339
Rainbow Warrior, 114n, 410
Rajoy, Mariano, 320
Ramírez, Pedro J., 208, 226n, 259, 297, 299, 300–1, 307, 314, 315, 319, 343, 344, 360, 370, 400n, 449–50
    and conspiracy to undermine PSOE, 350, 351, 357
    and Ruiz-Mateos case, 354n
    sex video, 348–9
Ramos, General Sánchez, 133
Rapú, Exuperancia, 348–9

Sartre, Jean-Paul, 37, 39
    Les Mains Sales, 407, 409
Savater, Fernando, 321
Schmidt, Helmut, 278n
Second Republic (1931), 29
Second World War, 179
self-defence network in response to GAL,
    143–4, 156–7
self-determination issue, 4, 22, 27, 28, 39, 51,
    58–9n
Selfe, James, 46–7
'Señor X' enigma, 200, 220–1, 222, 224, 231,
    263, 274, 399
Seoane, Alberto *see* Paesa, Francisco
Serra, Eduardo, 317–19, 320, 328, 332n
Serra, Narcís, 271, 273, 280n, 298, 299, 301,
    302, 303, 305, 312n, 317, 324, 326, 336,
    337, 338, 372, 450
Servicio Central de Documentación de
    Presidencia del Gobierno (SECED), 46,
    109
Seys, Judge Christophe, 203, 209, 210, 213
Sinn Féin, 137
Socialist Party (PSOE), 3, 5, 11, 13n, 26, 27,
    28, 42n, 65–9, 77, 95, 136, 152n, 177–96,
    253, 308, 317, 318, 319, 328, 343, 344–5,
    360, 442, 447, 452
    aftermath of Marey verdict, 381–2, 392–9,
        408–11, 413–14, 419
        ten-point statement on, 394
    annual congress (34th), 345
    apparatchiks, 185
    on Argentinian/Chilean dictatorships,
        349–50
    aversion to Conde, 298, 299
    campaign to choose prime ministerial
        candidate, 352
    deny paying Galindo's bail, 373
    in elections
        1979, 129
        1982, 6, 54, 55, 65, 69
        1984, 105
        1989, 69–70n, 246
        1993, 245–8, 250
        1996, 339–40, 341
        2000, 446
        European parliament, 252, 257n, 272
        improved performance in local
            elections, 272
    funding scandals, 354n
    hostility to judiciary, 321, 332n, 337, 340,
        341, 347, 354n, 413–14, 416
    implicated in corrupt practices, 214, 215,
        217–18, 259–76, 296, 301, 302, 303,
        330, 336, 340–1, 365, 389, 390
    media conspiracy to undermine, 315,
        350–1
    popularity drops in Galician regional
        elections, 347
    'reformed' administration, 231, 250, 447
        unravels, 250–2
    relationship with radical nationalism,
        124, 130

request pardon for Barrionuevo and Vera,
    419–20
'road of repression', 120
second absolute majority in legislature,
    228n
solidarity with Barrionuevo, 337–8, 339,
    356, 357
'social reinsertion', 64, 69n, 76, 104, 133,
    153n, 171, 182, 218, 228n, 364
Sofía, Queen, 130
Sogecable television company, 343–4
Sokoa factory, 81, 85n, 182, 360, 367, 369
Solana, Javier, 211, 227n, 248, 338
Solaun, Mikel, 103–4, 171
Somontes, Jesús, 315
Soriano, José Velázquez (*Txema*), 195–6
Sorozabal, Pablo, 98
Spanish empire 'disaster' (1898), 28
Spanish Socialist Workers' Party *see* Partido
    Socialista Obrero Español
Special Operations Groups *see* Grupos
    Especiales de Operaciones
Statute of Autonomy (Statute of Gernika),
    5–6, 12n, 50, 52, 54, 129, 130
Suárez, Adolfo, 47, 49, 56, 58n, 216, 219,
    309n, 310n, 450, 452
    and Conde blackmail case, 300–1, 302–3,
        306, 311n
    decrees amnesty, 127
    resigns as Prime Minister, 63–4
Suárez Partierra, Gustavo, 316
Sud-Oest, 118, 122
Sukarno, President of Indonesia, 223
Sullivan, John, 130
Svahn, Judge Michel, 86n, 111, 118, 184,
    187–8, 201, 411, 450
Sygma agency, 117

Tagle, Carmen, 283
Talbi, Mohand, 136, 188, 210, 212–13, 366
Tápies, Antonio, 39
taxation *see fueros*
Tejero, Antonio, 64, 103
    and '23-F', 268
terrorism, definition of, 9–10
Thomas, Dominique, 153n, 217, 224
Tiempo, 112, 116
Goñi Tirapu, José Ramón, 349
Tomás y Valiente, Francisco, 266, 339
Torres, Rafael, 240
torture, use of, 8, 11, 38, 74, 75, 76, 78, 120,
    149, 177, 186, 218, 247, 281, 282, 283,
    288, 291, 296, 305, 331n, 359, 412, 415,
    428n
    by Galindo's units, 286, 287
    international laws against, 349
tourism, 17, 113
Tourré, Alain, 123n, 188, 192
'triangle of death', 54, 67
Trinquet Txiki bar attack, 141–2, 432
'Triple A' (Alianza Anticomunista Argentina),
    47, 53, 128, 233
Tubau, Olga, 359, 373–4